T0188835

Communications in Computer and Information Science 1267

More information about this series at http://www.springer.com/series/7899

Zibin Zheng · Hong-Ning Dai ·
Xiaodong Fu · Benhui Chen (Eds.)

Blockchain and Trustworthy Systems

Second International Conference, BlockSys 2020
Dali, China, August 6–7, 2020
Revised Selected Papers

 Springer

Editors
Zibin Zheng 🆔
Sun Yat-sen University
Guangzhou, China

Xiaodong Fu 🆔
Kunming University of Science
and Technology
Kunming, China

Hong-Ning Dai 🆔
Macau University of Science
and Technology
Macau, China

Benhui Chen
Dali University
Dali, China

ISSN 1865-0929   ISSN 1865-0937 (electronic)
Communications in Computer and Information Science
ISBN 978-981-15-9212-6   ISBN 978-981-15-9213-3 (eBook)
https://doi.org/10.1007/978-981-15-9213-3

This Springer imprint is published by the registered company Springer Nature Singapore Pte Ltd.
The registered company address is: 152 Beach Road, #21-01/04 Gateway East, Singapore 189721, Singapore

Preface

Blockchain has become a hot research area in academia and industry. The blockchain technology is transforming industries by enabling anonymous and trustful transactions in decentralized and trustless environments. As a result, blockchain technology and other technologies for developing trustworthy systems can be used to reduce system risks, mitigate financial fraud, and cut down operational cost. Blockchain and trustworthy systems can be applied to many fields, such as financial services, social management, and supply chain management.

This volume contains the papers presented at the International Conference on Blockchain and Trustworthy Systems (BlockSys 2020). This conference was held as the second in its series with an emphasis on the state-of-the-art advances in blockchain and trustworthy systems. It was held virtually due to the COVID-19 pandemic. The main conference received 100 paper submissions, out of which 42 papers were accepted as regular papers and 11 papers were accepted as short papers. All papers underwent a rigorous peer-review process and each paper was reviewed by two to three experts. The accepted papers, together with our outstanding keynote and invited speeches, led to a vibrant technical program. We are looking forward to future events in this conference series.

The conference would not have been successful without help from so many people. We would like to thank the Organizing Committee for their hard work in putting together the conference. We would like to express our sincere thanks to the guidance from honorary chairs: Huaimin Wang and Jiannong Cao. We would like to express our deep gratitude to general chairs: Zibin Zheng, Yan Zhang, and Benhui Chen for their support and promotion of this event. We would like to thank the program chairs: Hong-Ning Dai, Shangguang Wang, and Xiaodong Fu for supervising the review process of the technical papers and compiling a high-quality technical program. We also extend our deep gratitude to the Program Committee members whose diligent work in reviewing the papers lead to the high quality of the accepted papers. We greatly appreciate the excellent support and hard work of publicity chairs: Wei Liang, Yongjuan Wang, Celimuge Wu, Kun Wang, and Wei Feng; publication chairs: Li Liu and Ke Zhang; organizing chairs: Haichao Yang, Yong Feng, Jiajing Wu, and Zhenpeng Li; and advisory board: Michael R. Lyu and Kuan-Ching Li. Most importantly, we would like to thank the authors for submitting their papers to the BlockSys 2020 conference.

We believe that the BlockSys conference provides a good forum for both academic researchers and industrial practitioners to discuss all technical advances in blockchain and trustworthy systems. We also expect that future BlockSys conferences will be as successful as indicated by the contributions presented in this volume.

August 2020

Zibin Zheng
Hong-Ning Dai
Xiaodong Fu
Benhui Chen

Organization

Honorary Chairs

Huaimin Wang   National University of Defense Technology, China
Jiannong Cao   The Hong Kong Polytechnic University, Hong Kong, China

General Chairs

Zibin Zheng   Sun Yat-sen University, China
Yan Zhang   University of Oslo, Norway
Benhui Chen   Dali University, China

Program Chairs

Hong-Ning Dai   Macau University of Science and Technology, Macau, China
Shangguang Wang   Beijing University of Posts and Telecommunications, China
Xiaodong Fu   Kunming University of Science and Technology, China

Organizing Chairs

Haichao Yang   Dali University, China
Yong Feng   Kunming University of Science and Technology, China
Jiajing Wu   Sun Yat-sen University, China
Zhenpeng Li   Dali University, China

Publicity Chairs

Wei Liang   Hunan University, China
Yongjuan Wang   Information Engineering University, China
Celimuge Wu   The University of Electro-Communications, Japan
Kun Wang   University of California, Los Angeles, USA
Wei Feng   Tsinghua University, China

Publication Chairs

Li Liu   Kunming University of Science and Technology, China
Ke Zhang   University of Electronic Science and Technology of China, China

Advisory Board

Michael R. Lyu   The Chinese University of Hong Kong, Hong Kong,
                                China
Kuan-Ching Li   Providence University, Taiwan, China

Special Track Chairs

Yongjuan Wang   Henan Key Laboratory of Network Cryptography
                                Technology, China
Ao Zhou   Beijing University of Posts and Telecommunications,
                                China
Wei Liang   Hunan University, China
Fei Dai   Southwest Forestry University, China
Qian He   Guilin University of Electronic Technology, China

Program Committee

Alexander Chepurnoy   IOHK Research, Sestroretsk, Russia
Ali Vatankhah   Kennesaw State University, USA
Andreas Veneris   University of Toronto, Canada
Ao Zhou   Beijing University of Posts and Telecommunications,
                                China
Bahman Javadi   Western Sydney University, Australia
Bu-Qing Cao   Hunan University of Science and Technology, China
Chang-Ai Sun   University of Science and Technology Beijing, China
Claudio Schifanella   University of Turin, Italy
Debiao He   Wuhan University, China
Fangguo Zhang   Sun Yat-sen University, China
Gerhard Hancke   City University of Hong Kong, Hong Kong, China
Guobing Zou   Shanghai University, China
Han Liu   Tsinghua University, China
Jan Henrik Ziegeldorf   RWTH Aachen University, Germany
Jiwei Huang   China University of Petroleum, China
Kai Lei   Peking University, China
Kenneth Fletcher   University of Massachusetts Boston, USA
Laizhong Cui   Shenzhen University, China
Mario Larangeira   IOHK and Tokyo Institute of Technology, Japan
Pengcheng Zhang   Hohai University, China
Qianhong Wu   Beihang University, China
Qinghua Lu   CSIRO, Australia
Shangguang Wang   Beijing University of Posts and Telecommunications,
                                China
Shizhan Chen   Tianjin University, China
Shuiguang Deng   Zhejiang University, China

Sude Qing	China Academy of Information and Communication Technology, China
Tao Xiang	Chongqing University, China
Ting Chen	University of Electronic Science and Technology of China (UESTC), China
Tsuyoshi Ide	IBM, USA
Wei Luo	Zhejiang University, China
Wei Song	Nanjing University of Science and Technology, China
Weifeng Pan	Zhejiang Gongshang University, China
Xiaodong Fu	Kunming University of Science and Technology, China
Xiaoliang Fan	Xiamen University, China
Yucong Duan	Hainan University, China
Yutao Ma	Wuhan University, China
Zhihui Lu	Fudan University, China
Quanqing Xu	Alibaba, China
Yiming Zhang	National University of Defense Technology, China

Contents

Blockchain and Internet of Things

Blockchain and Mobile Edge Computing

Blockchain and Smart Contracts

Trustworthy System Development

Theories and Algorithms for Blockchain

Modeling and Verification of the Nervos CKB Block Synchronization Protocol in UPPAAL

Qi Zhang, Yuteng Lu, and Meng Sun[(✉)]

School of Mathematical Sciences, Peking University, Beijing 100871, China
{zhang.qi,luyuteng,sunm}@pku.edu.cn

Abstract. The Nervos CKB (Common Knowledge Base) is a public permission-less blockchain designed for a peer-to-peer crypto- economy network. The CKB block synchronization protocol is an important part of the Nervos CKB, which provides a set of rules that participating nodes must obey while synchronizing their blocks. The protocol contains three stages: Connecting Header, Downloading Block and Accepting Block. In this paper, we develop the formal model of the CKB block synchronization protocol and verify some important properties of the protocol using the UPPAAL model checker. Based on the formal model, the reliability of CKB can be guaranteed.

Keywords: CKB · Block synchronization protocol · Modeling · Verification · UPPAAL

1 Introduction

The notion of *blockchain* was first proposed by Satoshi Nakamoto in 2008 to support the Bitcoin cryptocurrency [14], which has numerous benefits such as decentralization, persistency and anonymity. Blockchain provides a continuously growing ledger of transactions which is represented as a chained list of blocks, distributed and maintained over a peer-to-peer network [16]. In the past decade, blockchain has become a popular technology and has been applied in many scenarios due to its ability to create, transfer and own assets in a peer-to-peer crypto-economy network. Bitcoin is the first public permission-less blockchain. Later Ethereum [11] was proposed, which extends the application range of block-chain and allows developers to write smart contracts and create all kinds of decentralized applications.

Bitcoin and Ethereum have shown an exciting possibility for building a future crypto-economy. However, both of them have suffered from the scalability problem. To alleviate this problem, the Nervos team proposed Common Knowledge Base (CKB) [15], which is designed for long-term sustainability, uses a decentralized and secure layer, and provides common knowledge for the peer-to-peer network. CKB consists of a Proof-of-Work based consensus, a RISC-V instruction set based virtual machine, a state model based on cells, a state-oriented

Z. Zheng et al. (Eds.): BlockSys 2020, CCIS 1267, pp. 3–17, 2020.
https://doi.org/10.1007/978-981-15-9213-3_1

economic model, and a peer-to-peer network. A family of important protocols are used in CKB together to build the secure and optimal crypto-economy system, such as the block synchronization protocol, CKB consensus protocol, and so on.

Because CKB is the decentralized trust root of the secure and optimal crypto-economy system, ensuring the correctness of its protocols has been of vital importance. In fact, many protocols are error-prone, and vulnerabilities have been discovered in some protocols that have been considered to be correct for many years [5]. To ensure the security and correctness of CKB protocols, manually checking and testing are not enough as people usually cannot cover all possible situations of protocols. Model checking [8] is a typical formal verification technique, which aims to guarantee the correctness of systems automatically. Meanwhile, model checking approach also makes it easier to find and fix bugs in the design process, which can avoid detours for protocol users and designers. There are some literature for analysis and verification of Blockchains. For example, [7] provides Bitcoin protocol's formal model and verifies the protocol using UPPAAL [4, 9]. A novel formal modeling method to verify properties of Ethereum smart contracts is proposed in [1], where a concrete smart contract example is analyzed using the statistical model checking approach.

In this paper, we propose the formal model of CKB block synchronization protocol and verify its important properties using the UPPAAL model checker, which has been applied successfully in many industrial case studies [2,7,12]. To our knowledge, this is the first work to model and verify a CKB protocol with model checking techniques. Based on the formal model of the CKB block synchronization protocol, we can verify the protocol's important properties with mathematical rigor and make probabilistic analysis for double-spending attacks. The model can also be used in future to further analyze other properties that are useful for CKB developers.

The rest of this paper is organized as follows: The Nervos CKB and block synchronization protocol are briefly described in Sect. 2. Section 3 presents the formal model of the block synchronization protocol. Then the verification of properties in UPPAAL is provided in Sect. 4. Some related works are provided in Sect. 5. Finally, Sect. 6 concludes the paper and discusses possible future works.

2   A Primer on CKB and Block Synchronization Protocol

This section gives a brief introduction on Nervos CKB and the block synchronization protocol.

Nervos CKB is a layer 1 blockchain, designed as a public permission-less blockchain for a layered crypto-economy network. The crypto-economy network is served by the CKB and all layer 2 protocols together. The states are stored and defined in layer 1, and layer 2 is the generation layer processing most transactions and generating new states. Different methods can be used for state generation, such as local generators on the client, traditional web services, state channels,

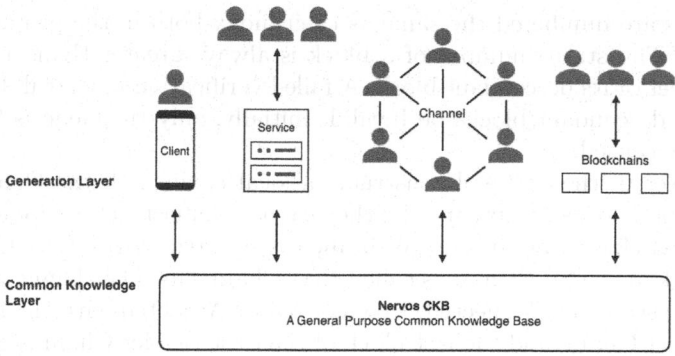

Fig. 1. The CKB layered architecture

and generation chains. The layered architecture, as shown in Fig. 1, separates state and computation, providing each layer more flexibility and scalability. For example, blockchains on layer 2 may use different consensus algorithms. CKB is the lowest layer with the broadest consensus and provides the most secure consensus in the network. Applications can choose the proper generation methods based on their particular needs. CKB provides common knowledge custody for the crypto-economy network and its design target focuses on states. The significance of common knowledge is that it refers to states verified by global consensus. Crypto-assets are examples of common knowledge. CKB can generate trust and extend this trust to layer 2, making the whole crypto-economy network trusted. Furthermore, CKB can also provide the most secure consensus in the Nervos network.

The block synchronization protocol is one of the most important protocols in Nervos CKB. The protocol describes how blocks are synchronized between peers, and commits to make all the peers agree with the consensus that the Best Chain is the chain with the most PoW and starting with a common genesis block. As the cost of downloading and verifying the whole chain is huge, the CKB block synchronization protocol is divided into three parts: *connecting header*, *downloading block* and *accepting block*. These three parts are executed one by one and a chain can enter the next stage only if it passes the current stage. A block has five status according to the three execution stages:

1. *Unknown*: we know nothing about a new block before Connecting Header.
2. *Invalid*: once a block's verification fails during any of the above steps, this block as well as its descendant blocks should be marked as Invalid.
3. *Connected*: the header of a block is successfully achieved in stage Connecting Header, and none of its ancestor blocks are in a status of Unknown or Invalid.
4. *Downloaded*: the content of a block is successfully obtained in stage Downloading Block, and none of its ancestor blocks are in the status Unknown or Invalid.
5. *Accepted*: the rest of the block verification is done and the block is accepted by a peer.

Those status are numbered the same as their index both in the protocol and in our models. The status number of a block is always greater than or equals to status number of its descendant block. A failed verification block will lead to the status of its descendant blocks be Invalid. Initially, only the Genesis block is in the status Accepted.

Every peer in the protocol constructs a local chain with the Genesis block being the root. Blocks are discarded if they cannot connect to the root eventually. In every local chain, the most PoW branch is referred to the Best Chain, and the last block of the Best Chain is called Best Chain Tip. The chain composed of blocks in the status of Connected, Downloaded or Accepted with the most PoW is Best Header Chain, and the last block of the Best Header Chain is called Best Header Chain Tip. Next, we introduce the three steps of block synchronization process and the new block announcement part of the protocol.

Connecting Header. Only the block header is synchronized in this stage, and it is expected that not only the topological structure of the global blockchain can be obtained with the minimum cost, but also the possibility of maximum evil is ruled out. When Alice connects to Bob, Alice asks Bob to send all the block headers that are in Bob's Best Chain but not in Alice's Best Header Chain. Then those blocks are verified. After that, we could determine whether the status of these blocks is Connected or Invalid. First, Bob can get the latest common block between these two chains according to his own Best Chain and the last common block observed from Alice. Such block can always be found because the Genesis block is identical. Bob is supposed to send all block headers from the last common block to Alice. If there are too many blocks to be sent, pagination is required. After a round of Connecting Headers, peers should keep up-to-date using new block notification. The status tree of a local blockchain is explored and extended in the Connecting Header stage.

Downloading Block. After the Connecting Header stage, a status tree ending with one or more Connected blocks can be obtained. Then the protocol schedules synchronization to avoid useless work. Only when the local Best Chain is shorter than the Best Chain of the observed peer, blocks could be downloaded. The Connected chain with more PoW should be processed first. When a branch is verified to be Invalid, or the download process times out, the branch should be switched to another lower PoW branch.

Accepting Block. If the Best Chain Tip's cumulative work is less than those chains', it is supposed to perform the complete validation in the chain context. If there are multiple chains satisfied, the protocol performs the chain with the most work first. Once the verification result of a block fails, both the block itself and the descendant blocks in its Downloaded chain are considered as Invalid.

New Block Announcement. When the local Best Chain Tip is updated, the peer should push an announcement to other peers. The best header with most cumulative work sent to each peer should be recorded to avoid sending duplicate blocks.

3   The Formal Model of the Block Synchronization Protocol

In this section, we propose a formal model of the CKB block synchronize protocol based on the UPPAAL model checker. The model consists of two types of automata: *blockmaker* and *peer*. A blockmaker creates blocks and broadcasts them to all peers. Meanwhile, it can process the request of the headers or whole block content from other peers. A peer conducts the three-stages synchronizing process. Based on the process, the behavior of this protocol is accurately characterized.

3.1   The Global Declaration

We first introduce the global declaration of the formal model. In the model, two global integer constants are set: PEER_NUM and MAX_BLOCK. PEER_NUM is the number of peers which participate in the block synchronization process. MAX_BLOCK is the maximum number of blocks that blockmaker could create. The concrete value of both constants are adjustable according to experimental needs.

Declaration 1. Block Datatype in UPPAAL

---

const int PEER_NUM = 3;
const int MAX_BLOCK = 100;
typedef int [1,5] STATUS;
typedef struct{
    int [0, MAX_BLOCK-1] id;
    int [0, MAX_BLOCK-1] pre;
    int [0, MAX_BLOCK-1] len;
    STATUS status;
}Block;
Block GENESIS;

Declaration 1 shows the structure of a block. Each block consists of four variables: id, pre, len and status. id is a unique integer indicating its identification. pre is the id of father block that this block follows, len records the length of the chain ended by the block. Initial status of a block is set to 5 (i.e. Accept status) by its creator. GENESIS, which is a global declaration, is an instance of this data type, as shown in Declaration 1. The values 1, 0, 1 and 5 are assigned to the four variables of GENESIS. So its own identification and its parent block's identification are 1 and 0, respectively. Its len equals to 1 because the Genesis block is the first block in the chain. According to the protocol, the Genesis block is born acknowledged by all peers, so its status equals to 5 (Accepted Status).

In the protocol, every peer maintains a local blockchain according to the blocks they received, so we set up a local blockchain for each peer in the model.

Each local blockchain is made up of blocks mentioned above. We adopt the following data structure as shown in Declaration 2 to record a blockchain.

Declaration 2. Blockchain Datatype in UPPAAL

```
typedef struct{
    Block chain[MAX_BLOCK];
    Block BC_tip;
    Block BHC_tip;
    int [0, MAX_BLOCK-1] Other_BC_tip[PEER_NUM+1];
    int [0, MAX_BLOCK-1] Best_Send_Header[PEER_NUM+1];
}BLOCKCHAIN;
BLOCKCHAIN blockchain[PEER_NUM+1];
```

A blockchain consists of five parts: a `chain`, a Best Chain Tip named `BC_tip`, a Best Header Chain Tip named `BHC_tip`, `Other_BC_tip` and `Best_Send_Header`. `Other_BC_tip` represents the Best Chain Tip of the other peers observed by this peer, and `Best_Send_Header` denotes the Best Chain Tip sent to the other peers by this peer. These variables are kept updated during each round of synchronization.

3.2   The Peer Automaton

The peer automaton, as shown in Fig. 2, starts from the location *idle*, taking a transition *init_chain()* to location *wait*. This transition makes the peer catch the Genesis block and get ready to execute the block synchronize process to build its own local blockchain. This transition is set to make sure that the Genesis blocks of the nodes participating in synchronization must be the same, and all the blocks must form a tree rooted by the Genesis block. A peer executes the three-stages synchronizing process periodically and perpetually. Each stage is strictly described in our model according to the three-stages synchronization process in the protocol. The process is triggered either spontaneously or stimulated by the new block announcement from a blockmaker.

In the *Connecting Header* stage, a peer requests block headers within the largest possible range to locally build a global graph of the whole blockchain with high credibility. This stage starts from location *wait* and transits to the location *connect* either by spontaneously taking a transition *gettid()* or stimulated by the signal *sendhead?* within a time interval [3,5] before taking a transition *gettid()*.

In *gettid()*, an adjacent peer is selected, and the variable *flag* is initially set to *true* and change to *false* when every peer has already been selected in this stage. When *flag* is *true*, the transition *getsendhead()* should be conducted and the automaton transit to location *sample*. In the protocol, the last common block should be found first. Then there are three situations waiting for acceptance. These processes are implemented in *getsendhead()*. In the*sample* location, two choices can be made. If there are still some blocks left to be sent (*clen* > 0 in

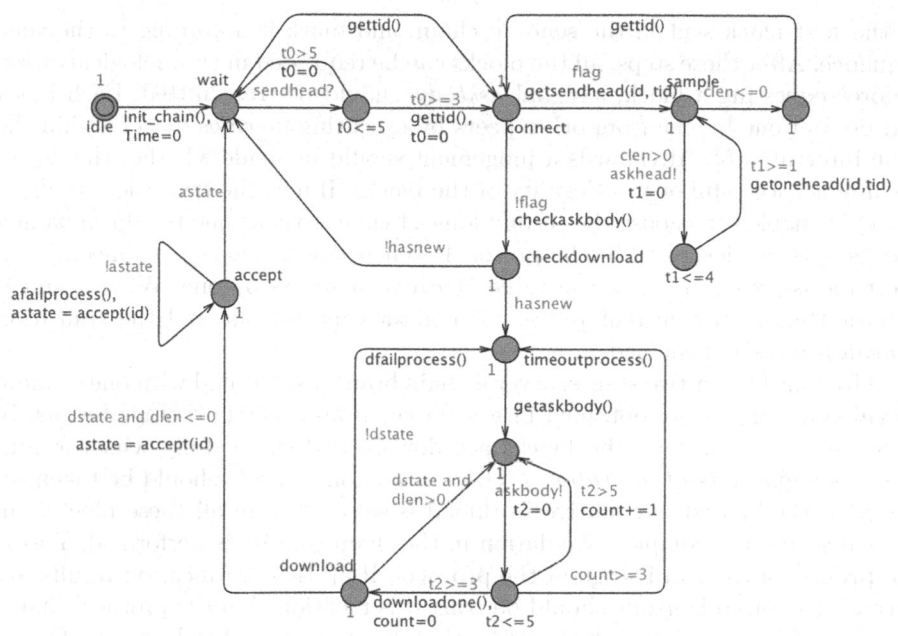

Fig. 2. The Peer Automaton

Fig. 2), the transition *getonehead()* should be executed. If there are too many blocks to be sent, the paging process needs to be done. Thus, the transition *getonehead()* is set to analogize the paging process. However, for simplicity, we set the capacity of each page to one block. If all blocks have been received (*clen* <= 0 in Fig. 2), another peer that have not been selected ever is selected and the automaton transit back to the location *connect*. Then a new round of Connecting Header begins.

When *flag* turns to *false*, the first stage is ended and the transition *check-askbody()* is enabled. In this transition, the longest chain branch is found first according to the Best Chain Tip of other chain observed in the connecting header stage. Then the model will judge whether there are new blocks to be synchronized and set the value of the variable *hasnew*. It is mentioned in the protocol that an effective optimization can be made when download blocks. Specifically, only when the cumulative workload of other peers Best Chain is greater than the current local Best Chain. This is reflected in the model by using*checkaskbody()* to check and *hasnew* variables to control. When *hasnew* is *false*, there is no need to move on the next Downloading block stage. So we take a transition from *checkdownload* to *wait*.

The second stage begins when *hasnew* is *true*. In the second stage, a peer asks for the whole content of blocks which exists on the longest chain. When downloading a branch, the earlier block should be downloaded first due to block dependencies. Therefore, *getaskbody()* is executed to trace from the latest block to the first block sent in the sending chain, and mark it according to the time sequence. After these steps, all the blocks can be requested in chronological order. Before requesting a block, a signal *askbody!* should be transmitted. Each block can be sent one by one from other peers by executing *downloadone*() within the time interval $[3,5]$. Afterwards a judgement should be made whether the downloading is successful or not (legality of the block). If not, the transition *dfailprocess*() is enabled to choose the second longest chain to continue the downloading process just as described in the protocol. When *downloadone*() is timeout, i.e., the time is greater than 5, the value of *count* increases by one. When *count* is greater than 3, the current process is regarded as timeout and the transition *timeoutprocess*() is enabled.

After the former two stages, several chain branches that end with one or more downloaded blocks are obtained in a local chain and the third stage begins. In location *download*, if all the blocks are downloaded successfully which formulated as a guard *dstate and dlen* $<= 0$, a transition *accept*() should be taken. In *accept*(), the highest cumulative workload is selected from all these blockchain branches, and the complete validation in the chain context is performed. This is the process of the third stage in the protocol. If all their verification results are correct, the variable *astate* should be *true*. It is mentioned in the protocol that if there is a failure during a block verification, the remaining blocks on the Downloaded Chain are all in the Invalid state and do not need to be downloaded. At this time, if the current Best Chain Tip is lower than the previous tip, the workload of the Best Chain should rollback. If there are other Downloaded Chain with higher workload, this branch should be chosen to execute Downloading block process. This process is accurately described in the transition *afailprocess*(). If any block is illegal, *astate* should change to *false* and the transition *afailprocess*() is enabled to discard the received block. Then the second longest chain would be selected to carry out the connect stage. When there are no new blocks or the accept blocks are all legal, the guard *astate* is satisfied and the automaton transits back to the state *wait* to get ready for a new synchronizing process.

3.3 The Blockmaker Automaton

Blockmakers can be formally modeled by the automaton as shown in Fig. 3. It has three functions:

- create new blocks and broadcast to other peers,
- receive and process *askhead?* signals,
- receive and process *askbody?* signals.

Both *askhead* and *askbody* are broadcasting channels. Starting from the location *start*, each blockmaker could monitor signals *askhead?* and *askbody?*. The corresponding signals *askhead!* and *askbody!* are elicited by a peer to ask for the head and body of a block respectively.

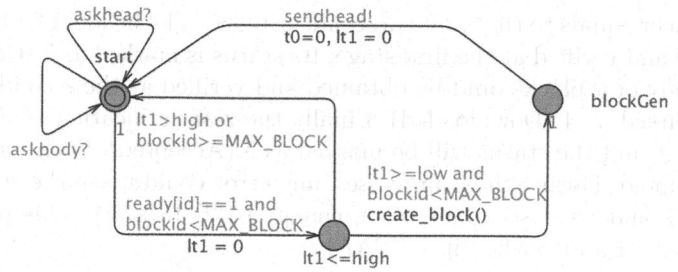

Fig. 3. The Blockmaker Automaton

Each blockmaker can create new blocks within the range of 2 to *MAX_BLOCK* (1 for genesis block). For the sake of representing different computing power, each blockmaker generates blocks in different rate, which is controlled by the parameter *low*. Every blockmaker can create block in the time interval $[low, low + 1]$, so the period of generating blocks can be approximately formulated as $low + 1$. When the transition *create_block()* is enabled and the automaton transits to the location *blockGen*, a block is successfully created, then the blockmaker could send out a signal *sendhead!* to inform other peers to synchronize this new block.

4 Verification in UPPAAL

In this section we conduct substantial experiments to ensure the correctness and consistency of the protocol model, assuming that each peer is honest. All the results suggest the fact that the model, if not attacked, would arrive at a consensus state. Even when attacked, they are resistant to those attacks on certain conditions. We performed some experiments to simulate how the model behave in real situations. In our experiments, we set three peers, three blockmakers and checked the properties for different number of blocks in the system. These experiments are conducted in two situations: 1) every peer follows the protocol (see Sect. 4.1); 2) one of the peers is malicious (see Sect. 4.2).

4.1 Correctness and Consistency Analysis Without Maliciousness

Above all, the CKB block synchronization process will never stop, because every peer should monitor whether new blocks are generated for synchronization at any time. This property is expressed in UPPAAL as P1, which means that the model will never deadlock. We verify the property in UPPAAL and the result shows that the model satisfy P1.

$$A[]\ not\ deadlock \tag{(P1)}$$

We have mentioned that every block has a status number, i.e., *status* according to the CKB block synchronization protocol. The status number of a block is greater than or equals to that of its descendent block. The header of a block must be obtained and verified at the first stage. Its status is marked as 3 (Connected), then the body of a block could be obtained and verified at the second stage. Its status is marked as 4 (Downloaded). Finally the rest verification could be done at third stage and the status will be marked as 5 (Accepted). Such order should not be disrupted. During those processes, any error could make the status value of this block and its descendant block change to 2 (Invalid). This property is formalized as P2 and verified in UPPAAL.

$$A[] forall(j : int[1, PEER\_NUM]) forall(i : int[2, MAX\_BLOCK - 1])$$

$$blockchain[j].chain[i].status <=$$

$$blockchain[j].chain[blockchain[j].chain[i].pre].status \qquad ((P2))$$

When there are no attacks, according to the protocol, all peers should maintain a stable local blockchain after certain rounds, and those local blockchains all together can restore a global blockchain. When the system finally reaches a stable state, the Best Chain of every local blockchain should be the same, i.e., every peer reaches a consensus. But there is an exception. A blockchain has many legal forks and every honest peer should work on the longest forks. However, it is still possible that two or more Best Chains with equal length exist at the same time. This phenomenon is caused by the unavoidable block transmission delay. Hence, we first estimate the probability that every local blockchain can reach a same length after a certain time units described as P3. The verification in UPPAAL shows that this property is accepted with a strong probability of [0.95,1] with 95% level of significance in 738 runs. It means that every local blockchain can achieve a consensus after a certain round of synchronization.

$$Pr(<> [1500, 2000](forall(i : int[1, PEER\_NUM - 1])$$

$$(blockchain[i].BC\_tip.len == blockchain[i + 1].BC\_tip.len))) \qquad ((P3))$$

Furthermore, the property P4 estimates the probability that every local blockchain has the same Best Chain after a certain time units. Compared with property P3 which explores the length consensus, the correctness of P4 ensures the chain consensus. Therefore, we call property P4 the strict consensus state. This property is accepted with the probability of [0.94729, 1] with 95% level of significance in 738 runs. It is worth noting that the result is slightly less than [0.95, 1] as the result of P3. Evidently, this state could not be achieved within only 100 blocks in this experiment. When the number of blocks is increased to 200, the result changes to [0.95, 1].

$$Pr(<> [1500, 2000](forall(i : int[1, PEER\_NUM - 1])$$

$$blockchain[i].BC\_tip.id == blockchain[i + 1].BC\_tip.id)) \qquad ((P4))$$

Table 1. Verification results of property P3 and P4 based on the block number.

Block number	Time bound	P3 verification results	P4 verification results
10	100–500	0.95,1	0.84–0.94
50	500–1000	0.95,1	0.92–1
100	1000–1500	0.95,1	0.947,1
150	1500–2000	0.95,1	0.95,1
200	2000–2500	0.95,1	0.95,1

Table 1 shows the experiment results for verification of P3 and P4 with different number of blocks. These experiments are firmly devised to make sure that these blocks can reach a steady state in their corresponding provided time bound. The experiments indicate that a consensus state would be reached for any number of blocks. In the previous experimental settings (200 blocks), the following two statements are confirmed to be hold by the UPPAAL model checker.

$$A <> Time > 2000 \, imply \, (forall(i : int[1, PEER\_NUM - 1])$$

$$(blockchain[i].BC\_tip.len == blockchain[i + 1].BC\_tip.len)) \qquad ((P5))$$

$$A <> Time > 2000 \, imply \, (forall(i : int[1, PEER\_NUM - 1])$$

$$(blockchain[i].BC\_tip.id == blockchain[i + 1].BC\_tip.id)) \qquad ((P6))$$

Hence the verification results confirm that our model is consistent with the CKB block synchronize protocol.

4.2 Consistency and Robustness Analysis with Maliciousness

In reality, malicious attacks are always inevitable. Thus, we add attacks to our model. As mentioned previously, a block goes through the three-stages synchronization process until it is accepted, and each stage tries to preclude a type of attacks. In the first stage, the Connecting Header step tries to validate PoW and the correctness of the block header format. The error discovered in this step is named as *header error*. In the second stage, the matching of transaction lists and block header is verified. The corresponding error is named as *body error*. In the third stage, the rest verification should be completed, including all rules that depend on historical transactions. The corresponding error is named as *UTXO error* because it involves UTXO (unspent transaction outputs) indexes.

The header error normally means one malicious peer has created a block whose PoW is calculated incorrectly or header format is wrong. This error could be checked out by other peers that do not acknowledge the malicious block. Under the circumstances, we attempt to explore the probability that the system reaches a consensus. By running property P3 we get the result [0.46626, 0.56626] with confidence 0.95 in 738 runs. By running property P4 we get the result [0.448645, 0.548645] with confidence 0.95 in 738 runs. When the malicious block does not exist in the Best Chain, it becomes an orphan block so its effect is neglected. Thus the probability of this situation is not 0. When we preclude the malicious peer, the property is modified as follows:

$$Pr(<> [2000, 2500](exists(j : int[1, PEER\_NUM]) \, !malicious[j] \, and$$
$$forall(i : int[1, PEER\_NUM])$$

$$(malicious[i] \, or \, blockchain[i].BC\_tip.id == blockchain[j].BC\_tip.id))) \quad ((P7))$$

The verification result turns to [0.95, 1] with confidence 0.95 in 738 runs. Except for the malicious peer, other honest peers can correctly and easily find out the error caused by the malicious peer, which meets our expectation.

The body error regularly consists of the following situations: transaction id is repeated, transaction list is empty, inputs and outputs are blank simultaneously, the generation transaction is not unique or the first, etc. We make an analogy for this situation and explore the probability that the system reach a consensus. By running property P3 we got the result [0.49336, 0.59336] with confidence 0.95 in 738 runs. By running property P4 we got the result [0.489295, 0.589295] with confidence 0.95 in 738 runs. By running property P7, the result is [0.95, 1] with confidence 0.95 in 738 runs. This result meets our expectation that the cause of body error is similar to that of the header error. Those errors are more associated with carelessness rather than maliciousness. In addition to the peer who makes the mistake, other peers can recognize this error easily and maintain the consistency of the chain.

The UTXO is involved with the notorious Double Spending attack. In the attack, the attacker deliberately creates two or more transactions of which all the inputs are from the same UTXO id. In other words, the attacker attempts to spend the same asset twice or more in different transactions. When the first expense is acknowledged by the blockchain, one can purchase an equivalent product successfully, later he is able to take back this expense by making another longer chain than the current Best Chain. Such attacks make the entire system untrustworthy. In fact it is impossible to prevent double spending totally. The payee is suggested to confirm the payment after 6 confirmation blocks in the official method, because the probability of double spending is very low at this time.

The impact of this attack is explored. We first investigate the probability of successful attacks. We choose peer 1 as the malicious peer, and the two blocks it creates in succession are attack blocks, denoted by transactions 1 and 2 respectively. Transaction 1 exists in the Best Chain. Once the branch where transaction 2 exists is longer than the current Best Chain, it becomes the new Best Chain. By this time, transaction 1 is no longer valid and transaction 2 is acknowledged. Thus, the Double Spending occurs. We have checked the consistency on the experiment setting. By running property P3 we get the result $[0.813144, 0.913144]$ with confidence 0.95 in 738 runs. By running property P4 we get the result $[0.775203, 0.875203]$ with confidence 0.95 in 738 runs. Then we check the probability of the Double Spending attack as described in property P8 and property P9. Here $ds1$ represents the successful confirmation of transaction 1 and $ds2$ represents the successful confirmation of transaction 2. The property P8 specifies that $ds1$ and $ds2$ hold simultaneously, and the property P9 describes the probability that $ds2$ holds under the condition that $ds1$ holds. By running the property P8 the result is $[0, 0.05]$ with confidence 0.95. By running the property P9 the result is $[0.536721, 0.636721]$ with confidence 0.95 in 738 runs.

$$Pr(<> [2000, 2500](ds1 \, and \, ds2)) \qquad ((P8))$$

$$Pr(<> [2000, 2500](ds1 \, imply \, ds2)) \qquad ((P9))$$

This results implies the fact that when the computing power is evenly distributed, the possibility that transaction 2 Double Spending attack succeeds is more than 50%.

5   Related Works

Even though there is no work on verification of CKB, there exists some results on verification of blockchain and smart contracts. Model checking approaches have been successfully applied in both hardware and software verification, and also adopted in verification of blockchain models. A probabilistic model for smart contract is studied in [6] and the PRISM model checker is used to verify its properties. The UPPAAL model for the Bitcoin Protocol is proposed in [7], where the probability of success of double spending attacks based on the formal model is also investigated. In [2], timed automata is used to provide a framework for modeling the Bitcoin contracts. A runtime verification approach has been proposed in [10], in which finite state machine is used to model contracts. In [3], smart contracts are modeled in Promela and the SPIN model checker is adopted to verify whether the logic of a contract is correct. The interface automata model of computation is used in [13] as a semantic domain to formalize smart contracts for detecting violations of the contract agreements. In [1], the BIP framework is used to model blockchain behavior and statistical model checking is used to analyze the results.

6   Conclusion and Future Work

In this paper we formally model the CKB block synchronization protocol in the UPPAAL model checker, and verify a family of important properties related to the correctness and consistency of the protocol for different cases with or without maliciousness. Potential malicious attacks are simulated in the experiments, and their impacts are investigated.

The CKB block synchronization protocol also contains some parallel algorithm optimization to make full use of bandwidth and computation resource. We have only modeled and verified the simplified version in this paper. In the future, we hope to make it possible to model and verify the optimized protocol to provide enhanced assurance for protocol trustworthy. In addition, we are also planning to use the model checking approach to verify other protocols in CKB, such as the transaction filter protocol and the CKB consensus protocol.

Acknowledgments. This work was partially supported by the Guangdong Science and Technology Department (Grant no. 2018B010107004) and the National Natural Science Foundation of China under grant no. 61772038 and 61532019. The authors are grateful to the members of Cryptape and the Nervos team for their helpful discussions.

References

1. Abdellatif, T., Brousmiche, K.-L.: Formal verification of smart contracts based on users and blockchain behaviors models. In: 2018 9th IFIP International Conference on New Technologies, Mobility and Security (NTMS), pp. 1–5. IEEE (2018)
2. Andrychowicz, M., Dziembowski, S., Malinowski, D., Mazurek, Ł.: Modeling Bitcoin contracts by timed automata. In: Legay, A., Bozga, M. (eds.) FORMATS 2014. LNCS, vol. 8711, pp. 7–22. Springer, Cham (2014). https://doi.org/10.1007/978-3-319-10512-3_2
3. Bai, X., Cheng, Z., Duan, Z., Hu, K.: Formal modeling and verification of smart contracts. In: Proceedings of ICSCA 2018, pp. 322–326. ACM (2018)
4. Behrmann, G., David, A., Larsen, K.G.: A Tutorial on UPPAAL. In: Bernardo, M., Corradini, F. (eds.) SFM-RT 2004. LNCS, vol. 3185, pp. 200–236. Springer, Heidelberg (2004). https://doi.org/10.1007/978-3-540-30080-9_7
5. Bhargavan, K., Blanchet, B., Kobeissi, N.: Verified models and reference implementations for the TLS 1.3 standard candidate. In: 2017 IEEE Symposium on Security and Privacy, pp. 483–502. IEEE (2017)
6. Bigi, G., Bracciali, A., Meacci, G., Tuosto, E.: Validation of decentralised smart contracts through game theory and formal methods. In: Bodei, C., Ferrari, G.-L., Priami, C. (eds.) Programming Languages with Applications to Biology and Security. LNCS, vol. 9465, pp. 142–161. Springer, Cham (2015). https://doi.org/10.1007/978-3-319-25527-9_11
7. Chaudhary, K., Fehnker, A., van de Pol, J., Stoelinga, M.: Modeling and verification of the bitcoin protocol. In: Proceedings of MARS 2015, EPTCS, pp. 46–60. Open Publishing Association, November 2015
8. Marques-Silva, J., Malik, S.: Propositional SAT solving. Handbook of Model Checking, pp. 247–275. Springer, Cham (2018). https://doi.org/10.1007/978-3-319-10575-8_9
9. David, A., Larsen, K.G., Legay, A., Mikuăionis, M., Poulsen, D.B.: Uppaal SMC tutorial. Int. J. Softw. Tools Technol. Transfer **17**(4), 397–415 (2015)
10. Ellul, J., Pace, G.J.: Runtime verification of ethereum smart contracts. In: Proceedings of EDCC 2018, pp. 158–163. IEEE Computer Society (2018)
11. Ethereum. https://github.com/ethereum. Accessed 2 May 2020

12. Lu, Y., Sun, M.: Modeling and verification of IEEE 802.11i security protocol in UPPAAL for internet of things. Int. J. Softw. Eng. Knowl. Eng. **28**(11–12), 1619–1636 (2018)
13. Madl, G., Bathen, L.A.D., Flores, G.H., Jadav, D.: Formal verification of smart contracts using interface automata. In: Proceedings of Blockchain 2019, pp. 556–563. IEEE (2019)
14. Nakamoto, S.: Bitcoin: a peer-to-peer electronic cash system (2008). https://bitcoin.org/bitcoin.pdf
15. Nervos CKB: A Common Knowledge Base for Crypto-Economy. https://github.com/nervosnetwork/rfcs/blob/master/rfcs/0002-ckb/0002-ckb.md
16. Zheng, Z., Xie, S., Dai, H., Chen, X., Wang, H.: Blockchain challenges and opportunities: a survey. Int. J. Web Grid Serv. **14**(4), 352–375 (2018)

A Blockchain Consensus Mechanism for Marine Data Management System

Ziqi Fang[1], Zhiqiang Wei[1,2], Xiaodong Wang[1], and Weiwei Xie[1,2(✉)]

[1] Department of Computer Science and Technology, Ocean University of China,
Qingdao 266100, China
`fangziqi@stu.ouc.edu.cn`,{`weizhiqiang,wangxiaodong`}`@ouc.edu.cn`,
`wwxie@qnlm.ac`
[2] Qingdao National Laboratory for Marine Science and Technology,
Qingdao 266237, China

Abstract. As the underlying technology of Bitcoin, blockchain has become increasingly mature in financial, medical, logistics and other commercial fields, and has great application potential in the marine field. Its "decentralized" feature can maintain data security and reliability through decentralized methods. Marine data management system is one of the specific application scenarios that blockchain technology is used to protect marine network data information. The consensus algorithm and decentralized idea possessed by the blockchain technology can effectively guarantee the information collaboration of the marine network, and help to improve the collaboration efficiency among multiple parties involved in the safe sharing of marine data. In this paper, according to the analysis of the construction demands of the marine data management system, based on the blockchain technology, a distributed cross-chain transaction, called the global blockchain, is structured, which integrates the marine data collaborative heterogeneous blockchain network. On this basis, aimed at the problems of the existing PBFT consensus algorithm, such as poor dynamic addition and deletion of nodes, and large communication overhead, etc., a global consensus algorithm adapted to the marine data global blockchain network is designed for optimization of the checkpoint mechanism and view change mechanism as well as reduction of the amount of transmitted information in these two processes of the system. The simulation results show that the algorithm can effectively guarantee the consensus efficiency and the trustworthiness of the proxy nodes, realize the efficient sharing of marine data, and support the design and implementation of the blockchain-based marine data management system.

Keywords: Blockchain · Marine data · Consensus mechanism · PBFT · Election mechanism

1 Introduction

Marine science is rapidly entering the digital age. The expansion of the scope and scale of ocean observations, the emergence of automated sampling and smart

Z. Zheng et al. (Eds.): BlockSys 2020, CCIS 1267, pp. 18–30, 2020.
https://doi.org/10.1007/978-981-15-9213-3_2

sensors, and the marine stereoscopic observation system consisting of space-based, air-based, land-based, sea-based in the marine field has spawned exponentially increasing high-precision, multi-frequency, and multi-source heterogeneous marine data. Marine data is the accumulation of a large number of data at different times, scales, and regions, reflecting the spatiotemporal processes in ocean phenomena.

Marine data sharing is the foundation of data management in the marine field. The security and integrity of data sharing directly affect the quality and efficiency of the entire marine data management system. Compared with traditional data security, security and privacy protection of marine data are obviously different, showing typical structure-based features, including "one-to-many" structure, "many to one" "structure" and "many to many" structure. The biggest problem faced by traditional marine data management systems is data privacy security and easy manipulation, so data information in the marine field cannot be reliably shared among enterprises, laboratories, scientific research units and even public groups. Characteristics of multi-source and multi-category, spatiotemporal sensitivity, real-time responsiveness, random errors increase the difficulty of marine data in the process of effective management and efficient application services. It presented new challenges to hardware and file system, which require data storage to be more scalable. Adaptive algorithms and models should be selected based on data types and analysis goals to efficiently process marine data.

The marine data management system needs to have financial attributes that encourage sea-related units to break the "data island", as well as security attributes that ensure that data shared by sea-related units cannot be stolen or modified at will. The blockchain technology integrates with multiple technologies such as distributed ledger, consensus protocol, and smart contract to achieve the characteristics of transparency, credibility, reliability and immutability [1]. It provides the possibility of re-architecting the underlying technology foundation for data protection and sharing in the marine field. The novelty of blockchain is a genuine combination of well-known research results taken from distributed computing, cryptography and game theory [2].

In 2009, Satoshi Nakamoto released "Bitcoin: a peer-to-peer electronic cash system", where he expounded the principles and characteristics of blockchain technology as the underlying layer of Bitcoin, making Bitcoin the first practical application using blockchain technology [3]. Blockchain is the key supporting technology of digital cryptocurrency system [4]. In a special sense, blockchain is a decentralized database [5], which are shared and maintained among distrustful nodes [6]. A blockchain transaction can be regarded as a public static data record showing the token value redistribution between sender and receiver [7].

Blockchain technology has been used in cryptocurrencies [8], digital assets [9], education [10], energy [11], medical care [12]and other fields. It is also an innovative application method to promote the efficient management of marine data. Applying blockchain technology to the marine data management system can make the marine data in the blockchain more valuable, and ensure that the marine data information has high credibility and is not easy to be tampered with. Besides, it brings low-cost trust methods, efficient and safe data collaboration methods as well as decentralized and trusted data sharing systems to sea-related units. Then, a new model combining the marine field with blockchain technology is established to mine the "wisdom" hidden in the marine data.

The marine data management system based on blockchain technology has many nodes, involving many sea-related units and a certain scale of marine data management personnel, so a fast and accurate blockchain consensus mechanism is the key to the implementation of the system. If they become participants in the blockchain consensus of the marine data management system, the network maintenance cost of the system will increase greatly, which is not conducive to the effective operation of the marine data management system. Therefore, according to the different roles of various sea-related departments in the marine data management system, selecting the nodes trusted by the users of the marine data management system to generate information blocks is the basic principle based on the consensus of the marine data management system. The blockchain PBFT consensus mechanism reaches consensus through inter-node negotiation to generate blocks, and its characteristics are more compatible with the marine data management system. It is the first choice for the blockchain-based marine data management system consensus mechanism. Based on the above analysis, a global consensus framework applied to the marine big data sharing system is established, combined with the election mechanism to improve the consensus algorithm, ensures the validity of the main node election and the credibility of the system data.

2   Related Work

The consensus mechanism including distributed computing, load balancing, and transaction validation in blockchains [13] is the core support technology for stable operation and orderly derivation of the blockchain, which is used to solve the consistency problem of distributed systems. It guarantees the persistence of the ledger data [2]. The goal of a blockchain consensus protocol is to ensure that all participating nodes agree on a common network transaction history, which is serialized in the form of a blockchain [14]. In recent years, people have continuously researched on consensus algorithms and made certain progress. From incremental modifications of Nakamoto consensus protocol to innovative alternative consensus mechanisms, many consensus protocols have been proposed to improve the performance of the blockchain network itself or to accommodate other specific application needs [15]. At present, the consensus algorithms of blockchain mainly consist of: POW [3], POS [16], DPOS [17], Raft [18], BFT [19], PBFT [20]and Paxos [21]. These consensus algorithms have their own advantages and disadvantages, so they can be applied in different scenarios.

The POW and POS algorithms are mainly used in public chains; the POS consensus mechanism eases the waste of resources caused by the competition of computing power, but still does not get rid of the mining process; In order to further improve the efficiency of consensus and improve the solution to the waste of hash power, Bitshares proposed the delegated POS (DPOS) consensus algorithm [17], where all nodes jointly select a group of witnesses, and these witnesses sequentially generate new blocks.

Although POW, POS and DPOS can tolerate Byzantine nodes, they may cause a bifurcation of the blockchain network and rely on tokens, which are not used in many commercial applications. In this case, the Super Ledger Project launched by the Linux Foundation [22] reached consensus across the entire network by adopting PBFT.

The PBFT algorithm is used to solve the Byzantine problem and is a deterministic consensus algorithm without bifurcation. It does not depend on tokens and is mainly used in alliance chains [23]. In the PBFT algorithm, consensus is reached through negotiation among nodes, which can ensure that the blockchain network can still operate normally when no more than one-third of the nodes have Byzantine errors. Therefore, PBFT can be regarded as an ideal consensus algorithm, and its consensus mechanism for blockchain has high reliability.

In specific applications, the nodes participating in the consensus process have their own characteristics. It is necessary to further study how to select the most suitable verification node for the blockchain network and determine the number of verification nodes. Besides, PBFT cannot work in a dynamic network. When the main node fails, such as a Byzantine node that behaves arbitrarily or network failure [24], the replica nodes would start a process of view change. However, view change is expensive, which should be avoid as much as possible. It takes a lot of communication overhead to reach consensus, and there are some loopholes in system security. Based on the application of blockchain in the marine data sharing model, a consensus framework is designed based on the marine data management system, which introduces the idea of the election mechanism, improves the accuracy of the main node selection, and solves the defect in the consensus mechanism that cannot delete the wrong node in time.

3   Marine Data Sharing Model Based on Blockchain Technology

Aiming at the needs of cross-chain data sharing and transactions between sea-related departments, a cross-chain sharing model of marine data that can achieve independent parallel blockchain interconnection is built, as shown in Fig. 1.

Combined with the diversified characteristics of various sea-related departments, a distributed transaction structure called Global Blockchain is designed. Based on cross-chain technology, the global blockchain is the main chain, and the rest are side chains. According to the degree of decentralization of different types of blockchain architecture, a heterogeneous global blockchain network of marine data sharing and cooperation is constructed, as shown in Fig. 2. The global blockchain network contains many different types of nodes, supporting the access of many independent parallel blockchain networks. In this way, the problem of "data islands" existing between sea-related departments will be effectively resolved.

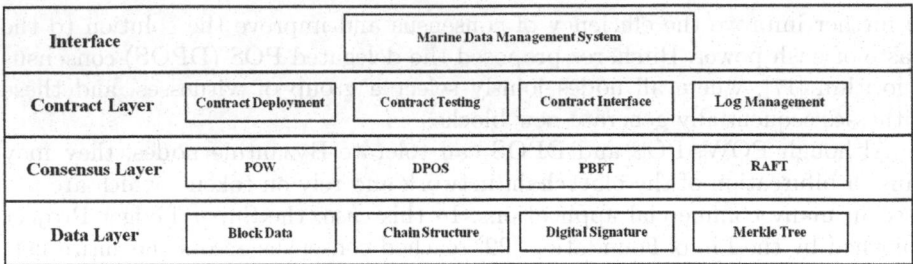

Interface	Marine Data Management System			
Contract Layer	Contract Deployment	Contract Testing	Contract Interface	Log Management
Consensus Layer	POW	DPOS	PBFT	RAFT
Data Layer	Block Data	Chain Structure	Digital Signature	Merkle Tree

Fig. 1. Heterogeneous global blockchain network of marine data cooperation.

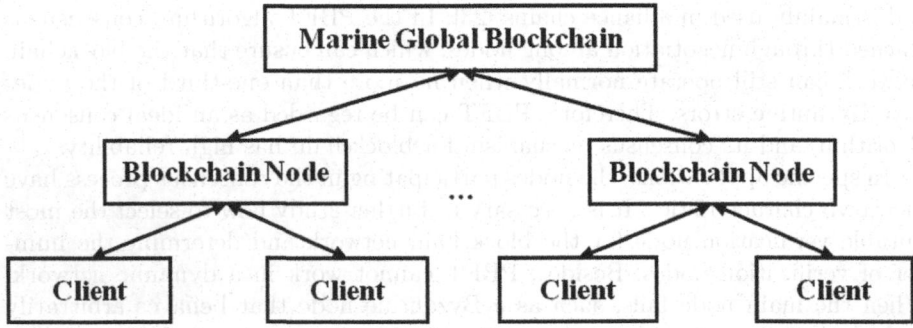

Fig. 2. Heterogeneous global blockchain network of marine data cooperation.

3.1 Design Principles of Marine Global Blockchain Network

(1) Entensibility: Each node of the marine global blockchain network should be loosely coupled, and it is easy to add new nodes and delete eliminated nodes.

(2) Scalability: If a large number of users access a node, it will inevitably bring down the service of the node. So when faced with the request pressure of many users, the nodes of the marine global blockchain network need to quickly achieve horizontal expansion.

(3) Privacy: Data from participants of all parties in the marine global blockchain ecological network, which are various data providers, such as enterprises, laboratories, and scientific research units, can be protected, and participants can selectively open their data according to their own needs.

3.2 Marine Global Blockchain Consensus Mechanism

Based on the marine data sharing model, a global blockchain consensus mechanism is further proposed to ensure the effectiveness of cross-chain transactions between independent parallel blockchains, the versatility of the entire global blockchain and the security of transactions.

The global blockchain is an architecture that can access all parallel chains in the marine data management system, and there will be many accounting nodes in the network. If all the nodes added to the blockchain network participate in the consensus process, the network bandwidth requirements and dynamics are difficult to meet. In this research plan, many different parallel chains can access the global blockchain, and some parallel blockchains may have a higher frequency of cross-chain transaction generation. Therefore, the global blockchain must have a very high transaction processing speed to be able to match the parallel chain with high transaction generation frequency, so as to forward transactions from each parallel chain in time.

In PBFT consensus, information such as blocks is only released by the "main node", and other nodes reach a consensus on the information issued by the main node by broadcasting confirmation messages. Without sacrificing security, the PBFT mechanism can effectively reduce the consensus delay. Therefore, PBFT consensus can guarantee a high transaction processing speed.

Aimed at the problems that the PBFT algorithm cannot support nodes to dynamically join or launch the network and the consensus timeout for low view change efficiency, based on the application of the blockchain in the marine data management system, the defects of the PBFT algorithm are improved to design the marine global blockchain consensus mechanism combined with the idea of voting, and these problems are solved by simplifying the three-phase protocol.

4   Description of PBFT Consensus Algorithm

The PBFT [20] proposed by Miguel Castro and Barbara Liskov in 1999 is composed of a consensus protocol, a view replacement protocol, and a checkpoint protocol. It is an algorithm specifically designed to solve the Byzantine Generals problem and ensure the consistency and correctness of the final decision when there are malicious nodes in the entire network. PBFT is a copying algorithm of state machine copy, that is, modeling the service as a state machine. In a distributed system, the state machine copies at different nodes, so the PBFT algorithm was originally used in the field of distributed systems, but not in the field of blockchain.

All nodes in the PBFT algorithm are divided into two types: main node and vice node. In the PBFT algorithm, a consensus process led by a main node is in a view v. Views are consecutively numbered integers. There are three roles in each view. In addition to the main nodes and vice nodes, there are also clients that send requests. A main node is mainly responsible for receiving the requests from the client, sorting and numbering these requests, and then broadcasting to the vice nodes in the network. A vice node, however, is mainly responsible for receiving messages from the main node and other vice nodes, performing corresponding verification, performing the corresponding operation, and finally sending the consensus result to the client.

Each node has the right to be elected and the right to vote. The probability of each node in the election process is equal. The consensus process of the PBFT algorithm in one view can be roughly divided into the following steps (as shown in Fig. 3):

(1) Request: The client initiates a consensus request to the main node of the consensus network.
(2) Pre-prepare: After receiving the request from the client, the main node broadcasts the request to other vice nodes through the network.
(3) Prepare: All the vice nodes need to perform a preparing and committing process in pairs.
(4) Commit: All copies need to execute the request and return the result to the client.
(5) Reply: Since the maximum number of Byzantines in the network is f, the client needs to wait for f+1 different nodes to return the same result before it thinks that the entire network has reached consensus.

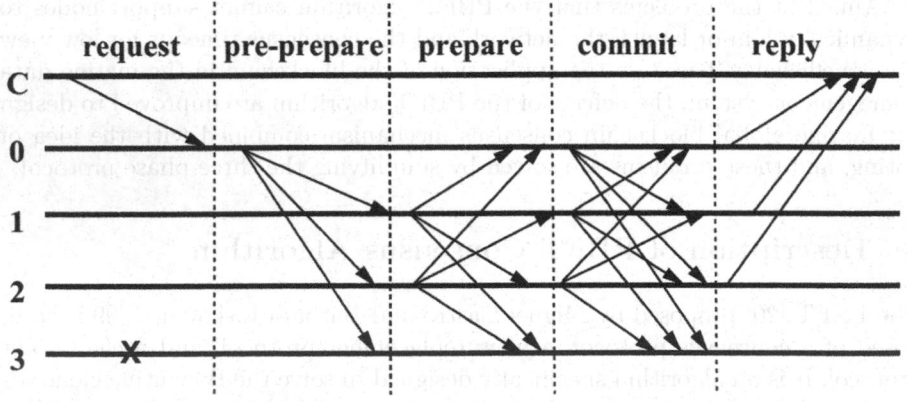

Fig. 3. The operation process of PBFT.

5   Global Consensus Algorithm Based on PBFT

5.1   Ideas of Algorithm Improvement

Considering that consensus nodes in mature systems have no subjective and malicious motivation, there will be no Byzantine nodes with malicious actions. The probability of a Byzantine node appearing in the network transmission is extremely low. Usually, the Byzantine node will only appear when the network is down or the communication is disconnected. There have already been lots of mature means to avoid and solve this problem in distributed networks, so there is no need to perform a three-stage broadcast every time to reach consensus. In order to ensure that high performance can be maintained even when there are many nodes, the traditional PBFT algorithm is simplified, and an election mechanism is introduced in the selection of the main nodes. The three-phase protocol is optimized to a two-step broadcast communication method to reach the consensus and reduce one-step full-node broadcast in the process. When the consensus is not reached, the process will be switched to the classic PBFT algorithm.

5.2   Global Algorithm Design

Main Node Election Mechanism. Considering the importance of the main node in the PBFT algorithm, in order to reduce the probability of the abnormal node being the main node, in the global consensus algorithm, the election mechanism of the Raft consensus algorithm is used for reference. In the process of selecting accounting nodes, an election mechanism is introduced, and the candidate node set R is added as a buffer to receive newly added nodes and main nodes eliminated from the consensus set.

First build a global construction group, start the first round of elections, randomly select some nodes, which is only allowed to participate in the consensus process to reduce the number of accounting nodes in the consensus, from the many accounting nodes in the network, and then send the selection result to other nodes in the network. Other nodes in the network that have not participated in the candidate still have certain rights. They can elect the nodes on the candidate node list, and the top N nodes elected become the accounting nodes of the blockchain network.

After the node selection process is completed, the second round of elections is entered and the nodes of the entire network will vote on the historical performance of the candidate nodes. The number of votes of the candidate nodes will be stored in a priority queue. After the voting, according to the needs of the system, the first n representative nodes are selected as new accounting nodes to participate in the consensus. The node with the most votes will be regarded as the main node and has the authority to generate global blocks. Finally, the main node constructs the global block and sends it to other parallel blockchain nodes for verification. Each parallel blockchain node will verify the legality of the global block after receiving the global block. If the global block is valid, it will be sent to other nodes in the network where the parallel blockchain node is located, and the main node continues to build the next global block; if invalid, the global block will be deleted, and a new main node is selected to restart this process.

Main Node Rotation Mechanism. After completing the process of electing accounting nodes from the blockchain network, the elected accounting nodes will take turns as the main node and participate in the consensus of all information in the entire network.

However, when a certain accounting node is responsible for completing consensus for a long time as the main node, it may cause certain security risks. For example, a group of accounting nodes may collude and interfere with transactions sent from the parallel blockchain to the global blockchain. Under the condition of multi-centralization, in order to exclude some main nodes from cheating and participate in the consensus of the entire network for a long time, it must ensure that the main node allocation process is random and verifiable. Therefore, a rotation mechanism is designed to periodically rotate different accounting nodes as main nodes.

A target value t is set in advance. At the i(th) time to rotate, a global blockchain with block of height of i is selected, and the hash value h_i of its block header is found. If the account address of this accounting node is addr, an integer n needs to be found from the accounting node to satisfy the following inequality:

$$O = hash(h_i \parallel addr \parallel n) \le t \qquad (1)$$

In order to perform the consistency process, a combined arrangement of the nodes in the system is called a view, and the view number is a continuous integer, denoted by v. Suppose there are $|R|$ nodes in the view, that is, there are currently R blocks connected to the global blockchain, and each parallel blockchain is numbered $\{1, 2, 3...|R|\}$, the number of the main node is noted as p. Then calculate

$$p = O \bmod |R| \qquad (2)$$

The main node in PBFT encapsulates and signs the message that needs to be consensus and broadcasts it among the elected nodes. The format of the encapsulated and signed message $<i, n, addr, p>$. Subsequently, this main node will be responsible for parallel blockchain transaction verification for the next period of time. Because the hash function has a one-way characteristic, it is impossible to speculate the input of the hash function given the target value in advance. Therefore, this method can ensure that a certain node cannot specify the responsible parallel blockchain in advance. In addition, any node can verify the validity of the distribution result according to the broadcast message.

Consensus Process. A two-stage agreement is used to reach consensus when all blockchain nodes are honest nodes. In the case of Byzantine nodes, switch to the PBFT algorithm. The specific consensus process is as follows:

(1) The system selects a main node P according to the node election mechanism, and P initiates the consistency protocol.
(2) The main node packages the transaction records, verifies the transaction signature, and sends a verified broadcast message to the vice nodes.
(3) After receiving the message from the main node, the vice nodes verify the message and send a confirmation message to the main node.
(4) After receiving the verification messages from all vice nodes, the main node packages the transaction records into blocks and adds them to the blockchain, while sending broadcast messages to the remaining nodes.
(5) The other vice nodes verify the block and synchronize the block to the chain, delete the transaction stored in their own memory, and set the view to 0. The main node remains unchanged, and starts the next round of consensus.

In the process of the main node verifying the validity of transactions, the most accurate verification method is that the accounting nodes all store a complete block chain copy, but this will increase the storage burden of the accounting nodes. Based on this problem, only the block headers of each parallel blockchain are stored in the accounting node, and the Merkle tree mechanism of the blockchain is used for transaction verification. If necessary, branches of the Merkle tree can be obtained to help complete the verification. When each parallel blockchain generates a new block, it sends the block header to the corresponding accounting node through the data sending and receiving node, and the accounting node broadcasts the block header to the global blockchain network. In this way, the block header is finally included in the global blockchain, and each accounting node contains the block headers of all parallel blockchains. Since each block header is relatively small, this method can significantly reduce the storage burden of the accounting node relative to saving a complete parallel blockchain copy.

View Change Protocol. If the main node does not respond within the specified time and the consensus process is not completed or the main node has a Byzantine error during the two-stage protocol execution process, the vice node will think that the main node is the problem node. It will switch the process to the PBFT algorithm, trigger the view change protocol, re-select the main node and generate blocks to continue the two-phase consistency process. At the same time, the main node which has the Byzantine error exits the consensus set, and a candidate node elected by the alternate set R enters the consensus set, and is added to the position of the eliminated node. Give a certain reward to the main node that has reached consensus. At the same time, abolish the right of eliminated nodes to participate in the election of candidate nodes and impose a certain deduction of account funds. The finally confirmed consistency block will be added to the blockchain, and then the next block proposal will be triggered to continue to the next consistency verification process.

6 Experimental Analysis and Summary

This algorithm uses docker virtualization technology to build blockchain nodes, deploying each node in an independent docker container, each of which 2G of independent memory. In the simulation experiment, 1, 2, 4, 6, and 8 nodes were deployed for testing, comparing the throughput and transaction delay of the PBFT algorithm and the improved global consensus algorithm in different node environments.

Throughput TPS generally refers to the number of transactions processed by the system per unit time. The level of throughput shows the load on the system, the ability to process transactions or request transactions. As shown in Fig. 4(a), as the number of nodes in the network increases, the throughput of both algorithms shows a downward trend, but overall, the throughput of the global consensus algorithm based on PBFT is much higher than that of the PBFT algorithm.

Transaction latency refers to the time required from block generation to confirmation of a new block. This time is mainly generated by the consensus process and the view change process in the consensus mechanism. Under the same conditions, the delays of the two algorithms are shown in Fig. 4(b). The global consensus algorithm based on PBFT will execute the optimized consistency protocol in the absence of Byzantine nodes. It can be seen that the transaction delay is better than the PBFT algorithm. And as the number of nodes increases, the transaction delay of the PBFT algorithm grows faster, while the transaction delay of the global consensus algorithm is more stable and grows slower. Therefore, in the case of many nodes, the advantages of the global consensus algorithm are more obvious.

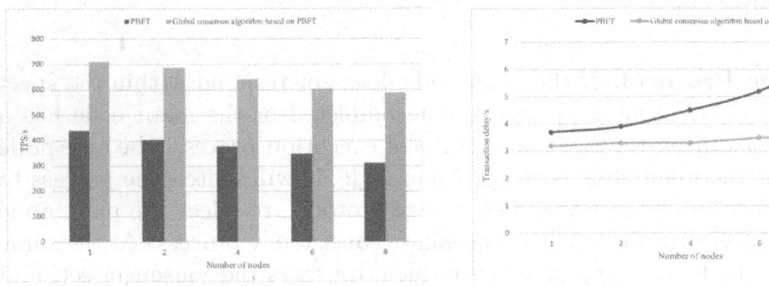

(a) Comparison of the throughput   (b) Comparison of the transaction delay

Fig. 4. Comparison of PBFT algorithm and global consensus algorithm.

Focusing on the actual demand and development trend of blockchain technology, in the application scenario of marine data management system, a cross-chain transaction architecture called global blockchain is proposed. And a global Byzantine fault-tolerant algorithm based on the PBFT algorithm in the global blockchain scenario is designed to achieve efficient and real-time sharing of marine data based on the combination of the global blockchain and the global consensus algorithm. The consistency process of the PBFT algorithm is improved, and the three-phase consistency verification process is simplified to a two-stage consistency process. The PBFT main node confirmation protocol is optimized, and the Raft algorithm election mechanism is used to confirm the main node of each round of consensus, making the elected main node more trustworthy. A main node rotation mechanism is introduced to reduce the possibility of abnormal nodes acting as main nodes. Besides, the consistency protocol is optimized, the submission process in the consistency process is eliminated, and the network communication time broadcast by the nodes is reduced. In addition, the view change protocol is optimized, and a timeout retransmission mechanism is added to the consensus network to further reduce the number of view changes, improve the consensus efficiency of the network, and maintain the stability of the entire blockchain network.

In the future work, it will be continued to optimize algorithm details and further reduce network traffic. The node credit integration mechanism can be introduced to select the optimal node comprehensively. Apply the algorithm to the blockchain system in the marine field to contribute to the application and popularization of the blockchain.

References

1. Yuan, Y., Wang, F.Y.: Blockchain and cryptocurrencies: model, techniques, and applications. IEEE Trans. Syst. Man Cybern. Syst. **48**(9), 1421–1428 (2018)
2. Gramoli, V.: From blockchain consensus back to Byzantine consensus. Future Gener. Comput. Syst. **107**, 760–769 (2020)
3. Nakamoto, S., Bitcoin, A.: A peer-to-peer electronic cash system (2008). Bitcoin https://bitcoin.org/bitcoin.pdf
4. Linnhoff-Popien, C.: Blockchain-the next big thing? (2018)
5. Zheng, P., Zheng, Z., Luo, X., Chen, X., Liu, X.: A detailed and real-time performance monitoring framework for blockchain systems. In: 2018 IEEE/ACM 40th International Conference on Software Engineering: Software Engineering in Practice Track (ICSE-SEIP), pp. 134–143. IEEE (2018)
6. Dinh, T.T.A., Liu, R., Zhang, M., Chen, G., Ooi, B.C., Wang, J.: Untangling blockchain: a data processing view of blockchain systems. IEEE Trans. Knowl. Data Eng. **30**(7), 1366–1385 (2018)
7. Wang, W., et al.: A survey on consensus mechanisms and mining strategy management in blockchain networks. IEEE Access **7**, 22328–22370 (2019)
8. Tschorsch, F., Scheuermann, B.: Bitcoin and beyond: a technical survey on decentralized digital currencies. IEEE Commun. Surv. Tutor. **18**(3), 2084–2123 (2016)
9. Hasan, H.R., Salah, K.: Proof of delivery of digital assets using blockchain and smart contracts. IEEE Access **6**, 65439–65448 (2018)
10. Turkanović, M., Hölbl, M., Košič, K., Heričko, M., Kamišalić, A.: EduCTX: a blockchain-based higher education credit platform. IEEE Access **6**, 5112–5127 (2018)
11. Aitzhan, N.Z., Svetinovic, D.: Security and privacy in decentralized energy trading through multi-signatures, blockchain and anonymous messaging streams. IEEE Trans. Depend. Secure Comput. **15**(5), 840–852 (2016)
12. Shae, Z., Tsai, J.J.: On the design of a blockchain platform for clinical trial and precision medicine. In: 2017 IEEE 37th International Conference on Distributed Computing Systems (ICDCS), pp. 1972–1980. IEEE (2017)
13. Bamakan, S.M.H., Motavali, A., Bondarti, A.B.: A survey of blockchain consensus algorithms performance evaluation criteria. Expert Syst. Appl. **154**, 113385 (2020)
14. Xiao, Y., Zhang, N., Li, J., Lou, W., Hou, Y.T.: Distributed consensus protocols and algorithms. In: Blockchain for Distributed Systems Security, vol. 25 (2019)
15. Xiao, Y., Zhang, N., Lou, W., Hou, Y.T.: A survey of distributed consensus protocols for blockchain networks. IEEE Commun. Surv. Tutor. **22**(2), 1432–1465 (2020)
16. King, S., Nadal, S.: PPcoin: peer-to-peer crypto-currency with proof-of-stake. self-published paper (2012)

17. Larimer, D.: Delegated proof-of-stake white paper (2014)
18. Ongaro, D., Ousterhout, J.: In search of an understandable consensus algorithm. In: 2014 USENIX Annual Technical Conference (USENIXATC 2014), pp. 305–319 (2014)
19. Belotti, M., Božić, N., Pujolle, G., Secci, S.: A Vademecum on blockchain technologies: when, which, and how. IEEE Commun. Surv. Tutor. **21**(4), 3796–3838 (2019)
20. Castro, M., Liskov, B., et al.: Practical Byzantine fault tolerance. In: OSDI, vol. 99, pp. 173–186 (1999)
21. Lamport, L., et al.: Paxos made simple. ACM SIGACT News **32**(4), 18–25 (2001)
22. Cachin, C., et al.: Architecture of the hyperledger blockchain fabric. In: Workshop on Distributed Cryptocurrencies and Consensus Ledgers, vol. 310, p. 4 (2016)
23. Platania, M., Obenshain, D., Tantillo, T., Amir, Y., Suri, N.: On choosing server-or client-side solutions for BFT. ACM Comput. Surv. (CSUR) **48**(4), 1–30 (2016)
24. Liu, S., Viotti, P., Cachin, C., Quéma, V., Vukolić, M.: XFT: practical fault tolerance beyond crashes. In: 12th USENIX Symposium on Operating Systems Design and Implementation (OSDI 2016), pp. 485–500 (2016)

A Complete Anti-collusion Mechanism in Blockchain

Xiangbin Xian[✉], Zhenguo Yang, Guipeng Zhang, Tucua Miro de Nelio S.,
and Wenyin Liu

Web Identity Security Lab, Guangdong University of Technology, Guangzhou 510006, China
1245549353@qq.com, zhengyang5-c@my.cityu.edu.hk,
zhguipeng@outlook.com, mtucua@hotmail.com, liuwy@gdut.edu.cn

Abstract. Collusion attack is an issue existing in most blockchains, especially for token-based decentralized applications using voting as consensus mechanism and incentive method. Malicious users may collude others to get more votes, in order to get rewards. We present a complete anti-collusion mechanism (CACM), aiming to cheat the malicious users who want to collude others. Each vote will be committed on smart contract and consumes the commitment for last vote. Zero knowledge Succinct Non-interactive Argument of Knowledge (zkSNARKs) is used to ensure the correctness of the voting and tallying operations in CACM. We implement CACM on the Ethereum test network, and the CACM circuit on local machine. The experiments show the low cost of time and gas respectively in generating zkSNARKs proof and interactions with smart contract, which proves CACM is efficient.

Keywords: Blockchain · Collusion attack · Zero-knowledge proofs · Voting mechanism · Decentralized application

1 Introduction

In recent years, blockchain has been applied to different fields. People use smart contracts to write and build a variety of applications, benefiting from the decentralized and tamper-proof characteristics of blockchain, which can guarantee the credibility and transparency of applications. Moreover, people can indirectly regulate the behaviors of participants by designing token-based incentive mechanisms through smart contracts. In blockchain, the incentive mechanisms are designed to secure the blockchain itself, encouraging miners and staking users to participate honestly.

The incentive mechanisms have been also applied into quadratic voting [3], quadratic financing [4], and FOMO game, etc. Recently, using token-based incentive mechanisms to encourage high-quality posts in social media [1, 2] becomes popular. However, these mechanisms which are usually constructed in smart contract, rarely take the collusion of users into consideration. Smart contracts automatically running on blockchain systems can only handle the logic of the code that has been deployed, such as accepting or rejecting an operation. They cannot judge the behavioral motives of offline participants.

© Springer Nature Singapore Pte Ltd. 2020
Z. Zheng et al. (Eds.): BlockSys 2020, CCIS 1267, pp. 31–44, 2020.
https://doi.org/10.1007/978-981-15-9213-3_3

For example, people may collude to do the same operation, forming a community of shared interests or even an attacker group, which can be called as collusion attack and can harm the profit of other participants. This kind of attack is very covert and all operations are legal. It will not directly cause fatal damage to the system, but it will affect the ecology of the blockchain.

Vitalik has used two examples to explain how collusion attacks exist in most of today's token-based blockchain applications, both using voting mechanism. On BIHU [1], users can post articles and vote for an article to show their like or approval. The weight of each vote is proportional to the number of tokens the voting user has. Within each epoch, the system limits the number of votes per user without consuming the user's token. Finally, the system counts the total weight of votes gained by each author within the epoch and awards the author accordingly. Ethereum trading subreddit [2] uses a similar mechanism, but each vote has the same weight and the system awards based on the number of votes it receives. Assuming that a user always only votes for his articles or colludes other users by bribing to vote for his articles, as long as the cost of bribe lower than the reward from system after tallying. This kind of behavior can be called Self-interested Voting, and he can achieve long-term stable earnings, even if his articles are of poor quality. Self-interested Voting is also found in many blockchains that use PoS (Proof of Staking) kind of consensus mechanisms, such as EOS, under more euphemistic names such as "staking pool" that shares mining rewards. It should be noted that collusion can occur wherever voting mechanism is used, usually by bribing others.

Furthermore, most of the voting mechanisms assume that the user is independent, but a user can create multiple blockchain accounts in fact, which always carry risk of collusion attack even without bribing others. There have been many projects deployed to map real identities into blockchain account. In WeIdentity [20], every user has a unique electronic identity in the blockchain, by converting their identity-card or passport into blockchain accounts after some calculations. While it may require a centralized identity authority, it's still a necessary premise to prevent collusion attacks in the form of bribery. Our method also relies on the unique identity. That is, each blockchain account that can participate in the voting is controlled by an independent person in reality.

In this paper, we propose a complete anti-collusion mechanism against collusion, which makes collusion incredible inspired by Vitalik. Since blockchain and smart contracts cannot avoid the appearance of rich users and cannot know how they bribe other users, we can try our best to help other users cheat the bribers, so as to curb the collusion attack. CACM is a concise framework that can be extended to fit a variety of voting mechanisms including quadratic voting. In this mechanism:

1. Each vote will be committed on smart contract and consumes the commitment for last vote, which prevent the attacker from forging the vote of other users. Therefore, all votes of a user can be chained and traced with commitments.
2. Users can provide real voting messages to briber to prove that they voted for the briber, but users can send another voting message to revote, or delegate other users to revote, which will not be detected by the briber.

The whole paper is organized as follow. In Sect. 2, we introduce the related work including some voting mechanisms proposed for blockchain and several solutions to collusion attack. In Sect. 3, we introduce the notations of the algorithms used in CACM and in Sect. 4, we describe the structure of CACM in detail. Implement and evaluation of the CACM circuit and the interactions with smart contract are shown in Sect. 5.

2 Related Work

To resist collusion attacks, Vitalik proposed two well-known solutions, i.e., collusion-safe with identity-free, and collusion-safe with identity. The difference between them is whether requires that a real-world person can only register one account in the application or blockchain. In fact, the first approach only achieves 50% collusion-safe at most, while a wealthy attacker can create and manipulate any number of blockchain accounts to vote without bribing other users. For blockchain systems using the POW consensus algorithm, they still suffer from 51% attacks. Even if the power of a single miner (like a blockchain account in a voting mechanism) is limited, super-rich users can buy a large number of miners to form a pool larger than half of the power of the blockchain system.

Furthermore, Vitalik [6] have proposed a solution based on secret key update. The vote is valid only if the secret key carried by the vote message is the same as the secret key of the user held by the smart contract currently, and the secret key can be changed by owing user. The user can show the briber with a real vote message, but the briber may not know whether the vote is valid or whether the user has previously changed the secret key. If the briber is smart enough, he will ask the user for proof of validity, not just a vote message, e.g., the briber may require the user to provide the secret key that is currently stored in the system. Thus, it cannot resist collusion attack. Barry WhiteHat extended it and implemented a Minimum anti-collusion Infrastructure [7] (MACI) based on Vitalik's thought. A role called "operator" is introduced in MACI, which is responsible for validating each user's voting message, updating the system state of each user, and tallying. Operator needs to generate zero-knowledge proofs to prove the correctness of all the computing processes, while the smart contract needs to verify the proof, which can also prove that the user's voting message is not censorshiped by operator. Regarding the censorship attack, Vitalik [21] and Xiangbin [22] have focused on resolving the censorship with malicious purpose and rejection of certain users' votes. MACI cannot prevent collusion attacks completely, because the key fraud method for users is to show the attacker a real but invalid voting message. Therefore, a savvy attacker can only pay the user after confirming that the user's vote is valid. Besides, MACI uses quadratic voting model [3], so Barry WhiteHat pointed out that it cannot prevent "deposit", a special kind of collusion attack. Because the quadratic voting model does not limit the weight of a vote, thus rich user can use a large number of tokens which can be lent from other users, to vote for themselves.

3 Preliminaries

In this section, we introduce the cryptographic primitives and the public security parameters used in CACM. We use λ to denote the security parameter. Let GroupGen be a polynomial-time algorithm that on input 1^λ outputs (p, g, G) where $p = \theta(\lambda)$, p is prime, G is a group of order p, g is a generator of G, and the decisional Diffie-Hellman

(DDH) assumption holds in G. The below cryptographic primitives all use the same public security parameters.

Pseudorandom function. Informally speaking, a pseudorandom function $PRF : A \rightarrow B$ is indistinguishable from a random function that maps A to B, and also denote that B is sampled uniformly at random from a set A. We use SHA256-compress function as pseudorandom function [16] to generate random number for commitment and nullifier in CACM.

Group hash function. Given a group G, a group hash function $GroupHash_G : d \rightarrow G$ maps a random number d to a group element. Let $GroupHash_G^* : d \rightarrow g$ denotes a special group hash function that maps a random number d to a generator g of G. We use group hash function in one-time key pair generation.

Commitment schemes. A commitment scheme is the compound of two algorithms (Com, Vf) such that:

- $Com_r(m)$: given message m and randomness r, returns commitment cm;
- $Vf(cm, m, r)$: given commitment cm, message m and randomness r, checks whether $cm \leftarrow Com_r(m)$ and accepts if that is the case.

The commitment scheme is statistically binding if no attacker, even computationally unbounded, can produce commitment cm and two openings (m, r), (m', r'), such that $cm \leftarrow Com_r(m) = Com_{r'}(m')$ and is computationally hiding if for every m, m', the probability distributions of $Com_r(m)$ and $Com_{r'}(m')$ are computationally indistinguishable over the choice of randomness r, r'. In CACM, we use Perderson Commitment algorithm to commit the random number known by users.

Key Agreement & Key Derivation. A key agreement scheme is a cryptographic protocol in which two parties agree a shared secret, each using their private key and the other party's public key. A key agreement scheme KA defines a type of public keys $KA.Public$, a type of private keys $KA.Private$, and a type of shared secrets $KA.SharedSecret$. There is the agreement function as:

$$KA.Public \leftarrow KA.Derive(KA.Private)$$
$$KA.SharedSecret \leftarrow KA.Agree(KA.Private, KA.Public)$$

A key derivation function is defined for a particular key agreement scheme and authenticated one-time symmetric encryption scheme; it takes the shared secret produced by the key agreement and additional arguments, and derives a key suitable for the encryption scheme. Let

$$Sym.K \leftarrow KDF(KA.SharedSecret, KA.Public)$$

be the key derivation function. Let $Sym.Encrypt_{Sym.K}$ and $Sym.Decrypt_{Sym.K}$ denote the one-time symmetric encryption algorithm. We use the above algorithms as same in Zcash [16], which have been proved to be safe.

zkSNARK [13, 14]. A zkSNARK can be used to prove/verify statements of the form *"given a public predicate F and a public input x, I know a secret input w such that F(x, w) = true"*. It consists of three algorithms: the *setup*, *prover*, and *verifier*. The *setup* takes predicate F and security parameter λ as inputs, and outputs a common reference string (CRS) *crs* along with a trapdoor *td*. The part of *crs* used for proving statements is sometimes called proving key and denoted crs_p, and the part necessary for their verification is called verification key and denoted crs_v. The *prover* receives the proving key crs_p, a public input x for F, and a secret input w for F, and outputs a proof π. The *verifier* receives the verification key crs_v, a public input x for F, and a proof π, and outputs a decision bit ("accept or", "reject"). Anyone can run the *verifier*.

4 Overview of CACM

In this section, we provide an overview of the CACM. There are three roles in CACM, including operator, user and smart contract (verifier). Specifically, a user can be an honest voter, attacker, and candidate (voting option). The operator uses the circuit implemented for CACM to generate zkSNARKs proof (zk-proof) π, and the smart contract verifies it with public input x and common reference string (CRS) crs. Note that the zkSNARKs algorithm Groth16 we used needs a trusted setup for circuit to generate crs, and the crs_v will be stored in smart contract after trusted setup.

Assume that an identity authentication institution has issued a unique pair of keys {sk, pk} to each legitimate user and the operator, and the user needs to use the keys to join in CACM. The key pairs are zkSNARKs friendly [24]. In short, users make their votes by sending transactions with voting messages to smart contract. The operator gets M messages at a time from smart contract and tally them after validating. Likewise, operator will return messages to users through smart contract. In the meantime, operator needs to make a zk-proof to prove the correctness of his operations. Finally, smart contract only needs to verify the zk-proof and update the voting result. The whole progress and interactions are shown in Fig. 1. The following subsection describes the building of smart contract (Sect. 4.1), the encryption scheme used in sending message and getting message (Sect. 4.2), and the specific voting process (Sect. 4.3), respectively. We show how CACM can completely achieve collusion-safe by analyzing specific scenarios as well (Sect. 4.4).

4.1 Building of Smart Contract

The smart contract not only serves as verifier, but also provides a message tunnel for users and the operator. As shown in Fig. 1, the smart contract provides several functions {*deposit, sendmessage, getmessage, insert, update, withdraw*} that can be called by users and operator. Besides, smart contract stores the global state data including Message Merkle tree (MTree), Commitment Merkle tree (CTree), Nullifier pool (NPool), Message pool (MPool) and User pool (UPool).

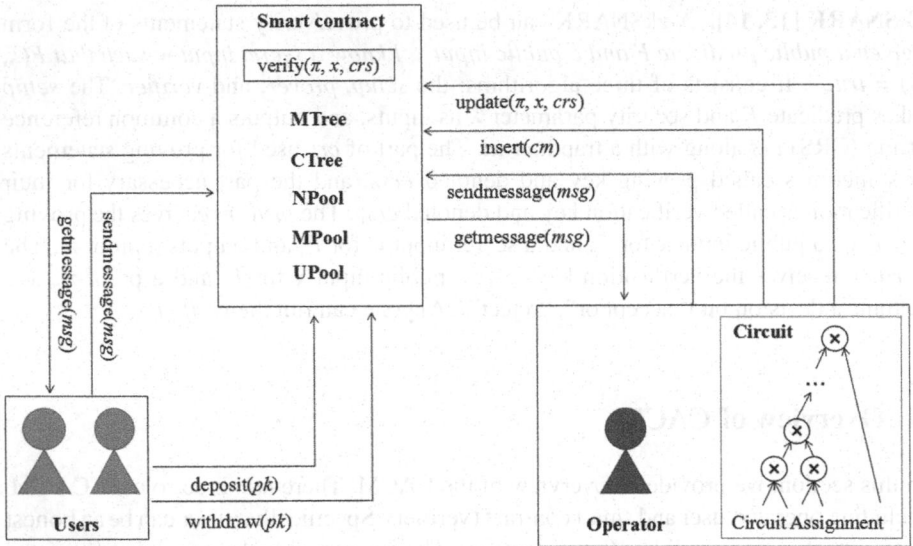

Fig. 1. Overview of CACM

The Merkle trees constructed in smart contract use MIMC as hash function and are initialized with zero values as their leaf nodes. For a tree of depth d, it contains $2^{d+1} - 1$ nodes. The operator needs to prove that the Merkle path from a specific leaf to root is valid when tallying. The Merkle path of a leaf can be got from smart contract when inserting it into the Merkle tree. The pool in smart contract are implemented as array of length *len*, which is cheaper than Merkle tree in inserting new element and storing.

- Message Merkle tree (MTree), a message Merkle tree is used to store the hash of messages in leaf nodes. Let $hash_{msg}$ denote the hash of message text *msg* sent by user.
- Commitment Merkle tree (CTree), a commitment Merkle tree is used to store the commitments in leaf nodes. Let $m = \{\{pk_i\}, nf\}$ denote a commitment text, $\{pk_i\}$ denote the public keys of candidates, and *cm* denote the commitment with trapdoor r for the vote, which can be calculated as $cm \leftarrow Com_r(m)$.
- Nullifier pool (NPool), is used to store the nullifier *nf* contained in commitment, which have been used and disclosed. Nullifier is a random number and used to prevent double-use of commitment. If a user makes a new vote, it will consume the commitment of the last vote and the operator will create a new commitment for it. The nullifier of the consumed commitment will be inserted to NPool.
- Message pool (MPool), is used to store the message sent by users and operator. The user and operator can also get the messages through scanning the array, which provide a message channel between users and operator.
- User pool (UPool), is used to store the *pk* of users who have signed up and the amount of total votes they get if someone has voted for them. A person can sign up the voting application by depositing a certain amount of tokens. Let $(pk : value)$ denote an element in UPool array.

4.2 Message Encryption Scheme

The message is sent by a user including a ciphertext decrypted by operator, and the returned message from operator can only be decrypted by that user. Therefore, other users cannot know the secret information including commitment. We take a common scenario to show how to achieve it. Let pt denote the plaintext that contains secret information known by a user and operator. A user's key pair is $\{sk_{user}, pk_{user}\}$, and the operator's key pair known by all users is $\{sk_{oper}, pk_{oper}\}$. We use the curve babyJubJub [23] built on BN254 in key agreement and key derivation, which is different from Zcash, because the curve JubJub using in Zcash does not fit the base curve BN254. BabyJubJub is a curve with equation as $ax^2 + y^2 = 1 + dx^2y^2$, where $a = 168700$ and $d = 168696$. The order p of babyJubJub is of 251bits.

Encryption. The user sends a voting message to smart contract by calling function *sendmessage(msg)*. The user firstly encrypts the pt with steps in Table 1.

Table 1. Encryption.

Encryption
1. generate a new KA key pair $(epk, esk) \leftarrow KA(public, private)$
2. $SharedSecret \leftarrow KA.Agree(esk, pk_{oper})$
3. $Sym.K \leftarrow KDF(SharedSecret, epk, pk_{oper})$
4. $ct \leftarrow Sym.Encrypt_{Sym.K}(pt)$

Let sig be the signature of ct under secret key sk_{user}. The resulting message text send to smart contract is $msg = \{ct, epk, sig, pk_{user}\}$.

Decryption. The operator gets a voting message from smart contract by calling function *getmessage(msg)*, then extract the components $\{ct, epk, sig, pk_{user}\}$ from msg and decrypt the ct with steps in Table 2.

Table 2. Decryption.

Decryption
1. $SharedSecret \leftarrow KA.Agree(sk_{oper}, epk)$
2. $Sym.k \leftarrow KDF(SharedSecret, epk, pk_{oper})$
3. $pt \leftarrow Sym.Decrypt_{Sym.K}(ct)$

If the returning result pt is not valid, which means this message is not for operator, then the operator gets other messages.

Note that, a user can use the same message encryption scheme to send message to another user, just replacing the operator's key pair. The operator firstly detects whether he is the receiver of a message rather than verifying the signature of a message, which will save a lot of time. Likewise, if operator return messages to user, he will use the same progress to encrypt the message, and then the receiving user can extract the message out.

4.3 Voting Process

A complete voting process includes four stages {Signup, Vote, Tally, Withdraw}. We denote the incentive settlement period of an application as an epoch, and the results of voting in each epoch will be reset at the beginning of the next epoch. Considering an application like BIHU, once a user has registered, he can vote many times within the rules until signing out. Thus, the Vote stage and Tally stage repeat many times between deposit stage and Withdraw stage. Unlike some traditional voting mechanisms [10, 12], in which the operator or smart contract execute tallying only once after all users voting, tallying can be executed many times for the new voting messages since last tallying in our mechanism. Moreover, a new user can sign up at any time of an epoch and can vote or be voted after then.

Signup stage. Besides depositing tokens, user also need to send their public key pk to smart contract by calling function $deposit(pk)$, which will add an element ($pk : value$) in UPool array. The $value$ denotes the total amount of votes that the user with public key pk get, so a user can also be a candidate after signing up. Compared to MACI, in which the candidates are fixed since set up the smart contract, our method is more flexible. For every new user, the operator respectively generates initial commitment with steps in Table 3.

Table 3. Generate initial commitment

Generate initial commitment
1. select a random number r
2. $nf \leftarrow PRF_{pk_{user}}(r)$
3. let $m = \{pk, nf\}$
4. initial commitment $cm \leftarrow Com_r(m)$
5. insert the cm in CTree by calling function $rt_{CTree} \leftarrow insert(cm)$
6. let $pt \leftarrow \{r, cm, nf, rt_{CTree}\}$
7. encrypt with message encryption scheme $ct \leftarrow Sym.Encrypt_{Sym.K}(pt)$

At last, the operator puts the ct in a message and sends to smart contract by calling $sendmessage(msg)$ function, which will insert the hash of msg $hash_{msg}$ to MTree.

Vote stage. The user firstly get message from smart contract send by operator and can extract $\left\{r^{old}, cm^{old}, nf^{old}, rt^{old}_{CTree}\right\}$ after decrypting message. In particular, the new vote will consume the initial commitment or the commitment for the last vote, so the user need to put it in the new voting message. But in traditional voting mechanisms and MACI, there is no relationship between the new voting message and last voting message from same user. Let

$$pt = \left\{\left\{pk_i^{old}\right\}, \left\{pk_i^{new}\right\}, r^{old}, cm^{old}, nf^{old}, rt^{old}_{CTree}\right\}$$

The user encrypts it in a message text msg and send to smart contract by calling $sendmessage(msg)$ function. $\left\{pk_i^{old}\right\}$ are the public keys of candidates the user previously voting to, and $\left\{pk_i^{new}\right\}$ are the public keys of candidates they want to vote. We limit the total number of voting messages a user can send, which can prevent DOS attack, but don't limit the total number of candidates a user can vote in a voting message.

Tally stage. The operator gets M new voting messages every once and decrypt them. Compared to MACI, M is not fix, but it is restricted by the gas of verifying a zk-proof (seeing in the fifth section). The operator can choose a suitable M in every tallying. For every new message, the operator respectively validates the old commitment and create a new commitment with steps in Table 4.

Table 4. Validate old commitment and create new commitment

Validate old commitment and create new commitment
1. let $m^{old} = \left\{\{pk_i^{old}\}, nf^{old}\right\}$
2. $cm \leftarrow Com_{r^{old}}(m^{old})$
3. if ($cm \neq cm^{old}$ or NPool.contain(nf^{old})) then abort endif
4. if (! $CTree.validate(cm)$) then abort endif
5. select a random number r^{new}
6. $nf^{new} \leftarrow PRF_{pk_{user}}(r^{new})$
7. let $m^{new} = \left\{\{pk_j^{new}\}, nf^{new}\right\}$
8. $cm^{new} \leftarrow Com_{r^{new}}(m^{new})$
9. for $pk^{old} \in \{pk_i^{old}\}$ do UPool.$pk^{old} --$
10. for $pk^{new} \in \{pk_i^{new}\}$ do UPool.$pk^{new} ++$
11. insert the cm^{new} in CTree by calling function $rt^{new}_{CTree} \leftarrow insert(cm^{new})$
12. let $pt = \{r^{new}, cm^{new}, nf^{new}, rt^{new}_{CTree}\}$
13. encrypt with message encryption scheme $ct \leftarrow Sym.Encrypt_{Sym.K}(pt)$

Note that, function $validate$ in step4 is pseudocode in smart contract which validate the Merkle path from leaf cm to rt^{old}_{CTree}. At last, the operator put the ct in a message and send to smart contract by calling $sendmessage(msg)$ function, which will insert the hash of $msg\ hash_{msg}$ to MTree. The operator can deal with multiple voting messages and create initial commitments for multiple new users in the meantime. After processing the above steps for all messages and new users, operator generate a zk-proof π and send to smart contract calling function *update* (π, x, crs), which will verify the π with primary input x and *crs*.

Withdraw stage. If a user wants to sign out, he can call the function *withdraw(pk)* to bring back tokens. Note that, there is a time window between the user calling the function *withdraw* and the smart contract sending tokens to user. In the time window, the operator deletes the corresponding element $(pk : value)$ in UPool array, and deduct some tokens from the user's deposition if he has violated the rule, such as sending too much invalid message. Traditional voting mechanisms rarely consider users to be evil and punishing malicious users.

4.4 Discussions on Collusion-Safe

Assume that all encryption and zkSNARKs algorithms are secure, which gives a promise that all information that the user can get from smart contract are the number of votes of candidates in UPool and messages in MPool. When an attacker named Tom bribes a user named Alice, Alice can show Tom the vote message text *msg,* the plaintext *pt* and the one-time symmetric encryption key *Sym.K*, which can be verified by Tom that the ciphertext *ct* in *msg* is encrypted by *pt* with *Sym.K*. Therefore, Tom can believe Alice who have voted for him after checking the pk_i^{new} in *pt*, and give Alice money. As noting before, Alice can make vote again to invalidate the vote for Tom (subtract one from the value of Tom's *pk* in UPool). In addition, for some applications using voting to express agreement with an article like BIHU, the user can make vote again to cancel agreement.

Considering Tom may ask Alice to give him a consumable commitment rather than to show him the vote message, Tom can use that commitment to vote for himself. So, we can limit the number of messages that a user can send in an epoch, which also benefits the CACM in preventing Dos attack. Besides, Alice can entrust another user named Bob to vote just by telling Bob the secret information of a voting commitment which can be consumed. Specifically, Alice sends Bob the $pt = \left\{ \left\{ pk_i^{old} \right\}, \left\{ pk_j^{new} \right\}, r^{old}, cm^{old}, nf^{old}, rt_{CTree}^{old} \right\}$ and Bob can make a voting message for that plaintext. Therefore, the attacker cannot know whether Alice keeps the promise by monitoring voting messages in MPool and the transactions on blockchain.

5   Implementation & Evaluations

In this section we describe the implementation of CACM including zkSNARKs circuit used by operator, and evaluate the cost of time that the operator generates a zk-proof. We also evaluate the cost of total gas of each function calling. Our implementation relies on the libsnark and ethsnark library and makes use of the precompiled contracts for the elliptic curve operations on BN254, a pairing friendly curve introduced in Ethereum after the Byzantium hard fork. The trusted setup can be held by a trusted third party or be carried out by multi-party computation ceremonies [17, 18] in practice, but we take a centralize method to generate the CRS for simplicity. All measurements were performed on a laptop running Ubuntu 18.04 equipped with 4 cores, 2.3 GHz Intel Core i7 and 16 GB DDR3 RAM. Our implementation of smart contract was deployed on Ethereum's test network that mimics the production network. We use the Web3 framework to facilitate communication between the web browser and the Ethereum daemon.

5.1 CACM Circuit

The circuit is deployed in c++ with some gadgets mainly including Pederson commitment gadget, MIMC hash gadget and Merkle tree gadget. The gadget is a constructed constraint for specific function and CACM circuit consist of above constraints. To ensure the correctness of the operations of operator, some operations including generating initial commitment for new user and tallying are compiled in constraints. Therefore, the smart contract only needs to verify the proof that generated by the circuit, which is equal to verify all the operations of operator. At the code level, the proof is to prove a pair of primary input x and auxiliary input w that satisfy the given constraints.

Let $cmAddr$ and $msgAddr$ respectively denote the Merkle address of a node in CTree and MTree; $mkPath_{CTree}^{leaf}$ and $mkPath_{MTree}^{leaf}$ respectively denote the Merkle path from a leaf to root of CTree and MTree; $mkPath_{CTree}^{rt}$ denotes Merkle path from rt_{CTree}^{old} to rt_{CTree}^{new}; $value_{pk}^{old}$ and $value_{pk}^{new}$ respectively denote the amount of total votes that a candidate get in UPool before tallying and after tallying; M denote the amount of voting messages and N denote the amount of new users that the operator handle at a time. Given the primary input:

$$x = \left\{ M, N, \left\{ cm^{old}, cm^{new}, nf^{old}, hash_{msg}, msg \right\}_{k, k \in M}, \left\{ cm_l^{init}, pk_l^{init} \right\}_{l \in N} \right\}$$

and auxiliary input: $w = \{w_1, w_2\}$

$$w_1 = \left\{ \begin{array}{c} r^{old}, r^{new}, nf^{new}, rt_{CTree}^{old}, rt_{CTree}^{new}, rt_{MTree}^{old}, cmAddr^{old}, msgAddr^{old}, \\ mkPath_{MTree}^{leaf}, mkPath_{CTree}^{leaf}, mkPath_{CTree}^{rt}, \left\{ pk_i^{old} \right\}, \left\{ pk_j^{new} \right\} \end{array} \right\}_{k, k \in M}$$

$$w_2 = \left\{ r_l^{init}, nf_l^{init} \right\}_{l \in N}$$

the logic of constraints in circuit are shown in Table 5.

Note that function $generateRoot$ is pseudocode in circuit which computes a Merkle root from a list of nodes. After preparing the primary input x and auxiliary input w, the operator can generate a zk-proof with proving key crs_p on his machine, and smart contract can verify it with verifying key crs_v and primary input x online. As shown in Table 6, with four voting messages ($M = 4$) and four new users($N = 4$), generating a zk-proof only cost 3.9913 s, and the zk-proof is of 1996 bits long. Importantly, increasing M and N in the inputs will increase the size of the circuit, which also increase the proving time and verification time. The circuit can be more complex to prove more operations, but the current circuit is enough to ensure that the operator working properly and maintain the security of CACM.

Table 5. Constrains of CACM Circuit

CACM Circuit

for each voting message $msg_k, k \in M$,

let $m^{old} = \left\{\{pk_i^{old}\}, nf^{old}\right\}, m^{new} = \left\{\{pk_j^{new}\}, nf^{new}\right\}$

Constraint I: $cm^{old} = Com_{r^{old}}(m^{old})$

Constraint II: $cm^{new} = Com_{r^{new}}(m^{new})$

Constraint III: $rt_{CTree}^{old} = generateRoot\left(cm^{old}, cmAddr_{leaf}^{old}, mkPath_{CTree}^{leaf}\right)$

Constraint IV: $rt_{CTree}^{new} = generateRoot(rt_{CTree}^{old}, cmAddr_{rt}^{old}, mkPath_{CTree}^{rt})$

Constraint V: $hash_{msg} = Sha256(msg)$

Constraint VI: $rt_{MTree}^{old} = generateRoot\left(hash_{msg}^{old}, msgAddr_{leaf}^{old}, mkPath_{MTree}^{leaf}\right)$

Constraint VII: $nf^{old} = PRF_{pk_{user}}(r^{old})$

    for each pk in $\{pk_i^{old}\}$:

    Constraint VIII: $value_{pk_i}^{old} - 1 = value_{pk_i}^{new}$

    for each pk in $\{pk_j^{new}\}$:

    Constraint IX: $value_{pk_j}^{old} - 1 = value_{pk_j}^{new}$

for each new user $pk_l^{init}, l \in N$

let $m_l^{init} = \left\{\{pk_l^{init}\}, nf_l^{init}\right\}$

Constraint X: $cm_l^{init} = Com_{r_l^{init}}(m_l^{init})$

Table 6. Time of generating zk-proof

M&N	M = 0, N = 1	M = 1, N = 0	M = 1, N = 1	M = 2, N = 2	M = 3, N = 3	M = 4, N = 4
Time(s)	0.175	1.1068	1.1663	2.1442	3.0965	3.9912

5.2 Gas Cost

Each function calling is wrapped in an Ethereum transaction, and we record the gas cost of each transaction. We measure the gas cost of the functions {*deposit, sendmessage, getmessage, insert, update, withdraw*} mentioned in 4.1, which are used by the users and operator in the whole process, and the results are shown in Table 7.

Table 7. Gas cost of each function

Function	*deposit*	*sendmessage*	*getmessage*	*insert*	*update*	*withdraw*
Gas	8634	14221	752	11856	240311	10174

As described in voting process, the function *deposit* and *withdraw* are only used once by each user, and the function *sendmessage* and *getmessage* are used by users and operator respectively for each voting and tallying. Besides, the function *update* and *insert* are only used by operator for each tallying and commitment respectively. Note that, the main cost of gas in calling function *update* is from verifying a zk-proof, so function *update* always cost more than other functions. In an Ethereum block which has a capacity of approximately 4.7 million gas, therefore a block can hold more than 330 times of voting or 19 times of tallying. We also measure the gas cost of the function *update* when the operator deals with different amounts of new user and new voting message. The results are shown in Table 8.

Table 8. Gas cost of verifying zk-proof

M&N	$M = 0, N = 1$	$M = 1, N = 0$	$M = 1, N = 1$	$M = 2, N = 2$	$M = 3, N = 3$	$M = 4, N = 4$
Gas	223850	231977	240311	273649	310255	367365

The overall gas cost of function update is dominated by the gas cost of a zk-proof verification, which can be express as the gas cost of key operations such as point addition, scalar multiplication and pairings equality checks on bn256 curve, seeing in ZETH [19] for details. Although increasing M and N in the inputs will increase the verification gas cost and the number of modifications made in the Ethereum storage at each function calling, it can reduce the frequency of generating and verifying the zk-proof. Thus, there exist a trade-off and it affected by the number of voters and voting messages in practice. Furthermore, if the smart contract maintains very deep Merkle tree will also cost a lot every time when insert a leaf. So, we can add a function *clear* calling by operator to clear the MTree, CTree NPool and MPool before next epoch, but keep the users' keypairs in UPool.

6   Conclusion

In this paper, we have proposed CACM to solve the collusion problem, which exist in most of decentralized applications using voting mechanism. We not only introduce the concrete structure of CACM, but also test the implement of CACM on Ethereum test network, which have shown the feasibility of it. Never the less, CACM can be extend to use in consensus mechanism of blockchain. Based on the knowledge gained from this paper, we can't avoid the existence of the operator currently, which need to execute some heavy arithmetic tasks to generate zk-proof. In future work, we will investigate the feasibility of eliminating the operator, and improve the privacy of voters.

Acknowledgments. This work is supported by the National Natural Science Foundation of China (No. 91748107), Guangdong Basic and Applied Basic Research Foundation (No. 2020A1515010616), Guangdong Innovative Research Team Program (No. 2014ZT05G157).

References

1. Bihu (2017). https://bihu.com/whitePaper.pdf
2. Eth.: Ethereum Trading Subreddit. http://reddit.com/r/ethtrader
3. Buterin, V.: Quadratic Payments: A Primer. Vitalik Buterin's website, (2019) https://www.vit alik.ca/general/2019/12/07/quadratic.html
4. https://medium.com/gitcoin/gitcoin-grants-50k-open-source-fund-e20e09dc2110
5. Buterin, V.: On Collusion. Vitalik Buterin's website (2019). https://vitalik.ca/general/2019/04/03/collusion.html
6. Buterin, V.: Minimal anti-collusion infrastructure. Ethereum Research (2019) https://ethres ear.ch/t/minimal-anti-collusion-infrastructure/5413
7. WhiteHat, B., Tan, K., Gurkan, K., WeiJie, K.: Minimal anti-collusion infrastructure (2019) https://github.com/barryWhiteHat/maci/blob/master/SPEC.md
8. Sean, B., Ariel, G.: Making groth's zk-snark simulation extractable in the random oracle m-odel. IACR Cryptol. ePrint Arch. pp. 187 (2018)
9. Groth, J., Maller, M.: Snarky signatures: minimal signatures of knowledge from simulation-extractable snarks. In: Katz, J., Shacham, H. (eds.) CRYPTO 2017. LNCS, vol. 10402, pp. 581–612. Springer, Cham (2017). https://doi.org/10.1007/978-3-319-63715-0_20
10. Jens, G.: On the Size of Pairing-based Non-interactive Arguments. Cryptology ePrint Archive:Report 2016/260 (2016). https://eprint.iacr.org/2016/260
11. Daira, H., Sean, B., Taylor, H., Nathan, W.: Zcash Protocol Specification, Version 2019.0.6 [Overwinter + Sapling + Blossom]. Accessed 22 Feb 2019 https://github.com/zcash/zips/blob/master/protocol/protocol.pdf
12. Abdolmaleki, B., Baghery, K., Lipmaa, H., Zajac, M.: A subversion-resistant snark. In: Takagi, T., Peyrin, T. (eds.) ASIACRYPT 2017. LNCS, vol. 10626, pp. 3–33. Springer, Cham (2017). https://doi.org/10.1007/978-3-319-70700-6_1
13. Fuchsbauer, G.: Subversion-zero-knowledge snarks. In: Abdalla, M., Dahab, R. (eds.) PKC 2018. LNCS, vol. 10769, pp. 315–347. Springer, Cham (2018). https://doi.org/10.1007/978-3-319-76578-5_11
14. Antoine, R., Michal, Z.: ZETH: On Integrating Zerocash on Ethereum (2019). https://arxiv.org/pdf/1904.00905.pdf
15. WeBank. WeIdentity. https://fintech.webank.com/developer/docs/weidentity
16. Xiangbin, X., Zhenguo, Y., Wenyin, L.: Improved consensus mechanisms against censorshi-p attacks. In: 2019 IEEE International Conference on Industrial Cyber Physical Systems (ICPS) (2019)
17. Buterin, V.: Automated Censorship Attack Rejection (2017). https://github.com/ethereum/res earch/tree/master/papers/censorship_rejection
18. WhiteHat, B.: baby_jubjub_ecc. https://github.com/barryWhiteHat/baby_jubjub_ecc
19. Loopring.: New Approach to Generating Layer-2 Account Keys (2020). https://blogs.loo pring.org/new-approach-to-generating-layer-2-account-keys-cn

The Framework of Consensus Equilibria for Gap Games in Blockchain Ecosystems

Lan Di[1], Fan Wang[2], Lijian Wei[2], George Yuan[2,3,4(✉)], Tu Zeng[4], Qianyou Zhang[5(✉)], and Xiaojing Zhang[6]

[1] School of Artificial Intelligence and Computer Science, Jiangnan University, Wuxi 214122, China
[2] Business School, Sun Yat-Sen University, Guangzhou 510275, China
george_yuan99@yahoo.com
[3] School of Fintech, Shanghai Lixin University of Accounting and Finance, Shanghai 201209, China
[4] BBD Technology Co., Ltd. (BBD), No. 966, Tianfu Avenue, Chengdu 610093, China
[5] Business School, Chengdu University, Chengdu 610106, China
zhangqianyou@163.com
[6] Military Science Press, Military Academy of Science, Xianghongqi, Haidian District, Beijing 100091, China

Abstract. The goal of this paper is to establish the general framework of consensus equilibria for Mining Pool Games in Blockchain Ecosystems, and in particular to explain the stable in the sense for the existence of consensus equilibria related to mining gap game's behaviors by using one new concept called "Consensus Games" under the environment of Blockchain Ecosystems, where, the Blockchain Ecosystem mainly means the economic activities by taking into the account of three fundamental factors which are "Expenses, Reward Mechanism and Mining Power" for the work on blockschain by applying the key consensus called "Proof of Work" due to Nakamoto in 2008 and related ones.

Keywords: Consensus equilibrium · Nakamoto consensus · Mining gap game · Blockchain ecosystems

1 Introduction

The goal of this paper is to explain the stable in the sense for the existence of consensus equilibria for mining gap games by using one new concept called consensus games (CG) under the framework of Blockchain Ecosystems which mainly mean the economic activities by taking into the account of three types of different factors which are expenses, reward mechanism and mining power for the work on blockschain by applying consensuses including the Proof of Work due to Nakamoto in 2008 as a special case.

By a fact that both equity and currency tokens are typically two kinds of initial coin offerings (ICOs) like Bitcoin or Ethereum based on the platform of

© Springer Nature Singapore Pte Ltd. 2020
Z. Zheng et al. (Eds.): BlockSys 2020, CCIS 1267, pp. 45–53, 2020.
https://doi.org/10.1007/978-981-15-9213-3_4

Blochchains to provide a particular product or service, it is very important to study the mechanism of Blockchain Ecosystems. It is well known that in the Bitcoin world, all miners following the so-called Nakamoto's consensus protocol (2008), and work in a number of different groups (pools) to mine for Bitcion. Work on the block in a process called "mining" is successfully and approved due to the majority of miners applying key consensus called "Proof of Work", as each miner or pool may work in different ways, we need to thus deal with the so-called "Pool-Games" of miners (also use the term, "Mining Pool Game") with their working (mining) behaviors as an individual or in a group (pool) by following either cooperative or non-cooperative ways. In order to so do, we will introduce a new notion called "Consensus Games" which will be used to establish the general existence of equilibria for consensus games to describe mining behavior for Blockchain Ecosystems in Fintech. In particular, we will focus on the general discussion for the mechanism of the phenomenon called "Mining Gap Behavior" (in short, "Gap Games") for miners under the framework of general incentives consensus in which miners would avoid mining blocks when the available fees are insufficient (in particular, if incentives come only from fees, then a mining gap behavior would happen, for more in details, see Carlesten et al. [3], Tsabary and Eyal [25] and related references wherein).

The idea to consider the mixture of both Nash and cooperative equilibria together was originally studied by Zhao [29] under the name called "Hybrid Solution", and supported by recently work under Yang and Yuan [27], we are able to establish a new tool by "Consensus Games" in topological vector spaces without ordered preferences from the viewpoint of Blockchain in Fintech (see also Di et al. [9,10])

Briefly, the "Consensus Game" is a new concept which allows us to discuss if there exists an acceptable (may or not be "optimal") collaborative strategy which consists of a partial cooperative strategy and a partial noncooperative strategy under a given consensus rule in which some participants are based on cooperative, or non-cooperative game strategies by following such as mining "Longest Chain Rules (LCR)" due to Nakamoto [20] consensus (see also Biais et al. [1], Nyumbayire [22] and reference wherein) for the discussion with or without occurring forks for blockchain acting as a platform called the "Blockchain Ecosystems" or "Consensus Economics"). Thus, when comparing with the traditional cooperative and non-cooperative game, the consensus game is a natural extension for a consensus economy, especially under the framework of the Bitcoin ecosystem associated with Nakamoto's consensus protocol. We note that mining pool games were extensively studied by Bonneau et al. [2], Eyal [11], Eyal and Sirer [12], Kroll et al. [18], Sapirstein et al. [23] and references wherein. By applying the new concept called "Consensus Game" discussed by Di et al. [9,10], the aim of this paper is to discuss he following issue which is one of the most fundamental questions for consensus economics in Fintech:

"Is it possible to have a general consensus (for example, the Nakamoto's one) to lead the Mining-Pool Game stable in supporting the Blockchain ecosystem to run (even with existing attacker) in terms of two issues below:

(1) there always exists honest miners maintaining the Mining Longest Chain Rules (LCR) (given the plausibility of mining pool attacking); and

(2) Bitcoin ecosystem always works (or, majorities of miners do not collude to break it; here the term "collusion" means an attempt to violate the LCR and for a high reward block)?"

2   The Meaning for the New Concept "Consensus Games"

By following the consensus protocol due to Nakamoto in year 2008, it is expected that the way to follow a set of rules formulated by the consensus protocol truthfully for each miners (agents) from mining pools should correspond a preference mapping (e.g., see the profit function discussed in next section) under the framework of so-called the abstract economy model (see Yuan [28] and references wherein), it thus is very important to study the existence (and stability) of Blockchain consensus in the perspective of the existence for equilibria of miners (from mining pools) to follow the so-called "LCR" (see the discussion in Sect. 3 below) while with or without occurring of forks for blockchain of Bitcoin ecosystems.

Based on the idea of the consensus mechanism associated with blockchains, a mining pool game can be regarded as a problem to find a (game) strategy under which some group of miners (called, "honest miners") in the mining pools (for Bitcoins) to apply for "LCR" consensus respect to either non-cooperative or cooperative game's behaviors though maybe some miners may take "selfish mining" or "mining pool with attacking" strategies, this situation by the mixing of both cooperative and non-cooperative game behaviors is indeed the concept for so-called a "Consensus Game".

For a given consensus $\mathbf{G}$, by following Di et al. [10], let $N = \{1, 2, \cdots, n_0\}$, the set of players (or say, agents), and $p = \{N_1, \cdots, N_{k_0}\}$, the partition of N. For each $i \in N$, the mapping $u_i : X \rightrightarrows R$ is a payoff function for i associated with the rules of the consensus $\mathbf{G}$, a normal form of a "Consensus Games" is defined by the form: $CG := (\mathbf{G}, N, p, (X_i, u_i)_{i \in N})$. Thus, a consensus game (in short, CG) is defined by

$$CG := (N, p, (X(t))_{t \in N}, P)$$

where N is the set of players (miners); $p := \{N_r | r \in R\}$, a partition of N; $X(t)$ is the strategy space of player t; and $X := \prod_{t \in N} X(t), X(S) = \prod_{t \in S} X(t), X(-S) = \prod_{t \notin S} X(t), \forall S \in \mathcal{N}$; and $P(t, \cdot) : X \rightrightarrows X$ is its preference mapping of player t.

A point $x^* \in X$ is a consensus equilibrium of CG if for any $N_r \in p$ and any $S \in \mathcal{N}_r$, there exists no $y(S) \in X(S)$ such that

$$\{y(S)\} \times X(N_r - S) \times \{x^*(-N_r)\} \subset P(t, x^*), \ \forall t \in S.$$

We will use the consensus equilibria for consensus games in Sect. 4.

3   The Consensus Equilibria of Mining Gap Games

In order to discuss the general existence and stability problems related the study from a number of literatures for mining pool games of Bitcoins consensus principle introduced by Nakamoto [20] in Year 2008, we first give the description for the Mining Gap Game.

1) The Concept of General Gap Games for Miners

As discussed by Tsabary and Eyal [25], the repeated search for the blocks becomes a series of independent one-shot competitions, in each only one miner gets the reward but all miners pay expenses. The reason to consider the expected revenues, rather than considering the individual iterations we consider a one-shot game played by the miners. A player's strategy is the choice of start times of all of her rigs: when each rig is turned on. The choice of start times are made a-priori by all players. We define the profit function $P_i(t)$ for the miner i (but the corresponding utility of a player to be her/his expected profit), which is her/his expected income minus her/his expected expenses at a given time t.

Here we recalled that a "Gap Game (GP)" indeed is a set of miners $N :=$ $\{1, 2, \cdots, n\}$ with a partition $N_1, N_2, \cdots, N_k$ of N which is a system (consisting of n mining rigs controlled by k players), each N_j is a player, where $j \in K =$ $\{1, 2, \cdots, k\}$: The player j controls the set of rigs with indices R_j.

We use "Block-Interval" to denote the expected block time interval achieved by the protocol, let s_j be the start time of each rig j, and using $\hat{s}_j :=$ $\frac{s_j}{Block-Interval}$ to represent the normalized start time.

Throughout of this paper, for the convenience, we assume that once a rig is turned on, the time the rig requires to find a block following an independent exponentially distributed with parameter $\mu(\hat{s}))$, and $\hat{s}$ denotes the vector of increasing order n rigs' start times. By assuming all rigs are identical (i.e., with the computing power), thus each mining rig costs "C_{cap}" per time unit for the ownership explained as the capital cost (for example), and "C_{op}" per time unit if it is turned on explained as operation cost.

Without loss of the generality, we assume that the fees reward accumulation over time to use a linear regression to model (see Tsabary and Eyal [25]). Thus, total block reward is modelled as a linear function and denoted by λ_t as the "fees accumulation rate", and λ_0 as the "base reward", we have following notations by defining "Expected-Total-Fees" being the expected total fees accumulating during the expected time to find a block, namely,

$$\text{Expected-Total-Fees} := \text{Block-Interval} \cdot \lambda_t,$$

and also define $\text{EBRR} := \dfrac{\lambda_0}{\text{Expected-Total-Fees}}$.

By the fact that we assume any miner has only one option either joining or leaving the system, and for the simplicity, we may suppose the cost of C_{op} and C_{cap} are a fixed amount.

Next we discuss the profit function $P_i(t)$ for each $i = 1, 2, \cdots, k$ at time t, which allow us to establish the general existence of consensus equilibria for Gap Games described in next section.

2) The Miner's Profit Function for Mining Gap Games

For a given miner $i = 1, 2, \cdots, k$, assume a single rig $j \in R_i$ with start time s_j, the random variable in time for this rig to find a block is denoted by B_j, then B_j is drawn from the shifted exponential distribution with parameters s_i and $\mu((s))$. For any time t and any player i, the active sets $\text{active}_i(t)$ and $\text{active}(t)$ are defined by $\text{active}_i(t) := \{j \in R_i : s_j \leq t\}$ and, $\text{active}(t) := \cup_{i=1}^{k} R_i$. By defining $\alpha_i(t) := \frac{|\text{active}_i(t)|}{|\text{active}(t)|}$ as the ratio of player $i's$ active rigs out of all the active rigs at time t, then we know that the ratio $\alpha_i(t)$ is continuous in t, and is also the expected factor of player $i's$ portion of the total reward.

We also recall that players in general have two kind of expenses: The first one may be called "Capex", would be explained for the capital cost such as for "owning a rig"; and the second one called "Open", for example, which would be explained for the operation cost such as for "keeping a rig active". By a fact that the Capex for all rigs is controlled by the player (whether turned on or not), it follows for each rig, the Capex it imposes by time t is the quantity: $C_{\text{cap}} \cdot t$.

Then for each miner i, we have the following profit function (e.g., see Tsbary and Eyal [25]):

$$P_i(t) = \alpha_i(t)(\lambda_0 + \lambda_t \cdot t) - C_{\text{cap}} \cdot |R_i| \cdot t - C_{\text{op}} \cdot \Sigma_{j \in \text{active}_i(t)}(t - s_j) \qquad (1)$$

4   The Consensus Equilibria of Gap Games

Now for a given mining gap game, where $i \in N = \{1, 2, \cdots, n\}$, without loss of generality we may assume that T_i assigned a big enough value in the real line R for time, and we define $X_i := [0, T_i]$ and $X := \prod_{i=1}^{n} X_i$. Then X_i and X are both compact and convex subsets of the real line R and R^n for $i \in N$. Based on the notations of a gap game introduced above, and incorporating with the profit function $P_i(t)$ for $i \in N$ at time t defined in X_i, then it is easy to see that a gap game indeed is a consensus game $CG := (N, K, (X_i, P_i)_{i \in N})$, where $N = \{1, 2, \cdots, n\}$, $K = \{1, 2, \cdots, k\}$ with the $k's$ partition $N_1, \cdots, N_2, \cdots, N_k$ of N as mentioned above.

We now have the following general existence results for consensus equilibria of Gap Games in supporting the stability for Blochchain Ecosystems as applications of general consensus game model established in Sect. 2 above.

Theorem 4.1 (The Consensus Equilibria for Mining Gap Games). For a given general Mining Gap Game (which is indeed a consensus game (in short, CG) if the profit function P_i (defined above) is concave from $[0, T_i] \mapsto R$ for each $i \in N = \{1, 2, \cdots, n\}$, then the Gap Game CG has at least one consensus equilibrium.

Proof. Note that for each $i \in N$, P_i is continuous in t, plus we assume that P_i is concave, thus P_i is continuous and concave. All assumptions of Theorem 2.2 of Di et al. [10] are satisfied, and the conclusion follows and the proof is complete.

Theorem 4 says that for a given consensus and a miner i, if its Profit function P_i is reasonable well (see below for each special case), the consensus game theory allows us to deal with the general framework for Gap games, thus we are able to claim the existence for honest miners to keep "Mining Longest Chain Rules (LCR)" under a reasonable consensus (e.g., such as Nakamoto [20]) which indeed answer the following question in affirmatively:

"The stability for Blockchain ecosystems is there due to the existence of the honest miners keeping "Mining Longest Chain Rules (LCR)" under a given reasonable consensus, and thus we would claim the following statements:

(1): there always exists honest miners keeping "Mining Longest Chain Rules (LCR)" (though maybe with or without either "Occurring Gap Behavior, or Fork Chain" for blockchains), plus the plausibility of mining-pool attacking; and

(2): Bitcoin ecosystem always works (as the majorities of miners do not collude to break it)."

As applications of Theorem 4, we have the following Remark 4 by assuming the operation cost for the Gap Game's system being zero.

Remark 4.1 (The Mining Pool Game is Stable without Operational Cost).

Indeed, for each miner i, by (1) it follows that the Profit function $P_i(t)$ has the following form:

$$P_i(t) = \alpha_i(t)(\lambda_0 + \lambda \cdot t) - C_{\text{cap}} \cdot |R_i| \cdot t.$$

By the fact that the term "$-C_{\text{cap}} \cdot |R_i| \cdot t$" play a huge negative role for player i's income in terms of profit function P_i at time t, thus one way to reduce the loss for the system (in terms of $P_i(t)$) is to make the ratio $\alpha_i(t)$ as bigger as possible at time t. If assume miner i's computing power is m_i for $i \in N$, then one of the possible best options (strategies) for player i is to run all rigs, and thus $\text{active}_i(t) = m_i$ and so we have $\alpha_i(t) = \frac{m_i}{\Sigma_{j=1}^{k} m_j}$ for any time $t \in [0, T_i]$. Thus the ratio $\alpha_i(t)$ is independent of t and thus concave, therefor the concavity assumption is satisfies, which implies that the system for the gap game without operational cost always has at least one equilibrium with the mining's starting time for miners at zero (thus in the situation without operational cost, the pool games in general has no "Gap" phenomenon as all miners like to start mining with starting time zero (due to the fact without any expense of the operational cost).

When the system of mining pool games has no capital and operational cost, then we have the following general result for mining pool game without the phenomenon of the Gap game behavior to occur.

Theorem 4.2 (The Ming Gap Games without Capital and Operational Cost). For a given general Gap Game with both Capital and Operational Costs are zero, if assume the ratio function $\alpha_i(t)$ is concave in t for each $i \in N = \{1, 2, \cdots, n\}$, then the mining pool game has at least one consensus equilibrium, and no phenomenon of gap game behavior.

Remark 4.2. When both $C_{\text{OP}} = 0$ and $C_{\text{cap}}(t) = 0$, by considering the Profit function $P_i(t) = \alpha_i(t)(\lambda_0 + \lambda_t \cdot t)$. The best way to increase the value of $P_i(t)$ is to fully run rigs, thus it is best at the beginning to have $\alpha_i = \frac{m_i}{\Sigma_{j=1}^{k} m_j}$, where m_i

is the mining power for miner $i \in \{1, 2, \cdots, n\}$. In this way, $\alpha_i(t)$ is a constat, thus all assumptions of Theorem 4 are satisfied, which leads the system has at least one equilibrium.

5 The Conclusions

We wish to point out that the study on the existence of Mining Gap games and related stability for mining-pools games by applying consensus games show that the concept of consensus equilibria would play a key role for the development of fundamental theory for consensus economics. Indeed, the concept of consensus games can also be used to establish the general fundamental results in supporting existence and related stability for mining pool games of Bitcoin economics, and the study for data trading of IoTs and related consensus management (see Di et al. [10], Kang et al. [16] and references wherein).

We also note that problems related to smart contracts related Blockchains, bigdata and related topics in fintech have been studied by Chen et al. [4], Chiu and Koeppl [5], Cong and He [6], D'Acunto et al. [7], Dai and Vasarhelyi [8], Di et al. [9]–[10], Foley et al. [13], Fuster et al. [14], Goldstein et al. [15], Narayanan et al. [21] Tang [24], Vallee and Zeng [26], Zhu [30] and references wherein.

The Acknowledgements. All authors thank the professional service and hardwork provided by the organization committee for Blocksys'2020. This research was supported in part by the National Natural Science Foundation of China under the grant numbers U1811462 and 11501349.

References

1. Biais, B., Bisire, C., Bouvard, M., Casamatta, C.: The blockchain folk theorem. Review Finan. Stud. **32**(5), 1662–1715 (2019)
2. Bonneau, J., Miller, A., Clark, J., Narayanan, A., Kroll, A., Felten, E.: Research perspectives and challenges for Bitcoin and cryptocurrencies. In: Proceedings of the 36th IEEE Symposium on Security and Privacy, San Jose, California, USA, 18–20 May 2015
3. Carlsten, M., Kalodner, H., Weinberg, S.M., Narayanan, A.: On the instability of Bitcoin without the block reward. In: Proceedings of the 2016 ACM SIGSAC Conference on Computer and Communications Security, ACM, pp. 154–167, Vienna, Austria, 24–28 October 2016
4. Chen, M., Wu, Q., Yang, B.: How valuable is FinTech innovation? Rev. Financial Stud. **32**(5), 2062–2106 (2019)
5. Chiu, J., Koeppl, T.: Blockchain-based settlement for asset trading. Rev. Financial Stud. **32**(5), 1716–1753 (2019)
6. Cong, L.W., He, Z.: Blockchain disruption and smart contracts. Rev. Financial Stud. **32**(5), 1754–1797 (2019)
7. D'Acunto, F., Prabhala, N., Rossi, A.G.: The promises and pitfalls of Robo-Advising. Rev. Financial Stud. **32**(5), 1983–2020 (2019)
8. Dai, J., Vasarhelyi, M.A.: Toward blockchain-based accounting and assurance. J. Inf. Syst. **31**, 5–21 (2017)

9. Di, L., Yang, Z., Yuan, G.X.: The consensus games for consensus economics under the framework of blockchain in Fintech. In: Li, D.-F. (ed.) EAGT 2019. CCIS, vol. 1082, pp. 1–26. Springer, Singapore (2019). https://doi.org/10.1007/978-981-15-0657-4_1

10. Di, L., Yuan, G.X., Tu, Z., Zhang, Q., Zhang, X.: The existence of consensus equilibria for data trading under the framework of Internet of Things (IoT) with Blockchain ecosystems. In: Bie, R. Sun, Y. Yu, J. (eds.) 2019 International Conference on Identification, Information and Knowledge in the Internet of Things, Procedia Computer Science, vol. 174, pp. 55–65. Springer, Heidelberg (2020)

11. Eyal, I.: The Miners Dilemma. In: Proceedings of the 36th IEEE Symposium on Security and Privacy, San Jose, California, USA, 18–20 May 2015

12. Eyal, I., Sirer, E.: Majority is not enough: Bitcoin mining is vulnerable. In: Proceedings of the 18th International Conference on Financial Cryptography and Data Security, FC'14, pp. 436–454. Springer, Heidelberg (2014)

13. Foley, S., Karlsen, J.R., Putnins, T.: Sex, drugs, and Bitcoin: how much illegal activity is financed through Cryptocurrencies? Rev. Financial Stud. 32(5), 1798–1853 (2019)

14. Fuster, A., Plosser, M., Schnabl, S., Vickery, J.: The role of technology in mortgage lending. Rev. Financial Stud. 32(5), 1854–1899 (2019)

15. Goldstein, I., Jiang, W., Karolyi, G.: To FinTech and beyond. Rev. Financial Stud. 32(5), 1647–1661 (2019)

16. Kang, J., Xiong, Z., Niyato, D., Ye, D., Kim, D.I., Zhao, J.: Toward secure blockchain-enabled internet of vehicles: optimizing consensus management using reputation and contract theory. IEEE Trans. Veh. Technol. 68(3), 2906–2920 (2019)

17. Kiayias, A., Koutsoupias, E., Kyropoulou, M., Tselekounis, Y.: Blockchain mining games. In: 2016 ACM Conference on Economics and Computation, Maastricht, The Netherlands, 24–28 July 2016

18. Kroll, J., Davey, I., Felten, E.: The economics of Bitcoin mining, or Bitcoin in the presence of adversaries. In: Proceedings of The Twelfth Workshop on the Economics of Information Security (WEIS 2013), Georgetown University, Washington DC, USA, 11–12 June 2013)

19. Kwon, Y., Kim, D., Son, Y., Vasserman, E., Kim, Y.: Be selfish and avoid Dilemmas: fork after withholding (FAW) attacks on Bitcoin. In: 2017 ACM CCS 2017, Oct. 30–Nov. 3, 2017, Dallas, TX, USA. 2017 ACM. ISBN 978-1-4503-4946-8/17/10 https://doi.org/10.1145/3133956.3134019

20. Nakamoto, S.: Bitcoin: a peer-to-peer electronic cash system. http://bitcoin.org/bitcoin.pdf (2008)

21. Narayanan, A., Bonneau, J., Felten, E., Miller, A., Goldfeder, S.: Bitcoin and Cryptocurrency Technologies: A Comprehensive Introduction. Princeton University Press, Princeton (2016)

22. Nyumbayire, C.: The Nakamoto Consensus (https://www.interlogica.it/en/insight-en/nakamoto-consensus). Insight, Interlogica, February 2017

23. Sapirshtein, A., Sompolinsky, Y., Zohar, A.: Optimal selfish mining strategies in Bitcoin. In: Grossklags, J., Preneel, B. (eds.) FC 2016. LNCS, vol. 9603, pp. 515–532. Springer, Heidelberg (2017). https://doi.org/10.1007/978-3-662-54970-4_30

24. Tang, H.: Peer-to-Peer lenders versus banks: substitutes or complements? Rev. Financial Stud. 32(5), 1900–1938 (2019)

25. Tsabary, I., Eyal, I.: The gap game. In: Proceedings of the 2018 ACM SIGSAC conference on computer and communications security (CCS 2018), pp. 713–728 (2018)

26. Vallee, B., Zeng, Y.: Marketplace lending: a new banking paradigm? Revi. Financial Stud. **32**(5), 1939–1982 (2019)
27. Yang, Z., Yuan, G.X.: Some generalizations of Zhao's theorem: hybrid solutions and weak hybrid solutions for games with nonordered preferences. J. Math. Econ. **84**, 94–100 (2019)
28. Yuan, G.X.: The study of equilibria for abstract economies in topological vector spaces-a unified approach. Nonlinear Anal. TMA **37**, 409–430 (1999)
29. Zhao, J.: The hybrid solutions of an N-person game. Games Econ. Behav. **4**, 145–160 (1992)
30. Zhu, C.: Big data as a governance mechanism. Rev. Financial Stud. **32**(5), 2021–2061 (2019)

Performance Optimization of Blockchain

DP-Hybrid: A Two-Layer Consensus Protocol for High Scalability in Permissioned Blockchain

Fulin Wen[1], Lei Yang[1(✉)], Wei Cai[2,3], and Pan Zhou[4]

[1] School of Software Engineering, South China University of Technology,
Guangzhou 510006, China
201921043987@mail.scut.edu.cn, sely@scut.edu.cn
[2] School of Science and Engineering, The Chinese University of Hong Kong,
Shenzhen 518172, China
caiwei@cuhk.edu.cn
[3] Shenzhen Institute of Artificial Intelligence and Robotics for Society,
Shenzhen 518172, China
[4] School of Cyber Science and Engineering, Huazhong University of Science
and Technology, Wuhan 430074, China
panzhou@hust.edu.cn

Abstract. The permissioned blockchain has attracted the attention of multiple industries like the supply chain due to its decentralization and data tamper resistance. In these industries applications, the permissioned blockchain maintained by multiple participants often has a large number of nodes. The PBFT consensus is commonly used in the permissioned blockchain, but it requires a large amount of message transmission to reach consensus, resulting in poor scalability. In this paper, we propose DP-Hybrid, a novel two-layer consensus protocol, to reduce the communication costs and improve scalability. Specifically, nodes use PBFT to establish K autonomous systems at the bottom layer, and then participate at the top layer with Constrained PoW consensus protocol. DP-Hybrid reduces the communication costs from PBFT's $O(N^2)$ to $O(N^2/K^2)$. The experiment results show that DP-Hybrid's throughput is always about 10 times that of PBFT when the number of nodes increases.

Keywords: Blockchain · Permissioned blockchain · Consensus protocol · Scalability · Throughput

1 Introduction

Blockchain utilizes special consensus protocols in a decentralized network to maintain data consistency between nodes and provide tamper-proof capability. The permissioned blockchain is a blockchain that provides node authentication. The Practical Byzantine Fault Tolerance (PBFT) [1] is widely used in permissioned blockchain. It achieves high throughput and low latency when the

© Springer Nature Singapore Pte Ltd. 2020
Z. Zheng et al. (Eds.): BlockSys 2020, CCIS 1267, pp. 57–71, 2020.
https://doi.org/10.1007/978-981-15-9213-3_5

number of nodes N is small. However, when N rises, its performance drops rapidly because of the $O(N^2)$ communication costs required to reach consensus.

Optimizations of PBFT were proposed in [2–4]. Researchers also proposed new consensus to achieve higher performance. In [5,6], fault tolerance is sacrificed for faster consensus speed. Hierarchical consensus protocols were proposed in [7–13], which reduce the number of nodes participating in consensus and sacrifice fault tolerance to improve scalability. [7–13] use a voting-based consensus at the high layer, and there are leader nodes which vote on behalf of ordinary nodes to reduce the communication costs, which inevitably reduces security. We believe that non-voting-based consensus, such as Proof of Work (PoW), is more suitable as a high-layer consensus protocol in hierarchical consensus protocols.

In this paper, we propose DP-Hybrid to achieve high throughput and scalability in permissioned blockchain. DP-Hybrid uses PBFT as the bottom-layer consensus protocol and Constrained PoW (CPoW) as the top-layer consensus protocol. In DP-Hybrid, nodes are divided into groups at the bottom layer. The nodes within the same group communicate with each other based on PBFT. All the nodes represent their own group to communicate with other participants' nodes based on CPoW at the top layer. The hierarchical structure reduces the communication costs and improves scalability. Meanwhile, DP-Hybrid's security is not sacrificed and it can be configured to meet requirements. In contrast to [7–13], there are no leader nodes to represent the ordinary nodes in DP-Hybrid and thus the Byzantine failure of leader nodes does not exist.

We conduct extensive experiments to evaluate DP-Hybrid's throughput. Results show that DP-Hybrid's throughput is about 10 times of PBFT in the experimental environment. As the number of nodes increases, throughput of both consensus protocols decreases, but DP-Hybrid's throughput is always about 10 times of PBFT. We summarize our contributions as follows:

- To the best of our knowledge, DP-Hybrid is the first consensus protocol that combines CPoW and PBFT to improve scalability of permissioned blockchain without sacrificing security.
- We evaluate DP-Hybrid's throughput using extensive experiments. The results show that DP-Hybrid's throughput is always higher than PBFT when the number of nodes increases.

The remainder of this paper is organized as follows. Section 2 introduces the preliminary knowledge of blockchain and consensus protocols. Section 3 describes our design of DP-Hybrid. Section 4 analyzes communication costs, security, liveness and latency of DP-Hybrid and comparative consensus protocols. Section 5 presents the experiment we conducted to evaluate DP-Hybrid. Section 6 discusses the related works. Section 7 concludes this paper.

2   Preliminary

2.1   Consensus Protocol

In a distributed system, consensus protocols are required to maintain consistent data across nodes. Blockchain is a special distributed system, whose data can

Table 1. Comparison of different consensus protocols

	Type	Scalability	Throughput	Latency	Node authorization	Fault tolerance
PoW	PCP	Good	Low	High	No	–
PoS	PCP	Good	Low	High	No	–
PBFT	DCP	Bad	High	Low	Yes	$\lfloor \frac{N-1}{3} \rfloor$

only be added but not deleted or modified. Therefore, consensus protocols in the blockchain mainly describe the rules or processes of adding new data.

There are two types of consensus protocols in the blockchain, i.e., Deterministic Consensus Protocol (DCP) and Probabilistic Consensus Protocol (PCP). The outcome of DCP is irreversible if consensus is reached between the nodes. Conversely, the outcome of PCP consensus is reversible, but will gradually strengthen over time, making the outcome a definitive result. We compare common consensus protocols in terms of type, latency, etc. The details are listed in Table 1.

PCP has better scalability, where nodes can freely enter or exit the blockchain. In contrast, node changes in DCP require modifications of the remaining nodes. DCP has higher throughput and lower latency than PCP but performance drop rapidly as the number of nodes increases. PCP can be used in public blockchain without node authorization and it's fault tolerance is independent of the number of nodes, but related to node's read-world assets. Conversely, DCP can only be used in permissioned blockchain with node authorization to resist the Sybil Attack. DCP can tolerate a fixed proportion of faulty nodes.

2.2   PBFT Consensus Protocol

In the PBFT, N nodes are numbered from 0 to $N-1$. The PBFT can tolerate $F = \lfloor \frac{N-1}{3} \rfloor$ faulty nodes. Nodes move through a succession of configurations called views. Views are numbered consecutively starting from 0. In each view v, the node i with $i = v\%N$ acts as the *primary node* and the others act as *backup nodes*. The *primary node* accepts clients' requests and initiates PBFT to reach consensus. Each node sends the result to the client after reaching consensus. The client waits for $F+1$ replies with the same result from different nodes.

If the client does not receive enough replies before timeout, it broadcasts the request to *backup nodes*. If the request has been processed, *backup nodes* resend the result. Otherwise, *backup nodes* initiate a *PBFT view change* to generate a new *primary node*. Each *backup node* broadcasts a *view change* message to the others. if a node receives $2 \times F$ same *view change* messages, it updates its $v = v + 1$. After that, nodes reprocess the client's request.

The protocol steps in the normal case of no *primary node* faults are as follows:
Step 1: Request. Client sends a request r to the *primary node*.
Step 2: Pre-Prepare (PP). The *primary node* broadcasts a pre-prepare message containing r to *backup nodes*.
Step 3: Prepare (P). Each *backup node* broadcasts a prepare message to the other nodes to confirm r's contents.

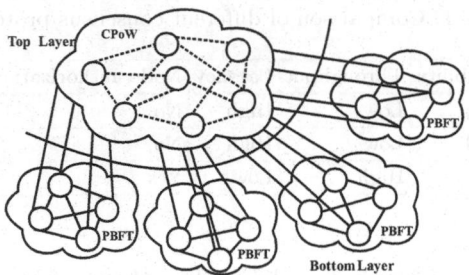

Fig. 1. Network model

Step 4: Commit (C). Each node broadcasts a commit message to the other nodes to confirm the execution of r.

Step 5: Reply. All the nodes execute r and reply to the client.

According to the above process, the communication costs required to reach consensus in PBFT are $O(N^2)$. As N increases, the number of messages increases rapidly, which results in decreased throughput and increased latency. For above reasons, we believe that PBFT is not suitable for industries scenarios where there are a large number of nodes. We propose DP-Hybrid, which combines CPoW and PBFT to reduce communication costs and imporves scalability.

3　Design of DP-Hybrid

3.1　DP-Hybrid Structure

As shown in Fig. 1, DP-Hybrid is divided into two layers, i.e., the bottom layer and the top layer. We assume that K participants jointly maintain a DP-Hybrid blockchain. The participants could be companies which join the blockchain for data sharing. There exists total N nodes in the blockchain and each participant has N/K nodes. The nodes within the same participant are called *internal nodes* and the other participants' nodes are called *external nodes*. The *internal nodes* of a participant forms a group at the bottom layer and communicate with each other based on PBFT. Meanwhile, all the nodes can represent their own groups to communicate with *external nodes* based on the CPoW at the top layer. The details of the consensus process will be discussed in Sect. 3.2.

We define notations as follows. P_i is the ith participant. N_i is the number of nodes in P_i. $F_i = \lfloor \frac{N_i-1}{3} \rfloor$ is the tolerable number of faulty nodes in P_i. n_i^j is the jth node in P_i. Every node knows all P_i, N_i and F_i ($i = 1 \ldots K$). They also know which participant each node belongs to. We list the notations in Table 2.

In the initialization, the *internal nodes* within P_i establish connections with each other and keep *external nodes'* communication addresses. After that, a *PBFT view change* occurs in P_i to generate a *primary node* and then each *internal node* in P_i broadcasts a message to the *external nodes*. The message is named by External View Changed (ext-VC) message, which includes the information of the new *primary node*. If a *external node* receives $2 \times F_i + 1$ same

Table 2. Notations in this paper

Notation	Meaning	Notation	Meaning
N	The total number of nodes	$\langle m \rangle_i^j$	Message m signed by n_i^j
K	The total number of participants	$\langle m \rangle$	Unsigned message m
P_i	The ith participant	v_i	The PBFT view number of P_i
N_i	The number of nodes in P_i	Tx	The transaction from client
F_i	The tolerable number of faulty nodes in P_i	B_a	The ath block in the CPoW blockchain
n_i^j	The jth node in P_i	l_i	The latest ID of Tx in P_i

ext-VC messages from P_i, it updates P_i's *primary node* information. With the ext-VC message, *external nodes* can identify P_i's *primary node*.

After finishing initialization, if a new node joins P_i or an existing node exits P_i, P_i's PBFT network system needs to be reconfigured. After that, except for the new node or the exited node, each *internal node* in P_i broadcasts a message to the *external nodes*. The message is named by External Node Changed (ext-NC) message, which includes the information of the new node or the exited node. If a *external node* receives $2 \times F_i + 1$ same ext-NC messages from P_i, it updates N_i, F_i and P_i's nodes information. With the ext-NC message, the *external node* can verify the new node's messages or ignore the exited node's messages.

In the operation of the DP-Hybrid blockchain, the client sends a transaction Tx to the *primary node* of a random P_i. The nodes in P_i reach local consensus on Tx via PBFT, and the local consensus is broadcast to other participants. Each participant collects local consensus from other participants. Meanwhile, all the participants compete to package both internal and external local consensus into CPoW blocks. To make a CPoW block valid, they need to find a nonce that makes the block's hash value less than a threshold. The valid CPoW blocks and transactions within the blocks are considered as global consensus.

3.2 Consensus Process

The following descriptions focus on the nodes of one participant P_i with N_i and F_i, while the nodes of the remaining participants are collectively referred to as *external nodes*. For simplicity, we use n_i^0 as the *primary node* and n_i^j ($j = 1, 2 \ldots N_i - 1$) as *backup nodes* in P_i to describe the consensus process.

At the bottom layer, each *internal node* acts as a PBFT state machine with an initial bottom state (*b_state*) of *Pre-Prepare* and performs state transitions as shown in Fig. 2. When a client sends a transaction to the *primary node*, the *primary node* triggers bottom state transitions. In each state, each *internal node* broadcasts confirmation message and waits for $2 \times F_i$ identical messages from other *internal nodes*. In the *Commit* state, the transaction is transformed into local consensus, and waiting to be packed into CPoW blocks.

The details of the bottom state transitions of the *primary node* and *backup nodes* are given in Algorithm 1 and Algorithm 2. We denote the message m signed by n_i^j as $\langle m \rangle_i^j$, the unsigned one as $\langle m \rangle$, the view number of P_i as v_i, the transaction as Tx, the assigned ID of Tx as l_i and the digest of Tx as d.

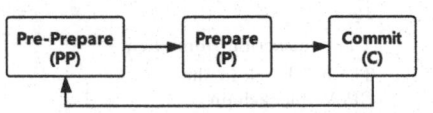

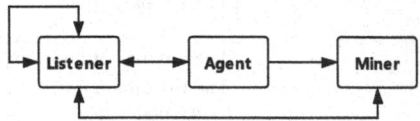

Fig. 2. State transitions of nodes at the bottom layer

Fig. 3. State transitions of nodes at the top layer

Algorithm 1. PBFT for primary node at the Bottom Layer

1: $l_i \leftarrow 1$, $b\_state \leftarrow PP$
2: **for** l_i=1,2,3... **do**
3:    **if** receive Tx from client & $b\_state = PP$ **then**
4:       broadcast $\langle \langle PP, v_i, l_i, d \rangle_i^0, Tx \rangle$ to *backup nodes*
5:       $b\_state \leftarrow P$
6:       wait for $2 \times F_i$ prepare messages with same v_i, l_i and d from different nodes
7:    **end if**
8:    **if** meet the above conditions & $b\_state = P$ **then**
9:       broadcast $\langle C, v_i, l_i, d, 0 \rangle_i^0$ to *backup nodes*
10:      $b\_state \leftarrow C$
11:      wait for $2 \times F_i$ commit messages with same v_i, l_i and d from different nodes
12:   **end if**
13:   **if** meet the above conditions & $b\_state = C$ **then**
14:      save $\langle P_i, l_i, Tx \rangle$ as local consensus
15:      reply to the client that Tx has been transformed into local consensus
16:      broadcast $\langle P_i, l_i, Tx \rangle_i^0$ to *external nodes*
17:      $l_i \leftarrow l_i+1$, $b\_state \leftarrow PP$
18:   **end if**
19: **end for**

After reaching local consensus, n_i^0 broadcasts $\langle P_i, Tx, l_i \rangle_i^0$ to *external nodes*. This allows Tx to be packed into CPoW block by other participants. Only the local consensus containing valid Tx, unused l_i and signature of P_i's *primary node* is valid and accepted. The *primary node* may send transactions that have not reached local consensus to *external nodes*, but this does not have benefit. Because invalid transactions will not be accepted anyway while valid transactions have more opportunities to be packed into CPoW block after reaching local consensus.

Algorithm 2. PBFT for backup node at the Bottom Layer

1: $l_i \leftarrow 1$, $b\_state \leftarrow PP$
2: **for** l_i=1,2,3... **do**
3:     **if** receive $\langle\langle PP, v_i, l_i, d\rangle_i^0, Tx\rangle$ from *primary node* & $b\_state = PP$ **then**
4:         broadcast $\langle P, v_i, l_i, d, j\rangle_i^j$ to the *primary node* and other *backup nodes*
5:         $b\_state \leftarrow P$
6:         wait for $2 \times F_i$ prepare messages with same v_i, l_i and d from different nodes
7:     **end if**
8:     **if** meet the above conditions & $b\_state = P$ **then**
9:         broadcast $\langle C, v_i, l_i, d, j\rangle_i^j$ to the *primary node* and other *backup nodes*
10:        $b\_state \leftarrow C$
11:        wait for $2 \times F_i$ commit messages with same v_i, l_i and d from different nodes
12:    **end if**
13:    **if** meet the above conditions & $b\_state = C$ **then**
14:        save $\langle P_i, l_i, Tx\rangle$ as local consensus
15:        reply to the client that Tx has been transformed into local consensus
16:        $l_i \leftarrow l_i+1$, $b\_state \leftarrow PP$
17:    **end if**
18: **end for**

While running PBFT to deal with transactions from client, each node communicates with *external nodes* according to the top-layer CPoW consensus protocol. We define the two constraints of CPoW:

– Confirmation Number (CN): If there are not less than CN blocks following the ath block B_a, the transactions in B_a become global consensus.
– Maximum number of Blocks in CN (MBC): A maximum of MBC blocks from the same participant are allowed in CN consecutive blocks.

These constraints reduce the competition of computing resources and make security not entirely dependent on the distribution of computing resources. Due to the MBC constraint, not all the nodes in a participant perform the Write Operation, which wastes computing resources. Therefore, we define three top states (t_state) of the nodes when participating at the top layer as follows:

– Listener: Only performs the Read Operation.
– Miner: Performs both Read and Write Operations.
– Agent: Determines whether to perform the Write Operation and broadcasts signed message containing the set S of miners' ID if needed.

The top state transitions are shown in Fig. 3. Algorithm 3 and Algorithm 4 describe the Write Operation and the Read Operation. The initial t_state of the nodes is *Listener*. We use the timestamp of the latest CPoW block, denoted as T, to generate the agent node and thus the agent node changes after receiving or generating new blocks. The n_i^j with $j = T\%N_i$ acts as the agent node and determines whether to perform the Write Operation according to the MBC constraint. If the MBC constraint is violated, the agent node broadcasts an empty set. Otherwise, the agent node generates a miner set S based on the incentive policy and broadcasts it to other *internal nodes*. The agent node soon changes its *t_state* based on S it generated. *Internal nodes* judge S based on the same incentive policy to change their *t_state*. If they find that S provides far smaller than the needed computing resources, they broadcast agent change message to

---

Algorithm 3. Write Operation at the Top Layer

1: **function** WRITEOPERATION()
2:     Generate a block B containing the hash of the previous block, local consensus from each participant, etc.
3:     find a *nonce* that makes B's hash start with D zeros
4:     add B to the CPoW blockchain
5:     broadcast B to both *internal* and *external nodes*
6:     *t_state* ← *Listener*
7:     execute ONRECEIVEBLOCK(B)
8: **end function**

---

replace the agent node. if a node receives $2 \times F_i$ same messages, it consider the n_i^q with $q = (T+1)\%N_i$ as the new agent node.

In the Algorithm 3, miner nodes find a *nonce* that makes B's hash start with D zeros. D is the difficulty factor of CPoW and it changes periodically. All the nodes in the network calculate the Average Block Interval (ABI) in a cycle and then adjust D based on the difference between the current ABI and the expected value. The expected value of ABI is a hyperparameter set before building the blockchain. ABI is negatively correlated with D, and the change in D always makes next cycle's ABI closer to the expected value. If the ABI is too high, the nodes reduce D in the next cycle, and the rest cases are similar.

Honest nodes only accept valid blocks from participants who do not violate the MBC constraint. A valid block should contain the hash of the previous block and a nonce that satisfies D and not contain any invalid transactions. When a valid block satisfies the CN constraint, the transactions in the block become global consensus and take effect.

3.3   Incentive Policy

There is no cryptocurrency in permissioned blockchain to motivate nodes to perform the Write Operation. To solve this problem, we limit the default amount of transactions from each participant contained in a CPoW block, denoted by Default Size (DS), and provide an additional amount of transactions to participant who generated blocks as a reward, denoted by Reward Size (RS). If P_i generated B_i, an additional RS transactions in each block from B_i to B_{i+CN-1} are allowed from P_i. Therefore, the Block Size (BS) can be expressed as $BS = DS \times K + RS \times CN$.

By setting the appropriate parameters, participants with large data volumes actively perform the Write Operation to obtain RS to meet the demand for writing data. Participants with less data volumes can meet the demand relying on DS without investing too much computing resources.

Algorithm 4. Read Operation at the Top Layer
_____
1: **function** ONRECEIVEBLOCK(B)
2:     **if** B is valid **then**
3:         add B to the CPoW blockchain
4:         **if** $t\_state = Miner$ **then**
5:             stop WRITEOPERATION()
6:         **end if**
7:         **if** ID $j \neq B.time\%N_i$ **then**
8:             $t\_state \leftarrow Listener$
9:         **else**
10:             $t\_state \leftarrow Agent$
11:             **if** the MBC constraint is violated **then**
12:                 generate miner set S
13:                 broadcast S to other *internal nodes*
14:                 execute ONRECEIVEMINERSET(S)
15:             **else**
16:                 broadcast empty set to other *internal nodes*
17:                 $t\_state \leftarrow Listener$
18:             **end if**
19:         **end if**
20:     **end if**
21: **end function**
22: **function** ONRECEIVEMINERSET(S)
23:     **if** ID $j \in S$ **then**
24:         $t\_state \leftarrow Miner$
25:         execute WRITEOPERATION()   ▷ on new thread
26:     **else**
27:         $t\_state \leftarrow Listener$
28:     **end if**
29: **end function**
_____

4   Theoretical Analysis and Comparison

4.1   Communication Costs

Communication costs are related to blockchain's performance and scalability. Lower communication costs can lead to better scalability and performance. We assume a total of K participants and N nodes, and each participant has N/K nodes in our proposed system. For a transaction from the client, the communication costs to reach consensus at the bottom-layer PBFT are $O(N^2/K^2)$. After that, the *primary node* broadcasts the local consensus to *external nodes*, leading to $O(N)$ communication costs. Broadcasting a CPoW block causes $O(N)$ communication costs, but it usually contains multiple transactions, so it can be ignored when considering only one transaction. According to the above analysis, the communication costs of DP-Hybrid are $O(N^2/K^2)$.

4.2 Security

Blockchains need to resist attacks that tamper with valid blocks or write invalid blocks to ensure security. 51% attacks[14] are commonly used attacks that damage the security of PoW-based blockchains. To launch 51% attacks, attackers have to generate a long enough blockchain to replace the original one. For example, an attacker's valid Tx_a was packed in B_a, and it takes effect after the generation of B_{a+CN}, which is the latest block now. If the attacker wants to destroy the record of Tx_a in B_a, he or she has to regenerate blocks B_a to B_{a+CN+1}, i.e., longer than the original one. In the other case, if an attacker wants to pack an invalid Tx_b in the latest CPoW B_b, he or she has to continuously generate blocks B_b to B_{b+CN+1}, because honest nodes refuse to follow B_b containing invalid Tx_b. However, due to the MBC constraint, it is impossible for any participant to continuously generate CN blocks.

To reflect the difficulty of attacks, we define the Minimum number of Attackers $MinA = CN/MBC$, which means that attackers need to control at least $MinA$ participants to generate CN consecutive blocks. We define the Attack Tolerance Factor $ATF = MinA/K$. A larger ATF means that the blockchain can tolerate more participants collusion.

4.3 Liveness

Liveness means that the blockchain can handle valid transactions. When the number of normal nodes is not enough to continuously generate blocks and extend the blockchain, the blockchain loses its liveness.

Similarly, we define the Minimum number of Crashed nodes $MinC = K - MinA + 1$, meaning that when the nodes of $MinC$ participants are crashed, the remaining participants cannot continue to extend the blockchain. We define the Crash Tolerance Factor $CTF = MinC/K$. A larger CTF means that the blockchain can tolerate more participants' nodes simultaneously crashed.

4.4 Latency

Latency is the time elapsed between the client sending the transaction and the transaction taking effect. In DP-Hybrid, transactions are transformed into local consensus by PBFT, and then packed into CPoW block. When there are CN CPoW blocks generated following B_a, the transactions in B_a become global consensus and take effect. The time required to generate a block is not fixed, but in the long-term operation of the CPoW-based blockchain, ABI is stabilized within a range. We assume that a transaction was submitted at time period $(ABI, 2 \times ABI)$, transformed into global consensus at time point $3 \times ABI$ and took effect at time point $(CN + 3) \times ABI$. The latency is between $(CN + 3) \times ABI - ABI$ and $(CN + 3) \times ABI - 2 \times ABI$ and the average latency is $(CN + 1.5) \times ABI$.

4.5 Comparison

We compared communication costs, security, liveness, latency of DP-Hybrid, PBFT, PoW, committee-based (CB) and leadership-based (LB) consensus protocols. The details are listed in Table 3.

We give a comparative analysis according to the table. DP-Hybrid has lower communication costs than PBFT but usually higher than CB and LB. The typical communication costs of both CB and LB are $O(NC)$ or $O(C^2)$, where C is the number of committee or leader nodes and smaller than N. In terms of security, DP-Hybrid is configurable and can achieve higher security than PBFT. But for CB and LB, the security is sacrificed for lower communication costs. The fault tolerance of CB is $F = \lfloor \frac{C-1}{3} \rfloor$ and LB even has a smaller F, because the leader node directly represents the subsidiary nodes below it. The consensus protocols mentioned above have good liveness, but for some implementations of CB and LB, view changes are often triggered to ensure liveness, which may reduce the actual performance. The latency of DP-Hybrid is stable and higher than the remaining consensus protocols. The latency of PBFT, CB and LB is low, but increases rapidly as the number of nodes increases.

Table 3. Comparison of different consensus protocols

	DP-Hybrid	PBFT	CB	LB
Communication costs	$O(N^2/K^2)$	$O(N^2)$	$O(NC)$	$O(C^2)$
Security	Configurable	$F < \lfloor \frac{N-1}{3} \rfloor$	Low	Low
Liveness	Configurable	High	High	High
Latency	High	Low	Low	Low

Latency is what DP-Hybrid sacrifices for other performance and scalability. We believe that sacrificing latency is better than sacrificing security.

5 Experiments

We have conducted experiments on throughput in permissioned blockchain. The experiments measure normal-case behavior without Byzantine failure to achieve the best performance. The experiments ran on one six-core twelve-thread desktop with a frequency of 3.2 Ghz and 8 GB RAM. We use Docker to simulate multiple nodes, and the nodes are connected through a physical wireless network. The client is deployed on another computer and sends transactions to the blockchain system over the same wireless network. The client sends transactions to the blockchain system at a sufficient rate, so it does not limit the throughput.

We developed a PBFT blockchain and developed the DP-Hybrid blockchain based on it. Signing and verification are omitted for simplicity. We conducted comparative experiments on the throughput of these two blockchains.

We define the throughput of the blockchain as the number of transactions that can be handled per second (Tx/s). We tested the throughput under a varying number of nodes, including $N = 4, 7, 10, 16, 28, 40, 52$. In DP-Hybrid, K is 4, CN is 6, MBC is 2 and BS is 10240. The experiments for DP-Hybrid were conducted only at $N = 16, 28, 40, 52$ and each participant has 4, 7, 10, 13 nodes.

The throughput of PoW-based blockchain is not a fixed value, because the interval between blocks is different. For simplicity, we simulate that a new CPoW block is generated every 15 s in DP-Hybrid, and thus the throughput is the number of transactions contained in the block divided by 15. As shown in Fig. 4, with an increase in N, the throughput of PBFT decreases rapidly because of the $O(N^2)$ communication costs. DP-Hybrid's throughput also decreases with the increase of N, but always has about 10 times the throughput of PBFT in the experimental environment.

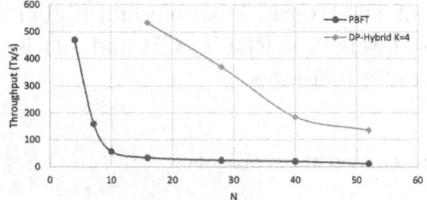

Fig. 4. Throughput of DP-Hybrid and PBFT under a varying N

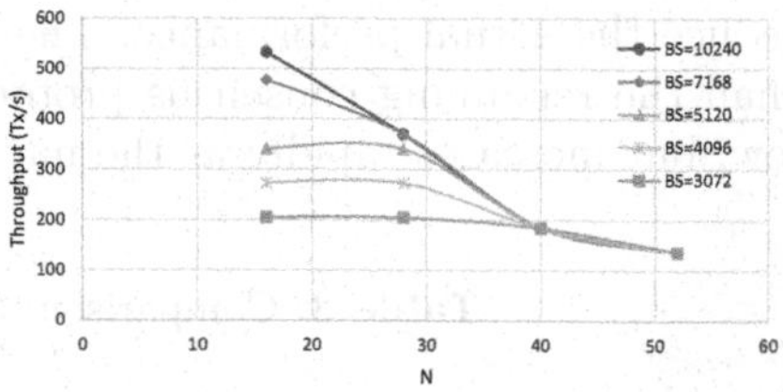

Fig. 5. Throughput of DP-Hybrid under a varying BS

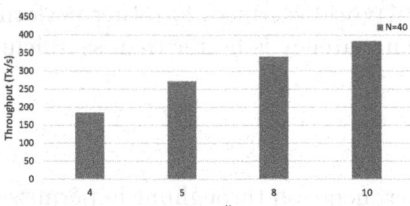

Fig. 6. Throughput of DP-Hybrid under a varying K

The BS is a factor that affects DP-Hybrid's throughput. We test DP-Hybrid's throughput under a varying BS, including $BS = 10240, 7168, 5120, 4096, 3072$. The remaining parameters are the same as the above experiments. As shown in Fig. 5, BS limits the maximum throughput of DP-Hybrid, which is reflected when the number of nodes is small. Larger BS allows larger CPoW blocks, but transferring these blocks consumes more network bandwidth. According to the incentive policy discussed above, BS is determined by the DS and the RS, so the BS should be configured properly in conjunction with the incentive policy.

The number of participants is also a factor that affects DP-Hybrid's throughput. We test the throughput of different K in the case of $N = 40$, including $K = 4$, 5, 8, 10, and each participant has 10, 8, 5, 4 nodes. We keep the BS at 10240 by changing RS and DS, and the remaining parameters are the same as the above experiments.

Figure 6 shows that a larger K results in higher throughput when N is fixed. This means that in industry applications, an increase in the number of participants does not degrade performance. Besides, more participants make the incentive policy and security configurations more flexible.

We conclude that DP-Hybrid has much higher throughput than PBFT when the number of nodes is large. With low reconfiguration overhead and configurable incentive policy and security, DP-Hybrid has better scalability for industry applications with many participants.

6   Related Work

As a core part of the blockchain, consensus protocols have been extensively studied. Researchers have proposed optimization on leader election [2], PBFT commit stage [3] and no view-change case [4] to speed up PBFT. The trade-off between the consensus speed and fault tolerance was discussed in [5,6], which sacrifices fault tolerance for faster consensus speed. Researchers also proposed new consensus protocols to speed up consensus by providing higher voting rights for honest nodes [15,16], but honest nodes may not remain honest in the future.

Another way to improve performance and scalability is to reduce the amount of message transmission. This is usually achieved through committee-based and leadership-based consensus protocols. Committee-based consensus protocols were proposed in [7–9]. Committee nodes are selected randomly [7,8] or by a combination of the latest consensus results and the node's authentication information [9]. Committee nodes participate consensus on behalf of other nodes, and the ordinary nodes accept the consensus results obtained by majority committee nodes.

Leadership-based consensus protocols were proposed in [10–13]. In [10], every several nodes form a committee at the bottom layer and select a leader node to participant in the upper layer and then recursively build a hierarchical structure. Consensus protocol is run on the committees and the local consensus are uploaded to the upper level by the leader node and then recursively reached global consensus. In [11–13], consensus protocol only runs on the leader nodes and the result are passed to the lower-layer nodes by the leader node. In contrast to committee-based consensus protocols, lower-layer ordinary nodes directly accept the consensus results obtained by their unique leader node.

However, both committee-based and leadership-based consensus are hard to solve Byzantine faults of committee nodes or leader nodes. In contrast, DP-Hybrid uses PoW-based consensus instead of voting-based consensus as a high-layer consensus, which can improve scalability without sacrificing security.

7 Conclusion

In this paper, we have studied the consensus protocols in permissioned blockchain. We found that the PBFT consensus protocol which is commonly used in permissioned blockchain leads to poor scalability and high reconfiguration overhead. To solve this problem, we proposed a two-layer consensus protocol called DP-Hybrid that combines PBFT and CPoW. DP-Hybrid reduces both communication costs and reconfiguration overhead and thus improves the scalability, while providing configurable incentive policy and security. We conducted experiments and results show that DP-Hybrid's throughput is always about 10 times that of PBFT when the number of nodes increases.

Acknowledgments. This work was supported in part by the National Natural Science Foundation of China (No. 61972161 and No. 61902333), and in part by the Fundamental Research Funds for the Central Universities, China (No. 2018MS53).

References

1. Castro, M., Liskov, B.: Practical Byzantine fault tolerance. In: Proceedings of the 3rd Symposium on Operating Systems Design and Implementation (OSDI), pp. 173–186 (1999)
2. Augustine, J., Pandurangan, G., Robinson, P.: Fast Byzantine leader election in dynamic networks. In: Moses, Y. (ed.) DISC 2015. LNCS, vol. 9363, pp. 276–291. Springer, Heidelberg (2015). https://doi.org/10.1007/978-3-662-48653-5_19
3. He, L., Hou, Z.: An improvement of consensus fault tolerant algorithm applied to alliance chain. In: 2019 IEEE 9th International Conference on Electronics Information and Emergency Communication (ICEIEC), pp. 1–4 (2019)
4. Jiang, Y., Ding, S.: A high performance consensus algorithm for consortium blockchain. In: 2018 IEEE 4th International Conference on Computer and Communications (ICCC), pp. 2379–2386 (2018)
5. Braud-Santoni, N., Guerraoui, R., Huc, F.: Fast Byzantine agreement. In: Proceedings of the Annual ACM Symposium on Principles of Distributed Computing, pp. 57–64 (2013)
6. Jalalzai, M.M., Busch, C.: Window based BFT blockchain consensus. In: 2018 IEEE International Conference on Internet of Things (iThings) and IEEE Green Computing and Communications (GreenCom) and IEEE Cyber, Physical and Social Computing (CPSCom) and IEEE Smart Data (SmartData), pp. 971–979 (2018)
7. Naif, A, Nirupama, B.: Block-supply chain: a new anti-counterfeiting supply chain using NFC and blockchain. In: Proceedings of the First Workshop on Cryptocurrencies and Blockchains for Distributed Systems, (CryBlock 2018), pp. 30–35 (2018)
8. Jalalzai, M.M., Busch, C., Richard, G.G.: Proteus: a scalable BFT consensus protocol for blockchains. In: 2019 IEEE International Conference on Blockchain (Blockchain), pp. 308–313 (2019)
9. Meng, Y., Cao, Z., Qu, D.: A Committee-Based Byzantine Consensus Protocol for Blockchain. In: 2018 IEEE 9th International Conference on Software Engineering and Service Science (ICSESS), pp. 1–6 (2018)
10. Chander, G., Deshpande, P., Chakraborty, S.: A fault resilient consensus protocol for large permissioned blockchain networks. In: 2019 IEEE International Conference on Blockchain and Cryptocurrency (ICBC), pp. 33–37 (2019)

11. Zou, J., Ye, B., Qu, L., Wang, Y., Orgun, M.A., Li, L.: A proof-of-trust consensus protocol for enhancing accountability in crowdsourcing services. IEEE Trans. Serv. Comput. **12**(3), 429–445 (2019)
12. Chen, C., Su, J., Kuo, T., Chen, K.: MSig-BFT: a witness-based consensus algorithm for private blockchains. In: 2018 IEEE 24th International Conference on Parallel and Distributed Systems (ICPADS), pp. 992–997 (2018)
13. Li, K. Li, H., Hou, H., Li, K., Chen, Y.: Proof of vote: a high-performance consensus protocol based on vote mechanism & consortium blockchain. In: 2017 IEEE 19th International Conference on High Performance Computing and Communications; IEEE 15th International Conference on Smart City; IEEE 3rd International Conference on Data Science and Systems, (HPCC/SmartCity/DSS), pp. 466–473 (2017)
14. Conti, M., Kumar E, S., Lal, C., Ruj, S.: A survey on security and privacy issues of bitcoin. IEEE Commun. Surv. Tutor. **20**(4), 3416–3452 (2018)
15. Lei, K., Zhang, Q., Xu, L., Qi, Z.: Reputation-based Byzantine fault-tolerance for consortium blockchain. In: 2018 IEEE 24th International Conference on Parallel and Distributed Systems (ICPADS), pp. 604–611 (2018)
16. Bahri, L., Girdzijauskas, S.: When trust saves energy: a reference framework for proof of trust (PoT) blockchains. In: Companion Proceedings of the The Web Conference 2018 (WWW 2018), pp. 1165–1169 (2018)

A Blockchain-Based Crowdsourcing System with QoS Guarantee via a Proof-of-Strategy Consensus Protocol

Xusheng Cai[1], Yue Wang[2], Feilong Lin[1], Changbing Tang[2(✉)], and Zhongyu Chen[1]

[1] School of Mathematics and Computer Science, Zhejiang Normal University, Jinhua 321004, China
{caixusheng,bruce_lin,czy}@zjnu.edu.cn
[2] College of Physics and Electronics Information Engineering, Zhejiang Normal University, Jinhua 321004, China
{wangyue,tangcb}@zjnu.edu.cn

Abstract. Crowdsourcing technology has been widely used in the online matching system, e.g., Uber and Airbnb, which provides an efficient matching service and enables a balance between service supply and demand. The current crowdsourcing platform generally leverages a centralized architecture through a third party for trust endorsement. However, this kind of architecture brings several challenges such as the quality of service (QoS) and trustability. In this paper, a novel blockchain-based crowdsourcing system (BCS) is proposed to guarantee QoS and fight with the malicious behaviors which employs a new consensus protocol *Proof-of-Strategy* to solve the well-known fork issue in the blockchain. Proof-of-Strategy also enables a fully distributed implementation of a crowdsourcing platform which prevents the damage of the information during the matching service. By this tamper-proof design, the task of matching supply and demand can prevent malicious behaviors, e.g., plagiarism and fraud. Moreover, a *Quality Rating Protocol* (QRP) is introduced to jointly work with *Proof-of-Strategy* for the guaranteed service quality. The existence of Nash equilibrium regards to BCS is given by the game theoretical analysis. The performance evaluation is presented to illustrate the effectiveness of our proposed method.

Keywords: Blockchain · Crowdsourcing · Quality of service · Consensus protocol · Incentive

1 Introduction

With an increasing number of mobile devices, crowdsourcing platform enjoys a great popularity from the online matching systems. Its inherent parallel computational power plays a significant role in cutting down the time in the task of the matching matter between publishment and acceptance [3]. Unlike the

© Springer Nature Singapore Pte Ltd. 2020
Z. Zheng et al. (Eds.): BlockSys 2020, CCIS 1267, pp. 72–86, 2020.
https://doi.org/10.1007/978-981-15-9213-3_6

traditional offline service market, crowdsourcing platform can offer an efficient matching service in large scale with a guaranteed service quality [1,5,14]. A typical crowdsourcing system consists of three different entities: the requester, the worker and the central coordinator [13]. A requester issues a task to the central coordinator. Once the central coordinator of crowdsourcing platform receives the task, it will publish this task and recruit workers who response to the task request for completing the task and returning the result to the crowdsourcing platform. In general, the crowdsourcing platform is responsible for the worker recruitment, the task allocation, the result collection, the data processing, and the evaluation on the trust of all workers. It returns the final report of the task execution to the requester.

However, the crowdsourcing confronts a series of challenges relevant to Quality of Service (QoS) and trustability [2,6]. The traditional crowdsourcing system generally leverages a centralized architecture which relies on a trustworthy service provider in the coordination centre. This architecture leads to two major disadvantages. First, it is easy for the crowdsourcing system to suffer from a single point of failure and the privacy leakage due to the matching service provided by the central platform. Second, workers may return a poor-quality result with little effort as the response to the task request. But these workers still claim that they have completed the task with a noticeable effort to ask for higher benefits. This kind of behaviour is called "free riding". The requester may claim a lower benefit to those workers who complete the task normally, regardless how well the workers have done. This kind of behaviour is called "false reporting". Because of these two typical cheating behaviours, it is difficult to guarantee QoS of crowdsourcing system.

The existing researches can partially address these challenges in crowdsourcing system. Various incentive mechanisms are developed to ensure QoS in the crowdsourcing system [10,15]. These incentive mechanisms can prevent from the cheating behaviours for both requester and the workers. Firstly, the requester will not cheat to falsely report the quality of the task result. Thus, no matter the workers complete the task honestly or not, the requester needs to pay the workers amounting at its true value. Then, the workers are motivated to make efforts spontaneously and complete the task with a high quality. This is because in the incentive mechanism, the workers without any noticeable effort will not obtain a profitable income. A batch allocation for tasks with overlapping skill requirements in crowdsourcing system is proposed in [7] where a better performance on the total payment of requesters, the average income of workers and the maintenance of the close successful probability of the task completion can be achieved. Moreover, there are existing researches that solves the security issues caused by the centralization. Encryption and differential privacy are used to protect data privacy [11]. New blockchain based crowdsourcing systems are introduced in [8]. In these systems, it is no longer a centralized system to provide services which can prevent the single point of failure and privacy disclosure risks.

Nevertheless, these incentive mechanisms require a credible central platform while these crowdsourcing systems cannot guarantee QoS effectively. To guarantee

QoS and solve the security issues simultaneously, it is essential to develop a new framework of incentive mechanism for solving these challenges in crowdsourcing system. In this paper, a blockchain based framework is introduced for a distributed crowdsourcing system where a Proof-of-Strategy consensus protocol is developed to address the fork issue of the blockchain. The *Quality Rating Protocol* (QRP) is proposed to jointly work with the Proof-of-Strategy consensus protocol for guaranteeing QoS. The main contributions of this paper are threefold:

– A novel blockchain crowdsourcing system (BCS) is proposed which can guarantee QoS and trustability in a distributed manner. Moreover, a new consensus protocol, namely Proof-of-Strategy, is designed for new block confirmation which ensures that only one unique block will be determined in each block period, and the security is further improved.
– Under the assumption of no centralized trusted third party existing in the system, a QRP is introduced to jointly coordinate with the Proof-of-Strategy protocol for motivating both the requester and the workers honestly making efforts to the task. This finally results in a high quality of matching service. Furthermore, the existence of Nash equilibrium regards to this BCS is verified by two game theoretical analyses.
– QoS of BCS is estimated through extensive performance evaluation. The numerical results show that the task results given by the workers in different scales are all of high quality. Moreover, the effect of important parameters, on the quality of the matching service system is given while the guideline on the design of system parameters are presented.

The rest of the paper is organized as follows. Section 2 introduces the BCS and analyzes the process of the completion of a crowdsourcing task briefly, as well as, details discussion of the modeling process. Section 3 analyses the worker's utility and verifier's utility by game theory to verify the existence of Nash equilibrium in BCS. In Sect. 4, the performance of the model is analyzed by simulations and experiments. Finally, Sect. 5 summarizes this paper.

2   Blockchain-Based Crowdsourcing Model

This section mainly explains the specific procedure of how BCS works in each stage with the key elements. The main symbols used in this paper have been listed, as shown in Table 1.

2.1   System Model

In BCS, two currencies, S-coin for service reward and R-coin for reputation evaluation, are designed. As a currency, S-coin is only issued as a reward when new blocks are generated by the system. Of course, real currency can be exchanged between agents by S-coin. As a value currency generated by reputation, R-coin is rewarded or deducted by the system according to the quality after the agent

Table 1. The notations of explanation

Notation	Explanation
r_i	The amount of R-coin owned by agent i
s_i	The amount of S-coin owned by agent i
r_i'	The amount of R-coin declared by the agent i when competing with the verifier
s_i'	The amount of S-coin obtained by the agent i when competing for verifier
a	The verifier's S-coin reward
b	The sum of S-coin rewards for participating in the verifier's competition
c	Cost per unit of completion effort
t_i	The time when the agent i completes the task
p_i	The percentage of tasks completed by the agent i
D	Task difficulty
T	Task working time interval, $T = T_{deadline} - T_{publish}$
h	The social threshold
$F(D)$	Task cost paid by S-coin
$k, \eta, \mu, \alpha, \beta, \lambda$	The constants given by the system designer

completes the task. In BCS, there are three roles: 1) the requester, 2) the worker, 3) the verifier. Each agent can become a requester or a worker according to the actual situation. In addition, the Proof-of-Strategy consensus protocol is proposed to select the verifier. Every agent can participate the verifier competition. In the process of competition, the agent will consume a number of R-coin and get a number of S-coin. If the agent becomes a requester, it needs to pay the workers who accept the task with a number of S-coins to publish the task. If the agent becomes worker, it can get a number of S-coins for completing the task, and the system will reward or deduct a number of R-coins according to the task completion quality.

As shown in Fig. 1, the agent that wants to publish the task becomes the requester and the task information is broadcast to all agents. After receiving the task, the agent that wants to make a profit from completing the task becomes the worker. The workers need to encrypt the results and broadcast them to the verifier when they complete the task. When the deadline comes, the verifier first checks whether the worker's R-coin balances, who has been sent the results, is higher than the social threshold. If so, it decrypts and reads the information of the time that the worker completed the task. After every worker has been checked, the verifier calculates the S-coin reward that the requester needs to pay through the function $F(x)$ and sends the payment requests to the requester. After the remunerations are paid by the requester and verified by the verifier, he will send results to the requester. The requester will receive the task result and generates the worker's R-coin reward and punishment results according to the Quality Rating Protocol (QRP). Then, the requester broadcasts it. Finally, the verifier will generate the new block, including the requester's payment to the worker, the R-coin information of the system rewards and punishments, and the task results, broadcasting to every agent.

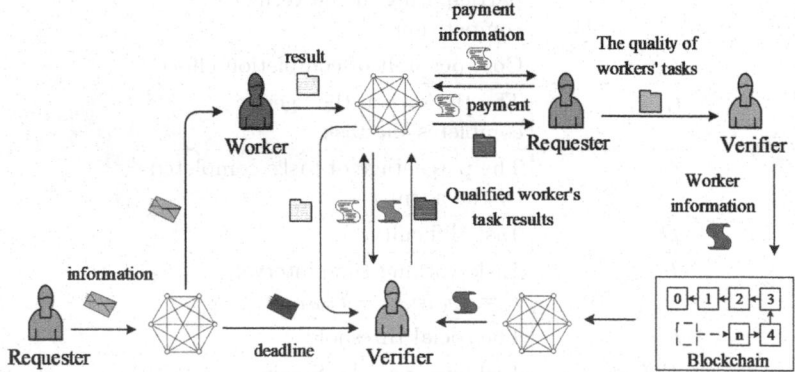

Fig. 1. Blockchain-based crowdsourcing system

2.2   Proof-of-Strategy Consensus Protocol

There are many problems in the traditional consensus protocol. For instance, a big waste of social resources is ubiquitousness in the consensus process of the *proof-of-work* (PoW) in regard to bitcoin. The fork problem of *proof-of-stake* (PoS) is not unusual. In order to solve this problem, a Proof-of-Strategy consensus protocol will be proposed in BCS. Each agent can choose a different strategy according to its own situation, which corresponds to a different success rate of becoming the verifier. The Proof-of-Strategy consensus is low-cost and can logically solve the fork problem, where a bribe attacks will be extremely expensive. At the same time, the "verifier" generates the next block can only be created by a selection policy that is competitive. Hence, it is hard to be predicted. The specific procedures of the proof-of-strategy consensus protocol are as follows.

First, the agent who wants to be a "verifier" is called the "competitor". It declares a certain amount of R-coin as its own strategy according to its own situation, and its declaration amount should not exceed its R-coin balance. After the declaration time is over, the system allocates S-coin according to the proportion of the declared R-coin in all declared R-coin, and deducts the declared R-coin, following the formula below:

$$s_i' = b \cdot \frac{r_i'}{\Sigma_{i=1}^n r_i'}, \tag{1}$$

where s_i' means the amount of S-coin obtained by the agent i when competing for the verifier. r_i' means the amount of R-coin declared by the agent i when competing with the verifier. b is a constant in the system, represents the total number of S-coins issued by the system during each competition to become the verifier. n is the total number of competitors.

Then, each newly allocated S-coin, with a minimum unit of "*satoshi*", has a continuous binary number of l_s in length. Every *satoshi* S-coin that a competitor gets can provide the system with a "bit" information, so the system will get mapping relationships between the new S-coin number and the value $\{0, 1\}$. Then it arranges the mapped $\{0, 1\}$ from small to large according to its corresponding s-coin number, and will obtain a string of binary numbers with the length of l_t. l_t is the newly allocated total amount of S-coins with the smallest unit "*satoshi*".

Finally, this binary number of length l_t is hashed to a binary number of the length l_s, and the competitor who has the same number S-coin becomes the verifier of this phase. The system awards an additional S-coin. It is worth noting that the proof-of-strategy consensus protocol splits the s-coin reward into two parts, i.e., $a + b$, so that agents that do not become the verifier will also have benefits. It can promote agents to actively participate in the verifier competition. In the competition, the "verifier" selection is based on the strategy of each competitor and is therefore unpredictable.

2.3   The Cost of Task

Generally, the type of tasks is not of single class, which may consist of a large number of classes. Different kinds of tasks have not only different complexities, but also the same kind of tasks with a different complexity. Considering that the complexity of a task is related to the time and the quantity of completion, we define the task complexity as follows:

Definition 1 (Task Complexity, D). *The complexity of the task published by the requester is determined by the linear combination of the average time of the worker completing the task and the reciprocal of the number of workers completing the task within the specified time, satisfying the condition:*

$$D = \begin{cases} \eta \cdot \frac{1}{N} \Sigma_{i=1}^N (t_i - t_{publish}) + (1 - \eta) \cdot \frac{1}{N} & N \geq 1, \\ 0 & N = 0, \end{cases} \tag{2}$$

where D is a numerical mapping of the task complexity. As a system parameter, η is used to control the effect on the average completion time and the number of workers completed on the complexity of the task. Of course, it may be different for different types of tasks. N represents the number of workers completing the task within the specified time. T_i represents the time taken by the ith worker to complete the task. $t_{publish}$ denotes the publish time of the task. When the average time to complete the task is long or the number of people completing the task within the specified time is small, it is said that the task is more difficult. otherwise it is simple.

After the task complexity is determined, according to the rule that the higher complexity, the higher cost. The task S-coin cost function $F(D)$ is given, which follows the formula:

$$F(D) = \begin{cases} F_{base} + k \cdot D & D \neq 0, \\ 0 & D = 0, \end{cases} \tag{3}$$

where, $F(D)$ represents the cost of S-coins required for the task, F_{base} represents the basic cost, and k is the system parameter.

2.4 Quality Rating Protocol

After accepting the task, a worker may has the incentive to take the payment and provides no effort to solve the task, a behavior commonly known as "free riding". In order to avoid this phenomenon and encourage workers to work honestly, two indexes of "task complexity: D" and "task completion degree: p" are introduced, and a rating agreement is constructed. The quality of work is quantified through $D \cdot p$, so as to allocate corresponding rewards and penalties.

Definition 2 (Task Completion Degree, p). *It is assumed that the degree of task completion is quantifiable and the cost per unit is c. This degree is denoted by p, $p \in [0, 1]$.*

p is also used to quantify the quality of the worker's completed tasks. The larger the p, the better the worker's working attitude and the higher the task quality.

Definition 3 (Quality Rating Protocol, QRP). *A quality rating protocol QRP is represented as a quadruple $\{r, \sigma, \tau, \varphi\}$, which consists of four components: a set of rating labels r, a social strategy σ, a rating scheme τ, and a pricing scheme φ.*

- $r \in R$ denotes the set of rating labels, where r represents the R-coin balance of each individual. If the r is too low, you will not respond to the task.
- $\sigma : r \rightarrow p$ is the social strategy adopted by each worker, where p represents the task completion degree of worker.

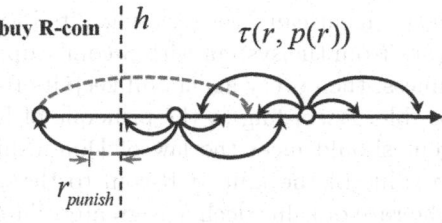

Fig. 2. Schematic representation of a rating protocol.

- $\tau : r \times p \to r$ specifies how a worker's R-coin balance should be updated based on its strategies. In this rating scheme, the higher the degree of completion of tasks, the more rewards to the worker, as follows:

$$\tau(r,p) = \begin{cases} r + \mu D(p - 0.6) & r \geq h \text{ and} \\ & r + \mu D(p - 0.6) \geq h, \\ r + \mu D(p - 0.6) - r_{punish} & r \geq h \text{ and} \\ & r + \mu D(p - 0.6) < h, \\ r & r < h \end{cases} \quad (4)$$

where $h > 0$ is the selected social threshold. When the r is less than h, the worker cannot accept the task. It is worth noting that when the R-coins balance of the worker changes from not less than h before the task to less than h after the task, the system will deduct its r_{punish} R-coins as the penalty. Therefore, the higher the R-coins balance, the more secure it is, and the higher the status it will be. μ is the system parameter, the designer can adjust μ to control the growth rate of R-coin in the whole system. A schematic representation of a proposed rating protocol is provided in Fig. 2.

- $\varphi : t \to s$ defines the rules that the designer uses to reward/punish workers in order to incentivize their service provision. In this pricing scheme, workers will get more rewards for completing tasks in a shorter time. Therefore, workers are encouraged to complete tasks quickly. Specific pricing scheme as follows:

$$\varphi(t_i) = S_{base} + [F(D) - N \cdot S_{base}] \cdot \frac{T_{deadline} - t_i + T_{base}}{T_{all}}, \quad (5)$$

where $S_{base} = \alpha \cdot F(D) \cdot \frac{1}{N}$, $T_{all} = \sum_{i=1}^{N}(T_{deadline} - t_i + T_{base})$. S_{base} represents basic rewards, $T_{deadline}$ represents task deadline. Parameter α is used to control the degree of incentive for the task completion time. The smaller α is, the stronger the desire of workers to complete the task in a short time will be.

3   Utility Analysis

This section mainly analyses the workers' utility by game theory to verify the existence of Nash equilibrium in BCS.

Considering that every agent can't get task when its R-coin is less than h, so it needs to purchase tasks from the system with S-coin. Supposed that all agents are rational and selfishness, then every agent will keep its R-coin from being less than h as much as possible. According to the principle of Economics, the value of R-coin to every agent should meet the law of Diminishing marginal utility, which means that the value of the unit of R-coin to the agent which has less R-coin is higher, and the rate of value decline is greater. Supposed that the value of a R-coin to every agent satisfies the utility function $Q(\cdot), Q(r_i) > 0, Q'(r_i) < 0, Q''(r_i) > 0, r_i \in (h, \infty)$.

3.1   Verifier's R-Coin Declaration Game

Considering a competition with a group of competitors to become the verifier. The agents denoted by $J = \{1, 2, ...\}$. The ith competitor declares a certain amount of R-coin, denoted by $r'_i, r'_i \leq r_i$. In the competition, the utility function of competitor i consists of 1) the expected revenue obtained from being the verifier, 2) S-coin revenue obtained from declaring R-coin, 3) the utility of deducting R-coin, which is formulated as follows:

$$w_i = a \cdot \frac{r'_i}{\Sigma_{i \in J} r'_i} + b \cdot \frac{r'_i}{\Sigma_{i \in J} r'_i} - Q(r_i) \cdot r'_i, \tag{6}$$

We employ the backward induction method to analyze the Stackelberg equilibrium of the utility function [9]. Given the utility function $Q(\cdot)$, the competitors compete to maximize their individual utilities by choosing their a certain amount of R-coin, which forms a noncooperative Verifier R-coin declaration Game (VRG) $G^v = \{J, R', \{w_i\}_{i \in J}\}$, where J is the set of competitors, R' is the strategy set of competitors, and w_i is the utility function of competitor i.

Definition 4. *A set of strategy profiles $R'^{ne} = \{r_1'^{ne}, ..., r_{|J|}'^{ne}\}$ is the Nash equilibrium of the VRG $G^v = \{J, R', \{w_i\}_{i \in J}\}$, if, for $\forall i \in J, w_i(r_i'^{ne}, R_{-i}'^{ne}, Q(\cdot)) \geq w_i(r'_i, R_{-i}'^{ne}, Q(\cdot))$, for $r'_i \geq 0$. Where $R_{-i}'^{ne}$ represents the Nash equilibrium set excluding r'_i .*

Theorem 1. *A Nash Equilibrium exists in VRG $G^v = \{J, R', \{w_i\}_{i \in J}\}$.*

Proof. By differentiating w_i defined in Eq. (6) with respect to r'_i, we have $\frac{\partial w_i}{\partial r'_i} = \frac{(a+b) \sum_{j \in J-i} r'_j}{(\sum_{j \in J} r'_j)^2} - Q(r_j)$, and $\frac{\partial^2 w_i}{\partial r_i'^2} < 0$. Where J_{-i} represents a group of miners excluding i. Noted that w_i is a strictly concave function with respect to r'_i. Therefore, given any $Q(r_i) > 0$ and any strategy profile $R_{-i}'^{ne}$ of the other competitors, the best response strategy of competitor i is unique when $r'_i \geq 0$. Accordingly, the Nash equilibrium exists in the noncooperative VRG G^v.

3.2   Worker's Attitude Game

Suppose that the working ability of the ith worker is v_i, which represents an inherent attribute of worker i. Considering a task with a group of workers (denoted by $J' = \{1, 2, ...\}$), the ith worker chooses an attitude (denoted by $p_i, p_i \in [0, 1]$) to complete the task. Therefore, the cost for the worker i to complete the task is $p_i \cdot c$, and the time interval for the worker i to complete the task is p_i/v_i. In this task, the utility function of the worker i consists of 1) basic remuneration of S-coin, 2) S-coin revenue obtained from the requester, 3) the utility of rewarding or deducting R-coin from system, 4) the cost of complete the task, which is formulated as follows:

$$U_i = S_{base} + A \cdot \frac{\triangle t - \frac{p_i}{v_i}}{\sum_{j \in J'} \triangle t - \frac{p_j}{v_j}} + Q(r_i) \cdot \triangle \tau(r_i, p_i) - p_i \cdot c, \qquad (7)$$

where $A = [F(D) - |J'| \cdot S_{base}]$, $\triangle t = t_{deadline} - t_{publish}$. We employ the backward induction method to analyze the Stackelberg equilibrium of the utility function. Given the utility function $Q(\cdot)$, the workers compete to maximize their individual utilities by choosing their attitude of completing the task, which forms a noncooperative Workers' attitude Game (WAG) $G^w = \{J', P, \{U_i\}_{i \in J'}\}$, where J' is the set of workers, P is the strategy set of workers, and U_i is the utility function of worker i.

Definition 5. *A set of strategy profiles $P^{ne} = \{p_1^{ne}, ..., p_{|J'|}^{ne}\}$ is the Nash equilibrium of the WAG $G^w = \{J', P, \{U_i\}_{i \in J'}\}$, if, for $\forall i \in J', U_i(p_i^{ne}, P_{-i}^{ne}, Q(\cdot)) \geq U_i(p_i, P_{-i}^{ne}, Q(\cdot))$, for $p_i \geq 0$. Where P_{-i}^{ne} represents the Nash equilibrium set excluding p_i*

Theorem 2. *A Nash Equilibrium exists in WAG $G^w = \{J', P, \{U_i\}_{i \in J'}\}$.*

Proof. By differentiating U_i defined in Eq. (7) with respect to p_i, we have $\frac{\partial U_i}{\partial p_i} = -\frac{A}{v_i} \cdot \frac{\sum_{j \in J'_{-i}} \triangle t - \frac{p_j}{v_j}}{(\sum_{j \in J'} \triangle t - \frac{p_j}{v_j})^2} - \mu DQ(r_i) - c$, and $\frac{\partial^2 U_i}{\partial p_i^2} < 0$. Where J'_{-i} represents a group of miners excluding i. Noted that U_i is a strictly concave function with respect to p_i. Therefore, given any $Q(r_i) > 0$ and any strategy profile P_{-i}^{ne} of the other competitors, the best response strategy of competitor i is unique when $p_i \geq 0$. Accordingly, the Nash equilibrium exists in the noncooperative WAG G^w.

Through the above analysis, the Nash Equilibrium exists in both games. Therefore, the system designer can adjust the parameters so that only when all workers choose a high work attitude can they reach the Nash equilibrium. It is worth noting that in Eq. (7), if the worker's ability v_i for completing the task is at a low level, he will find out through calculation that his optimal strategy is not to participate in the task. In other words, even if he is completely conscientious about the task in this case, he is so limited by his ability cannot to provide high-quality results that he is unable to reap the benefits.

4 Performance Evaluation

In this part, to analyze the QoS given by the blockchain-based crowdsourcing model, we provide numerical results to illustrate its characteristics. We use DiDi

Data set for experimental settings where a ride-hailing business of an enterprise edition is extracted [4]. Specifically, in a modern company, there are a large number of customers that require a ride-hailing service when working after hours every day. Thus, completing the ride-hailing service for a specific company is a task. DiDi platform is the requester while the car driver who accepts the request is the worker. The working ability v_i of each worker is considered an inherent trait that will not change in the short term, and measured by the overall driver-partner rating. The social threshold is set to $h = 30$, basic pay is set to $F_{base} = 10$, and the function $Q(\cdot)$ is set to $Q(r_i) = 100/(r_i - h)$. Under these conditions, by dynamic update system parameters a, b and α in different scales, which guarantee that the optimal policy $r_i'^{ne}$ in VRG and p_i^{ne} in WAG of all agents satisfy $r_i'^{ne} \epsilon (0, h), p_i^{ne} \epsilon (0, 1)$. In the experiment, we chose a set of ride-hailing service data for a similar distance as the same kind of crowdsourcing task. Meanwhile, set $\Delta t = 30$ min. If the driver arrives at the destination in Δt, his task completion degree p is 100%. If not, $p = \Delta t \times v_i$. Under these Settings, we analyze the task quality of the system in the following aspects.

4.1 QoS Comparison Between BCS and General Incentive Model

In order to facilitate the comparison, only used QRP to simulate the general incentive model (GIM) [12] without combining proof-of-strategy. In this case all workers will accept the task because they are profitable. Under the condition of keeping other parameters unchanged, agents with different working efficiencies are randomly selected for the system with total agents of 10–100, 100–1000 and 0.1–1 million respectively. The average task quality under the corresponding scale in BCS and general model is simulated, as shown in Fig. 3. The abscissa represents the total number of agents N, and the ordinate represents the QoS, which is the average task quality of the BCS and general model, and the number of workers participating in the task.

Obviously, compared with general incentive model, the QoS in BCS stay higher level, because workers who are not competitive in BCS will voluntarily give up accepting tasks. In the same scale, the more agents, the higher the QoS in BCS. In different scales, the larger the scale, the smaller the fluctuation of the QoS in BCS and the much stabler the system. Interestingly, under the same scale, the number of workers participating in tasks increases with the number of agents, but it tends to be flat after reaching at a certain large value. This shows that when the number of agents reaches a certain value, there will be a competition amongst agents. Some workers who do not have a competitiveness (the quality of completing tasks cannot reach a high level) will not accept tasks spontaneously.

4.2 The Effect of Parameters on QoS

1) **The Effect of T on QoS**
   As a linear mapping of the task difficulty, the larger Δt, the more drivers

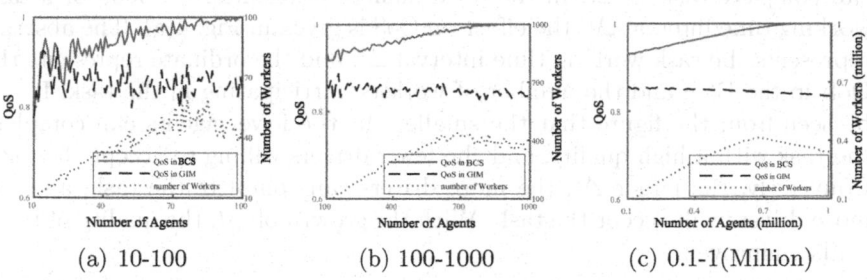

(a) 10-100   (b) 100-1000   (c) 0.1-1(Million)

Fig. 3. Average task quality of total agents under (a) 10–100 (b) 100–1000 (c) 100,000–1,000,000

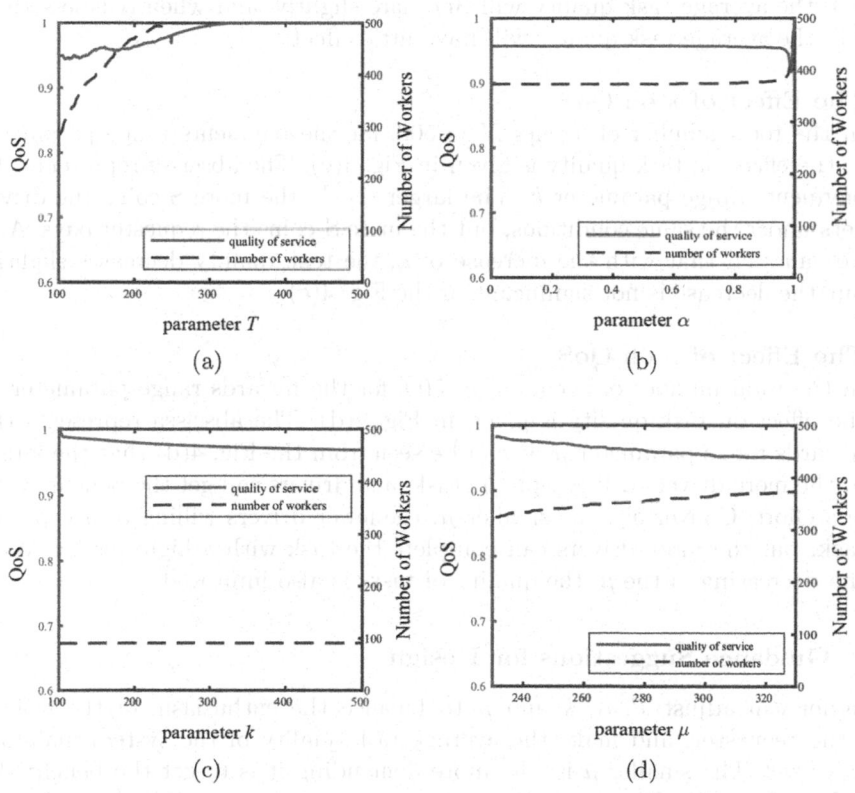

(a)   (b)

(c)   (d)

Fig. 4. The effect on (a) T, (b) α, (c) k and (d) μ on average task quality at $N = 500$

can complete the task with $p = 1$; otherwise, the smaller Δt, the less driver can complete task in Δt. In the total number of agents $N = 500$, for a task working time interval Δt, the effect on QoS is given in Fig. 4(a). The abscissa represents the task working time interval Δt, and the ordinate represents the QoS in the BCS and the number of workers participating in the task. It can be seen from the figure that the smaller Δt, the fewer agents can complete the task with a high quality, and the fewer drivers willing to accept the task; Conversely, the larger Δt, the more drivers can complete the task, and the more drivers will accept the task. With the growth of Δt, the quality of tasks is also improved.

2) **The Effect of α on QoS**
The parameter α affects the driver's base salary for completing the task. The driver will get more base salary if α increasing. In the total number of agents $N = 500$, for the importance parameter α of the task efficiency, the effect on the task quality is given in Fig. 4(b). The abscissa represents the importance parameter α of the task efficiency. It can be seen that when α is greater than 0.9, the average task quality will fluctuate slightly, and when α is less than 0.9, the average task quality will have little effect.

3) **The Effect of k on QoS**
In the total number of agents $N = 500$, for the payments range parameter k, the effect on task quality is given in Fig. 4(c). The abscissa represents the payments range parameter k. The larger the k, the more S-coins the driver gets under the same conditions, but the more S-coins the requester pays. And we can seen that with the increase of k, the task quality decreases slightly, but the decrease is not significant in the Fig. 4(c).

4) **The Effect of μ on QoS**
In the total number of agents $N = 500$, for the rewards range parameter μ, the effect on task quality is given in Fig. 4(d). The abscissa represents the rewards range parameter μ. It can be seen from the Fig. 4(d) that the larger μ, the more drivers will accept the task, and drivers can get the benefits with less effort; Conversely, the smaller μ, the fewer drivers willing to accept the task, but the more drivers can complete the task with a high quality. With the decreasing of the μ, the quality of tasks is also improved.

4.3   Guidance Suggestions for Design

Designer can adjust T, α, k and μ to balance the enthusiasm of the worker and the requester, and make the average task quality of the system maintain a high level. The smaller μ is, the more demanding it is to get the benefits by complete the tasks. The larger T, the more agents can complete the task, and the more agents can accept the task. The smaller α, the worker well use less time to complete the tasks, but the μ will be bigger. The larger k, the more S-coins the worker will get and this system will be able to attract more agents so that the QoS of this system will be easier to maintain a high level. However, the requester need to pay more S-coin.

5   Conclusion

To address the problem that the QoS and the trustablility of the central platform in the traditional crowdsourcing cannot be guaranteed, we have proposed a blockchain-based crowdsourcing system (BCS). By introducing the blockchain technique into a crowdsourcing scenario, the model can achieves the properties of centerless, irrevocable and nonrepudiation during the process of crowdsourcing, thus avoiding the risk of attacks and frauds.

In addition, we have proposed the Proof of Strategy consensus protocol to solve the fork problem and the high cost problem of blockchain operation. In this consensus protocol, each agent chooses its own strategy to compete for its best interests, and reaches a consensus, determining the only verifier, according to the strategy chosen by all agents.

In BCS, we combine the Proof of Strategy consensus protocol and the quality rating protocol to guarantee the QoS, and verify the existence of BCS. The simulation results show that the task results given by workers in different scales are of high quality. At the same time, we also give some guidance suggestions for the parameter design of BCS.

Acknowledgments. This work was partly supported by the National Natural Science Foundation of China (No. 61877055), the Zhejiang Provincial Natural Science Foundation of China (Nos. LY18F030013), and the National innovation and entrepreneurship program for college students (No. 201910345015).

References

1. Baba, Y.: Statistical quality control for human computation and crowdsourcing. In: Proceedings of the Twenty-Seventh International Joint Conference on Artificial Intelligence, IJCAI 2018, pp. 5667–5671. International Joint Conferences on Artificial Intelligence Organization (2018)
2. Checco, A., Bates, J., Demartini, G.: Quality control attack schemes in crowdsourcing. In: Proceedings of the 28th International Joint Conference on Artificial Intelligence, pp. 6136–6140. AAAI Press (2019)
3. Chittilappilly, A.I., Chen, L., Amer-Yahia, S.: A survey of general-purpose crowdsourcing techniques. IEEE Trans. Knowl. Data Eng. **28**(9), 2246–2266 (2016)
4. Dataset (2019). https://outreach.didichuxing.com/research/opendata/en/
5. Fang, Y., Sun, H., Chen, P., Huai, J.: On the cost complexity of crowdsourcing. In: Proceedings of the Twenty-Seventh International Joint Conference on Artificial Intelligence, IJCAI 2018, pp. 1531–1537. International Joint Conferences on Artificial Intelligence Organization (2018)
6. Feng, W., Yan, Z., Zhang, H., Zeng, K., Xiao, Y., Hou, Y.T.: A survey on security, privacy, and trust in mobile crowdsourcing. IEEE Internet of Things J. **5**(4), 2971–2992 (2017)

7. Jiang, J., An, B., Jiang, Y., Shi, P., Bu, Z., Cao, J.: Batch allocation for tasks with overlapping skill requirements in crowdsourcing. IEEE Trans. Parallel Distrib. Syst. **30**(8), 1722–1737 (2019)
8. Li, M., et al.: CrowdBC: a blockchain-based decentralized framework for crowdsourcing. IEEE Trans. Parallel Distrib. Syst. **30**(6), 1251–1266 (2018)
9. Li, Z., Kang, J., Yu, R., Ye, D., Deng, Q., Zhang, Y.: Consortium blockchain for secure energy trading in industrial internet of things. IEEE Trans. Industr. Inf. **14**(8), 3690–3700 (2017)
10. Peng, D., Wu, F., Chen, G.: Pay as how well you do: a quality based incentive mechanism for crowdsensing. In: Proceedings of the 16th ACM International Symposium on Mobile Ad Hoc Networking and Computing, pp. 177–186. ACM (2015)
11. To, H., Ghinita, G., Fan, L., Shahabi, C.: Differentially private location protection for worker datasets in spatial crowdsourcing. IEEE Trans. Mob. Comput. **16**(4), 934–949 (2016)
12. Wang, H., Guo, S., Cao, J., Guo, M.: Melody: A long-term dynamic quality-aware incentive mechanism for crowdsourcing. In: 2017 IEEE 37th International Conference on Distributed Computing Systems (ICDCS), pp. 933–943 (2017)
13. Xia, J., Zhao, Y., Liu, G., Xu, J., Zhang, M., Zheng, K.: Profit-driven task assignment in spatial crowdsourcing. In: Proceedings of the Twenty-Eighth International Joint Conference on Artificial Intelligence, IJCAI 2019, pp. 1914–1920. International Joint Conferences on Artificial Intelligence Organization (2019)
14. Xia, S., Lin, F., Chen, Z., Tang, C., Ma, Y., Yu, X.: A Bayesian game based vehicle-to-vehicle electricity trading scheme for blockchain-enabled Internet of vehicles. IEEE Trans. Veh. Technol. **69**, 6856–6868 (2020)
15. Zhang, Y., Van der Schaar, M.: Reputation-based incentive protocols in crowdsourcing applications. In: 2012 Proceedings IEEE INFOCOM, pp. 2140–2148. IEEE (2012)

PBFT Consensus Performance Optimization Method for Fusing C4.5 Decision Tree in Blockchain

Zhihong Liang[1], Yuxiang Huang[1], Zhichang Guo[1(✉)], Qi Liu[2], and Tiancheng Liu[3]

[1] School of Big Data and Intelligent Engineering, Southwest Forestry University, Kunming 650224, China
changg871@163.com
[2] Public Security Department of Yunnan Province, Kunming 650228, China
[3] Easy-Visible Supply Chain Management Company, Kunming 650100, China

Abstract. Data management methods using blockchain have the advantages of being traceable and not easy to tamper. Therefore, blockchain is widely used in supply chain finance, credit reporting and other fields. However, in the actual blockchain system application, there are two main problems in the Hyperledger Fabric license alliance chain based on the Practical Byzantine Fault Tolerance (PBFT) consensus mechanism: 1) The non-honesty node acts as the primary node to interfere with the consensus process; 2) The network bandwidth resource consumption caused by the flooded message broadcast of the consensus node is too large. To solve these problems, a blockchain PBFT consensus performance optimization method for fusing C4.5 decision tree is proposed. This method uses the C4.5 decision tree with high model classification accuracy to evaluate the trust degree of the consensus nodes in the blockchain network, and effectively reduces the non-honesty node as the primary node. On this basis, the voting weight is introduced. Consistency verification can be completed only by considering a small number of trusted nodes voting weights, thereby reducing the number of messages broadcasted in the network. The experimental results show that compared with the existing methods, the trust node classification and voting weights of the consensus nodes are improved in the consensus performance of throughput, delay and fault tolerance, and the effectiveness of the proposed method is verified.

Keywords: BlockChain · Hyperledger Fabric · PBFT · C4.5 decision tree · Node trust · Voting value

1 Introduction

In the traditional centralized data management mode, since the "trusted" third party completes the management and maintenance of the database, it has absolute control over the data [1]. However, it is impossible for other institutions or individuals to know the data update process. Taking supply chain finance enterprise financing as an example, each enterprise maintains a database that records its own business data independently,

Z. Zheng et al. (Eds.): BlockSys 2020, CCIS 1267, pp. 87–96, 2020.
https://doi.org/10.1007/978-981-15-9213-3_7

resulting in the fragmentation of information. For risk control, qualification and credit considerations, financial institutions are only willing to provide financing services to core enterprises. They are not willing to invest additional manpower and material resources to verify the authenticity of data information of SMEs. The emergence of blockchain provides a new solution. It can integrate multiple single-point databases that only maintain their own business, to achieve multi-party database maintenance [2]. Either party has no absolute control over the database. Only through a strict consensus mechanism can the database be updated to achieve the trusted storage of data [3].

The concept of blockchain [4] was first proposed by a scholar who changed his name to "Satoshi Nakamoto". According to the node access rules [5], the blockchain can be divided into three categories: public chain [6], private chain [7] and alliance chain [8]. Among them, Bitcoin [9] and Ethereum [10] are representative platforms of public chains. Hyperledger Fabric [11] is a widely used enterprise-level blockchain open source platform.

Hyperledger Fabric supports permission management, and is well designed to be pluggable and extensible. PBFT [12] reduced the complexity of the BFT algorithm from exponential level to polynomial level for the first time, enabling it to be widely used in distributed systems. However, in the specific application of the blockchain system, there are also pain points such as the dishonest node acting as the primary node to break the consensus process, serious network communication overhead, and low system fault tolerance. The crux of these problems lies in the shortcomings of the primary node selection method and the frequent verification of broadcast messages in the network. As a result, the Hyperledger Fabric licensing alliance chain system based on the PBFT consensus algorithm has poor performance and limited practical application.

In view of the above problems, this paper proposes a blockchain PBFT consensus performance optimization method fusing C4.5 decision tree. Specifically, the main contributions of this paper have the following three aspects:

1) Propose to use C4.5 decision tree with high model classification accuracy to classify the trust rating of consensus nodes in the blockchain network. In order to reduce the possibility of non-honest nodes acting as primary nodes.
2) On the basis of trust rating evaluation of consensus nodes in the blockchain network, it is proposed to introduce voting weights. Only by considering the voting weights of a few consensus nodes with a high degree of trust, the consistency verification is completed. The purpose of this is to reduce the number of messages broadcast in the network.
3) Based on the supply chain financial dataset, a Hyperledger Fabric simulation test experiment is designed. The experimental process and results are reported in detail. It shows that this method has better consensus performance than the existing blockchain consistency verification method.

2 Related Work

In 2002, Miguel Castro and Barbara Liskov proposed Practical Byzantine Fault Tolerance. It was applied to a distributed data management system to solve the Byzantine

Generals problem. In the actual system application process of PBFT, there are short-comings that the dishonest node acts as the primary node, which reduces the external service capability of the system and consumes too much network bandwidth resources. Therefore, a series of optimization and improvement work for this problem have been proposed successively. For instance, Kotla et al. [13] proposed a method for simplifying node request agreement. They believe that most of the nodes in the distributed network are in a stable and credible state. Only when there is a node failure, they need to request the agreement of all nodes before executing. Liu et al. [14] proposed a Cross Fault Tolerance mechanism that simplifies the BFT message model. They believe that it is difficult for a malicious attacker to control all the nodes of the entire network at the same time. It is possible to solve the Byzantine General's problem while tolerating the error of more than 33.33% of the nodes of the entire network. Cowling et al. [15] proposed a Hybrid Quorum to optimize PBFT, which divides the writing process into two stages. Since the HQ protocol has no competition for client requests, it was optimized when the server is running normally.

Bijun Li et al. [16] for the first time proposed a parallel sorting framework Sarek for the blockchain. It divides the service state into exploiting parallelism during the protocol and execution. Eventually, the throughput performance was doubled in half the delay time. Wenbing Zhao et al. [17] proposed an Optimistic BFT, which uses a weaker consistency model to achieve higher throughput and lower end-to-end latency. Zhihong Liang et al. [18] proposed to set a threshold to optimize the PBFT consensus mechanism. Each node votes by the number of notary unit references. The top ten nodes with the highest votes are regarded as notary nodes, which are refreshed after a period of time and then reselected. Wu Teng et al. [19] proposed the process of introducing corporate voting and two-stage submission in PBFT. This reduces the number of message transfers in the distributed network and improved the system's fault tolerance. However, these optimization methods are based on the simplified PBFT consensus process in exchange for execution efficiency. It does not guarantee the credibility of the mechanism consistency verification results.

In response to the above problems of the existing similar consensus mechanisms, this paper proposes a blockchain PBFT consensus performance optimization method that fuses C4.5 decision trees. Not only can it improve the consensus performance of the blockchain, but also ensure the validity of the consistency verification results.

3 PBFT Optimization Method Fusing C4.5 Decision Tree

Firstly, the supply chain financial dataset is used to test and analyze several common machine learning classification algorithms. The test data classification accuracy is used as the basis for selecting the classification algorithm. Secondly, this paper proposes optimization methods such as consensus node trust assessment and voting weight. Finally, the optimized PBFT execution process and algorithm description are given.

3.1 Selection of Machine Learning Classification Algorithm

Use WEKA open source software to build classification models for machine learning classification algorithms such as C4.5 decision tree, KNN, NBC, SVM, BN. 10-fold

Cross Validation test dataset. In addition, the supply chain financial dataset required for the establishment of the model is the real data provided by easy-visible (stock code: 600093), and the company's management personnel have initially processed the data. On this basis, some data results were given corresponding class labels, and the enterprise trust assessment results were divided into excellent, good, and qualified categories. Finally, the classification precision is calculated by formula (1):

$$Precision = \frac{TP}{TP + FP} \qquad (1)$$

Among them, TP and FP are examples of correct classification and incorrect classification. The classification accuracy of the test data set is shown in Table 1.

Table 1. Comparison of model classification accuracy of five classification algorithms.

Classification algorithm	Precision
C4.5	71.83%
KNN	70.14%
NBC	63.52%
SVM	69.43%
BN	67.32

From Table 1, the accuracy of model classification accuracy of the five machine learning classification algorithms is similar. However, the accuracy of the C4.5 decision tree classification algorithm is slightly higher than the other four. Therefore, this paper chooses it as the method for evaluating the trust rating of consensus nodes.

3.2 Classification of Trust Evaluation of Consensus Nodes

After the data attribute value is input into the C4.5 classification model, the enterprise trust level can be classified and evaluated. The following is the construction process of the consensus node classification model based on the supply chain financial dataset:

1) Calculate information entropy. Let set D be the data set of supply chain financial enterprises, and the proportion of the k sample in D is Pk. Because the labels of the supply chain financial data set classification in this paper are three categories of excellent, good and qualified. Therefore, the value of k here is {1, 2, 3}. Then, the category information entropy calculated according to set D is:

$$Info(D) = -\sum_{k=1}^{3} P^k \log^2 Pk \qquad (2)$$

2) *Calculate information gain.* In set D, select attribute feature vector a to divide it. Feature vector a total of 7 possible values {asset liability, account receivable turnover rate, total asset turnover rate, inventory turnover rate, sales profit margin, net value yield rate, net profit growth rate}. Then, when the v value is taken, the value selected in the sample set D is a^v, which is recorded as D^v. The information entropy of D^v can be calculated by formula (2). The branch node is given a weight $\frac{|D^v|}{|D|}$ to solve the problem of different number of samples contained in the branch node. Therefore, the information gain of dividing the set D using the attribute feature vector a can be expressed as:

$$Gain(D, a) = Info(D) - \sum_{v=1}^{7} \frac{|D^v|}{|D|} Info(D^v) \qquad (3)$$

However, the use of information gain will make it have a preference for more attribute selection values. Therefore, the C4.5 decision tree algorithm selects the gain ratio to select the partition attribute.

3) *Calculate the gain ratio.* The calculation of the gain rate in C4.5 is extended on the basis of information gain. The training set D uses the gain rate of the attribute feature vector a, as shown in formula (4):

$$Gain\_ratio(D, a) = \frac{Gain(D, a)}{IV(a)} \qquad (4)$$

among them:

$$IV(a) = - \sum_{v=1}^{7} \frac{|D^v|}{|D|} \log 2 \frac{|D^v|}{|D|} \qquad (5)$$

3.3 Introduce Voting Weight

Judging from the operation principle of C4.5 decision tree, it is a classification method tailored for data classification. Therefore, it is very meaningful to classify and evaluate all consensus nodes before applying it to the PBFT protocol. According to the trust rating of the consensus nodes, the $|R|$ consensus nodes in the blockchain network are sequentially numbered $\{0, ..., |R| - 1\}$. Based on the use of C4.5 decision tree to classify the trust rating of the consensus nodes in the blockchain network, this paper draws on the research ideas of the Tendermint algorithm: introducing the concept of voting weights [20]. The idea of "the better the degree of trust, the greater the voting weight" is adopted to reflect the differences between consensus nodes. For the convenience of research, the definition of voting weight of consensus nodes is given below:

Definition 1. In a blockchain network where the number of consensus nodes is $|R|$. During the consistency consensus verification process of node k, the reliability and response speed of the verification message provided is expressed in the form of voting weight. Let it be written as $Weight_k$, as shown in formula (6), and $Weight_k \in (0, \frac{1}{3}]$.

$$Weight_k = \frac{1}{k+3}, \quad \{k|0 \le k \le |R|-1\} \tag{6}$$

Then, the sum of the voting weights of all consensus nodes in the blockchain is denoted as SUM_{weight}, that is:

$$SUM_{weight} = \sum_{k=0}^{|R|-1} Weight_k \tag{7}$$

Here, this paper draws on the research method of PoW. Using the "minority obeys the majority" idea, the voting weight threshold $Weight_{threshold}$ is set to 0.5 times the total voting weight, that is:

$$Weight_{threshold} = \frac{SUM_{weight}}{2} \tag{8}$$

3.4 Optimized PBFT Execution Process

The optimized PBFT consensus mechanism in this paper adds an initialization process before the implementation of the three-phase protocol on the basis of keeping the original three-phase broadcast protocol unchanged, as shown in Fig. 1 below. Since the number of all consensus nodes is fixed during the operation of PBFT, it does not support dynamic free entry or exit. Therefore, the initialization phase (Init) only starts when new nodes are added or old nodes are exited.

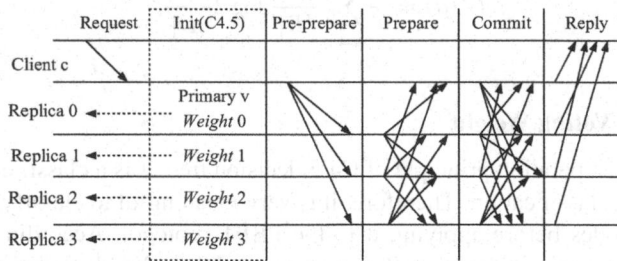

Fig. 1. Optimized PBFT execution process.

4 Experiment and Analysis

Experiment 1: compare the algorithm delay performance before and after optimization.

In order to compare with PBFT before optimization, this paper selects the number of transactions with block size in the range of [50, 1000] for simulation test. After 10 experiments, the average value is calculated, and the transaction delay under different block size is obtained. As shown in Fig. 2.

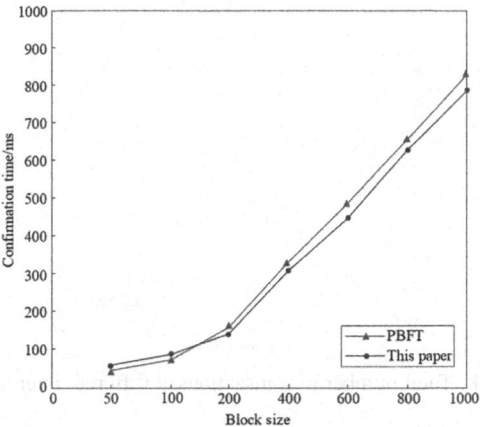

Fig. 2. Trading delay for different block sizes.

Experiment 2: compare the algorithm transaction throughput before and after optimization.

In order to compare the transaction throughput performance of the PBFT consensus mechanism of the blockchain before and after optimization, this paper simulates different time intervals during the operation of four blockchain systems: 5 s, 10 s, 20 s, 40 s. Each time interval has undergone 10 experiments, as shown in Figs. 3 and 4.

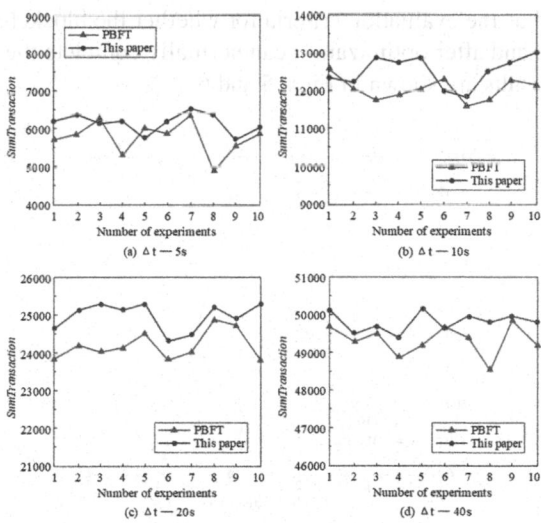

Fig. 3. Total number of transactions at different intervals.

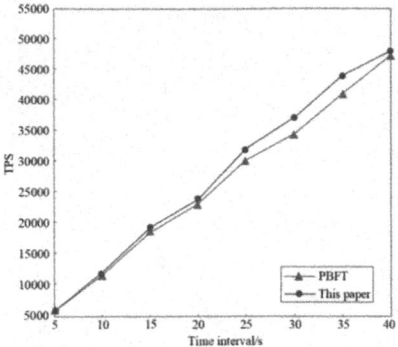

Fig. 4. Total number of transactions at different intervals.

Experiment 3: Comparison of algorithm fault tolerance before and after optimization. In the PBFT-based blockchain system, if the value range of $|R|$ is [4, 100], at most $f = \left\lfloor \frac{|R|-1}{3} \right\rfloor$ consensus nodes in the blockchain network can tolerate malicious errors. In order to verify the optimized PBFT fused with C4.5 decision tree, it has greater advantages in fault tolerance. In this paper, among the 8 consensus nodes on the Hyperledger Fabric blockchain simulation test platform, the values of f are simulated in order of 0, 1, 2, 3, 4, and 5 respectively for experimental comparison. Each value experiment is 10 times. The average value of the experiment is taken as the final processing result of the experiment, and compared with the experimental result of the PBFT before optimization. Among them, the system transaction confirmation time and transaction throughput are used as the evaluation criteria for whether the blockchain system based on the PBFT before and after optimization can normally complete the consensus work. The experimental results are shown in Figs. 5 and 6.

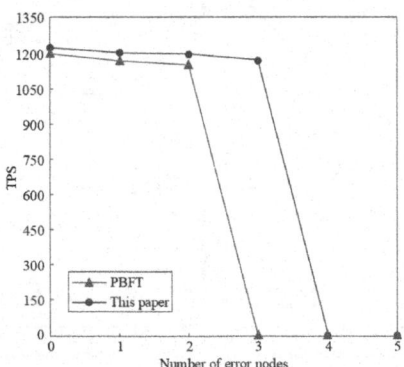

Fig. 5. The relationship between TPS and the number of faulty nodes.

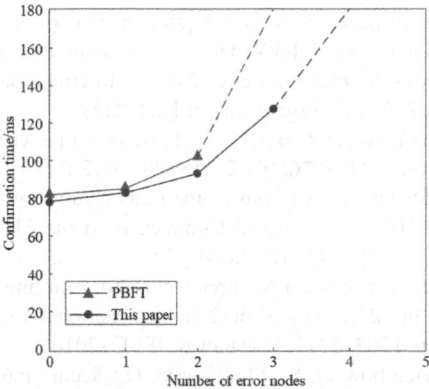

Fig. 6. The relationship between delay and number of faulty nodes.

Compared with PBFT, the method in this paper can tolerate more consensus node errors in the blockchain network.

5 Conclusion

The purpose of this paper is to optimize the performance of the blockchain PBFT. To achieve the improvement of system delay, throughput and fault tolerance with less time consumption. This paper mainly introduces the current research results of the PBFT consensus algorithm based on the current status of PBFT research. In view of the current weak research in the blockchain system, the research method of optimizing the blockchain PBFT by fusing C4.5 decision tree is established. Finally, a Hyperledger Fabric simulation test platform is used to test the optimization method, and the experimental results show the correctness and effectiveness of the method in this paper.

Acknowledgments. This work has been supported by the Major Project of Science and Technology of Yunnan Province under Grant No. 202002AD080002 and No. 2019ZE005.

References

1. Pass, R., Seeman, L., Shelat, A.: Analysis of the blockchain protocol in asynchronous networks. In: Coron, J.S., Nielsen, J.B. (eds.) EUROCRYPT 2017. LNCS, vol. 10211, pp. 643–673. Springer, Cham (2017). https://doi.org/10.1007/978-3-319-56614-6_22
2. Watanabe, H., Fujimura, S., Nakadaira, A., et al.: Blockchain contract: a complete consensus using blockchain. In: Proceedings of the 4th International Conference on Consumer Electronics. pp. 577–578, Piscataway,IEEE (2015)
3. Xiaolong, X., Liu, X., Zhanyang, X., Dai, F., Zhang, X., Qi, L.: Trust-oriented IoT service placement for smart cities in edge computing. IEEE IoT J. **7**(5), 4084–4091 (2020)
4. Huh, S., Cho, S.: Managing IoT devices using blockchain platform. In: Proceedings of the 2017 International Conference on Advanced Communication Technology. Piscataway, pp. 464–467, IEEE (2017)

5. Nakamoto, S.B.: A peer-to-peer electronic cash system. (2019)https://bitcoin.org/bitcoin.pdf
6. Kosba, A., Miller, A., Shi, E., et al.: Hawk: The blockchain model of cryptography and privacy preserving smart contracts. In: Proceedings of the 2016 International Conference on Security and Privacy (S&P). pp. 839–858, Piscataway, IEEE (2016)
7. Bu-Tian, H., Zheng-Guang, L., Jian-Hai, C., et al.: Behavior pattern clustering in blockchain networks. Multimed. Tools. Appl. **76**(19), 20099–20110 (2017)
8. Pass, R., Seeman, L., Shelat, A.: Analysis of the Blockchain protocol in asynchronous networks. In: Proc of the 2017 International Conference on the Theory and Applications of Cryptographic Techniques. pp. 643–673 ACM (2017)
9. Jin, H., Dai, X., Xiao, J.: Towards a novel architecture for enabling interoperability amongst multiple blockchains. In: Proceedings of 22nd International Conference on Distributed Computing Systems. pp. 1203–1211, Piscataway, IEEE (2018)
10. Andrychowicz, M., Dziembowski, S., Malinowski, D.: Secure multiparty computations on bitcoin. Communic. ACM **59**(4), 76–84 (2016)
11. Qifeng, S., Cheqing, J., Zhao, Z., et al.: Blockchain: architecture and research progress. Chinese J. Comput. **41**(05), 969–988 (2018)
12. Cachin, C.: Architecture of the Hyperledger blockchain fabric. In: Proceedings of the 7th Workshop on Distributed Cryptocurrencies and Consensus Ledgers. pp. 523–527, Piscataway, IEEE (2016)
13. Castro, M., Liskov, B.: Practical byzantine fault tolerance and proactive recover. ACM Trans. Comput. Syst. **20**(4), 398–461 (2002)
14. Kotla, R., Alvisi, L., Dahlin, M., et al.: Zyzzyva: speculative byzantine fault tolerance. In: Proceedings of the 21st ACM Symposium International Conference on Operating Systems Principles. pp. 45–58, New York, ACM (2007)
15. Liu, S., Viotti, P., Cachin, C., et al.: XFT: Practical fault tolerance beyond crashes. In: Proceedings of 12th International Conference on Operating Systems Design and Implementation (OSDI). pp. 485–500, Piscataway, IEEE (2016)
16. Cowling J, Myers D, Liskov B. HQ Replication: a hybrid quorum protocol for byzantine fault tolerance. In: Proceedings of the 7th International Conference on Operating Systems Design and Implementation. pp. 177–190, Stroudsburg, ACL (2006)
17. Li, B., Xu, W., et al.: SAREK: optimistic parallel ordering in byzantine fault tolerance. In: Proceedings of the 12th European Dependable Computing Conference. pp. 577–588 Piscataway, IEEE (2016)
18. Zhao, W.: Optimistic byzantine fault tolerance. Int. J. Parallel, Emergent Distributed Syst. **31**(3), 254–267 (2016)
19. Liang, Z., Huang, Y., et al.: Creativity in trusted data: research on application of blockchain in supply chain. Int. J. Perform. Eng. **15**(2), 526–535 (2019)
20. Qi, M., Wei, S., Fei, D., Leilei, L., Tong, L.: Development of collaborative business processes: a correctness enforcement approach. IEEE Trans. Serv. Comput. (2019)

Blockchain Security and Privacy

Identifying Illicit Addresses in Bitcoin Network

Yang Li[1,2], Yue Cai[1,2], Hao Tian[1,2], Gengsheng Xue[1,2], and Zibin Zheng[1,2(✉)]

[1] School of Data and Computer Science, Sun Yat-sen University,
Guangzhou 510275, China
{liyang99,caiy26,tianh23,xuegsh}@mail2.sysu.edu.cn
[2] National Engineering Research Center of Digital Life, Sun Yat-sen University,
Guangzhou, China
zhzibin@mail.sysu.edu.cn

Abstract. Bitcoin has attracted a lot of attentions from both researchers and investors since it was first proposed in 2008. One of the key characteristics of Bitcoin is anonymity, which makes the Bitcoin market unregulated and a large number of criminal and illicit activities are associated with bitcoin transactions. Therefore, it's necessary to identify the illicit addresses in the Bitcoin network for safeguarding financial systems and protecting user's assets. To identify the illicit addresses in the Bitcoin network, first, we collect a large dataset of illicit addresses. The illicit addresses come mainly from some specific websites, public forums, and research papers. Second, we make a careful design of the features of illicit addresses. The features include basic features that refer to the related papers and the novel proposed features (topological features and temporal features). Third, we apply various machine learning algorithms (RF, SVM, XGB, ANN) to evaluate our features, which indicates that the proposed features are discriminating and robust. Besides, the paper discusses the class imbalance problem and achieves a better enhancement when using the cost-sensitive approach. Moreover, the paper proposes a model that incorporates LSTM into auto-encoder to generate temporal features. Results show that the generated features are helpful for the illicit addresses identification. Finally, the dataset and code are released in Github.

Keywords: Bitcoin · Illicit addresses · Machine learning · Auto-encoder · Topological features · Temporal features

1 Introduction

Bitcoin has attracted extensive attention from both investors and researchers since it was first proposed by Nakamoto [1] in 2008. It is the first open-source and widest spread digital cryptocurrency that has no central authority to control or manage its supply. Bitcoin works on the principle of a public decentralized ledger called blockchain [2,3], which is the core mechanism and provides security for the Bitcoin network. A blockchain consists of the longest series of blocks from the genesis block to the current block that is linked using cryptography. The process of new coins created is known as Bitcoin mining [4,5], which is to solve a computation problem.

One of the key characteristics of Bitcoin is the high anonymity it provides for its participants [6]. Bitcoin addresses are the only information used to send or receive Bitcoins for participants who do not need to provide any information on identification. Although address' information (all historical transactions and balances) can be obtained through the public decentralized ledger once the address is used, it is still impossible to de-anonymize it. Thus, there exist a wide range of crimes such as murders for hire, funding terrorism, drug, weapon, organ trafficking, Ponzi schemes, forgeries, unlawful gambling, money laundering, illegal mining, computer hacking, spreading ransomware and outright theft [7–9]. Therefore, identifying illicit addresses play a critical role in safeguarding financial systems, which is helpful for the Bitcoin ecosystem.

In addressing the aforementioned problems, we construct a large dataset that includes more than 20,000 illicit addresses and applies machine learning methods to identify them. More specifically, first, we collect the illicit addresses from various sources such as bitcoin websites, public forums, and some related papers. We also verify some addresses through open websites. Second, we not only collect the features which are used in related papers that are evidenced effectively but also propose two types of novel features (topological features and temporal features) in this paper. Last, we apply various machine learning algorithms (RF, SVM, XGB, ANN) to evaluate the proposed features and achieve good performance. Besides, the paper discusses the class imbalance problem and achieves a better enhancement using a cost-sensitive approach. Furthermore, the paper proposes a model that incorporates LSTM into auto-encoder to generate temporal features. Results show that the generated features are helpful for the illicit addresses identification.

In summary, our main contributions are:

- Dataset: a dataset of illicit addresses are collected from various source.
- Features: two types of novel features (topological features and temporal features) are proposed to identify illicit addresses.
- Algorithm: an auto-encoder with an LSTM model is proposed to generate new temporal features.
- Experiments: various and sufficient machine learning methods are used to identify illicit addresses and the class imbalance problem is discussed in this paper.

The rest of this paper is organized as follows. Section 2 investigates the related work of identifying illicit addresses. Section 3 illustrates our methodology of collecting illicit addresses dataset and constructing three types of features. Section 4 compares the effectiveness of various machine learning methods and discusses the class imbalance problem. Besides, we propose a model that incorporates LSTM into auto-encoder to generate new features to enhance the prediction. Finally, Sect. 5 draws some conclusions.

2   Related Work

Identifying illicit addresses play a critical role in safeguarding financial systems. Studies can be divided into two categories for identifying illicit addresses in the Bitcoin network. The first is to detect anomalous users and transactions. The second is to focus on specific illicit addresses such as scam, ransomware, Darknet market, Hack.

For identifying anomalous users and transactions in the Bitcoin network, [10] proposes three main social network techniques to detect potential anomalous users and transactions in the Bitcoin transaction network. [11] recently proposes unsupervised learning approaches to detect anomalies in the Bitcoin transaction network. [12] proposes a supervised classification model for detecting abnormality of Bitcoin network addresses. [13] presents graph convolutional networks for financial forensics on the Elliptic dataset. The dataset is also used in our paper.

For the scam identification, [14] applies data mining techniques to detect Bitcoin addresses related to Ponzi schemes. [15] proposes a novel methodology for HYIP (high yield investment programs) operators' Bitcoin addresses identification. For the ransomware identification, [16] proposes a network topology to measure and analyze ransomware in the Bitcoin network. For the Darknet market identification, [9] builds a dynamic research model to examine the evolution of Bitcoin and Darknet markets. However, the illicit addresses used in the above researches are small.

We collect a large illicit addresses' dataset. To the best of our knowledge, there exist no works that learn a recognized model for all types of illicit addresses on a large illicit addresses' dataset with advanced supervised learning methods.

3   Dataset Construction

3.1   Tag Collection

We develop a web crawler for public forums, user profiles (e.g., Bitcointalk.com, Twitter and Reddit) and darknet markets (e.g.., Silkroad, The Hub Marketplace and Alphabay) with some keywords (e.g., drug, arms, Ponzi, investment, ransomware, blackmail scam, sextortion, bitcoin tumbler, darknet market, ...). Especially, we crawl and filter bitcoin addresses of Bitcoinica Hack in https://bitcointalk.org/index.php?topic=576337. The data crawled from these sites is called crawled data. We also extend our search by considering all addresses listed on www.blockchain.com/btc/tags, a website that allows users to tag Bitcoin addresses. Most of the tagged addresses also contain a link to the website where they are mentioned and the description of tags. We filter the illicit addresses by the tags mentioned above. www.bitcoinabuse.com is a public database of bitcoin addresses used by hackers and criminals, which tracks bitcoin addresses used by ransomware, blackmailers, fraudsters, and so on. We download all the illicit addresses from it, addresses are also classified. www.bitcoinwhoswho.com is a website which provides all available information about a bitcoin address and it will report some Bitcoin Scams. Thus, we crawl some Bitcoin scam addresses from it. The data tagged from these websites is called tagged data. Besides, we investigate some papers which are related to the identify illicit addresses. [14] releases a dataset of real-world Ponzi schemes. [17] releases the ransomware seed dataset. [13] releases an Elliptic dataset which includes 11,698 illicit addresses (scams, malware, terrorist organizations, ransomware, Ponzi schemes). However, they don't provide the specific labels of each illicit entity. The data collected from these papers is called paper data. Besides, we removed addresses without any transactions. These addresses may be used for scams or other illicit usages, but no one is fooled by them.

Overall, we find 24,720 illicit addresses which can be categorized as follows and the details we display in Table 1.

- **Ponzi scheme** is fraudulent investments that repay users with the funds invested by new users that join the scheme and implode when it is no longer possible to find new investments.
- **Ransomware** is spread to lock or encrypt the database, files, PC, or any electronic copy and demand ransoms in Bitcoin to enable access.
- **Blackmail** Bitcoin holder knowingly sends Bitcoin to criminals because of threatening or blackmail.
- **Darknet market** is a commercial website on the web that operates via darknets such as Tor or I2P. We collect the illicit addresses like arms trade, human trafficking, pornography and violence, drugs, etc.
- **Hack** wallets belonged to an exchange or a platform are hacked by outsiders, which led to the collapse of the exchange.

Table 1. Classes of illicit addresses

Class	Number	Source
Ponzi schemes	120	Tagged data, crawled data, papers data
Ransomeware	8979	Tagged data, crawled data, papers data
Blackmail	2884	Crawled data, tagged data
Darknet market	293	Crawled data, tagged data
Hack	406	Crawled data, tagged data
Unknown	11698	Only from paper [13]
Others	340	Tagged data
Total	24720	

3.2 Automatic Addresses Filtering

Some addresses may be inevitably misidentified as illicit addresses. We make an automatic address filtering, leveraging addresses clustering. Addresses clustering is based on a heuristic [18]. It can be described as if two or more addresses are inputs of the same transaction with one output, then, all these addresses are controlled by the same user. This heuristic is expected to be accurate since Bitcoin clients do not provide support for different users to participate in a single transaction.

The considerations of filtering licit addresses can be summarized into two parts. First, addresses may mix with some normal addresses like exchanges, services since there exist multiple services for multi-input transactions nowadays. It's hard to label them as normal addresses or illicit addresses. Secondly, addresses may be normal scams that live a long time. Thus, it's also hard to label them. Therefore, we remove these uncertain addresses. Overall, we remove 523 illicit addresses whose multi-input addresses are more than 1000 from our collected dataset.

3.3 Discriminating Features Extraction

Here, we extract various features from illicit addresses, which are used to detect with supervised learning algorithms. Features can be roughly categorized as follows: 1) basic features, they are obtained from existing literatures; 2) topological features, they are extracted from the topological structure of transactions; and 3) temporal features, they are obtained from the change of balance of addresses. The following subsections provide more details on each type of feature.

Basic Features (BaF). The basic information of an address is used for feature construction. It includes the sum of all the inputs and outputs transferred to (resp. from) the address and final balance.

Besides, some basic features are obtained from [12,14,19]. The features in [14] are used for detecting Bitcoin Ponzi schemes. We select the lifetime of the address, the activity days, the maximum number of daily transactions to/from the address, the Gini coefficient of the values transferred to (resp. from) the address, the sum of all the values transferred to (resp. from) the address, the number of incoming (resp. outgoing) transactions which transfer money to (resp. from) the address, the ratio between incoming and outgoing transactions to/from the address, the average (resp. standard deviation) of the values transferred to/from the address, the minimum (resp. maximum, average) delay between the time as a part of our basic features. The features in [19] are used to identify what kind of services are operated by Bitcoin addresses. We select the frequency of transactions, payback ratio, the average numbers of inputs and outputs in the spent transactions as a part of our basic features. The features in [12] are used to classify Bitcoin addresses. We select the transaction moments which are proposed to encode temporal information as a part of basic features, the details are described in this paper.

Topological Features (ToF). Figure 1 shows that addresses with the same structure of transactions are labeled differently due to the property of input

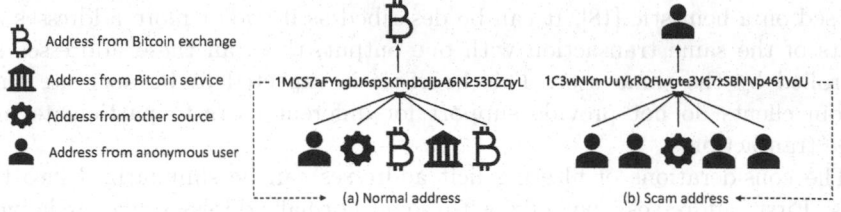

Fig. 1. A topological structure of a normal address and a scam address.

addresses and output addresses. More specifically, address a receives Bitcoins mainly from Bitcoin exchanges and services (provide bitcoin service for users) and sends to Bitcoin exchange. Thus, address a is a normal address with high probability and labeled as normal address since the KYC (Know Your Client, is the process of a business verifying the identity of its clients and assessing their suitability) is required by Bitcoin exchanges and some Bitcoin services. Instead, address b receives Bitcoins mainly from anonymous users and sends it to anonymous users. Thus, address b is an illicit address with some probability and labeled as a scam address. To solve this problem, we construct topological features to capture more information. At first, we characterize addresses into five categories (exchange, service, gambling, pool, and unknown user) followed by [20]. Then, each address will have a topological feature vector of length 10. For example, a topological feature vector is $[1{-}4, 7, 10]$, the first five number represents that one input address comes from the exchange, three input addresses come from service, four input addresses come from gambling, seven input addresses come from the pool, and ten input addresses come from the unknown user. The second five number represents that four output addresses come from the exchange, two output addresses come from service, ten output addresses come from gambling, two output addresses come from the pool, and three output addresses come from the unknown user.

Temporal Features (TeF). Apart from the BaF and ToF, each address has different time distributions of transactions. In order to capture the temporal information, the time series of each address's balance (B) is constructed. More specifically, the address's balance will be updated and appended to the time series when it has a new transaction.

Figure 2 shows an example of a ransomeware (12PEiX8JrYmpMRL6jkTK38pc-Dnq14NwVHB) and Ponzi scheme address (1Dgp5LqGZKWP7PrmxTG1Sitb88a-16HzwCy). It can be seen that the Ponzi address tends to receive bitcoins with the same amount every time and transfer a large number of bitcoins to other addresses at a time. To find some regular features, first, we apply the first difference method to the vector B and form a new vector C. Second, the mean and variance of C are calculated. Last, we define a time window of t, which is used to get a new vector V from C. The length of V is $len(C)/t$, and the values are the mean of C in the period of t. The mean and variance of V are calculated as features. Here, t is set to $2, 4, 6, 8$ respectively. Besides, the main difference between the ransomware addresses and normal addresses is that the number of bitcoins received from normal addresses may have irregular decimals. However, ransomware addresses may receive the number of bitcoins with regular decimals or integer due to the value of bitcoins. Therefore, if $mean(C) = 0$ and $Round(sum(a), 2) = a$, we set 1 as the feature, otherwise, we set 0 as the feature.

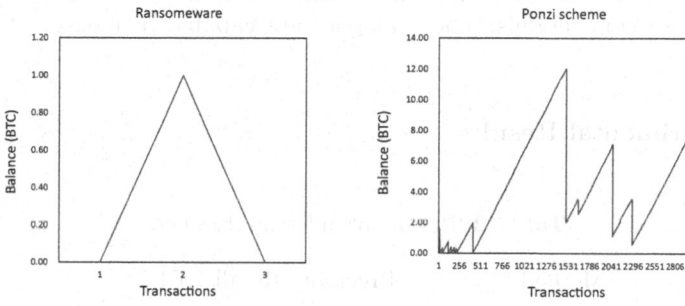

Fig. 2. An example of a ransomware address and a Ponzi scheme address.

4   Supervised Learning for Illicit Addresses Identifying

4.1   Data and Experimental Setup

The dataset includes 24,197 illicit addresses and other 1,209,850 licit addresses. The illicit addresses described in Sect. 3 are labeled as 1. The licit addresses sampled from WalletExplorer.com are labeled as 0. All 92 features described in Sect. 3 are used as model inputs. The imbalance ratio between two classes is 1:50 (1 illicit address every 50 instances of licit addresses). The main reason is that [14] proposes 1 Ponzi instance in every 200 instances of non-Ponzi and we expand to 1:50 in our illicit addresses compared to licit addresses because we have a lot of other types of illicit addresses. Besides, the dataset are divided into a training set (80% of the dataset), validate set (10% of the dataset), and testing set (10% of the dataset).

4.2   Classifiers and Evaluation Metrics

In this section, we evaluate the hand-crafted features (BaF, ToF, TeF) using several classic classifiers such as Random Forests (RF) [21], Support Vector Machine with RBF kernel (SVM) [22], XGBoost (XGB) [23], and Artificial neural networks (ANN) [24].

The implementation details are described as follows. We apply scikit-learn [25] which is a Python module for machine learning to SVM and RF. XGB is implemented with the XGB python library which is open source at github. The artificial neural networks are implemented with Keras [26]. The architecture of artificial neural networks is composed of three fully-connected hidden layers and an output layer. Each hidden layer incorporates batch normalization and dropout regularization. Besides, we normalize the input data with a max-min method which changes the values of numeric columns to a common value between 0 and 1 since the neural networks are sensitive to the input data.

Precision, recall, and F1 score are used to evaluate the performance of the presented detection models. These metrics are capable to measure the imbalanced data.

4.3   Experimental Results

Table 2. Results of different classifiers

Method	Precision	Recall	F1
RF^{BaF}	0.9263	0.7069	0.8019
$RF^{BaF+ToF}$	0.9297	0.7231	0.8135
$RF^{BaF+ToF+TeF}$	**0.9355**	0.7293	0.8196
SVM^{BaF}	0.7813	0.6512	0.7103
$SVM^{BaF+ToF}$	0.8197	0.6742	0.7399
$SVM^{BaF+ToF+TeF}$	0.8355	0.6983	0.7608
ANN^{BaF}	0.7802	0.7844	0.7823
$ANN^{BaF+ToF}$	0.8712	0.7302	0.7945
$ANN^{BaF+ToF+TeF}$	0.8662	0.7750	0.8181
XGB^{BaF}	0.9049	0.8453	0.8741
$XGB^{BaF+ToF}$	0.9063	0.8529	0.8787
$XGB^{BaF+ToF+TeF}$	0.9100	**0.8540**	**0.8811**

Table 2 shows the detailed testing results in terms of precision, recall, and F1 score for the illicit class. Each model is executed with different input features. BaF refers to the basic features, ToF refers to the topological features, and TeF refers to the temporal features.

Note that XGB, RF outperform SVM and ANN, indicating the usefulness of the tree-based methods compared to other methods. Besides, XGB achieves the best F1 score and recall with all the three types of features. The main reason is that we can tune the parameter Scale_pos_weight of XGB which can suit for imbalanced data to obtain a good recall. Scale_pos_weight is the ratio of the number of negative class to the positive class.

Another insight from Table 2 is obtained from the comparison between features trained on the same model. For XGB, it can be seen that the enhanced feature (ToF, TeF) can improve the accuracy of the model only with BaF.

4.4   Class Imbalance Problem

The ratio of illicit addresses to licit addresses is 1:50 in the previous experiments [14]. However, the real-world distribution may be not equal to this specific ratio. In this section, the class imbalance problem is discussed. We change the imbalance ratio of training set and apply RF to evaluate. The ratio is set 1:200, 1:100, 1:50, 1:20, and 1:5 respectively.

Table 3. Results of different imbalance ratio

Imbalance ratio	Precision	Recall	F1
1:200	0.8448	0.4900	0.6200
1:100	0.8286	0.5800	0.6824
1:50	0.9355	0.7293	0.8196
1:20	0.9411	0.767	0.8452
1:5	**0.9567**	**0.84**	**0.8946**

Table 3 shows that the results are different with different imbalance ratio. The results achieve best in precision, recall and F1 score when the imbalance ratio is 1:5. Besides, the larger the imbalance ratio, the lower the recall.

To improve the results of class imbalance problem, we investigate it in data mining [27]. The solutions can be divided into sampling-based approaches and cost-sensitive approaches. Sampling-based approaches [28] construct balanced training set and adjusting the prior distribution for minority class (under sampling) or majority class (over sampling). Cost-sensitive approaches [29] is another type which takes the misclassification costs into consideration in the training phase. More specifically, the cost-sensitive approaches use a cost matrix to penalize different misclassification. For example, CM5 represents the cost of a false negative error is 5 times larger than the cost of a false positive error. In this paper, we only consider the cost-sensitive approaches because the sampling-based approaches will change the distribution of the training set, and the imbalance ratio is 1:50.

Table 4. Results of different cost matrix

Cost matrix	Precision	Recall	F1
CM5	**0.9038**	0.7737	0.8337
CM10	0.8768	0.8032	**0.8384**
CM20	0.8522	0.7976	0.8240
CM40	0.8181	**0.8327**	0.8253

The details of RF that applies cost-sensitive approach can refer to [30]. Table 4 shows that different cost matrices are used for RF model with the dataset. The best F1 score are achieved with the CM10 cost matrix. All the four cost matrices perform better than the origin RF with F1 score. However, it also indicates that the performance is sensitive to the cost matrix, the design of the cost matrix is important when we want to get a good result with cost-sensitive approaches.

4.5   Auto-encoder with LSTM

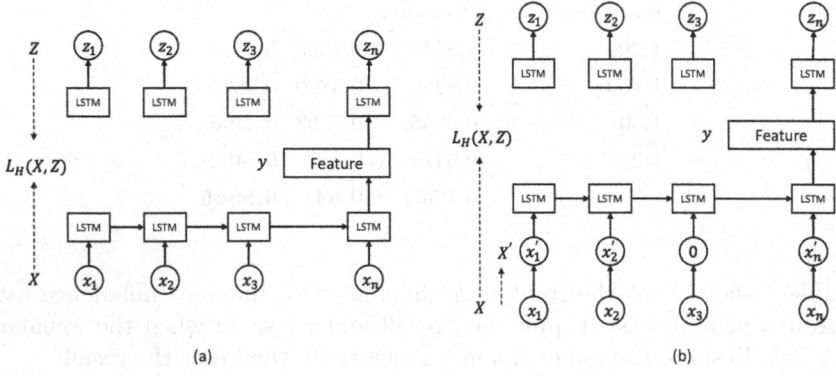

Fig. 3. Auto-encoder with LSTM.

The temporal features described in Sect. 3 are shallow and lack of hidden information since we only use a time window to obtain features. Thus, the regular rules or the trading behaviors in the transaction series are not included. In order to obtain more useful and discriminating temporal features, we apply an auto-encoder [31] method to generate it. An auto-encoder is a type of artificial neural network used to learn efficient features in an unsupervised process.

However, about 80% of all illicit addresses have less than 10 transactions. The main reason is that a lot of addresses are ransomware and blackmail, the extortioner (the address owner) may only use the address once when they black-mailed their users. For addresses with less than or more than 10 transactions, we adopt two different auto-encoders to obtain the hidden features. The first is an ordinary auto-encoder applied to addresses with less than 10 transactions, which is shown in Fig. 3(a), it includes three parts, encoder, decoder, and training. The main process of each part is described as follows.

- **Encoder.** The LSTM network [32] that transforms an input vector x into hidden representation y is called the encoder process. y is an encoder feature that is called generated features (GeF).
- **Decoder.** The hidden representation y is mapped back to a reconstructed dimensional vector z from a LSTM network. This mapping is called the decoder.

– **Training.** Autoencoder training consists of minimizing the reconstruction error, that is, carrying the following optimization:

$$\mathrm{argmin} L_H(X, Z) \tag{1}$$

For addresses which have a large number of transactions (>10), we adopt a denoising auto-encoder with LSTM (L-DAE) to obtain the hidden features since a large number of transactions may contain noise. The architecture of denoising auto-encoder with LSTM is shown in Fig. 3(b) and the main process is the same as auto-encoder with LSTM. The main difference is that the denoising auto-encoder uses a denoising criterion, which can be described as each time a training example x is presented, a different corrupted version $\tilde{x}$ of it is generated according to $q_D(\tilde{x}|x)$. $q_D(\tilde{x}|x)$ is a stochastic mapping.

Table 5. Comparison of GeF and TeF

Method	Precision	Recall	F1
$XGB^{BaF+ToF+TeF}$	0.9100	0.8540	0.8811
$XGB^{BaF+ToF+GeF}$	0.9273	0.8735	0.8996
$XGB^{BaF+ToF+TeF+GeF}$	**0.9348**	**0.8805**	**0.9069**

Table 5 shows that the generated features are better than the hand-crafted TeF. A combination of four types of features (BaF, ToF, TeF, GeF) achieves the best with XGB model. Besides, we compare the features generated only by L-AE and the features generated by both L-AE and L-DAE. The results in Table 6 shows that both L-AE and L-DAE performs better than L-AE.

Table 6. Comparison of L-AE and L-DAE

Method	Precision	Recall	F1
XGB L-AE	0.9211	0.8725	0.8961
XGB L-AE + L-DAE	**0.9348**	**0.8805**	**0.9069**

5   Conclusions

In this paper, we collect a new dataset for identifying illicit addresses in the Bitcoin network. Illicit addresses include ransomware, Ponzi schemes, darknet market, blackmail, hack and some unknown addresses which are not specifically categorized. We introduce three types of features for the illicit addresses classification problem. The basic features are based on some previous works, which are proved to be effective. The topological features contain extra information on addresses' inputs and outputs. The extra information can provide the trading behaviors and rules of the address. The temporal features are extracted from the change of addresses' balance. It can capture some regular patterns of addresses. Experimental results show that the performance of the proposed features and feature combinations improve the classification measurement. Besides, we make a sufficient discussion on the class imbalance problem because the amount of illicit addresses and licit addresses is a significant difference in the real world and we also apply cost-sensitive approaches to improve the results. Moreover, we provide a deep learning approach (auto-encoder with LSTM) to generate new temporal features and achieve better results than previous features.

Lastly, we hope the collected dataset and proposed methods in this field of identifying illicit addresses can attract more researchers and make the financial systems safer.

Acknowledgments. The work described in this paper was supported by the National Key Research and Development Program (2016YFB1000101), the National Natural Science Foundation of China (U1811462, 61722214) and the Key-Area Research and Development Program of Guangdong Province (2018B010109001).

References

1. Nakamoto, S., et al.: Bitcoin: A peer-to-peer electronic cash system (2008)
2. Zheng, Z., Xie, S., Dai, H., Chen, X., Wang, H.: An overview of blockchain technology: Architecture, consensus, and future trends. In: 2017 IEEE International Congress on Big Data (BigData Congress), pp. 557–564. IEEE (2017)
3. Zheng, Z., Xie, S., Dai, H.-N., Chen, X., Wang, H.: Blockchain challenges and opportunities: a survey. Int. J. Web Grid Serv. **14**(4), 352–375 (2018)
4. Chuen, D.L.K.: Handbook of Digital Currency: Bitcoin, Innovation, Financial Instruments, and Big Data. Academic Press, Cambridge (2015)
5. Eyal, I., Sirer, E.G.: Majority is not enough: bitcoin mining is vulnerable. Commun. ACM **61**(7), 95–102 (2018)
6. Reid, F., Harrigan, M.: An analysis of anonymity in the bitcoin system. In: Altshuler, Y., Elovici, Y., Cremers, A., Aharony, N., Pentland, A. (eds.) Security and Privacy in Social Networks, pp. 197–223. Springer, New York (2013). https://doi.org/10.1007/978-1-4614-4139-7_10
7. Hurlburt, G.F., Bojanova, I.: Bitcoin: Benefit or curse? It Professional, **16**(3), 10–15 (2014)
8. Foley, S., Karlsen, J.R., Putniņš, T.J.: Sex, drugs, and bitcoin: how much illegal activity is financed through cryptocurrencies? Rev. Financ. Stud. **32**(5), 1798–1853 (2019)
9. Janze, C.: Are cryptocurrencies criminals best friends? Examining the co-evolution of bitcoin and darknet markets (2017)
10. Pham, T., Lee, S.: Anomaly detection in bitcoin network using unsupervised learning methods. arXiv preprint arXiv:1611.03941 (2016)
11. Monamo, P., Marivate, V., Twala, B.: Unsupervised learning for robust bitcoin fraud detection. In: 2016 Information Security for South Africa (ISSA), pp. 129–134. IEEE (2016)

12. Lin, Y.-J., Wu, P.-W., Hsu, C.-H., Tu, I-P., Liao, S.: An evaluation of bitcoin address classification based on transaction history summarization. In: 2019 IEEE International Conference on Blockchain and Cryptocurrency (ICBC), pp. 302–310. IEEE (2019)
13. Weber, M., et al.: Anti-money laundering in bitcoin: experimenting with graph convolutional networks for financial forensics. arXiv preprint arXiv:1908.02591 (2019)
14. Bartoletti, M., Pes, B., Serusi, S.: Data mining for detecting bitcoin Ponzi schemes. In: 2018 Crypto Valley Conference on Blockchain Technology (CVCBT), pp. 75–84. IEEE (2018)
15. Toyoda, K., Takis Mathiopoulos, P., Ohtsuki, T.: A novel methodology for hyip operators' bitcoin addresses identification. IEEE Access **7**, 74835–74848 (2019)
16. Liao, K., Zhao, Z., Doupé, A., Ahn, G.-J.: Behind closed doors: measurement and analysis of cryptolocker ransoms in bitcoin. In: 2016 APWG Symposium on Electronic Crime Research (eCrime), pp. 1–13. IEEE (2016)
17. Paquet-Clouston, M., Haslhofer, B., Dupont, B.: Ransomware payments in the bitcoin ecosystem. J. Cybersecur. **5**(1), tyz003 (2019)
18. Androulaki, E., Karame, G.O., Roeschlin, M., Scherer, T., Capkun, S.: Evaluating user privacy in bitcoin. In: Sadeghi, A.-R. (ed.) FC 2013. LNCS, vol. 7859, pp. 34–51. Springer, Heidelberg (2013). https://doi.org/10.1007/978-3-642-39884-1_4
19. Toyoda, K., Ohtsuki, T., Takis Mathiopoulos, P.: Multi-class bitcoin-enabled service identification based on transaction history summarization. In: 2018 IEEE International Conference on Internet of Things (iThings) and IEEE Green Computing and Communications (GreenCom) and IEEE Cyber, Physical and Social Computing (CPSCom) and IEEE Smart Data (SmartData), pp. 1153–1160. IEEE (2018)
20. Jourdan, M., Blandin, S., Wynter, L., Deshpande, P.: Characterizing entities in the bitcoin blockchain. In: 2018 IEEE International Conference on Data Mining Workshops (ICDMW), pp. 55–62. IEEE (2018)
21. Breiman, L.: Random forests. Mach. Learn. **45**(1), 5–32 (2001)
22. Hearst, M.A., Dumais, S.T., Osuna, E., Platt, J., Scholkopf, B.: Support vector machines. IEEE Intell. Syst. Appl. **13**(4), 18–28 (1998)
23. Chen, T., Guestrin, C.: XGBoost: a scalable tree boosting system. In: Proceedings of the 22nd ACM SIGKDD International Conference on Knowledge Discovery and Data Mining, pp. 785–794. ACM (2016)
24. Jain, A.K., Mao, J., Moidin Mohiuddin, K.: Artificial neural networks: a tutorial. Computer **29**(3), 31–44 (1996)
25. Pedregosa, F., et al.: Scikit-learn: machine learning in python. J. Mach. Learn. Res. **12**, 2825–2830 (2011)
26. Gulli, A., Pal, S.: Deep Learning with Keras. Packt Publishing Ltd. (2017)
27. Longadge, R., Dongre, S.: Class imbalance problem in data mining review. arXiv preprint arXiv:1305.1707 (2013)
28. Nguyen, G.H., Bouzerdoum, A., Phung, S.L.: Learning pattern classification tasks with imbalanced data sets. In Pattern recognition, IntechOpen (2009)
29. Sun, Y., et al.: Cost-sensitive boosting for classification of imbalanced data. Pattern Recogn. **40**(12), 3358–3378 (2007)
30. Bahnsen, A.C.: Ensembles of example-dependent cost-sensitive decision trees (2015)
31. Kramer, M.A.: Nonlinear principal component analysis using auto associative neural networks. AIChE J. **37**(2), 233–243 (1991)
32. Hochreiter, S., Schmidhuber, J.: Long short-term memory. Neural Comput. **9**(8), 1735–1780 (1997)

Blockchain-Based Participant Selection
for Federated Learning

Keshan Zhang[1,2], Huawei Huang[1(✉)], Song Guo[3,4], and Xiaocong Zhou[1]

[1] School of Data and Computer Science, Sun Yat-Sen University, Guangzhou, China
zhangksh6@mail2.sysu.edu.cn, {huanghw28,isszxc}@mail.sysu.edu.cn
[2] National Engineering Research Center of Digital Life, Sun Yat-Sen University, Guangzhou, China
[3] Department of Computing, The Hong Kong Polytechnic University, Kowloon, Hong Kong
song.guo@polyu.edu.hk
[4] Shenzhen Research Institute, The Hong Kong Polytechnic University, Kowloon, Hong Kong

Abstract. Federated Learning (FL) advocates training a global model using a large-scale of distributed devices such that the collaborative model training can be benefited from the rich local datasets, while preserving the privacy of local training dataset in each participant. This is because only the training results, i.e., the updated model parameters and model weights are needed to report to the FL server for aggregation in each round of FL-training. However, during the model transmission of the original FL protocol, there is no security guarantee towards the training results. Thus, every step during model uploading phase can be attacked by malicious attackers. To address such threat, we propose a new federated learning architecture by taking the advantages of blockchain into account. The proposed architecture includes two-phase design. The first phase is a *numerical evaluation*, which can prevent the malicious devices from being selected. For the second phase, we devise a participant-selection algorithm that enables the FL server to select the appropriate group of devices for each round of FL-training. We believe that our study can shed new light on the joint research of blockchain and federated learning.

Keywords: Federated learning · Participant selection · Blockchain · Malicious attackers · Distributed devices

1 Introduction

When facing the problem of a large amount of training data of machine learning, which can not be handled by a single computing unit, distributed learning came into our vision. However, in traditional distributed machine leaning, it needs a central server which distributes data used to train model to the participating devices. This manner makes the data and the privacy behind the data potentially be exposed. In order to meet the demand of privacy preservation, federated learning (FL) [1–3] was proposed.

© Springer Nature Singapore Pte Ltd. 2020
Z. Zheng et al. (Eds.): BlockSys 2020, CCIS 1267, pp. 112–125, 2020.
https://doi.org/10.1007/978-981-15-9213-3_9

Federated learning is a new paradigm of distributed machine learning approach which enables different devices, like mobile phones and tablets, to training for a global model basing on their own local data without exposing their privacy [4]. The machine learning algorithms that can be used in federated learning are not limited to neural networks, but also include conventional algorithms such as random forests. Thus, FL is getting more and more attention.

Under FL, the participants need to periodically transfer their training results to a FL server [3], which has no guarantee for the credibility of the data according to the existing implementation of FL. However, there always exists the risks where the distributed training results will be tampered maliciously or unintentionally during model updating. For example, malicious nodes or bad transmission condition will change the bit stream of the participant devices. As a result, the FL server may receive the faulty data stream. Via an overview of the related work published recently, we did not find a practical solution to the problem aforementioned. For this reason, we introduce a new architecture that combines blockchain and federated learning mechanism, trying to offer a useful solution to the future federated learning. Blockchain [5–7] is a distributed ledger shared by a group of peers. In a blockchain, a certain amount of data can be stored, with the characteristics of being against tampering and easy traceability. Based on these characteristics, blockchain has built a solid trusted foundation and created a reliable collaboration mechanism. The blockchain itself is constructed in a decentralized manner. Due to all the advantages mentioned above, we believe that it is very suitable for the secure model updating under federated machine learning.

For a federated learning task, there is at least one server which is in charge of managing the FL tasks [4]. In detail, the FL server in our system is responsible for selecting appropriate devices for each round of machine learning training. In order to help the FL server make better choices, we propose an algorithm called Descending Weight Selection. The main contributions of this paper are as follows:

- We introduce a new system architecture combining federated learning and blockchain to protect the training results from changing during the model updating phase of FL.
- In our architecture, we first propose a scoring mechanism to deal with the malicious devices that may perform the data-injection attacks.
- We then propose a selection algorithm that can help the FL server make good choices when selecting participants to join in a training iteration of federated learning.

The rest of this paper is organized as follows. Section 2 reviews the state-of-the-art studies. Section 3 describes the system model and problem formulation. Then, Sect. 4 discusses the candidate selection algorithm. Section 5 shows the experiment results. Finally, Sect. 6 concludes this paper.

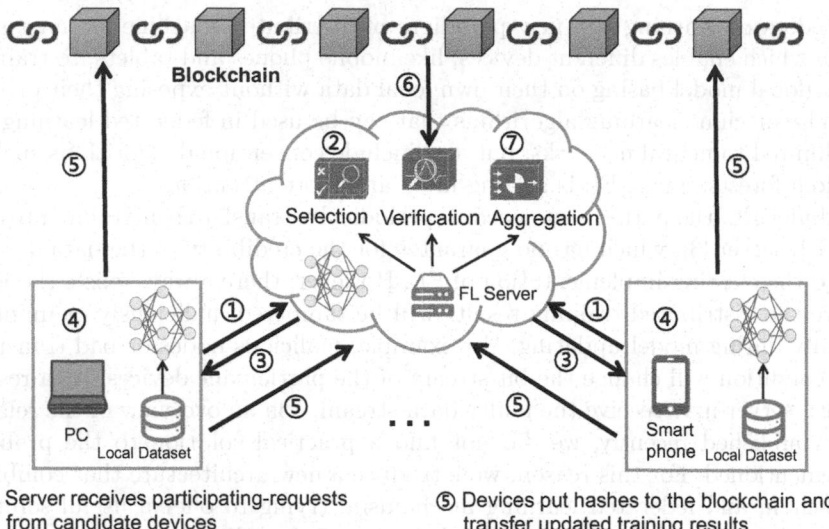

① Server receives participating-requests from candidate devices
② Server selects appropriate devices
③ Server sends configuration to devices
④ Devices train model and calculate hashes
⑤ Devices put hashes to the blockchain and transfer updated training results
⑥ Server varifies training updates
⑦ Server aggregates updated results into the global model

Fig. 1. Interactions between blockchain and federated learning framework under the proposed system model.

2   Related Work

Ensuring the security and reliability of candidate devices in federated learning has drawn substantially research attention recently. For example, to select the trusted and reliable candidate devices, Kang et al. [8] introduce the reputation-based concept for the utilization of blockchain, in which the authors adopted consortium blockchain as a decentralized approach for achieving efficient reputation management for workers. Geyer et al. [9] propose an algorithm for client-side towards the differential privacy-preserving federated optimization, which aims to hide clients' contribution during the training phase and the information about their dataset. Li et al. [10] proposed a secure energy trading system by utilizing the consortium blockchain technology.

On the other hand, new protocols and algorithms [1,2,4,5,8,11,12] have been proposed for the synchronous-fashioned federated learning in recent years. For example, Zhou et al. [5] proposed a byzantine-resilient distributed-learning framework by exploiting the sharding-based blockchain, under the decentralized 5G computing environment. McMahan et al. [1] presented a practical method for the federated learning of deep networks based on iterative model averaging. Based on those pioneer studies, we try to combine the blockchain technology with the federated learning to secure the model updating phases.

3   System Model and Problem Formulation

3.1   System Model

We call a complete procedure counting from device selection to model update during training an FL model a *round*, which includes three major phases *device selection*, *configuration*, and *reporting updated training results*.

Like the most federated learning [2,9,13,14], there are two types of participants in our system model, i.e., participating devices and FL servers. The main mission of participating devices is to train the local model using their local data and send the training results to the FL sever. The major task of the FL server is to select the participating devices to run a specified federated learning task and aggregate the updated gradients for the whole federated learning model in every FL round.

The general process of each round is shown in Fig. 1. At first step, a candidate device who intends to run a federated learning task will send a short *participating-request* message to the FL server. Then, the FL server will consider whether to select this candidate device. After the phase of selection, the FL server will send configurations of the federated learning task to the selected devices. Then the selected devices will start training using their local datasets. After the local training, the selected devices report their training results, i.e., the updated model parameters and weights of gradients, back to the FL server. Then, the participating devices calculate the corresponding hash values by taking their individual training results as inputs, and upload the hash values to the blockchain, which is used for detecting whether the training results are tampered during the subsequent transmission of models/parameters.

Table 1. Symbols and Notations

$\mathbb{T}$	The set of all FL-training rounds
$\mathbb{I}$	The set of all candidate devices anticipating to participate in FL
$\bar{M}_t$	The maximum number of selected participants at round t
N_t	The minimum number of selected participants at round t
$\bar{T}_t$	The tolerant time set by the FL server at round t
$X_{i,t}$	Whether device i is selected at round t
$E_{i,t}$	Time estimated by device i within round t
$R_{i,t}$	The time actually used corresponding to $E_{i,t}$ of device i within round t
$D_{i,t}$	The size of local dataset in device i at round t
$\Delta_{i,t}$	The integrated numerical evaluation of device i at round t
$W_{i,t}$	The weight of device i within round t
$\theta_{i,t}$	The numerical score of device i at round t

For the FL server, before aggregating the training results from the selected devices, it needs to check the trustworthiness of their training results [15]. Thus, it also calculates the hash values by invoking the training results reported from FL devices using the unified hash function of the whole system. When the FL server gets the hash values uploaded by the corresponding devices from the blockchain, their training results can be added to the *aggregation phase* only if the hash values are verified same. Once the training results are found tampered, i.e., the two hash values are different, the training results will not be used to the aggregation phase of global model in the an FL round.

Under the blockchain-assisted Federated Learning framework, even if the training results were tampered during the transmission phases, those falsified results will be quickly detected by the blockchain-based verification mechanism. In general, when the FL server receives all the local-training model updates and verifies them, it will aggregate the results and update the global FL model. After model aggregation, an FL round terminates for a synchronous-fashioned training.

3.2 Numerical-Evaluation Mechanism for All Participants

To help understand our formulation easily, we summarize the major symbols and their definitions in Table 1.

Under our system model, all FL rounds are recorded in a set denoted by $\mathbb{T}$, while all the participating devices are denoted by a set $\mathbb{I}$. For all participating devices $i \in \mathbb{I}$, we define a binary variable $X_{i,t}$ to represent whether device i is selected for training an FL model at round $t \in \mathbb{T}$. $X_{i,t}$ is decided by the FL server. The definition of $X_{i,t}$ is described as follows:

$$X_{i,t} \triangleq \begin{cases} 1, & \text{at round } t \in \mathbb{T}, \text{selector adopts} \\ & \quad \text{candidate device } i \in \mathbb{I} \\ 0, & \text{otherwise.} \end{cases} \tag{1}$$

At the very beginning of round t, the device i intended to run a FL task, will send a participating-request message to the FL server. We consider that the message is short enough such that the transmission latency is negligible. The short message includes necessary information like the numerical performance evaluation of a device $i \in \mathbb{I}$ denoted by $\Delta_{i,t}$, and the estimated timespan $E_{i,t}$ generated by this device itself in round t. The participating-request messages are finally sent to the FL server, which makes decision to decide whether a device should be selected to participate in an FL-training task. When the number of devices meets the lowest number of required and doesn't exceed the maximum workload capacity of the FL server, FL server will choose an appropriate group of devices by referring to their participating-request messages.

At each round t, every device i allowed to join in an FL task, i.e., $X_{i,t} = 1$, has an estimated timespan $E_{i,t}$, which is defined as follows:

$$E_{i,t} = \kappa_{i,t} + Max(\lambda_{i,t}, \rho_{i,t}), \forall t \in \mathbb{T}, \forall i \in \mathbb{I} \tag{2}$$

We explain each symbol appeared in this equation as follows. After being selected and receiving the FL-training configuration and the checkpoints about the global model from the FL server, device i starts to train its local model utilizing its local dataset. The timespan of the local training is denoted by $\kappa_{i,t}$.

When updated training results are transferred from the devices to the FL server, devices and the FL server will take advantages of blockchain to protect the results from tampering. The device i uses a hash algorithm like SHA-256 to calculate the target hash of an update. The input of the hash algorithm is the training results. Then the target hash will be uploaded to the blockchain to share with the FL server. The timespan for calculating a target hash and uploading the hash to the blockchain is represented by $\lambda_{i,t}$. We use another symbol $\rho_{i,t}$ to indicate the timespan spending on transferring the training results from device i to the FL server at round t. Because transferring the updated gradients, calculating target hashes and uploading them to the blockchain will not influence each other, they can perform in a parallel way. So we just focus on the longest timespan between the hash calculating and the transferring of training results, which is $Max(\lambda_{i,t}, \rho_{i,t})$.

Before aggregating the training results from different devices, the FL server needs to verify each model updates to ensure that they were not tampered. Firstly, the FL server puts the received results from device i as input to calculate a hash value using the same hash algorithm used by each device i. Next the hash result will be compared with the target hash that has been recorded in the blockchain by device i. If the two hash values are completely equal to each other, the FL server will permit the received training results to the aggregation of the global model. Otherwise, the FL server will notify the corresponding device that the training results will not be adopted for this round.

To make sure an FL task can be well trained with a guaranteed performance at each round, FL server requires a minimum number $\bar{N}_t$ of all participating devices during each round $t \in \mathbb{T}$. Once the number of selected devices is less than $\bar{N}_t$, FL server will cancel the round t and starts the next round.

For each round t, FL server sets a tolerable deadline $\bar{T}_t$ according to the actual situation of the computing environment. Once $E_{i,t}$ is longer than $\bar{T}_t$, FL server will not select device i at round t. On the contrary, if $E_{i,t}$ is shorter than $\bar{T}_t$, the FL server will take device i into further consideration with the following conditions:

$$X_{i,t} = \begin{cases} 0: & \text{if } E_{i,t} - \bar{T}_t > 0, \forall t \in \mathbb{T}, \forall i \in \mathbb{I} \\ 0/1: & \text{if } E_{i,t} - \bar{T}_t \leq 0, \forall t \in \mathbb{T}, \forall i \in \mathbb{I} \end{cases} \tag{3}$$

We then transfer the two-fold conditions shown in (3) into the following formalized constraints:

$$X_{i,t}(E_{i,t} - \bar{T}_t) \leq 0, \forall t \in \mathbb{T}, \forall i \in \mathbb{I} \tag{4}$$

Regarding the number of participating devices for each round of Federated Learning, we have introduced a minimum number of devices in round t, i.e., $\bar{N}_t$. On the other hand, the calculating capacity and the processing power of the FL server are resource-constrained [16]. This replies that the FL server can only handle a certain number of participating devices in each round. Thus, we set an upper bound number, denoted by $\bar{M}_t$, for the FL server to indicated the maximum number of devices it can handle in round t. Then, the FL server has to ensure the number of participating devices in round t is between $\bar{N}_t$ and $\bar{M}_t$. This constraint is described as follows:

$$\bar{N}_t \leq \sum_{i \in \mathbb{I}} X_{i,t} \leq \bar{M}_t, \forall t \in \mathbb{T} \tag{5}$$

For different devices, their hardware resources like CPU and battery are not the same in different FL rounds. Thus, we definite $C_{i,t}$ as the CPU level and $P_{i,t}$ as the power level of device i at round t. The size of local dataset is denoted by $D_{i,t}$. In our system model, we believe that the larger the training dataset is, the more valuable of the training results are. Then the integrated *numerical evaluation* of device i in round t, denoted by $\Delta_{i,t}$, which can represent the ability and efficiency of device i when training a local model using its local dataset. Thus, $\Delta_{i,t}$ could be expressed as follows:

$$\Delta_{i,t} = \eta C_{i,t} + \xi P_{i,t} + \gamma D_{i,t}, \forall t \in \mathbb{T}, \forall i \in \mathbb{I}, \tag{6}$$

where the coefficients of the three terms η, ξ, and γ can be tuned by the FL server according to a certain policy.

Inside the participating-request message, the device provides an estimated timespan by invoking Eq. (2), which is used as a reference for the FL server when selecting candidates. However, the time actually spent on the blockchain-assisted FL training is always not equal to the estimated one. In reality, some devices may deliberately send shorter estimated timespans that helps them increase the probability to be selected by the FL server. To avoid such malicious attacks, we set a particular *numerical score* for each device i at the end of a round t, which is expressed as $\theta_{i,t}$:

$$\theta_{i,t} = \mu(E_{i,t} - R_{i,t})X_{i,t} + \nu\theta_{i,t-1}, \forall t \in \mathbb{T}, \forall i \in \mathbb{I}, \tag{7}$$

where $R_{i,t}$ represents the total real timespan spending on the round t, which includes the time consumed on training the local FL model, and the maximum time between hash-computing and model-reporting of device i. We then interpret the Eq. (7) as follows. In the end of round t, the score of device i, i.e., $\theta_{i,t}$, is updated and stored in the FL server. Once device i is selected, its score at round t will be affected by the difference between the real execution time and the estimated timespan, i.e., $(E_{i,t} - R_{i,t})$. If the real time is shorter than the estimated timespan, device i will get a bonus[17], since the difference is a positive number, and vice versa. The term $(E_{i,t} - R_{i,t})$ can only influence the devices being selected at this round t. For all the devices including those are not selected at round t, their scores will inherit their partial of their previous numerical score calculated from the previous round, i.e., the term $\nu\theta_{i,t-1}$. Thus, $\theta_{i,t}$ is determined by both the term $(E_{i,t} - R_{i,t})$ and the term $\nu\theta_{i,t-1}$. For these two terms, we also define two factors μ and ν to represent their weights, respectively. The effect of varying the two factors will be shown in simulation results.

Algorithm 1: Weight-Descending Candidate Selection

Input : $t \in \mathbb{T}, i \in \mathbb{I}, \bar{N}_t, \bar{M}_t, \bar{T}_t, E_{i,t}, R_{i,t}$
Output: $X_{i,t}$

1 **for** $\forall i \in \mathbb{I}$ **do**
2 $\quad \theta_{i,0} = 0$

3 **while** *in each FL round t* **do**
4 $\quad$ The FL server receives participating messages from totally N_0 devices;
5 $\quad$ **for** $i = 1, 2, ... N_0$ **do**
6 $\quad\quad X_{i,t} \leftarrow 1$ /*Label all devices to 1 tentatively*/

7 $\quad \langle flag, X_{i,t} \rangle \leftarrow$ **Algorithm 2** $(\mathbb{I}, t, \bar{N}_t, \bar{M}_t, E_{i,t}, \bar{T}_t)$
8 $\quad$ **if** $flag == \text{'FURTHER-CHECK'}$ **then**
9 $\quad\quad$ **for** $\forall i \in \mathbb{I}$ **do**
10 $\quad\quad\quad W_{i,t} \leftarrow$ Eq. (8).
11 $\quad\quad \pi \leftarrow$ a descending list of all $W_{i,t}|_{X_{i,t}==1}$
12 $\quad\quad$ **for** $j = \sum_{i \in \mathbb{I}} X_{i,t} - \bar{M}_t + 1, ..., N_0$ **do**
13 $\quad\quad\quad k \leftarrow \arg\{\pi[j]|_{X_{k,t}==1}\}$
14 $\quad\quad\quad X_{k,t} \leftarrow 0$ /*Get rid of the stragglers*/

15 $\quad$ FL server sends FL-model to the selected devices i (where $X_{i,t} == 1$) and waits for receiving its reported model updates.
16 $\quad$ **for** $i \in \mathbb{I}$ **do**
17 $\quad\quad$ FL server updates $\theta_{i,t}$ by invoking Eq. (7)

As mentioned above, an FL server can only choose a limited number of candidate devices to participate in the Federated Learning. We define a weight function $W_{i,t}$ for each device i in round t. The expression of such weight function is shown as follows:

$$W_{i,t} = \alpha \Delta_{i,t} + \beta \theta_{i,t-1}, \forall t \in \mathbb{T}, \forall i \in \mathbb{I}, \tag{8}$$

where $\Delta_{i,t}$ and $\theta_{i,t}$ are two major components, and the factors α and β are set by the FL server according to different bias.

3.3 Problem Formulation

For each round t, the FL server always desires to select the group of candidate devices that have the maximum numerical total weights for the global FL model training. Thus, our objective function is defined as follows.

$$\max \quad \sum_{i \in \mathbb{I}} X_{i,t} W_{i,t}, \forall t \in \mathbb{T}$$

$$\text{s.t.} \quad (4), (5), (6), (7), (8)$$

$$\text{Variables: } X_{i,t} \in \{0, 1\}, \forall i \in \mathbb{I}, \forall t \in \mathbb{T}. \tag{9}$$

Algorithm 2: First-Step Filtering

Input : Device set $\mathbb{I}$
   The current index of round t
   Minimum # of devices for FL: $\bar{N}_t$
   Maximum # of devices for FL: $\bar{M}_t$
   The estimated timespan of device i: $E_{i,t}$
   The tolerant timespan of round t: $\bar{T}_t$
Output: Whether this Round can continue: $flag$,
   Partial decisions of variables $X_{i,t}$

1 **for** $i \in \mathbb{I}$ **do**
2   **if** $X_{i,t} == 1$ **then**
3   Further check device i by invoking Eq. (3), and update $X_{i,t}$ using $E_{i,t}$.

4 **if** $\sum_{i \in \mathbb{I}} X_{i,t} < \bar{N}_t$ **then**
5   **for** *each* $i \in \mathbb{I}$ **do**
6     $X_{i,t} \leftarrow 0$
7   $flag \leftarrow 0$
8 **if** $\bar{N}_t \leq \sum_{i \in \mathbb{I}} X_{i,t} \leq \bar{M}_t$ **then**
9   $flag \leftarrow 0$
10 **if** $\sum_{i \in \mathbb{I}} X_{i,t} > \bar{M}_t$ **then**
11 $flag \leftarrow$ 'FURTHER-CHECK'

---

4   Algorithm Design

The algorithms designed in this section include two, i.e., a main-frame algorithm Algorithm 1 *weight-descending candidate selection*, and an auxiliary one Algorithm 2 *First-Step Filtering*.

Algorithm 1 performs the candidate-selection for each round of FL-training task. As mentioned in system model, due to the limited capacity of the FL server, the number of participating devices that can be processed in each FL round is also limited. The specific number of devices that are able to participate in each FL-training round depends on the real-time capability of the FL server. Suppose that in total N_0 mobile devices intend to join in this round of FL-training by sending participating messages to the FL server. As the first step, FL server labels all participating devices to 1 tentatively. Then, FL server gets a $flag$ by invoking Algorithm 2 to know whether the current round of FL-training should continue or not. After that, this algorithm will perform the following steps.

1. $\forall i \in \mathbb{I}$, updating $W_{i,t}$ by invoking Eq. (8).
2. Establishing a descending list (denoted by π) of all $W_{i,t}$ where $X_{i,t} == 1$.
3. For the devices ranking in the end of list, i.e., a number of $\sum_{i \in \mathbb{I}} X_{i,t} - \bar{M}_t$ straggling devices in the rear of list π, algorithm sets the variables $X_{i,t}$ to 0.
4. FL server then sends FL-model to the selected devices i (where $X_{i,t} == 1$) and waits for receiving its reported model updates.
5. The FL server updates $\theta_{i,t}$ by invoking Eq. (7).

Note that, even though the *flag* returned from Algorithm 2 is 0, the above steps 4) and 5) will still be executed to update the scores of each candidate devices $\theta_{i,t}$ by invoking Eq. (7) at round t.

We then explain Algorithm 2. The purpose of Algorithm 2 is to decide whether to continue this round of FL-training and to make a fast filtering towards several unreasonable cases. The first step is to calculate the number of devices. When the number of devices that meets the conditions after filtering is less than the minimum number $\bar{N}_t$ required by the FL server in round t, the FL server will give up training at this round and begin the next round immediately. If so, the FL server will also broadcast a notification of starting the next round to every candidate device. There is another situation in which the number of candidate devices that meets the required FL conditions at round t is just between the maximum number $\bar{M}_t$ and the minimum number $\bar{N}_t$ set by the FL server. In this case, the FL server only needs to select all the qualified devices directly, and send the FL-model configurations to all the selected devices for training in this round.

Different from the previous two situations, when the number of devices that meets the required FL conditions exceeds the maximum number $\bar{M}_t$ set by the FL server at round t, a selection strategy is needed to meet the objective function Eq. (9). So, Algorithm 2 returns a 'FURTHER-CHECK' flag to the main Algorithm 1, i.e., Weight-Descending Candidate Selection, which will get rid of the undesired straggling candidates.

5   Simulations and Analysis

In simulation, we use the synthesized trace dataset generated that try to match the real-world situation. The data includes the traces of 200 devices in 20 rounds of FL-training. The attributes of data include the estimated timespan $E_{i,t}$ and the offline real-time $R_{i,t}$ of each device i at each FL round t. The Cumulative Distribution Function (CDF) of $E_{i,t}$ and $R_{i,t}$ are shown at Fig. 2. We also generate different maximum tolerant-timespan thresholds $\bar{T}_t$ for each round t and the upper bounded and the lower bounded numbers of selected devices ($\bar{M}_t$ and $\bar{N}_t$). For device i at round t, its numerical evaluation $\Delta_{i,t}$ is randomly generated between 1 and 20. Once a device is selected, we assume that it will train the local FL model honestly and send the training updates to the FL server finally.

To evaluate our proposed Weight-Descending Candidate Selection algorithm, we compare the results of our algorithm with those of the Random algorithm and offline optimal solutions solved by Gurobi [18]. In order to fairly examine these algorithms, when generating synthesized dataset, we let the number of candidate devices, i.e., N_0, be larger than the maximum number of required devices, i.e., $\bar{M}_t$, in most rounds of FL training. Thus, when selecting participating devices, most of them need to conduct a further check using both the proposed algorithms.

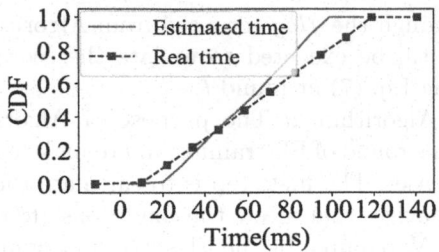

Fig. 2. The CDF of the estimated timespan and the offline execution-time of all participating devices in the synthesized dataset.

From Eq. (8), we see that $W_{i,t}$ plays a pivotal role in the results of our algorithm. $W_{i,t}$ is determined by $\Delta_{i,t}$ and $\theta_{i,t-1}$ and two coefficients α and β. Regarding those two coefficients, α and β can be set by the FL server. According to Eq. (7), $\theta_{i,t}$ is determined by other two factors μ and ν. Thus, we evaluate the proposed algorithm by tuning these 4 coefficients. For these four factors, we have designed contrast simulations to compare the results obtained from 3 algorithms. First, in the group of simulation shown in Fig. 3, we vary each of the four factors α, β, μ, ν from 0.1 to 1, respectively, and set the remaining three as 0.5. All results shown in Fig. 3 are the performance of the 20th round of FL-training.

We can observe how α affects the wight function from Fig. 3a. With the increase of α, the weight gaps between the proposed algorithm and the offline optimal solution calculated by Gurobi become smaller. Especially when α is equal to 1.0, the performance of the proposed algorithm is almost equal to that of Gurobi. This is because in Eq. (8), α denotes the weight of integrated *numerical evaluation* $\Delta_{i,t}$. When α is growing large, the proposed algorithm will prefer to choose the candidate devices that are with high integrated *numerical evaluation*. Thus, this preference drives the proposed algorithm approaches to the optimal solution solved by Gurobi. On the other hand, although the weights of Random algorithm increase, they are always lower than the proposed algorithm. **Insights:** This group of simulations indicate that a larger α helps the proposed algorithm approximates the offline optimal strategy.

We then evaluate the effect of coefficient μ. As know by Eq. 7, μ decides the weight of the timespan difference calculated by the estimated timespan and the offline real timespan of a device, i.e., $E_{i,t} - R_{i,t}$. According to the CDF of those two timespan shown in Fig. 2, 70% of all estimated timespans are less than the real offline timespan, i.e., $(E_{i,t} - R_{i,t}) < 0$ with 70% probability. Therefore, when μ grows larger, the total numerical score $\theta_{i,t}$ of a candidate device calculated by (7) decreases. Accordingly, the overall weight of the device $W_{i,t}$ declines, too. That is why we observe that all the wights of all algorithms reduce following the growth of μ in Fig. 3c. However, we see that when μ is equal to 1.0, the proposed algorithm and the Random algorithm have very low performance comparing with the offline optimal solution. **Insights:** The results of this group of simulations

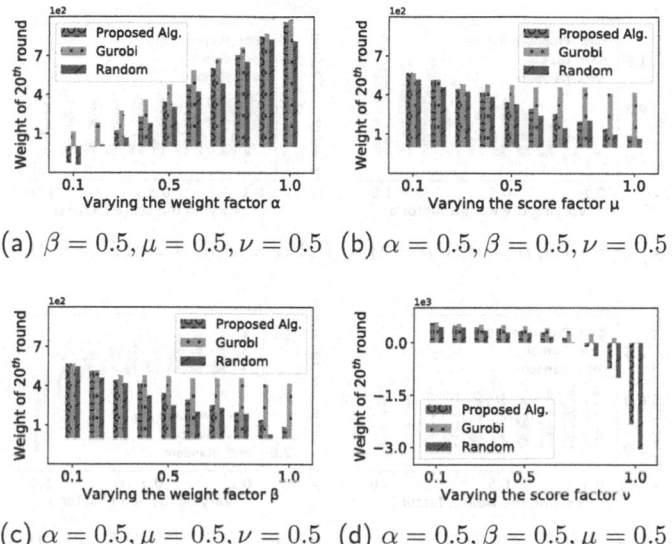

Fig. 3. Fix the three factors α, μ, β, ν to 0.5 and vary the last factor to compare the weight of 20th round calculated by algorithms.

tell us a smaller μ is preferred when setting in the real system implementation in our future work.

Next, we evaluate the impact of coefficients β and ν, which represent the contribution of the numerical scores $\theta_{i,t-1}$ defined in Eq. (8) and Eq. (7), respectively. From Fig. 3(c) and Fig. 3(d), we observe similar performance with that of Fig. 3(b). The insights behind those two figures are described as follows. Since 70% of the estimated timespans are less than the offline real execution-timespan, and the initial setting for the numerical score of each candidate device is 0, $\theta_{i,t}$ has 70% probability to be a negative number. Therefore, a larger β or a larger ν can help yield a smaller $W_{i,t}$. **Insights:** Similarly, in order to make the proposed algorithm approach the offline optimal solution, β and ν should be set with small values.

We also perform evaluation of the cumulative weights added up from all the 20 rounds of FL training. The results are shown in Fig. 4. Overall, the cumulative weights of all 20 rounds illustrate similar shapes with those of the 20th round shown in Fig. 3. The particular exception is that the proposed algorithm has a much closer total weights to the optimal solutions than the weights of the 20th round. This results demonstrate that the proposed algorithm can strive for near-optimal solutions if we set appropriate coefficients such as α, μ, β and ν in the blockchain-empowered Federated Learning framework.

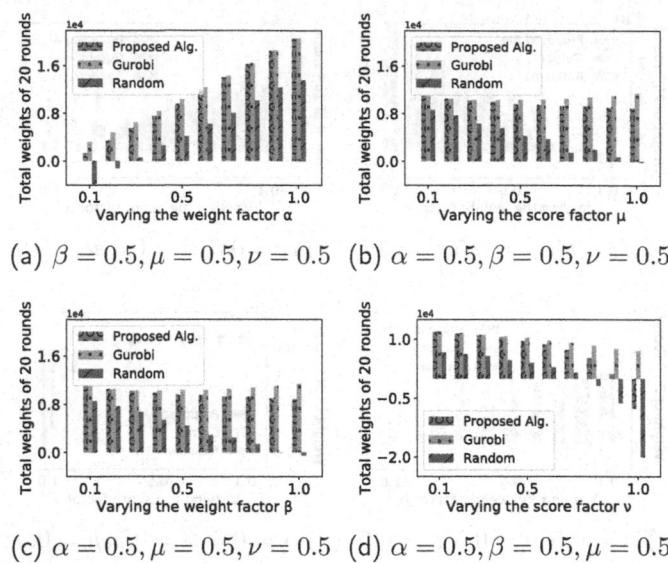

(a) $\beta = 0.5, \mu = 0.5, \nu = 0.5$ (b) $\alpha = 0.5, \beta = 0.5, \nu = 0.5$

(c) $\alpha = 0.5, \mu = 0.5, \nu = 0.5$ (d) $\alpha = 0.5, \beta = 0.5, \mu = 0.5$

Fig. 4. Fix the three factors α, μ, β, ν to 0.5 and vary the last factor to compare the cumulative weights of all 20 rounds calculated by algorithms.

6   Conclusion and Future Work

In this paper, we have introduced a system architecture combined federated learning with blockchain, in order to prevent devices' local training results from being tampered during the FL updating phases. To solve the problem that devices may behave dishonestly, we proposed a new evaluation mechanism, which can evaluate each participant fairly. Next, to help the FL server make a good selection of participating devices to join the distributed federated learning in each round, we proposed a *weight-descending candidate selection* algorithm. Through simulations, we compared the proposed algorithm with other baselines. The simulation results show that the proposed algorithm outperforms other baselines in terms of model updating efficiency. For the future work, we plan to design more efficient selection strategies to improve the practicality of the blockchain-assisted federated learning framework.

Acknowledgments. The work described in this paper was supported partially by the National Natural Science Foundation of China (61902445, 61872310, U1811462), partially by Key-Area Research and Development Program of Guangdong Province (2019B020214006), Fundamental Research Funds for the Central Universities of China (19lgpy222), Natural Science Foundation of Guangdong Province of China (2019A1515011798), and partially by the Shenzhen Basic Research Funding Scheme (JCYJ20170818103849343).

References

1. McMahan, H.B., Moore, E., Ramage, D., Hampson, S., et al.: Communication-efficient learning of deep networks from decentralized data. In: Proceedings of the 20th International Conference on Artificial Intelligence and Statistics (AISTATS 2017) (2017)
2. Li, T., Sahu, A.K., Talwalkar, A., Smith, V.: Federated learning: challenges, methods, and future directions. arXiv preprint arXiv:1908.07873 (2019)
3. Nishio, T., Yonetani, R.: Client selection for federated learning with heterogeneous resources in mobile edge. In: ICC 2019–2019 IEEE International Conference on Communications (ICC), pp. 1–7 (2019)
4. Bonawitz, K., et al.: Towards federated learning at scale: system design. arXiv preprint arXiv:1902.01046 (2019)
5. Zhou, S., Huang, H., Chen, W., Zheng, Z., Guo, S.: Pirate: a blockchain-based secure framework of distributed machine learning in 5g networks. arXiv preprint arXiv:1912.07860 (2019)
6. Mendis, G.J., Wu, Y., Wei, J., Sabounchi, M., Roche, R.: Blockchain as a service: a decentralized and secure computing paradigm. arXiv preprint arXiv:1807.02515 (2018)
7. Guo, S., Hu, X., Guo, S., Qiu, X., Qi, F.: Blockchain meets edge computing: a distributed and trusted authentication system. IEEE Trans. Ind. Informat. **16**(3), 1972–1983 (2019)
8. Kang, J., Xiong, Z., Niyato, D., Zou, Y., Zhang, Y., Guizani, M.: Reliable federated learning for mobile networks. arXiv preprint arXiv:1910.06837 (2019)
9. Geyer, R.C., Klein, T., Nabi, M.: Differentially private federated learning: a client level perspective. arXiv preprint arXiv:1712.07557 (2017)
10. Li, Z., Kang, J., Yu, R., Ye, D., Deng, Q., Zhang, Y.: Consortium blockchain for secure energy trading in industrial internet of things. IEEE Trans. Ind. Informat. (TII) **14**(8), 3690–3700 (2017)
11. Hard, A., et al.: Federated learning for mobile keyboard prediction. arXiv preprint arXiv:1811.03604 (2018)
12. Zhou, Q., Huang, H., Zheng, Z., Bian, J.: Solutions to scalability of blockchain: a survey. IEEE Access, pp. 1–10 (2020)
13. Khan, L.U., et al.: Federated learning for edge networks: resource optimization and incentive mechanism. arXiv preprint arXiv:1911.05642 (2019)
14. Lian, X., Zhang, W., Zhang, C., Liu, J.: Asynchronous decentralized parallel stochastic gradient descent. arXiv preprint arXiv:1710.06952 (2017)
15. Li, Z., Yang, Z., Xie, S., Chen, W., Liu, K.: Credit-based payments for fast computing resource trading in edge-assisted internet of things. IEEE Internet Things J. **6**(4), 6606–6617 (2019)
16. Zhan, Y., Li, P., Guo, S.: Experience-driven computational resource allocation of federated learning by deep reinforcement learning. In: Proceedings of IPDPS (2020)
17. Zhan, Y., Li, P., Qu, Z., Zeng, D., Guo, S.: A learning-based incentive mechanism for federated learning. IEEE Internet Things J. (2020)
18. "Gurobi," January 2020. https://www.gurobi.com/

PSM²: A Privacy-Preserving Self-sovereign Match-Making Platform

Chenyu Wu[1], Feng Yuan[2], Youshui Lu[2(✉)], and Saiyu Qi[3(✉)]

[1] School of Software Engineering, Xi'an JiaoTong University, Xi'an 710049, China
chenyuwu272@stu.xjtu.edu.cn
[2] School of Computer Science and Technology, Xi'an Jiaotong University, Xi'an 714000, Shannxi, China
yuanfeng@stu.xjtu.edu.cn, lucienlu@me.com
[3] Xidian University, Xi'an 710071, Shannxi, China
syqi@connect.ust.hk

Abstract. The scale of matchmaking market continues to grow rapidly. In the current fast pace of life, an online matchmaking platform is getting more popular, and users are only required to provide their personal information and preferences to match with others, which is accurate and efficient. However, as data privacy laws such as European Union(EU)'s General Data Protection Regulations(GDPR) aims to give control back to consumers over their personal data, current matchmaking platforms failed to fulfil the data transparency and data processing requirements, which raise privacy concerns by the society. To address this issue, in this paper, we proposed a self-sovereign blockchain-based privacy-preserving matchmaking platform namely PSM², which enables its users to treat their personal data as a digital asset and trade it according to the matching score with other users. By leveraging smart contract, we carefully designed a trading contract to ensure a fair and transparent trading process. In addition, we build a matching score calculation algorithm, according to which PSM² can determine the price for purchasing someone's contact information. Finally, we develop a proof of concept prototype on Hyperledger Fabric and conduct several experiments to demonstrate the performance of the matching algorithm and the feasibility of PSM².

Keywords: Matching-making · Privacy-preserving · Smart contract · Fair exchange · Blockchain

1 Introduction

The matchmaking market segment contains dating services for the systematic search for partners who are willing to enter into a long-term committed relationship through mathematical algorithms. Online dating is made up of online services which offer a platform where its members can flirt, exchange personal information or fall in love. A statistic [2] gives a forecast that the online revenue in the eServices segment Dating Services (DS) worldwide is expected to be 830.3 million U.S. dollars in 2024.

C. Wu and F. Yuan—These authors contributed equally to this work.

Most current existing matchmaking platforms rely on a centralized service provider. The process of matchmaking often involves the consumer's personal data which raise privacy concerns. On the one hand, the matchmaking platforms store consumer's private information, it may lead to data leakage risks. On the other hand, most platforms profit from their users' private information without their users' consent which [3] also infringes the user's right and interest. Both issues are not in compliance with the data protection laws (such as the GDPR [13]) in aspects of data transparency, data processing, and so on.

Although many pieces of research on the privacy-preserving platform have emerged, none of them focuses on the matchmaking field. Considering that the centralized platform is vulnerable to attacks and may maliciously use the user's private data for profiting, a centralized matchmaking solution cannot address these potential issues. Instead, our idea is to leverage blockchain technology [5] to build a self-sovereign matchmaking platform, which can enable its user to exchange personal contacting information with others in a private-preserving way. Unfortunately, directly using blockchain technology raises several challenges. First, putting user's personal data on a blockchain raises a high privacy leakage risk. Second, it is a challenge to implement matching algorithms in a privacy-preserving way. Third, it is also a challenge to achieve fair and efficient trading between online users without relying on a centralized party. In response, we design a privacy-preserving self-sovereign matchmaking platform, called PSM^2, which not only enables the users to match with each other over encrypted personal data, but also allows them to trade their contact information transparently and fairly by using carefully designed smart contact.

The design of PSM^2 mainly focuses on two aspects, (1) a privacy-preserved matchmaking algorithm, which calculates an accurate matching score to indicate the degree that a user's personal information matches the other's preferences. Importantly, the matching algorithm works on the encrypted personal data on the ledger; (2) a transparent and fair trading mechanism, which regards users' personal data as a digital asset and allows privacy-preserving and fire exchange while ensuring transparency and fairness by designing smart contract carefully. Secure systems [21–23] that provide practical cryptographic enforcement of access control will be considered in future work.

Concretely, PSM^2's matchmaking based on user's profile allows two users to match their profiles without disclosing their private information. The user first creates personal profiles which include his/her personal information such as age, education, hobbies, professions, and so on. Also, they will include a list of his/her preferences. Once the IAC verifies their personal information and preferences, the data will be encrypted and then recorded on the ledger in the blockchain network. Next, PSM^2's computing node will calculate the matching scores based on the user's profile and preferences. With the matching scores, the user then can purchase his/her desired user's contact information through the purchasing smart contract. Finally, we build a proof of concept prototype on Hyperledger Fabric, and we conduct several experiments to demonstrate the accuracy of the matching algorithm and the feasibility of PSM^2.

The main contributions of this paper are summarized as follows:

(1) We design a novel matching score calculating algorithm over encrypted data by using RSA, one-hot coding and pearson correlation similarities.

(2) We carefully design a trading smart contract which enables the user to exchange his/her contact information transparently and fairly without a third-party escrow.

(3) We demonstrate that PSM^2 can achieve an efficient privacy-preserved matchmaking process without revealing users' personal information.

(4) We build a proof of concept prototype on Hyperledger Fabric and also evaluates on the performance of PSM^2, and the experiment results indicate that PSM^2 is technically feasible.

2 Preliminaries

2.1 Blockchain

Since the birth of blockchain technology, its features of decentralization, open autonomy, anonymity and information tamper-proof [16] fit naturally with the social domain. Blockchain technology has received considerable attention from both academia and industry [15,17,20]. In Peilin Zheng et al. proposed a performance monitoring framework with a log-based method which can make detailed and real-time performance monitoring of blockchain systems [19]. The essence of the blockchain is a public distributed ledger that allows anyone to participate in. Once the blocks are recorded, it is not feasible to be modified or erased. In this way, the failure of a blockchain node does not affect other nodes. The consensus mechanism between blockchain nodes maintains the entire blockchain network, which allows each blockchain node to obtain a complete copy of the database. Therefore, the blockchain system can only be modified in accordance with strict rules and consensus. Blocks and transactions are the main components of the blockchain network. Each block stores transaction information in a certain organization. Each transaction records a specific set of operations. The cryptographic hash algorithm and the Merkle tree [6] structure ensure that the data cannot be tampered. Current applications of blockchain include many fields mainly concentrate on finance, IoTs and healthcare. In PSM^2, blockchain is mainly used to store the verified user's personal data in a decentralized manner.

2.2 Smart Contract

Smart Contract, first proposed by Nick in 1995, is a computer program that can be executed automatically according to its contents. In Yuan Huang, et al's work [18] support the update of a target smart contract. Ethereum [4] is a programming platform that enables developers to build distributed applications based on smart contracts. Specifically, Ethereum can be used for protocol programming, behavioural assurance and trading, such as voting, financial transactions, company management, and signing agreements. Compared to the Bitcoin system,

Ethereum has an innovative feature that enables programs to be executed on the blockchain. Once the smart contract is deployed, it can execute the contract without relying on any central authority. Ideally, the smart contract runs exactly as programmed, so the results are accurate and verifiable. On the social platform constructed by blockchain, the smart contract can replace the intermediary and perform automatic transactions.

Hyperledger Fabric, which supports smart contract, is a project hosted by the Linux Foundation as a cross-industry collaborative project. The system was designed with the enterprise architecture in mind with customizable networking rules that help different consensus protocols operate. It borrows the Unspent Transaction Output(UTXO) and script-based logic from Bitcoins, and uses Practical Byzantine Fault-tolerant (PBFT) consensus protocol instead of the PoW algorithm. PBFT is known to process thousands of requests per second with a latency increase of less than a millisecond.

2.3   One-Hot Coding

The OHC is usually used to address lookup tables (LUTs) and at the output of some linear circuits such as FIR filters [1]. One-hot coding is the representation of classification variables as binary vectors. With OHC, only one bit takes the value of one and the other as zero. It mainly uses n-bit state registers to encode N states, each state is its own independent register bit, and only one is valid at any time.

Most matching algorithms are calculated based on the metrics in vector space. To make the values of variables in the non-partial order relationship not have partial order. In classification, clustering and other machine learning algorithm, calculation of the distance between the characteristics of the calculation of similarity is significant. European space similarity calculation is often used, thus map the discrete characteristics through one-hot coding to European space is necessary and important.

2.4   Fair Exchange

Fair exchange is an efficient protocol for two users to exchange their information and money using smart contracts. A fair exchange allows Alice to sell her information x for a fixed price p to a receiver Bob. The protocol must be secure if Bob only pays if he receives the correct x from Alice. Fair exchange guarantees fairness by relying on smart contracts executed over decentralized cryptocurrencies, where the contract takes the role of an external judge that completes the exchange in case of disagreement [14].

Distribute payment system fair trade allows the platform to carry out by relying on smart contracts while avoiding costly zero-knowledge proofs. The platform also shows out a proof of misbehaviour, it can be short and it is verified by the underlying smart contract, which upon receiving such a proof penalizes the sender for cheating [14]. The trading process is non-interactive and involves only two parties. The witness stays hidden until the receiver has committed coins into the contract for paying the sender. The trading process also allowed a receiver to buy a large file x that matched with a particular hash value h. Here x may be many gigabytes large, but using the proofs of misbehaviour, we can reduce the data that has to be processed by the smart contract to a few 100 bytes, while still guaranteeing the fairness of the file exchange.

3   Problem Formulation

In this section, we formulate the system model, security model, and the design goals of this paper.

3.1   System Model

As shown in Fig. 1, there are three entities in PSM^2: 1) user, 2) information authentication center, and 3) computing nodes.

- 1) *User.* A user U_i, can upload his/her personal information and preferences to the blockchain network once his/her information is verified and certified by the information authentication center. The user can also purchase other user's contact information through a trading smart contract.
- 2) *Information Authentication Center.* An information authentication center IAC, acts as an identity authority which is responsible for verifying the user's personal information and then encrypts and records it on the ledger of the blockchain network. IAC can be a centralized third party or a decentralized consortium for identity verification.
- 3) *Computing Nodes.* In a blockchain network, the nodes can hold copies of ledgers and copies of smart contracts. Since the user's mobile devices have limited storage and computation power, PSM^2 uses computing nodes to calculate the matching scores between different users according to the encrypted user's information on the ledger.

At a high level, PSM^2 works as follows, users first register themselves to PSM^2. Each user uploads his/her personal information and preferences to IAC. After that IAC will verify the truthfulness and correctness of the information, then encrypts it before recording on the ledger. After that, a user can trade his/her contact information through the trading contract. The price of each user's contact information is determined by the matching scores calculated by the matching algorithm.

3.2   Security Model

As mentioned earlier, IAC can be a centralized third party or a decentralized consortium for identity verification. This is reasonable since the IAC could be a government agency responsible for the administration of citizens. A centralized IAC may be malicious, while the decentralized identity verification ecosystem can mitigate the shortcomings brought by the centralized IAC, but it is beyond

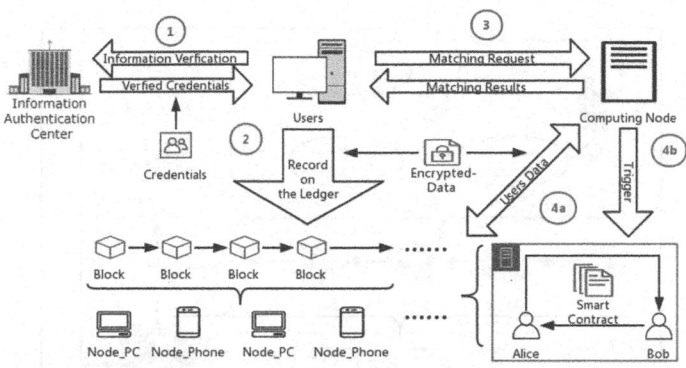

Fig. 1. Overview of PSM²

the scope of this paper. Therefore, for simplicity, we assume that the IAC is trustworthy in PSM². Some users can be malicious and upload incorrect information or preferences for profits. We further assume that the computing nodes are trusted, because if they are malicious in the consortium, PSM²'s reputation will be damaged and then nobody would user PSM². Service provider, non-profit making organization or government agency will hold different blockchain nodes after the system deployment. In addition, we require that an adversary cannot control the majority of the nodes in the blockchain system.

3.3 Design Goals

Under the security assumptions, we summarize the design goals of the PSM².

- 1) Correctness. The user's personal information should be true and correct.
- 2) Confidentiality. The user's private information should be kept private at any time in PSM².
- 3) Transparency. The trading process should be fair and transparent.
- 4) Accuracy. The matching score should be calculated accurately.
- 5) Efficiency. PSM² should be operating efficiently, the performance of PSM² should be practical and acceptable for real-life implementation.

4 PSM² System

In our work, we propose a self-sovereign match-making platform based on smart contracts, homomorphic encryption and Euclidean distance similarity techniques. Our system consists of three components: processing user's information, matching score calculation and trading contract. Table 1 lists the notations that will be used in PSM² system.

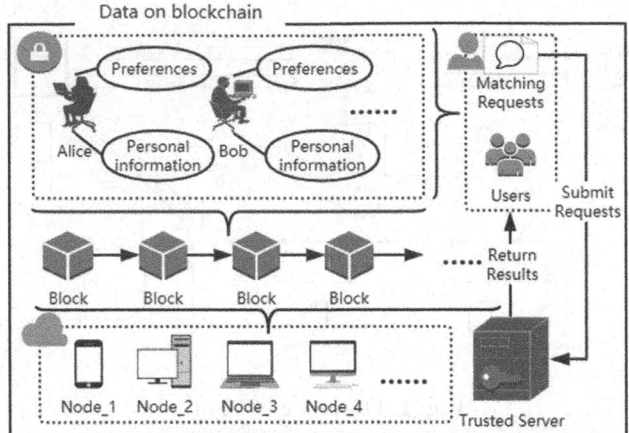

Fig. 2. Data flow

4.1   Processing User's Information

User's information consists of the user's personal information and the preferences, the types of attributes of the user's personal information and user's preferences are of the same, as shown in Fig.2. After the user uploads his information, his personal information is converted into a numerical vector by using OHC. We use vector $V_i^{Id} = [Att_1, Att_2, ..., Att_n]$ to denote a user's personal information, and vector $V_p^{Id} = [Att_1, Att_2, ..., Att_n]$ to denote a user's preferences. An example user's personal information is shown in Table 2. The example indicates user Alice has a personal information of [Female, 23; Master; Unmarried; Beilin District, Xi'an, Shaanxi; Beilin District, Xi'an, Shaanxi; Haidian District, Beijing; Volkswagen Golf, Fitness)] that can be converted into a vector of $V_i^{Alice} = [0, 23, 2, 0, 120905, 120905, 10904, 711, 10]$. Note that before recorded on the ledger in the blockchain network, all the information must be verified by the IAC. We omit the detailed explanation of the verification process as it is not the main contribution of this paper.

4.2   Matching Score Calculation

In PSM^2, we use the matching score to indicate how one user's personal attributes match the other's preferences. As shown in Fig. 4, each person has two sets of attributes, personal information and preferences, matching score is the percentage of the interaction of one's personal information and other's preferences out of the other user's preferences. For example, Alice's personal information attributes are denoted as V_i^A, and the preferences attributes are denoted as V_p^A. Bob's personal information attributes are denoted as V_i^B, and the preferences attributes are denoted as V_p^B. And the matching score will then be used to determine the price for one to purchase the other's contact information.

Table 1. Notation with nomenclature

Field	Use
V_i^A	The vector that represents Alice's personal information attributes;
V_p^A	Alice's preference attributes;
V_i^B	Bob's personal information attributes;
V_p^B	Bob's preference attributes;
S_{AB}	The degree to which Alice conforms to Bob;
S_{BA}	The degree to which Bob conforms to Alice;
a	The intersection of Alice's personal information attributes and Bob's preference attributes;
b	The intersection of Bob's personal information attributes and Alice's preference attributes;
$Score_{AB}$	The matching score of Alice to Bob;
$Score_{BA}$	The matching score of Bob to Alice;
$Score_{AB} = \frac{a}{V_p^B}$	As shown in Fig. 3a;
$Score_{BA} = \frac{b}{V_p^A}$	As shown in Fig. 3b;

One should pay (1-matching score) $\times \alpha$. α is an coefficient of the pricing index. For example:

- Alice meets 80% of Bob's preferences;
- Bob meets 60% of Alice's preferences;
- Charles meets the preferences of 90% Alice;
- Alice meets the 80% Charles' preferences.

If Alice wants to view Bob's and Charles' contact information, she has to pay $(1 - 80\%) \times \alpha$ to Bob and Charles respectively.
2If Bob wants to view Alice's contact information, he has to pay Alice $(1 - 60\%) \times \alpha$.
In this situation, compared to Alice, Bob has to pay more.
If Charles wants to view Alice's contact information, he has to pay Alice $(1 - 90\%) \times \alpha$.

4.3 Trading Protocol

Suppose that the Alice(buyer) A who want to view user Bob(seller) B 's contact information. $Info_A$ represents A's contact information and $Info_B$ is B's contact information. Fee represents the amount paid. PK_B is private key to encrypt B's contact information. As shown in Fig. 2, the detailed trading protocol is as follows.

- (Round 0). PSM² recommend user A a list of users $\{user_1, user_2, ..., user_n\}$, and $user_n = \{id, ad, Score_AB, Score_BA, Enc\{V_i, V_p\}, Enc(Info_n)\}$, in which the matching scores are calculated by the computing node (matching node), ad is the address of trading smart contract (T) deployed by the user.

Table 2. User's personal information example

Field	Use
Gender	Female→0
Age	23→23,
Education	Master→2,
Marriage status	Unmarried→0,
Place of birth	Beilin District, Xi'an, Shaanxi→120905,
Property location	Beilin District, Xi'an, Shaanxi→120905,
Residential Place	Haidian District, Beijing→10904,
Vehicles Model	Volkswagen Golf→306,
Hobbies	Fitness→10,

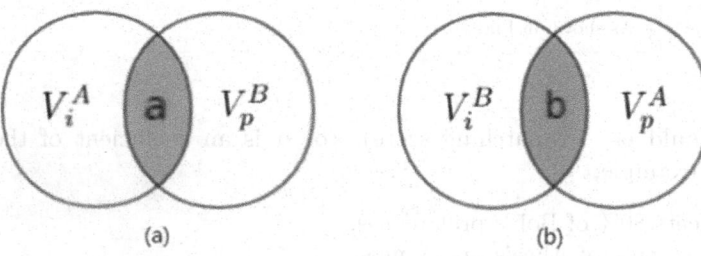

(a)   (b)

Fig. 3. Matching score calculation

- (Round 1). Assume user A finds user B is a perfect match for her and she decides to view B's contact information by sending a purchasing request to the computing node.
- (Round 2). The computing node will forward the request to user B, and wait for B to decide whether or not to accept the request. If B accepts, the trade process will continue to the next round. If B does not accept the request, the transaction will be terminated.
- (Round 3). B notifies A for acceptance of the trading.
- (Round 4). Then A requests B's contact information by sending a transaction to 'T' together with A's $Score_{AB}$, $Score_{BA}$ and $Enc\{V_i^A, V_p^A\}$.
- (Round 5). B sends $(id, Enc\{V_i^B, V_p^B\}, Enc(Info_B), PK_B)$ to 'T'.
- (Round 6). The contract program will then get the $Score_A B'$, $Score_B A'$ by calculating the Euclidean distance between $Enc\{V_i^A, V_p^A\}$ and $Enc\{V_i^B, V_p^B\}$, if

$$Score_{AB} = Score'_{AB}$$

$$Score_{BA} = Score'_{BA}$$

then 'T' will transfer the Fee from A's account to B's account, and B's $PK_B, Enc(Info)$ will be send to A.

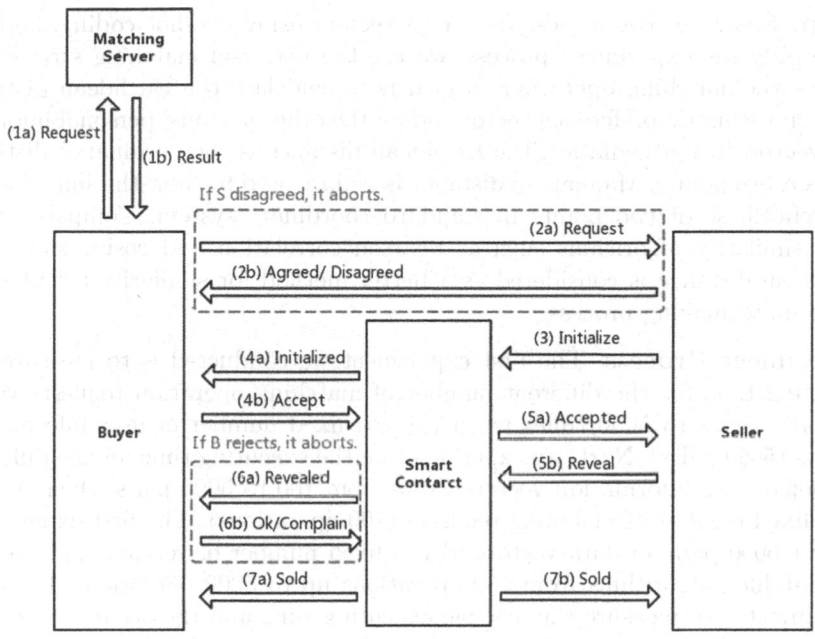

Fig. 4. The interactions of trading smart contract

– (Round 7). If
$$Score_{AB} \neq Score'_{AB}$$
or
$$Score_{BA} \neq Score'_{BA}$$
the trade will be canceled.

5   Experiment Implementation and Evaluation

To demonstrate the feasibility of our proposed platform PSM², we have implemented the design using Hyperledger Fabric 1.4.1. The chaincode APIs are written in Go and the client APIs written in NodeJS. Our prototype is built on a Ubuntu 16.04 virtual machine in a 2.10 Ghz Core 8 Duo Intel Xeon server with 64 GB of memory. We present the implementation details to evaluate the performance of the matching algorithm and the trading operations.

5.1   Experiment 1: Performance of Private-Preserving Matching Algorithm

Datasets. We collected 10362 persons' information including personal information and their preferences for matchmaking, the ratio between male to female is almost equal to 1.

Setup. First, we covert these data into vectors using one-hot coding. Second, to simplify the experiment process, we use the traversal matching strategy to process the matching operations, which is to calculate the Euclidean distance between the user's preference vector and all the other persons' personal information vector. In mathematics, the Euclidean distance is the "ordinary" distance between two points. Manhattan distance is mainly used to show the sum of absolute wheelbase of two points in standard coordinate system. Compared with other similarity algorithms such as Pearson correlation and cosine similarity, Euclidean distance is considered as a better method for similarity calculations in the matchmaking process.

Experiment Process. The first experiment we conducted is to measure the executing time for the different number of matching operation requests varies from 100 times to 5000 times when using a fixed number of user information vectors (5000 pairs). Next, we experiment on the executing time for the different number of user information vectors varies from 100 to 5000 pairs when executing a fixed number of matching requests (100 operations). The first experiment on over 5000 pairs of data vectors with a fixed number of vectors, and execute the matching algorithms from 100 operations up to 5000 operations. For both experiments, we measure the average executing time and the accumulated executing time for both unencrypted data and the encrypted data by using RSA homomorphic encryption.

Results and Evaluation

- In the first experiment, as shown in Fig. 5(a), the accumulated executing time is increasing linearly for both unencrypted data and the encrypted data. When executing different times of operations, the difference between the total accumulated time consumed for encrypted data and unencrypted data remains a fixed time value. The reason is that when processing encrypted data, it involves more computation overheads. However, for the average executing time, the difference between the unencrypted and encrypted data is getting smaller as the number of matching operations increases. It is also reasonable because when executing in parallel, the operations can share the cache for encryption and decryption, which can effectively reduce the negative impact of the extra overheads during encryption and decryption.
- In the second experiment, as shown in Fig. 5(b), as the matching requests increases, both the accumulated and average executing time for both unencrypted and encrypted data is increasing linearly. Compared with unencrypted data, the time consumed for encrypted data increased more rapidly as the matching requests increase. The result indicates that the computation overheads for encryption and decryption increases more sharply as the number of data vectors increases. It obviously become the system bottleneck.

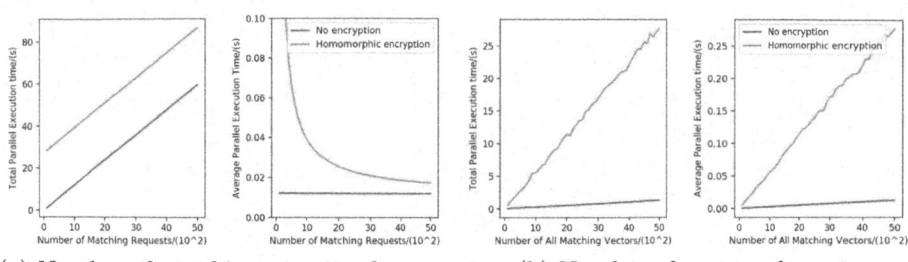

(a) Number of matching requests changes.   (b) Number of vectors changes.

Fig. 5. Time cost of matching algorithm

5.2   Experiment 2: Trading Performance

Next, we evaluate the overhead introduced by PSM²'s trading functionalities. We use the prototype described earlier in this section.

Setup. We deploy the prototype application in a Hyperledger Fabric network, where each organization owns 4 peers node acting as its endorser and committer, and two certificate authority (CA) nodes. We set up a Kafka-based ordering service with 4 Zoo-Keeper nodes, and one Fabric orderer.

Experiment Process. We use Hyperledger Caliper to measure the performance of Open and Query operations. The detailed performance metrics include the maximum latency, average latency, minimum latency, and throughput. During the experiment, first, we record the performance metrics of executing the Open functionality by increasing from 200 operations to 1,000 operations, and Query functionality from 2,000 operations to 10,000 operations. Second, we experiment on how the number of peers affects the performance of PSM² when executing a fixed number of Open(1,000 times) or Query (10,000) operations.

Throughput Evaluation: In the first experiment, as shown in Fig. 7, we observe that PSM²'s throughput for Open operations remains constant at a low level as the number of operations increases. But for the Query operations, as the number of operations increases, the throughput increases up to 1,350 transactions per second(tps).

Next, in the second experiment, as shown in Fig. 7, when executing a fixed number of Open operations, the throughput increases very slow as the number of peers increases. For the Query transactions, when there is only one machine with two peers, the throughput is very low, but by adding another machine, the throughput has a huge increase, and the throughput reaches to nearly 1400 tps. By adding more machines to the network will not lead to a significant increase to the throughput. From the results, we can see that the Open operation has poor concurrency, which is a performance bottleneck of PSM². However, it is still practical for a relatively low number of trading operations scenario.

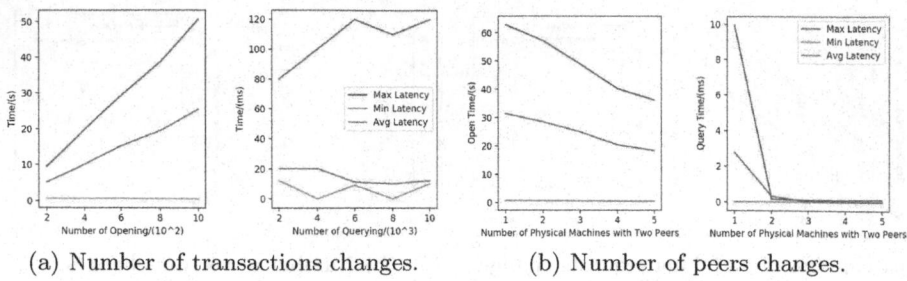

(a) Number of transactions changes.   (b) Number of peers changes.

Fig. 6. Latency of open and query

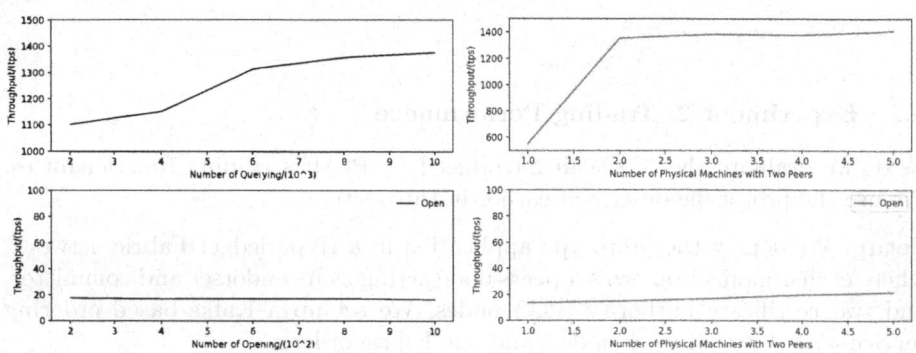

Fig. 7. Throughput of open and query operation

Latency Evaluation: In the first experiment, as shown in Fig. 6(a), for the Open operations, as the number of transactions increases, the average and max latency will also increase, the max latency increases much faster than the average latency. But the minimum latency remains a constant level of nearly to 0 s. In addition, for the Query operations, as the number of transactions increases, the maximum latency increases up to 120 ms(ms). Although the average and minimum latency fluctuates, the overall trend of average and minimum latency slightly decreases.

Next, in the second experiment, when executing a fixed number of Open operations, the latency decreases as the number of peers increases. As we can see from Fig. 6(b), the maximum latency has dropped from over 60 s(s) to 40 s, and the average latency has dropped from over 30 s to less than 20 s. In addition, for the Query transactions, when there are only one machine with two peers, the maximum latency and average latency is very high, but by adding another machine, the maximum latency and average latency drops dramatically, which from 10 ms to 0.05 ms and from 3 ms to 0.03 ms, respectively. From the results we can see that the Open operation has high latency. However, when the number of nodes in the blockchain network reaches a considerable amount, the latency will be practical enough for real life implementation.

5.3 Comparison with Related Work

The comparisons between PSM^2 and the traditional centralized matchmaking platform are as follows:

- Most of the traditional platforms i.e. FindU [10], have multi-party servers. The traditional third-party server encrypts, stores, matches and trades user information, but PSM^2 is a special node of blockchain which only stores the encrypted information of the user and matches the completed information.
- Some of the traditional matching schemes include trading operation i.e. Maggie [12] but most don't i.e. E-SmallTalker, FindU, VENETA [8,10,11]. The trading process is controlled by the smart contract which is implement on the blockchain ledger. In PSM^2, the information is trade as an asset and can use for transaction. Our third-party servers have no rights to interfere with the transaction process. However, to guarantee the accuracy, each transaction of smart contract will send 1% of the transaction amount to system administrator. The money will be used to maintain matching server nodes.
- Most traditional third-party server will complete the transaction process by controlling users, but in PSM^2, the transaction process is controlled by the smart contract directly. When the transaction is completed, it will be written into the super ledger. The successfully linked transaction information will be encrypted and packaged and sent to the banking system. The bank system decrypts and parses the transaction information package to complete the actual transfer operation.

6   Related Work

Friend matchmaking is not a difficult task, but it is challenging to protect the users' private information while ensuring accurate matching results. Various matching schemes in existing social networking application have proposed, and some of them are focusing on user's privacy protection.

Zhu et al. [7] proposed a privacy-preserving friend matching protocol, which aims to attain privacy and fairness assurance. This protocol runs with low overhead. However, their computation cost is quite high because it incurs much computation overheads at the blind transformation phase. Although the encryption part is expensive, it is still a relatively efficient approach that guarantees the matching fairness without sacrificing the user's privacy.

Besides, Yang et al. [8] proposed E-SmallTalker, which is a distributed mobile communication system for social networking in physical proximity among strangers. It employs Bluetooth as communication technology to enable its users to exchange information and match within a short-range locally. This system works best when there are few devices. However, as the number of devices increases, the discovery performance decreases dramatically. The weakness of this system is that it would not work beyond 10 m.

Another work named FindU [10] proposed by Li et al. is a privacy-preserving personal profile matching schemes for mobile social networking applications. FindU allows a user to find the best matching profile among all possible candidates for friending. The privacy-preserving nature makes FindU a reliable friend matching scheme. Although its computation complexity is small, its communication cost is relatively high.

Moreover, Dong et al. [9] presented various security issues that need to be addressed during friend matching. Mobile social networking applications involve joint computation between the datasets of two different nearby users based on their location and similarity. Under this scheme, two users will exchange their profile information before computing their similarities in-between. If the similarity value exceeds a threshold, they can be potential friends. Although This friend matching scheme provides privacy preservation feature, the communication and computation overheads are relatively high.

Moreover, Arb et al. [11] proposed a system named VENETA, which introduced a decentralized method that is able to explore the social neighbourhood of a user by detecting friends of friends. In this way, it has attempted to address the issue of lack of popular friendship exploration features in mobile social networks. The authors claim that they mitigated privacy issues by only exploiting information about real friends, however, real friends' information does also have privacy concerns, therefore this work does not efficiently address the privacy issues.

7 Conclusion

In this paper, we propose PSM^2, a private-preserving self-sovereign matchmaking platform based on blockchain. PSM^2 introduces a privacy-preserving matching score algorithm between different users, and a trading smart contract for the user to trade contact information in a transparent and fair way. We build a prototype by using Hyperledger Fabric, and we analyse the efficiency of privacy-preserving matching process, the performance of trading process, and we compare our scheme with the other existing matching and trading schemes. The results show that PSM^2 is practical for real life implementation.

Acknowledgments. This research is supported by the National key R&D Program of China under Grant No.2018YFB1402700. It is also partially supported by the National Natural Science Foundation of China under Grant No.61672421 and No.61602363.

References

1. Vun, C.H., Premkumar, A.B.: RNS encoding based folding ADC. (ISCAS). IEEE Int. Symposium Circuits Syst. **57**(1), 814–817 (2012)
2. Blumtritt, C.: Online revenue forecast for Dating Services worldwide until 2024. https://www.statista.com/statistics/891138/eservices-dating-services-online-revenue-by-segment-worldwide/. Accessed 15 March 2020
3. Opiria. Scope Of The General Data Protextion Regular. https://www.trustedintrading.com/articles/enabling-gdpr-compliant-trading-of-personal-data-on-the-blockchain/. Accessed 15 Apr 2019
4. Wood, G.: Ethereum: a secure decentralised generalised transaction ledger. Ethereum project yellow paper, 151, 1–32 (2014)

5. Dinh, T.T.A., Liu, R., Zhang, M., Chen, G., Ooi, B.B., Wang, J.: Untangling blockchain: a data processing view of blockchain systems. IEEE Trans. Knowl. Data Eng. **30**(7), 1366–1385 (2018)
6. Merkle, R.C.: A digital signature based on a conventional encryption function. In: Pomerance, C. (ed.) CRYPTO 1987. LNCS, vol. 293, pp. 369–378. Springer, Heidelberg (1988). https://doi.org/10.1007/3-540-48184-2_32
7. Zhu, H., Du, S., Li, M., Gao, Z.: Fairness-aware and privacy-preserving friend matching protocol in mobile social networks. IEEE Trans. Emerg. Top. Comput. **1**(1), 192–200 (2013)
8. Yang, Z., Zhang, B., Dai, J., Champion, A.C., Xuan, D., Li, D.: ESmallTalker: a distributed mobile system for social networking in physical proximity. In: IEEE International Conference on Distributed Computing Systems, pp. 468–477, June 2010
9. Dong, W., Dave, V., Qiu, L., Zhang, Y.: Secure friend discovery in mobile social networks.INFOCOM IEEE, Shanghai, China (2011)
10. Li, M., Cao, N., Yu, S., et al.: FindU: Privacy-Preserving Personal Profile Matching in Mobile Social Networks. INFOCOM IEEE, Shanghai (2011)
11. Arb, M.V., Bader, M., Kuhn, M., et al.: VENETA: serverless friend-of-friend detection in mobile social networking. In: International Conference on Networking & Communications IEEE (2008)
12. Maggie. http://www.maggiethefilm.com/. Accessed 18 Dec 2019
13. GDPR Compliance Personal Data-Selling Personal Data. https://www.trustedintrading.com/articles/enabling-gdpr-compliant-trading-of-personal-data-on-the-blockchain/. Accessed 15 Apr 2019
14. FairSwap: How to Fairly Exchange Digital Goods. https://blog.acolyer.org/2018/12/05/fairswap-how-to-fairly-exchange-digital-goods/. Accessed 5 Dec 2018
15. Lu, Y., Qi, Y., Qi, S., Li, Y., Song, H., Liu, Y.: Say no to price discrimination: decentralized and automated incentives for price auditing in ride-hailing services. IEEE Trans. Mob. Comput., 1–18 (2020). https://doi.org/10.1109/TMC.2020.3008315
16. Zheng, Z., Xie, S., Dai, H.N., Chen, X., Wang, H.: Blockchain challenges and opportunities: a survey. Int. J. Web Grid Serv. **14**(4), 352–375 (2018)
17. Hong-Ning, D., Zibin, Z., Yan Z.: Blockchain for Internet of Things: a survey. IEEE Internet Things J. (IoT-J), 6, 8076–8094 (2019)
18. Huang, Y., Kong, Q., Jia, N., Chen, X., Zheng, Z.: Recommending differentiated code to support smart contract update. In: IEEE/ACM 27th International Conference on Program Comprehension (ICPC), pp. 260–270 (2019)
19. Zheng, P., Zheng, Z., Luo, X., Chen, X., Liu, X.: A detailed and real-time performance monitoring framework for blockchain systems. In: IEEE/ACM 40th International Conference on Software Engineering: Software Engineering in Practice Track (ICSE-SEIP), pp. 134–143 (2018)
20. Qi, S., Lu, Y., Zheng, Y., Li, Y., Chen, X.: Cpds: enabling compressed and private data sharing for industrial IoT over blockchain. IEEE Trans. Ind. Informat. https://doi.org/10.1109/TII.2020.2998166
21. Qi, S., Zheng, Y.: Crypt-DAC: cryptographically enforced dynamic access control in the cloud. IEEE Trans. Dependable Secure Comput. p. 1 (2019)
22. Qi, S., Zheng, Y., Li, M., Liu, Y., Qiu, J.: Scalable industry data access control in RFID-enabled supply chain. IEEE/ACM Trans. Netw. (ToN) **24**(6), 3551–3564 (2016)
23. Qi, S., Lu, Y., Wei, W., Chen, X.: Efficient data access control with fine-grained data protection in cloud-assisted IIoT. IEEE Internet Things J. (IoT-J), 1–15 (2020). https://doi.org/10.1109/JIOT.2020.3020979

A Blockchain-Based Distributed Authentication and Dynamic Group Key Agreement Protocol

Zisang Xu[1]($\boxtimes$), Feng Li[1], Minfu Tan[2], and Jixin Zhang[3]

[1] Computer and Communication Engineer Institute, Changsha University of Science and Technology, Changsha 410114, Hunan, China
xzsszx111@sina.com, lif@csust.edu.cn
[2] Big data development and Research Center, Guangzhou College of Technology and Business, Guangzhou 528138, China
131173290002@163.com
[3] School of Computer Science, Hubei University of Technology, Wuhan 430068, Hubei, China
zhangjixin@hnu.edu.cn

Abstract. With the rapid development of mobile networks, there are more and more application scenarios that require group communication. Group communication can transmit messages to all group members with minimal resources. The security of group communication depends on the security of the group key. Most existing group key agreement protocols are often flawed in performance, scalability, or security. Therefore, this paper proposes a blockchain-based distributed authentication and dynamic group key agreement protocol. Based on blockchain technology, this protocol improves the scalability and makes it possible to track malicious members. In addition, comparison with related protocols shows that our protocol reduces computational and communication costs.

Keywords: Authentication · Blockchain · Cryptography · Group key agreement

1 Introduction

With the rapid development of mobile networks, the secure transmission of data is no longer limited to both parties in communication, but is required in group communication. Group communication can transmit messages to all group members with minimal resources [12]. This is because the sending of the message only needs to be broadcast once within the group, instead of sending the same message to all group members one by one, which results in a significant increase in communication efficiency. Therefore, group communication is widely used in mobile networks.

In order to provide a reliable and scalable group communication service, the most basic and critical security issue is access control [1,6]. In most cases,

© Springer Nature Singapore Pte Ltd. 2020
Z. Zheng et al. (Eds.): BlockSys 2020, CCIS 1267, pp. 142–151, 2020.
https://doi.org/10.1007/978-981-15-9213-3_11

access control can be achieved by encrypting or decrypting messages, because only legitimate group members can get the key and use this to decrypt the ciphertext to access the messages. This means that all members of the group need to perform mutual authentication and negotiate a same session key, which is also called the group key. Therefore, the security of group communication depends on the security of the group key, and designing an efficient group key agreement protocol is the key to ensuring the security of group communication.

In recent years, many researchers have proposed many authentication and distributed group key agreement protocols, but most of these protocols are flawed in performance, scalability, or security. Therefore, this paper designs a blockchain-based distributed authentication and dynamic group key agreement protocol to solve the above problems. The protocol has the following characteristics:

- Our protocol uses blockchain technology to manage the list of group members and the identities and public keys of each group member. This improves the scalability of the protocol and makes it possible to track malicious members.
- During the authentication phase of our protocol, each group member only needs to authenticate their neighboring group members once, which reduces computational and communication costs.
- In our protocol, when a group member joins or leaves a group, it only needs to update the parameters of an adjacent group member, which also reduces the computational and communication costs.

The rest of this article is arranged as follows. Section 2 describes the related works. The network model and threat model are introduced in Sect. 3. The proposed protocol is described completely in Sect. 4. Section 5 analyzes the security and performance of our protocol. Finally, we conclude the article in Sect. 6.

2 Related Works

In order to ensure the security of group keys, a large number of researchers have proposed many solutions. These solutions are generally divided into the following three types [1,12,13].

Centralized group key agreement protocol. There is usually only one entity for controlling the entire group in this type of protocol, which is called a Key Distribution Center (KDC). The KDC is responsible for key generation, distribution, and management. It also needs to be responsible for tasks such as group communication. The protocol proposed by Wong et al. [17] is a typical group key agreement protocol based on Logical Key Hierarchy (LKH). This type of protocol requires less space to store the keys, and when the keys need to be updated, the amount of communication is greatly reduced. Islam et al. [8] proposed a group key agreement protocol for Internet of Vehicles. In their protocol, TA plays the role of KDC.

Decentralized group key agreement protocol. This type of protocol divides all group members into subgroups, and each subgroup is managed by its own subgroup controller. This greatly reduces the load on KDC and solves the problem of single node failure. Mittra [10] proposed a scalable multicast framework, which divides large groups into multiple subgroups, and each subgroup has a controller called a group security intermediate node or a group security agent. In the protocol of Setia et al. [14], The group key is updated at regular intervals, rather than when group members join or leave. Naresh et al. [11] proposed a cluster-based hybrid group key agreement protocol, which divides large groups into a certain number of clusters, and specifies the last member of the cluster as the cluster head and group controller.

Distributed group key agreement protocol. All group members in this type of protocol are equal and there is no KDC or group controller. Without the base station, Wang et al. [16] proposed a device-to-device group key agreement protocol. The protocol guarantees the anonymity of each device and uses a signature scheme based on the Gap-Diffie-Hellman group [2]. Based on the hyper elliptic curve digital signature and Elgamal algorithm, Kavitha et al. [9] proposed a distributed group authentication protocol for the healthcare system in the Internet of Things. The protocol proposed by Zhang et al. [20] divides the entire authentication and key agreement protocol into two rounds. The first round is mutual authentication between members, and the second round is group key generation. In the above protocol, each group member only needs to perform mutual authentication with the other two group members. The protocol proposed by Zhang et al. [18] and Shi et al. [15] merge the two processes described above into one. In 2018, Zhang et al. [19] and Gupta et al. [7] respectively proposed a distributed group key agreement protocol where the key can be self-certified.

3 Network Model and Threat Model

There are two parts in our network model, namely KDC and General Node (GN). All nodes except KDC are considered as GNs. These GNs are equal and there is no hierarchy or subordinate relationship. In addition, GNs are usually fixed nodes, have no energy consumption restrictions, have certain computing and storage resources, and they can join or leave a group at any time. KDC and GNs form a blockchain network [4,21]. However, only KDC can use the proof-of-work mechanism to create a new block [3], and all GNs can only verify the correctness of the new block and read the information in the blockchain. KDC is considered a trusted node. The network model used in our protocol is shown in Fig. 1.

Before GN joins the blockchain network, it needs to submit its identity to KDC. The KDC will calculate a pair of keys based on the identity and distribute it to the GN. In addition, the KDC will generate a new block containing the identity and related information of the newly added GN, which will be verified by other GNs in the group. Note that KDC does not participate in group key agreement.

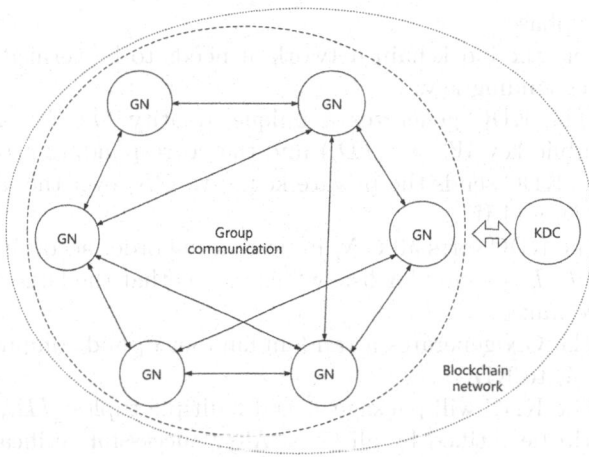

Fig. 1. The network model used by our protocol.

We define the threat model as follows:

- KDC is a trusted node.
- The adversary has the ability to intercept all data transmitted over unsecured channels, and he can inject new data and replace or replay the previously sent data.
- All GNs are semi-trusted parties, which means that they may misbehave themselves, but do not conspire with any other GN [5].

4 Proposed Protocol

In our protocol, each GN only needs to verify the identity of the left neighbor once and send a message to the right neighbor, and then the group key can be negotiated. In addition, when any GN joins or leaves the group, only the left neighbor of the GN needs to update parameters, which reduces the calculation and communication overhead. Our protocol has six parts: initialization phase, registration phase, mutual authentication phase, group key generation phase, GN join event, and GN leave event. Suppose there are $GN_i(1 \leq i \leq n)$ that need to generate the same group key, and their identities are $ID_i(1 \leq i \leq n)$, where n is the number of GN. The detailed description of the above six parts is as follows.

(1) Initialization phase
KDC generates $\{G_1, G_2, Q, e, p\}$, where G_1 is a cyclic additive group of order p, G_2 is a cyclic multiplicative group of order p, Q is a generator of G_1, and $e : G_1 \times G_1 \rightarrow G_2$ is a bilinear map. Then, the KDC generates a random private key s and calculates the corresponding public key $P_{pub} = sQ$. Finally, the KDC publishes parameters $\{p, G_1, G_2, Q, e, P_{pub}, h(.), E_k, D_k\}$ and stores s in its memory, where $h(.)$ is the hash function used by this protocol, E_k is the symmetric encryption algorithm, and D_k is the symmetric decryption algorithm.

(2) Registration phase

Before GN_i enters the blockchain network, it needs to be verified by KDC and receive the corresponding key.

Step R1: The KDC generates a unique identity ID_i for each GN_i and calculates its public key $W_i = h(ID_i)$ and the corresponding private key $S_i = sW_i$. Finally, the KDC sends the private key S_i to GN_i over the secure channel, and publishes ID_i and W_i.

Step R2: The KDC sorts all GN_i in descending order according to ID_i, and forms a GN list L. L is a circular list, which means that the largest ID_i and the smallest ID_i are linked.

Step R3: The GN generates a random number a_i and computes $A_i = a_iQ$. GN then sends A_i to KDC.

Step R4: The KDC will package L and multiple tuples (ID_i, A_i) into new blocks, which will be verified by all GNs. After successful verification, the new block will be linked to the blockchain.

(3) Mutual authentication phase

In this phase, GN_i will send a message to its right neighbor GN_{i+1}, and let GN_{i+1} authenticate GN_i. At the same time, GN_i will also receive a message from its left neighbor GN_{i-1} and will need to authenticate GN_{i-1}. The GN_i performs the following operations.

Step A1: Generates a random number m_i and a timestamp t_{1_i}, and get A_{i+1} from the blockchain.

Step A2: Computes $M_i = m_iQ$, $KT_{i+1} = a_iA_{i+1}$, $SE_{i+1} = E_{KT_{i+1}}(M_i)$, $C_i = h(SE_{i+1}, KT_{i+1}, t_{1_i})S_i$.

Step A3: Sends message (SE_{i+1}, C_i, t_{1_i}) to GN_{i+1}.

Step A4: GN_i received a message $(SE_i, C_{i-1}, t_{1_{i-1}})$ from GN_{i-1}, and get A_{i-1} from the blockchain.

Step A5: Checks that $t_{new} - t_{1_{i-1}} < \Delta t$ holds or not, where t_{new} is the time of the message was received and Δt is the maximum communication delay. If not, broadcast authentication failure message.

Step A6: Computes $KT_i = a_iA_{i-1}$.

Step A7: Checks whether the condition $e(Q, C_{i-1})? = e(P_{pub}, h(SE_i, KT_i, t_{1_{i-1}})W_{i-1})$ is satisfied. If the condition is not true, terminates the current session.

Step A8: Uses KT_i to decrypt SE_i and get M_{i-1}.

Step A9: Generates a random number b_i and a timestamp t_{2_i}.

Step A10: Computes $X_i = b_iW_iZ_i = e(M_i - M_{i-1}, Q)Y_i = (b_i + h(X_i, Z_i, t_{2_i}))S_i$.

Step A11: Broadcasts $R_i = (X_i, Y_i, Z_i, t_{2_i})$

(4) Group key generation phase

During this phase, GN_i receives the message $R_r(1 \le r \le n, r \ne i)$ from all other GNs. At this point, GN_i will perform a group authentication and then negotiate the group key. The execution steps of GN_i are as follows.

Step K1: Checks the timestamp $t_{new} - t_{2_r} < \Delta t, (1 \leq r \leq n, r \neq i)$ in each received message is valid. If the check fails, broadcasts an authentication failure message.

Step K2: After receiving the message from all other GNs, checks that

$$e(\sum_{r \neq i} Y_r, Q)? = e(\sum_{r \neq i} (X_r + h(Z_r, t_{2_r})W_r), P_{pub})$$

holds or not. If the check fails, broadcasts an authentication failure message.

Step K3: Computes $k = e(nM_i, Q)Z_{i+1}^{n-1} Z_{i+2}^{n-2} \cdots Z_{i-1}$, and group key $Ks = h(k, R_1, R_2, \cdots, R_n)$.

(5) GN join event

When a new GN_j wants to join the group, it first needs to be verified by the KDC. Second, the KDC inserts the identity ID_j of GN_j into the appropriate position in the list L. Third, the GN_j generates a random number a_j, computes $A_j = a_j Q$, and broadcasts A_j. Fourth, the GN_{j-1} regenerates a new random number a'_{j-1}, computers $A'_{j-1} = a'_{j-1}Q$, and broadcasts A'_{j-1}. Fifth, the KDC packages the updated L and tuples (ID_i, A_i) of all group members including GN_j and GN_{j-1} into new blocks, which will be verified by all GNs. After successful verification, the new block will be linked to the blockchain. Sixth, as in the mutual authentication phase, the GN_j sends (SE_{j+1}, C_j, t_{1_j}) to its right neighbor GN_{j+1}, and receives message $(SE'_j, C'_{j_1}, t'_{1_{j-1}})$ from GN_{j-1}. Seventh, after the messages received by GN_j and GN_{j+1} are successfully authenticated, all GNs broadcast $R_i = (X_i, Y_i, Z_i, t_{2_i})$ and perform the group key generation phase to complete the key update.

(6) GN leave event

When a GN_j wants to leave the group, it first submits an application to the KDC. Second, the KDC broadcasts GN's identity ID_j and deletes ID_j from the list L. Third, the GN_{j-1} regenerates a new random number a'_{j-1}, computers $A'_{j-1} = a'_{j-1}Q$, and broadcasts A'_{j-1}. Fourth, the KDC packages the updated L and tuples (ID_i, A_i) of all group members including GN_{j-1} into new blocks, which will be verified by all GNs. After successful verification, the new block will be linked to the blockchain. Fifth, as in the mutual authentication phase, the GN_{j-1} sends $(SE'_j, D'_{j-1}, t'_{1_{j-1}})$ to GN_{j+1}. Sixth, after U_{j+1} authenticates U_{j-1}, all GNs broadcast $R_i = (X_i, Y_i, Z_i, t_{2_i})$ and perform the group key generation phase to complete the key update.

5   Security and Performance Analysis

5.1   Correctness Analysis

Theorem 1. GN_i and GN_{i+1} can calculate the same symmetric key KT_{i+1}, so that GN_{i+1} can get M_i.

Proof. Since GN_i computes $KT_{i+1} = a_iA_{i+1}$ to get KT_{i+1}, and GN_{i+1} computes $KT_{i+1} = a_{i+1}A_i$ to get KT_{i+1}, then

$$KT_{i+1} = a_iA_{i+1} = a_ia_{i+1}Q = a_{i+1}A_i.$$

Since the same KT_{i+1} can be obtained by calculating a_iA_{i+1} and $a_{i+1}A_i$, GN_i and GN_{i+1} can use the symmetric key KT_{i+1} to encrypt or decrypt transmitted messages.   □

Theorem 2. *During the group key generation phase, GN_i is valid for batch authentication of other group members.*

Proof. In the group key generation phase, GN_i authenticates other group members in batches by verifying whether formula $e(\sum_{r\neq i} Y_r, Q) = e(\sum_{r\neq i}(X_r + h(X_r, Z_r, t_{2_r})W_r), P_{pub})$ holds. The correctness of the formula is proved as follows.

$$
\begin{aligned}
e(\sum_{r\neq i} Y_r, Q) &= e(\sum_{r\neq i}(b_r + h(X_r, Z_r, t_{2_r}))S_r, Q) \\
&= e(\sum_{r\neq i}(b_r + h(X_r, Z_r, t_{2_r}))sW_r, Q) \\
&= e(\sum_{r\neq i}(b_rW_r + h(X_r, Z_r, t_{2_r})W_r), sQ) \\
&= e(\sum_{r\neq i}(X_r + h(X_r, Z_r, t_{2_r})W_r), P_{pub}).
\end{aligned}
$$

Although the adversary can easily obtain $\sum_{r\neq i} Y_r$, Q, $\sum_{r\neq i}(X_r + h(X_r, Z_r, t_{2_r})W_r)$, and P_{pub}, due to the decisional Diffie-Hellman assumption, the adversary cannot determine whether the formula $e(\sum_{r\neq i} Y_r, Q) = e(\sum_{r\neq i}(X_r + h(X_r, Z_r, t_{2_r})W_r), P_{pub})$ is true in polynomial time. If the adversary wants to forge a GN_i^* to pass the above batch authentication, he needs to create valid X_i^* and Y_i^* to satisfy $e(Y_i^*, Q) = e((b_i + h(X_i^*, Z_i, t_{2_i}))sW_i, Q)$. First, the adversary cannot get b_i, so it is difficult for him to calculate $(b_i + h(X_i^*, Z_i, t_{2_i}))sW_i$ according to the Elliptic Curve Discrete Logarithm Problem (ECDLP). Second, suppose that $(b_i + h(X_i^*, Z_i, t_{2_i}))$ is revealed by the adversary, but the adversary cannot get s, so according to the ECDLP, he still cannot calculate valid X_i^* and Y_i^* in polynomial time.   □

Theorem 3. *If all GN_is participating in the group key generation phase are honest, then all GN_is can negotiate a same group key.*

Proof. According to the Theorem 1, as long as all GN_is participating in the group key generation phase are honest, each GN_i can obtain the parameter M_{i-1} sent by its left neighbor. Therefore,

$$
\begin{aligned}
k &= e(nM_i, Q)Z_{i+1}^{n-1}Z_{i+2}^{n-2}\cdots Z_{i-1} \\
&= e(m_iQ, Q)^n Z_{i+1}^{n-1}Z_{i+2}^{n-2}\cdots Z_{i-1} \\
&= e(Q,Q)^{nm_i+(n-1)(m_{i+1}-m_i)+(n-2)(m_{i+2}-m_{i+1})+\cdots+(m_{i-1}-m_{i-2})} \\
&= e(Q,Q)^{m_1+m_2+\cdots+m_i}.
\end{aligned}
$$

From the above, it can be found that all GN_is can calculate the same parameter k. Therefore, their group keys $Ks = h(k, R_1, R_2, \cdots, R_n)$ are also the same. □

5.2   Performance Analysis

We compare our protocol with the protocol of Zheng et al. [20], the protocol of Zhang et al. [19], and the protocol of Gupta et al. [7] in terms of computational costs, communication costs, and security.

In the mutual authentication phase and the group key generation phase of our protocol, the computational cost of each GN is $n + 7$ point multiplication operations on ECC, 4 bilinear pairing operations, $n + 3$ hash operations, and 2 symmetric encryption or decryption operations. The communication cost of each GN is sending 5 general parameters and 2 timestamps. Table 1 shows the comparison of computational cost and communication cost between our protocol and related protocols, where n is the number of GN and C is the length of the general parameter. We assume C is 160 bits and timestamp T is 64 bits. It can be found from Table 1 that our protocol has the lowest computational and communication costs. As for security, because after GN_j joins or leaves the group, neither its left neighbor nor its right neighbor updated the corresponding temporary secret parameter, the protocol of Zheng et al. [20] lacks forward or backward secrecy. The protocol of Zhang et al. [19] and Gupta et al. [7] have no obvious security issues.

Table 1. The comparison of computational cost and communication cost between our protocol and related protocols.

	Zheng et al. [20]	Zhang et al. [19]	Gupta et al. [7]	Our protocol
Point multiplication operations on ECC	$n+4$	$3n+2$	$4n$	$n+7$
Pairing	6	$2n$	0	4
Hash operation	$n+4$	0	5	$n+3$
Symmetric encryption or decryption	0	0	0	2
Point addition operations on ECC	0	0	$2n+1$	0
Communication cost	$9C+2T$	$(4n+8)C$	$7nC$	$5C+2T$

6   Conclusions

This paper proposes a blockchain-based distributed authentication and dynamic group key agreement protocol. In our protocol, each group member only needs to authenticate its left neighbor once to complete the authentication, which improved authentication efficiency. When a node joins or leaves a group, only the left neighbor of the node needs to update the data, which also greatly reduces the computational and communication costs. In addition, we use mathematics to prove the correctness and security of our protocol. Comparison with related protocols shows that our protocol reduces computational and communication costs.

Acknowledgments. This work was supported in part by National Natural Science Foundation of China under Grant 61872138 and Grant 61772185.

References

1. Barskar, R., Chawla, M.: A survey on efficient group key management schemes in wireless networks. Indian J. Sci. Technol. **9**(14) (2016)
2. Boneh, D., Lynn, B., Shacham, H.: Short signatures from the weil pairing. In: Boyd, C. (ed.) ASIACRYPT 2001. LNCS, vol. 2248, pp. 514–532. Springer, Heidelberg (2001). https://doi.org/10.1007/3-540-45682-1_30
3. Chen, W., Zheng, Z., Cui, J., Ngai, E., Zheng, P., Zhou, Y.: Detecting ponzi schemes on ethereum: towards healthier blockchain technology. In: Proceedings of the 2018 World Wide Web Conference, pp. 1409–1418 (2018)
4. Dai, H.N., Zheng, Z., Zhang, Y.: Blockchain for internet of things: a survey. IEEE Internet Things J. **6**(5), 8076–8094 (2019)
5. Franklin, M.K., Reiter, M.K.: Fair exchange with a semi-trusted third party. In: Proceedings of the 4th ACM Conference on Computer and Communications Security, pp. 1–5 (1997)
6. Gong, L., Shacham, N.: Multicast security and its extension to a mobile environment. Wireless Netw. **1**(3), 281–295 (1995)
7. Gupta, S., Kumar, A., Kumar, N.: Design of ECC based authenticated group key agreement protocol using self-certified public keys. In: 2018 4th International Conference on Recent Advances in Information Technology (RAIT), pp. 1–5. IEEE (2018)
8. Islam, S.H., Obaidat, M.S., Vijayakumar, P., Abdulhay, E., Li, F., Reddy, M.K.C.: A robust and efficient password-based conditional privacy preserving authentication and group-key agreement protocol for vanets. Future Generation Comput. Syst. **84**, 216–227 (2018)
9. Kavitha, S., Alphonse, P., Reddy, Y.V.: An improved authentication and security on efficient generalized group key agreement using hyper elliptic curve based public key cryptography for iot health care system. J. Med. Syst. **43**(8), 260 (2019)
10. Mittra, S.: Iolus: a framework for scalable secure multicasting. In: ACM SIGCOMM Computer Communication Review, vol. 27, pp. 277–288. ACM (1997)
11. Naresh, V.S., Reddi, S., Murthy, N.V.E.S.: A provably secure cluster-based hybrid hierarchical group key agreement for large wireless ad hoc networks. Hum. Centric Comput. Inf. Sci. **9**(1), 1–32 (2019). https://doi.org/10.1186/s13673-019-0186-5

12. Rafaeli, S., Hutchison, D.: A survey of key management for secure group communication. ACM Comput. Surv. (CSUR) **35**(3), 309–329 (2003)
13. Seetha, R., Saravanan, R.: A survey on group key management schemes. Cybern. Inf. Technol. **15**(3), 3–25 (2015)
14. Setia, S., Koussih, S., Jajodia, S., Harder, E.: Kronos: a scalable group re-keying approach for secure multicast. In: Proceeding 2000 IEEE Symposium on Security and Privacy. S&P 2000, pp. 215–228. IEEE (2000)
15. Shi, Y., Chen, G., Li, J.: Id-based one round authenticated group key agreement protocol with bilinear pairings. In: International Conference on Information Technology: Coding and Computing (ITCC 2005)-Volume II, vol. 1, pp. 757–761. IEEE (2005)
16. Wang, L., Tian, Y., Zhang, D., Lu, Y.: Constant-round authenticated and dynamic group key agreement protocol for d2d group communications. Inf. Sci. **503**, 61–71 (2019)
17. Wong, C.K., Gouda, M., Lam, S.S.: Secure group communications using key graphs. IEEE/ACM Trans. Networking **8**(1), 16–30 (2000)
18. Zhang, Q., Wang, R., Tan, Y.: Identity-based authenticated asymmetric group key agreement. J. Comput. Res. Develop. **51**(8), 1727–1738 (2014)
19. Zhang, Q., Gan, Y., Zhang, Q., Wang, R., Tan, Y.A.: A dynamic and cross-domain authentication asymmetric group key agreement in telemedicine application. IEEE Access **6**, 24064–24074 (2018)
20. Zheng, J., Yang, C., Xue, J., Zhang, C.: A dynamic id-based authenticated group key agreement protocol. In: 2015 4th National Conference on Electrical, Electronics and Computer Engineering. Atlantis Press (2015)
21. Zheng, Z., Xie, S., Dai, H.N., Chen, X., Wang, H.: Blockchain challenges and opportunities: a survey. Int. J. Web Grid Serv. **14**(4), 352–375 (2018)

Scalable and Communication-Efficient Decentralized Federated Edge Learning with Multi-blockchain Framework

Jiawen Kang[1], Zehui Xiong[2(✉)], Chunxiao Jiang[3], Yi Liu[4], Song Guo[5], Yang Zhang[6], Dusit Niyato[7], Cyril Leung[8], and Chunyan Miao[7]

[1] Energy Research Institute, Nanyang Technological University (NTU), Singapore 639798, Singapore
[2] Alibaba-NTU Joint Research Institute, NTU, Singapore 639798, Singapore
zxiong002@e.ntu.edu.sg
[3] School of Information Science and Technology, Tsinghua University, Beijing 100084, China
[4] Faculty of Information Technology, Monash University, Clayton, VIC 3800, Australia
[5] Department of Computing, Hong Kong Polytechnic University (HKPU), Hong Kong and Shenzhen Research Institute, HKPU, Shenzhen 518057, China
[6] School of Computer Science and Technology, Wuhan University of Technology, Wuhan 430070, China
[7] School of Computer Science and Engineering, NTU, Singapore 639798, Singapore
[8] The University of British Columbia and Joint NTU-UBC Research Centre of Excellence in Active Living for the Elderly, Singapore 639798, Singapore

Abstract. The emerging Federated Edge Learning (FEL) technique has drawn considerable attention, which not only ensures good machine learning performance but also solves "data island" problems caused by data privacy concerns. However, large-scale FEL still faces following crucial challenges: (i) there lacks a secure and communication-efficient model training scheme for FEL; (2) there is no scalable and flexible FEL framework for updating local models and global model sharing (trading) management. To bridge the gaps, we first propose a blockchain-empowered secure FEL system with a hierarchical blockchain framework consisting of a main chain and subchains. This framework can achieve scalable and flexible decentralized FEL by individually manage local model updates or model sharing records for performance isolation. A Proof-of-Verifying consensus scheme is then designed to remove low-quality model updates and manage qualified model updates in a decentralized and secure manner, thereby achieving secure FEL. To improve communication efficiency of the blockchain-empowered FEL, a gradient compression scheme is designed to generate sparse but important gradients to reduce communication overhead without compromising accuracy, and also further strengthen privacy preservation of training data. The security analysis and numerical results indicate that the proposed schemes

The original version of this chapter was revised: The funding information was removed from the acknowledgments section. The correction to this chapter is available at https://doi.org/10.1007/978-981-15-9213-3_54

can achieve secure, scalable, and communication-efficient decentralized FEL.

Keywords: Federated edge learning · Blockchain · Gradient compression · Communication efficiency · Security

1 Introduction

With the rapid advancement of Artificial Intelligence, a larger amount of emerging applications empowered by machine learning technologies significantly enhance the life quality of humans [1]. These applications, such as automatic driving and smart healthcare, utilize advanced machine learning algorithms to train different learning tasks on massive user data from various edge nodes, e.g., smart phones. For traditional machine learning approaches, user data needs to be gathered and centralised in a central server for model training, such as chest CT image analysis for COVID-19 diagnosis. However, the centralized learning approaches may bring serious data privacy leakage problems. The growing concerns about security and privacy of user data have intensified the demand for new solutions. A promising machine learning technique named Federated Edge Learning (FEL) is introduced to achieve privacy-preserving model training [2]. In FEL, the edge nodes collaboratively train a globally shared model by their local data, and only send their local model updates instead of raw data to a central server [3]. The central server gathers all the local model updates to generate an updated global model for the next training iterations.

Despite that FEL has great advantages for AI-based application with requirements of data privacy protection, there exist two major challenges for the wide deployment of FEL as follows: (I) The central server plays an important role to aggregate local model updates from edge devices and maintain global model parameters, but is vulnerable to security challenges, e.g.., single point of failure. An unstable central server may result in a system crash. A compromised central server may generate falsified global model to mislead model training and increase system resource consumption. (II) There lacks a communication-efficient FEL framework for scalable model training. In the existing FEL framework, edge devices need to frequently upload a large number of local model parameters to the central server for model aggregation, which causes excessive communication overhead and a high demand for network bandwidth [4].

For the security issues of a single central server, previous researchers have integrated blockchain into federated learning for secure model training [4–6]. Kim et al. presented a public blockchain-based federated learning framework, in which local model updates are exchanged and verified among miners running energy-hungry Proof-of-Work consensus algorithms [5]. Instead of public blockchain, Lu et al. [6] proposed a hybrid blockchain framework with an asynchronous learning scheme for secure and efficient federated learning. Similarly, Li et al. [4] designed a decentralized federated learning framework using permissioned blockchain. Although blockchain is an effective way to replace the central server with security guarantee, the process of sharing local model updates among miners brings data privacy leakage challenges to FEL, which is ignored in the existing work. Specifically, recent studies have shown that, even only sharing gradient parameters, a compromised miner may launch inference attack that infers features of private training data, even the training data of edge devices, from publicly shared gradients on blockchain [7].

For the communication efficiency issues, the existing study presented new consensus mechanisms for blockchain-based FEL to reduce communication cost [4] or developed communication-efficient stochastic gradient descent algorithms [2], e.g., gradient quantization and encoding [8]. However, the existing schemes cannot be straightforwardly applied to large-scale FEL because of high communication-overhead caused by lots of gradients exchanged between edge devices and a central server (or miners). The challenges drive the urgent need of developing secure, decentralized, privacy-preserving and communication-efficient FEL.

To address these challenges, we first propose a Blockchain-empowered Federated Edge Learning (BFEL) framework without relying on a trusted centralized server. In BFEL, a consortium blockchain acting as a trusted and decentralized ledger to manage model updates from edge devices. To filter out malicious or poisoning model updates, we then propose a Proof-of-Verifying (PoV) consensus scheme to collaboratively verify the quality of local model updates among predefined miners. Only the verified model updates can be stored into the block for decentralized federated learning. Since the communication efficiency is significantly important for BFEL, we further integrate a gradient compression scheme into PoV without lowering learning accuracy. This scheme also relieves inference attack to improve privacy protection of training data.

Moreover, after model training, learning task publishers can share their models to other entities without enough budget or resources to organize federated learning. For example, a map company can reuse and trade its traffic-prediction training model to vehicles for economic benefit. For the sake of security, the sharing records will be added in the blockchain. However, if both model updates and model sharing records are stored into a single blockchain, this will result in larger block size and higher consensus delay. The miners with limited resources cannot synchronize block data in real time. To avoid this dilemma, we design further a scalable and flexible framework consisting of a public blockchain as the main blockchain and multiple consortium blockchains as subchains for performance isolation [9]. Specifically, according to data characteristics and service demands (e.g., access control), the model updates from edge devices are respectively stored on individual subchains named "Model training subchains". Meanwhile, the model sharing records between the task publishers and other entities are stored in a subchain named "Model trading subchain".

The main contributions of this paper are summarized as follows.

- Unlike single blockchain-based systems, we design a hierarchical blockchain framework with a main blockchain and multiple subchains to manage model updates and model sharing records in a secure, scalable and flexible manner.
- For model training subchains, we design a PoV consensus scheme to filter out unreliable model updates by allowing miners to collaboratively verify the quality of model updates for secure BFEL.
- We propose a gradient compression scheme to improve the communication efficiency of BFEL without compromising learning accuracy, and also to enhance privacy preservation by mitigating inference attacks.

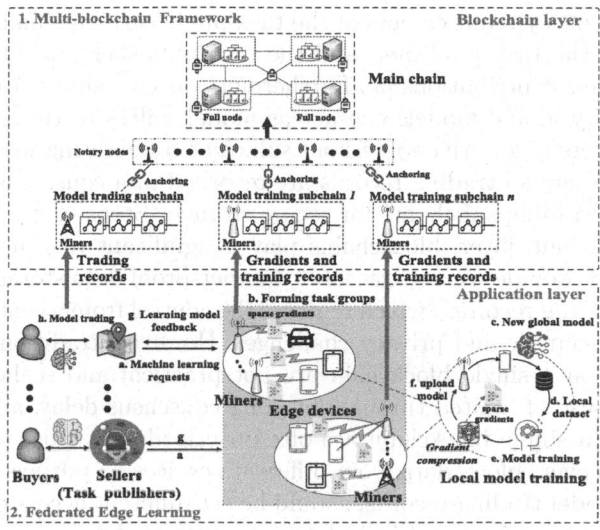

Fig. 1. The proposed federated edge learning framework with multi-blockchain.

2 Scalable Blockchain Framework for Decentralized FEL

2.1 Multi-blockchains for Secure Federated Edge Learning

As shown in Fig. 1, the considered federated edge learning system includes an application layer and a blockchain layer. In the application layer, each task publisher, e.g., a map company, sets a learning task (e.g., traffic prediction) and sends the collaborative machine learning request to nearby wireless communication infrastructures, e.g., RoadSide Units (RSUs) in vehicular networks or base stations in cellular networks (Step a in Fig. 1) [3,10]. These infrastructures broadcast the learning task to edge devices with suitable data (e.g., vehicles or smart phones). Legitimate edge devices can join in a task group and act as workers to train the learning task on their local datasets (Step b). Each dataset is generated from personal applications (e.g., navigation services) or collected from surroundings (e.g., sensors on vehicles). Each worker trains a given global model from its task publisher, and generates local model updates (Steps c, d, e). Considering large communication overhead of transmitting local model updates to miners, a gradient compression scheme is performed to transform the model updates into compressed model updates with sparse gradients (more details are given in Sect. 4). Here, the miners can be pre-selected RSUs or base stations to establish a consortium blockchain called "Model training subchain". Next, the workers upload their compressed model updates to the miners for model quality evaluation. After executing Proof-of-Verifying (PoV) consensus scheme (introduced in Sect. 3), the qualified model updates are included into a new block and stored in a model training subchain (Step f). Finally, the workers download the latest block data and calculate a new global model for the next iterations till meeting the accuracy requirements of the task publisher. The final global model is sent back to the task publisher, and the task publisher rewards the workers according to their contributions [3]. Furthermore, after training, task publishers with high-quality global models can act as model sellers to trade their models with model buyers (e.g., drivers) without sufficient cooperating workers or training budget. The model trading records are recorded in a consortium blockchain named "Model trading subchain" for secure storage (Steps g, h).

In the blockchain layer, blockchains play a significant role in the federated edge learning to provide secure, traceable, tamper-proof data storage (i.e., model updates and trading records), which removes the control from a centralized server suffering from security and privacy challenges. However, traditional blockchain systems based on a single blockchain are not practical and scalable for large-scale FEL because of limited throughput, long consensus delay, and large block size. Miners in a single blockchain are often overloaded because of constrained resources. Moreover, block data from different services or purposes, e.g., model training and model trading records, should be set different access permission for different entities, and is stored in isolation to protect data privacy [9]. To this end, we propose a multi-blockchain system including consortium blockchain-based subchains and a public blockchain-based main chain.

Specifically, by treating model updates as "transactions" between workers and task publishers, local model updates of workers and workers' contributions are securely stored in their corresponding model training subchains [9]. Each subchain is only accessible for a task publisher and its participating workers. Meanwhile, to enable secure and reliable model trading, the model trading records should be kept as tamper-proof records in the model trading subchain. Only the task publishers and their model buyers can access and obtain block data in this subchain. For different subchains, miners are randomly chosen from communication infrastructures with sufficient computation and storage resources to execute efficient consensus algorithms (e.g., DPoS and PBFT), respectively. These miners will be changed after each consensus round to reduce the effects of possible collusion among the miners. The miner selection schemes are out of scope here, but can refer to related work in [11].

To efficiently monitor all subchains and miner behaviors, all the subchains should be anchored to the main chain after a time interval for effective governance. To solve the trust problem among blockchains, the block data in the individual subchains can be easily verified by following the notary mechanism in [9,12]. The main chain periodically stores the Merkle tree root of the block data from different subchains, not the original bock data on the subchains for privacy protection and saving storage resources. This means that the main chain only manages and maintains network addresses of model updates and model trading records. The model buyers can search global models by the latest block data in the main chain, and thus send trading requests to finish the model trading. In short, compared with traditional single blockchain-based systems, the proposed framework can achieve: i) data privacy protection by setting access permission on individual subchains and ii) performance isolation through individual consensus algorithms. Each individual subchain maintains its own data locally, and all the subchains are anchored to the main blockchain periodically for publicly verifiable integrity of subchains as well as ensuring scalability and flexibility.

2.2 Attack Model for Federated Edge Learning

Although federated learning can solve data privacy issues to a certain extent, it is subject to new security threats, such as: i) poisoning attack and ii) inference attack. For poisoning attack, malicious edge devices may intentionally send malicious, poisonous or low-quality model updates to poison the global model, thus misleading model training process and increasing the probability of incorrect learning results [3]. The poisoning attacks degrade the accuracy of learning tasks, increase the convergence time of the global model, and the probability of erroneous learning results. For inference attack, recent studies have shown that a compromised central server (i.e., parameter server) can infer underlying training data by analyzing shared local gradients from edge devices when using gradient-based reconstruction. This intrudes the data privacy of edge devices illegally and silently [7,13]. This attack is becoming more serious because more entities may obtain shared gradients in blockchain-based federated learning systems. Therefore, it is important to defend against the poisoning attack and inference attack for secure and privacy-enhanced federated edge learning [3,7].

3   Proof-of-Verifying Consensus Scheme for Training Subchain

In this paper, inspired by the Delegated Proof-of-Stake (DPoS) consensus algorithm, we propose an efficient consensus scheme named Proof-of-Verifying (PoV) that integrates model updates and quality evaluation into the consensus process, which can defend against poisoning attacks and achieve secure model update and storage. The main steps involved in PoT are as follows.

- Step 1: Initialization: We adopt an elliptic curve digital signature algorithm and asymmetric cryptography for communication initialization in the system [21]. A Global Trust Authority (GTA) joins in the proposed PoV to perform identity verification and key manager. Each legitimate entity generates public & private keys and corresponding certificates for information encryption and decryption after passing GTA's checking.
- Step 2: Miner joining: Communication infrastructures send joining requests and submit their resource and identity-related information to the GTA. The GTA will verify the validity of the communication infrastructures based on records of historical behaviors. Only legitimate, reliable and resource-rich communication infrastructures can be miner candidates to establish subchains. The workers vote for their miner candidates. The candidates with high votes are chosen as delegates and join into a miner group with a randomly selected leader and other miners acting as verifiers. The verifiers will

execute quality evaluation of local model updates (described in Step 3). Meanwhile, the leader miner is responsible for aggregating all qualified local model updates and generating pending block. After each round of consensus, for the sake of safety, the leader and the verifiers will be changed randomly. Similar to DPoS, all miners should submit a deposit to a shared account under public supervision [21]. If a miner has malicious behaviors during PoV consensus process or causes damage to the global model, the blockchain system will confiscate the deposit and remove the miner.

- *Step 3: Quality evaluation of local model updates:* After finishing a local model training process, each worker (i.e., participating edge device) executes the gradient compression scheme to generate compressed local model updates. More details about the gradient compression scheme are given in Sect. 4. Then the worker sends its compressed model update to the nearest miner on the corresponding model training subchain. This miner (i.e., verifier) first evaluates the quality of the compressed model updates from nearby workers by using a testing dataset. This small testing dataset is verified and provided by the task publisher in each model training subchain, which is considered as a reliable dataset for verifying the training model. Only the qualified model updates, whose accuracy is higher than a given threshold, are picked up to store in a pending block later. The thresholds can be adjusted according to security requirements of different task publishers. In this way, the model evaluation can prevent poisoning attacks incurred by malicious participants, thus improving security of the proposed BFEL framework [4].

- *Step 4: Consensus process:* For mutual monitoring, the verifiers broadcast their model updates and verification results with signatures to each other for double-checking. Each verifier then compares the verification results with those of other miners, and sends the comparison results as a response to current leader miner for aggregation. The response includes qualified model updates, comparison results, a digital signature, and timestamp. The leader receives all the qualified local model updates and verifier responses, thus put them into a pending block and broadcasts this pending block to all verifiers. If and only if more than $\frac{2}{3}$ of verifiers agree on the pending block of this round of model updates, this block data will be added into the model training subchain and synchronized among the all the miners.

- *Step 5: Updating training model:* All the workers download the new block data from their corresponding subchains, and calculate the average of all qualified local model updates as their new global models, respectively. The workers will use the new global model for the next training iteration.

4   Gradient Compression Scheme for Communication-Efficient BFEL

In blockchain-empowered federated edge learning, workers need to send a large amount of gradient information (i.e., local model update parameters) to miners for aggregating model updates in each training iteration. The workers not only bear large communication overhead, but also suffer from the inference attack when sharing gradients. However, previous studies have shown that the sparseness degree of gradient is generally high, so only a few important gradients (i.e., gradients with large absolute values) have a positive effect on the accuracy of the model [13]. Inspired by this, we propose a gradient compression scheme to achieve communication-efficient and secure BFEL. Here, only the important gradients (with large absolute values) are uploaded to the miners to reduce the communication overhead. The importance of a gradient is indicated by its magnitude. Only the gradients, whose absolute values are larger than a given threshold, are transmitted. To maintain model performance, the gradient compression scheme utilizes the techniques of momentum correction and local gradient clipping on top of the gradient sparsification to ensure no loss of accuracy [7]. As a result, the gradient compression scheme not only reduces communication bandwidth problems by gradient sparsification (i.e., compressing the gradients), but also relieves the inference attack problems by only sharing limited gradient information [7, 13].

More specifically, the workers only send a part of gradients with large absolute values to their miners. To avoid information loss caused by gradient sparsification, the rest of gradients are stored in local buffer space of workers, and accumulated locally till becoming large enough to be uploaded [7]. Here, we use distributed stochastic gradient descent for iterative updates, and define the loss function to be optimized as follows [7, 14]:

$$F(\omega) = \frac{1}{D_k} \sum_{x \in D_k} f(x, \omega), \tag{1}$$

$$\omega_{t+1} = \omega_t - \eta \frac{1}{Nb} \sum_{k=1}^{N} \sum_{x \in \mathcal{B}_{k,t}} \nabla f(x, \omega_t), \tag{2}$$

where $F(\omega)$ is the loss function, $f(x, \omega)$ is the loss calculated from data sample $x \in D_k$ for workers, and ω is the weight of the neural network. The learning rate is denoted as η, and $\mathcal{B}_{k,t}$ is a sequence of N mini-batches sampled from D_k for the t-th round of training ($1 \leq k < N$), and b is size of each local data sample.

Note that the model convergence time will be affected when the sparsification degree of gradients reaches a large value, e.g., 99% [7]. To address the convergence problem, we employ a momentum correction mechanism proposed in [7, 14] to mitigate this effect. Using the momentum correction mechanism, the accumulated small gradients for each worker converge toward the direction of the gradients with a larger absolute value, thus accelerating the model convergence speed. Moreover, we also apply gradient clipping mechanism to overcome gradient explosion. Specifically, by following [14], the gradient clipping is executed locally before adding current gradients to the previous local gradient accumulation, thus the gradient explosion problem is alleviated [14, 15].

We prove the gradient compression scheme has no impact on the model convergence as follows [14]. We define $g^{(i)}$ as the i-th gradient, and $u^{(i)}$ is the sum of the gradients using the optimization algorithm in [2]. $v^{(i)}$ represents the sum of the gradients accumulated in local buffer space, and m is the ratio of the remaining gradients to all gradients. If the i-th gradient does not exceed threshold until the $(t-1)$-th iteration and triggers the model update, we have:

$$u_{t-1}^{(i)} = m^{t-2} g_1^{(i)} + \cdots + m g_{t-2}^{(i)} + g_{t-1}^{(i)}, \tag{3}$$

$$v_{t-1}^{(i)} = \left(1 + \cdots + m^{t-2}\right) g_1^{(i)} + \cdots + (1+m) g_{t-2}^{(i)} + g_{t-1}^{(i)}, \tag{4}$$

thus we can update $\omega_t^{(i)} = w_1^{(i)} - \eta \times v_{t-1}^{(i)}$ and set $v_{t-1}^{(i)} = 0$. If the i-th gradient is larger than the threshold at the t-th iteration, model update is triggered, then we have:

$$u_t^{(i)} = m^{t-1} g_1^{(i)} + \cdots + m g_{t-1}^{(i)} + g_t^{(i)}, \tag{5}$$

$$v_t^{(i)} = m^{t-1} g_1^{(i)} + \cdots + m g_{t-1}^{(i)} + g_t^{(i)}. \tag{6}$$

Next, we can obtain,

$$\begin{aligned}
\omega_{t+1}^{(i)} = \omega_t^{(i)} - \eta \times v_t^{(i)} &= \omega_1^{(i)} - \eta \times \left[\left(1 + \cdots + m^{t-1}\right) g_1^{(i)} + \cdots + (1+m) g_{t-1}^{(i)} + g_t^{(i)}\right] \\
&= w_1^{(i)} - \eta \times v_{t-1}^{(i)}.
\end{aligned} \tag{7}$$

Therefore, the result of using the local gradient accumulation is consistent with the usage effect of the optimization algorithm in [2]. The detailed implementation of the gradient compression scheme is given in Algorithm 1 with the following phases:

– **Phase 1: Local Model Training:** The workers train their local models on their own local datasets with momentum correction and local gradient clipping mechanisms. These mechanisms can solve the learning convergence and gradient explosion problems, respectively.
– **Phase 2: Gradient Compression:** Each worker executes the gradient compression process in Algorithm 1 to compress the gradients and upload sparse gradients (i.e., **only the gradients whose absolute values larger than a threshold are transmitted**) to the nearby miner. Note that the workers send the remaining local gradients in their buffer space to the nearby miner when the local gradient accumulation is greater than the threshold.
– **Phase 3: Gradient Aggregation:** The miner verifies and aggregates sparse gradients from local workers. Finally, the qualified gradients from all workers are put into a block, and then both the miners and the workers can obtain a new global model from the new block data in their corresponding model training subchains.

5   Security Analysis and Numerical Results

5.1   Security Analysis

Blockchain-Related Issues: The proposed decentralized federated learning framework with multi-blockchains is secure and reliable due to the following

---

Algorithm 1: Gradient compression scheme.

Input: A set of workers $\mathcal{N} = \{n_1, n_2, \cdots, n_i\}$, B is the local mini-batch size, D_k is the local dataset, η is the learning rate, and the optimization function SGD.

Output: ω.

1 Initialize ω_t;
2 $g^k \leftarrow 0$;
3 **for** $t = 0, 1, \cdots$ **do**
4     $g_t^k \leftarrow g_{t-1}^k$;
5   **for** $i = 1, 2, \cdots$ **do**
6   Sample data x from D_k;
7        $g_t^k \leftarrow g_t^k + \frac{1}{NB} \nabla f(x; \omega_t)$;

8   **if** *Gradient Clipping* **then**
9        $g_t^k \leftarrow$ Local_Gradient_Clipping (g_t^k);

10   **foreach** $g_t^{k_j} \in \{g_t^k\}$ *and* $j = 1, 2, \cdots$ **do**
11   Thr $\leftarrow |\text{Top } \rho\% \text{ of } \{g_t^k\}|$;
12   **if** $|g_t^{k_j}| > $ Thr **then**
13   Send this gradient to the nearby miner;
14   Send the remaining gradients to the buffer space of the worker;

15   **else if** *When accumulated local gradient* $>$ Thr **then**
16   Send this gradient to the nearby miner;

17   All-reduce $g_t^k : g_t \leftarrow \sum_{k=1}^{N} (\text{sparse } \tilde{g}_t^k)$;
18       $\omega_{t+1} \leftarrow$ SGD (ω_t, g_t).

19 **return** ω.

---

reasons: (I) The proposed BFEL framework can defend against traditional security attacks by standard cryptographic methods including asymmetric and symmetric key-based encryption, and digital signature schemes. (II) The hierarchical blockchain framework provides flexible authority control. The consortium blockchain-based subchains are established on authorized infrastructures with different access permissions according to security requirements and configuration. The model training subchains are isolated based on different federated learning tasks. Only authorized edge devices and miners can access their corresponding model training subchains. The model trading subchain is accessible for model buyers and sellers. The main chain based on public blockchain is open access for all the entities to check and monitor model training records and model training information. This framework enables performance isolation that each individual subchain maintains its own data locally without privacy concerns. All the subchains are anchored to the main blockchain periodically for publicly verifiable integrity of subchains. (III) Similar to the DPoS consensus algorithm, the proposed Proof-of-Verifying scheme is secure and reliable as long as the number of malicious miners does not exceed $\frac{1}{3}$ of the total number of miners [4]. The malicious miners will be punished and their deposit confiscated (mentioned in

Step 2 of the PoV consensus scheme), which deters the malicious behaviors of miners. (IV) The local model update records and model training records are secure because of tamper-proof, decentralization and traceability properties of blockchain technologies [16–18].

Federated Learning-Related Issues: With the help of PoV consensus scheme, both the local model updates and global model updates are reliable and secure for federated edge learning. The reason is that, for the i-th round of local model updates, miners will mutually verify the quality of the local model updates using a given testing dataset, and remove poisonous local model updates that may damage the global model. Only the high-quality model updates are added into model training subchains to generate a new and reliable global model for the next iteration. Therefore, the PoV consensus scheme can defend against poisoning attacks and ensure secure decentralized federated edge learning. Moreover, the gradients from workers contains the distribution of local training data. For inference attacks, the attackers analyze this distribution information and reconstruct the training data according to shared gradients by reverse engineering [7]. Thereby, we can utilize the gradient compression scheme to generate sparse gradients, and upload these gradients to the miners without compromising learning accuracy. Using this approach, we can prevent the attackers from obtaining the complete distribution of local training data, which can reduce gradient privacy issues during decentralized model learning. As a result, the gradient compression scheme not only improves the communication efficiency of BFEL, but also relieves inference attacks caused by gradient leakage problems.

5.2 Numerical Results

We evaluate the performance of the proposed BFEL framework and schemes by using real-world datasets including MNIST and CIFAR-10. The datasets are uniformly divided into a training set including 70% data and the rest data is included in a test set. We implement the proposed BFEL framework using Pytorch, PySyft, and a blockchain platform named EOSIO with DPoS scheme [3, 21], The experiment is conducted on a virtual workstation with the Ubuntu 18.04 operating system, Intel (R) Core (TM) i7-4500U CPU, 16 GB RAM, 512 GB SSD. There exist 2 task publishers, 22 miners, 20 workers, and also a model trading subchain and 2 model training subchains in the simulation. All of the subchains apply the DPoS scheme as their consensus algorithms.

In our Blockchain-based Federated Edge Learning (BFEL) framework, the gradient compression scheme plays an important role for system performance. We first evaluate effects of a hyperparameter ρ (i.e., the threshold of gradient absolute value in Algorithm 1) for the BFEL. A simple Convolutional Neural Network (CNN) network (i.e., CNN with 2 convolutional layers followed by 1 fully connected layer) is used to perform the classification tasks on MNIST and CIFAR-10 datasets, respectively. The pixels in all datasets are normalized into range of [0,1]. In the simulation, we take a model training subchain with 10 workers and 11 miners as an example. The learning rate is $\eta = 0.001$, and the training epoch is $E = 1000$. The mini-batch size is $B = 128$, and θ is set as 0.05. We compare the performance of different ρ thresholds for the learning accuracy, and thus find out the best threshold of the gradient compression scheme in our simulation.

Specifically, ρ takes value from the set $\{0.1, 0.2, 0.3, 0.5, 0.9, 1, 100\}$ to carry out simulation on the MNIST and CIFAR-10 datasets to observe the best threshold of the gradient compression scheme. As shown in Fig. 2, we observe that the larger ρ leads to the better accuracy performance of the proposed framework. For the MNIST task, the results demonstrate that the accuracy is 97.25% when $\rho = 0.3$, and the accuracy is 99.08% when $\rho = 100$. This means that although the gradient size has been raised more than 300 times as compared with $\rho = 0.3$, the learning accuracy is only improved 1.83% than that of $\rho = 0.3$. Furthermore, we observe a trade-off between the gradient threshold and accuracy. Therefore, to achieve the trade-off between the gradient threshold and the learning accuracy, we set $\rho = 0.3$ as the best threshold of the gradient compression scheme.

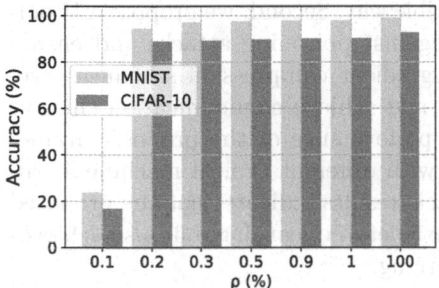
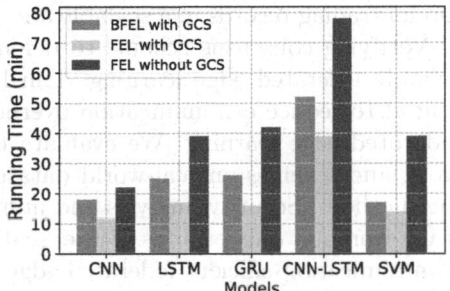

Fig. 2. The accuracy of BFEL framework with different gradient thresholds ρ.

Fig. 3. Comparison of communication efficiency in different scenarios and models.

For the communication efficiency of the BFEL framework, we compare the BFEL framework with the Gradient Compression Scheme (GCS) with the traditional centralized FEL framework with or without GCS. We apply typical CNN, Long Short-Term Memory (LSTM), Gate Recurrent Unit (GRU), CNN-LSTM, and Support Machine Vector (SVM) methods with an identical simulation configuration. For these methods, CNN is running on MNIST dataset to execute an image classification task, and the rest of methods are running on a power demand dataset with time series data to perform power consumption prediction task [19]. The gradient threshold ρ of the GCS is set as 0.3. Similar to DPoS in EOSIO platform, the consensus time of PoV scheme in each round is set as 0.5 s for the BEFL framework [20]. Considering the communication overhead of each round as a fixed value, we compare the running time of the above methods in three scenarios (i.e., BFEL with GCS, FEL with or without GCS) to indicate the communication efficiency. As shown in Fig. 3, we observe that the running time of FEL framework with GCS is less 50% than that of FEL without GCS.

The reason is that GCS can reduce the number of gradients exchanged between the workers and the cloud aggregator. Since there exists delay caused by PoV scheme in BFEL, the running time of BFEL framework with GCS in different scenarios is higher than that of FEL with GCS, but much lower than that of FEL without GCS. Moreover, the BFEL framework with GCS can defend against poisoning attacks by the PoV scheme and remove the centralization security challenges by blockchain technology. Furthermore, GCS can compress the gradient size by 300 times with almost no reduction in accuracy. Therefore, the proposed BEFL framework is more secure, communication-efficient and practical in real-world applications.

6   Conclusions

In this paper, we propose BFEL, a scalable, communication-efficient, blockchain-based framework for federated edge learning. First, we introduce a hierarchical blockchain framework with multiple blockchains to manage training models and model trading records in a scalable and flexible way. Second, we propose a Proof-of-Verifying consensus scheme to defend against poisoning attacks and ensure reliable federated edge learning. Third, a gradient compression scheme is presented to reduce communication overhead and achieve communication-efficient federated edge learning. We evaluate the performance of the proposed framework and schemes on real-world datasets with different typical machine learning methods. Security analysis and numerical results indicate that the proposed framework not only ensures secure, scalable federated learning, but also achieves communication-efficient federated edge learning.

Acknowledgments. This research is supported by the National Research Foundation (NRF), Singapore, under Singapore Energy Market Authority (EMA), Energy Resilience, NRF2017EWT-EP003-041, NRF2015-NRF-ISF001-2277, Singapore NRF National Satellite of Excellence, Design Science and Technology for Secure Critical Infrastructure NSoE DeST-SCI2019-0007, A*STAR-NTU-SUTD Joint Research Grant on AI for the Future of Manufacturing RGANS1906, Wallenberg AI, Autonomous Systems and Software Program and NTU under grant M4082187 (4080), Alibaba Group through Alibaba Innovative Research (AIR) Program and Alibaba-NTU Singapore Joint Research Institute (JRI), NTU, Singapore, and also the National Natural Science Foundation of China (Grant 61872310) and the Shenzhen Basic Research Funding Scheme (JCYJ20170818103849343), the Open Fund of Hubei Key Laboratory of Transportation Internet of Things, China (No. WHUTIOT-2019005), and the Open Research Project of the State Key Laboratory of Industrial Control Technology, Zhejiang University, China (No. ICT20044).

References

1. Zhou, Z., Chen, X., et al.: Edge intelligence: paving the last mile of artificial intelligence with edge computing. Proc. IEEE **107**(8), 1738–1762 (2019)

2. Konecnỳ, J., McMahan, H.B., et al.: "Federated learning: strategies for improving communication efficiency." arXiv preprint arXiv:1610.05492 (2016)
3. Kang, J., Xiong, Z., Niyato, D., Xie, S., Zhang, J.: Incentive mechanism for reliable federated learning: a joint optimization approach to combining reputation and contract theory. IEEE Internet Things J. **6**(6), 10700–10714 (2019)
4. Li, Y., Chen, C., et al.: "A blockchain-based decentralized federated learning framework with committee consensus. arXiv preprint arXiv:2004.00773 (2020)
5. Kim, H., Park, J., Bennis, M., Kim, S.: Blockchained on-device federated learning. IEEE Commun. Lett. **24**, 1279–1283 (2020)
6. Lu, Y., Huang, X., et al.: Blockchain empowered asynchronous federated learning for secure data sharing in internet of vehicles. IEEE Trans. Veh. Technol. **69**(4), 4298–4311 (2020)
7. Zhu, L., Liu, Z., Han, S.: Deep leakage from gradients. In: Advances in Neural Information Processing Systems, pp. 14747–14756 (2019)
8. Alistarh, D., Grubic, D., et al.: "QSGD: communication-efficient SGD via gradient quantization and encoding. In: Advances in Neural Information Processing Systems, pp. 1709–1720 (2017)
9. Weber, I., Lu, Q., Tran, A.B., et al.: "A platform architecture for multi-tenant blockchain-based systems." In: 2019 ICSA, pp. 101–110. IEEE (2019)
10. Liu, Y., Yu, J.J.Q., et al.: Privacy-preserving traffic flow prediction: a federated learning approach. IEEE Internet Things J. (2020, in press)
11. Zheng, Z., Xie, S., Dai, H., et al.: An overview of blockchain technology: architecture, consensus, and future trends. In: 2017 BigData congress, pp. 557–564. IEEE (2017)
12. Wang, R., Ye, K., Xu, C.-Z.: Performance benchmarking and optimization for blockchain systems: a survey. In: Joshi, J., Nepal, S., Zhang, Q., Zhang, L.-J. (eds.) ICBC 2019. LNCS, vol. 11521, pp. 171–185. Springer, Cham (2019). https://doi.org/10.1007/978-3-030-23404-1_12
13. Wei, W., Liu, L., Loper, M., et al.: "A framework for evaluating gradient leakage attacks in federated learning." arXiv preprint arXiv:2004.10397 (2020)
14. Lin, Y., Han, S., Mao, H., et al.: Deep gradient compression: reducing the communication bandwidth for distributed training. arXiv preprint arXiv:1712.01887 (2017)
15. Wangni, J., Wang, J., Liu, J., Zhang, T.: "Gradient sparsification for communication-efficient distributed optimization." In: Advances in Neural Information Processing Systems, pp. 1299–1309 (2018)
16. Dai, H.-N., Zheng, Z., Zhang, Y.: Blockchain for internet of things: a survey. IEEE Internet Things J. **6**(5), 8076–8094 (2019)
17. Zheng, Z., Xie, S., Dai, H.-N., et al.: Blockchain challenges and opportunities: a survey. Int. J. Web Grid Serv. **14**(4), 352–375 (2018)
18. Huang, Y., Kong, Q., et al.: Recommending differentiated code to support smart contract update. In: 2019 IEEE/ACM ICPC, pp. 260–270 (2019)
19. http://archive.ics.uci.edu/ml/datasets/Individual+household+electric+power+consumption
20. https://developers.eos.io/welcome/latest/protocol/consensus_protocol
21. Kang, J., Xiong, Z., Niyato, D., Ye, D., Kim, D.I., Zhao, J.: Toward secure blockchain-enabled internet of vehicles: optimizing consensus management using reputation and contract theory. IEEE Trans. Veh. Technol. **68**(3), 2906–2920 (2019)

PoW-Based Sybil Attack Resistant Model for P2P Reputation Systems

Biaoqi Li[1], Xiaodong Fu[1,2]($\boxtimes$), Kun Yue[3], Li Liu[1,2], Lijun Liu[1,2], and Yong Feng[1,2]

[1] Yunnan Provincial Key Laboratory of Computer Technology Application, Kunming 650500, China
xiaodong_fu@hotmail.com
[2] Faculty of Information Engineering and Automation, Kunming University of Science and Technology, Kunming 650500, China
[3] School of Information Science and Engineering, Yunnan University, Kunming 650091, China

Abstract. Peer-to-peer and other distributed systems are known particularly vulnerable to Sybil attack, so is P2P reputation systems. Reputation helps users to make better decisions in P2P systems, but Sybil attacker can obtain multiple identities and pretends to be multiple. It can control more than "one vote" to let others' reputation change just as the attacker wants. This paper presents a Sybil attacker resistant model for P2P reputation systems by introducing multiple rounds of PoW (Proof-of-Work) verification and dynamic difficulty adjustment. A savvy attacker usually doesn't carry out attacks without positive returns, so we minimize the expected profit of attackers through the using of puzzles. The costs and benefits are quantified as effectiveness in our model. We explore the effectiveness in two types of comparison, one is in dynamic or static difficulty adjustment, the other is executing once or multiple rounds of verification, and show the effectiveness of our model both analytically and experimentally.

Keywords: Sybil attack · P2P · Proof of work · Reputation system · Puzzle verification

1 Introduction

Peer-to-peer (P2P) systems generally employ reputation metric to help users to make good choices in many different resources or services. However, P2P as a type of identity-based system are vulnerable to those identity-management related attacks. For example, impersonation is a well-known attack that malicious peer portrays itself as another peer. Furthermore, attacker can also create multiple identities and use them in concert to defeat the system. This type of attack is Sybil attack [1, 2].

Sybil attack is an identity-based attack in distributed system. Sybil attacker can create many fake identities to manipulate target peer's rating score or reputation value in P2P reputation system. For example, attacker can interact with the target peer in multiple times through many fake identity peers. To improve target peer's reputation value, each fake peer will give it positive reviews. The higher reputation will provide more future requests to the target peer. That will destroy the reputation system of P2P network.

© Springer Nature Singapore Pte Ltd. 2020
Z. Zheng et al. (Eds.): BlockSys 2020, CCIS 1267, pp. 166–177, 2020.
https://doi.org/10.1007/978-981-15-9213-3_13

How to effectively resist Sybil attack becomes an important problem. This problem can be mitigated by two main types of methods, called resources proofing and behavior detecting. Resource proofing requires peer performing a task which a single entity could not complete in a certain time. Behavior detecting such as *SybilGuard* [3] and *SybilLimit* [4] detects suspected peers through relationship network or graph theory, and isolates these peers with normal peers to eliminate the effect of attacker. Therefore, behavior detecting usually depends on specific scenarios, and resources proofing is more suitable to P2P reputation systems under general scenarios.

Considering how to suppress Sybil attack from the source, we envisage making the attack uneconomical to attacker. In other words, it is to minimize the effectiveness of Sybil attack. Given that behavior detecting takes effect after the attack and relies on specific scenarios, we employ resource proofing to minimize attacker's effectiveness. In this paper, we introduce a robust task for verification before the identity of peer is accepted by system, and we design a multiple-round verification mechanism to further decrease the effectiveness of Sybil attack.

The contribution of this paper can be summarized as follows.

- We explore the problem of resisting Sybil attack in P2P reputation system by introducing proof-of-work, and verify the effectiveness through experiment and theoretical analysis.
- We propose a verification model with dynamical-adjust difficulty. Let the verification time change dynamically with the current reputation of peer, that will give a stronger constrain to attacker.
- We evaluate the performance with different parameter settings of our resistant model.

The rest of paper is organized as follows. In Sect. 2 we review related work. In Sect. 3 we introduce the methods used in this model and illustrate our model with formal proof and flow diagram. In Sect. 4 we show our experimental study and comparison of methods. In Sect. 5 we conclude and discuss the future work.

2 Related Work

Sybil attack generally aims at tampering reputation value of the target peer in reputation system. Due to its identity-based feature, existing methods can only suppress rational attacker who consider the benefits of attack. It is difficult to be completely defended, so our goal is to minimize the impact of the attack. The methods to resist Sybil attack in distributed systems can be divided into two categories, one is registration strategy, the other is authentication strategy.

1. Registration strategy. Centralized certificate requires a trusted third party as a certificate authority (CA) to issue certificates to peers before they participant in the system. It ensures each peer in the system is a single entity. CA may also require proof of real-world identity to ensure that each peer receives only one system identifier, perhaps use credit card verification [5]. These solutions are necessarily centralized. They are difficult to scale up due to their high maintenance cost. Centralized network structure is vulnerable to single point attack or single point failure [6]. Resource proofing

referred by John R. Douceur [1] can be classified in registration strategies, when peer only be required to proof during registration. Pradhan. S [7] proposed a security framework based on blockchain for P2P file sharing system. They use miners of blockchain to monitor peers' activity and record the activity logs in blockchain. That means all of the activity logs open to every peer and no one can tamper them. If attacker try to implement Sybil attack, the abnormal activity will be discovered by any peer in system. E. Friedman [8] introduced deposits or admission fee in registration part. Deposits will be refunded when the peer has no bad history record. The registration process will bring a huge cost, and weaken attacker's motivation to continue attacking.

2. Authentication strategy. Haifeng Yu [2] proposed *SybilGuard* based on social network. They use characteristics that malicious peer can create many identities but few trust relationships, then the graph between the Sybil peers and normal peers could be cut to separate the effect of attacker. Haifeng Yu also proposed improve version of *SybilGuard* named *SybilLimit* [3]. It uses graphs to represent social network features to further limiting the number of Sybil peers. Tianyu Gao [9] detected Sybil peers by using content-based method with deep learning technology in online social networks. Martin Byrenheid [10] proposed a leader election algorithm to distinguish between Sybil peers and normal peers. G. Danezis [11] combined social networks and Bayesian theory to come up with *SybilInfer*. Given the relationship structure between peers, they use Bayes to mark peers as honest or dishonest. These authentication models try to defend against the attack by detecting Sybil peers during or after the Sybil attack.

Due to respective characteristics, current Sybil attack resistant models have some incompatibilities with P2P reputation systems under general scenarios. For example, centralized methods will encounter problems of scalability and single point failure. Behavior detecting requires specific scenarios such as social network. In this paper, we consider that how to resist the attack for general P2P reputation system. Providing a higher cost of psychological expectation can largely suppress the attack from the source, so we can take some mechanisms to make the attack less economical.

The effectiveness of any solution relies on a cost scale like time or money. An adversary with infinite resources can compromise any property [6]. For example, if Sybil attacker owns infinite resources, it can tamper any peer's reputation no matter how high cost in registration process, but the vast majority of attackers are rational to attack. To make Sybil attack uneconomical and resist the attack with registration strategy, one idea is to verify the legitimacy by requiring peers to complete tasks that consume resources. Due to Sybil attacker controlling many Sybil peers in system, the total cost for each peer to complete the task will be very large. The task can be a storage puzzle or a computational puzzle. Storage puzzle like requiring peers to store a large amount of unique, uncompressible data, and computational puzzle need to compute a time-consuming problem like math or cryptography problem. They both demand peer to spend storage space or computing power to proof it is not a fake identity. Although resource tests cannot eliminate Sybil attack altogether [12], we can employ it to substantially reduce the impact of Sybil attack.

3 Preliminaries

In P2P systems, there are many services or resources to choose. The reputation based on members' rating to help users making good choices. Higher reputation means better services or resources, it is also the purpose of Sybil attacker.

Formally, we consider a P2P file sharing model with a Sybil attacker. The resource providers are defined as a finite set $P = \{p_1, p_2, \ldots\}$, and receivers are defined as a finite set $R = \{r_1, r_2, \ldots\}$. Each peer in the system can be either provider or receiver. The set of Sybil attacker is $S = \{s_A, s_1, s_2, \ldots, s_n\}$, s_A is attacker, and $s_1, s_2, \ldots, s_n$ are Sybil peers controlled by s_A. n is less than the total number of peers in the system. We assume that the cost of s_A to manage an attack with $s_1, s_2, \ldots, s_n$ is C, and the benefit of s_A is B. The best expectation of s_A is making B as large as possible, and making C as small as possible. In order to quantify the effect of s_A, here we define an effectiveness function:

$$E_A = \frac{B}{C} \tag{1}$$

As E_A increasing, the attack will be more effective. However, our purpose is to decrease E_A. There are two ways to achieve that, one is promoting C, the other is reducing B. For registration strategies, most of existing puzzle-based methods only implement one-time verification. That means $s_1, s_2, \ldots, s_n$ only spend one-time cost, and the cost can be shared in future benefits of attack. Margolin [13] pointed that charging a recurring fee for each participating identity is quantitatively more effective than charging a one-time fee. Therefore, if it wants to improve C to enlarge the cost of s_A, we need to use a multi-round solution instead of a single round solution. For reducing B, behavior detecting can find $s_A, s_1, s_2, \ldots, s_n$ and their relationships to limit B of s_A. However, these methods depend on specific scenarios, and are not suitable for general P2P systems. Here we need to consider an improved puzzle-based method to minimize E_A of s_A. In other words, we need to find possible B and C that satisfies function E to reach the possible minimum value m:

$$m = \underset{B,C}{\arg\min} \frac{B}{C} \tag{2}$$

4 PoW-Based Sybil Attack Resistant Model

Jochen Dinger [14] referred when there are no resource consuming proofs, there is no verification counterpart, and peer's identity cannot be verified. Dewan [15] also pointed out that we can resist Sybil attack by making the identity generation extremely resource intensive, such that the peer cannot afford to generate multiple identities. We need to employ resource consuming puzzle to prevent one entity to create multiple fake identities. John R. Douceur [1] pointed out, the puzzle used to verify peer's identity should satisfied the following two principles.

- The puzzle must be issued to all identities simultaneously.
- The puzzle is difficult to solve and easy to verify.

Storage verification requires peers store a large amount of unique, uncompressible data to defend Sybil attacker due to resources restricting. But large amount of data will put pressure on network transmission, this will be detrimental to the efficiency of the P2P network. Computational puzzle executes calculation on local that will not bring a large load to the network. The result of calculation is just a value and easy to check it is true or not. Inspired by this decentralized verification, we think of verification methods in blockchain. Bitcoin [16] and many similar blockchains use PoW (Proof of Work) or PoS (Proof of Stake) to verify peer's workloads or shareholdings. These consensus protocols also protect the blockchain from the threat of Sybil attack [17]. Especially PoW based on hash function, ensuring peers to complete computational puzzle before they are accepted by the system. Additionally, if the puzzle is a computational puzzle, it also needs robustness that attacker can hardly crack the algorithm to reduce C. PoW aims to find target hash, it is based on SHA256 hash function which has sufficient collision resistance and unidirectionality, so that s_A can hardly crack PoW to reduce verification time.

4.1 Framework of Sybil Attack Resistant Model

We proposed a Sybil resistant verification model based on PoW. Here is the process diagram of this model (see Fig. 1).

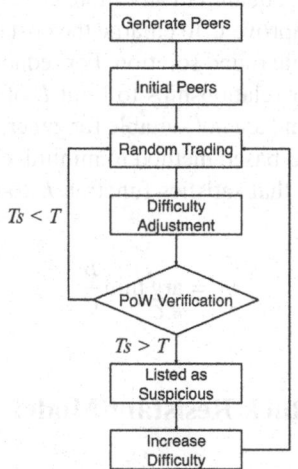

Fig. 1. Process of sybil resistant model

We use P2P filesharing system as our research object. Each peer in the system can both provide and receive files from others. Firstly, we randomly generate peers in the system. As assumed in Preliminaries, there are two set of different roles of peers in filesharing process, $P = \{p_1, p_2, \ldots\}$ and $R = \{r_1, r_2, \ldots\}$. Secondly, we initialize peers' reputation value. In order to avoid potential whitewashing attack, we need to set different initial reputation between newcomers and participants which showing good for a long time [18]. As we use boolean values as representation for reputation (if r_j download successfully, the reputation value of p_i will increase by 1, otherwise will increase by 0), and use averaging as the aggregation of reputation values [19]. The most suitable initial value is the average of 0 and 1. On the other hand, to make all peers fairly accumulate reputation from the initial value, we assume the initial reputation value of all peers is 0.5:

$$Rep_{normal} = Rep_{attacker} = Rep_{Sybil} = 0.5 \tag{3}$$

Then, peers will randomly combine into a pair to form a transaction. Each transaction has both two roles. The set of transactions of peers is $TX = \{tx_1, tx_2, \ldots\}, tx = (p_i, r_j)$. Each tx will generate a reputation value Rep from p_i to r_j. Rep will accumulate on p_i and take the average to update reputation value in real time.

As we use averaging to indicate current reputation value of peer, if a peer e participate in forming m transaction pairs as provider, in each transaction e gets $Rep_i(i = 1, 2, 3, \ldots, m)$ points of reputation value, the current reputation value of e is:

$$Rep_e = \frac{\sum_{i=1}^{m} Rep_i}{m} \tag{4}$$

It's important to quantify attack effects before evaluating the performance of resistant method, so we define E_A before to represent the effectiveness of s_A, and we assume that t_i is the average verification time for one peer, s_A will spend nt_i to complete the whole verifications. In our model, E_A is a ratio of reputation increment $\Delta Rep_{attacker}$ to verification time consumption. E_A can be equivalent to:

$$E_A = \frac{B}{C} = \frac{\Delta Rep_{attacker}}{nt_i} \tag{5}$$

As $\Delta Rep_{attacker}$ increases or t_i decreases, E_A would increase. That means effect of attack is good. On the other hand, the resistant method has a poor performance. In P2P filesharing system, $\Delta Rep_{attacker}$ as B of s_A, because the higher reputation means the more future requirements of resources from others. Reputation is positively correlated with influence, that s_A can benefit from through attack. The C of s_A is the computing power to control Sybil peers to complete verifications. To sum up, E_A indicates whether the attack is cost-effective.

Generally, C increases linearly as the number of Sybil peers increases. In order to prevent Sybil attack more effectively, we adopted multi-rounds and adaptive PoW verification.

We use PoW to perform verification simultaneously on all peers with regular interval time T, and dynamically adjust the difficulty of verification based on peer's current reputation. It can be obtained from theory analysis, that t_i increases approximately linearly with n (the number of $s_1, s_2, \ldots, s_n$ controlled by s_A), so we set different gradients of reputation value to make the difficulty of PoW increasing with reputation. Due to the purpose of s_A is improving reputation value of target peer. As the reputation increases, C is promoted, then E_A will drop to some extent. For non-Sybil peers, it only adds little time consumption in reasonable range.

The time interval T between verifications is set more than the maximum time of one-time verification. This will greatly reduce the impact on normal peers. For s_A, Sybil peers are almost impossible to complete verification during T, that causes some of Sybil peers fail to verify. These peers will be treated as suspicious peers in our model. To further increase the difficulty of Sybil peers and promote C of s_A, suspicious peers' difficulty will be raised by one unit, this will give s_A greater burden at the next round verification and form a vicious attack circle.

4.2 Theoretical Analysis of Sybil Attack Resistant Model

We will analyze this process in following part. We assumed the total number of peers in P2P file sharing system is N, the proportion of Sybil peers (including s_A) is S, t_i satisfied the puzzle function $f(d)$, d is the difficulty of verification, so the average time for s_A to complete a verification is:

$$T_s = NSt_i = NS \cdot f(d) \tag{6}$$

Considering extreme cases, t_i should satisfied:

$$f(d) \le t_i \le NS \cdot f(d) \tag{7}$$

This round for s_A, the number of Sybil peers which cannot complete verification in t_i is:

$$S_u = \left\lfloor \frac{NS \cdot f(d) - t_i}{f(d)} \right\rfloor \tag{8}$$

For suspicious peers, their difficulty will be raised one unit in next round, if their current difficulty is d, the next round difficulty is $d + 1$, the total average time spent by s_A in next round is:

$$T_s' = (NS - S_u) \cdot f(d) + S_u \cdot f(d + 1) \tag{9}$$

Compared to the average time of verification without introducing time interval, the time consumption increasing by:

$$\Delta T = T_s' - T_s = S_u(f(d + 1) - f(d)) \tag{10}$$

As the difficulty function here is PoW, it is approximately an index distribution. The same as $f(d + 1) - f(d)$, with increasing of difficulty, s_A will spend exponential time to verify Sybil peers.

For optimization function $\arg\min_{B,C} \frac{B}{C}$, considering that $0 \le B, C < \infty$, there is no certain minimum value m of E, and B is a randomly changing parameter in our model. It mainly aims to let C as large as possible in unit time. We provide a PoW-based mechanism to make C reach exponential growth. The general methods [6–8] employ one-time verification to peers, so C of these method increases linearly. Compared with them, we can achieve the possible smaller E.

Here we will analyze that why function $f(d)$ (PoW) approaches an exponential distribution. The PoW scheme we employ is based on SHA-256 which use hexadecimal representation. We assume that the Hash value has ℓ bits in total, and the difficulty of target finding is d (the first d bits of target Hash is 0). Supposing the process of find- ing the target Hash follows a uniform distribution. Then, the probability of finding the target Hash $\mathcal{H}$ is:

$$\mathcal{H} = \frac{16^{\ell-d}}{16^{\ell}} = \frac{1}{2^{4d}} \tag{11}$$

Considering extreme cases:

- Found the target Hash on the first try, it takes 1 time to search.
- Found the target Hash after going through the possible result set, it takes $2^{4\ell} - 2^{4(\ell-d)}$ times to search.

The average times of finding target Hash is $\frac{1}{2} + 2^{4\ell-1} - 2^{4(\ell-d)-1}$, Here we set the problem scale function $f(n)$, let parameter replace ℓ, n and d is a parameter restricted by: n

$$f(n) = \frac{1}{2} + 2^{4n-1} - 2^{4(n-d)-1}, d\epsilon(1,n) \tag{12}$$

So, the time complexity function $T(n)$ of PoW algorithm is:

$$T(n) = O(f(n)) = O\left(\frac{1}{2} + 2^{4n-1} - 2^{4(n-d)-1}\right) = O(2^n), d\epsilon(1,n) \tag{13}$$

Therefore, PoW is an exponential algorithm, and time scale grows exponentially with difficulty. That can provide more differences of time consumption between normal peers and Sybil attacker. On the other hand, SHA256 provide enough robustness to PoW algorithm. It is almost impossible for an attacker to reduce time consumption by cracking the PoW.

5 Experimental Study

In this section, we report our experimental results to test the effectiveness of the proposed resistant model. All experiments were conducted on a PC with Intel Core i7 3.6 GHz CPU and 16 GB RAM. The algorithms are implemented in PyCharm.

We study the resilience of our model against Sybil attack with E_A and C of s_A. There are 10000 peers in our experiment to simulate Sybil attack under P2P file sharing system. In the attack model, we assume only one Sybil attack happens at a time. For a simple Sybil strategy, the Sybil peers are not connected to each other.

In our experiment, first we generated 10000 peers including normal peers, attacker and Sybil peers. Referring Tien Tuan [20] 's parameter setting of Sybil attack model, we assume there is only one attacker s_A, and the proportion of Sybil peers S is var- ied from 1% to 5%. After reputation initialization, we randomly selected two peers to construct a transaction pair $tx = (p_i, r_j)$, and generate reputation value for provider $P = \{p_1, p_2, \ldots\}$.

At the same time of tx generating, each peer will execute PoW verification every fixed time. We assume the interval time T is 50 times of t_i (t_i should more than the maximum time of one-time verification) to ensure that each non-Sybil peer can complete verification in legal time. The value of t_i is obtained from the average of multiple experiments: The solid line is time-growth change trend fitted by liner regression, R^2 approaches 1.0 indicates that the relationship between difficulty of PoW and t_i approaches index distribution (see Fig. 2).

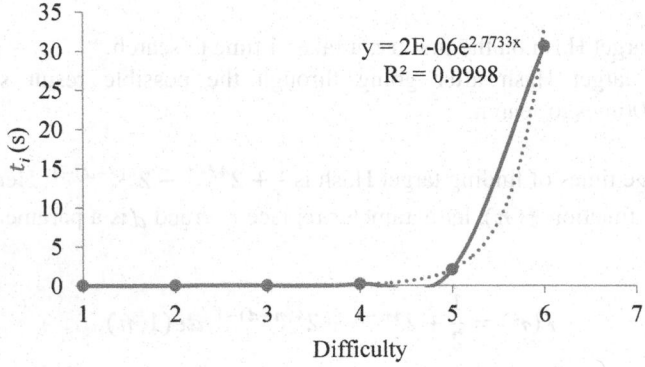

Fig. 2. The difficulty of PoW verification

5.1 Resistance Effect

As S increasing, E_A (ratio of reputation increments to verification time consumption) showed a significant downward trend (see Fig. 3). Because each Sybil peer have to execute the verification puzzle, and the time consumption of Sybil peers will add to s_A. C will increase linearly with S, but the reputation changes of s_A cannot be linear growth as time consumption, that E_A will show a downward trend.

5.2 Dynamical Difficulty Adjustment

When we introduce the dynamic adjustment of puzzle's difficulty, we need to avoid a significant impact on normal peers. As the experiment indicate, the time consumption in verification of normal peers keeps stable lower value as S raising, but Sybil peers' consumption has significantly increased (see Fig. 4).

Figure above has proofed the effect of dynamic-adjust difficulty on normal peers is negligible. On the other hand, we need to search whether the dynamic mechanism is effective to defend s_A. Here we use verification under static difficulty and our dynamic difficulty to compare. In dynamic difficulty circumstance, we assume that if current reputation value is greater or equal to 0.5, the verification difficulty of the peer will be increased by 1 unit. Static difficulty will keep the difficulty as a constant. As the result, dynamic difficulty has a significantly effect on E_A (see Fig. 5).

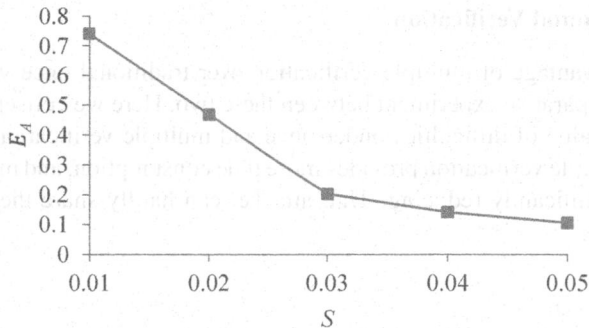

Fig. 3. E_A decreasing while S growing

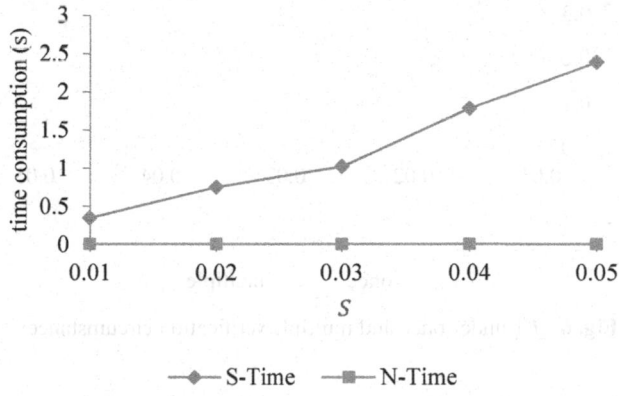

—◆—S-Time   —■—N-Time

Fig. 4. Time consumption of Sybil peers and non-Sybil peers with S raising.

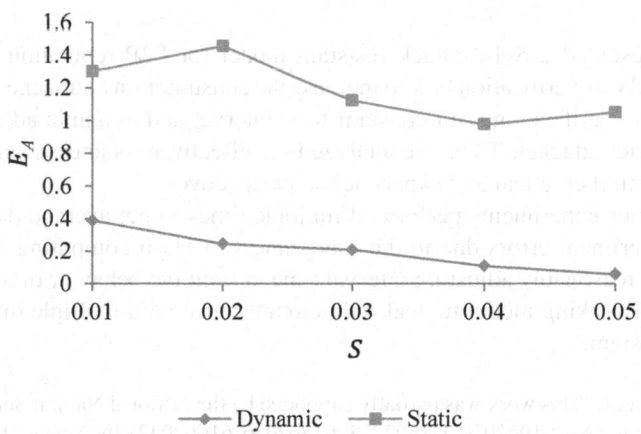

—◆—Dynamic   —■—Static

Fig. 5. Dynamic and static difficulty's impact on E_A

5.3 Multiple Round Verification

To verify the advantage of multiple verification over traditional once verification, we performed a comparative experiment between these two. Here we collected the average E_A at different value of difficulties under once and multiple verification circumstance (see Fig. 6). Multiple verification provides more time consumption, and makes attacker's effectiveness significantly reducing. That attacker can hardly share the cost in future benefits of attack.

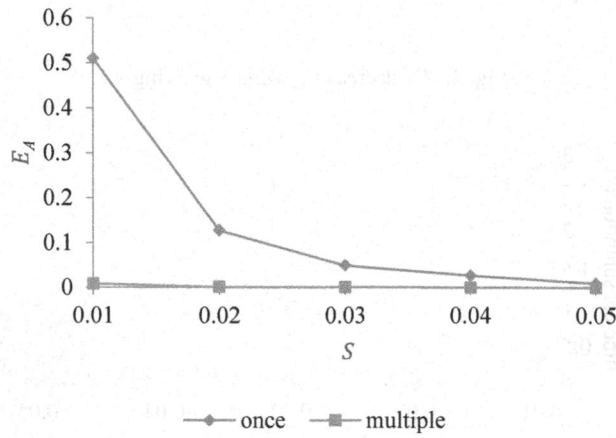

Fig. 6. E_A under once and multiple verification circumstance.

6 Conclusion

This paper presented a Sybil attack resistant model for P2P reputation systems, by introducing PoW as verification task to increase the consumption of attacker. We employ multiple rounds verification with constant time interval and dynamic-adjust difficulty to further restrict attacker. Then, we analyzed the effectiveness and advantages of our model from both theoretical and experimental perspectives.

Although our experiments performed multiple times to get average data, there are still some experiment errors due to the randomness of Hash computing. Other future work includes reasonably adjusting interval time to limit the behavior of attacker more effective, and tweaking model to deal with circumstance with multiple different Sybil attackers in system.

Acknowledgement. This work was partially supported by the National Natural Science Foundation of China (Grand No. 61962030, U1802271, 61862036, 61662042), the Science Foundation for Distinguished Young Scholars of Yunnan Province (Grand No. 2019FJ011), and the Foundation for Young Academic and Technical Leader of Yunnan Province (Grand No. 202005AC160036).

References

1. Douceur, J.R.: The sybil attack. In: Druschel, P., Kaashoek, F., Rowstron, A. (eds.) IPTPS 2002. LNCS, vol. 2429, pp. 251–260. Springer, Heidelberg (2002). https://doi.org/10.1007/3-540-45748-8_24
2. Koutrouli, E., Tsalgatidou, A.: Taxonomy of attacks and defense mechanisms in P2P reputation systems—Lessons for reputation system designers. Comput. Sci. Rev. 6(2–3), 47–70 (2012)
3. Yu, H., Kaminsky, M., Gibbons, P.B., Flaxman, A.: Sybilguard: defending against sybil attacks via social networks. IEEE/ACM Trans. Netwk. 16(3), 576–589 (2008)
4. Yu, H., Gibbons, P.B., Kaminsky, M., Xiao, F.: SybilLimit: a near-optimal social network defense against sybil attacks. IEEE/ACM Trans. Netwk. 18(3), 885–898 (2010)
5. Castro, M., Druschel, P., Ganesh, A., Rowstron, A., Wallach, D.S.: Secure routing for structured peer-to-peer overlay networks. SIGOPS Oper. Syst. Rev. 36, 299–314 (2002)
6. Marti, S., Garcia-Molina, H.: Taxonomy of trust: categorizing P2P reputation systems. Comput. Netwk. 50(4), 472–484 (2006)
7. Pradhan, S., Tripathy, S., Nandi, S.: Blockchain based security framework for p2p file-sharing system. In: 2018 IEEE International Conference on Advanced Networks and Telecommunications Systems (ANTS), pp. 1–6. IEEE, Indore, India (2018)
8. Friedman, E.J., Resnick, P.: The social cost of cheap pseudonyms. J. Econ. Manage. Strategy 10(2), 173–199 (2001)
9. Gao, T., Yang, J., Peng, W., Jiang, L., Sun, Y., Li, F.: A content-based method for sybil detection in online social networks via deep learning. IEEE Access 8, 38753–38766 (2020)
10. Byrenheid, M., Strufe, T., Roos, S.: Attack resistant leader election in social overlay networks by leveraging local voting. In: 21st International Conference on Distributed Computing and Networking (ICDCN 2020). Article 7, pp. 1–10. ACM, New York, USA (2020)
11. Danezis, G., Mittal, P.: Sybilinfer: Detecting sybil nodes using social networks. NDSS. pp. 1–15. San Diego, CA (2009)
12. John, R., Cherian, J.P., Kizhakkethottam, J.J.: A survey of techniques to prevent sybil attacks. In: 2015 International Conference on Soft-Computing and Networks Security (ICSNS). pp. 1–6. IEEE, Coimbatore, India (2015)
13. Levine, B.N., Shields, C., Margolin, N.B.: A survey of solutions to the sybil attack. Univ. Massachusetts Amherst, Amherst, MA 7, 224 (2006)
14. Dinger, J., Hartenstein, H.: Defending the sybil attack in P2P networks: taxonomy, challenges, and a proposal for self-registration. In: 1st International Conference on Availability, Reliability and Security (ARES 2006). pp. 8, IEEE, Vienna, Austria (2006)
15. Dewan, P., Dasgupta, P.: P2P reputation management using distributed identities and decentralized recommendation chains. IEEE Trans. Knowl. Data Eng. 22(7), 1000–1013 (2009)
16. Nakamoto S.: Bitcoin: A peer-to-peer electronic cash system. Manubot (2019)
17. Liu, Y.Z., Liu, J.W., Zhang, Z.Y., Xu, T.G., Yu, H.: Overview on Blockchain consensus mechanisms. J. Cryptol. Res. 6(4), 395–432 (2019)
18. Hoffman, K., Zage, D., Nita-Rotaru, C.: A survey of attack and defense techniques for reputation systems. ACM Comput. Surv. (CSUR) 42(1), 1–31 (2009)
19. Hendrikx, F., Bubendorfer, K., Chard, R.: Reputation systems: a survey and taxonomy. J. Parallel Dist. Comput. 75, 184–197 (2015)
20. Tuan, T., Dinh, A., Ryan, M.: Towards a Sybil-resilient reputation metric for P2P applications. In: International Symposium on Applications and the Internet. pp. 193–196. IEEE, Turku, Finland (2008)

Phishing Detection on Ethereum via Learning Representation of Transaction Subgraphs

Zihao Yuan[1,2], Qi Yuan[1,2], and Jiajing Wu[1,2(✉)]

[1] School of Data and Computer Science, Sun Yat-Sen University,
Guangzhou 510006, China
wujiajing@mail.sysu.edu.cn
[2] National Engineering Research Center of Digital Life, Sun Yat-sen University,
Guangzhou 510006, China

Abstract. With the widespread application of blockchain in the financial field, blockchain security also faces huge challenges brought by cybercrimes, especially phishing scams. It forces us to explore more efficient countermeasures and perspectives for better solution. Since graph modeling provides rich information for possible downstream tasks, we use a surrounding graph to model the transaction data of a target address, aiming to analyze the identity of an address by defining its transaction pattern on a high-level structure. In this paper, we propose a graph-based classification framework on Ethereum. Firstly we collect the transaction records of some verified phishing addresses and the same number of normal addresses. Secondly we form a set of subgraphs, each of which contains a target address and its surrounding transaction network in order to represent the original address on graph-level. Lastly, based on the analysis of the Ether flow of the phishing scam cycle, we propose an improved Graph2Vec, and make classification prediction on the subgraphs we built. The experimental results show that our framework has achieved a great competitiveness in the final classification task, which also indicate the potential value of phishing detection on Ethereum via learning the representation of transaction network.

Keywords: Blockchain · Ethereum · Phishing detection · Graph classification

1 Introduction

Blockchain is a distributed ledger technology that implements trusted intermediary transactions in an environment of mutual distrust [19]. It could be described as a distributed and trusted database maintained by a peer-to-peer network based on a creative consensus mechanism. Blockchain technology has the characteristics of anti-counterfeiting, immutability, and the ability to expand application scenarios through smart contracts, with which it is regarded as the

© Springer Nature Singapore Pte Ltd. 2020
Z. Zheng et al. (Eds.): BlockSys 2020, CCIS 1267, pp. 178–191, 2020.
https://doi.org/10.1007/978-981-15-9213-3_14

next generation of disruptive core technology. With the underlying support of blockchain technology, blockchain platforms such as Bitcoin and Ethereum have also taken this opportunity to flourish and be famous around the world as new digital currency trading platforms [17]. Among them, Ethereum is the most lag blockchain platform that provides a Turing-complete language to supports smart contracts, which will be executed in the Ethereum virtual machine (EVM). Due to the adaptability of the above characteristics of Ethereum, it has gained great development support in the field of economics and finance, and become a widely used platform for financial applications [9].

With the increasing prosperity of e-commerce, more and more people trade goods or services online, which also gives phishing scams more opportunities. Phishing scams refer to scammers illegally forge official websites or contact information to obtain users' private information, such as user names, passwords, and address numbers, for further gains [10]. The usual method is to send the victim a fake email that appears to come from the official, informing him to click on the link to modify relevant information, and the link actually points to a fake webpage for fraud, on which the information victim leaked will finally be obtained by scammers. In real cases, these fake information are generally spread through emails, Google ads, forums, and chat apps, and due to the low cost, they have great lethality in most of the time [1]. Nowadays, phishing scams have become one of the most widely used scams on Ethereum, which forces us to attach more attention to research in this field for adopting correct and efficient countermeasures [5,13,17].

In order to detect phishing addresses, we usually crawl their transaction records to extract distinguishing features [11]. Then we can form a directed graph according to the corresponding transaction records of those addresses. Note that in the Ethereum transaction network, each node represents an Ethereum address, while each edge indicates a certain Ether transfer between the addresses. Different types of addresses always exhibit different characteristics in transaction patterns, which could also be reflected in the network structure. And conversely, we can also evaluate the label of users through the relevant network information of corresponding addresses. In view of the development of research in the field of graph classification, we are increasingly able to mine valuable information via learning the embedding of network. Thus we use a surrounding transaction network to represent the target address, expecting to analyze identity of the address by defining its transaction pattern on a high-level structure. On the one hand, comparing with forming a large-scale network connected by all of those target addresses, using a second-order transaction subgraph to represent the original address costs less. We could easily extract the transaction records of a certain address on the Ethereum and build up a corresponding transaction network for it. On the other hand, through the graph embedding algorithm, the second-order transaction subgraph could also be used to extract meaningful information as representation features from the surrounding transaction network.

Summarily, from the perspective of transaction network, our proposed detection strategy could have the following advantages:

1. Representing the addresses with the second-order transaction subgraphs costs little and could analyze the characteristics of transaction patterns for identifying in an effective and direct way.
2. Using graph classification methods for anomaly detection on Ethereum is a new perspective of related research, which could extract high-level information as features for classification from the transaction network. It makes up for the lack of information from a perspective of network in other methods.
3. Considering the analysis of the transaction network on Ethereum, the proposed framework is designed specifically for the phishing detection issues, in order to boost its competitiveness in final classification performance.

In this paper, we propose a novel framework to detect phishing scams on Ethereum from the perspective of the transaction network. First, we extract the labeled phishing addresses and corresponding transaction records from an authorized platform. According to the collected transaction records, we build several corresponding subgraphs. Second, we mainly focus on extracting features from the corresponding subgraphs. According to the analysis of the transaction pattern of phishing scammers, we adopt an improved graph embedding method to extract the latent features of the subgraphs as addresses' features for subsequent phishing classification. Finally, we adopt SVM(Support Vector Machine) to distinguish whether the address is a phishing scammer.

The following chapter of the paper is organized as follows. Section 2 provides related work about phishing scam detection on Ethereum and anomaly detection by graph classification methods. In Sect. 3, the proposed framework is discussed in detail. Sections 4 summarize experimental results and the analysis of them. Lastly, we conclude our work in Sect. 5.

2   Related Work

2.1   Phishing Detection

Since phishing scams have received much research attention, traditional phishing detection methods based on virtual similarity, association rule learning, and support vector machines have been proposed and used in various fields [1]. With continuous research, a variety of features related to phishing scammers have also been confirmed and summarized, such as the source code of phishing websites [20], the characteristics of link URLs [14], and the CSS characteristics of websites [12]. And as traditional phishing scams obtain the victims' private information mainly through phishing emails and websites, the above traditional detection methods are basically based on the detection of phishing content.

However, phishing frauds on Ethereum not only obtain key information via phishing websites, but also spread phishing addresses via emails, chatting apps and other ways [10]. Thus due to the diversity of phishing approaches on Ethereum, current traditional detection methods are unsuitable to be applied here directly.

Analysis of phishing scams on Ethereum can be conducted from its whole life cycle and the difference of behaviors between confirmed phishing addresses and normal addresses. Considering that a complete fraud attack is a dynamically changing process, we can build multi-angle features based on the different behavioral characteristics displayed in each stage [1]. After scientific and rigorous quantitative analysis of these features, the most effective and sufficient key indicators are extracted to help the subsequent models to classify the correct labels of users. In the previous work [16], we built the classification model by feature engineering from the perspectives of address features, network features, and Ether flow characteristics. Among them, through the selection of indicators that can fully show the specificity of phishing addresses, the model has better performance in the final downstream tasks. And our work is more focused on the transaction network, trying to explore the potential information available for classification tasks from a new perspective.

2.2 Development and Applications of Graph Classification

Recently, we have witnessed an increasing number of applications involving objects with structural relationships, for which graph-structured data become more and more ubiquitous in many domains such as social networks [3], cybersecurity [6], bio- and chemo-informatics [7]. In such applications, graph is proved to be a natural and powerful tool for modeling and capturing dependency relationships between objects in the network structure. Different from conventional methods, we focus on using the entire-network structural relationships to explore information by graph classification algorithms, instead of representing data in a feature-value vector format directly. In other word, in the processing of this kind of graph-structured data, model based on a high-level structure may acquire additional valuable information missed by regular methods.

With the rapid development of graph applications and more challenges from different fields, the research field of graph classification algorithms has gradually become more diversified. The current graph classification methods can be summarized into the following categories: graph kernel [15], deep learning [4], and factorization [2].

The cases of different application scenarios are also constantly proving that the embedded representation learned from network structure will obtain a better performance than handcrafted features. While the transaction network is also a typical graph analytics scenario, it is also suitable to explore the information on it from the perspective of high-level structure. According to the above, we decide to integrate ideas of graph classification into solving phishing detection problems on Ethereum.

3   Proposed Model

3.1   Problem Definition

Given a set of addresses on Ethereum $\mathbb{A} = \{A_1, A_2, ...\}$, we build a set of representation transaction graphs for each target address $\mathbb{G} = \{G_{A_1}, G_{A_2}, ...\}$.

$G_{A_x} = (V, E, Y)$ is a transaction network centered on the target address A_x, where V represents the set of addresses that are transaction neighbors of the center address, E represents the set of transactions between those addresses, with $Y \in \mathbb{R}^{|A| \times |\gamma|}$ where γ is the set of labels of the target addresses and the corresponding graphs. For the scenario of phishing address identification, γ includes two kinds of labels that $+1$ for phishing address and -1 for normal address. Our goal is to predict the missing values in γ. We intend to learn the embeddings for all the representation transaction graphs $X \in \mathbb{R}^{|V| \times d}$, where d represents the number of embedding dimension. And these embeddings will be used as features of addresses for the downstream phishing detection task (Fig. 1).

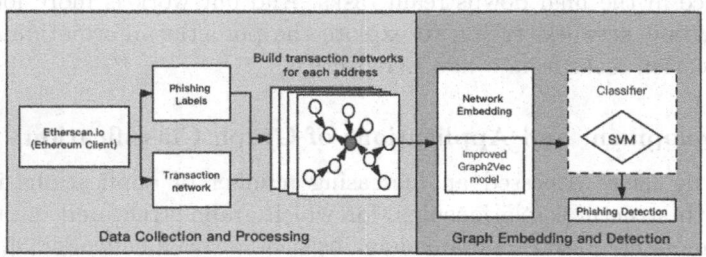

Fig. 1. Our proposed framework.

3.2   Data Collection and Processing

Because of the openness of public blockchain, each client on Ethereum is able to obtain all the transaction records, through which we could get the Ethereum dataset for model transaction network. In order to detect phishing scams, we need to get enough sufficient verified phishing addresses as our positive samples. As a block explorer and analytics platform for Ethereum, *Etherscan*[1] provide a growing list of phishing addresses labeled by the serious audit based on a majority of reports on the platform. We obtain 1660 verified phishing addresses which were reported in the list before October 17th, 2019 [18]. And then we randomly choose the same number of normal addresses to construct the sample list.

According to the list of addresses, we crawl the transaction network information for each target address through APIs offered by Etherscan. The transaction network information here consists of first-order transaction information between the target address and their first-order transaction neighbors, and the second-order transaction information that between first-order transaction neighbors and their next-order transaction neighbors. Note that the specific transaction records include: the address that initiated and accepted the transaction, the transaction timestamp, and the transaction amount. Based on the obtained information,

---

[1] https://etherscan.io/.

we can construct a second-order transaction subgraph centered on the target address. In this graph, each node represents a transaction neighbor of central address. A directed edge represents an Ether transfer transaction from the initial address to the recipient address. In the following work, we will use this kind of transaction subgraph to represent the original address.

Addresses with various functions in a transaction network may exhibit different patterns with their neighbors, and thus behave differently in terms of network structure. So we assume that the embedding of second-order transaction subgraph of the target address retains the feature information of transaction behavior pattern. This is also the main motivation for us to use the graph classification algorithm for phishing detection in our proposed model.

At the same time, we need to note that there is often a lot of redundant data in the Ethereum transaction records, i.e. a considerable number of addresses have little value for our research target because of their extreme situation. For example, addresses act as wallet interact with other addresses frequently, for which their numbers of neighbor addresses are too large for analysis of transaction network. This kind of data increases the burden of data processing, and even cause unexpected deviations to the results of model training. Thus it is necessary to set standards to clean the obtained dataset. According to previous work, we consider the addresses with the number of transactions less than 10 as inactive addresses and the addresses with the number more than 300 as overactive addresses, filtering them after transaction records collecting [16].

3.3 Improved Graph Classification Algorithm

Then we focus on how to analyze and process the extracted transaction network of the target addresses. Firstly, we introduce the key tool for processing from the field of graph classification, named Graph2Vec, which has shown great improvement in classification over substructure embedding methods. Graph2Vec is inspired by Doc2Vec, an extension to Word2Vec algorithm in NLP (Natural Language Processing) direction. Doc2Vec uses a derived model of skipgram named paragraph vector-distributed bag of words (PV-DBOW) to learn representations of word sequences [2]. Likewise, Graph2Vec learns the embeddings of a set of graphs based on rooted subgraphs extracted from them, actually expressing the potential connections between addresses in the transaction network. The major steps of Graph2Vec consist of the following two parts: 1) extract rooted subgraphs in order to represent all of the graphs in the form of a set of subgraphs. 2) learning embeddings of graphs by skip-gram model.

First, let H be the maximum height of rooted subgraphs, which means that for each node in the graph, Graph2Vec extract $(H + 1)$ rooted subgraphs whose root is it. Then the t-th subgraph $(0 < t < H)$ of the certain node is considered as the surroundings around it within t hops. In a word, for a graph G with n nodes, Graph2Vec generates $n(H + 1)$ subgraphs denoted by $c(G) = \{sg_1^{(0)}, sg_2^{(0)}, ..., sg_n^{(0)}, ..., sg_1^{(H)}, sg_2^{(H)}, ..., sg_n^{(H)}\}$. To extract these rooted subgraphs and quantize them into subgraph IDs, Graph2vec adopt the WL relabeling strategy that lays the basis for WL kernel [15].

After extracting rooted subgraphs from all the graphs, Graph2Vec learns the graph embeddings by skip-gram model. At the input layer of skip-gram model, the input graphs are encoded as one-hot vectors. And at the output layer, the predicted probability distribution is output over the substructure of inputted graphs. In the process of model training, the only hidden layer is able to gradually obtain the representation vector for the corresponding graph. Given a set of graphs $\{G_1, G_2, ..., G_n\}$ expected to be classified consist of subgraphs $c(G_1), c(G_2), ..., c(G_n)$, skip-gram model simultaneously learns embedding $f(G)$ for graph G and embedding for each rooted subgraph in $c(G)$. Then the model considers the probability that subgraph in $c(G)$ is contained in the graph G, maximizing the log-likelihood:

$$\sum_{j=1}^{n_i(H+1)} \log P_r(sg_j | G_i), \tag{1}$$

$$\frac{exp(f(G_i) \cdot f(sg_j))}{\sum_{sg \in V_{OC}} exp(f(G_i) \cdot f(sg))}, \tag{2}$$

n_i in Eq. 1 is the number of nodes in G. And V_{OC} in Eq. 2 means the vocabulary of subgraphs across all the graphs in the dataset. Given a pair of graphs G_1 and G_2, their final embeddings trained by the model get closer in the vector space if they are composed of many common rooted subgraphs, i.e graphs with analogous network structure will be embedded to similar representation vectors.

Then we put our attention to the analysis of the transaction network on Ethereum. As mentioned above, various of addresses exhibit different behavior patterns in the transaction networks formed with their neighbors. For example, financial applications, such as exchange markets, usually interact with a large amount of addresses frequently, for which the extracted network of this kind of address may contain many neighbor addresses with bilateral transactions. Intuitively, we could also summarize the typical behavior patterns of such abnormal addresses through the analysis of phishing life cycle. According to the previous work [10], The ultimate goal of scammers is to defraud Ether from other normal addresses, so their corresponding nodes will be connected to more in-degree neighbor nodes in the transaction network. Moreover, the phishing address usually completely cuts off the contact with the victim after it succeeds, for which there is often only exists a single transaction record between the phishing address and the victim address.

After visualization of the network as Fig. 2, we find that most of the transaction networks around the phishing addresses present like a converging star chart, i.e the Ether flow for most transactions is gathered from the outside to the central phishing address. We attach great importance to the value of this feature in our idea of detecting phishing addresses through the representation transaction subgraphs. The current graph classification algorithms, including Graph2Vec, which could only identify the label of address, are rarely able to handle the label of edge, so the improvement method we propose tries to integrate direction information of edge into Graph2Vec model. To achieve this goal, we try to use the edge label as the carrier of the transaction direction information, for which we label each edge of the network according to the Ether flow's direction of the corresponding transaction record.

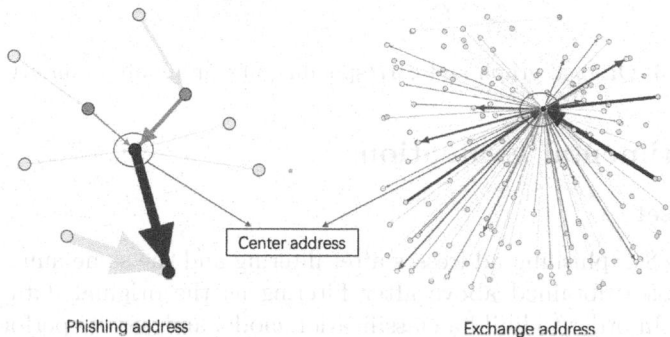

Fig. 2. Visualization of the transaction network of phishing address and exchange address.

In order to make full use of the feature information brought by the edge direction, we convert the original network based on address nodes and transaction edges into line graphs with the original transaction edge as the core analysis object of the model. In detail, the specific process is described as follows:

- In the process of constructing the transaction graph of each target address through the collected information, the direction information of each transaction is recorded at the same time, and stored in the network through the label of the edge. There are two edge labels respectively correspond to deposit transactions and transfer transactions.
- In order to take into address both the structural information of the original graph and the importance of the edge information, we intend to transform the original graph to a new form named line graph. To build up the line graph, we covert the original edges to the nodes of the new graph, and connect the nodes that share the common endpoint node while they act as edges in the original graph. Then we keep the label of the original edge as the label of its corresponding node in the new graph, so we could make use of the information carried by the original edge in Graph2Vec model by the edge-to-node conversion.
- At last, we put the converted corresponding line graph into Graph2Vec model to acquire the representation vectors for all the graphs. It not only retains the original network structure information, but also incorporate edge direction information as one of the important elements into the process of model training. After acquiring the embeddings of graphs, we utilize general classifiers to perform downstream classification tasks (Fig. 3).

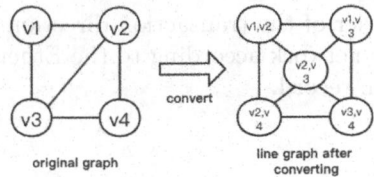

original graph

line graph after converting

Fig. 3. Original graph and corresponding line graph after converting.

4   Experimental Evaluations

4.1   Dataset

We used the 801 phishing addresses after filtering and the same number of unlabeled addresses obtained above after filtering as the original data set of the experiment. In order to build a classification model and test its performance, we divided the original data set into two parts. The first part occupies 80% of the original dataset and is used as the training dataset of the classifier. The other part is the remaining 20% of the original data set, which will be used as the test dataset. After the training of the classifier is completed, the test dataset will be used as its input to obtain the experimental prediction results for subsequent comparative analysis.

4.2   Metric

For the evaluation of the results of the binary classification model, we have adopted three evaluation metrics commonly used in machine learning here: Precision, Recall, and F1-score.

$$Precision = \frac{true\ positive}{true\ positive\ +\ false\ positive} \tag{3}$$

$$Recall = \frac{true\ positive}{true\ positive\ +\ false\ negative} \tag{4}$$

$$F1 - score = 2 \times \frac{Precision \times Recall}{Precision\ +\ Recall} \tag{5}$$

Precision indicates how many predictions are accurate, from the perspective of prediction results. Recall indicates how many of the true positive classes were successfully recalled, i.e classified as predicted positive classes by model. F1-score is a comprehensive metric that combines the impact of precision and recall.

4.3   Baselines and Experimental Setup

Specifically, we intend to show the value and potentiality of our proposed framework from figuring out the following research questions: 1) Whether the proposed framework can extract latent feature information of the transaction network as addresses' features for subsequent phishing classification. 2) Whether the proposed model reflects stronger adaptability for the phishing detection on Ethereum through more consideration on transaction records. So we compare our model with several baseline methods including Node2Vec, WL-kernel, and original Graph2Vec. Node2Vec is derived from the Word2Vec algorithm in the field of natural language processing. It samples through a specific random walk, generating a corresponding sequence of context for each node. Then treat these sequences as text and import them into the Skip-gram model in Word2Vec to get the embedding of central node. In the experiments, we set parameters of Node2Vec as recommended by the original paper [8] with walks per node $r = 10$, context size $k = 10$, walk length $l = 5$, while $p = 0.25$ and $q = 0.75$ for random walk.

WL-kernel is a method inspired by the Weisfeiler-Lehman test of graph isomorphism. Its key idea is iterate over each labeled node in graph and its neighbors to build a multiset label. In the end, we compare the similarity of graphs by counting the co-occurrences of labels in them after iteration. And the parameter settings is height parameter $h = 3$.

For all the methods, we all use a common embedding dimension of 256. And the hyperparameters of classifier are adjusted well based on 5-fold cross validation on the training set.

4.4   Results and Discussions

Table 1. Performance comparison of various methods.

Method	Metric		
	Precision	Recall	F1-measure
node2vec	0.57	0.58	0.58
WL-kernel	0.65	0.62	0.63
Graph2Vec	0.68	0.67	0.68
Line_Graph2Vec	**0.69**	**0.77**	**0.73**

Classification Performance. Figure 1 shows the performance comparison of various methods. We can find out some interesting phenomenon that meets our expectation. First, we pay attention to low-order substructure embedding technique, Node2vec. According to the result, using Node2vec to obtain graph embeddings performs the worst among all methods. We can find out the proposed approach outperforms it by more than 15%. Note that Node2vec is a representation learning method based on a lower-dimensional structure, i.e at the node level. It utilizes the similarity information of the neighbor node to train the representation vector, which means that the embeddings acquired by this kind of method could only extract local information. Thus it is hard to satisfy our demand for mining deeper structure information in the transaction network.

Secondly, WL-kernel is a graph classification strategy based on graph kernel. As a graph classification algorithm, it also learns representation vectors based on graph substructure information. Compared with the Node2vec method, as a method considered at the network level, WL-kernel can further obtain relatively global structural information, so it could have better performance in the classification task. However, it is still not as good as the results of the Graph2Vec model, for the reason that Graph2Vec is more scalable and meticulous in the way of generating rooted subgraphs, extracting more precise features in the end. Moreover, it cannot deal with the label information of nodes or edges, so the behavioral characteristics that we have summarized according to the transaction patterns of phishing scammers could never play the role we expect.

Lastly, we compare the proposed framework incorporating the transaction direction information and the original Graph2Vec model, observing the impact that the transaction records may cause on the classification effect. As can be seen from the Table 1, our framework has better performance in all evaluation metrics, especially the recall has been greatly improved, which indicates that framework is provided with certain practical value. It shows the fact that the transaction pattern of phishing scammers we consider about is actually an important feature for identifying the addresses. So integrating the transaction direction information into the training of subgraphs representations could contribute to boosting the performance of framework. In addition, it shows that in the process of training, if more features of the transaction network can be considered, the training results of the model can give us more help in solving the anomaly detection problem. Moreover, it also reflects that the research perspective is still worth more exploring.

Starting from the motivation inspired by the strategy in the field of graph classification, we propose a framework to solve the problem of phishing detection via learning features from the representation transaction subgraphs. After designing based on the analysis of the transaction network and the patterns of phishing behavior, our proposed framework showed great competitiveness in the final experimental results. And the superiority and differences revealed by the prediction results presented in performance comparison also strongly illustrate that our idea of using transaction network to represent certain addresses can indeed uncover richer valuable information from the different dimensions of phishing detection problem.

Impact of Transaction Graph. In the first step of our proposed framework, according to the transaction records, we build a second-order transaction graph for each target address to represent it. To evaluate whether the second-order graph could certainly contribute to providing adequate information on the transaction network surrounding the target address, we set a comparison between it and the first-order transaction graph. Note that the first-order transaction graph only contains the first-order transaction information between the target address and its first-order transaction neighbors. As shown in Table 2, the framework applying the second-order transaction graph has much better performance in all metrics. The result indicates that because of the limited topology of the first-order graph, our model based on Graph2Vec fails to extract enough features for the downstream classification task. Moreover, the second-order transaction graph remains more information of those transaction neighbors, which contributes to defining the transaction behavior pattern of the target address. Thus the second-order transaction graph is the best choice for our framework.

Table 2. Performance Comparison of different order of transaction graph.

Graph setting	Metric		
	Precision	Recall	F1-measure
First-order	0.57	0.52	0.54
Second-order	**0.69**	**0.77**	**0.73**

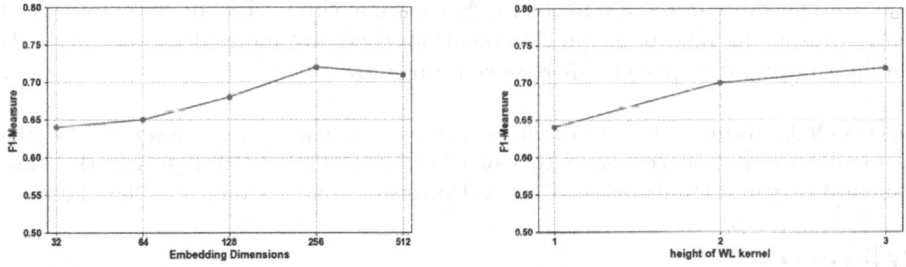

Fig. 4. Parameter sensitivity

Parameter Sensitivity. For the proposed framework, there are some parameters that influence the results. In Fig. 4, considering F1-Measure as the performance metric, we evaluate the effects of the chosen key parameters: embedding dimension and height of the WL kernel. When a parameter is adjusted for evaluating, other parameters are set as default. In order to evaluate how embedding dimensions could impact the detection performance, we gradually increase the dimensions from 32 to 512. From Fig. 4, we can observe that, as the increasing of embedding dimension, our framework has achieved better performance for classification. It indicates that larger dimensions could retain richer information that explored by the algorithm for the classification task. Besides for height of the WL kernel, we similarly adjust it from 1 to 3 and compare the detection results. Referring to Fig. 4, increasing the height of WL kernel can apparently boost the final performance. Note that the height of WL kernel actually means the degree of rooted subgraphs that used to represent all the graphs. The results indicate that with a larger degree of rooted subgraphs, more features of network structure can be considered for representation learning.

5   Conclusion

In this paper, we presented a new perspective to solve the problem of phishing detection on Ethereum. Firstly we utilized the surrounding transaction network of the addresses to characterize their positions and behaviors in the transaction network. Then through the analysis of the behavior pattern of the phishing scammers, we integrated the Ether flow feature information and build up an improved verification framework. In the final experiment, we found out from the comparison and analysis of the results that the network representation has the potential to extract more meta information from transaction network. Undoubtedly, the conclusion shows great potential value of the representation features extracted by graph embedding from the surrounding transaction network. In the follow-up work, we will make more use of transaction records collected, introducing attention mechanisms that could redistribute the weight of information in transaction network, to make the model better adapt to the Ethereum environment and phishing detection problem. At the same time, with the development of algorithms in the field of graph classification, there are more ideas and methods worthy of new attempts in this research direction.

Acknowledgements. The work described in this paper was supported by the National Natural Science Foundation of China (61973325, 61503420) and the Fundamental Research Funds for the Central Universities under Grant No.17lgpy120.

References

1. Abdelhamid, N., Ayesh, A., Thabtah, F.: Phishing detection based associative classification data mining. Expert Syst. Appl. **41**, 5948–5959 (2014)
2. Adhikari, B., Zhang, Y., Ramakrishnan, N., Prakash, B.A.: Distributed representations of subgraphs. In: Proceedings of the 2017 IEEE International Conference on Data Mining Workshops, New Orleans, LA, USA, pp. 111–117. IEEE (2017)
3. Backstrom, L., Leskovec, J.: Supervised random walks: predicting and recommending links in social networks. In: Proceedings of the 4th ACM International Conference on Web Search and Data Mining, New York, NY, USA, pp. 635–644. Association for Computing Machinery (2011)
4. Cao, S., Lu, W., Xu, Q.: Deep neural networks for learning graph representations. In: Proceedings of the Association for the Advance of Artificial Intelligence, Phoenix, Arizona, USA, pp. 1145–1152. AAAI Press (2016)
5. Chang, T., Svetinovic, D.: Improving Bitcoin ownership identification using transaction patterns analysis. IEEE Trans. Syst. Man Cybern. Syst. **50**, 1–12 (2020)
6. Chau, D.H., Nachenberg, C., Wilhelm, J., Wright, A., Faloutsos, C.: Polonium: tera-scale graph mining and inference for malware detection. In: Proceedings of the 2011 SIAM International Conference on Data Mining. Mesa, Arizona, USA, pp. 131–142 (2011)

7. Duvenaud, D., et al.: Convolutional networks on graphs for learning molecular fingerprints. In: Proceedings of the 28th International Conference on Neural Information Processing Systems, pp. 2224–2232. MIT Press, Cambridge (2015)
8. Grover, A., Leskovec, J.: Node2vec: scalable feature learning for networks. In: Proceedings of the 22nd ACM SIGKDD International Conference on Knowledge Discovery and Data Mining, New York, NY, USA, pp. 855–864. Association for Computing Machinery (2016)
9. Han, Q., Wu, J.W., Zheng, Z.Z.: Long-range dependence, multi-fractality and volume-return causality of Ether market. Chaos Interdisc. J. Nonlinear Sci. **30**, 011101 (2020)
10. Khonji, M., Iraqi, Y., Jones, A.: Phishing detection: a literature survey. IEEE Commun. Surv. Tutor. **15**, 2091–2121 (2013)
11. Lin, D., Wu, J., Yuan, Q., Zheng, Z.: Modeling and understanding Ethereum transaction records via a complex network approach. IEEE Trans. Circ. Syst. **67**, 1 (2020). II-Express Briefs
12. Moghimi, M., Varjani, A.Y.: New rule-based phishing detection method. Expert Syst. Appl. **53**, 231–242 (2016)
13. Monamo, P., Marivate, V., Twala, B.: Unsupervised learning for robust Bitcoin fraud detection. In: Proceedings of the Information Security for South Africa, Johannesburg, South Africa, pp. 129–134. IEEE (2016)
14. Sahingoz, O.K., Buber, E., Demir, O., Diri, B.: Machine learning based phishing detection from URLs. Expert Syst. Appl. **117**, 345–357 (2019)
15. Shervashidze, N., Schweitzer, P., van Leeuwen, E.J., Mehlhorn, K., Borgwardt, K.M.: Weisfeiler-lehman graph kernels. J. Mach. Learn. Res. **12**, 2539–2561 (2011)
16. Wu, J., et al.: Who are the phishers? Phishing scam detection on Ethereum via network embedding. arXiv preprint arXiv:1911.09259 (2019)
17. Xie, S., Zheng, Z., Chen, W., Wu, J., Dai, H.N., Imran, M.: Blockchain for cloud exchange: a survey. Comput. Electric. Eng. **81**, 106526 (2019)
18. Zheng, P., Zheng, Z., Dai, H.: Xblock-ETH: extracting and exploring blockchain data from Ethereum. arXiv preprint arXiv:1911.00169 (2019)
19. Zheng, Z., Xie, S., Dai, H., Chen, X., Wang, H.: An overview of blockchain technology: architecture, consensus, and future trends. In: Proceedings of the 2017 IEEE International Congress on Big Data, Los Alamitos, CA, USA, pp. 557–564. IEEE (2017)
20. Zouina, M., Outtaj, B.: A novel lightweight URL phishing detection system using SVM and similarity index. Hum. Centric Comput. Inf. Sci. **7**, 17 (2017)

Detection of Smart Ponzi Schemes Using Opcode

Jianxi Peng[1($\boxtimes$)] and Guijiao Xiao[2]

[1] Foshan Polytechnic, Foshan 528137, GuangDong, China
309719939@qq.com
[2] South China Business College, Guangdong University of Foreign Studies,
Guangzhou 510006, China
250761680@qq.com

Abstract. Blockchain is becoming an important infrastructure of the
next generation of information technology. But now, the fraud on
blockchain is serious which has affected the development of blockchain
ecology. Smart Ponzi scheme which realized by smart contract is a new
type of Ponzi scheme and running on Ethereum. It would cause more
serious damage to society in less time than other Ponzi schemes. Timely
and comprehensive detection of all smart Ponzi schemes is the key to constructed an automatic detection model of smart Ponzi scheme. A model
that effectively detect smart Ponzi scheme in its full lifecycle is proposed
in this paper. The model only uses features based on operation codes
(i.e., opcodes) of smart contract on Ethereum. The systematic modeling
strategy realizes the efficient automatic detection model of smart Ponzi
scheme step by step. Precision, Recall and F1-score of the model are 0.98,
0.93 and 0.95 respectively by experiments. Smart Ponzi schemes hidden
on Ethereumaredetectedeffectivelyby the model. More importantly, the
performance of model is guaranteed at any moment in the lifecycle, even
at the birth of a smart Ponzi scheme.

Keywords: Ponzi scheme · Smart contract · Ethereum · Opcode ·
Modeling

1 Introduction

Blockchain has the characteristics of distributed, decentralized, and data can
not be tampered with [1]. It is the underlying technology of Bitcoin. Since its
appearance in 2008, it has attracted wide attention. Ethereum which supports
smart contract [2] expands the application of blockchain. The application scenarios of blockchain have been extended from digital currency to finance, industry,
social governance and other fields [3–5]. Blockchain is becoming an important
infrastructure of the next generation of information technology [6].

However, the blockchain technology is a new technology, its regulatory technologies need to be improved and the regulatory mechanism is not perfect [7].

© Springer Nature Singapore Pte Ltd. 2020
Z. Zheng et al. (Eds.): BlockSys 2020, CCIS 1267, pp. 192–204, 2020.
https://doi.org/10.1007/978-981-15-9213-3_15

Illegal and criminal activities using the flaws of blockchain technology are emerging one after another [8,9]. How to enhance the security of blockchain and prevent the illegal and criminal behaviors on blockchain has become one of the key researches on the healthy and sustainable development of blockchain. The security and privacy of blockchain have been studied in [10]. The illegal price manipulation of blockchain has been studied in [11]. The illegal activities such as money laundering [12], gambling [13], trafficking in contraband [14] and frauds [15] have been explored respectively using the analysis of the data on the blockchain. Various attacks on blockchain system, such as double blossom attack [16] and selfish mining [17], have been studied. Defect detection tools for smart contracts have also been developed [18].

Ponzi scheme is a typical financial fraud in these illegal activities. Vasek and Moore, after studying the frauds on Bitcoin, pointed out that 13,000 victims fell into the Ponzi scheme and lost $11 million [15]. Bernie Madoff's Ponzi scheme defrauded investors of 64.8 billion USD [20]. Ponzi schemes on blockchain have seriously damaged the reputation of blockchain. The development of blockchain technology has been seriously affected by Ponzi schemes. Identification of Ponzi scheme on the blockchain has attracted the concern of scholars.

Based on the dataset of Bitcoin_based Ponzi scheme, a detection model was constructed based on features extracted from the historical data of transactions [21]. Toyoda et al. [22] proposed a detection model of Bitcoin_based Ponzi scheme using features extracted from the historical data of transactions. Bartoletti et al. [25] first found the Ponzi scheme running on Ethereum in the form of smart contract, and named it as smart Ponzi scheme. They built a dataset, and studied the life time of smart Ponzi scheme from the social interaction between victims and fraudsters. A framework of automatic detection model of smart Ponzi scheme was proposed, and three detection models were constructed using features of opcode and account [23,24].

But, there are two weaknesses in the previous work [21–24]. One of them is that the models using features of historical data [21–24] or hybrid features [23] can not detect Ponzi schemes in time. Only Ponzi schemes which have accumulated sufficient data can be detected by these models. Network features allow Ponzi scheme on the blockchain to spread faster. The characteristics of the smart contract that it can not be tampered with and automatically execute make the smart Ponzi scheme easier to attract investors [25,26]. When these models detect a fraud, the fraud has been widely spread and the harm has been caused. The other one is that the Recall of the model [23] using features of opcode is only 0.73%. However, the Recall is the key metric of the automatic detection model of smart Ponzi scheme. Besides, it is necessary to consider sampling methods since the detection of smart Ponzi scheme is a typical problem of imbalanced data detection [27].

In order to detect all frauds timely, comprehensively and precisely, a systematic modeling strategy was used to model the detection of smart Ponzi scheme on Ethereum in this paper. The strategy only uses the opcode sequence of smart contract as the feature to model the detection of smart Ponzi scheme. The data on blockchain cannot be tampered with. So the automatic detection model based on opcode can detect the smart Ponzi scheme in time. Based on the features of opcode sequence, the strategy uses a systematic method to construct the detection model of smart Ponzi scheme step by step. Each step of modeling applies some main factors that affect the performance of the model. Finally, an efficient automatic detection model of smart Ponzi scheme is obtained.

The experimental results show that the model obtained by the proposed strategy is better than others. Precision, Recall and F1-score predicted by the model increased by 0.01, 0.20 and 0.13 compared with the best in [23], respectively. The most important thing is that the performance of the detection model is guaranteed at any time in the lifecycle of smart Ponzi scheme.

Contributions:

1. A detection model of smart Ponzi scheme in the full lifecycle on Ethereum, which can detect smart Ponzi scheme timely, comprehensively and precisely. Precision, Recall and F1-score predicted by the model are 0.98, 0.93 and 0.95 respectively. The performance is guaranteed at any moment in the lifecycle of smart Ponzi scheme.

2. A systematic modeling strategy for detection of smart Ponzi scheme. The model was constructed with a systematic approach that considers the main factors of the model. The factors include feature type, calculation method of the value of features, proportion of oversample, the key feature and classifier, etc. The strategy can obtain an efficient model in fewer iterations.

The rest of the paper is organized as follows. In Sect. 2, Detection of Ponzi scheme on blockchain is briefly reviewed. Section 3 describes the systematic strategy was used to model the detection of smart Ponzi scheme on Ethereum. Section 4 verifies the proposed strategy by experiments. Finally, the conclusions of the paper are given in Sect. 5.

2   Related Work

Compared with other financial frauds, Ponzi scheme has more victims, wider influence, deeper harm, stronger concealment and more severe social harm [19]. It is an important research topic in the field of finance. Moore et al. [28] first studied the online Ponzi schemes, collected nearly 1,000 schemes and created a tracking website to monitor the operation of the frauds. Vasek et al. [15] studied the lifetime of Ponzi scheme on bitcoin blockchain from inflow and outflow of bitcoin addresses. Bartoletti et al. [25] used the standardized Levenshtein Distance [29] of the contract's bytecode as the differentiation to identify the Ponzi scheme, and found 55 smart Ponzi schemes on Ethereum that hidden the source code. These works laid the foundation for the establishment of an automatic detection model of Ponzi scheme on the blockchain.

The models were proposed by [21,22] which used to detect the Bitcoin_based Ponzi schemes. They use data mining techniques and machine learning to build these models. Features of the model are extracted from historical data of transactions. Performance of [21] has 1% of false positives and identifies 31 Ponzi schemes out of 32. True Positive Rate, False Positive Rate and Accuracy of [22] are 0.95, 0.049 and 0.9375 respectively. One weakness of these models is that they can not identify Ponzi schemes as early as possible. Some of these features take time to produce their own value, and others only are accumulated to enough quantity in a period of time can they take effect.

Three types of models that detect smart Ponzi schemes on Etereum are proposed in [23,24]. They all use data mining techniques and machine learning to build the model for detecting smart Ponzi schemes. One of them uses the data related to the account (i.e., account) as features to detect smart Ponzi scheme. The best performance of this type is that Precision, Recall and F1-score are 0.64, 0.76 and 0.61 respectively. The other uses hybrid features of account and opcode to detect smart Ponzi schemes. Precision, Recall and F1-score of the best model of this type are 0.95, 0.69 and 0.79 respectively. The data related to the account is also the historical data of transactions. These two types of models have the same weakness as those proposed by [21,23]. The third model detects smart Ponzi schemes by using opcode features. But it only uses a single opcode as the feature, and uses the frequency of a single opcode in the contract to calculate the value of features. Precision, Recall and F1-score of the best model in this type are 0.94, 0.73 and 0.82 respectively. The Recall of the model is not ideal.

Smart Ponzi scheme is more harmful to society than other Ponzi schemes in a shorter time which has the characteristics of Ethereum. The data on blockchain can not be tampered with and is transparent [1], the participants of the smart Ponzi scheme would think that it is impossible for the lawbreakers to cheat their input. According to the pre-defined rules, smart contracts will run automatically and permanently. It makes participants believe that they will get their expected profits. Moreover, the network virtualization and user anonymity of the blockchain make it difficult to identify the scammers [25]. The smart Ponzi scheme is deeply deceptive, full of strong temptation, and spreads quickly. It is easy to attract a large number of investors in a short time, which would make the victims wider and cause more serious losses. Detection of financial fraud is a typical problem of detecting imbalanced data detection. In the problem of detecting imbalanced data detection, more attention is paid to the Recall and F1-score of the model [27]. Therefore, the detection of smart Ponzi schemes should detect all scams in time and comprehensively.

All the models proposed by the prior works [21–24] can not meet the needs of automatic detection model of smart Ponzi scheme at the same time. Models based on historical data of transactions can not detect frauds in time. It takes time to collect these historical data. These models can only detect the smart Ponzi schemes that have been for some time. The other model based on bytecode can not detect the Ponzi scheme very well. And the Recall and F1-score of the model used features of opcode are only 0.73 and 0.82. This would certainly lead to very serious consequences in society.

The goal of constructing a model is to detect all smart Ponzi scheme timely, comprehensively, and precisely, next section explored a systematic modeling strategy for detecting the smart Ponzi scheme automatically. The strategy only uses features extracted from the opcode of smart contract to build model. Different from [23], features used in the strategy are opcode sequences whose length is from 1 to 5. Section 3.1 first illustrates that the opcode-based detection model can detect a smart Ponzi scheme at any point in its lifecycle. Then the method of extracting features from opcode and the calculation method of the value of features are described. Section 3.2 describes the three steps of systematic modeling strategy. The main factors that affect the performance of the model are allocated to each step, and build an efficient automatic detection model of smart Ponzi scheme step by step.

3   Methodology

Smart Ponzi schemes should be detected timely, comprehensively, and precisely. This section explores a strategy for systematically modeling detection of smart Ponzi scheme. Firstly, methods of feature extraction and calculating the value of features are introduced. These solve the problem that the model cannot detect smart Ponzi schemes as early as possible. Then, it describes a systematic modeling process of detecting smart Ponzi scheme. In this process, the main factors that affect the performance of the model are applied step by step. This would improve the performance of the model.

3.1   Feature Extraction and Value of Feature Calculation

To deploy a smart contract on Ethereum, the bytecode of the smart contract is required. All the logical functions of the smart contract are encapsulated in its bytecode. Once a smart contract is released on Ethereum, the bytecode of it will be saved on blockchain and cannot be tampered with. The data on blockchain is transparent and public, so the bytecode of smart contract is easy to obtain. And the bytecode of a smart contract can be decompiled to the opcode. Therefore, the results of data analysis and mining on the opcode can be used in the full lifecycle of smart contract.

After removing operands and numeric suffixes of the opcode, number of the different opcodes (i.e., NOP) is 74. Then, they are sorted by the sorts in dictionary, and an ordered set of opcode (i.e., OPS) is gotten. So, a smart contract can be expressed as $SC = (op_1, op_2, \ldots, op_i, \ldots, op_l), op_i \in OPS$, where l is the number of the opcode for the smart contract. The $ops_{N,i}$ is used to represent the ith opcode sequence of all opcode sequences with length N. The SV_N is used to represent the feature vector generated by the opcode sequence of length N, it shows as formula 1.

$$SV\_N = (ops_{N,0}, ops_{N,1}, \cdots, ops_{N,(NOP-1)^N}) \tag{1}$$

The opcode sequence of smart contract is essentially a text language and the opcode sequence is regarded as a term. Term frequency (i.e., TF) shown in formula 2 is widely used for information retrieval and malicious code detection [31]. In this formula, $n_{i,j}$ is the number of times the term i appears in the file

j. In order to prevent bias to longer documents, normalization $\sum_k n_{k,j}$ is used. $\sum_k n_{k,j}$ is the sum of the times of all terms in the jth sample document. Term frequency inverse document frequency (i.e., TF-IDF) shown in formula 3 is an improved TF calculation method, $IDF_i = \log \frac{|D|}{|\{j:t_i \in d_j\}|}$, $|D|$ is the total number of files in the dataset, and $|\{j : t_i \in d_j\}|$ is the number of files in the dataset in which term i appears. TF-IDF performs better than TF in information retrieval and classification [32], but it uses the number of files in the dataset to calculate the value, and its value will change with the change of the dataset.

$$TF_{i,j} = \frac{n_{i,j}}{\sum_k n_{k,j}} \tag{2}$$

$$TF - IDF_{i,j} = TF_{i,j} \cdot IDF_i \tag{3}$$

The method of N-gram to calculate the value of features [31] is simplified here. The simplified calculation method is shown in formula 4, $TF'_{i,j}$ is the number of times of the maximum prefix term for term i appears in file j, and we name it TF-OUR.

$$TF - OUR_{i,j} = \frac{TF_{i,j}}{TF'_{i,j}} \tag{4}$$

3.2 Systematic Modeling Strategy

Systematic modeling is a way to improve the performance of the model. There are many factors that will affect the performance of the model. In this paper, it mainly considers the following factors: the type of feature, the calculation method of the value of features, the key features, the distribution of samples, classifier and so on. The systematic model strategy is divided into three steps, and these factors are applied step by step in the systematical modeling process. The strategy of systematically modeling is shown as Fig. 1.

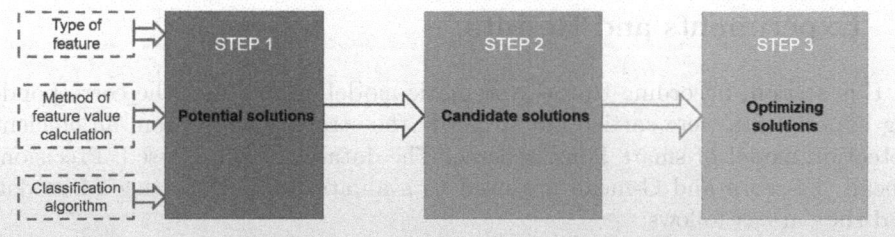

Fig. 1. Strategy of systematically modeling.

The first step is to choose candidate solutions from the potential solutions. As shown in Fig. 1, a potential solution is a combination of type of feature, calculation method of the value of features and classifier. Each solution is trained and cross validated to produce a potential model. The potential solution uses the prediction dataset to predict, and generates the Precision, Recall, F1-score and G-mean of the model. Each metric of all potential models is ranked and then four TopNs are obtained. The candidate solutions are selected according to the results of comprehensive consideration of three aspects: the number of potential solutions appearing in the four TopNs, the specific ranking and the specific value of metric. The results of this step are the better combinations of feature type, calculation method of the value of features and classifier.

The second step is to choose the better solutions from the candidate solutions. Financial fraud detection is a typical imbalanced data detection. Resampling is a common method to improve the performance of the model. In this step, over-sampling technology is used to improve the performance of the candidate solutions. The proportion of positive and negative sample gradually increased from the original proportion to 1. The best proportions are obtained by comparing the peak values of the curve of the four metrics: Precision, Recall, F1-score and G-mean. When the peak values are the same, the minimum proportion is chosen. The results of this step are the better combinations of feature type, calculation method of the value of features, classifier and proportion of oversampling.

The third step is to optimize the better solutions and get the best model with minimal features. In this step, filtered feature and embedded feature are used to select important features. After each iteration, the contribution values of the features are sorted, and then the features with non-zero contribution value are filtered to enter the next iteration. The best model is obtained by comparing the curve peaks of the four metrics. When the peak values are the same, the maximum number of iterations is chosen. The features used in this iteration are the key features, and the resulting model is the best model. The results of this step are the features used in this iteration and the resulting model.

This strategy can obtain a model which has a better performance with less training time. What needs to be improved is that there is no quantitative evaluation when choosing solutions.

4   Experiments and Results

In this section, according to the systematic modeling strategy, the corresponding experiments were carried out to verify the strategy and obtain an efficient detection model of smart Ponzi scheme. The dataset of [23] is used. Precision, Recall, F1-score and G-mean are used to evaluate the performance of model, and they are as follows:

$$Precision = \frac{TP}{TP + FP} \tag{5}$$

$$Recall = \frac{TP}{TF + FN} \tag{6}$$

$$F1 - score = 2 \cdot \frac{Recall \times Precision}{Recall + Precision} \qquad (7)$$

$$G - mean = \sqrt{Recall \cdot Precision} \qquad (8)$$

Firstly, experiments were conducted to determine which solutions are more suitable for the detection of Ponzi scheme. Secondly, based on the above results, experiments were conducted to determine which solutions and which proportions of oversampling are more suitable for detection model. Finally, experiments were conducted to optimize the solution.

Note that the values of performance are the result of the model's prediction on dataset of prediction. The dataset used for model prediction had not participated in model training and testing. The layered 10 fold cross validation method was used to train and test the model.

4.1   Experiment 1: Which Solutions Are Better?

Experiments were conducted to determine which solutions are more suitable to detect smart Ponzi scheme. In these experiments, eight classification algorithms such as Logistic Regression (i.e., LR) [33], Decision Trees (i.e., DT) [34], Support Vector Machine (i.e., SVM) [35], Random Forests (i.e., RF) [36], Extremely randomized trees (i.e., ET) [37], Gradient Boosting Machines(i.e., GDB) [38], XGBoost (i.e., XGB) [39] and LightGBM (i.e., LGB) [40] were used. The default parameters of the classifier were used during model training. The calculation methods of feature are TF, TF-IDF and TF-OUR. The types of features are five opcode sequences of different lengths (1 to 5).

The Top5 of the four evaluation metrics of experimental results are shown in Fig. 2, where No. is the number of solution, method is the calculation method of features value, and length is the length of opcode sequence. From Fig. 2 it can be seen that No. 124 and No. 39 are more suitable for modeling than others. No. 124 and No. 39 appear 3 times. No. 124 has twice ranked first and once ranked second. No. 39 has once ranked first, second and fourth respectively. The candidate solutions are No. 124 and No. 39.

4.2   Experiment 2: Which Proportion Is Better?

Experiments were carried out on the candidate solutions to determine the best proportion of oversampling and the best solution. SMOTE resampling technique was used. The proportion of negative sample to positive sample was started from 0.06 and increased by 0.01 each time until the proportion was 1. The results of the experiments are shown in Fig. 3.

As shown in Fig. 3, the performance of No. 124 is better than that of No. 39. When the proportion is 0.16 and 0.39, the three metrics (Precision, F1-score and G-mean) of No. 124 all reach the same maximum value (0.98, 0.94 and 0.94 respectively), while Recall is 0.91. When the proportion is 0.63 and 0.93,

Top 5 Precision

No.	Method	Length	Classifier	Precision	Recall	F1-score	G-mean
124	TF-OUR	3	ET	0.97	0.83	0.89	0.90
13	TF	1	GDB	0.97	0.79	0.85	0.88
185	TF	5	SVM	0.97	0.53	0.54	0.72
47	TF-IDF	1	LGB	0.96	0.83	0.88	0.89
164	TF-OUR	4	ET	0.96	0.83	0.88	0.89

Top 5 Recall

No.	Method	Length	Classifier	Precision	Recall	F1-score	G-mean
37	TF-IDF	1	GDB	0.82	0.89	0.85	0.85
38	TF-IDF	1	XGB	0.80	0.88	0.83	0.84
0	TF	1	LR	0.69	0.88	0.74	0.78
39	TF-IDF	1	LGB	0.93	0.87	0.90	0.90
112	TF-OUR	3	LR	0.91	0.86	0.88	0.88

Top 5 F1-score

No.	Method	Length	Classifier	Precision	Recall	F1-score	G-mean
39	TF-IDF	1	LGB	0.93	0.87	0.90	0.90
124	TF-OUR	3	ET	0.97	0.83	0.89	0.90
55	TF	2	LGB	0.94	0.85	0.89	0.89
35	TF-IDF	1	RF	0.95	0.85	0.89	0.90
103	TF	3	LGB	0.94	0.83	0.88	0.88

Top 5 G-mean

No.	Method	Length	Classifier	Precision	Recall	F1-score	G-mean
124	TF-OUR	3	ET	0.97	0.83	0.89	0.90
39	TF-IDF	1	LGB	0.93	0.87	0.90	0.90
35	TF-IDF	1	RF	0.95	0.85	0.89	0.90
55	TF	2	LGB	0.94	0.85	0.89	0.89
126	TF-OUR	3	XGB	0.95	0.84	0.88	0.89

Fig. 2. Top 5 metrics .

the three metrics (Recall, F1-score and G-mean) of No. 39 all reach the same maximum value (0.93, 0.94 and 0.94 respectively), while Precision is 0.96.

In fraud identification, when F1-score and G-mean are the same, Recall is more important than Precision. In addition, the larger the proportion is, the more expensive the training model will be. Therefore, 0.63 is the best proportion, No. 124 is a more suitable solution for identification of smart Ponzi scheme.

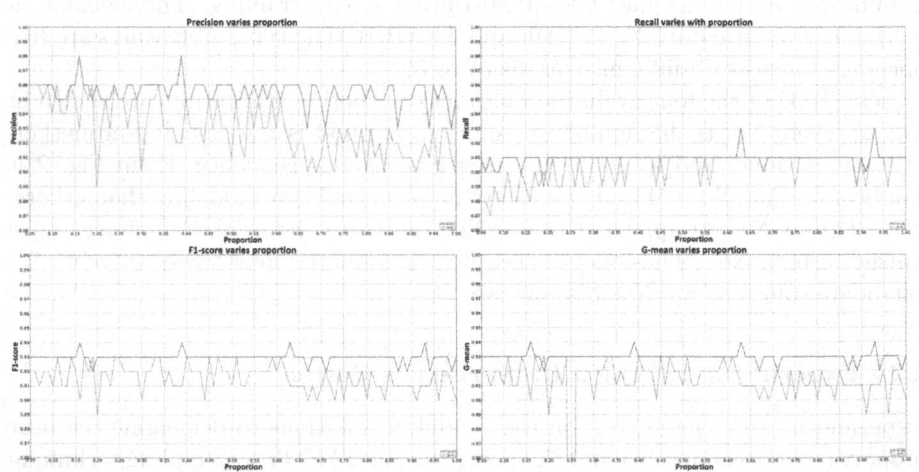

Fig. 3. Metrics vary with proportion.

4.3 Experiment 3: Optimizing the Solution

This time, the No. 124 solution (the value calculation method is TF-OUR, the length of opcode sequences is 3, the classifier is ET, and the proportion of over-sampling is 0.63) was optimized through multiple iterative experiments. At the end of each iteration, features have been processed according to their contribution value, and features were re-selected for the next iteration experiment. The way of feature processing is to clear up the features whose contribution value is 0, and carry out descending according to the contribution value. In this way, a descending list of non-zero features was obtained by contribution value, and the next iteration experiment is conducted. After 1000 iterations, the experimental results are shown in Fig. 4.

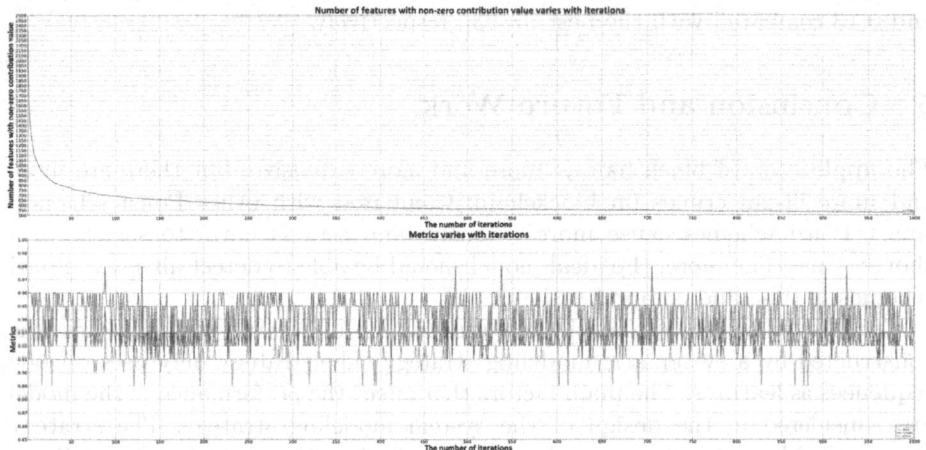

Fig. 4. Number of features with non-zero contribution value and metrics vary with iteration.

As shown in Fig. 4, after 1000 iterations, the curve of the number of features with non-zero contribution value tends to be stable. At the 88th and 130th iterations, Precision, Recall, F1-score and G-mean reach their maximum values at the same time, and their values are 0.98, 0.93, 0.95, 0.95, respectively. The 88th iteration uses 704 features, and the 130th iteration uses 669 features. The model obtained in the 128th iteration is the best.

4.4 Results and Comparison

The best automatic detection model of smart Ponzi scheme is obtained. 669 opcode sequences of length 3 are used as features in the model, and the calculation method of the value of features is TP-OUR. The classification algorithm of the model is the extremely randomized trees. Precision, Recall, F1-score and

Table 1. A performannce comparison

Model	Precision	Recall	F1-score
Account [23]	0.64	0.20	0.30
Opcode [23]	0.94	**0.73**	**0.82**
Opcode+Account [23]	**0.95**	0.69	0.79
Opcode (this paper proposed)	0.98	0.93	0.95

G-mean of the model is 0.98, 0.93, 0.95 and 0.95 respectively. The comparison with other models is shown in Table 1.

From Table 1 it can be seen that the proposed model in this paper is better than prior work [23]. Precision, Recall and F1-score They increased by 0.01, 0.20 and 0.13 compared with the best in [23], respectively.

5   Conclusion and Future Work

The application of blockchain is more and more extensive, but there are more and more illegal crimes on blockchain. Compared with other Ponzi schemes, smart Ponzi schemes cause more extensive and serious harm to society in a shorter time. Therefore, the ideal model should be able to detect all smart Ponzi schemes in time and comprehensively.

In this paper, an automatic detection model of smart Ponzi schemes was constructed by a systematic modeling strategy. The strategy only uses opcode sequences as features. The main factors that affect the performance of the model are considered in the design of the system modeling strategy. The strategy was verified by experiments, and an automatic detection model of smart Ponzi scheme is obtained. The model uses the extremely randomized trees algorithm as the classifier and 669 opcode sequences whose length is 3 as the features. The calculation method of the value of features is TF-OUR. More importantly, the performance of the model is the same at any moment from birth to death of smart Ponzi scheme. This can put an end to smart Ponzi schemes.

In the future, our research will focus on the following aspects. Firstly, to expand the dataset, not only add smart Ponzi scheme, but also add smart contracts for other frauds on Ethereum. Secondly, to extend the proposed model to detect other types of frauds on Ethereum. Thirdly, to construct a unified model to detect different types of fraud on Ethereum.

Acknowledgments. This work was supported in part by the Guangdong Provincial Key R&D Program under Grant No.2020B010166005, in part by the Characteristic innovation Program in Universities and Colleges of Guangdong Province, in part by the Youth Innovation Talent Program in Universities and Colleges of Guangdong Province(2018WQNCX301), in part by the General Research Program of South China Business College, Guangdong University of Foreign Studies(19-025B).

References

1. Nakamoto, S.: Bitcoin: a peer-to-peer electronic cash system [OL]. https://bitcoin. org/bitcoin.pdf
2. CoinDesk. (2017). Understanding Ethereum-blockchain Research Report. www. coindesk.com/research/understandingethereum-report/
3. Swan, M.: Blockchain: Blueprint for a New Economy. O'Reilly Media, Inc., Sebastopol (2015)
4. Chen, W., Zheng, Z.: Blockchain data analysis: a review of status, trends and challenges. J. Comput. Res. Dev. **55**(9), 1853–1870 (2018)
5. Yli-Huumo, J., Ko, D., Choi, S., Park, S., Smolander, K.: Where is current research on blockchain technology?-a systematic review. PLoS ONE **11**(10), e0163477 (2016)
6. Buterin, V.: A next-generation smart contract and decentralized application plat-form (2014)
7. Gandal, N., Hamrick, J.T., Moore, T., et al.: Price manipulation in the Bitcoin ecosystem. J. Monetary Econ. **95**, 86–96 (2018)
8. Brito, J., Castillo, A.: Bitcoin: a primer for policymakers. Mercatus Center at George Mason University (2013)
9. Slattery, T.: Taking a bit out of crime: Bitcoin and cross-border tax evasion. Brook. J. Int. L. **39**, 829 (2014)
10. Atzei, N., Bartoletti, M., Cimoli, T.: A survey of attacks on ethereum smart con-tracts (SoK). In: Maffei, M., Ryan, M. (eds.) POST 2017. LNCS, vol. 10204, pp. 164–186. Springer, Heidelberg (2017). https://doi.org/10.1007/978-3-662-54455-6_8
11. Chen, W., Wu, J., Zheng, Z., Chen, C., Zhou Y.: Evidence from Mining the Mt. Gox Transaction Network, Market Manipulation of Bitcoin (2019)
12. Moser, M., Bohme, R., Breuker, D.: An inquiry into money laundering tools in the Bitcoin ecosystem. Proceedings of the APWG Symposium on Electronic Crime Research. San Francisco, USA, pp. 1–14 (2013)
13. Tasca, P., Hayes, A., Liu, S.: The evolution of the bitcoin economy: extracting and analyzing the network of payment relationships. J. Risk Finan. **19**(2), 94–126 (2018)
14. Christin, N.: Traveling the silk road: a measurement analysis of a large anony-mous online marketplace. In: Proceedings of the International World Wide Web Conference. Rio de Janeiro, Brazil, pp. 213–224 (2013)
15. Vasek, M., Moore, T.: There's no free lunch, even using bitcoin: tracking the popu-larity and profits of virtual currency scams. In: Böhme, R., Okamoto, T. (eds.) FC 2015. LNCS, vol. 8975, pp. 44–61. Springer, Heidelberg (2015). https://doi.org/10. 1007/978-3-662-47854-7_4
16. Karame, G.O., Androulaki, E., Roeschlin, M., et al.: Misbehavior in bitcoin: a study of double-spending and accountability. ACM Trans. Inf. Syst. Secur. (TISSEC) **18**(1), 2 (2015)
17. Eyal, I., Sirer, E.G.: Majority is not enough: Bitcoin mining is vulnerable. Commun. ACM **61**(7), 95–102 (2018)
18. Bhargavan, K., Delignat-Lavaud, A., Fournet, C., et al.: Formal verification of smart contracts: Short paper. In: Proceedings of the 2016 ACM Workshop on Programming Languages and Analysis for Security, pp. 91–96. ACM (2016)

19. Moore, T., Han, J., Clayton, R.: The postmodern ponzi scheme: empirical analysis of high-yield investment programs. In: Keromytis, A.D. (ed.) FC 2012. LNCS, vol. 7397, pp. 41–56. Springer, Heidelberg (2012). https://doi.org/10.1007/978-3-642-32946-3_4

20. Szabo, N.: Smart contracts: building blocks for digital markets, September 1996. http://www.fon.hum.uva.nl/. Accessed 1 Oct 2017

21. Bartoletti, M., Pes, B., Serusi, S.: Data mining for detecting bitcoin Ponzi schemes (2018). http://arxiv.org/abs/1803.00646

22. Toyoda, K., Mathiopoulos, P.T., Ohtsuki, T.: A novel methodology for hyip operators' Bitcoin addresses identification. IEEE Access 7, 74835–74848 (2019). https://doi.org/10.1109/ACCESS.2019.2921087

23. Chen, W., Zheng, Z., Ngai, E., et al.: Exploiting Blockchain data to detect smart ponzi schemes on ethereum. IEEE Access 1, 37575–37586 (2019)

24. Chen, W., Zheng, Z., Cui, J., et al.: Detecting ponzi schemes on ethereum: towards healthier blockchain technology. In: The 2018 World Wide Web Conference (2018)

25. Bartoletti, M., Carta, S., Cimoli, T., Saia, R.: Dissecting Ponzi schemes on Ethereum: identification, analysis, and impact (2017). https://arxiv.org/abs/1703.03779

26. Smith, F.: Madoff ponzi scheme exposes the myth of the sophisticated investor. U. Balt. L. Rev. 40, 215 (2010)

27. Davis, J., et al.: The relationship between precision-recall and ROC curves. In: ICML (2006)

28. Moore, T., Han, J., Clayton, R.: The postmodern ponzi scheme: empirical analysis of high-yield investment programs. In: Keromytis, A.D. (ed.) FC 2012. LNCS, vol. 7397, pp. 41–56. Springer, Heidelberg (2012). https://doi.org/10.1007/978-3-642-32946-3_4

29. Yujian, L., Bo, L.: A normalized Levenshtein distance metric. IEEE Trans. Pattern Anal. Mach. Intell. 29(6), 1091–1095 (2007)

30. S. C. A. Chamber of Digital Commerce, "Smart contracts - Is the law ready," no. September 2018

31. Abou-Assaleh, T., Keselj, V., Sweidan, R.: N-gram based detection of new malicious code. In: Proceedings of the 28th Annual International Computer Software and Applications Conference, IEEE Computer Society, 41–42 (2004)

32. Salton, G., Wong, A., Yang, C.S.: A vector space model for automatic indexing. Commun. ACM 18, 613–620 (1975)

33. Kleinbaum, D.G., Klein, M.: Logistic Regression. SBH. Springer, New York (2010). https://doi.org/10.1007/978-1-4419-1742-3

34. Quinlan, R.J.: Induction of decision trees. Mach. Learn. 1(1), 81–106 (1986)

35. Hearst, M.A., Dumais, S.T., Osman, E., et al.: Support vector machines. IEEE Intell. Syst. 13(4), 18–28 (1998)

36. Breiman, L.: Random forests. Mach. Learn. 45(1), 5–32 (2001)

37. Geurts, P., Ernst, D., Wehenkel, L.: Extremely randomized trees. Mach. Learn. 63(1), 3–42 (2006)

38. Natekin, A., Knoll, A., et al.: Gradient boosting machines. a tutorial. Front. Neurorobotics, 7, 21 (2013). https://doi.org/10.3389/fnbot.2013.00021

39. Chen, T., Guestrin, C., et al.: XGBoost: A Scalable Tree Boosting System, pp 785–794 (2016). https://doi.org/10.1145/2939672.2939785

40. Qi, M.: LightGBM: A Highly Efficient Gradient Boosting Decision Tree (2018)

Towards on Blockchain Data Privacy Protection with Cryptography and Software Architecture Approach

Zexu Wang[1,3], Bin Wen[1,2,3(✉)], and Ziqiang Luo[1,2]

[1] School of Information Science and Technology,
Hainan Normal University, Haikou, China
z.x.wang1060@qq.com, binwen@hainnu.edu.cn
[2] Cloud Computing and Big Data Research Center,
Hainan Normal University, Haikou, China
[3] Key Laboratory of Data Science and Intelligence Education of Ministry of
Education, Hainan Normal University, Haikou 571158, China

Abstract. The essence of blockchain is to solve trust problems and realize value transfer. The traditional centralized processing method adopts centralized transmission and storage of users' data privacy, which improves the security and reliability of processing. The non central blockchain technology uses distributed ledger technology to realize the characteristics of disintermediation, data tampering, traceability, work audit, etc. encryption algorithm is used to encrypt the data, and consensus mechanism makes the data sharing of blockchain system more fair and stable. The current passive data privacy schemes are basically based on cryptography. On the premise of satisfying the constraint mechanism of blockchain, this paper studies the technical framework, encryption mechanism and empirical analysis of blockchain, and discusses the information privacy protection method of hiding the original big data as much as possible, so as to improve the system performance and protect the security and privacy of user data. At the same time, we study data privacy protection from the perspective of software architecture, and propose a data privacy protection scheme through algorithm decomposition multi center collaboration method, which provides guidance for big data sharing and transaction based on blockchain.

Keywords: Blockchain technology architecture · Cryptography · Cryptographic hash function · Privacy protection · Software architecture

1 Introduction

Blockchain is a computing infrastructure to realize value transfer in the digital economy era, because of its features of decentralization and anonymity, the traditional transmission of various types of value has a subversive improvement

© Springer Nature Singapore Pte Ltd. 2020
Z. Zheng et al. (Eds.): BlockSys 2020, CCIS 1267, pp. 205–217, 2020.
https://doi.org/10.1007/978-981-15-9213-3_16

[1, 2]. As an integrated system with point-to-point network, cryptography, consensus mechanism, smart contract and other technologies, blockchain provides a trusted channel for information and value transfer and exchange in untrusted networks. With its unique trust building mechanism, blockchain technology has cross innovation with new technologies and applications such as cloud computing, big data, artificial intelligence, etc., and has integrated and evolved into a new generation of network infrastructure to reconstruct the industrial ecology of digital economy [3–5].

Blockchain is the result of the integration of cryptography, consensus mechanism, computer science and other disciplines. Bitcoin [6] is one of blockchain's most successful apps, but blockchain isn't just about issuing coins. Just as the real value of blockchain lies in the safer and more efficient transfer of value than the traditional [11, 13]. Its system is composed of the storage layer and the network layer of the protocol layer, including all kinds of scripts,[1] and the intelligent contract extension layer, which encapsulates the application layer of all kinds of applications. All levels coordinate with each other to maintain the stability of the system [5].

The lack of data privacy is one of the main limitations of blockchain services. The current protection measures mainly include coin shuffle, ring signature, zero knowledge proof and so on.

Bitcoin is the first application of blockchain and also a very successful practice. As a kind of digital currency based on blockchain, it is precisely because the mechanism of block chain cryptography guarantees that the security of products based on blockchain technology such as bitcoin and litecoin has been greatly improved. The rest of the article is organized as follows. In the second 2, we will introduce the basic architecture of the blockchain and how to interact with each other to complete the daily work. Section 3 introduces how the digital currency represented by bitcoin can guarantee the security of the transaction through the cryptography mechanism in the blockchain. In the Sect. 4, we will verify and analyze the script examples to illustrate the significant advantages of the blockchain in decentralization. In the Sect. 5, the method of block chain privacy protection based on software architecture is proposed. Conclusions with main contributions of proposed approach and further work plans are also touched upon in Sect. 6.

2 Technical Architecture

2.1 Protocol Layer

This layer consists of a storage layer and a network layer. The storage layer is the lowest technology of the block chain, which mainly ensures the security and tradability of data while storing data. Data storage is mainly realized by using Markle tree [6], block chain storage and other data structures, and the high efficiency of data storage greatly determines the performance of the upper layer. Of course, there are certain requirements for programming ability, but the

---

[1] https://bitcoin.org/bitcoin.pdf.

logical structure of data storage can be achieved in most languages, such as Java, Python, GO, and so on.

The main task of the network layer is to realize the information exchange between users through distributed storage, asymmetric encryption, digital signature, multi-signature and other technologies in the point-to-point network. The network layer also includes a common algorithm for encapsulating network node voting and an incentive mechanism for mining and other economic factors to jointly guarantee the security of each node. Distributed network data transmission system verification algorithm, consensus algorithm, incentive mechanism together constitute the content of the protocol layer.

2.2 Extensions Layer

The problem of "intelligent contract" is the most important content in this aspect. The contract is embodied in the form of programming, which can only be executed after certain conditions are met, and finally some requirements can be intelligently realized.This level allows for more sophisticated intelligent contract types and value delivery using more complete scripting languages, allowing the development of the extension layer to be unconstrained [7,8]. The main task of this layer is to realize intelligent operation by extending the intelligent contract of the layer.

2.3 Application Layer

The application layer, as the name implies, is the layer to realize business applications. On the basis of the block chain, online shopping, games, digital assets, ownership certificates, digital currency and so on are realized. It can not only realize the function of traditional centralized server, but also has remarkable characteristics on the security guard of user information through anonymity [9].

3 Cryptography Mechanism in Blockchain

3.1 Key Pair

Blockchain uses asymmetric encryption to encrypt and decrypt data. The private key and the corresponding public key derived from the private key form a group of key pairs. In the bitcoin system, the private key determines the ownership of the bitcoin address property generated by the corresponding public key. The private key is mainly used for signature verification during the transaction. When the verification passes, the corresponding bitcoin address has the corresponding asset, otherwise it cannot be owned [10,12]. The private key must be well preserved, and once lost, the property on the corresponding bitcoin address cannot be recovered.

The private key is just a 256-bit binary number, and you can find a random number from 0 to 2^{256}. However, in order to exclude personal factors [5,14]: for example, the selected number is special, such as 123456789, etc., it is recommended to use a pseudo-random number generator $(CSPRNG)$ to generate a random number as the private key is more secure, but it must be backed up, otherwise the asset will be lost with the loss of the private key.

Using elliptic curve cryptography (ECC), the private $key(m)$ can be generated into the public $key(M)$, $M = m * G$, G is the constant point of the generation point of the elliptic curve. This process is one-way and irreversible [15]. Since G is the same, the relationship between the private key and the public key is fixed. Due to the irreversibility of the operation, the private key cannot be obtained from the public key. Thus, it is guaranteed that the address generated by the public key will not expose the private key to anyone. Asymmetric encryption uses the key pair, which greatly improves the security, enables the value to be transferred between users, and achieves anonymity and security.

3.2   Address

A bitcoin address can be seen by anyone, including anyone who wants to give you bitcoin. In the transaction of bitcoin, only the receipt address is needed, but no information about the payment address is known. The address of bitcoin represents the direction of capital inflow and issuance. The appearance of bitcoin address makes bitcoin very flexible, which can be put in various occasions to achieve the purpose of collection, without worrying about whether their private key will be exposed.

The address of bitcoin is obtained from the public key through k→SHA256→ RIPEMD160(double hash) to get a 160-byte public key hash, and then the public key hash is obtained through BaseCheck58 encoding to get the address of bitcoin. Basecheck58 encoding enables Base58 encoding with version, validation format, and explicit encoding format. Combining the 160-byte public key hash (data) with the version prefix, we get a 32-byte hash value through the double hash SHA256 (SHA256 (prefix+data)), we take the first 4 bits as our check code. Prefix + public key hash + check code, together with Base58 encoding to get the bitcoin address. The version prefix is used to indicate the type of encoded data, and the checksum is used to avoid and detect whether there are any errors caused by transcription and input. When coding Basecheck58, the checksum of the original data will be compared with the checksum in the result. If it is the same, the checksum will be successful, otherwise it will fail. It is the version prefix, checksum, and so on that makes the results of the Basecheck58 encoding easier to classify.

3.3   Wallet

There are no bitcoins in the wallet. It's a collection of private keys (See footnote 1). The owner of the wallet uses a key to sign the transaction, enabling the transfer of assets. According to the relationship between private keys in wallets, wallets can be divided into two categories: non-deterministic wallets and deterministic wallets.

The first kind of wallet: the non-deterministic wallet. This kind of wallet is just a collection of randomly generated private keys, each private key is generated by a random number, there is no relationship between the two private keys, is a discrete existence. The discrete existence of private keys in such wallets makes the loss of one private key not a threat to others. However, because the number of private keys in a wallet is limited, the number of bitcoin addresses generated is also limited. If frequently traded on a few addresses, the user's property will be threatened. Some people will say: we generate a lot of private keys can not it? Because of a large number of private keys, a large number of backups are required, but since there is no association between the private keys, it is difficult to backup and manage the private keys. Therefore, this kind of wallet is only suitable for special situations, but not suitable for general situations.

The second kind of wallet: the certainty wallet, also known as the seed wallet. Through the combination of random Numbers, indexes and chain codes, the subprivate keys can be derived, which in turn can be derived from the grandson private keys, forming a tree structure. (Merkle tree) thus, the entire purse can be recovered from a single seed. With the seed wallet, key transfer and management is very convenient, See Fig. 1 for details.

Determine that the wallet is currently using the $bip - 32$ standard HD wallet. The result generated by the root seed (512bits) through the one-way HMAC-SHA512 hash function is 512 bytes, and the left 256 bits are used as the main private key m, and the remaining 256 bytes are used as the right The bit-byte portion is encoded as the main chain. The main purpose of the chain code is to introduce random Numbers into the generation of this subkey. The corresponding master public key (M) is obtained by using elliptic curve cryptography $(ECC)m * G$.

From Parent Key to Child Key. The parent private key (m), the main chain code and the index number are combined to obtain a 512-bit Hash value after the three-hash of the one-way HMAC-SHA512 hash function. Where the right 256 bits encode the child chain, the remaining left 256 bits act with the index value on the parent private key (m) to generate the child private key. The subprivate key can be obtained by using elliptic curve cryptography $M = m*G$, and then the address can be generated by using the subpublic key.

Expanded Key. In the process of generating and secret key, we add 256-bit private key and 256-bit chain code together to form a sequence of 512 bytes. We call it the extension key, that is, the private key and chain code are combined to form the extension key.

Keys include public and private keys, so there are two types of extended keys: extended private keys and extended public keys. The chain code and the private key are combined to form the extended private key, which can be used to generate the sub-private key. The chain code and the public key are combined to form the extended public key, which can be used to generate the child public key. An extended private key can derive an entire branch, whereas an extended public key can only create a branch containing a public key because it cannot produce a

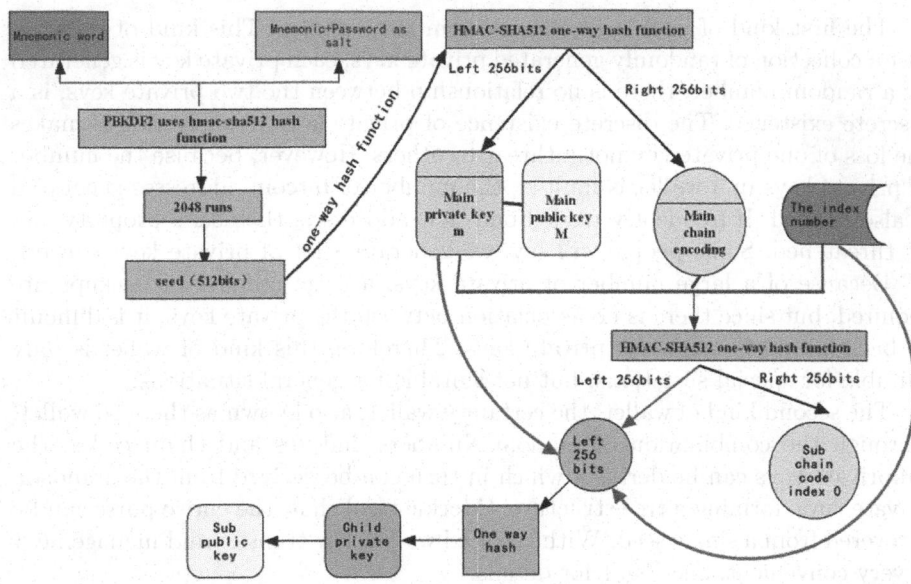

Fig. 1. Tree structure of HD wallet.

private key. As shown in the Fig. 2, the 512-bit bytes generated by combining the extended public key and index number together through the one-way HMAC-SHA512 hash function, the right 256 bit bytes are encoded as the child chain, while the left 256 bit bytes act on the parent public key to generate the child public key. However, since the extended public key contains chain code, if a child private key is exposed or lost, it will cause the insecurity of other brother private keys and even make the parent private key leak.

In this case, you can use the enhanced derivation of the child key: the method of generating the child chain code by the parent private key to solve the problem. Because we can't know the parent private key, we can't infer the parent or the brother private key by exposing the operator private key. In general, the extended public key is generally used, and the enhanced derivation method of using the child key on the parent node is generally used to ensure security, while the extended public key method is used for other nodes.

Generate Subpublic Key. To sum up, there are two ways to generate the subpublic key: one is to generate the subprivate key and then regenerate it into the subpublic key; Second, the public key can be generated directly by extending the public key. Using the extended public key to derive the HD wallet can be very convenient and secure value transfer. Using the extended public key, you can create a large number of addresses online, use the private key to sign and trade offline, and then complete the transaction by broadcasting. This ensures that safe transactions can be made even in unsafe situations.

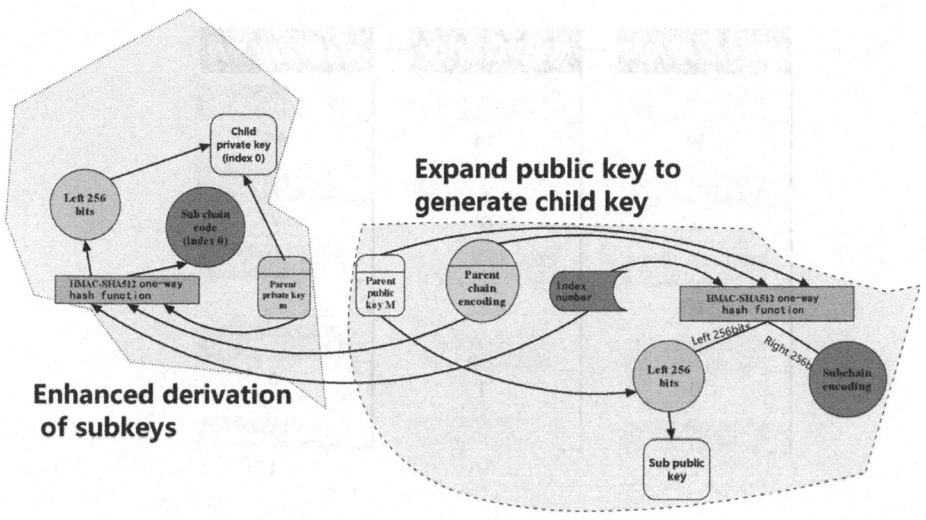

Fig. 2. Derivation of child key.

Path of Tree-Like Structure of HD Wallet. The tree structure of the HD wallet can be very large, each parent key can be composed of 4 billion subkeys: 2 billion regular subkeys, 2 billion enhanced derived subkeys. The same is true for each subkey, and so on. The tree structure of the HD wallet is huge. It is difficult to identify and manage a particular branch. A solution is provided through the bitcoin protocol BIP0044: the protocol specifies a structure consisting of five predefined tree hierarchies [6]:

$$M/purpose'/coin\_type'/'account'/change/address\_index$$

As shown in Fig. 3, purpose of the first layer is set to $44'$; The "$cion\_type''$ of the second layer specifies the currency, such as: Bitcoin uses $m/44'/0'$, Bitcoin Testnet uses $m/44'/1'$, Litecoin uses $m/44'/2'$; The third layer is "account". Users can create multiple sub-accounts to facilitate management and statistics. For example, $m/44'/0'/0'$ and $m/44'/0'/1'$ are two sub-accounts of bitcoin. The fourth layer is "change". Each HD wallet has two subtrees here, one for creating a collection address and one for creating a change address. The fifth layer is the child of the fourth layer, and "$address\_index$" is the available address for the HD wallet.

4   Empirical Analysis of Trading Scripts

P2KH ($pay-to-public-key-hash$) is the most widely used bitcoin transaction. When trading, by typing the private key of digital signature and public key that can unlock by the output of the locking P2KH script will unlock script and locking in end-to-end form combination script can be verify, structure as

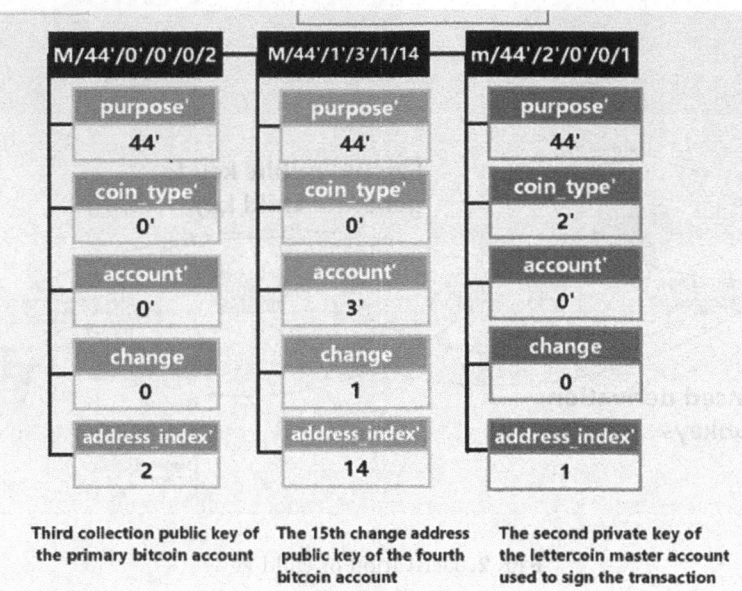

Fig. 3. BIP0044 HD wallet structure.

shown in Fig. 4, apply combination script combining stack implementation of transaction security authentication, is the realization of the programmability of the currency of important step.

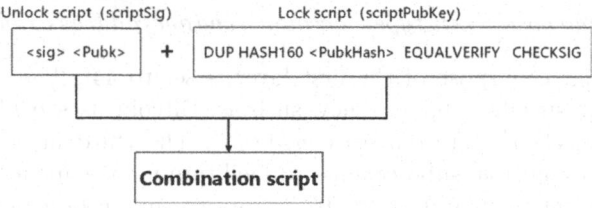

Fig. 4. Combination script.

A locking script is a constraint placed on an expense that can be unlocked and used when certain conditions are met, the process is shown in Fig. 5. Unlocking script: a script that, as the name implies, satisfies the constraints of the locking script so that it can be expensed. The implementation of the script depends on the data structure of the stack, which is a last in, first out queue. Numbers are pushed onto the stack, opcodes push or pop one or more parameters from the stack, manipulate them, and push the results onto the stack.

The p2sh script code is as follows:

```
def is_pay_to_script_hash(class_, script_public_key):
    return (len(script_public_key)==23 and
    byte2int(script_public_key)==OP_HASH160 and
    indexbytes(script_public_key,-1)==OP_EQUAL)
```

The code implements a double-level hash encoding of HASH160 for the length of the public key script, compares the result with the public key hash in the source code, and finally returns the type value of a bool.

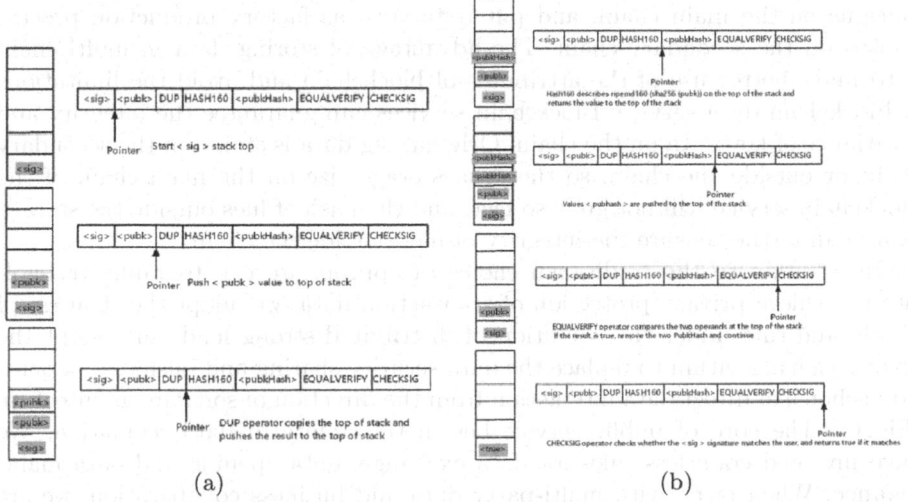

Fig. 5. P2KH combined script verification

When faced with wallets, blockchain browsers, and other applications, we see information like addresses and balances, and the transaction itself does not contain the address of bitcoin, but locks and unlocks the UTXO corresponding to the face value. When part of the UTXO is locked, only the unlocking script that meets the unlocking body condition can control the corresponding UTXO. The locking script and the unlocking script are constructed by a series of constraints, which are guaranteed by the security of cryptographic algorithms, which greatly improves the spontaneity and security of transactions.

5   Software Architecture Approach of Data Privacy Protection

Blockchain based application services may have sensitive data, which should only be available to some blockchain participants. However, the information on the blockchain is designed to be accessible to all participants, and there is no privileged user in the blockchain network, no matter whether the blockchain is public, federated or private [16]. At the same time, the storage capacity of the blockchain network is limited, because it contains the complete history of all transactions of all participants in the blockchain network (once written, it cannot be tampered with). As a result, sensitive data privacy protection of blockchain data services is a problem, data ownership affects data transaction effect, and high redundant data storage results in huge growth of storage space. Therefore, not all data are put on one chain, only sensitive and small data are stored on the main chain. For example, food quality traceability system can store traceability information (such as traceability number and results) required by traceability laws and regulations on the main chain, and put data such as factory production process photos on the secondary chain. The advantage of storing data in multi chain is to make better use of the attributes of blockchain and avoid the limitations of blockchain data service. Blockchain services can guarantee the integrity and invariance of key data on the chain. Original big data is stored in the secondary chain or outside the chain, so the data storage size on the main chain of the blockchain service will not grow so fast, and the hash of files outside the storage chain can further ensure the integrity of files outside the chain.

In addition to the traditional choice of appropriate cryptography technology to achieve privacy protection of transaction data, we adopt the strategy of divide and rule under the condition of distributed strong load, and adopt the transaction algorithm to replace the data security sharing and business cooperation scheme of direct data interaction from the direction of software architecture (Fig. 6). The core of public service lies in the ability of data regulation. We have invented countless rules for data exchange, data opening and data maintenance. When faced with multi-party data and business collaboration, we are often unable to do our best. Establish the main technical concept of trusted, transparent and traceable blockchain data exchange and business collaboration services - data three rights separation, that is, to realize data three rights separation by technical means, to solve the most core trust problem of the digital economy.

Data owner (seller): with local data (big data), data is increasingly becoming a core asset; data executor: a trusted execution service environment for data exchange to fill the gap between data owner and user; data user (buyer): it is conducive to data analysis and processing, and can only get analysis results without necessarily obtaining source data.

From Fig. 6, under the traditional centralized data management mode, the distributed data processing process is as follows:

1. Obtain data (transactions) from all participants (sellers);
2. Perform relevant data analysis algorithm for all aggregate data (big data). Data is essentially copied from the data owner. As a result, the network traffic is large, the data privacy risk of data owners is increased, and the data transaction efficiency is low.

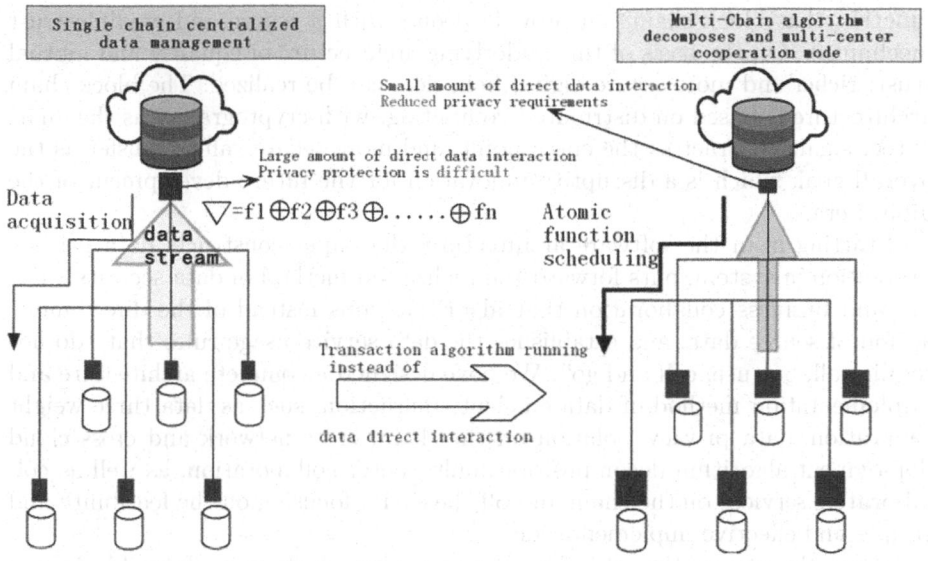

Fig. 6. Algorithm decomposition multi-center collaboration

Thus, the rules of data service usage are established, which are "do not require all, but use, call and go". By confirming the right of data and clarifying the relationship between the responsibility and right of data, the compliance exchange and capitalization of data under the compliance scenario are realized. The specific data service operation process adopts the scheme of privacy protection data sharing and collaborative implementation, establishes the privacy isolation method of the primary and secondary chain data on the chain, provides the connection function of the directory chain (main chain or on the chain) small data to the data provider (sub chain or off chain) big data, sets the directory chain pre drive contract to access the data provider to complete the data transaction, and calculates the pre drive Sub algorithm of data processing (transaction) for machine distribution.

6   Conclusions and Further Works

In this paper, we focus on the cryptography mechanism in blockchain and how to ensure the security of blockchain. Through the analysis of specific examples of bitcoin, From the perspective of security, transaction generation, broadcast, verification, block and other links are closely linked, and these links are inseparable from the calculation of multiple types and high frequency password hash functions. Cryptographic hash function plays an important role in digital signature, password protection, integrity verification, information compression and proof of work. It is precisely because of the anti-collision, antigenic attack, antigenic second attack, high sensitivity and other characteristics of cryptographic hash function that block chain can provide people with a secure and credible trust mechanism. On the basis of this underlying architecture of equality and mutual trust, richer and more secure digital behaviors can be realized. The block chain architecture is based on distributed computing, with cryptography as the guarantee, smart contract as the entry point, and more secure value transfer as the overall goal, which is a disruptive innovation for the future development of the digital era.

Starting from the software architecture, the paper constructs data privacy protection in system, puts forward the realization method of data security sharing and business collaboration that algorithm runs instead of the direct interaction of source data, and establishes the data service usage rules that "do not require all, but use, call and go". We have designed a complete architecture and implementation method of data efficient transaction, such as data three weight separation, data privacy isolation on the chain, cross network and cross cloud deployment algorithm decomposition multi center collaboration, as well as collaborative services on the chain and off the chain, focusing on the feasibility and simple and effective implementation.

From the perspective of software architecture, further work on blockchain privacy protection includes:

1. Research and application of security-oriented block chain platform abnormal attack defense deployment.
2. Research and implementation of block chain security audit auxiliary tools.
3. Analysis and response of block chain security vulnerabilities.
4. Research on the implementation mechanism of block chain application threat intelligence (BTI) collection and feedback.
5. Optimize and quantify the resource sharing capability of data transaction services through the cooperative implementation mechanism of privacy protection data sharing.

Acknowledgments. This research has been supported by the Natural Science Foundation of China (No. 61562024, No. 61463012).

References

1. Zheng, Z., Xie, S., Dai, H., Chen, X., Wang, H.: An overview of blockchain technology: architecture, consensus, and future trends. In: IEEE International Congress on Big Data (BigData Congress), pp. 557–564. IEEE (2017)
2. Aitzhan, N.Z., Svetinovic, D.: Security and privacy in decentralized energy trading through multi-signatures, blockchain and anonymous messaging streams. IEEE Trans. Dependable Secure Comput. **15**(5), 840–852 (2018)
3. Zheng, Z., Xie, S., Dai, H.N., Chen, X., Wang, H.: Blockchain challenges and opportunities: a survey. Int. J. Web Grid Serv. **14**(4), 352–375 (2018)
4. Hu, L., Song, L.: Review and development of cryptographic hash function. Commun. China Comput. Assoc. **15**(7), 23–28 (2019)
5. Zhu, L., et al.: Survey on privacy preserving techniques for blockchain technology. J. Comput. Res. Dev. **54**(10), 2170–2186 (2017)

6. Andreas, M.: Antonopoulos. Mastering Bitcoin. The United States of America (2010)
7. Luu, L., Chu, D.-H., Olickel, H., Saxena, P., Hobor, A.: Making smart contracts smarter. In: Proceedings of the 2016 ACM SIGSAC Conference on Computer and Communications Security, Vienna, Austria, pp. 254–269. ACM (2016)
8. Reyna, A., Martin, C., Chen, J., Soler, E., Diaz, M.: On blockchain and its integration with IoT: challenges and opportunities. Future Gener. Comput. Syst. Int. J. Escience **88**, 173–190 (2018)
9. Tosh, D.K., Shetty, S., Liang, X., Kamhoua, C.A., Kwiat, K.A., Njilla, L.: Security implications of blockchain cloud with analysis of block withholding attack. In: 2017 17th IEEE/ACM International Symposium on Cluster, Cloud and Grid Computing (CCGRID), p. 458 (2017)
10. Dorri, A., Steger, M., Kanhere, S.S., Jurdak, R.: BlockChain: A distributed solution to automotive security and privacy. IEEE Commun. Mag. **55**(12), 119–125 (2017)
11. Barnas, N.: Blockchains in national defense: trustworthy systems in a trustless world. Blue Horizons Fellowship, Air University, Maxwell Air Force Base, Alabama (2016)
12. Hurich, P.: The virtual is real: an argument for characterizing bitcoins as private property. Bank. Finance Law Rev. **31**, 573 (2016)
13. He, Z., Cai, Z., Yu, J.: Latent-data privacy preserving with customized data utility for social network data. IEEE Trans. Veh. Technol. **67**, 665–673 (2018). https://doi.org/10.1109/TVT.2017.2738018.CrossRef
14. Solat, S., Potop Butucaru, M.: Zeroblock: preventing selfish mining in bitcoin. Ph.D. thesis, University of Paris (2016)
15. Zheng, X., Cai, Z., Li, Y.: Data linkage in smart IoT systems: a consideration from privacy perspective. IEEE Commun. Mag. **56**(9), 55–61 (2018)
16. Zheng, W., Zheng, Z., Chen, X., Dai, K., Li, P., Chen, R.: NutBaaS: a blockchain-as-a-service platform. IEEE Access **7**, 134422–134433 (2019)

Research and Implementation of Cross-Chain Transaction Model Based on Improved Hash-Locking

Bingrong Dai[1,2(✉)], Shengming Jiang[1], Menglu Zhu[2], Ming Lu[2], Dunwei Li[2], and Chao Li[2]

[1] College of Information Engineering, Shanghai Maritime University, Shanghai 201306, China
dbr@sscenter.sh.cn
[2] Shanghai Development Center of Computer Software Technology, Shanghai 201112, China

Abstract. Blockchain is a decentralized, trust-free distributed ledger technology which has been applied in various fields such as finance, supply chain, and asset management. However, the network isolation between blockchains has limited their interoperability in asset exchange and business collaboration since it forms blockchain islands. Cross-chain is an important technology aiming to realize the interoperability between blockchains, and has become one of the hottest research topics in this area. This paper proposes a cross-chain transaction model based on improved hash locking consulted by the notary and users, which can solve the security problems in traditional hash locking. It can prevent malicious participants from creating large traffic blocking channels based on the key of unlocking condition. At the same time, the scheme of notary multi-signature is designed to solve the problem of lack of trust in traditional model. The transaction process of cross-chain, key agreement, cooperation mechanism of cross-chain, and security analysis based on the model is given in detail. Experiments of cross-chain transactions are implemented in Ethereum private chain, and prove that the proposed model has good application abilities.

Keywords: Blockchain · Cross-chain · Blockchain interoperability · Hash-locking · Notary schemes · Diffie-Hellman algorithm

1 Introduction

Blockchain is a decentralized, trust-free distributed ledger technology, which allows all nodes in the network to join in and manage the same data together through consensus algorithms and cryptographic algorithms [1, 2]. It has been applied in various fields such as finance, supply chain and asset management etc. However, the application of blockchain is still restricted by many factors, such as throughput, scalability, and network isolation [3]. Among these problems, the network isolation directly limits the interoperability of asset exchange and business collaboration. Users and developers have to choose which blockchain to use in each application scenario, since each blockchain

© Springer Nature Singapore Pte Ltd. 2020
Z. Zheng et al. (Eds.): BlockSys 2020, CCIS 1267, pp. 218–230, 2020.
https://doi.org/10.1007/978-981-15-9213-3_17

acts as a chain-island and cannot connect to the blockchain internet, which hinders the integration and development of blockchain [4].

Blockchain interoperability is the key to achieve the interconnection and value exchange between isolated blockchains [5–7, 9]. Cross-chain assets exchange needs to satisfy atomicity [4–6]. That is, transactions are either completely successful or completely failed, and there is no third intermediate state. Notary schemes, sidechains/relays, and hash-locking are currently popular cross-chain technologies [8].

The notary scheme is a centralized or multi-signature-based model, in which a party or a group of parties agree to carry out an action on blockchain B when some event on blockchain A takes place. Interledger's original solution was to use the notary scheme to ensure the atomicity of cross-chain transactions, and hashlock was also used into subsequent development to improve the protocol [7, 10]. Corda proposed parties of transaction to select a common notary as the supervisor to verify the transaction data, which can provide a safer notary selection mechanism [11].

The sidechain/relays refer to another blockchain that fully owns the functions of the main chain, which can collect data from the main chain and trigger the smart contract on the sidechain/relay chain. Pegged Sidechains is the original technical prototype of sidechains [7]. Currently, the most popular cross-chain solutions based on sidechain/relays chain are PolkaDot and Cosmos, which respectively designed the cross-chain platform structure of Relay Chain-Bridges-Parachains and Hub-Zone [12, 13]. Borkowski et al. [16] present a cross-chain transfer protocol Dextt to record a token transfer on any number of blockchains simultaneously, in which the chain selected by the arbitration consensus plays the role of relay chain. Philipp et al. [17] improve the relay contract by applying a content-addressable storage pattern to further reduce operating cost.

Hash-locking is to achieve the atomic exchange of assets through time difference and hidden hash value. Nolan's atomic transfers is the technical prototype of hash lock [14]. It is first used by lighting network in the BTC off-chain transfer expansion solution [15], with operations including contract locking, unlock execution, and ensures the atomicity of cross-chain transactions. Off-chain payment networks [8, 9] and state channels use hashed time-lock contracts to circumvent the scalability limits of existing blockchains. Herlihy [9] proposed a new method to construct complex distributed computing to manage cross-chain asset transactions with a time-lock commit protocol.

Each of these cross-chain technologies has its own advantages and disadvantages. For the notary schemes, the value transfer or information exchange mainly depends on the notary, which is highly centralized. Multi-signature enhances the security of notaries to a certain extent, but it still has a risk of conspiracy. For hash-locking, a certain amount of assets must be locked during the opening phase of the transaction channel, and there may be a risk of asset loss when timeout. Many transactions created by malicious participants will block channels and affect normal transactions.

This paper proposes a new cross-chain transaction model based on an improved hash locking, which combines the characteristics of decentralization of hash lock and the simplicity of the notary schemes. Based on the transaction synchronization mechanism of the notary node, users do not need to maintain the long-time connection to sign transactions. The main contributions of our work are summarized as follows.

- A novel architecture of cross-chain transaction system is proposed to consider different roles such as users, independent blockchain and cross-chain systems, with descriptions on the transaction processing mechanism of asset locking, key agreement and transaction processing.
- An algorithm is devised to generate a key negotiated by the notary and the user as the unlocking condition. The notary of cross-chain system supervises the execution of asset transactions between users to prevent malicious participants from creating a large number of channels to block transactions.
- A smart contract is designed for cross-chain asset exchange based on hash-locking such that the notary can coordinate the transaction through using the negotiated key.
- Finally, the paper analyzes the security of the model in several normal and abnormal transaction scenarios to verify the feasibility of the system through experiments.

The remainder of this paper is organized as follows. We first discuss the architecture of the proposed cross-chain transaction model in Sect. 2, which covers each process module of the cross-chain approach. Secondly, the security analysis of the model in normal and abnormal trading scenarios is given in Sect. 3 with an evaluation given in Sect. 4. The paper is concluded in Sect. 5.

2 Architecture of the Proposed Cross-Chain Transaction Model

2.1 Overview

This model involves three roles, including users, individual blockchains and the cross-chain system as illustrated in Fig. 1. Users have their own address and key in each individual blockchain that needs to perform cross-chain transactions. The cross-chain system acts as an intermediary to coordinate the transaction process, lock and unlock assets, and provide candidate notary node to monitor transactions in each blockchain. Users can select notary nodes, negotiate the keys of the transaction process, and lock assets by cross-chain contracts. Users will negotiate keys with selected notary nodes and lock assets through cross-chain contracts. During the transaction process, the notary nodes monitor strictly, listen to contract calls, and participate in the transaction according to users' behavior. Each role is described below.

The users need to share information, negotiate keys with the cross-chain system, and finish operations between individual blockchain, such as transaction processing, asset locking, etc.

Cross-chain system's notary nodes are responsible for communicating information and negotiate keys with users, monitoring events between individual blockchains, synchronizing data and processing transactions etc.

Each individual blockchain is responsible for locking assets and executing transactions via anchoring with the cross-chain system [11], which shares individual blockchains' data and transaction information with users, thereby coordinating the process of transactions. Individual blockchains A and B are responsible to perform transactions between blockchains.

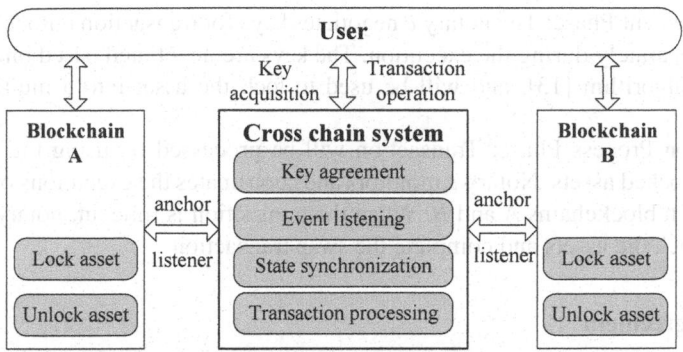

Fig. 1. Cross-chain system model

2.2 Cross-Chain Transaction Process

Both transaction parties need to lock their assets to a new multi-signature address provided by the system, and agree on the contract lock time [12]. The cross-chain transaction process is divided into three phases: assets locking, key agreement and transaction process, as illustrated in Fig. 2, which are described below.

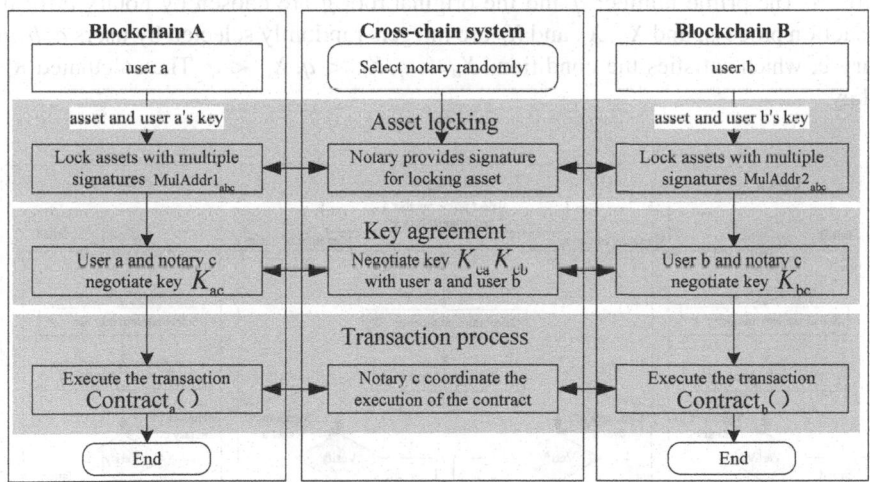

Fig. 2. Transaction processes based on the improved hash-locking

– Asset Locking Phase: Users a and b respectively lock assets with the key provided by the notary, which is selected by the cross-chain system. When the users need to start a transaction, the cross-chain system selects a specific notary c randomly, and sends its key to blockchains A and B. Then the lock asset contract in blockchains A and B will uses their keys to lock assets into multi-signature addresses $MulAddr1_{abc}$ and $MulAddr2_{abc}$.

- Key Agreement Phase: The notary c negotiates keys for transaction unlock with users a and b separately during the execution. The keys are negotiated based on the Diffie-Hellman algorithm [13], and will be used to lock the asset into a multi-signature contract.
- Transaction Process Phase: Transaction will be processed by using the negotiated keys and locked assets. Notary c monitors and coordinates the executions of the smart contracts in blockchains A and B. When the transaction is timeout, notary c and the users unlock the assets and complete the swap transaction.

2.3 Key Agreement

In order to supervise the subsequent execution process, the notary nodes selected by the cross-chain system need to negotiate keys only known to the transaction parties for the follow-up transactions before start. The Diffie-Hellman algorithm is introduced for key negotiations. The security of this algorithm is based on the discrete logarithms [18]. It assumes that when q is big enough, shared keys cannot be calculated by public values g^a mod q and g^b mod q, which is

$$K = g^{ab} mod\ q \tag{1}$$

The tripartite keys negotiation process between notary c, users a and b are illustrated in Fig. 3. The prime number q and the original root g are chosen by notary c for the transaction process, and X_a, X_b and X_c are integers randomly selected by users a, b and notary c, which satisfies the conditions $X_a < q, X_b < q, X_c < q$. The calculated K is the key.

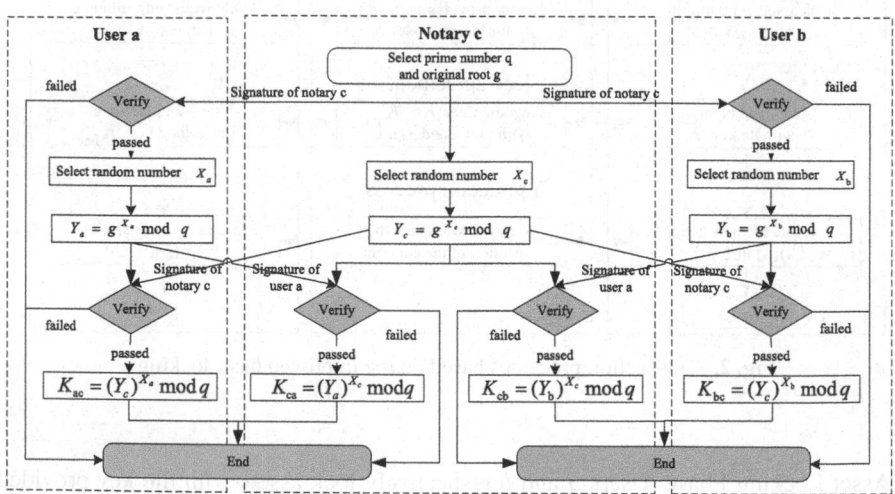

Fig. 3. Algorithm of key negotiations by notary c, users a and b

In Fig. 3, the prime number q and one of its original roots g is selected by notary c and sent to users a and b, who will verify q and g with the public key of notary c. After verification is completed, users a, b and notary c select random number X_A, X_b and X_c separately, then calculate Y_a, Y_b and Y_c. Notary c sends Y_c to users a and b, who then send Y_a and Y_b to notary c. Then K_{ac}, K_{bc}, K_{ca} and K_{cb} are calculated using formula (2), where $K_{ac} = K_{ca}$ and $K_{bc} = K_{cb}$ can be proved. This allows the notary c to obtain mutual authentication keys K_{ca}, K_{cb} with users a and b.

$$
\begin{aligned}
K &= (Y_c)^{X_a} \bmod q \\
&= (g^{X_c} \bmod q)^{X_a} \bmod q \\
&= (g^{X_c})^{X_a} \bmod q \\
&= g^{X_c X_a} \bmod q \\
&= (g^{X_a})^{X_c} \bmod q \\
&= (g^{X_a} \bmod q)^{X_c} \bmod q \\
&= (Y_a)^{X_c} \bmod q
\end{aligned}
\tag{2}
$$

A signature algorithm is used to verify the authenticity during the negotiation process. A hacker m wants to launch an attack, and intercepts the information and encrypted signature that notary c sent to user a, but he cannot forge a notary c's signature because of lack of the notary's private key C_a. User a will find that the signature verification fails after receiving the message, and be aware that the protocol exchange process is not secure. Then the user stops the key exchange process to cause the hacker m's attack to fail. The algorithm of *lockAsset* based on DHE is described in Algorithm 1, which mainly depends on the value of X_a, X_b and X_c with time complexity of $O(\log n)$.

Algorithm 1. Algorithm of *lockAsset*

Input: Y_a: user a's public number, Y_b: user b's public number, q: prime number, g: original root, K_a: user a's key, *ownerAddress*: address of assets transferred from, *userAddress*: address of assets transferred to, *myAddress*: fail-safe address, *account*: assets count, *dataHash*: key hash array

Output: Mul_{acd}(address of locked asset), Y_c(notary c's public number)
1. Initial transaction
2. **IF** $HASH(Input\ data)$ == dataHash
3.   Select random number $c \leftarrow Random()$
4.   Calculate shared key $K_{a'} \leftarrow DHE(Y_a{}^c, g, q)$
5.   Calculate shared key $K_{b'} \leftarrow DHE(Y_b{}^c, g, q)$
6. $KeyStore[ownerAddress] \leftarrow K_{a'}$
7. $Mul_{acd} \leftarrow LockAsset(ownerAddress, account, K_a, K_{b'})$
8. $Y_c \leftarrow g^c \bmod q$
9.   RERUN Mul_{acd}, Y_c
10. **ELSE**
11.   RERUN NULL
12. **END**

2.4 Cross-Chain Contract Execution

Assume that the parties of users a, b and notary c exist. Users a and b have locked their assets in the system-provided multi-signature addresses $MulAddr1_{abc}$ and $MulAddr2_{abc}$ using keys K_{ca}, K_{cb} negotiated with notary c. The system has provided multi-signature addresses $MulAddr1_c$, $MulAddr2_c$ to handle abnormal transactions, and users' addresses $Addr1'_b$, $Addr2'_a$ are used for normal transaction processes, as illustrated in Fig. 4.

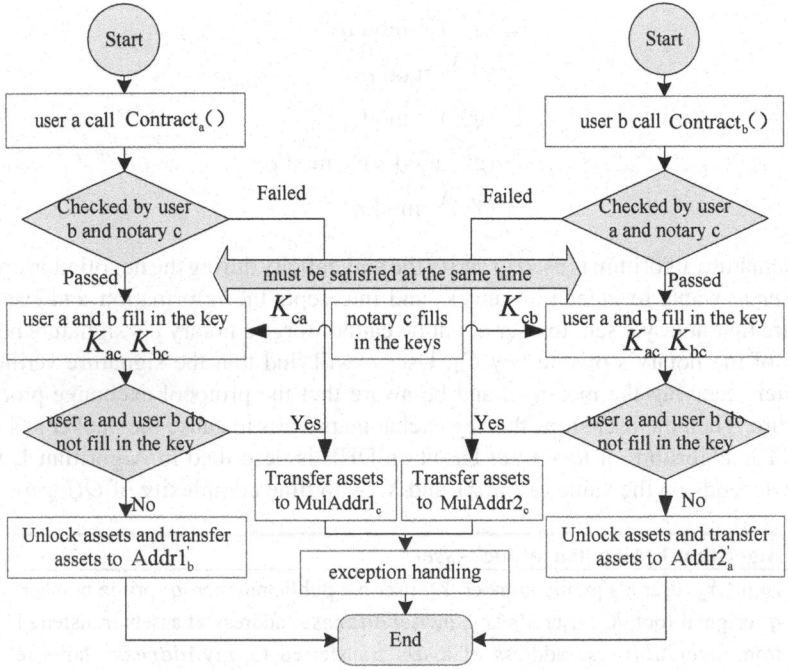

Fig. 4. Transaction contract calling process

User a deploys smart contract $Contract_a$ on blockchain A, and sets lock time $Time_{lock}$. If the transaction is successful within the lock time, the assets in the contract will be transferred to $Addr1'_b$. Otherwise, they will be transferred to $MulAddr1_c$, and the contract will set unlock conditions (see formula (3)). If the user or system uploads unlock keys K_a, K_b negotiated by users a, b and the notary c and satisfies more than one unlock condition through the contract built-in hash function, the contract will be unlocked automatically.

$$\begin{cases} Condition_1 = hash(K_a) \\ Condition_2 = hash(K_b) \end{cases} \tag{3}$$

User b deploys the same contract $Contract_b$ on blockchain B, and sets the same lock time $Time_{lock}$. After deployment, user a will check the parameters, such as multi-signature addresses. If any party presents an error, no follow-up action will be executed and the transaction will be cancelled. When the contract execution is started, as long as one party successfully meet the unlock conditions, notary c would unlock the contract for another to ensure the atomicity of the transaction. When the lock time $Time_{lock}$ is over, $Contract_a$ and $Contract_b$ will automatically transfer assets to the corresponding addresses. The algorithm of *executeTransaction* is described in Algorithm 2. The *executeTransaction* depends on the lock time $time_{lock}$ and the number of confirmed blocks $blockCount$ with time complexity of $O(n^2)$.

Algorithm 2. Algorithm of *executeTransaction* of $Contract_a$

Input:K_a: user a's key, K_b: user b's key, $MulAddr1_{abc}$: address of assets locked in, $userAddress$: address of assets transferred to, $myAddress$: fail-safe address, $account$: assets count, $time_{lock}$: transaction timeout, $blockCount$: count of block confirmed, $dataHash$: key hash array

Output: $Address$(address of unlocked asset)
1. Initial transaction
2. $K_x' \leftarrow KeyStore[\text{fromAddress}]$
3. $K_y' \leftarrow KeyStore[\text{userAddress}]$
4. $Addr1_b' \leftarrow userAddress$
5. **IF** $HASH(Input\ data) ==$ dataHash
6.   RETUN NULL
7. **FOR** $i \leftarrow 0$ *to* $time_{lock}$
8.   **IF** $K_x\ != $ NULL AND $K_y\ != $ NULL
9. $Addr1_b' \leftarrow UnLock(MulAddr1_{abc}, account, K_a, K_b)$
10.   **FOR** $j \leftarrow 0$ *to* $blockCount$
11.   Call $SynchronizeStatus()$
12.   RETURN $Addr1_b'$
13.   **ELSE** CONTINUE
14. **IF** $K_x\ != $ NULL AND $K_y\ ==$ NULL
15. $Addr1_b' \leftarrow UnLock(MulAddr1_{abc}, account, K_a, K_{b'})$
16.   **FOR** $j \leftarrow 0$ *to* $blockCount$
17.   Call $SynchronizeStatus()$
18.   RERUN $Addr1_b'$
19. **ELSE IF** $K_x\ ==$ NULL AND $K_y\ != $ NULL
20. $Addr1_b' \leftarrow UnLock(MulAddr1_{abc}, account, K_{a'}, K_b)$
21.   **FOR** $j \leftarrow 0$ *to* $blockCount$
22.   Call $SynchronizeStatus()$
23.   RERUN $Addr1_b'$
24. **ELSE IF** $K_x\ ==$ NULL AND $K_y\ ==$ NULL
25. $MulAddr1_c \leftarrow UnLock(MulAddr1_{abc}, account, K_{a'}, K_{b'})$
26.   **FOR** $j \leftarrow 0$ *to* $blockCount$
27.   Call $SynchronizeStatus()$
28.   RERUN $MulAddr1_c$
29. **ELSE** RERUN NULL

---

3 Security Evaluation

3.1 Normal Transaction

Users a and b start the transaction after preparing the conditions mentioned above. The steps of the normal process are described below.

- Step 1: User a deploys a smart contract $Contract_a$ as illustrated in Fig. 5(a) on blockchain A. Notary c monitors $Contract_a$, checks the settings of the smart contract and confirms that it is correct, then informs user b. In the same way, user b deploys the smart contract $Contract_b$ as illustrated in Fig. 5(b) for blockchain B.

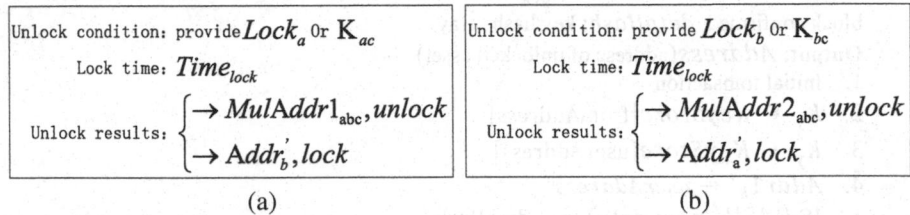

(a)   (b)

Fig. 5. Smart contract on blockchain A and B

- Step 2: Notary c monitors $Contract_b$ deployed in step 1, checks the settings of the smart contract and confirms that it is correct, then informs user a. After receiving the notification from notary c during $Time_{lock}$, user a calls $Contract_a$ and fills the parameter to unlock the assets.
- Step 3: Notary c notifies user b after listening to the behavior of user a in step 2. After receiving the notification during $Time_{lock}$, user b calls $Contract_b$ and fills the parameter to unlock the assets.
- Step 4: After the lock time $Time_{lock}$ is over, the contract automatically executes the transaction of assets to the parties' addresses $Addr1'_b$ and $Addr2'_a$.

3.2 Unexpected Situations

Generally, there are the following three unexpected situations in transaction processes. i) One party unlocks the assets within the specified time but the other does not; ii) One party conspired with the notary to defraud assets of the other; iii) Both parties do not unlock the assets. The contract proposed in this paper is equal for both parties in the transaction. There are two unlock conditions, which are the key set by the transaction parties and the key negotiated by the transaction parties and the system. Each situation is described below.

- Only one party unlocks the assets: Notary c will actively coordinate the party that has not unlocked the assets and notify him to transfer. If the contact fails, notary c will actively fill in the decryption key to force the assets to be unlocked. For example, if user a unlocks the smart contract on blockchain A while user b does not, notary c will call the smart contract on blockchain B and fill K_{bc}, which is negotiated with user b to unlock the assets.

- One party conspired with the notary: For instance, user a executes the smart contract on blockchain A to unlock the assets, but notary c and user b do not on blockchain B during the lock time. Therefore, user a's assets have been transferred to user b's address but user a has not received user b's assets. In this case, the system will force transfer out user b's assets from multi-signature address, freeze the assets, and remove notary c from the system.
- Both parties do not unlock the transaction: After users a and b deploy the transaction contract, if they reach a consensus to cancel the transaction, notary c and all users will not perform any follow-up operations, and the contract will transfer the assets to $MulAddr1_c$ and $MulAddr2_c$ when the lock time is over. Finally, the assets in $MulAddr1_c$ and $MulAddr2_c$ will be refunded to users a and b.

4 Experiment Evaluation

Here Ethereum is used for experimental evaluation and Go-Ethereum for the deployment. The experimental environment configuration is listed in Table 1.

Table 1. Experimental environment configuration

Name	Parameter
Geth version	1.8.11
Solidity version	0.5.0
System	Centos7.5
SDK	Python3.6

A simple example of users a and b performing cross-chain transactions with notary c is used to verify the cross-chain transaction model. User a located in blockchain A calls the contract, whose parameters are listed in Table 2. The contract's calling result is shown in Fig. 6, which indicates the contract data has been successfully uploaded.

Table 2. Parameters of user a's transaction

Variables	Parameter values	Explanation
uuid	0x681afa780d17da29203322b473d3f210a7d621259a4e6ce9e403f5a266ff719a	Transition unique id
owner_address	0x0832e2256a2fd1f1a35a43c07545c757c0796529	From user a's address
user_address	0x1d54f8a84a889dd89f6514a9489ace6e217d4b38	To user b's address
my_address	0x83c2e825832c83a06ec0350a66229cad4fd9f634	Fail-safe address
time_number	40	Timeout
hash_one	fcc5ba1a98fc477b8948a04d08c6f4a76181fe75021370ab5e6abd22b1792a2a	User a's private encryption key
hash_two	9787eeb91fe3101235e4a76063c7023ecb40f923f97916639c598592fa30d6ae	User a's and notary encryption key

{'uuid': '0x681afa780d17da29203322b473d3f210a7d621259a4e6ce9e403f5a266ff719a', 'owner_address': '0x0832e2256a2fd1f1a35a-3c07545c757c0796529', 'user_address': '0x1d54f8a84a889dd89f6514a9489ace6e217d4b38', 'my_address': '0x83c2e825832c83a06e-0350a66229cad4fd9f634', 'time_number': 40, 'hash_one': 'fcc5ba1a98fc477b8948a04d08c6f4a76181fe75021370ab5e6abd22b1792a2-', 'hash_two': '9787eeb91fe3101235e4a76063c7023ecb40f923f97916639c598592fa30d6ae', 'account': 10}
{'blockHash': '0xb5ffbc558bf07ffc03871a5fe4cb8593c5f6ee7633a32e27e2231fc289abb8d6', 'blockNumber': '0x2c', 'contractAdd-ess': '0x00000000000000000000000000000000000000000', 'from': '0x95198b93705e394a916579e048c8a32ddfb900f7', 'gasUsed': '0-e20b', 'input': '0xfbf53cd70000000000000000000000000000000000000000000000000000000000000001000000000000000000000000832-2256a2fd1f1a35a43c07545c757c0796529000000000000000000000001d54f8a84a889dd89f6514a9489ace6e217d4b3800000000000000000000000-00083c2e825832c83a06ec0350a66229cad4fd9f634000000000000000000000000000000000000000000000000000000000000002800000000000000-000000000000000000000000000000000000000000000000000000000fcc5ba1a98fc477b8948a04d08c6f4a76181fe75021370ab5e6abd22b1792a2a9787-eb91fe3101235e4a76063c7023ecb40f923f97916639c598592fa30d6ae0000000000000000000000000000000000000000000000000000000000000-0423078363833161666137383064313764613293230333332326234373364336632313061376436323132353963134653663653965343033663561326-63666663731396100000000000000000000000000000000000000000000000000000000', 'logs': [], 'logsBloom': '0x00000000000000000-00000000000000000000000000000000000000000000000000000000000000000000000000000000000000000000000000000000000000000000000-00000000000000000000000000000000000000000000000000000000000000000000000000000000000000000000000000000000000000000000000000-00000000000000000000000000000000000000000000000000000000000000000000000000000000000000000000000000000000000000000000000000-00000000000000000', 'output': (3002,), 'root': '0x3ae41abdb6f66e1def636dd53c961072ffd8a6a337f46c5b72278ef3b02e6056', '-status': '0x0', 'to': '0x4fb700f036dbd8a80940a88df8d9e55705a8ac97', 'transactionHash': '0x9fb9bc241be228415f3600670022ec-4739d1fd7c8f253a6a0ed20056e56b82d', 'transactionIndex': '0x0'}

Fig. 6. Example of user a's transaction results

User *b* located in blockchain *B* deploys the same contract, and the result of calling the contract is shown in Fig. 7. After the contract's parameters are jointly reviewed by the notary and the user, user *a* calls the contract to unlock the assets within the specified time. If the specified time is not over, the system will call the contract to view the transaction result. The output result 3002 represents that both parties have unlocked their respective transactions, and the transactions have been successfully executed. However, the output result 3001 represents that the contract data unlock failed, and the assets will be refunded to the original owner.

{'uuid': '0x3d5dca32b04c088dbea884d9d0d5f974c85782e0d26b8f3777bf69620bae6ce2', 'owner_address': '0x1d54f8a84a889dd89f651-1a9489ace6e217d4b38', 'user_address': '0x83c2e825832c83a06ec0350a66229cad4fd9f634', 'my_address': '0x0832e2256a2fd1f1a35-r43c07545c757c0796529', 'time_number': 40, 'hash_one': 'acb8d954e2cfef495862221e91bd7523613cf8808827cb33edfe4904cc51bf29-', 'hash_two': 'd833147d7dc355ba459fc788f669e58cfaf9dc25ddcd0702e87d69c7b5124289', 'account': 10}
{'blockHash': '0x0674e661eb95166203d945bbc263d74e2140e5be0ab01ac647a525a4cf551f34', 'blockNumber': '0x2d', 'contractAddr-ess': '0x00000000000000000000000000000000000000000', 'from': '0x95198b93705e394a916579e048c8a32ddfb900f7', 'gasUsed': '0x-27c33', 'input': '0xfbf53cd70000000000000000000000000000000000000000000000000000000000000083c2e825832c83a06ec0350a66229cad4fd9f634000000000000000000000001d54-r8a84a889dd89f6514a9489ace6e217d4b3800000000000000000000000083c2e825832c83a06ec0350a66229cad4fd9f634000000000000000000000-000000832e2256a2fd1f1a35a43c07545c757c0796529000000000000000000000000000000000000000000000000000000000002800000000000000-000000000000000000000000000000000000000000000000000000000acb8d954e2cfef495862221e91bd7523613cf8808827cb33edfe4904cc51bf29d833-147d7dc355ba459fc788f669e58cfaf9dc25ddcd0702e87d69c7b5124289000000000000000000000000000000000000000000000000000000000000-0423078363456463613332623034633038386462656518383364643964306435663937346538353537383265306643366238663337373726663639363-30626165366365532000000000000000000000000000000000000000000000000000000000', 'logs': [], 'logsBloom': '0x00000000000000000-000000000000000000000000000000000000000000000000000000000000000000000000000000000000000000000000000000000000000000000000-00000000000000000000000000000000000000000000000000000000000000000000000000000000000000000000000000000000000000000000000000-00000000000000000000000000000000000000000000000000000000000000000000000000000000000000000000000000000000000000000000000000-000000000000000000', 'output': (3002,), 'root': '0xf80174448c56a4dfa5567da6e2a621acfff089b011334a831dd8354eb7370a5d', '-status': '0x0', 'to': '0x4fb700f036dbd8a80940a88df8d9e55705a8ac97', 'transactionHash': '0x2af9f2e513e5b22a4f35f0d8789d87-t556eed9656f03c799527bb974429aa629', 'transactionIndex': '0x0'}

Fig. 7. Example of user b's transaction results

To evaluate the performance of the proposed algorithm, the experiments are conducted from two aspects: iterative execution and concurrent execution. Figures 8 (a) and (b) show the time and resource usage for iterative execution with transaction number on the x-axis and execution time or resource usage on the y-axis. It can be observed that as the transaction number increases, the average time of transaction executions and the usage of CPU and memory remain essentially the same, which shows the stable performance of the transaction execution of the model. Figures 8(c) and (d) shows that, as the number of concurrent transactions increases, the execution time and CPU usage also increase, while memory utilization remains stable. This result because a large number of concurrent transactions have to be processed so that the CPU usage increases rapidly, and the execution time of a single transaction also increases.

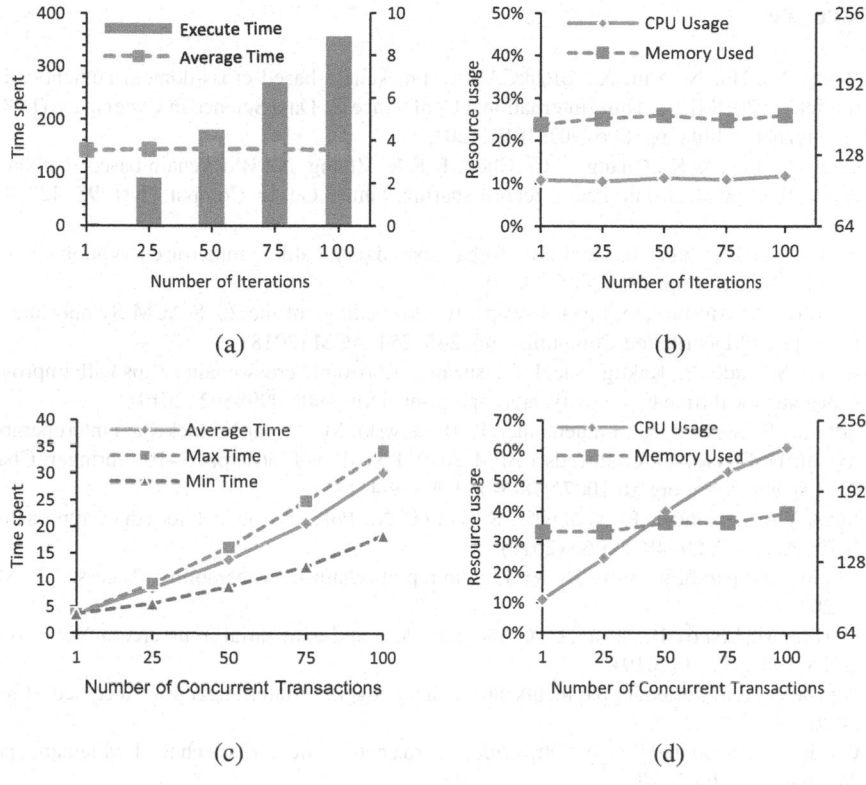

Fig. 8. Performance of the proposed model

5 Conclusion

This paper proposes a cross-chain transaction model based on an improved hash locking, which jointly exploits the decentralization of the hash locking and the simple operation of the notary schemes. This model provides a novel method of cross-chain key agreement and the execution of cross-chain contract, which can establish a safe and reliable mechanism about cross-chain trading. The experimental results show that the proposed model can ensure the security of cross-chain transactions while keeping the execution time and resource usage at a stable level. With the large-scale growth of blockchain applications, there will be more and more cross-chain concurrent transactions, and performance will become the key issue of cross-chain system. Future research will focus on the performance of cross-chain, in order to achieve efficient cross-chain data communication and value transaction on the basis of security assurance.

Acknowledgments. This work was supported by Shanghai Science and Technology Innovation Action Plan Project (No. 18DZ1112101) and Major Projects of Shanghai Zhangjiang National Innovation Demonstration Zone (No. ZJ2020-ZD-003).

References

1. Wang, W., Hu, N., Liu, X.: BlockCAM: a blockchain-based cross-domain authentication model. In: 2018 IEEE Third International Conference on Data Science in Cyberspace (DSC), Guangzhou, China, pp. 896–901. IEEE (2018)
2. Chen, L., Lee, W.K., Chang, C.C., Choo, K.K.R., Zhang, N.: Blockchain based searchable encryption for electronic health record sharing. Future Gener. Comput. Syst. **95**, 420–429 (2019)
3. Li, H., Tian, H., Zhang, F., He, J.: Blockchain-based searchable symmetric encryption scheme. Comput. Electr. Eng. **73**, 32–45 (2019)
4. Herlihy, M.: Atomic cross-chain swaps. In: Proceedings of the 2018 ACM Symposium on Principles of Distributed Computing, pp. 245–254. ACM (2018)
5. Imoto, S., Sudo, Y., Kakugawa, H., Masuzawa, T.: Atomic cross-chain swaps with improved space and local time complexity. arXiv preprint arXiv:1905.09985v2 (2019)
6. Schulte, S., Sigwart, M., Frauenthaler, P., Borkowski, M.: Towards blockchain interoperability. In: Di Ciccio, C., et al. (eds.) BPM 2019. LNBIP, vol. 361, pp. 3–10. Springer, Cham (2019). https://doi.org/10.1007/978-3-030-30429-4_1
7. Siris, V.A., Nikander, P., Voulgaris, S., Fotiou, N., Polyzos, G.C.: Interledger approaches. IEEE Access **7**, 89948–89966 (2019)
8. Chain Interoperability. https://www.r3.com/reports/chain-interoperability. Accessed 31 Mar 2020
9. Herlihy, M., Liskov, B., Shrira, L.: Cross-chain deals and adversarial commerce. arXiv preprint arXiv:1905.09743 (2019)
10. A protocol for interledger payments. https://interledger.org/interledger.pdf. Accessed 31 Mar 2020
11. Corda: A distributed ledger. https://docs.corda.net/_static/corda-technical-whitepaper.pdf. Accessed 31 Mar 2020
12. Wood, G.: Polkadot: vision for a heterogeneous multi-chain framework. https://polkadot.network/PolkaDotPaper.pdf. Accessed 31 Mar 2020
13. Kwon, J., Buchman, E.: Cosmos: a network of distributed ledgers. https://cosmos.network/whitepaper. Accessed 31 Mar 2020
14. Alt chains and atomic transfers. https://bitcointalk.org/index.php?topic=193281.0. Accessed 31 Mar 2020
15. The Bitcoin lightning network: Scalable off-chain instant payments. https://lightning.network/lightning-networkpaper.pdf. Accessed 31 Mar 2020
16. Borkowski, M., Sigwart, M., Frauenthaler, P., Hukkinen, T., Schulte, S.: DeXTT: decentralized cross-chain token transfers. IEEE Access **7**, 111030–111042 (2019)
17. Philipp, F., Marten, S., Spanring, C., Stefan, S.: Leveraging Blockchain Relays for Cross-Chain Token Transfers (2020). https://www.researchgate.net/publication/339400544
18. Ameri, M.H., Delavar, M., Mohajeri, J., Salmasizadeh, M.: A key-policy attribute-based temporary keyword search scheme for secure cloud storage. IEEE Trans. Cloud Comput. **8**, 660–671 (2020)

A Security Problem in Small Scale Private Ethereum Network

Zhen Gao[✉], Dongbin Zhang, and Jiuzhi Zhang

School of Electrical and Information Engineering, Tianjin University, Tianjin 300072, China
zgao@tju.edu.cn

Abstract. Ethereum is taken as the representative of the 2nd generation of blockchain system, and has been widely used in many applications. Different from Bitcoin system, Ethereum introduces the concept of *account*, so that the balance inquiry and transaction validation could be performed with lower complexity. Since the information of each account is not stored in the blockchain but in the local database, it is prone to be modified. This paper studied the balance inquiry process in Ethereum based on the source code, and found that the balance of an account could be easily modified, and the value will not be validated based on the state root in the block header when used for transaction validation. Tests based on a small scale private Ethereum network show that if the balance of an account is modified in the database on all participating nodes, the invalid transaction based on the modified balance would be taken as a valid one and packed in the blockchain. This could be a big problem for the application where a private blockchain is built based on Ethereum with small number of nodes.

Keywords: Ethereum · Balance · State database · Inquiry · Security

1 Introduction

Ethereum is proposed by Vitalik Buterin in 2013 [1], and is taken as the second generation of blockchain system [2]. Relative to Bitcoin system, Ethereum introduces the 'account' concept and smart contract [2, 3]. The former one improves the efficiency for different kinds of inquiry, and the latter one broadens the application scenarios of Ethereum greatly [3, 4]. Currently, many new applications have been implemented based on Ethereum. For example, InsureChain applied Ethereum to reduce the cost and enable automatic contract execution in the insurance business [5]; SecureChain applied Ethereum for valid user registration and access controlling in software defined networks [6]; Thankscoin applied Ethereum to build a platform between the post writers and the readers for reward purpose [7]; RightMesh applied Ethereum to form a sharing platform of communication resources among individuals [8]; The Everledger platform applied Ethereum to enable buyers and sellers of high value assets to trade with confidence [9]. Most of these applications applied Ethereum to build private blockchain system that is operated by the service provider.

© Springer Nature Singapore Pte Ltd. 2020
Z. Zheng et al. (Eds.): BlockSys 2020, CCIS 1267, pp. 231–242, 2020.
https://doi.org/10.1007/978-981-15-9213-3_18

Although the development of Ethereum and other blockchain systems are in full swing, related technologies are still in the preliminary exploration stage, facing complex security threats in the data layer, network layer, contract layer, etc. The data layer encapsulates the underlying data and related security modules like data encryption [10]. There are also various security issues in the data layer, including the threat of quantum computing to encryption algorithms, security issues caused by improper key management, and code defects in cryptographic components [11]. This paper analyzes the data storage security and query reliability of Ethereum by tampering with the local database of the node, and finds a new data layer security problem.

Ethereum is essentially a transaction-based state machine, in which the state of each account, including mainly the balance and the transaction counter, can only be updated by transactions between valid accounts. Each transaction will be verified by all nodes independently. The verification involves two parts [12]. One is to check the digital signature of the transaction to make sure it is transmitted by a valid account. The other is to check the balance of the transmitted account to make sure that the account has enough Ether for that would be transferred to the receiving account and the transaction fee. Once a transaction is verified and packed in a block that is accepted by all nodes, it is assumed to be non-modifiable. This tamper-proof property is mainly guaranteed by the way that the transactions are packed in the blockchain. Each block is divided in two parts, the header and the body. All transactions are packed in the block body, and the Markel root of all these transactions is included in the header. In addition, the header also includes the hash of the previous block, the time stamp of current block and a nonce. The nonce is a random number that could make the hash value of the block header smaller than a threshold determined by the Ethereum system dynamically. The process of finding such a random number is called 'mining', which is very resource consuming. If someone want to modify a transaction that is already packed in the blockchain, he needs to do a lot of work. First, if a transaction is modified, the Merkle root stored in the block head would be invalid, so it should be recalculated. Second, the change of the Merkle root would fail the mined nonce, so a new random number needs to be re-mined to make current block legal. Third, the new nonce will change the hash value of current block which is stored in the next block. If the hash value in the next block is updated, the nonce in the header needs to be re-mined. So to modify a transaction in the blockchain, the person needs to repeat the mining work for all the blocks following the block to which the transaction belongs. But this is just a start. To make the nodes in the blockchain network reach consensus about the modified transaction, the person needs to repeat the work above on more than half of the nodes in the network, which is usually called the 51% attack. This would consume huge amount of computation resources, so that it is more valuable to contribute this effort to mine the new blocks. Based on such economic principle behind, the transactions stored in the blockchain is assumed to be tamper-proof, even in a small or middle scale private blockchain system with tens or hundreds of full nodes.

In the Ethereum implementation, each account is a <key, value> pair stored in local database of each node. The key is the public address, and the value includes the balance, the transaction counter and the code hash. The last one is only meaningful for contract account. So an interesting question is that whether it is possible to modify the balance information? If possible, we can be rich in a second, and could transmit any number of *valid* transactions. This seems impossible because the block header includes a 'State Root', which is the root for all account states. If the root is verified during the check of the balance information for a transaction validation, the balance modification would be impossible due to the same reason for the transaction tamper-proof. But our analysis of the Ethereum code shows that this is not the case. We can easily modify the account balance and make valid transactions based on the modified account. This would be a big security problem for small scale private blockchain system based on Ethereum, especially when the network is fixed.

The remainder of this paper is organized as follows. Section 2 describes the balance inquiry process in Ethereum based on the source code. Section 3 discusses the possibility to modify the balance in the local database. In Sect. 4, we performed the balance modification in a small scale private blockchain based on Ethereum, and introduce the tests for enabling *valid* transactions based on the modified balance information. The paper is concluded in Sect. 5.

2 Balance Inquiry in Ethereum

This section will first introduce the general process of the balance inquiry in Ethereum based on the source codes of the Golang version Ethereum (*geth-windows-amd64-1.9.10* [13]). Then two related structures MPT and *StateDB* are introduced in the second part. Finally, the details of the two main steps for the balance inquiry are introduced in the last two parts, respectively.

2.1 General Process of Balance Inquiry in Ethereum

The balance inquiry may be direct or indirect. On the one hand, the user can directly initiate query requests to the node through JavaScript Console, web3, JSON-RPC, etc. On the other hand, as mentioned above, the balance of the transmitting address is also checked indirectly during the transaction confirmation, but this process is a subset of the former.

In the Golang source code of Ethereum, the structure *PublicBlockChainAPI* is defined in *go-ethereum/internal/ethapi/api.go*. This structure includes a backend interface providing the common API services with access to necessary functions, and *GetBalance* is one of them. Figure 1 shows the simplified calling process and returning process in *GetBalance* when the user directly queries the balance. In Ethereum, the inquirer could get the account balance information at different time, which is usually denoted as the block height in blockchain, so there are two steps involved in the *GetBalance* function. First, the a new *stateDB* corresponding to the designated block is built by calling the method *StateAndHeaderByNumberOrHash*. Then the *GetBalance* method of *stateDB* (*s.GetBalance* defined in *go-ethereum/core/state/statedb.go*) is called to return the balance information of the inquired address for the designated block. It should be noted that a new *StateDB* would be rebuilt for each balance inquiry by calling *GetBalance*.

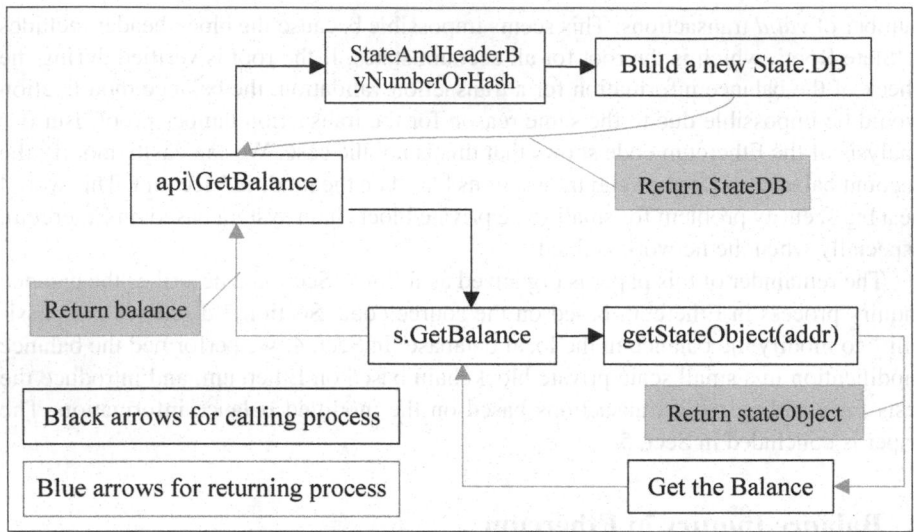

Fig. 1. General process for balance inquiry in Ethereum

2.2 MPT and StateDB

Two main structures are used in the balance inquiry process, including MPT (Merkle Patricia Tree) and StateDB. They are introduced briefly as follows.

(1) MPT structure

MPT is the combination of Merkle Tree and Patricia Trie. The root node in Patricia Trie is empty, but the root node in MPT stores the root hash of the whole tree. The generation process of the root hash in MPT is same as that in Merkle Tree. There are three kinds of nodes in MPT.

1) Leaf Nodes (corresponding to the valueNode in the source code)
   Each value node stores the value for an address, including balance, transaction counter and code hash (only for contract account).
2) Branch Nodes (corresponding to the fullNodes in the source code)
   Each full node stores a list with 17 items, including 16 characters 0~F and a value. The branch nodes could be the intermediate nodes on the search path or a terminating node. For the latter case, the value would be returned.
3) Extension Nodes (corresponding to the shortNodes in the source code)
   Such node stores the hash of another node as the value, and the key corresponds to one of the 16 characters in a branch node.

Figure 2 shows an example for MPT in Ethereum [14]. In addition to the above three kinds of nodes, another node type, hashNode, is used in the implementation of Ethereum for efficient nodes loading. The hashNode stores a root hash of a sub-tree growing from it. When a MPT is rebuilt in the cache, only part of the fullNodes and shortNodes would be loaded, and other nodes are 'folded' in hashNodes. The nodes would be unfolded only when the related hashNode is reached during the node searching. Essentially speaking, the root hash value for state, transactions and receipt that are included in the block header could be taken as hashNodes.

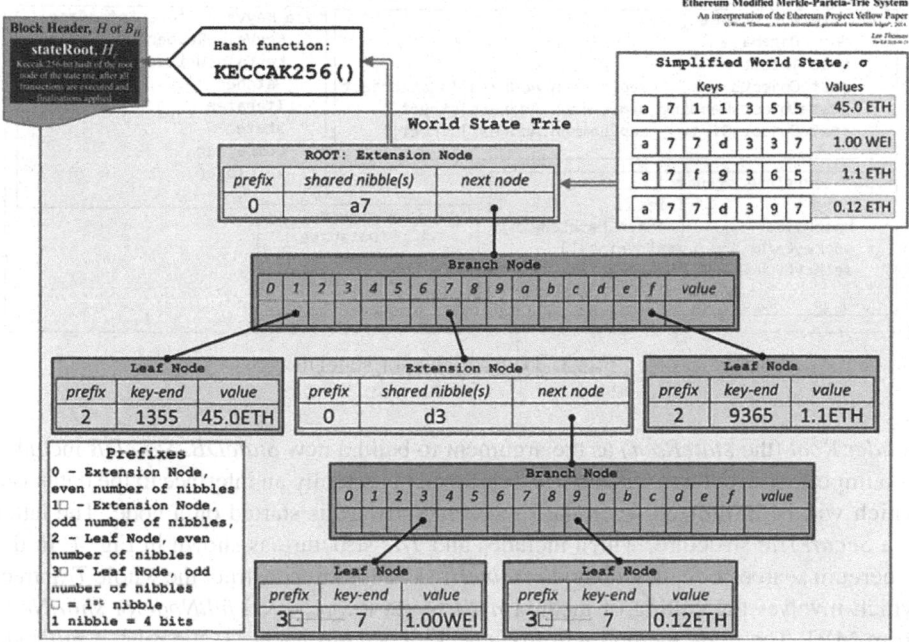

Fig. 2. An example of MPT

(2) StateDB

The structures involved in *StateDB* is shown in Fig. 3. *StateDB* is connected to the underlying databases *Database* and *Trie*. These two structures both include an interface *KeyValueStore*, which contains all the methods required to allow handling different key-value data stores backing the high level database. The *stateObjects* is the map caching of the account information for all the loaded nodes in the *Trie* (MPT), and the RLP coded version of the account information is stored in the leaf node of the MPT. If an account is not found in *stateObjects*, *StateDB* would search in *Trie*, and add the result in *stateObjects*. This process is performed by the *getStateObject* function in Fig. 1.

2.3 Building of New StateDB

The process of building a new *StateDB* is shown in Fig. 4. First, the API function *GetBalance* calls the method *StateAndHeaderByNumberOrHash* to get the block *header* based on the block height or the block hash. Then the method *StateAt* is called with

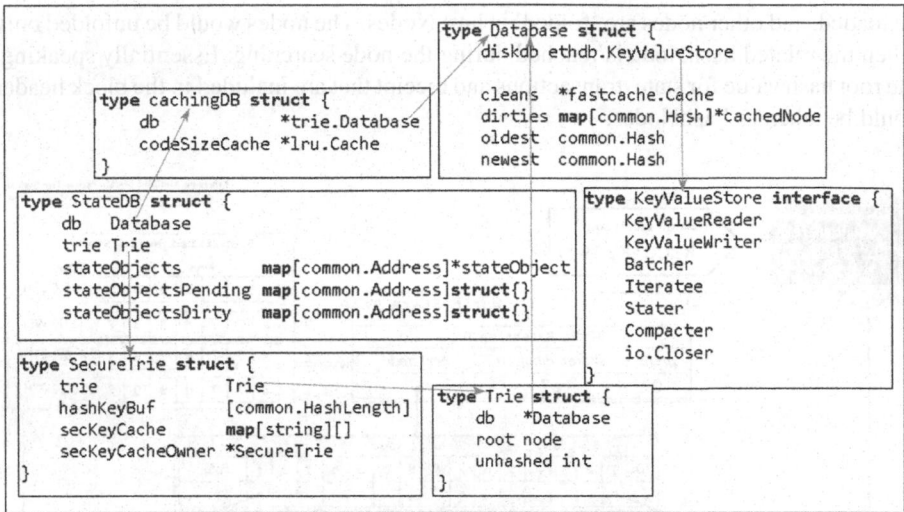

Fig. 3. Data structure of StateDB

header.Root (the *stateRoot*) as the argument to build a new *StateDB*. *StateDB* includes two important structures, *db* and *trie*. For former is actually an interface to the database, which will be initialized when the Ethereum software is started on a node. The latter is a *SecureTrie* structure, which includes and *Trie* structure as shown in Fig. 4. In the Ethereum source code, the method *resolveHash* is used to construct the whole *Trie* tree, which involves the calling of method *node* to get the required *fullNode* or *shortNode* from MPT. The *node* method will first check the *cleans* cache. If the related *fullNode* or *shortNode* does not exists in the cleans cache, the levelDB *distdb* would be searched with the target hash as the key.

2.4 Balance Inquiry from StateDB

After building a new *StateDB*, its method *GetBalance* would be called to get the balance with the account address as the argument. The process in shown in Fig. 5. Based on the structure of *StateDB* introduced in Sect. 2.2, the *stateObjects* in *StateDB* includes the account information of all the loaded nodes in the MPT. So the *GetBalance* will first call the method *getStateObject* to check whether the inquired address exists in *stateObjects*. If not, the *Tire* (MPT) will be searched through the method *tryGet*, which will perform a recursive search downward through the *fullNodes* and *shortNodes* with the hash of the account address as the key. Finally, the balance of the account stored in a *valueNode* would be returned.

When building a new *Trie*, only the part of the nodes would be loaded in the cache, and other nodes would be loaded only when needed. During the searching of an address through the MPT, if an *hashNode* is reached, the folded *fullNodes* and *shortNodes* would be resolved by calling the method *resolveHash*. In this case, the *Trie* would be updated with the resolved *fullNodes* and *shortNodes*.

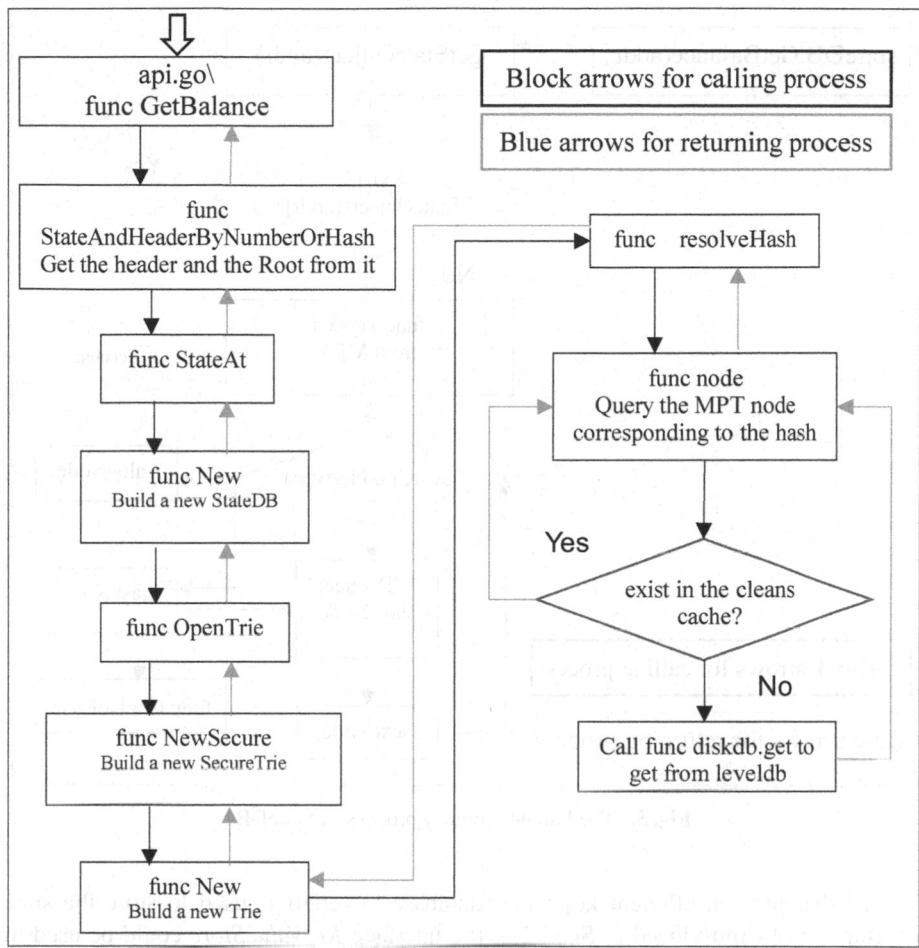

Fig. 4. The process for building a new StateDB in Ethereum

3 Feasibility of Modification of Balance in Ethereum

Based on the balance inquiry process analysis in Sect. 2, we find that the balance information is read out directly from the state database, and there is no verification mechanism to check whether the returned balance has been tampered with or not. In other words, since the root hash of the state database is not recalculated by recursive hashing of all the related valueNodes, shortNodes and fullNodes, although the root hash of the state information for a block is stored in the header, it is not compared with the recalculated one to validate the returned balance value. Similarly, for the inquiring involving hashNodes, there is no recalculation of the hash root for the folded fullNodes and short-Nodes, so the hash of the hashNode is not compared with the recalculated one for verification. In this case, it is possible in principle to modify the balance value of any account in the database without leaving any trace.

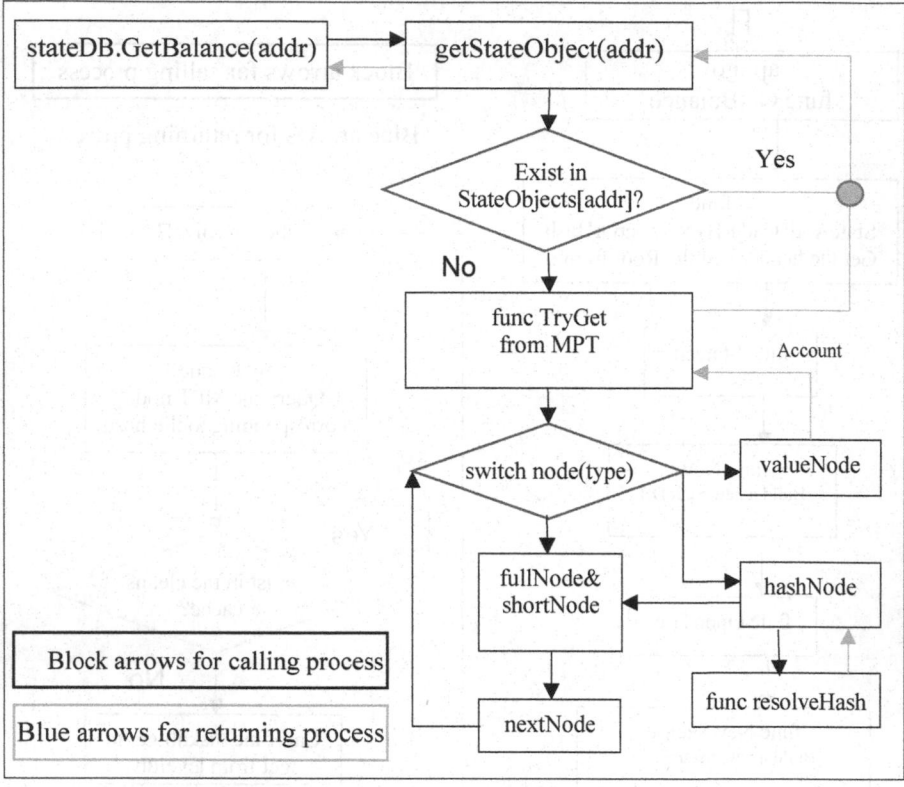

Fig. 5. The balance inquiry process in StateDB

In Ethereum, an efficient key-value database LevelDB is used to store the state information. As introduced in Sect. 2.2, the interface *KeyValueStore* could be used to read/write (modify) the data stored in levelDB directly through the *get/put* function.

4 Experiments for Balance Modification

4.1 Testing Platform and System Initialization

The Golang version of Ethereum *geth-windows-amd64-1.9.10* is used in following tests. A simple private Ethereum system with 3 nodes are established on a PC. The hardware and software configuration of the platform is listed in Table 1. Each node is started by executing '*geth*' in the command window, and running as a process in the system. Each node is assigned a different port number, and is connected with the other two nodes directly. After issuing of some normal transactions and mining of some valid blocks, the block height of the blockchain achieves 7, and the balance of each account is listed in the last column of Table 2.

Table 1. System configuration

Item	Descriptions
CPU	Intel(R) Core(TM) i7-7500U CPU
RAM	8.00 GB
Operation system	Microsoft Windows 10 Home Edition 64-bit

Table 2. Account information for block height of 7

Node	Addresses of accounts	Initial balance
node 0	"0xdb44c914972e0de3b706726e8e70be05e3591878"(etherbase) "0x7257d9476fed1e7421fd57ecffd55c20e45f1678"	11 ether 3 ether
node 1	"0x2f125dccacc4fcf6269c0520a8145554618cb6b0"(etherbase) "0xe7ad34c84d75d86a7f3233d75cab46872b01b6f8"	0 0
node 2	"0x748a0459f4fcb75c4b83c04304f63b64ecbb0bd0"(etherbase)	0

4.2   Experiment Results and Analysis

(1)   Modify the balance of an account on one node

The balance for the address "0x7257d9476fed1e7421fd57ecffd55c20e45f1678" on node 0 is changed from 3 ethers to 10 ethers through the *KeyValueStore* interface. As shown in Fig. 6, the *GetBalance* API would return 10 ethers without any error or warning message on node 0, but the same balance on other two nodes are still 3 ethers.

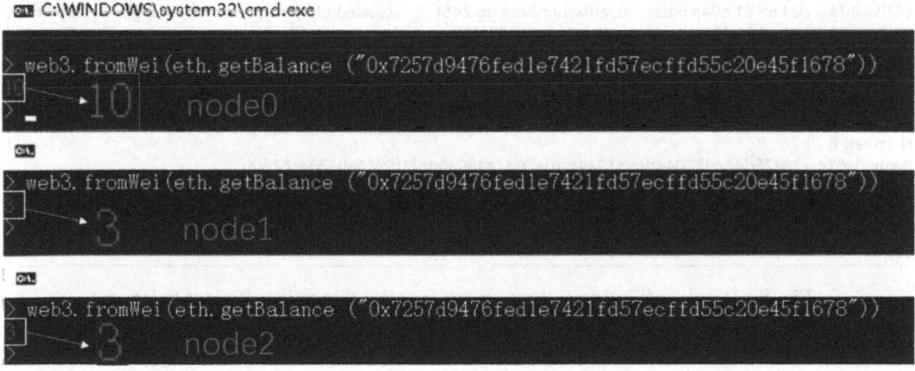

Fig. 6. Balance information for the same account on three nodes

Then node 0 issues a transaction from the modified account "0x7257d9476fed1e742 1fd57ecffd55c20e45f1678" to address "0xe7ad34c84d75d86a7f3233d75cab46872b01b6f8". First, the amount of the transaction is set to be 5 ethers as shown in Fig. 7. This transaction is verified to be valid, and packed in a new block on node 0. After node 0 mined the block, it broadcasts it to the other two nodes. But the block is not accepted due to "insufficient Balance for transfer" (as shown in Fig. 8). This is expected because each node will verify a received transaction based on the local stored state information. The balance of node 0 is modified to 10, which meets the transaction requirement. But the balance of the node 1 and 2 is 3 which is not enough to make a transaction of 5 ethers. Then we repeat the transaction with amount of 1 ether (as shown in Fig. 9). This time the error message changes to "invalid merkle root" during the block validation on the other two nodes (as shown in Fig. 10). This is because each node will recalculate the state root hash stored in the block header based on the local stored state information. In our case, the state root hash included in the new block is based on the modified state information, so the state root in the header would be different from the recalculated one on another node.

Fig. 7. Transaction based on the modified account (amount of 5 ethers)

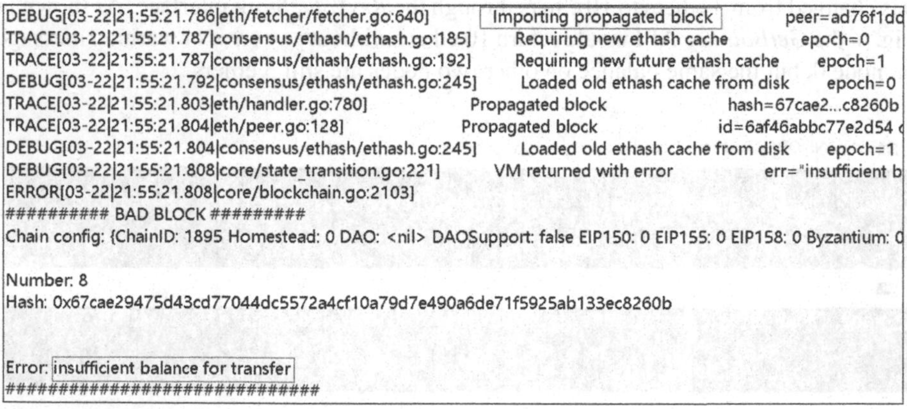

Fig. 8. Block validation failure on other nodes due to insufficient balance

(2) Modify the balance of an account on three nodes

We repeat the account modification on three nodes in the same way. The same transaction in Fig. 7 (with amount of 5 eithers) is issued by node 0. Then we find the new block is

```
> amount = web3.toWei(1,'ether')
"1000000000000000000"
> personal.unlockAccount("0x7257d9476fed1e7421fd57ecffd55c20e45f1678")
Unlock account 0x7257d9476fed1e7421fd57ecffd55c20e45f1678
Password:
true
> eth.sendTransaction({from:"0x7257d9476fed1e7421fd57ecffd55c20e45f1678", to: "0xe7ad34c84d75d86a7f3233d75cab46872b01b6f8
,value:amount})
"0x36765b5670ac8cd8b7b6b5e637389801f8b8663c542ce0d01606c74d928343bd"
> miner.start(1);admin.sleepBlocks(1);miner.stop();
```

Fig. 9. Transaction based on the modified account (amount of 1 ethers)

```
DEBUG[03-22|21:37:04.173|eth/fetcher/fetcher.go:640]      Importing propagated block            peer=ad76f1dd
TRACE[03-22|21:37:04.173|consensus/ethash/ethash.go:185]       Requiring new ethash cache            epoch=0
TRACE[03-22|21:37:04.173|consensus/ethash/ethash.go:192]       Requiring new future ethash cache       epoch=1
DEBUG[03-22|21:37:04.177|consensus/ethash/ethash.go:245]       Loaded old ethash cache from disk     epoch=0
DEBUG[03-22|21:37:04.189|consensus/ethash/ethash.go:245]       Loaded old ethash cache from disk     epoch=1
TRACE[03-22|21:37:04.191|eth/handler.go:780]        Propagated block            hash=df98ae...b742e3
TRACE[03-22|21:37:04.191|eth/peer.go:128]        Propagated block            id=6af46abbc77e2d54 c
ERROR[03-22|21:37:04.197|core/blockchain.go:2103]
########## BAD BLOCK #########
Chain config: {ChainID: 1895 Homestead: 0 DAO: <nil> DAOSupport: false EIP150: 0 EIP155: 0 EIP158: 0 Byzantium: 0

Number: 8
Hash: 0xdf98ae5761a55e24e505a625a2bdfcbdd13ab4f95647ecac500cc27783b742e3
    0: cumulative: 21000 gas: 21000 contract: 0x0000000000000000000000000000000000000000 status: 1 tx:

Error: invalid merkle root (remote: 652ac3a8397d16ce9e0b17af652996007fc7ed369c4ba7e3c1c1afd292fa4e1c local:
##############################

DEBUG[03-22|21:37:04.197|eth/fetcher/fetcher.go:668]       Propagated block import failed      peer=ad76f1dd
```

Fig. 10. Block validation failure on other nodes due to invalid merkle root

accepted by all nodes, which means the invalid transaction is verified. This result means that if we can modify the balance of an account on all participating nodes, the related transactions would be taken as valid ones and packed in valid blocks.

On this basis, we introduced a new node to the current network, then the new node starts to synchronize the whole blockchain. During the synchronization process the error message "insufficient Balance for transfer" comes again. This is because the new node builds the local state database by applying all the transactions in all the blocks. The balance for the address "0x7257d9476fed1e7421fd57ecf fd55c20e45f1678" for the block height of 7 would be 3. Then the transaction that transfer 5 ethers from the account would be found to be invalid (Fig. 11).

```
DEBUG[03-22|23:27:54.310|core/state_transition.go:221]     VM returned with error        err="insufficient balance for transfer"
ERROR[03-22|23:27:54.310|core/blockchain.go:2103]
########## BAD BLOCK #########
Chain config: {ChainID: 1895 Homestead: 0 DAO: <nil> DAOSupport: false EIP150: 0 EIP155: 0 EIP158: 0 Byzantium: 0 Constantinople:

Number: 8
Hash: 0x718d9ccea8b005c6e55b8f2bc7d041f75b273884021ac951b6273214bc9530f8

Error: insufficient balance for transfer
##############################
```

Fig. 11. Block validation failure during the block synchronization on a new node

5 Conclusions

This paper reports a potential security problem of the data storage and inquiry in the small scale Ethereum system. We first analyzed the balance inquiry process during the transaction validation, and found that the balance information is obtained by reading a local database, and the returned value will not be validated using the state root hash that is stored in the block header. On this basis, we find the interface that could access the local database directly. Based on a testing Ethereum network with three nodes, we proved that the balance of any account could be easily modified through the database interface. If the account is modified on only one node, the transaction based on the modified account will not accepted by other nodes due to the reason of "insufficient Balance for transfer" or "invalid merkle root". However, if the account is modified on all the nodes, the invalid transaction based on the modified account could be accepted by the system. In this case, the modification will not be noticed until new nodes join the network. In the Ethereum system with huge number of nodes, such attack would not be a big problem because it is almost impossible to modify an account information on most of the nodes. However, for a small scale private Ethereum network with tens or hundreds of nodes, the current transaction validation mechanism based on local database would be a big security problem, especially for the case that the nodes are fixed.

Acknowledgments. This work is supported by the Tianjin Natural Science Foundation (19JCY-BJC15700).

References

1. Buterin, V.: Ethereum white paper, June 2019. https://github.com/ethereum/wiki/wiki/White-Paper
2. Kehrli, J.: Blockchain 2.0 - from bitcoin transactions to smart contract applications (2016). https://goo.gl/CcDx4J
3. Chen, T., Zhu, Y., Li, Z., et al.: Understanding ethereum via graph analysis. In: IEEE INFO-COM 2018 - IEEE Conference on Computer Communications, Honolulu, HI, pp. 1484–1492 (2018)
4. Wang, S., Ouyang, L., Yuan, Y., et al.: Blockchain-enabled smart contracts: architecture, applications, and future trends. IEEE Trans. Syst. Man Cybern.: Syst. **49**(11), 2266–2277 (2019)
5. https://www.reply.com/en/content/insurechain
6. https://www.reply.com/en/content/securechain
7. https://thankscoin.org/about/
8. www.rightmesh.io
9. https://www.everledger.io/our-technologies/
10. Yuan, Y., Wang, F.-Y.: Blockchain: the state of the art and future trends. Acta Automatica Sinica **42**(4), 481–494 (2016)
11. Han, X., Yuan, Y., Wang, F.-Y.: Security problems on blockchain: the state of the art and future trends. Acta Automatica Sinica **45**(1), 206–225 (2019)
12. Wood, G., Antonopoulos, A.M.: Mastering Ethereum, Sebastopol, California. O'Reilly Medica Inc, Sebastopol (2018)
13. https://github.com/ethereum/go-ethereum
14. Wood, G.: Ethereum: a secure decentralised generalised transaction ledger. Ethereum Project Yellow Paper, vol. 151, pp. 1–32 (2014)

An Attack Detection and Defense Method for SDWN Oriented Blockchain Network

Lijun Xiao[1](✉), Yulian Gao[1], Bin Liu[2], and Tianke Fang[2]

[1] The Department of Accounting, Guangzhou College of Technology
and Business, Guangzhou 510850, Guangdong, China
ljxiaoxy@126.com, 592512904@qq.com
[2] The School of Software Engineering, Xiamen University of Technology, Xiamen 361024,
Fujian, China
lqq01863@163.com, Rock_FTK@163.com

Abstract. With the development of SDN, the problems of low efficiency of file transfer and limited network capacity in traditional network will be solved. However, due to the lack of protection mechanism in SDN application layer, data is easy to be lost and attacked. In this paper, the application layer and blockchain are combined to make full use of the unchangeable characteristics of blockchain data. A method of SDWN attack detection based on blockchain is proposed. The control layer controls the function of data distribution and access control. Then, the existing security problems are analyzed. Through the comparison between the methods in this paper and attack defense methods, several SDWN network security check methods are analyzed. It is found that this paper has better performance in the quality of experience (QoE) and network security performance, which will improve the controllability, flexibility and security of the network.

Keywords: Software-defined wireless network (SDWN) · Blockchain · Access control · Quality of experience (QoE)

1 Introduction

With the continuous development of Internet, but the Internet users still have the problem of low security awareness, which will lead to the increasing number of network attacks in recent years [1, 2]. The leakage and loss of user privacy data are becoming more and more serious [3]. For example, in 2018, in April, the number of Facebook privacy leaks rose to 87 million, and users were mainly concentrated in the United States; in May, researchers from the Kromtech Security Center found that information leaks caused by improper configuration of AWS buckets: led to the personal information leakage of tens of thousands of India cricket players; in August, a 16 year old high school student in Australia repeatedly invaded the Apple Corp server and downloaded about 90G of heavy In December, the French Ministry of Foreign Affairs said that the emergency contact information database had been hacked, and about 540000 personal file information had been stolen in the incident, including information such as name, telephone number and

© Springer Nature Singapore Pte Ltd. 2020
Z. Zheng et al. (Eds.): BlockSys 2020, CCIS 1267, pp. 243–252, 2020.
https://doi.org/10.1007/978-981-15-9213-3_19

email address; in February 2019, hackers from dub smash, Armor Games, 500px, white pages, Share this and other companies 16 Six websites collected 620 million accounts and sold them on the dark Internet; in April, 540 million Facebook related records collected by two third-party companies were exposed on AWS servers and opened to the world, including important privacy information such as name, ID card and password; in October, 7.5 million Adobe creative cloud The details of customers are stored in an insecure online database, which can be accessed by anyone without authentication; in the same month, more than 20 million tax records of Russian citizens are saved in an open database, which can be viewed online, with a time span from 2009 to 2016. In order to protect the security of user data and the network, researchers have proposed a series of security technologies, such as identity authentication [4], intellectual property protection [5], etc. However, from the numerous network attacks in recent years, we can know that: in the future network security applications, the number of blackmail attacks will be reduced, and the attack intensity will continue to increase; more targeted network attacks will gradually increase, and have a stronger purpose; this makes personal privacy information and important data protection need to be further enhanced.

The main factors restricting wireless networks development is the high complexity of data transmission and control. In order to solve this problem, Mckewown team [6] of American Stanford University firstly propose the concept of Software-defined network, which separate the control layer and the data layer, there are more efficient and convenient of network management. In view of the low utilization rate of traditional wireless networks, Salvatore [7] and other scholars from the University of Catania in Italy combined wireless networks with software defined networks to form software defined wireless networks. Although SDWN has more excellent characteristics of network resources and network structure, the research on network security detection and defense and SDWN architecture based on SDWN is still weak.

In this paper, the attack detection and defense method for SDWN is analyzed. Firstly, we introduce the basic concept of SDN, the basic concept of SDWN and the network architecture of SDWN. Secondly, we analyze the possible security threats in the software defined wireless network, discusses the network security detection and attack defense methods of SDWN, and puts forward a network attack detection and defense method for SDWN. Finally, we conclude the network attack detection and defense method for SDWN and the future work is prospected.

2 Software-Defined Network

2.1 SDN Technology Introduction

The earliest predecessor of SDN concept is programmable network. The most successful project in many research projects of programmable network is clean slate project, which mainly realizes a scheme of separating interaction mode and routing decision between network nodes. In 2006, the Martin Casado team of Stanford University began to study the ethane project. The project envisages to separate the control plane and data plane through a centralized processing mode, and the communication between networks is controlled by a secure control strategy. Through the centralized processing of the control layer, the network equipment is managed and configured safely and efficiently.

As shown in Fig. 1, the basic architecture of SDN is mainly divided into application layer, control layer and forwarding layer from top to bottom.

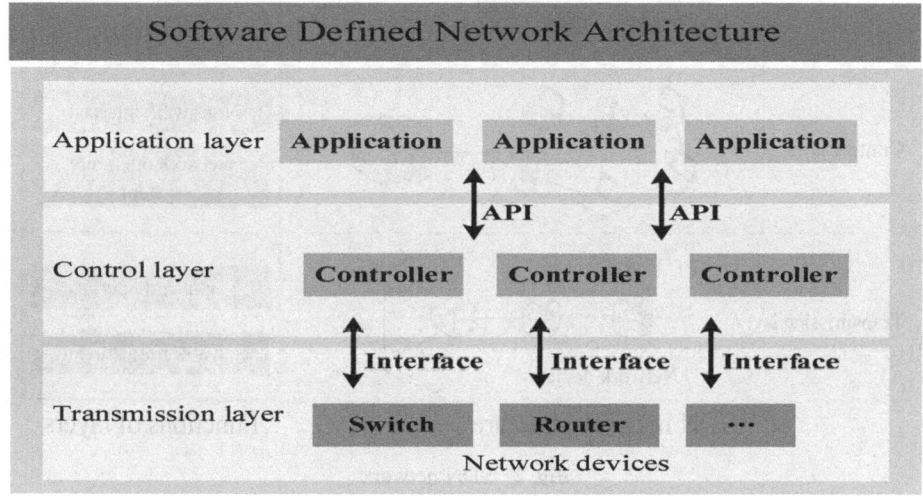

Fig. 1. Architectures of SDN

The core idea of SDN is to separate the control and forwarding of data, which makes the structure of the network more simplified and the operation more convenient, and improves the standardization and specialization of the whole network. Decoupling the control plane and the forwarding plane greatly reduces the load of the control plane and makes the network structure clearer. Then through the centralized control and management of the control plane, the resources in the network can be more balanced to achieve the maximum utilization of resources.

As shown in Fig. 2, the network structure and functions of each layer of SDN are as follows:

(1) The application layer mainly provides the application interface between various application layers and various networks, which is developed by various service manufacturers on the application layer, and ensures the efficient use of the network to the maximum extent. The communication mode between the application layer and the control layer is to use the north interface API. Service manufacturers can operate user data and provide virtualization services through various standardized APIs.

(2) The control layer is mainly responsible for network decision-making, the realization of programmable network through network operating system, and the realization of network control and management. The main function is to translate the instructions sent by the application layer through the South interface to the transmission layer for execution.

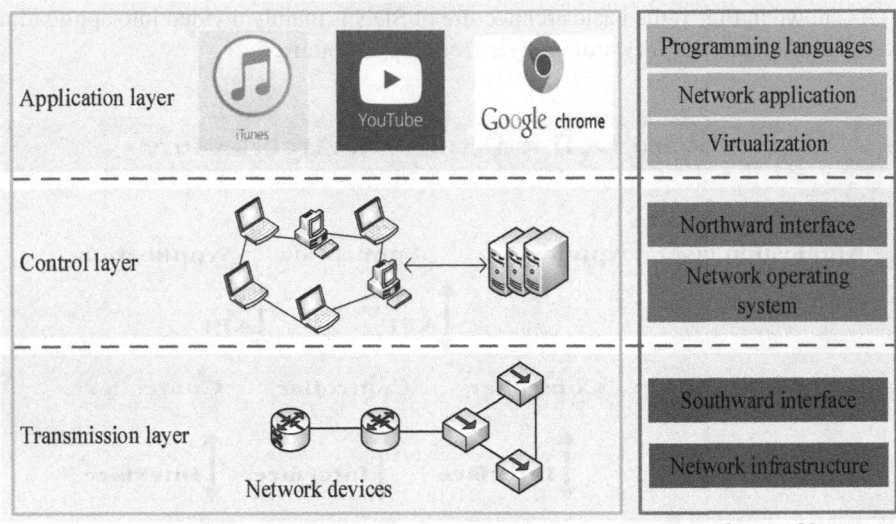

SDN network structure   Functions of layers

Fig. 2. SDN network

(3) The transmission layer mainly includes switches, routers and other basic network devices, which are only responsible for data forwarding, which greatly reduces the overall network load.

Martin Casado et al. [8] introduced the concept of OpenFlow in detail in 2008, which also marked the official arrival of SDN era. Casado and others believe that OpenFlow is a practical compromise: on the one hand, it allows researchers to run experiments on heterogeneous switches in a unified way, with line speed and high port density; on the other hand, suppliers do not need to disclose the internal work of their switches. And OpenFlow is based on an Ethernet switch, an internal traffic table and a standardized interface to add and delete traffic entries, and the implementation is very simple, without too much operation.

Because each service provider gathers the data center in its SDN network to the maximum extent, it makes it possible for virtualization technology. How to provide a safe, energy-saving and high-quality SDN service has become one of the urgent problems to be solved. The software defined network has become an efficient network communication technology, and can ensure sufficient network dynamic characteristics and reduce costs to improve network performance. Kreutz et al. [9] proposed how to implement a successful carrier level network with a software defined network. Kreutz et al. paid special attention to the challenges of network performance, scalability, security and interoperability, and proposed potential solutions. But efficient management network needs to support multiple concurrent tasks, from routing and forwarding and traffic monitoring to data access control and server load balancing. SDN platform can solve the problems of routing and traffic monitoring, but it is rare to create modular applications. Monsanto et al. [10] introduced the abstract model of building application program from many independent modules that jointly manage network traffic, which separated control plane and data plane to a great extent, and made network management more efficient. The control plane in the network defined by software is managed in the way of distributed cluster, and the consistency of the whole network must be guaranteed through cluster management, but this often produces large data. Aiming at the dynamic and network programmability of SDN, the security of cluster becomes a big security problem. Aiming at this problem, Wu et al. [11] of Shanghai JiaoTong University put forward an optimized control plane security cluster management architecture based on big data analysis, and an ant colony optimization method and control plane optimization implementation system which can realize big data analysis scheme. The simulation and experimental results show that the scheme is feasible and effective, and it is of great significance to improve the safety and efficiency of SDN control plane.

2.2   SDWN Architecture

With the continuous development of wireless networks, SDN has been applied to more and more diverse forms of wireless networks, such as mobile cellular networks, WLAN, WSNs, etc., which brings great flexibility to wireless networks, and greatly improves the efficiency between networks. However, the shortcomings of wireless network, software defined wireless network also have, such as low utilization rate of network resources, channel easily occupied and network transmission limitations, although it brings many problems to wireless network, but also provides more opportunities and challenges for software defined wireless network.

The birth of SDWN enables network service providers to deploy infrastructure and network services more efficiently, and take into account key technologies of distributed networks such as virtualization. However, the deployment and implementation of SDWN have some difficulties. Bernardos et al. [12] adopted a method similar to sdn applied to wireless mobile network, and used some representative use cases to illustrate the advantages of the architecture, and explained the modules, interfaces and advanced signaling aspects of the architecture in detail. They also reviewed ongoing standardization efforts and discussed potential strengths and weaknesses, as well as the need for a coordinated approach. This work has made great contribution to the following researchers of SDWN. With the increasing number of mobile devices such as mobile phones and tablets, the Internet will be defined by wireless networks to a large extent in the future. Zhou et al. [13] focused on the development of SDWN architecture, mainly including the virtualization strategy of SDWN's core control plane and the Semantic Ontology Applied in network resource description. They also proposed a new SDWN architecture, which can be used for resource description It describes autonomously and two kinds of semantic subjects for the description scheme. According to the current research situation of SDWN, the prospect is made. For the next generation wireless network, the research of in grid caching technology is the most important. Liang et al. [14] proposed a new software defined wireless network scheme, which mainly uses the bandwidth supply to improve the perceived experience quality (QoE) of wireless edge caching. In this scheme, firstly, we design a mechanism to provide active cache, bandwidth supply and adaptive video stream together, and cache the retrieved data dynamically in advance. According to the retrieved data, we propose a bandwidth optimized allocation scheme based on QoE. The experimental results show that the scheme can effectively reduce the system delay and greatly improve the cache utilization. Shu et al. [15] analyzed the three-tier architecture of SDN from the basic protocol, and proposed a security model of SDN, which contains a technology that can detect and defend some network attacks. The experimental results show that the model can effectively resist some network attacks and has low overhead. With the continuous progress and development of the Internet, from the era of 2G telephone network to the era of 3G and 4G high-speed network, to the era of 5G network, people's life experience is gradually improved, but there is no research on SDN architecture under 5G network. So far, Yan et al. [16] proposed a software defined wireless network security framework based on 5G network, which is based on adaptive trust The evaluation and management method fully guarantees the trust mechanism on SDWN platform to realize the network security under the software defined wireless network. The framework can meet the security deployment of virtual network and all kinds of standardized security services in cloud computing. The method has good universality, flexibility and security in 5G network.

In view of the above-mentioned security problems between networks based on SDWN, Pablo et al. [17], University of Frankfurt, Maine, Germany, proposed a network topology management method for wireless edge devices based on dynamic role assignment, which combines the centralized control of the controller with the virtualization of network functions, and integrates the network topology transformation, network services and application services into a single In the mechanism. Experimental results show that this method has the advantages of low power consumption and less bandwidth. Henrique et al. [18], Federal University of Minas Gerais, Brazil, proposed a software defined wireless network architecture for 802.11 wireless LAN, called ethanol. Ethanol can not only extend the control plane to the user's equipment, but also allow the software test of the smart white box, which will be more refined than the previous technology. The experimental results show that the memory and CPU occupied by the embedded Linux nodes are very low, which can be almost ignored, and the throughput of the network can be increased by 2 times through the dynamic optimization processing of data through ethanol, and the result of this method is about 45% higher than that of the traditional signal-based switching process by setting different control switching time Experimental results. In order to reduce the burden brought by the explosive growth of network traffic, Bomin et al. [19] of Sendai Northeastern University in Japan proposed a kind of SDWN routing strategy based on unsupervised deep learning. They used the convolutional neural networks (CNN) as the deep learning architecture, and ran CNN through the control plane to select the best path combination and used it in the forwarding layer The switch and other basic network devices are used for packet forwarding. The data flow between networks is tracked by control plane, and CNN is trained regularly to adapt to the latest network flow model. The experimental results show that the scheme can retain the previous security attack experience and has better routing functions.

3 SDWN Network Attack Detection and Defense Key Technologies

With the continuous expansion of SDN wireless network, it will be more difficult to judge the credibility of the nodes in the wireless network. If a large number of untrusted nodes are added to the network, it may lead to large-scale network paralysis, a large number of privacy data stolen from the server and other network security events. The security detection technology can solve the problem of insufficient network defense to some extent [20]. Therefore, the network security detection and attack defense of SDWN will become the top priority of SDWN's next research.

SDWN supports a new security protocol, which is expected to bring greater benefits to the operation, maintenance and management of wireless networks. However, because the wireless network defined by software separates the data plane from the control plane, the separation of the control plane from the data plane and the centralized data processing using the control plane will produce some new security threats. He et al. [21] discussed the security threat vector and its security design based on SDWN, analyzed the security requirements of SDWN, and summarized the security attacks and corresponding countermeasures of SDWN. At present, the main threats to SDWN are: the illegal node initiates DoS attack and intrusion system by forging identity; the illegal attacker attacks the forwarding device in the network, which will greatly damage the normal operation of the whole network; as we all know, the core of SDWN is the control layer, which can attack the data in the network through denial of service attack Stealing or destroying the controller through some design holes in the control layer will have a great impact on the whole network. When an illegal node attacks the resource management station in the network, the consequences are more threatening than the consequences of the controller being attacked, because it is easier to reprogram the whole network through one node (Management station); when the network is attacked And when the network needs to be repaired after being attacked, there is a lack of reliable resources for forensics and remediation in the network, which can help detect the root cause of the problem. In the absence of such resources, it is almost impossible to identify security incidents.

However, the threats in SDWN based networks are not only those mentioned above. In this paper, the following problems will be considered in the design of SDWN security access mechanism:

Overhead, the SDWN network built with OpenFlow will generate a lot of overhead, and the data sample information using open flow is less, which is difficult to be used for forensics and remediations.

The variability of users and the mobility of users in the network often lead to frequent switching of user data between base stations. Once there is abnormal user behavior, it will be difficult to detect, and there are different operators responsible for the existence of users in the network, which will make the compatibility of the network worse, the communication negotiation between networks will become complicated, and may lead to privacy disputes Problems and conflicts of service quality requirement. The SDN technology proposed in this paper separates the control plane from the data plane. Through the centralized control of the wireless network by the controller, not only can the structure of the wireless network be clearer, but also can ensure that the network structure can run more safely. Figure 3 shows the basic workflow of the controller in SDN. To send data to another node, the nodes in the network need to go through the following steps: the node sends the data packet to the switch in the network. If the corresponding flow table in the switch does not exist, the switch accesses the controller, the controller sends the flow table to the switch, and the switch can send the data The packet is forwarded to the network of the target node. If the switch in the network where the target node is located does not have the flow table corresponding to the target node, repeat the previous steps to obtain the flow table, and then forward the packets to the target node. At this point, the basic workflow of SDN is finished. In Algorithm 1, the above process is briefly described.

Algorithm 1: Centralized control algorithm of SDN controller

Input: node $P_1, P_2, \ldots, P_n$ in wireless, controller *Controller*, switch $T_1, T_2, \ldots, T_n$

1. The node P_1 send the packet $Packet_1$ to the wireless network.

2. **if** (there is no corresponding match in the flow table in switch T_1) {

3. T_1 send packet $Packet_1$ to controller *Controller* through Packet-In();

4.   Controller *Controller* obtains the flow table information through the whole network topology information;

5.   Controller *Controller* sends the flow table to switch T_1 through PacketOut(); }

6. After the switch T_1 obtains the flow table, it forwards the packet $Packet_1$ sent by the node P_1 to the switch t.

7. **Repeat:** step2, step 3, step 4, step 5

8. Switch T_2 forwards packet $Packet_1$ to target node P_2.

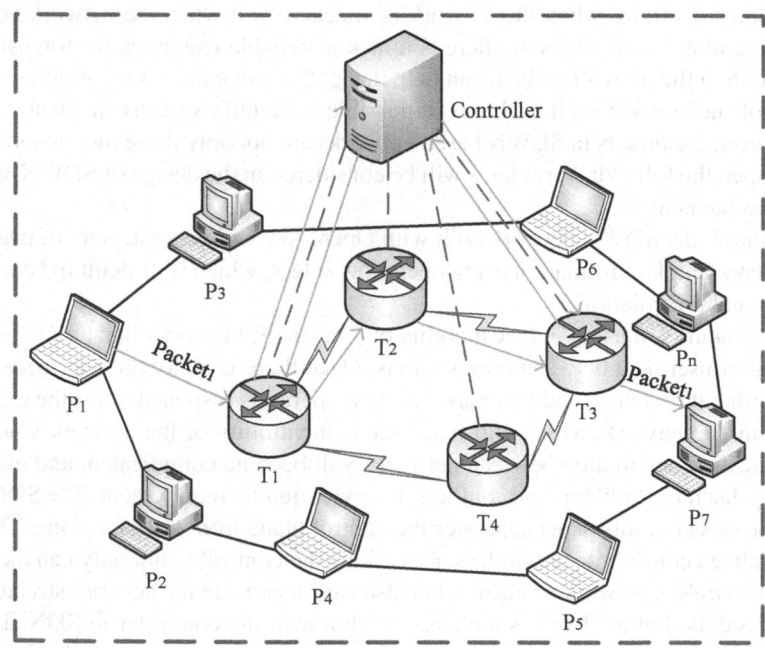

Fig. 3. Controller workflow

As shown in Table 1, literature [6] is the concept of OpenFlow proposed by McKeown team of Stanford University. It introduces a campus network system based on OpenFlow.

However, due to the lack of consideration of service quality and security at the early time of publication, document [9] has good experimental results, but the consideration of security is not enough. Although document [11] does not use the method of OpenFlow, but Taking into account the effect of QoE and security, the algorithm proposed in this paper uses OpenFlow, and takes into account the level of QoE and network security.

Table 1. A comparison of various SDN algorithm

Algorithm	Use OpenFlow	QoE	Traceability
Literature [6]	Yes	Weak	Medium
Literature [9]	Yes	Strong	Medium
Literature [11]	No	Strong	Strong
Ours	Yes	Medium	Strong

4 Conclusion

In this paper, software defined wireless network security detection and attack defense methods are studied. According to the major security events of network attacks and the trend of network security in recent years, this paper introduces the basic concept of SDN technology, including the three-layer network structure of SDN, the detailed functions of each layer and the interaction between each layer; then, it introduces the network structure of SDWN, and proposes a method of network attack detection and defense for SDWN. Through the analysis and comparison, we can see that the method in this paper has better advantages compared with the security performance of QoE (quality of experience) network. Finally, the paper analyzes the possible security threats in the software defined wireless network, discusses some network security detection and attack defense methods for SDWN, and makes a detailed analysis.

Although SDWN has made a lot of perfect research results so far, with the rapid development of the next generation Internet technology, SDWN still faces more challenges. How to carry out efficient cooperative control, load balance and emergency repair measures for controller node failure, and how to switch between different networks and the corresponding network virtualization technology under multi controller SDWN network are also our next research work.

References

1. https://www.anquanke.com/post/id/169720
2. https://cloud.tencent.com/developer/news/492018
3. Liang, W., Fan, Y., Li, C., Zhang, D., Gaudiot, J.-L.: Secure data storage and recovery in industrial blockchain network environments. IEEE Trans. Ind. Inform. **16**(10), 6543–6552 (2020). https://doi.org/10.1109/tii.2020.2966069

4. Liang, W., Xie, S., Long, J., et al.: A double PUF-based RFID identity authentication protocol in service-centric internet of things environments. Inf. Sci. **503**, 129–147 (2019)
5. Liang, W., Huang, W., Long, J., Zhang, K., Li, K., Zhang, D.: Deep reinforcement learning for resource protection and real-time detection in loT environment. IEEE Internet Things J. 1 (2020). https://doi.org/10.1109/jiot.2020.2974281
6. McKeown, N.: Software-defined networking. INFOCOM Keynote Talk **17**(2), 30–32 (2009)
7. Costanzo, S., et al.: Software defined wireless networks: unbridling SDNs. In: 2012 European Workshop on Software Defined Networking. IEEE (2012)
8. McKeown, N., et al.: OpenFlow: enabling innovation in campus networks. ACM SIGCOMM Comput. Commun. Rev. **38**(2), 69–74 (2008)
9. Kreutz, D., Ramos, F.M.V., Verissimo, P.: Towards secure and dependable software-defined networks. In: Proceedings of the Second ACM SIGCOMM Workshop on Hot Topics in Software Defined Networking (2013)
10. Monsanto, C., et al.: Composing software defined networks. In: 10th {USENIX} Symposium on Networked Systems Design and Implementation {NSDI} 2013 (2013)
11. Wu, J., et al.: Big data analysis-based secure cluster management for optimized control plane in software-defined networks. IEEE Trans. Netw. Serv. Manag. **15**(1), 27–38 (2018)
12. Bernardos, C.J., et al.: An architecture for software defined wireless networking. IEEE Wirel. Commun. **21**(3), 52–61 (2014)
13. Zhou, Q., et al.: Network virtualization and resource description in software-defined wireless networks. IEEE Commun. Mag. **53**(11), 110–117 (2015)
14. Liang, C., et al.: Enhancing QoE-aware wireless edge caching with software-defined wireless networks. IEEE Trans. Wirel. Commun. **16**(10), 6912–6925 (2017)
15. Yan, Z., Zhang, P., Vasilakos, A.V.: A security and trust framework for virtualized networks and software-defined networking. Secur. Commun. Netw. **9**(16), 3059–3069 (2016)
16. Shu, Z., et al.: Security in software-defined networking: threats and countermeasures. Mob. Netw. Appl. **21**(5), 764–776 (2016)
17. Graubner, P., et al.: Dynamic role assignment in software-defined wireless networks. In: 2017 IEEE Symposium on Computers and Communications (ISCC). IEEE (2017)
18. Moura, H., et al.: Ethanol: a software-defined wireless networking architecture for IEEE 802.11 networks. Comput. Commun. **149**, 176–188 (2020)
19. Mao, B., et al.: A novel non-supervised deep-learning-based network traffic control method for software defined wireless networks. IEEE Wirel. Commun. **25**(4), 74–81 (2018)
20. Liang, W., Li, K., Long, J., Kui, X., Zomaya, Y.: An industrial network intrusion detection algorithm based on multifeature data clustering optimization model. IEEE Trans. Industr. Inf. **16**(3), 2063–2071 (2019). https://doi.org/10.1109/TII.2019.2946791
21. He, D., Chan, S., Guizani, M.: Securing software defined wireless networks. IEEE Commun. Mag. **54**(1), 20–25 (2016)

Blockchain and Cloud Computing

BPS-VSS: A Blockchain-Based Publish/Subscribe Video Surveillance System with Fine Grained Access Control

Qian He[1,2]($\boxtimes$), Bingcheng Jiang[1,2], Dongsheng Cheng[2], and Rengang Liang[1,2]

[1] State and Local Joint Engineering Research Center for Satellite Navigation and Location Service, Guilin University of Electronic Technology, Guilin 541004, China
heqian@guet.edu.cn
[2] Guangxi Key Laboratory of Cryptography and Information Security, Guilin University of Electronic Technology, Guilin 541004, China

Abstract. In recent years, the video surveillance system has become an indispensable management tool for cities. The surveillance system can improve the effectiveness of management and supervision and reduce the possibility of crime. Video surveillance as a service is a type of cloud service that can reduce redundant information and communications technology (ICT) facilities. Users use video surveillance services through a publish/subscribe (P/S) model. In this paper, we propose a blockchain-based publish/subscribe video surveillance system with fine grained access control. A P/S service model for the video surveillance is given and the matching efficiency is improved using a multi-level index mechanism. Ciphertext-policy attribute-based encryption (CP-ABE) is adopted to encrypt the access control policy for a published video surveillance, and only the subscriber with satisfied attributes can decrypt and subscribe video services. In traditional CP-ABE schemes, access policy is stored and granted by the cloud, which lacks credibility due to centralization. We use blockchain to record the access policy, realizing user self certification. The video received from the camera is encrypted and stored in InterPlanetary File System (IPFS) node connected to the blockchain network. The decrypted key of the video is encrypted by CP-ABE. Finally, the access policy, decrypted key, video metadata, the hash value returned by IPFS are recorded in the blockchain.

Keywords: Video surveillance · Blockchain · Publish/subscribe · Attribute-based encryption · Service matching

1 Introduction

With the continuous development of smart cities, intelligent transportation, and the increasing security awareness of users in various industries such as finance, education, and property, the video surveillance market has maintained steady growth in recent years [1]. Traditional video surveillance systems, such as the

© Springer Nature Singapore Pte Ltd. 2020
Z. Zheng et al. (Eds.): BlockSys 2020, CCIS 1267, pp. 255–268, 2020.
https://doi.org/10.1007/978-981-15-9213-3_20

closed circuit television (CCTV) system, have served vast security applications in everyday life. However, most cameras can not get rid of the traditional method of manual monitoring, which results in a large amount of video data accumulation occupying storage resources, poor real-time video monitoring, and difficulty in video retrieval [2].

The cloud computing-based system architecture is designed for remote access, enabling user systems to have smooth video access and streaming access capabilities. In addition, through the encryption of the video transmission and access process, it is very convenient for general web browsers and mobile devices to access the video surveillance cloud system. Therefore, video surveillance and cloud computing are combined to form a new cloud service model for video surveillance as a service (VSaaS) [3,4]. VSaaS has obvious advantages, video data can be shared across regions and agencies. Video surveillance services serve different institutions with a unified platform, thereby reducing redundant ICT facilities. For example, in the security industry, VSaaS is a functional video hosting service, which means that a professional operating service company is responsible for the security system instead of the user. Users can host their own security systems on professional operating service platforms.

There are thousands of cameras in the existing video surveillance network, each camera is a producer of surveillance video services [5]. Generally, users directly select specialized cameras to view, but it is time-consuming and not flexible enough. It is necessary to introduce a new mechanism to improve the flexibility of the access control of the monitoring system. The pub/sub paradigm is an event-driven, asynchronous and loosely coupled multicast communication between the publishers and subscribers of messages. The complete decoupling of publishers and subscribers in space, time and synchronization makes it very suitable for deploying large scale distributed video surveillance services [6].

However, when applying publish-subscribe model onto cloud storage, data security and privacy have become a major issue since the cloud provider is not a fully trusted entity [7].

CP-ABE is known as one of the sophisticated encryption technologies for fine-grained access control. In a CP-ABE system, user's private key is associated with his own attributes, each ciphertext is labeled with an access control policy, which is defined by data owner. A user is able to decrypt a ciphertext only his attributes satisfy the access control policy. In most situations, the encrypted data and access control policy are uploaded to the cloud service providers (CSP), CSP as a third party is not fully trusted. Therefore, the traditional CP-ABE schemes are insecure. Blockchain is an emerging decentralized architecture and distributed computing paradigm. It is feasible to record the access control policy on the blockchain to realize user self-certification and cloud non-repudiation [8].

Additionally, with the development of artificial intelligence (AI) and deep learning methods, the presence of advanced counterfeiting has multiplied in recent years [9]. Now, deepfakes [10] have the capability of modifying reality, as long as sufficient data (or material) related to existing themes can be provided, deepfakes algorithm can be used to manipulate and modify video content, which is almost indistinguishable to human beings. Since the distributed ledger of the blockchain records the metadata of the surveillance video, it is cut off the chance of forgery of the data. We can also record the hash value of data to resist data tampering attack. Therefore, blockchain technology helps to discriminate fake videos from original one and to make sure that surveillance video are authentic [11].

In this paper, we propose a publish/subscribe Video Surveillance system with fine grained access Control, which is based on both CP-ABE and blockchain. In our scheme, A P/S service model for the video surveillance is given and a multilevel index mechanism is designed for improving matching efficiency. We use CP-ABE to realize fine grained access Control, blockchain is used to record the access policy of the data, realizing user self-certification. What's more, Considering the advanced video forgery ability of AI, Our scheme also supports video traceable and anti-tampering. The main contributions are given as follows.

1) We propose a publish/subscribe video surveillance system to realize one-to-many video sharing, P/S is realized on JXTA, camera owner can publish the surveillance video as a service and define the access policy.
2) We propose a proxy based CP-ABE method for P/S based video surveillance. Computational overhead of decryption is outsourced to the cloud proxy server, improve the decryption efficiency of the mobile user. We adopt blockchain to record the access policy of the video surveillance, realizing user self-certification.
3) We structure a procedure that can detect video forgery by applying blockchain technology. The video received from the camera is encrypted and stored in an IPFS [12], and then, the access policy, decryption key, video metadata and the hash value returned by IPFS are recorded in the blockchain.

The remainder of this paper is organized as follows. Section 2 introduces the related work. System architecture is presented in Sect. 3. In Sect. 4, we describe P/S model for video surveillance services and propose service matching algorithm. The experimental results and discussions in Sect. 5. Section 6 draws the conclusion.

2 Related Work

Hassan M et al. [13] proposed distributed subscriptions to different groups to improve IPTV video surveillance subscriptions. The release subscription middleware has the characteristics of loose coupling, asynchronous and multi-point communication and scalability. The use of publish/subscribe middleware can effectively improve the initiative of mobile cloud video surveillance service management [14]. However, the video surveillance terminal cloud service system has a large number of service advertisements and matching events, and the characteristics of the video surveillance object and the properties of the video surveillance user are matched to the requirements, and there are difficulties in the mobile cloud monitoring service publishing subscription. In the video surveillance domain, a video contains meaningful information and is beneficial to share among organizations. However, sharing raw videos can reach to sharing information that is not intended. Upmanyu et al. [15] proposed a method to protect the privacy of surveillance video. Each image frame is divided into random small images, which do not contain any information. Then the secret sharing algorithm is used to allocate and store small images among participants. However, this method is computationally intensive and not flexible.

Sahai et al. proposed attribute-based encryption (ABE) in the literature [16]. ABE mainly includes key strategy ABE (KP-ABE) [17] and ciphertext strategy ABE (CP-ABE) [18]. The CP-ABE integrates the access control policy into the ciphertext, which allowed a data owner to implement access control by setting up access policy. It is very suitable for publishing many-to-many data sharing methods in the subscription scene. Green et al. [19] proposed an outsourced decryption scheme, which divides the user's key into attribute key and decryption key. In the decryption phase, the main computing overhead is outsourced to the cloud server provider. However, the access structure for publishing the subscription message contains the sensitive information of the user. Zhong et al. [20] proposed a cloud storage strategy based on multi-attribute attribute hidden encryption access control scheme, which is computationally intensive. Fan et al. [21] proposed an efficient and privacy-protected ABE scheme, but the data owner needs to convert the access strategy through attribute authorization before encryption. In the traditional ABE scheme, only the security of the data can be guaranteed, and the access structure cannot be protected. Therefore, how to realize the hiding of the access policy will be a key issue for the ABE solution to protect the user's private information in the publishing and subscription system. Blockchain is a new technology system derived from the underlying technology of Bitcoin. The earliest definition came from a paper published by Takoshi Takemoto in 2009 [22]. Blockchain has the technical characteristics of decentralization, anti-tampering, and non-forgery. Compared with other traditional technologies, it has more advantages in ensuring information credibility, security and traceability. Blockchain technology provides new technical ideas and methods for data sharing and data trace. Recording the integrity of videos on the blockchain has been studied in the context of individual videos. Gipp et al. [23] proposed to record integrity of videos from a car's dashboard in the event of a collision, for using the video with provable integrity in court. In their android-phone-based system, when a collision is detected automatically using built-in accelerometers, the current video is cryptographically hashed, and the hash is recorded on bitcoin blockchain via the OriginStamp protocol. Similarly, Hemlin et al. [24] also explored an android-phone-based system where hashes of videos are recorded on a blockchain to preserve their integrity.

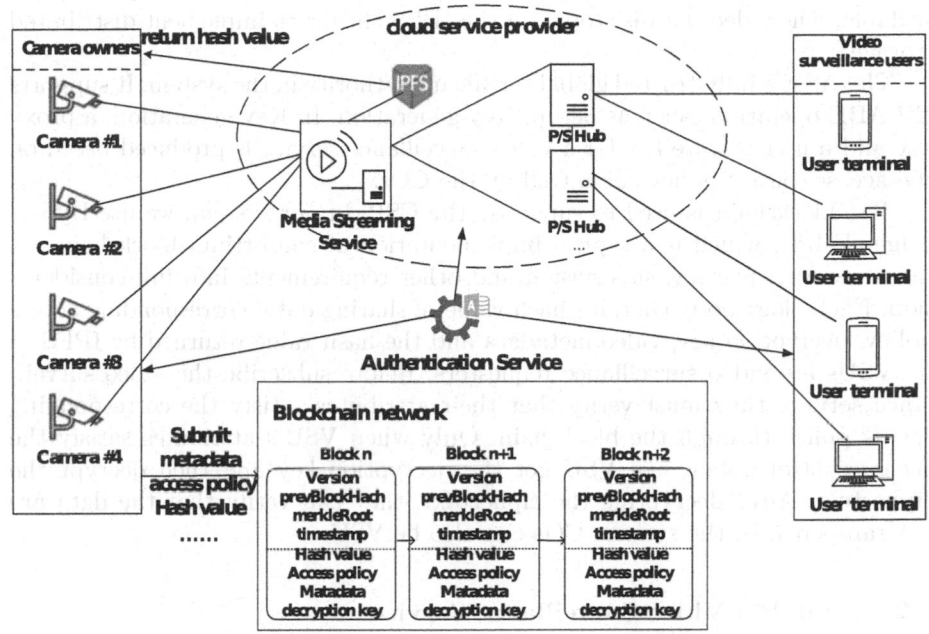

Fig. 1. System architecture of BPS-VSS

3   Architecture and Components

3.1   System Architecture

As shown in Fig. 1, our blockchain-based publish/subscribe video surveillance system with Fine Grained Access Control (BPS-VSS) consist of six entities: camera owners (COs), a cloud service provider (CSP), authentication service (AS), a video surveillance P/S overlay network, a blockchain and video surveillance users (VSUs).

COs are camera owners, also video data owners, and can define access control policies to decide who can access. COs can publish a video surveillance service to the CSP, and send the encrypted data to store in CSP. Meanwhile, COs need to verify that the ciphertext are received correctly by the CSP. If the hash value return from the CSP is equal to the hash value for ciphertext, the blochchain packs the access control policy, hash value of the data and video's metadata and the decryption key as a transaction. All COs jointly maintain the blockchain.

The CSP provides publish/Subscribe service and data storage service. CSP consists of media streaming services (MSS), P/S overlay network based on JXTA and IPFS. MSS is responsible for forwarding data, and the advertisement of the subscription is the URL of the camera published in the MSS. MSS need to validate the authentication before providing service to the user terminal. The P/S overlay network consists of thousands of smart cameras, users and P/S hubs. The overlay network protocol is based on JXTA whose is fully distributed and scalable. The video data is stored on the IPFS cluster to implement distributed storage.

The AS is a fully trusted global certificate authority in the system. It supports CP-ABE operations such as Setup, Key-generation. In Key-generation, a proxy key and a user private key for a video surveillance service is produced based on the access control policy submitted by the COs.

The blockchain is used to supervise the CSP. In our system, we use Hyperledger Fabric, which is a typical implementation of consortium blockchains. It takes security, privacy, supervision and other requirements into full consideration. Each block body contains hash value of sharing data, corresponding access policy, decryption key, video metadata and the hash value returned by IPFS.

VSUs are video surveillance requesters. Before subscribe the video surveillance service, they must verify that their attributes satisfy the corresponding access policy through the blockchain. Only when VSU's attributes satisfy the access control policy, can VSU get the decryption key and then decrypt the ciphertext. After decrypting the ciphertext, they can verify that the data are not tampered. In the system, COs can also be VSUs.

3.2 Publish a Video Surveillance Service

In order to protect the access permission of the video surveillance, the owner of smart cameras uses the constraint condition and the user's required attribute as an access control policy to encrypt an access permission message and publish it to P/S overlay network as video advertisement message. Only the VSUs satisfy the corresponding attribute, advertisement information can be decrypted. Therefore, the access control for effectively protecting the user's private information and the video surveillance service is achieved. The detail procedure of publishing a video surveillance service is as follows.

Step 1: a newly installed smart camera c^i is going to be published as video surveillance service. The camera owner publishs the video surveillance of c^i as a cloud service to P/S overlay network, and record the service Uniform Resource Locator (URL) address: VS_URL_i. And then generate a hash based global unique identifier for VS_URL_i using SHA(VS_URL_i).

Step 2: function characters of c^i are described and published to P/S overlay network. The function characters are described in the P/S model given in Sect. 4, which will combine with VS_URL_i together.

Step 3: access policy of c^i is defined and used for CP-ABE. The access policy will be convert to a LSSS matrix for CP-ABE. The video surveillance service VS_URL_i is encrypted based on the proxy based CP-ABE [25]. The access policy and SHA(VS_URL_i) is recorded on the blockchain.

After a video surveillance service is published on BPS-VSS successfully, it can be subscribed and monitored remotely by VSUs with the satisfied requirements of access policy.

3.3   Access a Video Surveillance Service

The main purpose of BPS-VSS is to provide a flexible and secure access mechanism for the manager and the authorized users. The authorized users should be marked attributes by the authentication service and fetch their private key SK firstly. The private key SK is generated through Key-Generation algorithm by the authentication service. Just these users having satisfied attributes can decrypt the ciphertext encrypted by the proxy based CP-ABE using their SK. Since CP-ABE can realize many-to-many data sharing, the access control of BPS-VSS can work well in an open environment. The procedure of accessing a video surveillance service is as follows.

Step 1: an access request is started by a user terminal u_i who wants to subscribe or monitor a video surveillance service provided by a smart camera c_j. u_i sends a request message consisting of SHA (VS_URL_i) and the attribute set S to the P/S hub using JXTA protocol.

Step 2: u_i query the access policy from blockchain according to SHA (VS_URL_i), and then the ciphertext of VS_URL_i is decrypted partly by the connected P/S hub. The P/S hub executes the $Proxy - Decrypt$ algorithm taking input ciphertext CT, transformation key TK and attribute set S. If S is accepted by the defined access policy, the semi-decrypted cipher text CT' is generated and sent to the requesting user terminal u_i with a randomly temporal session key ts_i for accessing the media streaming service. Otherwise, a null message is responded to u_i.

Step 3: the destination video surveillance service VS_URL_i is gotten by the requesting user terminal u_i. For an authorized VSU, u_i can download the semi-decrypted CT' from the P/S hub. Then, u_i does the Decrypt algorithm taking input CT' and his private key SK, which produces VS_URL_i.

Step 4: u_i access VS_URL_i from the media streaming service using the temporal session key ts_i.

Based on the above procedure, the subscribing or monitor procedure for the authorized user u_i can continue, and the access control with CP-ABE for the video surveillance is realized.

4   P/S Video Surveillance Service Description and Matching

4.1   P/S Model for Video Surveillance Services

The P/S model for video surveillance services is composed of an attribute description of surveillance service and a constraint description of access policy. A video surveillance service has two types of attributes: function and performance. The function attributes of a video surveillance service include location, service type, description keyword, and so on. The performance attributes include resolution, frame rate, and so on. An attribute of the video surveillance service is represented as a triple (*property, type, value*). Where, *property* is the name of the property, represented by a string, and *type* indicates the type of the attribute,

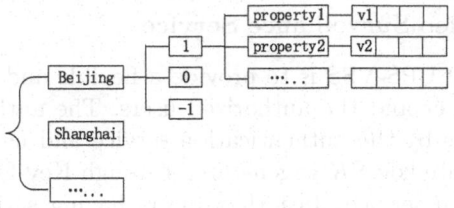

Fig. 2. Example of Multilevel index linked list

represented by an integer data. The value of *type* for a positive attribute equal to 1, whereas the value for a negative attribute equals to -1, and the value for a neutral attribute equal to 0. The parameter of *value* represents the value of that attribute, which is a string or number depending on the use case.

The service description and constrains matching is based on attribute matching rules. According to two video surveillance service attributes: $A_1 = (p_1, t_1, v_1)$ and $A_2 = (p_2, t_2, v_2)$, A_2 is matched by A_1 in three cases: 1) $type = 1$ and $v_1 \leq v_2$, 2) $type = 0$ and $v_1 == v_2$, 3) $type = 1$ and $v_1 \geq v_2$. Otherwise, A_1 is dominated by A_2. A video surveillance service VSC is represented by a set $\{A_1, A_2, \ldots, A_n, id, mark\}$. The variable $A_i (1 \leq i \leq n)$ represents a certain attribute of the video surveillance service, and the variable id is a globally unique identifier. The value of id is specified by the publisher of that video surveillance service. The variable mark represents the structure of the video surveillance service with a fixed-length string. For example, a video surveillance service $VSC = \{(Location, Beijing), (Definition, Medium), (Frame, 25), 10001\}$ indicates that the video surveillance service is located in Beijing, the resolution is medium, the frame rate is 25 fps, and id is equal to 10001.

A video surveillance constraint model $VSCC$ consists of a set of requirements $\{C_1, C_2, C_3, \ldots, C_n, mark\_s\}$ which is normally proposed by the video surveillance subscriber. Among them $C_i (1 \leq i \leq n)$ represents a constraint in the constraint model. $mark\_s$ indicates the structure of the subscription, represented by a fixed-length string.

Definition 1: Assuming VSC has a property $P_i = \{property, type, value\}$ and a single constraint $C_i = \{a, p, v\}$ of the video surveillance constraint model $VSCC$ subscribed by the user, if $\{property = a\} \bigcap \{value = v\} \bigcap \{match(type, value, v)\}$ is true, then the attribute P_i of the video surveillance service is matched with the constraint C_i, which is denoted as matched (P_i, C_i).

Definition 2: For any constraint C_i of the video surveillance constraint models $VSCC = \{C_1, C_2, C_3 \ldots, C_n, mark\_s\}$, There is at least one attribute can match, that is, $\forall C_i \in VSCC, \exists P_j \in VSC$, so that the attribute P_j can match the constraint C_i, and no attribute and constraint contradict, then VSC is matched with $VSCC$. That is: $\forall C_i \in VSCC, \exists P_j \in VSC$, so that matched (C_i, P_j) is true, and $\forall P_j \in VSC$. If there is no P_j to make conflicted (C_i, P_j) is true, then VSC is matched with $VSCC$, recorded as matched $(VSC, VSCC)$.

4.2   Multi-level Index List

The service advertisements published by the user are pre-processed, where a multi-level index should be generated and saved. Service advertisements generated by user should be operated according to the attribute dominated rules, and then constructs a multi-level index list based on their attribute type: location, service type, property name, and value, as shown in Fig. 2.

The multi-level index is a cascade of multi-level linked lists. Since the geographic location of video surveillance is most important, the first level of the linked list is designed as the attribution of the location of the smart camera, such as Beijing and Shanghai. The second level is the functional attribute (1: positive attribute; 0: neutral attribute, −1: negative attribute). If the value of types is 1 or −1, it is sorted according to the matching rules, so that the binary search method can be used to quickly find and match index entries. If the attribute constraint of the video surveillance advertisement matches the attribute of an advertisement in the linked list, the constraint of the video monitoring advertisement attribute to the end of the linked list matches the advertisement attribute. If the value of types is 0, the link may be a hash value. These hash values, arranged in their lexicographic order, only needs to match once in the hash table each time.

4.3   Service Matching Algorithm

The matching of the video surveillance service is mainly implemented by the peer group creation module and the service constraint matching module in the P/S hub. The peer group creation module creates a peer group and wait for the publisher and subscriber of the service to join, and the publishers and subscribers within the group can publish the subscription. As a core module, the service constraint matching module matches the published services and subscription constraints to obtain a video surveillance service that meets the requirements of the subscriber.

According to the mobile video monitoring and publishing subscription model, based on event filtering and multi-level index structure matching, the multi-level index based matching algorithm is given in Algorithm 1:

$mark\_s$ and $mark\_p$ are represented by a binary integer, each digit of the integer represents an attribute if the attribute is 1 in the subscribed or published advertisement. Otherwise, the position is 0. $MatchPS$ is a set to collect all the matched video services.

First, the $mark\_s$ of the service subscription and the type of $mark\_p$ in the published service set are compared one by one by the integer data. If the attribute in $mark\_p$ contains all the attributes in $mark\_s$, the pairing is successful; otherwise, the pairing fails. The service Id corresponding to the successfully paired $mark\_p$ is added to the temporary matching set $MatchPS$.

The attribute constraint of the service subscription advertisement is taken out, and the matching value is searched in the multi-dimensional index table in order according to its region, type, attribute name, and attribute value. Firstly, the geographical location of the video subscription is matched in the index. If

---

Algorithm 1. Multi-level service based matching algorithm

Input: $mark\_s, VSCC$
Output: $MatchPS$
 1: **for** $mark\_p$ in VSC **do**
 2:    **if** $mark\_p \leq mark\_s$ **then**
 3:       $MatchPS$ add cs
 4:    **end if**
 5: **end for**
 6: **if** $markPS ==$null **then**
 7:    **return** null
 8: **else**
 9:    **for** $mark\_p$ in $MatchPS$ **do**
10:       **if** $mark\_p$ don't matched $mark\_s$ **then**
11:          remove $mark\_p$ from $MatchPS$
12:       **end if**
13:       **return** $MatchPS$
14:    **end for**
15: **end if**

---

there is no match, the service is deleted from the $MatchPS$, then, the attribute-based matching is performed based on the multi-level index. After the matching is completed, the $MatchPS$ is a cloud service set that satisfies the subscription of the video user.

5   Implementation and Evaluation

5.1   Monitoring Performance of Video Surveillance Services

First, we tested the function of remotely accessing the smart camera cloud service through a user terminal. The video surveillance cloud service VSC and the attribute-based access control policy are issued on the smart camera implemented on the Android system to the authorization and proxy server, that is, the video surveillance cloud service advertisement. The terminal users, including PC or Android mobile phone, join into the JXTA network and submit the interested video surveillance cloud service to the authorization and proxy server, and various video monitoring services are subscribed according to the attributes of the video. The terminal that satisfies the requirements of the attribute-based access control policy will play the video according to the RTSP address parsed from the service advertisement.

In the case of one smart camera and one terminal user, the time cost of a complete publish and subscribe process is 498.88 ms. With a resolution of 176×144, a frame rate of 25 fps, and an access bandwidth of 86 Mbps, the video playback process is smooth. The delay of the video surveillance cloud service is less than 1.5 s.

5.2   P/S Performance of Video Surveillance Services

The video surveillance service release experiment tests the response time when 1,000–20,000 mobile terminal publishers concurrently publish video service advertisements to the authorization and P/S hub. The publish performance is shown in Fig. 3. When there are 20,000 publishers simultaneously publishing video surveillance service advertisements to the P/S hub, the total response time is 5,860.75 ms, and the average time for a single release record is 0.293 ms. The average release time of a single record of 1,000 publishers is 2 ms, which may be the initialization process of the concurrent release is performed simultaneously on each P2P node, so the time average of the single release after the accumulation is slightly decreased.

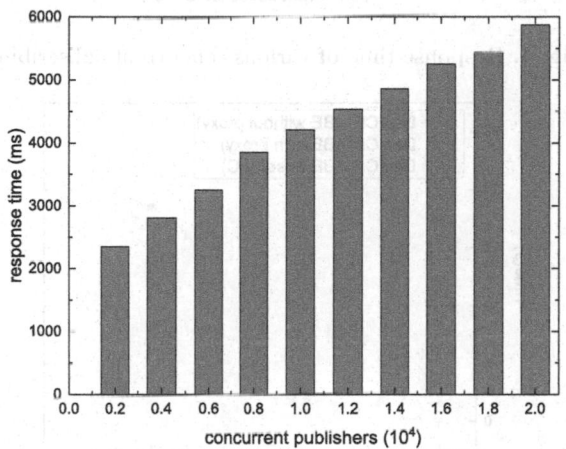

Fig. 3. Response time of various concurrent publishing

5.3   Video Surveillance Service Subscription

The video surveillance service subscription experiment tested the response time when 50–1,000 mobile terminal subscriptions simultaneously subscribed to the P/S hub, and its subscription performance is shown in Fig. 4. When 1,000 subscribers subscribe to the video service published by the same mobile terminal at the same time, the response time is 1372.25 ms, and the average time of a single subscription record is about 1.372 ms, which can meet the concurrent requirements. However, after subscribing to BPS-VSS, because there are multiple clients watching the same video surveillance at the same time, if data transmission methods such as multicast are not used, it will cause great traffic pressure on media streaming services.

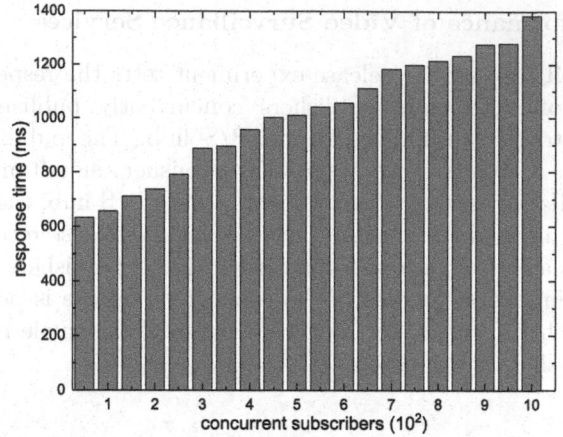

Fig. 4. Response time of various concurrent subscribing

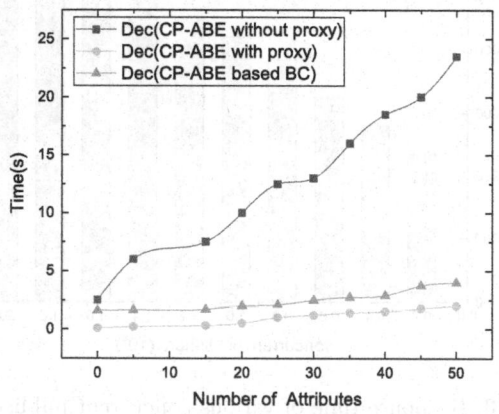

Fig. 5. Decryption time under various attributes

5.4   Decryption Performance of Proxy Based CP-ABE

In this part, the proxy-decrypt CP-ABE scheme based on blockchain is compared with the traditional CP-ABE scheme with proxy or not, and the time overhead of decryption in the case of different number of attributes is tested, time-consuming comparison is shown in Fig. 5.

It can be seen from the experimental results that the CP-ABE algorithm can effectively reduce time overhead of decryption phase by introducing a decryption proxy. As the number of attributes in the cipher text increases, the decryption time of the traditional CP-ABE scheme increases linearly, while the decryption time cost of the proxy-decrypt CP-ABE scheme is not obvious. In our scheme, there exist a time overhead when query the access policy from blockchain, but the overhead is slight. Therefore, our solution has less impact on BPS-VSS while ensuring data security, and is very suitable for application in the system.

6   Conclusion

In order to achieve active adaptation and fine-grained access control for massive video surveillance provided by cameras, a blockchain-based publish/subscribe video surveillance system based on CP-ABE is proposed in this paper. We use blockchain to record the access policy, realizing user self certification. The video received from the camera is encrypted and stored in InterPlanetary File System (IPFS). The access policy, decryption key, video metadata, the hash value returned by IPFS were recorded in the blockchain. The video surveillance is encapsulated as a cloud service, and the distributed publish/subscribe overlay network is built based on JXTA, which connecting the terminal user, the P/S hub and the smart camera. Considering characteristics of video surveillances, a multi-level index algorithm is designed to faster service attributes and constraints matching given by the terminal user. A fast and proxy based CP-ABE algorithm is constructed for the resource constrained application. The proxy technology can effectively improve the decryption efficiency of mobile terminals.

Acknowledgments. This work is supported in part by the National Natural Science Foundation of China (61661015,61967005), Guangxi Innovation-Driven Development Project (AA17202024), Guangxi Key Laboratory of cryptography and information security Found (GCIS201701), Guangxi Collaborative Innovation Center of Cloud Computing and Big Data Found (YD1901), CETC Key Laboratory of Aerospace Information Applications Found, Young and middle-aged backbone teacher of Guangxi colleges and universities Found and High Level of Innovation Team of Colleges and Universities in Guangxi Outstanding Scholars Program Funding.

References

1. Jararweh, Y., Obaidat, I., Gupta, B.B.: Automated wireless video surveillance: an evaluation framework. J. Real-Time Image Process. **13**, 1–20 (2016)
2. Hossain, S.M., Muhammad, G., Abdul, W., Song, B., Gupta, B.: Cloud-assisted secure video transmission and sharing framework for smart cities. Future Gener. Comput. Syst. **83**, 596–606 (2017)
3. Dašić, P., Dašić, J., Crvenković, B.: Service models for cloud computing: video Surveillance as a Service (VSaaS). Bull. Transilvania Univ. Brasov Ser. I: Eng. Sci. **9**(2), 83–90 (2016)
4. CloudSurveillance. http://www.cloud-surveillance.com/
5. Chen, Z., He, Q., Mao, Z., Chung, H.-M., Maharjan, S.: A study on the characteristics of douyin short videos and implications for edge caching. In: Proceedings of the ACM Turing Celebration Conference (2019)
6. Zhang, Y., Li, D., et al.: A cross-layer security solution for publish/subscribe-based IoT services communication infrastructure. In: 2017 IEEE International Conference on Web Services (ICWS). IEEE (2017)

7. Zhao, W., Dong, X., Cao, Z., Shen, J.: A revocable publish-subscribe scheme using CP-ABE with efficient attribute and user revocation capability for cloud systems. In: 2019 IEEE 2nd International Conference on Electronics and Communication Engineering (ICECE), Xi'an, China, pp. 31–35 (2019)

8. Fan, K., et al.: A secure and verifiable data sharing scheme based on blockchain in vehicular social networks. IEEE Trans. Veh. Technol. https://doi.org/10.1109/TVT.2020.2968094

9. Khan, P.W., Byun, Y.-C., Park, N.: A data verification system for CCTV surveillance cameras using blockchain technology in smart cities. Electronics **9**, 484 (2020)

10. Li, Y., Lyu, S.: Exposing DeepFake Videos By Detecting Face Warping Artifacts. arXiv, Computer Vision and Pattern Recognition (2018)

11. Li, X., He, Q., Jiang, B., Qin, X., Qin, K.: BTS-PD: a blockchain based traceability system for P2P distribution. In: BlockSys 2019: Blockchain and Trustworthy Systems, pp. 607–620 (2019)

12. Benet, J.: IPFS-content addressed, versioned, P2P file system. arXiv preprint arXiv:1407.3561 (2014)

13. Hassan, M.M., Hossain, M.A., Abdullah-Al-Wadud, M., Al-Mudaihesh, T., Alyahya, S., Alghamdi, A.: A scalable and elastic cloud-assisted publish/subscribe model for IPTV video surveillance system. Cluster Comput. **18**(4), 1539–1548 (2015)

14. Yang, J., Fan, J., Li, C., Jiang, S.: A novel index structure to efficiently match events in large-scale publish/subscribe systems. Comput. Commun. **99**, 24–36 (2016)

15. Upmanyu, M., Namboodiri, A.M., Srinathan, K., Jawahar, C.V.: Efficient privacy preserving video surveillance. In: 2009 IEEE 12th International Conference on Computer Vision, Kyoto, pp. 1639–1646 (2009)

16. Sahai, A., Waters, B.: Fuzzy identity-based encryption. In: Proceedings of EURO-CRYPT, pp. 457–473 (2005)

17. Goyal, V., Pandey, O., Sahai, A., Waters, B.: Attribute-based encryption for fine-grained access control of encrypted data. In: Proceedings of ACM CCS, pp. 89–98 (2006)

18. Bethencourt, J., Sahai, A., Waters, B.: Ciphertext-policy attribute-based encryption. In: Proceedings of IEEE Symposium on Security and Privacy (SP 2007), pp. 321–334 (2007)

19. Matthew, G., Hohenberger, S., Waters, B.: Outsourcing the decryption of ABE ciphertexts. Presented at Proceedings of Usenix Conference on Security USENIX Association 2011 (2011)

20. Hong, Z., et al.: Multi-authority attribute-based encryption access control scheme with policy hidden for cloud storage. Soft. Comput. **22**(1), 1–9 (2016)

21. Fan, K., et al.: Efficient and privacy preserving access control scheme for fog-enabled IoT. Future Gener. Comput. Syst. **99**, 134–142 (2019)

22. Nakamoto, S.: Bitcoin: a peer-to-peer electronic cash system (2008)

23. Gipp, B., Kosti, J., Breitinger, C.: Securing video integrity using decentralized trusted timestamping on the bitcoin blockchain. In: MCIS, p. 51 (2016)

24. Kosba, A., Miller, A., Shi, E., Wen, Z., Papamanthou, C.: Hawk: the blockchain model of cryptography and privacy-preserving smart contracts. In: 2016 IEEE Symposium on Security and Privacy (SP), pp. 839–858, May 2016

25. He, Q., Zhang, N., Wei, Y., Zhang, Y.: Lightweight attribute based encryption scheme for mobile cloud assisted cyber-physical systems. Comput. Netw. **140**, 163–173 (2018)

SDABS: A Secure Cloud Data Auditing Scheme Based on Blockchain and SGX

Hong Lei[1], Zijian Bao[1], Qinghao Wang[2]($\boxtimes$), Yongxin Zhang[2], and Wenbo Shi[2]

[1] Oxford-Hainan Blockchain Research Institute, Chengmai 571924, China
{leihong,zijian}@oxhainan.org
[2] Department of Computer Science and Engineering, Northeastern University, Shenyang 110001, China
1286579221@qq.com, silence_yongxin@163.com, shiwb@neuq.edu.cn
https://www.oxhainan.org

Abstract. With the continuous growth of data resources, outsourcing data storage to cloud service providers is becoming the norm. Unfortunately, once data are stored on the cloud platform, they will be out of data owners' control. Thus, it is critical to guarantee the integrity of the remote data. To solve this problem, researchers have proposed many data auditing schemes, which often employ a trusted role named Third Party Auditor (TPA) to verify the integrity. However, the TPA may not be reliable as expected. For example, it may collude with cloud service providers to hide the fact of data corruption for benefits. Blockchain has the characteristics of decentralization, non-tampering, and traceability, which provides a solution to trace the malicious behaviors of the TPA. Moreover, Intel SGX, as the popular trusted computing technology, can be used to protect the correctness of the auditing operations with a slight performance cost, which excellently serves as the of the blockchain-based solution. In this paper, we propose a secure auditing scheme based on the blockchain and Intel SGX technology, termed SDABS. The scheme follows the properties of storage correctness, data-preserving, accountability, and anti-collusion. The experiment results show that our scheme is efficient.

Keywords: Blockchain · Intel SGX · Cloud storage · Data auditing · Data preserving

1 Introduction

With the development of big data, the Internet of things, 5G, and other new technologies, data have grown explosively and become a strategic resource. As the local storage and computing capacities of users are very limited, which can not meet the users' storage and computing needs, users normally store massive data in a remote cloud storage service provider with a low cost. However, cloud storage service providers are not fully trusted, and they may modify or even

© Springer Nature Singapore Pte Ltd. 2020
Z. Zheng et al. (Eds.): BlockSys 2020, CCIS 1267, pp. 269–281, 2020.
https://doi.org/10.1007/978-981-15-9213-3_21

delete users' data for commercial interests. Besides, natural disasters (such as earthquakes and fires, etc.) may also cause damage to the data integrity. Incomplete or wrong data in the big data analysis will lead to the error of results, and even cause huge economic losses, so we need to ensure the data integrity.

The traditional data integrity auditing method needs to download the cloud data to the local for verification, which will consume a lot of bandwidth resources, and also bring huge waste of storage space and computing resources to users. A smarter approach relies on a third-party auditor (TPA) for verification (i.e., calculating the auditing task) instead of the user. But audit institutions may collude with cloud service providers to give back false results to users to obtain benefits.

Blockchain, which has the characteristics of decentralization, non-tampering, and traceability, provides a new solution to the cloud data auditing [22–24]. Some schemes [9,10] used blockchain to eliminate the TPA hypothesis and improved the reliability of data audit results. However, these schemes employed smart contracts to complete the audit of user data, which increased the computation of blockchain, with the high cost and low efficiency [25]. Other schemes [11,16] made use of the blockchain to assist in recording audit results and realized the regulatory function for malicious roles. However, it can only guarantee the responsibility after the event and cannot directly ensure the reliability of audit results.

Intel software guard extensions (SGX), as a new trusted computing technology, can provide the trusted execution environment (TEE) for applications, which protects the confidentiality and security of internal data and provides runtime security [26]. In this paper, we propose a cloud data auditing scheme based on SGX and blockchain, named SDABS. We use SGX to ensure the correct implementation of audit work, and blockchain to ensure the traceability of audit results. Finally, we analyze the security of SDABS, and implement the simulation experiment to evaluate its performance. The experiment results illustrate the effectiveness of the scheme.

The rest of the paper is organized as follows. Section 2 presents the blockchain and Intel SGX technology. Section 3 explains the related research works of the cloud data auditing. Then, we introduce the system model, the threat model, and the design goals of SDABS in Sect. 4. Our scheme is described in Sect. 5. We analyze the security of our scheme in Sect. 6, and present the simulation results in Sect. 7. We discuss the application of TEE technology in Sect. 8. Finally, we give the conclusion in Sect. 9.

2   Background

2.1   Blockchain Technology

Blockchain is the underlying technology of Bitcoin [17], which aims to provide a decentralized and tamper-proof digital ledger in an untrusted environment. Essentially, blockchain is a chain of blocks, and each block consists of many transactions. Cryptography technology is used to link the two blocks. A slight change in one block will affect blocks following it. Besides, nodes in the blockchain network jointly maintain this ledger using certain consensus algorithm (e.g., PoW [17], PBFT [18], PoS [19], etc.). Thus, it is very difficult for malicious attackers to modify the data on the blockchain, which ensures the credibility of blockchain data. One of the dilemmas of big data is how to deal with data sharing in an untrusted environment due to the doubt among different profit-driven entities [21]. In this scenario, blockchain technology can deals with this trust issue gracefully.

2.2 Intel SGX

Intel software guard extensions (SGX) is one of the most popular TEE technologies, which has been integrated into the commodity CPU of Intel [26]. It provides the new CPU instructions to help users create the secure container called enclave in an SGX-enabled platform. The confidentiality of programs in the enclave is protected by some hardware modules, even the privileged softwares (e.g., kernel, hypervisor, etc.) are malicious. Specifically, an external program cannot access the data in the enclave directly, and the data in the enclave are also encrypted until being brought to the processor.

SGX provides the remote attestation mechanism to help an enclave communicate with a remote party securely. Before information is exchanged, two parties perform the attestation protocol, which can prove that the particular code is running securely in this enclave and this enclave is on a real SGX-enabled platform. Moreover, the remote attestation mechanism can help two parties build a secure communication channel by the additional key exchange protocol. We refer the readers to read [27] for a detailed description.

3 Related Work

To ensure the integrity of data stored on an untrusted cloud server, Ateniese et al. [1] first proposed the concept of provable data possession (PDP), realizing that the user can verify the integrity of remote data without downloading. However, it made users keep online for verification, which was unfriendly to them. Then, Wang. et al. [2] introduced the concept of Third Party Auditor (TPA) into the PDP scheme, where users were liberated from the heavy burden of auditing. The introduction of TPA has brought privacy concerns, so Wang et al. [3,4] used proxy re-signature for the group users to hide the identity of the individual within the group. Wang et al. [5] adopted the homomorphic authenticable ring signature for protecting the user's privacy, but it was not suited to large-scale users due to the computation cost. Liu et al. [6] further extended the TPA hypothesis to the malicious one, pointing out that the audit scheme should be able to deal with malicious TPA. Huang et al. [7] used matrix calculation to invoke multiple TPAs for auditing, but it introduced extra and large useless calculations.

Blockchain, as the underlying technology of the digital cryptocurrency, implements the tamper-proof storage, which meets the need of auditing scheme for solving the problem of TPA. Consequently, many blockchain-based auditing schemes have emerged in recent years. Suzuki et al. [8] adopted blockchain as the information channel among users, TPA, and cloud service providers. Liu et al. [9] proposed a private IoT data auditing framework, using smart contracts to verify the data integrity. Yu et al. [10] used smart contracts instead of the TPA. Wang and Zhang [11] proposed a Blockchain and Bilinear mapping based Data Integrity Scheme (BB-DIS) for large-scale IoT data. Huang et al. [12] and Hao et al. [13] put the blockchain nodes as the auditor to verify the data integrity. Indeed, these schemes increased the computing overhead of blockchain. Zhang et al. [14] proposed the first certificateless public verification scheme against procrastinating auditors (CPVPA) by using blockchain technology to address the procrastinating attack of auditors. Xu et al. [15] proposed an arbitrable data auditing protocol, adopting the commutative hash technique, for the dishonest parties. Lu et al. [16] adopted Hyperledger Fabric [20] as a platform for the auditing and proposed two algorithms for choosing TPA. Blockchain technology is better suited as a tool for accountability in hindsight, but a more secure and reliable tool is needed at runtime when verifying the integrity.

4   Problem Statement

In this section, we describe the system model of SDABS and then describe the relevant threat model. Finally, we indicate the design goals of our scheme.

4.1   System Model

We show the architecture of our scheme in Fig. 1, which consists of four roles: Users, Cloud Storage Service Provider (CSP), Third Party Auditor (TPA), and Blockchain (BC). Users are resource-constrained individuals, who are unable to store big data and perform onerous auditing tasks. The CSP provides storage service for uses and responds to auditing challenges of users' data. The TPA is an auditing service provider, which maintains an SGX-enabled platform to perform auditing operations. The BC is a blockchain system (e.g., Bitcoin, Ethereum, Hyperledger Fabric), which serves as the bridge between users and the TPA. To ensure the quality and integrity of the data, users synchronize auditing requests to the BC. The TPA will obtain the requests from the blockchain and send auditing challenges to the CSP to check the integrity of users' data. Finally, the auditing results will be synchronized to the blockchain network, which can be acquired by users.

4.2   Threat Model

In our assumption, the CSP is an unreliable party. It will try to remove the less-used data of users to reduce the cost of storage. More seriously, the CSP may

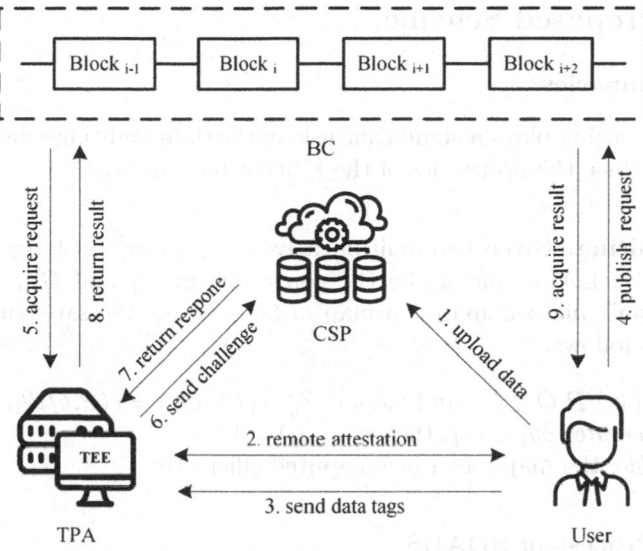

Fig. 1. The architecture diagram of SDABS.

tamper with partial data for some malicious purpose. We assume that the TPA is untrusted, and can control the communication of the enclave or terminate the enclave. Specially, the TPA may collude with the CSP to fraud users. Moreover, we assume the SGX technology is normally trustworthy. Security and confidentiality of data can be protected by the enclave and the remote attestation can prove the reliability of the remote SGX-enabled platforms. We also assume that over 50% of nodes in the BC are honest and hence the blockchain can not be arbitrary tempered.

4.3 Design Goals

As SDABS is designed to operate with untrusted entities, it is designed to achieve the following goals, including storage correctness, data-preserving, accountability, and anti-collusion.

(1) *Storage Correctness*: the data is stored by the CSP. For the data challenge proposed by the TPA, the CSP can only pass the auditing if it provides correct data proof.
(2) *Data-Preserving*: during the auditing process, based on the tag from the user and the data proof from the CSP, the TPA cannot infer the user's real data.
(3) *Accountability*: in our scheme, once an entity violates the agreement, it will be found and blamed.
(4) *Anti-Collusion*: it is difficult for the CSP and the TPA to deceive users by colluding.

5   The Proposed Scheme

5.1   Preliminaries

The bilinear pairing plays a significant role in the data auditing schemes [2–4, 8]. We will introduce the properties of the bilinear pairing briefly.

Bilinear Pairing. Given two multiplicative cyclic groups of large prime order q, G_1 and G_T. Let g_1 and g_2 be the generators of G_1 and G_T, respectively. A cryptographic bilinear map is a map $e: G_1 \times G_1 \to G_T$ satisfying the three properties as follows.

(1) *Bilinear*: for $\forall P, Q \in G_1$ and $\forall x, y \in Z_q^*$, $e(P^x, Q^y) = e(P, Q)^{xy}$;
(2) *Non-degenerate*: $\exists g_1 \in G_1$, then $e(g_1, g_1) \neq 1$;
(3) *Computable*: the map e can be computed efficiently.

5.2   The Process of SDABS

SDABS includes three phases in a typical circumstance: tag generation, storage, and auditing.

Tag Generation Phase. In order to audit data correctly, the user needs to generate the tags of the data. The user first generates the relevant parameters as follows. Two multiplicative cyclic groups are denoted as G_1 and G_T, respectively. p is the prime order of the groups and g is the generator of the group G_1. Thus, the cryptographic bilinear map e can be expressed as $G_1 \times G_1 \to G_T$. $H_1 : \{0,1\}^* \to G_1$ is the hash function that maps a string data to a point in G_1. Similarly, $H_2 : G_1 \to Z_q^*$ denotes the other hash function, which maps a point in G_1 to a point in Z_q^*. The user selects a secret key $x \in Z_q^*$ randomly and then calculates the public key $PK = g^x$. It is worth noticing that the part of parameters need to be published to all parties, including e, H_1, H_2, PK. Then the user splits the data into data blocks denoted as $D = \{d_1, d_2, \cdots, d_n\}$ and chooses a random element $r \in G_1$ to calculate the tag $\sigma_i = (H(d_i) \cdot r^{(d_i)})^x$ for each data block d_i. At this point, the user holds the data blocks $\{d_1, d_2, \cdots, d_n\}$ and the corresponding tags $\{\sigma_1, \sigma_2, \cdots, \sigma_n\}$.

Storage Phase. This phase is divided into two steps: (1) The user uploads data to the CSP and deletes the local data. (2) The user sends the corresponding tags to the TPA and removes them from the local. The details of the two steps are as follows.
    Step1. The user sends a request to the CSP for storage service and then uploads the data blocks $\{d_1, d_2, \cdots, d_n\}$. After the successful upload, the user can delete the local data to save storage.
    Step2. To establish trust with the enclave in the TPA platform, the user must receive assurance that the enclave is running in a real SGX-enabled platform and

that the auditing codes are correctly loaded in the enclave. This is implemented through remote attestation provided by SGX. Note that the remote attestation protocol has the self-defined data field, which can be used to build a secure communication channel by the key exchange protocol (e.g., Diffie-Hellman key agreement method [33]). In this step, the user first employs the remote attestation protocol to verify the enclave in the TPA platform and to build a secure channel with it. Thus, if the user transmits the message through the secure channel, the message can only be decrypted by the enclave. Then, the user sends the tags $\{\sigma_1, \sigma_2, \cdots, \sigma_n\}$ to the TPA using the secure channel. The tags correspond to the data blocks in the Step1 of this phase. The tags will be delivered to the enclave and be stored securely. The enclave then returns the storage result to the user by the secure channel. Finally, the user removes the local tags to save storage.

Auditing Phase. In this phase, the user issues the auditing request in the BC. Then, the TPA obtains the request from the BC and constructs a challenge in the enclave to the CSP. When the CSP receives the challenge, it computes the response and sends it to the TPA. After verification, the TPA will publish the auditing results in the BC.

Step1. The user issues the auditing request in the form of a blockchain transaction and synchronizes the transaction to the blockchain network. A request includes the identifiers of the data blocks to be audited such as $\{id_2, id_9, \cdots, id_{20}\}$ (id_i is the unique identifier of d_i), the expected time T, the rewards R, and the signature of the request. Due to the user has built the secure channel through the remote attestation, the user can use the exchanged key to encrypt the request as the signature, which can only be verified by the enclave.

Step2. The TPA real-time synchronizes the blockchain to the enclave. The enclave identifies the relevant transactions in the blockchain and verifies the signatures. It then acquires the identifiers of the data blocks such as $\{id_2, id_9, \cdots, id_{20}\}$, and the corresponding tags $\{\sigma_2, \sigma_9, \cdots, \sigma_{20}\}$. To construct the challenge, the also need to generate a random number for each data block, which is denoted as v_i. The challenge $C = (\{id_2, id_9, \cdots, id_{20}\}, \{\sigma_2, \sigma_9, \cdots, \sigma_{20}\}, \{v_2, v_9, \cdots, v_{20}\})$ will be deliver to the CAP and be sent to the CSP.

Step3. After receiving C, the CSP first verifies the tags $\{\sigma_2, \sigma_9, \cdots, \sigma_{20}\}$ to ensure that C is initiated by the enclave. Then the CSP computes $t_i = d_i \cdot v_i$ for each data blocks and aggregates all results as the respond $respond_{CSP}$. As the above example, $respond_{CSP} = t_2 + t_9 + \cdots + t_{20}$. The CSP final returns $respond_{CSP}$ to the TPA.

Step4. The TPA delivers $respond_{CSP}$ to the enclave, and the enclave calculates $verification_{TPA} = \sigma_2{}^{v_2} \cdot \sigma_9{}^{v_9} \cdots \sigma_{20}{}^{v_{20}}$. Then the enclave computes Formula (1) to verify $respond_{CSP}$, where I indicates the number of the audited data blocks. If the equation is true, the enclave will hold that the CSP stores the user's data correctly and completely. Otherwise, the CSP will be regarded as dishonest. After verification, the enclave returns the auditing report, which includes the auditing result and the signature of the result. The signature is generated by the exchanged key, similar to the process in the Step1 of this phase. Finally, the TPA constructs a blockchain transaction and synchronize it to publish the report.

$$e(\prod_{i \in I} \sigma_i^{v_i}, g) = e(\prod_{i \in I} H_1(d_i)^{v_i} \cdot r^{\sum_{i \in I} d_i \cdot v_i}, PK) \tag{1}$$

Step5. The user acquires the auditing report from the blockchain to perceive whether its data is corrupted. As the blockchain is public and tamper-proof, the TPA can provide the proof (i.e., the transaction with auditing request and the transaction with the auditing result in the blockchain) to the user and gets the rewards R. Moreover, the user can refuse to pay the rewards, if the auditing time exceeds the expected time T. It's easy to calculate the auditing time because each block in the blockchain involves the timestamp that denoting its confirmed time.

6   Security Analysis

In this section, we analyze the following security features of SDABS, namely: storage correctness, data-preserving, accountability and anti-collusion.

Storage Correctness: If all roles execute the protocol correctly and the data stored in the CSP is integrated, the storage correctness can be ensured.

Proof. We prove the correctness of our scheme as follows:

$$e(\prod_{i \in I} \phi_i^{v_i}, g)$$
$$= e(\prod_{i \in I} (H(d_i) \cdot r^{d_i})^{x v_i}, g)$$
$$= e(\prod_{i \in I} (H(d_i) \cdot r^{d_i})^{v_i}, g^x) \tag{2}$$
$$= e(\prod_{i \in I} H(d_i)^{v_i} \cdot r^{\sum_{i \in I} d_i v_i}, g^x)$$
$$= e(\prod_{i \in I} H(d_i)^{v_i} \cdot r^{\sum_{i \in I} d_i v_i}, PK)$$

Data-Preserving: The TPA cannot recover the real data from the auditing information.

Proof. It is difficult for the TPA to recover user's data by computing $\prod_{i \in I} \phi_i^{v_i}$ or $\sum_{i \in I} d_i v_i$, where $\phi_i = (H(d_i) \cdot r^{(d_i)})^x$. The original data d_i is protected by $H : \{0, 1\}^* \rightarrow G_1$, r and the user's secret key x. Besides, in the $\sum_{i \in I} d_i v_i$, All of the d_i is blinded by v_i generated by the enclave. Based on the hardness of Computational Diffie-Hellman (CDH) problem in G_1, it is hard for probabilistic polynomial time adversary to compute d_i.

Accountability: The party who breaks the protocol can be blamed.

Proof. In SDABS, the results of auditing will be sent to the blockchain by the SGX. SGX provides a secure runtime environment that makes it difficult for an adversary to tamper with its contents, making data transmitted to the blockchain believable. Blockchain is a kind of decentralized database, which uses cryptography technology to realize the non-tampering characteristics, which ensures the credibility of the data in the blockchain. Both off-chain and on-chain ensure that the data is credible, which ensures the credibility of the audit results kept on the blockchain. Any breach of the agreement by either party can be determined by the audit results. In this way, SDABS realizes the accountability.

Anti-Collusion: The TPA with SGX can hardly collude with the CSP to fraud users.

Proof. If the TPA wants to collude with the CSP to defraud the user, either the CSP falsifies the data or the TPA falsifies the results. For the former, CSP needs to construct data d'_i without the user's private key, so as to satisfy $e(\prod_{i \in I} H(d'_i)^{v_i} \cdot r^{\sum_{i \in I} d'_i v_i}, PK) = e(\prod_{i \in I} \phi_i^{v_i}, g)$. Similarly, based on the hardness of Computational Diffie-Hellman (CDH) problem in G_1 and the collision resistance of hash function, it is hard for probabilistic polynomial time adversary to realize this equation. Hence, the CSP is incapable of forge the results. For the latter, the auditing process is carried in the enclave, including the storage of data tags, the generation of random numbers, and the verification of proof, which are not controlled by the TPA. Therefore, the TPA cannot falsify the results.

7   Performance Evaluation

We implement the simulation experiment to evaluate the performance of our scheme. The three roles (i.e., the user, the CSP, and the TPA) run on the same PC with Ubuntu 16.04 LTS operating system, a 2.40 GHz Intel(R) Core(TM) CPU i7-8700T, and 16GB RAM. Specially, the program of the TPA is loaded in an enclave on the PC to perform, and the programs of the user and the CSP are performed in the normal memory.

Figure 2 illustrates the computation time of the three roles with different numbers of audited data blocks. To show the results clearly, we fix the size of the data block to 1 KB. We can see that the computation time of all roles is increased linearly with the numbers of audited data blocks. Specially, the user has a higher computation time overhead than other roles, because the user needs to generate the tags for each data block, which contains map-to-point hash functions involving expensive computation. The tags of data blocks are only calculated once in the whole scheme, thus the time overhead is acceptable.

We also test the performance overhead caused by the use of SGX. Specifically, we compare the computation time of the auditing operations executed in the enclave with the time of the same operations performed out of the enclave.

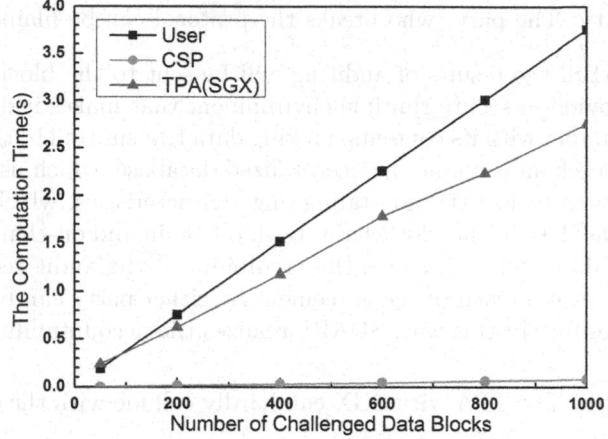

Fig. 2. The computation time of the different roles.

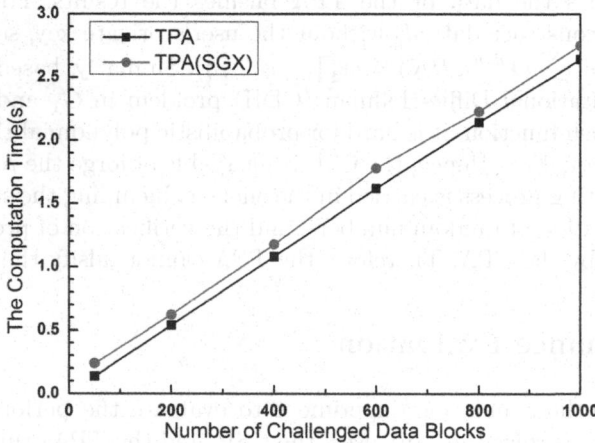

Fig. 3. The performance of the auditing operations performed in and out of the SGX enclave.

Figure 3 shows that the former is slightly more than the latter, which is because the programs in the enclave need to execute the additional encryption, decryption, and scheduling operations. However, all operations are limited on time scales of seconds, which is applicable to real scenarios. Thus, it is an efficient way to protect the audit process using the SGX technology.

8 Discussion

SGX can be applied into many fields, smart grid, blockchain, etc. Li et al. [30] leverages the SGX to protect the privacy of users when grid utilities are executing rich functionalities on customers' private data. Lind et al. [31] adopt TEE as a safe treasury to execute off-chain transactions asynchronously, prevent misbehavior of parties and maintain collateral funds. Bentov et al. [32] design a kind of exchange that offers real-time cross-chain cryptocurrency trades and secure tokenization of assets based on the SGX. And many application can be ported to the other TEE technologies if conditions permit. Arm TrustZone technology is also a famous TEE technology, offering an efficient, system-wide approach to security with hardware-enforced isolation built into the CPU [28]. However, TrustZone is focused on the mobile side [29], not the server side. TrustZone is a good choice in the future if edge computing can be used to offload the data integrity auditing to the mobile side.

9 Conclusion

The quality and reliability of data are greatly significant in the age of big data. In this paper, we propose SDABS, a new cloud data auditing scheme, based on the SGX and the blockchain technology. The scheme employs SGX to improve the reliability and stability of the auditing process and to eliminate the trust to the TPA. By introducing the blockchain, SDABS implements the accountability, which can trace the inappropriate behavior of any entities. We analyze the security of SDABS, which demonstrates that the proposed scheme has the features of storage correctness, data-preserving, accountability, and anti-collusion. The performance evaluation shows that our scheme is feasible and efficient.

Acknowledgements. This study is supported by Oxford-Hainan Blockchain Research Institute, the National Science Foundation of China (No. 61472074, U1708262) and the Fundamental Research Funds for the Central Universities (No. N172304023).

References

1. Ateniese, G., et al.: Provable data possession at untrusted stores. In: Proceedings of the 14th ACM Conference on Computer and Communications Security 2007, pp. 598–609. ACM (2007)
2. Wang, Q., Wang, C., Li, J., Ren, K., Lou, W.: Enabling public verifiability and data dynamics for storage security in cloud computing. In: Backes, M., Ning, P. (eds.) ESORICS 2009. LNCS, vol. 5789, pp. 355–370. Springer, Heidelberg (2009). https://doi.org/10.1007/978-3-642-04444-1_22
3. Wang, B., Li, H., Li, M.: Privacy-preserving public auditing for shared cloud data supporting group dynamics. In: 2013 IEEE International Conference on Communications (ICC), pp. 1946–1950. IEEE (2013)
4. Wang, B., Li, B., Li, H.: Panda: public auditing for shared data with efficient user revocation in the cloud. IEEE Trans. Serv. Comput. 8(1), 92–106 (2015)
5. Wang, B., Li, B., Li, H.: Oruta: privacy-preserving public auditing for shared data in the cloud. IEEE Trans. Cloud Comput. 2(1), 43–56 (2014)
6. Liu, C., et al.: Authorized public auditing of dynamic big data storage on cloud with efficient verifiable fine-grained updates. IEEE Trans. Parallel Distrib. Syst. 25(9), 2234–2244 (2014)

7. Huang, K., Xian, M., Fu, S., Liu, J.: Securing the cloud storage audit service: defending against frame and collude attacks of third party auditor. IET Commun. **8**(12), 2106–2113 (2014)
8. Suzuki, S., Murai, J.: Blockchain as an audit-able communication channel. In: 2017 IEEE 41st Annual Computer Software and Applications Conference (COMPSAC), vol. 2, pp. 516–522. IEEE (2017)
9. Liu, B., Yu, X., Chen, S., Xu, X., Zhu, L.: Blockchain based data integrity service framework for IoT data. In: 2017 IEEE International Conference on Web Services (ICWS), pp. 468–475. IEEE (2017)
10. Yu, H., Yang, Z., Sinnott, R.: Decentralized big data auditing for smart city environments leveraging blockchain technology. IEEE Access **7**, 6288–6296 (2019)
11. Wang, H., Zhang, J.: Blockchain based data integrity verification for large-scale IoT data. IEEE Access **7**, 164996–165006 (2019)
12. Huang, P., Fan, K., Yang, H., Zhang, K., Li, H., Yang, Y.: A collaborative auditing blockchain for trustworthy data integrity in cloud storage system. IEEE Access **8**, 94780–94794 (2020)
13. Hao, K., Xin, J., Wang, Z., Wang, G.: Outsourced data integrity verification based on blockchain in untrusted environment. World Wide Web **23**(4), 2215–2238 (2020). https://doi.org/10.1007/s11280-019-00761-2
14. Zhang, Y., Xu, C., Lin, X., Shen, X.S.: Blockchain-based public integrity verification for cloud storage against procrastinating auditors. IEEE Trans. Cloud Comput. (to be published). https://doi.org/10.1109/TCC.2019.2908400
15. Xu, Y., Ren, J., Zhang, Y., Zhang, C., Shen, B., Zhang, Y.: Blockchain empowered arbitrable data auditing scheme for network storage as a service. IEEE Trans. Serv. Comput. **13**(2), 289–300 (2020)
16. Lu, N., Zhang, Y., Shi, W., Kumari, S., Choo, K.: A secure and scalable data integrity auditing scheme based on hyperledger fabric. Comput. Secur. **92**, 101741 (2020)
17. Nakamoto, S.: Bitcoin: a peer-to-peer electronic cash system (2008)
18. Castro, M., Liskov, B.: Practical byzantine fault tolerance. In: The Third USENIX Symposium on Operating Systems Design and Implementation (OSDI), USA, vol. 99, pp. 173–186 (1999)
19. Seijas, P.L., Thompson, S.J., McAdams, D.: Scripting smart contracts for distributed ledger technology. IACR Cryptology ePrint Archive (2016)
20. Androulaki, E., et al.: Hyperledger fabric: a distributed operating system for permissioned blockchains. In: Proceedings of ACM 13th EuroSys Conference (EuroSys), USA (2018)
21. Xu, C., Wang, K., Li, P., Guo, S., Luo, J., Ye, B., Guo, M.: Making big data open in edges: a resource-efficient blockchain-based approach. IEEE Trans. Parallel Distrib. Syst. **30**(4), 870–882 (2019)
22. Zheng, Z., Xie, S., Dai, H., Chen, X., Wang, H.: Blockchain challenges and opportunities: a survey. Int. J. Web Grid Serv. **14**(4), 352–375 (2018)
23. Zheng, Z., Xie, S., Dai, H., Chen, X., Wang, H.: An overview of blockchain technology: architecture, consensus, and future trends. In: International Congress on Big Data (2017), pp. 557–564 (2017)
24. Dai, H., Zheng, Z., Zhang, Y.: Blockchain for internet of things: a survey. IEEE Internet Things J. **6**(5), 8076–8094 (2019)
25. Huang, Y., Kong, Q., Jia, N., Chen, X., Zheng, Z.: Recommending differentiated code to support smart contract update. In: International Conference on Program Comprehension (2019), pp. 260–270 (2019)

26. Intel. 2017. Software Guard Extensions (Intel SGX) (2017). https://software.intel.com/en-us/sgx
27. Costan, V., Devadas, S.: Intel SGX Explained. IACR Cryptology ePrint Archive (2016)
28. ARM. Arm TrustZone Technology. https://developer.arm.com/ip-products/security-ip/trustzone
29. Kwon, D., Seo, J., Cho, Y., Lee, B., Paek, Y.: PrOS: light-weight privatized secure OSes in ARM TrustZone. IEEE Trans. Mob. Comput. **19**(6), 1434–1447 (2020)
30. Li, S., Xue, K., David, W., Yue, H., Yu, N., Hong, P.: SecGrid: a secure and efficient SGX-enabled smart grid system with rich functionalities. IEEE Trans. Inf. Forensics Secur. **15**, 1318–1330 (2020)
31. Lind, J., Naor, O., Eyal, I., Florian Kelbert, F., et al.: Teechain: a secure payment network with asynchronous blockchain access. In: Proceedings of the 27th ACM Symposium on Operating Systems Principles(SOSP), pp. 63–79 (2019)
32. Bentov, I., Ji, Y., Zhang, F., Breidenbach, L., Daian, P., Juels, A.: Tesseract: real-time cryptocurrency exchange using trusted hardware. In: Proceedings of the 2019 ACM SIGSAC Conference on Computer and Communications Security (CCS), pp. 1521–1538 (2019)
33. Rescorla, E..: Diffie-Hellman key agreement method. RFC 2631 (1999)

Privacy-Preserving Multi-keyword Search over Outsourced Data for Resource-Constrained Devices

Lin-Gang Liu[1], Meng Zhao[2], Yong Ding[1,5(✉)], Yujue Wang[1], Hua Deng[3],
and Huiyong Wang[4]

[1] Guangxi Key Laboratory of Cryptography and Information Security,
School of Computer Science and Information Security,
Guilin University of Electronic Technology, Guilin 541004, China
`stone_dingy@126.com`
[2] School of Mechanical and Electrical Engineering,
Guilin University of Electronic Technology, Guilin 541004, China
[3] College of Computer Science and Electronic Engineering,
Hunan University, Changsha 410082, China
[4] School of Mathematics and Computing Science,
Guilin University of Electronic Technology, Guilin 541004, China
[5] Cyberspace Security Research Center, Peng Cheng Laboratory,
Shenzhen 518055, China

Abstract. With the rapid development of cloud computing, a variety
of cloud-based applications have been developed. Since cloud computing has the features of high capacity and flexible computing, more and
more users are motivated to outsource their data to the cloud server
for economic savings. Users are able to search over outsourced data
according to some keywords with the help of the cloud server. During
data searching, the confidentiality of the relevant data could be compromised since the keywords may contain some sensitive information.
However, existing privacy-preserving keyword search proposals have high
computation complexity, which are not applicable to IoT-related scenarios. That is, the data processing and search trapdoor generation procedures require the users to take resource-intensive computations, e.g.,
high-dimensional matrix operations, which are unaffordable by resource-
constrained devices. To address this issue, we propose a light-weight
privacy-preserving multi-keyword search scheme. The security and performance analyses demonstrate that our scheme outperforms existing
solutions and is practical in applications.

Keywords: Cloud computing · Outsourced data · Keywords search ·
Data privacy · Internet of Things

1 Introduction

With the advent of cloud computing, the users with limited local resources do
not need to purchase expensive hardware to support massive data storage. Thus,

Z. Zheng et al. (Eds.): BlockSys 2020, CCIS 1267, pp. 282–294, 2020.
https://doi.org/10.1007/978-981-15-9213-3_22

for economic savings, more and more individuals and enterprises engage cloud servers to maintain their data. However, users would lose control of outsourced data, which may leak some sensitive information, for example, in the cases where health records and private emails are hosted on cloud servers. Therefore, to protect data privacy, user data should be stored on the cloud server in ciphertext format.

For retrieving the interested data, users can request the cloud server to search over outsourced dataset with some specific keywords. However, the keywords may contain some sensitive information of outsourced data, which means these keywords cannot be presented to the cloud server in plaintext format, otherwise the users' private information could be deduced by the cloud server. To address this issue, privacy-preserving keyword search has recently gained attention, and many solutions have been proposed [8, 10, 17, 26].

However, existing solutions require users to take heavy computations in both phases of data processing and search trapdoor generation. For example, in [4], users need to perform high-dimensional matrix operations, such as multiplications and inversion, where the matrix dimension is determined by the cardinality of the keyword set. While in [20], users have to compute many exponentiation operations for generating searchable indexes and search trapdoor. To deploy in the Internet of Things setting, existing works are not suitable since those heavy computation operations are not affordable by resource-constrained devices.

1.1 Our Contributions

To address the above issue, this paper proposes a light-weight scheme supporting privacy-preserving ranked multi-keyword search over outsourced data, where the search results are determined by the similarity score between the search query and the keyword index of outsourced data. Our contributions are summarized as follows.

- The proposed scheme allows the user to search for outsourced data with multiple keywords, and the search results can be ranked so that the cloud server only needs to return the results satisfying the given threshold.
- The proposed scheme can guarantee the privacy of searchable index of outsourced data and queries. That is, the cloud server cannot deduce any private information of outsourced data from the encrypted index and queries.
- The proposed scheme can guarantee the unlinkability of search trapdoors. That is, for two search trapdoors submitted by the user, the cloud server is unable to identify whether they are generated for the same query.
- In both data processing and query generation phases, the user only needs to take light-weight computation operations.

Performance analysis demonstrates that our scheme is much more efficient than existing solutions, thus it can be deployed in IoT setting to support resource-constrained devices.

1.2   Related Works

The first single keywords searchable encryption scheme over outsourced encrypted data was proposed by Song et al. [21] in the symmetric key setting. Subsequently, a lot of this type schemes [2,6,15,23] were designed. David et al. [5] proposed a scheme supporting single-keyword boolean search over large outsourced dataset. However, the single keyword search mechanism cannot provide accurate search results. Since the cloud server usually stores massive data, there would be many match data satisfying the search condition of a single keyword, and most of the search results may have no relation with the expected data.

To support more sophisticated outsourcing search methods, many multi-keyword search schemes have been proposed [4,9,11,14]. These schemes can allow the cloud server to return the most relevant data, thus, they are more practical than the single keyword search mechanism in supporting real-world applications. Multi-keyword search can allow complicated search conditions on outsourced data, for example, the works [1,16] support multi-keyword search with fully homomorphic encryption, [11,14] support conjunctive keyword search, [9] supports multi-keyword fuzzy search, and [4] supports ranked multi-keyword search.

In the public-key setting, the first searchable encryption scheme was proposed by Boneh et al. [3], where anyone can outsource encrypted data to the cloud server, but only the user holding the private key can issue search queries. Xu et al. [25] constructed a searchable public-key ciphertexts scheme with hidden structures to achieve fast search. Hu et al. [13] presented a public-key encryption scheme with keyword search from obfuscation, where the cloud server is given an obfuscated simple decrypt-then-compare circuit with the secret key to perform keyword search. Xu et al. [24] designed a public-key multi-keyword searchable encryption scheme with a hidden structures model, which also supports boolean search over encrypted e-mails. Wang et al. [22] proposed a tree-based public-key multi-dimensional range searchable encryption scheme from the predicate encryption method and leakage function.

To enrich the functionality of searching over remote data, various practical schemes have been designed. He and Ma [12] proposed a fuzzy search scheme over encrypted data using bloom filter. Zhang et al. [27] noticed that He and Ma's proposal [12] cannot resist the sparse non-negative matrix factorization based attacks, and further presented a multi-keyword fuzzy search scheme using random redundancy method. Fu et al. [10] designed a semantic-aware search scheme, where both the index and search trapdoor contain two vectors.

Cao et al. [4] proposed an efficient multi-keyword ranked search scheme over encrypted cloud data, where coordinate matching was introduced to capture the relevance between data documents and the search query. In Raghavendra et al.'s solution [19], the index for keywords was generated using split factor, and to save computation overheads, the index tree was constructed to store keywords. Ren et al. [20] studied multi-keyword ranked search, where the search trapdoor is generated using a polynomial function. Ding et al. [7] constructed a keyword set using k-grams and Jaccard coefficient, and also built searchable index of small size. In Liu et al.'s scheme [17], the user is allowed to update the outsourced data and verify the search result.

1.3 Paper Organization

The remainder of this paper is organized as follows. Section 2 describes our system model, threat model, and design goals. Section 3 presents our scheme, which security and performance are evaluated and compared in Sect. 4. Section 5 concludes the paper.

2 Problem Formulation and Design Goals

2.1 System Model

As shown in Fig. 1, a multi-keyword search system consists of three types of entities, that is, data owner, data user and cloud server. There is a secure communication channel between data owner and data user. The data owner outsources a collection of documents to the cloud server. Since the documents may contain sensitive information, they cannot be directly uploaded to the cloud server. Thus, to protect the privacy of outsourced documents, they should be outsourced in ciphertext format.

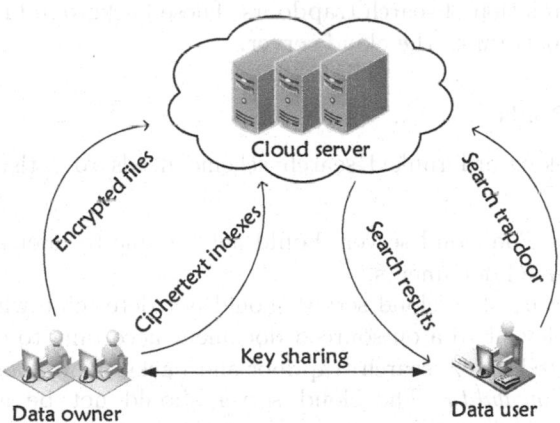

Fig. 1. The system model

To facilitate data searching, the outsourced documents should be attached with a list of keywords. All keywords are contained in a keyword dictionary. To guarantee that the keywords cannot leak the privacy of outsourced documents, in the data processing phase, the data owner is able to produce an encrypted searchable index for each document. The searchable index is outsourced to the cloud server along with the document.

In the search phase, data user can generate a search trapdoor of its query vector with multiple keywords to enable the cloud server to search over outsourced documents. The keywords in the query vector are also contained in the keyword dictionary, which should be transformed into search trapdoor to protect the privacy of outsourced data. Upon receiving the search trapdoor, the cloud server computes the similarity score between each encrypted searchable index and the search trapdoor, and returns the document if its similarity score satisfies the given search threshold.

2.2   Threat Model

In the honest-but-curious model, the cloud server can perform multi-keyword search according to the user's request, but it is curious about the sensitive information of outsourced documents. That is, the cloud server may try to deduce some information from the outsourced documents, ciphertext indexes, and search trapdoors. This paper assumes the adversary is able to launch known ciphertext attacks and known background attacks on outsourced documents.

Known ciphertext attack: The cloud server only knows some ciphertext information including encrypted documents, ciphertext indexes and search trapdoors. With these information, the cloud server aims to get the sensitive information of outsourced documents.

Known background attack: The cloud server may also know more background information of outsourced documents, such as statistic information of documents and relation of search trapdoors. These background information may leak the search pattern to the cloud server.

2.3   Design Goals

A secure multi-keyword ranked search scheme needs to satisfy the following requirements.

- *Data privacy*: The cloud server should not be able to infer any information about outsourced documents.
- *Keyword privacy*: The cloud server should not determine whether a specific keyword is relevant to a outsourced document according to encrypted document, encrypted index, search trapdoor and background knowledge.
- *Trapdoor unlinkability*: The cloud server should not be able to identify whether two search trapdoors are generated from the same query.
- *Efficiency*: Due to the limited computation capability of data owner and data user, the data processing and query generation phases cannot contain resource-intensive computations.

3   Concrete Construction

This section introduces a light-weight and privacy-preserving multi-keyword search scheme based on the inner product similarity computing scheme [18]. Some notations and the corresponding descriptions are given in Table 1.

Table 1. Notations and descriptions

Notations	Descriptions
F	Document set $F = \{F_1, F_2, ..., F_m\}$
$\overline{F}$	Encrypted document set $\overline{F} = \{\overline{F}_1, \overline{F}_2, ..., \overline{F}_m\}$.
W	Keyword dictionary
$\overline{W}$	A set of search keywords
$\overline{I}$	A plaintext index vector $\overline{I} = (\overline{I}_1, \overline{I}_2, ..., \overline{I}_m)$
$\hat{I}$	A ciphertext index vector $\hat{I} = (\hat{I}_1, \hat{I}_2, ..., \hat{I}_m)$
$Q_{\overline{W}}$	Query vector $Q_{\overline{W}} = (Q_{\overline{W}_1, \overline{W}_2, ..., \overline{W}_n})$ constructed from $\overline{W}$
$\hat{Q}_{\overline{W}}$	Search trapdoor in ciphertext format
S	The secret key of data owner
N_i	The filename of document F_i
d_i	The file size document F_i
γ_i	The hash value with regard to document F_i

- **System setup:** With input security parameters $\lambda_1, \lambda_2, \lambda_3, \lambda_4$, the data owner constructs a dictionary W, which contains n keywords. The data owner randomly picks a large prime numbers p such that $|p| = \lambda_2$, $S \in_R Z_p^*$, and a cryptographic one-way hash function $H : \{0,1\}^* \rightarrow \{0,1\}^{\lambda_1}$. Thus, the public parameters are $para = (\lambda_1, \lambda_2, \lambda_3, \lambda_4, p, n, H)$, and the data owner keeps W and S secret.

- **Index generation:** For each document F_i ($i = 1, ..., m$), the data owner encrypts it as ciphertext document $\overline{F}_i$ using some secure symmetric encryption, randomly picks a unique file name N_i, and calculates the length d_i of document F_i. The data owner computes $\gamma_i = H(N_i, d_i)$ and constructs the index vector $\overline{I}_i$ such that if the document F_i contains the jth keyword in the dictionary W, then $\overline{I}_{i,j} = 1$, otherwise $\overline{I}_{i,j} = 0$. The data owner further sets $\overline{I}_{i,n+1} = 0$ and $\overline{I}_{i,n+2} = 0$, chooses $n + 2$ random number m_j such that $|m_j| = \lambda_3$ for $1 \leq j \leq n + 2$, and encrypts each $\overline{I}_{i,j}$ as follow:

$$\hat{I}_{i,j} = S \cdot (\overline{I}_{i,j} \cdot \gamma_i + m_j) \mod p \tag{1}$$

Then for document F_i, the data owner outsources the ciphertext index vector $\hat{I}_i = (\hat{I}_{i,1}, \hat{I}_{i,2}, \cdots, \hat{I}_{i,n+2})$ and the processed file $\hat{F}_i = (\overline{F}_i, \gamma_i)$ to the cloud server, and keeps (N_i, d_i) at local.

- **Trapdoor generation:** Data user picks a large random number δ such that $|\delta| = \lambda_1$, and computes $S^{-1} \mod p$. From the query keyword set $\overline{W}$, data user constructs query vector $Q_{\overline{W}}$, where $Q_{\overline{W}_j} = 1$ if the query keyword set $\overline{W}$ contains the jth keyword in the dictionary W, otherwise $Q_{\overline{W}_j} = 0$. Data user then sets $Q_{\overline{W}_{n+1}} = 0$ and $Q_{\overline{W}_{n+2}} = 0$, and randomly chooses $n + 2$ numbers t_j such that $|t_j| = \lambda_4$ for $1 \leq j \leq n + 2$. Data user constructs the search trapdoor $\hat{Q}_{\overline{W}}$ as follows.

$$\hat{Q}_{\overline{W}_j} = S^{-1} \cdot (Q_{\overline{W}_j} \cdot \delta + t_j) \mod p \qquad (2)$$

Data user sets search threshold τ, and submits the search trapdoor $\hat{Q}_{\overline{W}} = (\hat{Q}_{\overline{W}_1}, \hat{Q}_{\overline{W}_2}, \cdots, \hat{Q}_{\overline{W}_{n+2}})$ and (τ, δ) to the cloud server.

- **Search**: Once received the encrypted search trapdoor $\hat{Q}_{\overline{W}}$, the cloud server computes the similarity score $Score(\overline{I}_i, Q_{\overline{W}})$ with each $\hat{I}_i$ as follows. The cloud server computes

$$E_i = Score(\hat{I}_i, \hat{Q}_{\overline{W}}) = \hat{I}_i \cdot \hat{Q}_{\overline{W}} \mod p \qquad (3)$$

By properly choosing the elements under the given security parameters $\lambda_1, \lambda_2, \lambda_3, \lambda_4$, we assume both the following conditions hold

$$\hat{I}_i \cdot \hat{Q}_{\overline{W}} < p$$

and

$$\rho = \sum_{j=1, I_{i,j} \neq 0, Q_{\overline{W}_j} \neq 0}^{n+2} (\gamma_i t_j \overline{I}_{i,j} + m_j \delta Q_{\overline{W}_j} + m_j t_j) +$$

$$\sum_{j=1, I_{i,j}=0, Q_{\overline{W}_j} \neq 0}^{n+2} (m_j \delta Q_{\overline{W}_j} + m_j t_j) + \sum_{j=1, I_{i,j} \neq 0, Q_{\overline{W}_j}=0}^{n+2} (\gamma_i t_j \overline{I}_{i,j} + m_j t_j) +$$

$$\sum_{j=1, I_{i,j}=0, Q_{\overline{W}_j}=0}^{n+2} m_j t_j$$

$$< \gamma_i \delta.$$

Then, the cloud server computes

$$Score(\overline{I}_i, Q_{\overline{W}}) = \sum_{j=1}^{n} \overline{I}_{i,j} \cdot Q_{\overline{W}_j} = \frac{E_i - (E_i \mod \delta \cdot \gamma_i)}{\delta \cdot \gamma_i} \qquad (4)$$

If the following search condition is satisfied

$$Score(\overline{I}_i, Q_{\overline{W}}) \geq \tau$$

then the cloud server returns the corresponding document $\overline{F}_i$.

Theorem 1. *The proposed multi-keyword search scheme is correct.*

Proof. To compute the similarity score $Score(\overline{I}_i, Q_{\overline{W}})$, it is required that both $\overline{I}_{i,j} \neq 0$ and $Q_{\overline{W}_j} \neq 0$ are satisfied for $1 \leq j \leq n$. Let

$$E_i' = \sum_{j=1, I_{i,j} \neq 0, Q_{\overline{W}_j} \neq 0}^{n+2} \gamma_i \delta \overline{I}_{i,j} Q_{\overline{W}_j} \mod p$$

Note that

$$E_i = \hat{I}_i \cdot \hat{Q}_{\overline{W}}$$

$$= \sum_{j=1, I_{i,j}\neq 0, Q_{\overline{W}_j}\neq 0}^{n+2} (\gamma_i \delta \overline{I}_{i,j} Q_{\overline{W}_j} + \gamma_i t_j \overline{I}_{i,j} + m_j \delta Q_{\overline{W}_j} + m_j t_j) +$$

$$\sum_{j=1, I_{i,j}=0, Q_{\overline{W}_j}\neq 0}^{n+2} (m_j \delta Q_{\overline{W}_j} + m_j t_j) + \sum_{j=1, I_{i,j}\neq 0, Q_{\overline{W}_j}=0}^{n+2} (\gamma_i t_j \overline{I}_{i,j} + m_j t_j) +$$

$$\sum_{j=1, I_{i,j}=0, Q_{\overline{W}_j}=0}^{n+2} m_j t_j$$

$$= E_i' + \rho \mod p$$

If $E_i < p$ and $\rho < \gamma_i \delta$ hold, then we have

$$Score(\overline{I}_i, Q_{\overline{W}}) = \frac{E_i - (E_i \mod \delta \cdot \gamma_i)}{\delta \cdot \gamma_i}$$

$$= \frac{E_i - \rho}{\delta \cdot \gamma_i}$$

$$= \frac{\sum_{j=1, I_{i,j}\neq 0, Q_{\overline{W}_j}\neq 0}^{n+2} (\gamma_i \delta \overline{I}_{i,j} Q_{\overline{W}_j})}{\delta \cdot \gamma_i}$$

$$= \sum_{j=1, I_{i,j}\neq 0, Q_{\overline{W}_j}\neq 0}^{n+2} (\overline{I}_{i,j} Q_{\overline{W}_j})$$

$$= \overline{I}_i \cdot Q_{\overline{W}} \mod p$$

Thus, the proposed scheme is correct.

4   Analysis and Comparison

4.1   Security Analysis

The proposed multi-keyword search scheme can guarantee the privacy of outsourced data in the known ciphertext attack model and the known background attack model.

Resistance of the Known Ciphertext Attacks. In the dada processing phase, the cloud server can get the encrypted documents and ciphertext indexes, while in the search phase, it is given the search trapdoors. These information are submitted to the cloud server in ciphertext format, where one-time parameters are used for processing each document, index and search query. Thus, the cloud server cannot deduce any sensitive information of outsourced documents and the private key of data owner even though it holds a lots of outsourced materials.

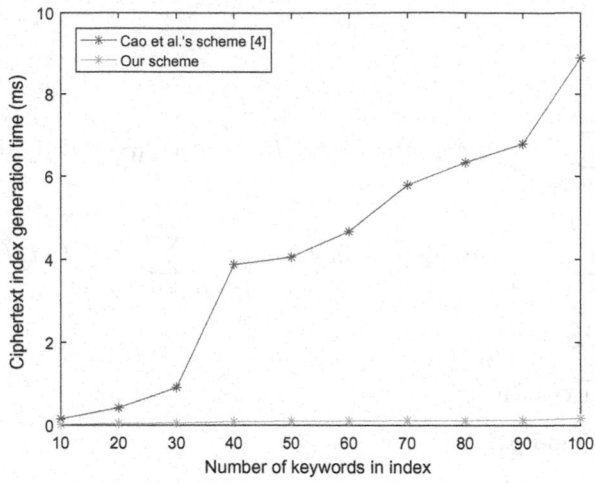

Fig. 2. Time cost on ciphertext index generation.

Resistance of the Known Background Attacks. Under this type of attacks, the cloud server can also get some background information of outsourced documents, for example, keyword frequency. In our scheme, for generating a search trapdoor, the one-time elements t_j and δ are randomly picked, which means that the same search query vector will be mapped to different search trapdoors in different round of searching requests. Moreover, the cloud server is unable to infer the real search query vector from these search trapdoors.

4.2   Performance Evaluation

We conduct experimental evaluation of our scheme and compare with Cao et al.'s scheme [4]. The experiments are implemented using Matlab on a Windows 10 operation system with Intel(R) Core(TM) i5-6500 Processor 3.20 GHz and 8 GB memory. In experiments, we compare the performance of each procedures, that is, ciphertext index construction, search trapdoor generation and cloud search. In experiments, the parameters satisfy $n \leq 2^{32}$, $|\gamma_i| = |\delta| = \lambda_1 = 200$, $|p| = \lambda_2 = 512$, $|m_j| = \lambda_3 = 128$, and $|t_j| = \lambda_4 = 128$.

As shown in Fig. 2, we set the size of the vector from 10 to 100 to evaluate the performance of generating ciphertext index. It can be seen that the time costs of our scheme are less than 1 ms for all cases, while the costs of Cao et al.'s scheme [4] rapidly increase as the number of keywords increases. As shown in Fig. 3, the time costs of both schemes are linear with the number of keywords in the query. Note that Cao et al.'s scheme [4] needs to perform matrix multiplications in generating search trapdoor. Thus, our scheme is more efficient than their scheme in all cases. For the search by the cloud server, our scheme does not involve complicated computation operations. Thus, as shown in Fig. 4, the performance of keyword search of our scheme keeps roughly the same for all cases. Whereas

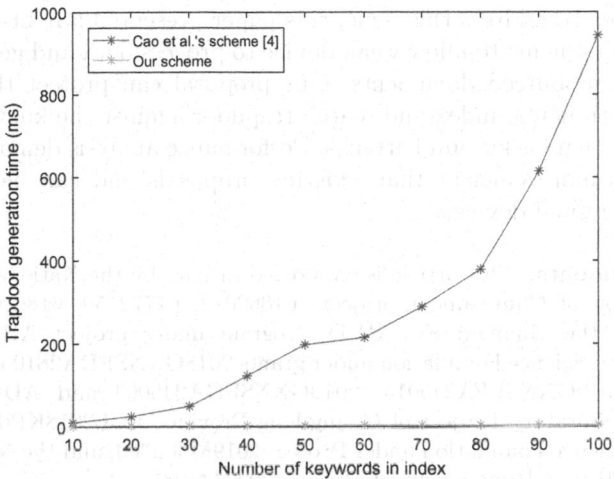

Fig. 3. Time cost on search trapdoor generation.

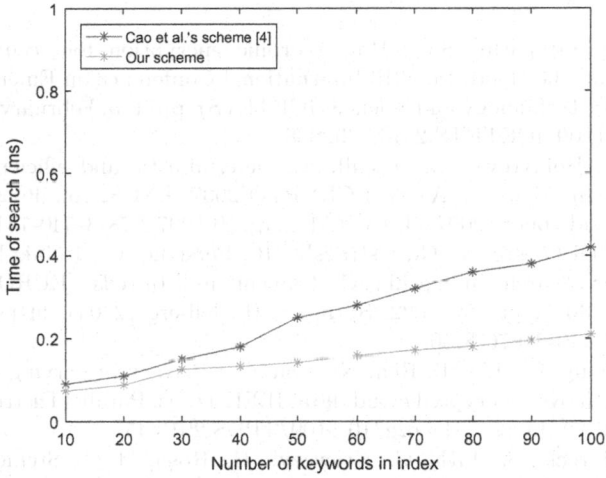

Fig. 4. Time cost on search process.

for Cao et al.'s scheme [4], the performance decreases greatly as the number of keywords in the query vector increasing. Thus, our scheme is more efficient than their scheme.

5   Conclusion

Existing privacy-preserving multi-keyword search schemes cannot be deployed on resource-constrained devices due to the complicated computation operations at the device side. To address this issue, this paper presented a light-weight multi-keyword search scheme to allow weak device to process data and generate search trapdoors of outsourced documents. Our proposal can protect the privacy of outsourced documents, index and search trapdoor against the known ciphertext attacks and known background attacks. Performance analysis demonstrated that our scheme is more efficient than existing proposals and can be deployed on resource-constrained devices.

Acknowledgements. This article is supported in part by the National Natural Science Foundation of China under projects 61862012, 61772150, 61862011, 61962012 and 61902123, the Guangxi Key R&D Program under project AB17195025, the Guangxi Natural Science Foundation under grants 2018GXNSFDA281054, 2018GXNS-FAA281232, 2019GXNSFFA245015, 2019GXNSFGA245004 and AD19245048, the Peng Cheng Laboratory Project of Guangdong Province PCL2018KP004, the China Postdoctoral Science Foundation under Project 2019M662769, and the Natural Science Foundation of Hunan Province under Project 2020JJ5085.

References

1. Anand, V., Satapathy, S.C.: Homomorphic encryption for secure information retrieval from the cloud. In: 2016 International Conference on Emerging Trends in Engineering, Technology and Science (ICETETS), pp. 1–5, February 2016. https://doi.org/10.1109/ICETETS.2016.7602988
2. Bellare, M., Boldyreva, A., O'Neill, A.: Deterministic and efficiently searchable encryption. In: Menezes, A. (ed.) CRYPTO 2007. LNCS, vol. 4622, pp. 535–552. Springer, Heidelberg (2007). https://doi.org/10.1007/978-3-540-74143-5_30
3. Boneh, D., Di Crescenzo, G., Ostrovsky, R., Persiano, G.: Public key encryption with keyword search. In: Cachin, C., Camenisch, J.L. (eds.) EUROCRYPT 2004. LNCS, vol. 3027, pp. 506–522. Springer, Heidelberg (2004). https://doi.org/10.1007/978-3-540-24676-3_30
4. Cao, N., Wang, C., Li, M., Ren, K., Lou, W.: Privacy-preserving multi-keyword ranked search over encrypted cloud data. IEEE Trans. Parallel Distrib. Syst. **25**(1), 222–233 (2014). https://doi.org/10.1109/TPDS.2013.45
5. Cash, D., Jarecki, S., Jutla, C., Krawczyk, H., Roşu, M.-C., Steiner, M.: Highly-scalable searchable symmetric encryption with support for boolean queries. In: Canetti, R., Garay, J.A. (eds.) CRYPTO 2013. LNCS, vol. 8042, pp. 353–373. Springer, Heidelberg (2013). https://doi.org/10.1007/978-3-642-40041-4_20
6. Chang, Y.-C., Mitzenmacher, M.: Privacy preserving keyword searches on remote encrypted data. In: Ioannidis, J., Keromytis, A., Yung, M. (eds.) ACNS 2005. LNCS, vol. 3531, pp. 442–455. Springer, Heidelberg (2005). https://doi.org/10.1007/11496137_30
7. Ding, S., Li, Y., Zhang, J., Chen, L., Wang, Z., Xu, Q.: An efficient and privacy-preserving ranked fuzzy keywords search over encrypted cloud data. In: 2016 International Conference on Behavioral, Economic and Socio-cultural Computing (BESC), pp. 1–6, November 2016. https://doi.org/10.1109/BESC.2016.7804500
8. Ding, X., Liu, P., Jin, H.: Privacy-preserving multi-keyword top-k k similarity search over encrypted data. IEEE Trans. Dependable Secure Comput. **16**(2), 344–357 (2019). https://doi.org/10.1109/TDSC.2017.2693969

9. Fu, Z., Wu, X., Guan, C., Sun, X., Ren, K.: Toward efficient multi-keyword fuzzy search over encrypted outsourced data with accuracy improvement. IEEE Trans. Inf. Forensics Secur. **11**(12), 2706–2716 (2016). https://doi.org/10.1109/TIFS.2016.2596138

10. Fu, Z., Xia, L., Sun, X., Liu, A.X., Xie, G.: Semantic-aware searching over encrypted data for cloud computing. IEEE Trans. Inf. Forensics Secur. **13**(9), 2359–2371 (2018). https://doi.org/10.1109/TIFS.2018.2819121

11. Golle, P., Staddon, J., Waters, B.: Secure conjunctive keyword search over encrypted data. In: Jakobsson, M., Yung, M., Zhou, J. (eds.) ACNS 2004. LNCS, vol. 3089, pp. 31–45. Springer, Heidelberg (2004). https://doi.org/10.1007/978-3-540-24852-1_3

12. He, T., Ma, W.: An effective fuzzy keyword search scheme in cloud computing. In: 2013 5th International Conference on Intelligent Networking and Collaborative Systems, pp. 786–789, September 2013. https://doi.org/10.1109/INCoS.2013.150

13. Hu, C., Liu, P., Yang, R., Xu, Y.: Public-key encryption with keyword search via obfuscation. IEEE Access **7**, 37394–37405 (2019). https://doi.org/10.1109/ACCESS.2019.2905250

14. Hwang, Y.H., Lee, P.J.: Public key encryption with conjunctive keyword search and its extension to a multi-user system. In: Takagi, T., Okamoto, E., Okamoto, T., Okamoto, T. (eds.) Pairing 2007. LNCS, vol. 4575, pp. 2–22. Springer, Heidelberg (2007). https://doi.org/10.1007/978-3-540-73489-5_2

15. Li, J., Wang, Q., Wang, C., Cao, N., Ren, K., Lou, W.: Fuzzy keyword search over encrypted data in cloud computing. In: 2010 Proceedings IEEE INFOCOM, pp. 1–5, March 2010. https://doi.org/10.1109/INFCOM.2010.5462196

16. Liu, J., Han, J., Wang, Z.: Searchable encryption scheme on the cloud via fully homomorphic encryption. In: 2016 Sixth International Conference on Instrumentation Measurement, Computer, Communication and Control (IMCCC), pp. 108–111, July 2016. https://doi.org/10.1109/IMCCC.2016.201

17. Liu, Q., Nie, X., Liu, X., Peng, T., Wu, J.: Verifiable ranked search over dynamic encrypted data in cloud computing. In: 2017 IEEE/ACM 25th International Symposium on Quality of Service (IWQoS), pp. 1–6, June 2017. https://doi.org/10.1109/IWQoS.2017.7969156

18. Lu, R., Zhu, H., Liu, X., Liu, J.K., Shao, J.: Toward efficient and privacy-preserving computing in big data era. IEEE Network **28**(4), 46–50 (2014). https://doi.org/10.1109/MNET.2014.6863131

19. Raghavendra, S., et al.: IGSK: index generation on split keyword for search over cloud data. In: 2015 International Conference on Computing and Network Communications (CoCoNet), pp. 374–380, December 2015. https://doi.org/10.1109/CoCoNet.2015.7411213

20. Ren, Y., Chen, Y., Yang, J., Xie, B.: Privacy-preserving ranked multi-keyword search leveraging polynomial function in cloud computing. In: 2014 IEEE Global Communications Conference, pp. 594–600, December 2014. https://doi.org/10.1109/GLOCOM.2014.7036872

21. Song, D.X., Wagner, D., Perrig, A.: Practical techniques for searches on encrypted data. In: Proceeding 2000 IEEE Symposium on Security and Privacy, SP 2000, pp. 44–55, May 2000. https://doi.org/10.1109/SECPRI.2000.848445

22. Wang, B., Hou, Y., Li, M., Wang, H., Li, H.: Maple: scalable multi-dimensional range search over encrypted cloud data with tree-based index. In: Proceedings of ACM ASIACCS (2014). https://doi.org/10.1145/2590296.2590305

23. Wang, C., Cao, N., Li, J., Ren, K., Lou, W.: Secure ranked keyword search over encrypted cloud data. In: 2010 IEEE 30th International Conference on Distributed Computing Systems, pp. 253–262, June 2010. https://doi.org/10.1109/ICDCS. 2010.34

24. Xu, P., Tang, S., Xu, P., Wu, Q., Hu, H., Susilo, W.: Practical multi-keyword and boolean search over encrypted e-mail in cloud server. IEEE Trans. Serv. Comput. (2019). https://doi.org/10.1109/TSC.2019.2903502

25. Xu, P., Wu, Q., Wang, W., Susilo, W., Domingo-Ferrer, J., Jin, H.: Generating searchable public-key ciphertexts with hidden structures for fast keyword search. IEEE Trans. Inf. Forensics Secur. **10**(9), 1993–2006 (2015). https://doi.org/10. 1109/TIFS.2015.2442220

26. Zhang, L., Zhang, Y., Ma, H.: Privacy-preserving and dynamic multi-attribute conjunctive keyword search over encrypted cloud data. IEEE Access **6**, 34214–34225 (2018). https://doi.org/10.1109/ACCESS.2018.2823718

27. Zhang, Q., Fu, S., Jia, N., Tang, J., Xu, M.: Secure multi-keyword fuzzy search supporting logic query over encrypted cloud data. In: Li, J., Liu, Z., Peng, H. (eds.) SPNCE 2019. LNICST, vol. 284, pp. 210–225. Springer, Cham (2019). https://doi. org/10.1007/978-3-030-21373-2_17

Blockchain-Based Secure Cloud Data Deduplication with Traceability

Hui Huang[1,3]($\boxtimes$), Qunshan Chen[1], Yuping Zhou[1], and Zhenjie Huang[2]

[1] College of Computer, Minnan Normal University, Zhangzhou 363000, China
hhui323@163.com
[2] Lab of Granular Computing, Minnan Normal University, Zhangzhou 363000, China
[3] Key Laboratory of Financial Mathematics (Putian University), Fujian Province University, Putian 351100, China

Abstract. Data deduplication technology makes the same data only keep one physical copy in the cloud, which can effectively eliminate data redundancy and achieve efficient storage. Data deduplication, especially encrypted data duplication, has become a research hotspot. Convergent encryption can effectively solve the existing problem of encrypted data deduplication. However, the cloud server cannot access plaintext data in the ciphertext environment, and it cannot check the consistency of the ciphertext and file label. Therefore, when the duplicate faking attack occurs, how to effectively trace malicious users becomes a critical problem. In this paper, we firstly introduce the blockchain technology into the scenario of secure data deduplication, and construct a specific deduplication scheme to solve the problem of malicious user tracing. We make use of the traceability of the blockchain to form a tamper-proof data chain. When the duplicate faking attack occurs, we can trace the identity of the malicious user and find out all the data files stored in the cloud server.

Keywords: Blockchain · Data deduplication · Traceability · Data updating

1 Introduction

With the rapid development of cloud computing technology, more and more enterprises and individuals outsource the massive data storage to the cloud. And thus reduce the burden of data maintenance and management. However, the repeated storage of a large number of data causes a vast waste of cloud storage resources. Therefore, how to efficiently manage increasing massive data has been a considerable challenge. Data Deduplication technology [1,5] is a critical large-scale data storage optimization technology, and it makes the same data only keep one physical copy in the cloud, which can effectively eliminate data redundancy and achieve efficient storage. However, data Deduplication technology is facing new challenges in the cloud environment.

© Springer Nature Singapore Pte Ltd. 2020
Z. Zheng et al. (Eds.): BlockSys 2020, CCIS 1267, pp. 295–302, 2020.
https://doi.org/10.1007/978-981-15-9213-3_23

Data encryption is the most effective way to protect data privacy. That is, the user encrypts the data locally and uploads the encrypted ciphertext data to the cloud server. Thus, even the cloud server cannot know the plaintext information because it does not know the private key. But in the traditional encryption scheme, the user uses the random key to encrypt the uploaded data. Different users encrypt the same data, and they get different ciphertexts. Moreover, the encrypted data has a strong randomness, which makes it impossible to realize cross-user data deduplication in the ciphertext environment.

Blockchain technology is a rising technology in recent years [4,6,7]. It is a kind of distributed ledger system, which combines the data blocks in a chain way to form a specific data structure. The data stored on the blockchain can not be tampered and forged through the technology of cryptography. And the data also has the advantages of timing and traceability. And the data also has the advantages of scheduling and traceability. Therefore, it is suitable for constructing a secure data deduplication scheme with user traceability.

1.1 Contributions

In this paper, we firstly introduce the blockchain technology into the scenario of secure data deduplication. Then we propose a specific deduplication scheme to solve the problem of malicious user tracing. And our solution also can solve the audit problem of data updating. The contributions of this paper are as follows:

1. Based on blockchain technology, we build a distributed audit center called public auditors (PA). We store the relevant information of the data on the blockchain, which maintained by the nodes of the audit center. Then, we make use of the traceability of the blockchain to form a tamper-proof data chain. When the duplicate faking attack occurs, the PA can trace the identity of the malicious user and find out all the data files stored in the cloud server;
2. Based on the idea of side-chain on the blockchain, we construct a side chain from the original data block on the main chain to record the relevant information of data modification. Thus, each data update has a record, which solves the audit problem of data updating.

2   The Concrete Construction

Cloud data deduplication is a special technology of data compression. In this work, the convergence encryption is used to protect the privacy of user's data and prevent the data from being uploaded repeatedly. However, there may be malicious users. They may upload incorrect data. The encrypted data cannot be validated. When malicious behavior occurs, the malicious users should be tracked. The data files uploaded by the malicious user, including the modified data files also should be tracked. To solve the above problems, the main idea of our solution is to adopt blockchain technique, all the data can be traced and the data updating can be done in an orderly manner. Then the convergence encryption and provable ownership technology are used to ensure that the integrity of the data can be verified. If there is incorrect data, we can trace the real identity of the data owner.

In this section, we discuss the detail of our secure cloud deduplication scheme based on Blockchain. The specific process is as follows.

- **Initialization**
  - Parameter Initialization: Assume $p(p > 3)$ is a prime. $E(F_p)$ is a cycle group. Randomly choose G of the prime order n as a generator of $E(F_p)$. Choose a Hash function $h : Z_q^* \to Z_q^*$.
  - User Registration: User U wants to join the system. He randomly chooses an integer $d, 1 < d \le n - 1$. Then computes the public key $PK_U = dG$.
- **Data Encrypt**: Assume user U wants to upload a data file M. In order to ensure the security of data, U needs to encrypt the data file. In this work, we adopt randomized convergent encryption (RCE) algorithm [8,9] to encrypt M. Besides, we introduce proof of ownership technology to help users provide ownership certification of data to the CSP. U chooses a random key k, runs Algorithm 1 and obtains the ciphertext C_M.

Algorithm 1. E-RCE()

Input: k, M;
Output: C_M;
1: Invoke the encryption algorithm Enc, where Enc is a symmetric encryption scheme;
2: Compute $C_1 = Enc(k, M)$;
3: Compute $k_M = H(M)$. H is a collision-resistant hash function;
4: Compute $C_2 = k \oplus k_M, Tok_M = H(k_M)$;
5: Divide M into n equal blocks denoted by the set $\{M_i\}$;
6: Compute $Tok_{M_i} = H_1(k_{M_i})$, generate a preudorandom value $Enc_{M_i} = P(Tok_{M_i}, i)$, P is a pseudorandom function;
7: Initialize the bloom filter B_M, store Enc_{M_i} into B_M;
8: Set $C_M = (C_1, C_2, Tok_M, B_M)$
Return C_M.

- **Sign.** After the data file is encrypted, the user U runs the sign Algorithm 2 to generate a signature σ_M on the ciphertext C_M.

Algorithm 2. Sign Algorithm

Input: C_M, (p, a, b, n, h, G);
Output: σ_M;
1: Choose a random number $l, 1 < l < n - 1$, compute $L = lG = (X_1, Y_1)$;
2: Compute $r = X_1 \bmod n$, if $r = 1$, return to 1;
3: Compute $e = h(C_M)$ and $s = l - e - rd$, if $s = o$, return to 2;
4: Let $\sigma_M = (r, s)$;
5: Return σ_M.

Algorithm 3. Verification Algorithm

Input: σ_M, C_M, PK_U;
Output: "Success" or "Fail";
1: Check if $1 < s < n - 1$ and $1 < r < n - 1$, compute $e = h(C_M)$;
2: Compute $R = (s + e)G + rPK_U = (X_1, y_1)$, if $R = O$, return "Fail". Otherwise, let $v = X_1 mod n$.
3: If $v = r$, return "Success". Otherwise, return "Fail".

- **Data Upload.** The user U sends an upload request to the cloud server. After receiving the data tag Tok_M, the cloud server checks whether the data tag is unique. Then, the cloud server performs the following operation.
- (1) If the data tag is unique, there is no duplicate in the cloud.
  - (a) The user U sends the data ciphertext C_M and the signature σ_M to the cloud server. The cloud server runs the signature verification Algorithm 3, so as to ensure the integrity of the upload data. If the verification passes, the cloud server stores the data ciphertext and signature and returns the corresponding data link to the user. The cloud server build a transaction that contains the data tag oken Tok_M, the data cipertext C_M and the signature σ_M. Then send the transaction to the PA. The PA generates a block for the new data file.

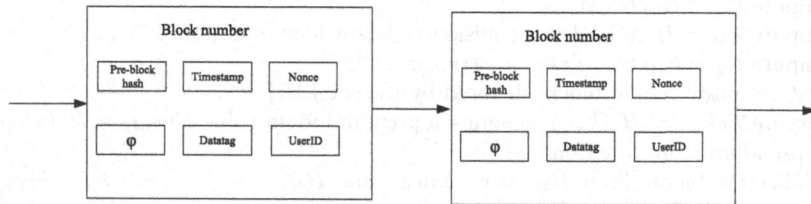

Fig. 1. Data chain

  - (b) Upon receiving the transaction, the PA runs the block generation algorithm described in Algorithm 4. After running the consensus algorithm, the nodes in the blockchain produce a new block to record the data information for the new data file M. The structure of the block is shown in Fig. 1 and 2. The value of ϕ is set as 0, which means the data uploaded has not been updated. The PA also maintains a user list L recorded the file tags and user public keys.

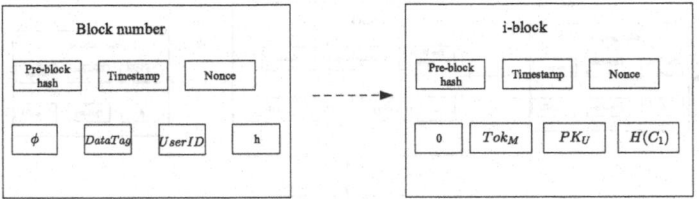

Fig. 2. Designation of data structure

(c) Upon the PA returns the result "Success", the cloud server returns a link of the data M and the data information in the blockchain to the user U.

Algorithm 4. Block Generation Algorithm

Input: Tok_M, C_M, σ_M, PK_U;
Output: "Success" or "Fail" or "Update";
1: Verify the signature σ_M, if verification failed, then return "Fail";
2: If verification success, check Tok_M has already existed in the blockchain and the value of ϕ;
3: If Tok_M has already existed in the blockchain and $\phi \neq 0$, then return "Update";
4: If Tok_M no exist in the blockchain, then build a new block. Let $UserID = PK_U$, $DataTag = Tok_M$, $h = H(C_1)$, $\phi = 0$, then return "Success";
5: Add Tok_M, PK_U into user list L.

---

(2) There is a duplicate of the data tag in the cloud. In this case, user and the cloud server are authenticated in two-way. That is, the user proves to the cloud server that he has a complete data ciphertext, and the cloud server also needs to provide stored ciphertext information to the user. The user verifies the ciphertext's correctness.

(a) The user performs the proof of ownership protocol. First, the cloud server randomly chooses l data block denoted by the set B_i and sends the address set of the blocks $A = 1, 2, \ldots, l$ to the user. After receiving the address set A, the user computes $Tok_{M_i} = H_1(B_i)$, where $i \in [1, l]$. Final, the cloud server computes $Enc_{M_i} = P(Tok_{M_i}, i)$ and checks whether these values belong to B_M. If the validation is successful, the cloud server returns the data link to the user. Otherwise, terminate data upload.

(b) After the proof of ownership checking, the user sends a request to the PA to obtain the value $h = H(C_1)$ and C_2 for the corresponding data file. Then, the user computes $k' = C_2 \oplus K_M$ and $h' = H(Enc(k', M))$. If $h = h'$, the user no longer upload data and he receives a data link from the cloud server. Otherwise, the user sends $H(M)$ to the PA to trace the identity of the encipherer.

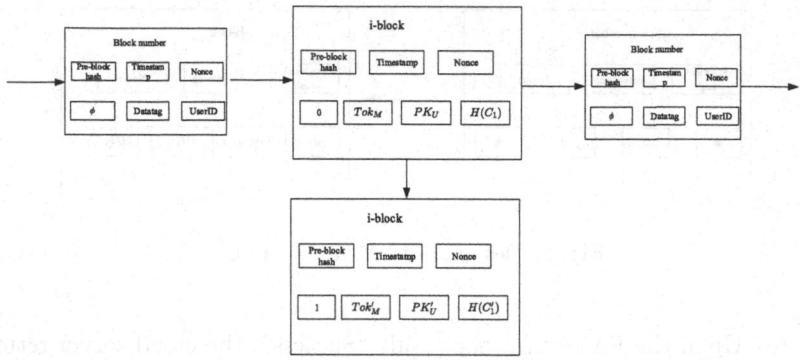

Fig. 3. Updating block

- **Data Update.** The user U sends an update request to the cloud server. After receiving the data tag Tok_M and the new data tag $Tok_{M'}$. The cloud server performs the following update operation. Firstly, check whether the data tag Tok_M label exists in the cloud server. If not, the cloud server performs data upload operation. If the tag exists, the cloud server updates the data tag and the data ciphertext. At last, The cloud server sends the update transaction to the PA. The PA generates a new block for the updated data file.

  Upon receiving the transaction, the PA runs the block update algorithm described in Algorithm 5. After running the consensus algorithm, the nodes in the blockchain produce a new block to record the updated data information for the new data file M'. Additionally, it is essential to note that we use the idea of sidechain in the blockchain to update the data block. The newly generated block is not linked to the main chain, but to the block where the updated data is located, to generate a new sidechain. The structure of the block is shown in Fig. 3.

Algorithm 5. Block Update Algorithm

Input: Tok_M, Tok'_M, $C_{M'}$, σ'_M, PK'_U;
Output: "Success" or "Fail";
1: Verify the signature σ'_M, if verification failed, then return "Fail";
2: If verification success, check Tok_M has already existed in the blockchain and the value of ϕ;
3: Check wether Tok_M has already existed in the blockchain, $PK'_U = PK_U$ and $\phi = 0$. If not, return "Fail";
4: If yes, generate a new block, and let $DataTag = Tok'_M$, $h = H(C'_1)$, $\phi = 1$, then return "Success";
5: Add Tok'_M, PK_U into user list L.

- **Trace**. When the PA receives a tracing request, the PA determines whether the user is honest by checking the correctness of the ciphertext because the user who submits tracing requests should be dishonest. The PA performs the following operations. 1) the PA computes $Tok'_M = H(H(M))$ and retrieves the corresponding ciphertext from the cloud server. 2) Recovery data encryption key $k' = C_2 \oplus H(M)$ and decrypt ciphertext to obtain data $M' = Dec(k', C_1)$. 3) Check if the equation $H(M') = H(M)$ holds. If does, the PA declares that the data stored by the server is correct. If not, the PA checks the list and finds out all the data tag and corresponding identities PK, containing the updated data. 4) The PA sends the results to the cloud server, and the cloud server deletes all links of the malicious user.
- **Data Retrieve**. To obtain the data file, the user sends the data link to the cloud server. The cloud server performs the searching operation and returns corresponding ciphertext data to users. Then, the user use his key to decrypt C_M and obtains M.

3   Security Analysis

In our proposed scheme, each uploaded data is signed by the elliptic curve signature algorithm, whose security is based on the intractability of the elliptic curve discrete logarithm problem. Each uploaded data is signed by the elliptic curve signature algorithm, whose security is based on the intractability of the elliptic curve discrete logarithm problem. The adversary could not forge the individual signature, so the uploaded encrypted data file is secure from tampering. If one user uploads an incorrect encrypted, another user can discover the malicious behavior in time. Therefore, the security of the user's data should not be affected.

We use randomized the randomized convergent encryption (RCE)algorithm to encrypt the uploaded data. According to [3], RCE is secure under the privacy against chosen distribution attack. When the adversary can not obtain the encryption key of RCE or break the RCE successfully, our scheme can meet the security requirements of data confidentiality.

Based on blockchain technology, we build a distributed audit center called public auditors (PA). We store the relevant information of the data on the blockchain, which maintained by the nodes of the audit center. When the duplicate faking attack occurs, the PA can trace the identity of the malicious user and find out all the data files stored in the cloud server. The data stored on the blockchain can not be tampered and forged. Therefore, the PA can be seen as a trusted third party.

4   Conclusion

In this paper, we consider how to trace the malicious user in the data deduplication scenario. To solve the problem, we design a blockchain-based data deduplication scheme. Our solution takes advantage of the traceability of blockchain to realize the malicious user traceability. We use the convergence encryption and provable ownership technology to ensure that the integrity of the data can be verified. To solve the audit problem of data updating, we construct a side chain from the original data block on the main chain to record the relevant information of data modification. Besides, our solution doesn't need complex computation.

Acknowledgments. This work is supported in part by the Natural Science Foundation of Fujian Province of China under Grant (No. 2019J01750, No. 2019J01752); the Research Project of Fujian Provincial Education Department of China under Grant (No. JAT170345, No. JAT170346, and No. JK2017031); the Project of Key Laboratory of Financial Mathematics of Fujian Province University (Putian University) under Grant (No. JR201806); and the presidential research fund of Minnan Normal University (No. KJ18024).

References

1. Abadi, M., Boneh, D., Mironov, I., Raghunathan, A., Segev, G.: Message-locked encryption for lock-dependent messages. In: Canetti, R., Garay, J.A. (eds.) CRYPTO 2013. LNCS, vol. 8042, pp. 374–391. Springer, Heidelberg (2013). https://doi.org/10.1007/978-3-642-40041-4_21
2. American Bankers Association and others. Public key cryptography for the financial services industry: the elliptic curve digital signature algorithm (ECDSA), pp. 62–1998. ANSI X9 (1999)
3. Bellare, M., Keelveedhi, S., Ristenpart, T.: Message-locked encryption and secure deduplication. In: Johansson, T., Nguyen, P.Q. (eds.) EUROCRYPT 2013. LNCS, vol. 7881, pp. 296–312. Springer, Heidelberg (2013). https://doi.org/10.1007/978-3-642-38348-9_18
4. Ghoshal, S., Paul, G.: Exploiting block-chain data structure for auditorless auditing on cloud data. In: Ray, I., Gaur, M.S., Conti, M., Sanghi, D., Kamakoti, V. (eds.) ICISS 2016. LNCS, vol. 10063, pp. 359–371. Springer, Cham (2016). https://doi.org/10.1007/978-3-319-49806-5_19
5. González-Manzano, L., Orfila, A.: An efficient confidentiality-preserving proof of ownership for deduplication. J. Netw. Comput. Appl. **50**, 49–59 (2015)
6. Huang, H., Chen, X., Wang, J.: Blockchain-based multiple groups data sharing with anonymity and traceability. Sci. China Inf. Sci. **63**(3), 1–13 (2019). https://doi.org/10.1007/s11432-018-9781-0
7. Huang, H., Chen, X., Wu, Q., Huang, X., Shen, J.: Bitcoin-based fair payments for outsourcing computations of fog devices. Fut. Gener. Comput. Syst. **78**, 850–858 (2018)
8. Wang, J., Chen, X., Li, J., Kluczniak, K., Kutyłowski, M.: A new secure data deduplication approach supporting user traceability. In: 2015 10th International Conference on Broadband and Wireless Computing, Communication and Applications (BWCCA), pp. 120–124. IEEE (2015)
9. Wang, J., Chen, X., Li, J., Kluczniak, K., Kutyłowski, M.: TrDup: enhancing secure data deduplication with user traceability in cloud computing. Int. J. Web Grid Serv. **13**(3), 270–289 (2017)

Blockchain and Internet of Things

PCN-Based Secure Energy Trading in Industrial Internet of Things

Yong Feng$^{(\boxtimes)}$, Yao Xiao, Dunfeng Li, and Xiaodong Fu

Yunnan Key Laboratory of Computer Technology Applications,
Kunming University of Science and Technology, Kunming 650500, Yunnan, China
fybraver@163.com

Abstract. The application of blockchain cryptocurrency in the field of
energy transactions has attracted wide attention because it supports
complex communication interactions of a large number of distributed
energy entities. Due to the high degree of autonomy of distributed systems, it is very important to use trusted encryption technology to ensure
the security of user information in the network. In order to avoid the
problem of user privacy leakage in the Peer-to-Peer (P2P) energy trading
scheme in the Industrial Internet of Things (IIOT), this paper adopts the
signature scheme based on Elliptic Curve Cryptography-based Threshold
Cryptography (ECC-TC) to complete the anonymous process of energy
nodes and ensure the traceability of pseudonyms. In addition, in order to
solve the problem of transaction restrictions caused by high transaction
costs and long confirmation time of energy block chain, we proposed
a payment scheme based on payment channel network (PCN) to support fast and frequent small energy transactions. We conducted security
analysis and feasibility assessment in the context of security and privacy
protection requirements and the conclusion proves that proposed scheme
enables peer to communicate anonymously in a P2P manner and quickly
complete small energy transactions while using blockchain technology to
protect basic transactions. In addition, the cost of communication and
calculation of the scheme is much less than that of traditional transaction
mode which proves that proposed scheme can be applied in practice.

Keywords: Industrial Internet of Things · Secure energy trading ·
Blockchain · Payment channel network · Threshold signature scheme

1 Introduction

In the past of years, the explosive growth of electric vehicles (EVs) has brought
about tremendous changes in the transportation sector and driving the rebuild-
ing of traditional energy structures. EVs users realize vehicle-to-vehicle (V2V)
and vehicle-to-grid (V2G) to achieve the balance between the energy demand
side and the supply side, which has become an important part of the energy
Internet. However, due to the decentralized, intensive and autonomous nature
of transactions, it also causes a huge burden on energy management and user

© Springer Nature Singapore Pte Ltd. 2020
Z. Zheng et al. (Eds.): BlockSys 2020, CCIS 1267, pp. 305–318, 2020.
https://doi.org/10.1007/978-981-15-9213-3_24

management. In this regard, blockchain has been studied and applied in energy transactions in recent years due to its advantages of decentralization, trustless, distributed sharing and non-tampering with transaction records.

Blocks of distributed structure weaken the function of the traditional centralized organization, in the energy of the Internet. Generally, trusted centers verify, store and manage the identity information of users, and store all transaction information. This single-point operation mode is easy to be attacked, resulting in the disclosure of users' privacy, and the attacker may manipulate the transaction information to infringe users' rights and interests. Blockchain-based cryptocurrency is an add-only distributed ledger shared between individuals who do not trust each other. It provides a distributed storage mechanism, in which each node in the blockchain network can download a complete ledger copy and all nodes can verify the Block information when the network generates a new Block, which is known as the consensus mechanism. Consensus algorithms are not widely used because they require huge storage space for copying data and high calculated load for adding blocks. In order to solve the scalability problem, the off-chain mechanism has been proposed to eliminate the need of have to submit every private transaction to the blockchain, currently, PCN is the most promising method. In this paper, PCN-based trading scheme [1] is adopted to support fast and frequent energy trading, users only need to register the first and last balance to the blockchain after multiple hop transactions, the time and cost of using PCN for small transactions is much less than that of block chain transactions.

Energy nodes in the blockchain network can conduct residual energy transactions with other nodes in a P2P way to meet local energy needs, improve energy efficiency, reduce transfer losses and promote green industrial systems. Considering the typical P2P energy trading scenario in IIOT, we propose a unified energy trading framework, including energy nodes, energy stations, several edge computing servers and certification centers. The edge computing server serves as the complete node of the block chain, providing energy nodes with matching and pricing of energy demand and supply, operating the block chain and resolving transaction disputes.

However, the privacy leakage caused by frequent energy transactions is becoming more and more serious. If the attacker analyzes the transaction information for a long time, which may steal the user's identity information or working mode as well as other private information that can be used by others, exposing the user's information to the public environment. Based on this, the transaction mode based on blockchain should hide the identity information and transaction records of the transaction nodes as much as possible. For this reason, we propose to apply the threshold signature scheme [2,3] to the IIOT energy trading system. Through integration with the PCN trading scheme, users can be allowed to conduct anonymous P2P transactions on the Blockchain. Proposed system uses threshold signature scheme for each node to provide authentication and generate a pseudonym to complete secret distribution, and each energy node uses the pseudonym to conduct transactions to protect its private information. In case of any dispute, t+1 participants can jointly restore the private keys to complete identity authentication, which can guarantee their privacy and be traceable at the same time.

Section 1 of this paper analyzes the deficiencies of the existing energy trading scheme, and then proposes the scheme based on the improvement. Section 2 summarizes relevant work; Sect. 3 introduces the main technologies in the system. In Sect. 4, anonymous scheme and PCN-based energy trading scheme are proposed. Section 5 analyzes the security and performance of the scheme; Sect. 6 gives the conclusion of this paper.

2   Related Work

Based on current smart grid architecture of distributed energy trading system deployment there are some kinds of security and privacy concerns, that the network entities involved in a P2P energy transactions needs to communicate at any time, such as there is demand response optimization, energy price negotiation and publish energy contracts and executive pay deals. This will expose users in the system to various security and privacy issues, including information confidentiality, message integrity, and availability attacks. In addition, the location privacy of users of plug-in-electric vehicles (PEV) mobile entity is crucial, because the location of PEV can be identified according to the location of charging stations [4]. Therefore, the system of P2P distributed energy trading (DET) should be equipped with necessary security, privacy and payment transaction mechanisms to ensure normal operation and fairness. Although some researchers have discussed the security and privacy of existing smart grid systems, only a few papers have considered the security and privacy of P2P DET [5,6].

[7] formalized the multi-commodity flow problem in the direct energy transaction between electric vehicles and charging stations, and proposed a payment network optimization model for determining the payment channels between charging stations. However, the scheme does not give a specific solution process to its model, nor does it involve the energy transaction in the network, nor does it solve the privacy protection problem in the energy transaction.

In [8], a credit-based payment scheme is proposed to support fast and frequent energy transactions between energy nodes through credit payment. However, it relies too much on the energy agent, and the energy node does not participate in the consensus process, so the energy agent node may control the entire block chain. The transaction scheme based on credit payment has some security risks, and its transaction speed is still limited. The use of multiple wallet addresses does not achieve complete anonymity because the wallet address is limited and will run out, and all transactions on the energy node are not anonymous to the energy broker.

[9] the author uses the concept of EnergyCoin to attract electric vehicles to participate in energy transactions to stabilize the local electricity market, and uses blockchain to conduct secure energy transactions. The author embraces Cooperative Games Theory to further solve the problem of energy trading, while

protecting the privacy of participating electric vehicles and guaranteeing energy trading. Similar to this scheme, the strategy of buying and selling electric vehicle energy [10] is modeled on the basis of blockchain. However, these plans ignore the huge cost and long confirmation time of blockchain transactions, which cannot meet the demands of the energy market. Considering the above problems, we use PCN and threshold encryption technology to realize a high-throughput and secure IIOT energy transaction scheme.

3   Core System Components

3.1   PCN

Blockchain technology can be used to realize real-time settlement between different currencies, but the transaction processing rate is limited because the transaction broadcasting and workload proof mechanism are too expensive to be widely used. To overcome the scalability problem, the proposed PCN enables instant payments without through expensive and slow blockchain transactions, where users simply register the initial and final balances of each channel to the Blockchain. In the PCN, senders can send payments to recipients through multiple hops, and users in the payment route can charge transfer fees through their channels, which are significantly less than Blockchain transaction fees.

The two users who participate in the transaction need to establish a transaction channel in advance, deposit a certain amount of Bitcoin into the joint account and add the transaction to the blockchain. The transaction is essentially an update of the channel balance agreed by both parties, when no further transfers are required or bitcoin deposits are depleted and to close the channel, a transaction closure message is broadcast to the Blockchain and a bitcoin balance notification is sent to the user based on the latest balance. As shown in "Fig. 1", Alice and Bob created a payment channel with an initial capacity of 5 bitcoins by instantiating a third-party account and storing 5 bitcoins, then they made two transactions in the off-chain payment channel, paying Bob1 bitcoins and 2 bitcoins respectively. When the channel is closed, the remaining 2 bitcoins and the received 3 bitcoins are submitted to Alice and Bob, respectively, and the balance information is written to the blockchain.

PCN is different from the traditional computer temporary network in two aspects: First, the transaction needs to be sent to the receiver together with the transfer fee and the cost of using the channel, when the intermediate node collects the fees according to the transaction routing order that will cause the balance requirement on different routes, namely the feasibility constraint. For example, in the payment example shown in "Fig. 2", if Alice wants to pay 2 bitcoins to Bob through the three nodes C, D and E, assuming the capacity of each channel is 5 bitcoins, she will initially pay 3 bitcoins (2 bitcoins for payment plus 1 bitcoin charged by the user in the path). Then the payment is settled in the following way: capacity in the link Alice→C is reduced by 3. In addition, if 0.25 bitcoins is required for channel use fee, C charges by reducing the capacity of link C→D by 2.75 instead of 3 bitcoins. Follow the same principle and set the

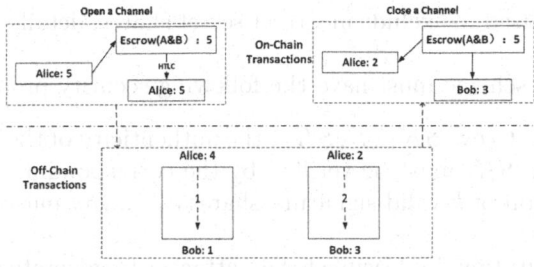

Fig. 1. An example of payment channel

capacity of link D—→E to 2.75, and the capacity of link E→Bob to 3. Secondly, the transaction time is determined by the number of hops, the user's tolerance of the transaction time leads to the timeliness constraint. The user stipulates the maximum tolerance time in the hash time lock contract (HTLC).

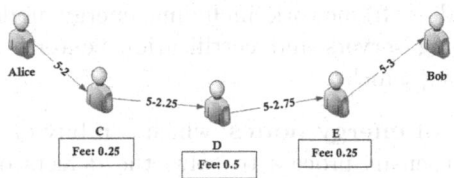

Fig. 2. Example of multi-hop transaction channel capacity in PCN

3.2 Threshold Signature Encryption Scheme

(t, n) threshold secret sharing scheme is shared secret information is divided into n pieces were assigned to the n legitimate participants, that is, a secret sharing by n participants, iff *tort* more participants can restore the secret and $(t - 1)$ or less participants cannot get any information of the secret. The scheme proposed by Shamir. [2] as follows: suppose there are n participants $(P_1, P_2..., P_n)$ in P, P is the large prime number of Z^*_p. The secret distributor constructs the polynomial of order $t - 1$, $f(x) = s + \sum_{j=1}^{t-1} a_j x^j$, where s is a constant. Each participant P_i gets a secret number b_i and generates a secret share $S_i = f(b_i)$. Then any k participants can cooperate to recover the Shared secret s through formula (1):

$$f(x) = S + \sum_{i=1}^{t-1} a_i x^i \tag{1}$$

Which $S = f(0)$. Dishonest participants may submit incorrect secret shares during secret refactoring, but the scheme is reliable because the share validation algorithm can be used to exclude incorrect secret shares, details will be described in Sect. 4.1.

The signature scheme must have the following security properties:

- By a set of secret keys SK_1, ..., SK_k, the authenticity of the digital signature σ generated by SK_i must be verified by the corresponding public key PK_i, The combination of k valid signature shares σ_1, ..., σ_k must generate a valid signature σ;
- It is not computationally feasible for an attacker to generate a valid signature without knowing the k or more secret key SK that generate the signature.

4   PCN-based Secure Energy Trading

Energy nodes in the blockchain network can trade residual energy with other nodes in a P2P way, so as to meet the local energy demand, improve the energy transaction efficiency, reduce the transfer loss and promote the green industrial system. Considering the typical P2P energy trading scenario in IIOT, we propose a unified energy trading framework including energy nodes, energy stations, several edge computing servers and certification centers, which communicate with each other, among which:

- **A large number of energy nodes**: which can buy or sell energy and participate in the consensus process to solve the defects of the entire system controlled by a small number of nodes in the alliance blockchain.
- **Energy station:** mainly provides energy supply and also accepts energy sales from energy nodes.
- **Edge distributed computing server (DC):** as a complete block chain node, it provides energy nodes with matching and pricing of energy demand and supply, operates block chain, and resolves transaction disputes.
- **Certificate Authority (CA):** complete the authentication and key distribution of all nodes in the whole system.

In addition, as the core privacy protection scheme of the system, threshold signature provides a reliable anonymous mechanism for energy nodes. As long as a certain number of participating nodes in the system are honest, the real identity and transaction information of each user will not be disclosed. Due to the tamper proof mechanism of the blockchain, all users can trust the data recorded on the blockchain, and in the event of a dispute, the edge server can efficiently perform pseudonym tracking to complete the authentication work. In order to introduce the working process of the system, we use the above energy entities as general examples, in which energy nodes are users and divided into applicant P_0 and n participants $P_i(\ P_1, \ldots,\ P_n)$. Assume that user P_0 needs to apply for a pseudonym PID from the energy network. First, P_0 sends a pseudonym application request to the CA, and the CA authenticates its identity and generates a pseudonym. Then DC as the distributor randomly distributed the P_0 private key as the main secret S to n participants, and participant P_i

received corresponding secret share S_i after verification, which get a secret share participants P_i cannot get any information about S. When there is a dispute during the transaction, a reconstruction request is initiated by the CA. If and only if t or more participants P_i respond and return the correct answer, then the real identity information of the requester P_0 can be secretly reconstructed by the DC. The system architecture is shown in "Fig.3":

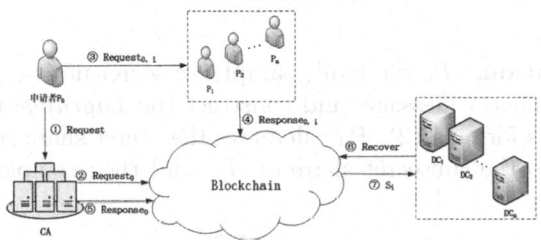

Fig. 3. System architecture based on Threshold Cryptography scheme

4.1 Threshold Cryptography-Based Identity Authentication Scheme

This paper focuses on the privacy issues in the energy trading system based on blockchain. In this section, the process of anonymization of energy nodes will be introduced. System parameters include: p is a large prime number, $q \in Z_p^*$ is a large prime factor of $p - 1$, $g \in Z_p^*$ is an element of order q; $h(\ )$ is a HASH function; $h_k(.)$ is a HASH function with a secret key; (E_k, D_k) is a pair of symmetric encryption and decryption algorithms; CA randomly selected the private key SK_{CA}, the corresponding public key as $PK_{CA} = g^{SK_{CA}} \ mod \ q$; Applicant P_0 private key is SK_0, and the public key $PK_0 = g^{SK_0} \ mod \ q$; $(SK_i, PK_i = g^{SK_i} \ mod \ q)$ is the participants' P_i public-private key pairs. In this scheme, the private key SK_0 of the applicant is distributed as the main secret share S. The specific design of the scheme is as follows.

PID Application. The applicant P_0 initiates a pseudonym application to the CA. The message contains its public key PK_0 and the private key SK_0 and the real identity information ID_0, as well as the used pseudonym $PIDused_i$, which is encrypted with the CA public key and sent. Where, the pseudonym PID is generated in the following format when the message is sent: $PID_0 = h(SK_0 + Timestamp)$.

$$P_0 \rightarrow CA : Request = \{ENC_{PK_{CA}}(PIDused_1,...PIDused_n); PK_0;$$
$$ENC_{PK_0}(SK_0||ID_0); Timestamp; PID_0\}$$

CA verifies the identity of P_0 after decrypting the message with its private key. If the information is verified to be correct then call the energy nodes in the network to participate in secret sharing. Assuming that n nodes are confirmed to participate, the request for pseudonym construction is broadcast to the Blockchain:

$$CA \rightarrow BLOCK : \ Request_0 = \{P_0, PK_0; P_1, PK_1; P_2, PK_2;$$
$$\ldots; P_n, PK_n; \ Timestamp\}$$

Secret Distribution. P_0 randomly samples n secret numbers $b_1, \ldots, b_n$ after receiving the broadcast message, and construct the *Lagrange* polynomial $f(x)$ of degree $t-1$ as formula (2). P_0 calculates the secret share $S_i = f(b_i)$, where b_i corresponds to the subsecret share of P_i, and then complete the following work:

$$f(x) = S + \sum_{i=1}^{t-1} a_i x^i \tag{2}$$

- P_0 randomly samples $x_i \in Z_p^*$, and calculates $k_i = (k_{i,1}, k_{i,2}) = h(\ PK_i{}^{x_i} \ \text{mod } p)$;
- Calculates $r_i = h_{k_{i,2}}(s_i)$, $c_i = E_{k_{i,1}}(s_i\|r_i)$, $R_i = g^{r_i}$, $M_i = x_i/(r_i + SK_0) \ mod \ q$;
- P_0 sends $(r_i, R_i, \ M_i)$ to the corresponding shared P_i.

$$P_0 \rightarrow P_i : Request_{0,i} = (ENC_{PK_i}\ (r_i, R_i, M_i)\ ; Timestamp)$$

Authentication. Without loss of generality, assumed that t honest participants $P_1, \ldots, \ P_t$ receive the message $Request_{0,i}$, which first needs to verify whether the data is acquired. The authentication process is as follows:

- Calculates $k_i = (k_{i,1}, k_{i,2}) = h((PK_0 R_i)^{SK_i M_i} \ mod \ p)$;
- Decryption to obtain $s_i\|r_i = D_{k_{i,1}}(c_i)\ h_{k_{i,2}} \ and \ (s_i)$;
- To determine if the equation holds $h_{k_{i,2}}(s_i) = ri$, if equal P_i accepts the message and return a receipt to the CA, otherwise submit an error report.

$$P_i \rightarrow CA : \ Response_{0,i} = (\ SIGN_{SK_i}(b_i\|Timestamp))$$

Add Block. CA will send the authentication completion message to the Blockchain after receiving the correct receipt from t honest participants $P_1, \ldots, \ P_t$ and construction block, then broadcast the result of this pseudonym application: $CA \rightarrow BLOCK : Response_0 = (P_0, PID; Timestamp)$ Then P_0 can use the pseudonym PID to trade in the energy network. All nodes in the system can obtain the pseudonym through the above steps and anonymous and safe energy trading can be conducted after verification.

Secret Refactoring. When the transaction is disputed and the real identity information of the node needs to be verified, DC initiates a refactoring request.

- P_i responds to the request, calculates $S_i = f(b_i)$ and sends the result to DC;
- DC verifies S_i after receiving it; After obtaining at least t different and correct secret share answers, DC reconstruction Lagrange polynomial $F(x)$ is as follows:

$$F(x) = \sum_{i=1}^{t} S_i \prod_{j=1, j \neq i}^{k} \frac{x - b_j}{b_i - b_j} \tag{3}$$

- Calculate the miner secret share $S = F(0)$, that is, the private key SK_0 of P_0, and DC will encrypt the result and send it to CA;
- CA obtains SK_0 and gets SK_0 after decrypting the encrypted information in $Request_0$.

4.2 PCN-based Energy Trading Scheme

PCN is defined as a directed graph $G = (V, E)$, where vertex V represents the set of bitcoin accounts and E is the set of currently open payment channels. Energy node $u \in V$, where u_0, u_s represents the payor and receiver respectively, and $0 \leq i < j \leq s$; The weight on each directed edge $(u_i, u_j) \in E$ represents the amount of remaining bitcoins $b_{i,j}$ that the transferor u_i can pay to the transferee u_j; There is a HTLC tolerance $\tau_{i,j}$ on each edge $(u_i, u_j) \in E$, which is the maximum waiting time for the random number R to be submitted. The success of the payment between two users depends on the capacity available γ on the path connecting the two users and the fee f charged by the intermediate nodes. Assuming that u_0 pay α bitcoin to the u_s through the path $u_0 \to u_1 \to u_2 \to \ldots \to u_n \to u_s$, for the payment to be successful, which must have each channel capacity $\gamma_i \geq \alpha'_i$, where $\alpha'_i = \alpha - \sum_{j=1}^{i-1} f(u_j)$ in which the initial payment amount is subtracted from the charge charges charged by the intermediate node on the path. To ensure that u_s successfully receives α bitcoin, the initial payment of u_0 is $\alpha_0 = \alpha + \sum_{j=1}^{n} f(u_j)$.

System Initialization. Proposed uses Threshold Cryptography scheme to initialize the system, and each node becomes a legal entity after the CA registration. After the energy node with real identity ID_i is added to the system then gets its public and private key $PK_i \& SK_i$ and the authenticated pseudonym PID_i, PID_i is used to uniquely identify the node with each binding registration information. Assume that the path $(u_1, u_2 \ldots u_n)$ from sender u_0 to receiver u_s is the standard scheme for indirect payments.

Before the transaction starts, u_0 executes HTLC locally and the contract locks x bitcoins that can only be released after the contract is fulfilled as scheduled. The sender u_0 randomly selects n random strings x_i and defines $y_i = H(\oplus_{j=1}^{n} x_j), j \geq i$. Then u_0 sends (x_i, y_i) to each intermediate user u_i, where τ_i is the HTLC tolerance that used to represent the biggest tolerance time to using the current channel. for all $i \in [n]$, $\tau_{i-1} = \tau_i + \Delta(\Delta > 0)$. The contract is defined as follows:

Algorithm 1. HTLC

Input: The original signal x, HTLC tolerance τ_i
Output: n random strings u_i, y_i
   $\forall i \in [n]$
   $x_i \in 0, 1^*; y_i \leftarrow \text{H}(\oplus_{j=1}^n x_j)$
   return $((x_1, y_1) \ldots (x_n, y_n))$
   HTLC $(u_i, u_{i+1}, y_{i+1}, \tau_i)$

OpenChannel $(u_i, u_j, \beta, \tau, f)$**.** The energy node u_0 needs to create an initial account $Acc = (PID_0, Addr_0, \beta, \tau, PID_l, Addr_l, \beta, \tau, f, account)$ before making a payment to the energy station u_s, which includes the wallet address of both parties $(Addr_0, Addr_l)$, initial channel capacity β, HTLC tolerance τ, channel transfer fee f and current account balance, etc. Both parties verify the account information and output a channel identifier $\delta(u_0, u_s)$ after verification. Establish payment channels $CH_{ij} = (\delta_{u_i, u_j}, \beta, \tau, f, amount) \in E$, then upload the account balance to Blockchain.

Transaction $((\delta_{u_0, u_1}, ..., \delta_{u_n, u_s}), v)$**.** If there is a payment route from sender u_0 to receiver u_s in PCN, and each channel $\delta u_i, u_{i+1}$ in the path has at least a balance $\gamma_i \geq v_i'$, where $v_i' = v - \sum_{j=1}^{i-1} f(u_j)$. then the transaction can start. The algorithm descripted as Algorithm 2.

Algorithm 2. Transaction

Input: $(\delta_{u_{i,i+1}}, v)$
Output: Decision
   $v_1 := v + \sum_i^n f(u_j)$
   if $v_1 \leq Cap (\delta_{u_0, u_1})$ **then**
      Cap $(\delta_{u_0, u_1}) := Cap(\delta_{u_0, u_1}) - v_1$;
      $\tau_0 := \tau_n ow + \Delta * n$;
   $\forall i \in [n]$
      $v_i := v_1 - \sum_{j=1}^{t-1} f(u_j)$;
      $\tau_i := \tau_{i-1} - \Delta$;
   Send $(u_i, (x_i, y_i, y_{i+1}, \delta_{u_{i-1,i}}, \delta_{u_{i,i+1}}, \tau_i, \tau_{i+1}, v_{i+1})$ **HTLC** $(u_0, u_1, y_1, \tau_1, v_1)$
   Send $(u_{n+1} (x_{n+1}, y_{n+1}, \delta_{u_{n,n+1}}, \tau_{n+1})$
   end if
   if $v_{i+1} \leq Cap (\delta_{u_i, u_i+1})$ and $\tau_{i+1} = \tau_i - \Delta$ **then**
      Cap $(\delta_{u_i, u_i+1}) := Cap(\delta_{u_i, u_i+1}) - v_{i+1}$;
      HTLC $(u_i, u_{i+1}, y_{i+1}, \tau_{i+1}, v_{i+1})$
      $H_{x_{n+1}} = y_{n+1}$ and $\tau_{n+1} = \tau_n ow + \Delta$
      Store $(x_{n+1}, y_{n+1}, \delta_{u_n}, u_{n+1})$
      Accept
   else
      Abort
   end if

---

u_0 calculate the total cost of sending v bitcoins to u_l: $v_1 = v + \sum f(u_i)$ and the cost associated with each intermediate node in the payment path before sends a payment. If u_0 does not have enough bitcoin and the payment is waived, otherwise the contract is sent to each transferor. Each intermediate node verifies whether the HTLC associated value is less than or equal to the channel capacity in the subsequent payment path, and that the difference Δ between the timeout of the incoming HTLC and the outgoing HTLC is positive. If all relevant verifications are correct, the corresponding HTLC will be generated for subsequent users in the payment path; Otherwise, payment will be suspended.

If each intermediate user in the path completes the contract within the specified time, and the payment finally reaches the receiver u_s, that is, once the contract between u_n, u_{n+1} is established then the receiver u_s can draw v bitcoins by publishing x_n. Once the value of x_n is known, u_{n-1} can deduce the random number of the contract between u_{n-2} and u_{n-1} by simply calculating $x_{n-1} \oplus x_n$ and publishing it, and so on. This mechanism will make all intermediate nodes in the route receive their transfer fees after the payer receives the transfer.

closeChannel $((\delta_{u_0,u_l}), v)$. For the two users u_0, u_l of the Shared payment channel CH_{ij} will close the channel when the account balance is locked after the agreed transaction is completed and update the account balance on the Blockchain, returning 1 if and only if the transaction is correctly added to the Blockchain.

5 Performance Analysis

5.1 Guarantee of Anonymity

Privacy of Energy Nodes. All energy nodes can obtain a pseudonym after the authentication of participating nodes in the Blockchain network, and conduct energy transactions under this pseudonym. Since the real identity of the applicant is signed by the private key of the applicant P_0 before it is sent to the CA for authentication, except the owner of the pseudonym, none of node including the energy station participating in the verification can associate the pseudonym with the real ID of P_0 until fewer than t participants cooperate to restore the secret. Therefore, this scheme has strong anonymity.

Traceability of Pseudonyms. SK_0 is used as the main secret share for distribution and the real identity information ID_0 is encrypted with the private key and sent to CA when applying for pseudonyms. When the private key of P_0 is recovered by $t + 1$ users in the event of a dispute, the private key can be used to decrypt the public key encrypted information in the message $Request_0$ and obtain its real identity ID_0. In addition, in order to avoid the possibility of dishonest nodes using inconsistent pseudonym generation method. Therefore, PID_0 is required to generate the following format when sending the pseudonym application message: $PID_0 = h(SK_0 + Timestamp)$

5.2 Safety Analysis

Different from the traditional communication security and privacy protection, proposed IIOT system uses PCN and Threshold Cryptography scheme to ensure the security and privacy protection of energy transactions. The security performance related to blockchain is as follows:

Decentralization. In proposed energy trading system, IIOT nodes conduct transactions in a P2P manner which is different from the traditional centralized energy trading method that relies on completely trusted intermediaries. All IIOT nodes have the right to anonymously trade energy after obtaining their pseudonyms after being authenticated by participating nodes in the network. The Blockchain network is scalable by using PCN transactions, and none of globally trusted intermediaries are required to participate.

Integrity. All transaction information is publicly reviewed and authenticated by other entities in the Internet (including IIOT nodes and trusted CA). The completely distributed Blockchain nodes are combined with Threshold Cryptography technology to ensure that any attacker cannot forge identity and damage the network. An attacker who controls one or more IIOT nodes in a blockchain network cannot track or steal any content of the relevant transaction because all IIOT nodes trade under a pseudonym and no one can associate the transaction information with the energy node until the identity information is recovered by t participants. Two users using PCN transactions can make multiple payments and only upload the first and last balances, that preventing the attacker from obtaining more transaction information from the public blockchain network.

Non-repudiation. PCN transaction need to upload the joint account balances at the beginning and the end to block chains, According to HTLC regulation, the transferee can only withdraw the payment after publishing the correct HASH random number, and no one can accept the transfer and deny the receipt. The transferor and the intermediate node shall not receive any remuneration before the payee receives the transfer, so as to ensure that both parties cannot deny the existence and rationality of transaction records.

5.3 Scheme Comparison

Table 1 compares the proposed PCN-based energy trading scheme with some of the proposals in the literature based on functionality. [5] proposed a private decentralized energy trading system based on Token which allows peers to anonymous negotiations in energy prices and use Blockchain technology, multi-signature and anonymous encrypted messages provide privacy protection to realize secure transactions, but due to the system to produce the problem such as communication message redundancy and routing insufficient that led to the scalability problems. As described in Chap. 2, authors used various schemes in [7–9] which could not guarantee the timeliness and security of transactions at the same time and did not provide complete anonymity mechanism for all energy nodes in IIOT. The Blockchain-based energy transaction scheme proposed in [11] using the miner node as the auxiliary node to verify all network transactions, and the miner node is selected according to various factors (such as energy demand, pricing, etc.), which increases the overall security of the system while incurs huge overhead and does not provide anonymous mechanism for the node to complete safe energy transactions. In this paper, the PCN-based transaction scheme is used to solve the un-scalability problem of Blockchain and providing authentication of energy nodes in the anonymous mechanism.

Table 1. Comparative analysis of Proposed Scheme with other competing approaches

Scheme	Techniques	Authentication	Scalability	Anonymity
[5]	Blockchain	✓	×	✓
[7]	PCN	×	✓	×
[8]	Blockchain	✓	✓	×
[9]	Blockchain	✓	×	✓
[11]	Blockchain	✓	×	×
Proposed	PCN	✓	✓	✓

6 Conclusion

This paper proposes a PCN-based energy trading scheme that supports the energy nodes in IIOT to trade quickly and frequently in P2P way, overcomes the limitation problem caused by the long confirmation time in the Blockchain network and supports transaction parties to make multi small scale payments by off-chain mechanism, in which HTLC ensures the security of its trading funds and the non-repudiation of transactions. In addition, the threshold sign-secret scheme is adopted to provide an anonymous mechanism for energy nodes. All nodes in IIOT use the authenticated pseudonym to conduct transactions, and the real identity information of nodes cannot be reconstructed by cooperation with less than t users. Dishonest nodes in the network cannot obtain any node information related to transactions. The security analysis shows that the proposed scheme provides an effective anonymous mechanism for each energy node. Compared with other schemes, proposed scheme effectively solve the problem of traceability of pseudonyms while allowing users to complete transactions anonymously.

Acknowledgments. This work is supported by the National Natural Science Foundation of China under Grants no. 61662042, 61262081, and 61462056; the Yunnan Provincial Key Project of Applied Basic Research Plan under Grants no. 2014FA028.

References

1. Poon, J., Dryja, T.: The Bitcoin Lightning Network: Scalable Off-chain Instant Payments (2016)
2. Shamir, A.: How to share a secret. Commun. ACM **22**(11), 612–613 (1979)
3. Blakley, G.R.: Safeguarding cryptographic keys. In: 1979 International Workshop on Managing Requirements Knowledge (MARK), pp. 313–318. IEEE (1979)
4. Han, W., Xiao, Y.: Privacy preservation for V2G networks in smart grid: a survey. Comput. Commun. **91**, 17–28 (2016)
5. Aitzhan, N.Z., Svetinovic, D.: Security and privacy in decentralized energy trading through multi-signatures, blockchain and anonymous messaging streams[J]. IEEE Trans. Dependable Secur. Comput. **15**(5), 840–852 (2016)
6. Hong, Y., Goel, S., Liu, W.M.: An efficient and privacy-preserving scheme for P2P energy exchange among smart microgrids. Int. J. Energy Res. **40**(3), 313–331 (2016)
7. Erdin, E., Cebe, M., Akkaya, K., et al.: Building a private bitcoin-based payment network among electric vehicles and charging stations. In: 2018 IEEE International Conference on Internet of Things (iThings) and IEEE Green Computing and Communications (GreenCom) and IEEE Cyber, Physical and Social Computing (CPSCom) and IEEE Smart Data (SmartData), pp. 1609–1615. IEEE (2018)
8. Li, Z., Kang, J., Yu, R., et al.: Consortium blockchain for secure energy trading in industrial internet of things. IEEE Trans. Ind. Inf. **14**(8), 3690–3700 (2017)
9. Kang, J., Yu, R., Huang, X., et al.: Enabling localized peer-to-peer electricity trading among plug-in hybrid electric vehicles using consortium blockchains. IEEE Trans. Ind. Inf. **13**(6), 3154–3164 (2017)
10. Liu, C., Chai, K.K., Lau, E.T., Chen, Y.: Blockchain based energy trading model for electric vehicle charging schemes. In: Chong, P.H.J., Seet, B.-C., Chai, M., Rehman, S.U. (eds.) SmartGIFT 2018. LNICST, vol. 245, pp. 64–72. Springer, Cham (2018). https://doi.org/10.1007/978-3-319-94965-9_7
11. Chaudhary, R., Jindal, A., Aujla, G.S., et al.: BEST: blockchain-based secure energy trading in SDN-enabled intelligent transportation system. Comput. Secur. **85**, 288–299 (2019)
12. Aggarwal, S., Chaudhary, R., Aujla, G.S., et al.: Energychain: enabling energy trading for smart homes using blockchains in smart grid ecosystem. In: Proceedings of the 1st ACM MobiHoc Workshop on Networking and Cybersecurity for Smart Cities, pp. 1–6 (2018)
13. Jindal, A., Aujla, G.S., Kumar, N.: SURVIVOR: a blockchain based edge-as-a-service framework for secure energy trading in SDN-enabled vehicle-to-grid environment. Comput. Netw. **153**, 36–48 (2019)

A Data Trading Scheme
Based on Payment Channel Network
for Internet of Things

Dunfeng Li[1], Yong Feng[1(✉)], Yao Xiao[1], Mingjing Tang[2], and Xiaodong Fu[1]

[1] Yunnan Key Laboratory of Computer Technology Applications,
Kunming University of Science and Technology, Kunming 650500, Yunnan, China
fybraver@163.com
[2] Yunnan Normal University, Kunming 650500, Yunnan, China

Abstract. In recent years, the Internet of Things has developed rapidly. With the popularity of 5G, the Internet of Things is about to enter every corner of our lives. With the popularization of IoT devices, a large amount of data will be generated, which includes all aspects of people's lives. Therefore, data has become one of the important commodities. This paper proposes a solution for Internet of Things data transactions through the "payment channel network" (PCN) technology based on blockchain. The use of PCN technology based on blockchain not only guarantees the security of data, conforms to the characteristics of IoT data decentralization, but also ensures the transaction rate, and solves the problem of long delay and slow transaction rate in traditional blockchain technology. In this article, we constructed a PCN-based transaction model, and compared the transaction delay based on blockchain and the transaction delay based on PCN through experiments.

Keywords: Internet of Things · Data trading · Blockchain · Payment channel network

1 Introduction

With the rapid development of 5G technology, in the near future we will witness the rapid spread of the Internet of Things to all aspects of our lives. The popularization of the Internet of Things is inseparable from the IoT devices all over life, which constantly produce a variety of data. Different IoT devices share these data to make your life more convenient. For example, smart home can automatically arrange your home scene in advance according to your travel data, and smart electricity meter can automatically allocate power according to your living habits. The above behaviors involve data exchange between IoT devices. In fact, data exchange between IoT devices needs to be carried out continuously. Therefore, we must establish the IoT data transaction market to supervise and manage these data transactions.

The traditional electronic transaction system has been quite mature, but the traditional e-commerce platform involve third parties. Moreover, IoT data has distinct personal characteristics, and each person's data reflects their personal privacy and characteristics, so how to protect the security of data is also an urgent problem to be solved. Obviously, blockchain technology is very consistent with the characteristics of IoT data transactions. It is also decentralized and ensures the security and privacy of data. But blockchain technology also has certain problems, that is, the transaction rate is too slow. Blockchain technology can only achieve 7 transactions per second [1], Ethereum can conduct 15 transactions per second, and visa can conduct 45000 transactions per second [1].

In order to solve this problem, paper uses the "payment channel network" (PCN) technology based on blockchain, which establishes a blockchain separated from the main chain of the blockchain, and completes the transaction at least association with the blockchain. Specifically, users use the deposited funds to establish peer-to-peer payment channels,and each transaction is actually readjusting the distribution of funds on the chain to transfer value [2]. All transactions during the establishment of payment channel will be recorded and published in the public blockchain when the payment channel expires. All operations involving blockchain only include the establishment, closure of payment channels and rare events requiring arbitration in case of disputes under non-cooperative behaviors. It can be predicted that the distributed network composed of these payment channels, that is, payment channel networks (PCNs), can enable most transactions to be conducted off-chain, which can greatly reduce the cost of payment, reducing the payment delay, and increase the class expansion of the payment system [1]. We will design a PCN-based smart contract to make the transaction process reasonable and have the following characteristics:

- **Flexibility.** Each IoT device can independently conduct IoT data transactions according to the smart contract, which is itself the seller and buyer of data. It can also trade with ordinary users according to the smart contract. All transactions are based on PCN to guarantee the security and privacy.
- **Efficient.** The transaction can be based on low trust, and without the participation of third parties, people greatly reduce the time spent on the exchange, improve the trading speed, reduce the transaction delay.
- **Low-cost.** The IoT devices use decentralized PCN trading mode, which eliminates the participation of third parties. In addition, the correlation between transaction and blockchain is low, and the resources of blockchain are less occupied. Devices can only save smart contracts to their own storage modules without storing the entire blockchain.

This paper is organized as follows: Sect. 2 introduces the current research progress of related work, and explains the necessity and enthusiasm of the research in this paper; Sect. 3 analyzes the IoT data transaction model in detail, describes the detailed process of data transaction, and introduces how to use PCN technology to ensure the security and privacy of the transaction in the case of low trust; Sect. 4 introduces the design and code implementation of smart contract; Sect. 5 will present the experiment and analyze the results; Sect. 6 will make a summary and outlook.

2   Related Work

With the application of big-data in various aspects, huge data from different sources have become an economic commodity [3]. Although the research on economics of data products is still in its infancy, many researchers have proposed effective methods that can be used to solve the transaction mechanism and data evaluation, and some data transactions platforms based on the third party have been established. According to the identities of different participants, Cao et al. [4] proposed an iterative data transaction mode, and coordinated the transactions through social optimal way, without access to personal information. Niu et al. [5] guarantee the privacy and authenticity of data through homomorphic encryption and digital identity signature. However, most of the IOT devices have very limited computing resources, but there are a lot of transaction requests, so their scheme is not suitable for IOT data transaction.

At present, many researchers have combined the blockchain technology with the Internet of Things, so that the IoT technology can be put into practice as soon as possible. Kang et al. [6] studied the application of blockchain technology in the energy trading of the industrial Internet of Things, proposed a safe energy trading system using the alliance blockchain technology, and priced through the Steinberg game, so as to ensure the safety and efficiency of the system. Lu et al. [7] studied the application of blockchain in the Internet of Vehicles, and implemented an anonymous authentication scheme with asymmetric encryption based on blockchain, which solves the problems of expansion and authentication efficiency in anonymous authentications. Liu et al. [3] put forward a blockchain-based IoT data transaction model, which uses edge computing and cloud servers to verify blockchain storage and smart contracts, and uses a Steinberg game model for pricing. But these studies are directly coupled with the blockchain main chain, and the research focuses on the pricing strategy in the market. With development of off-chain technology, there are lightning network, PCN and other off chain transaction technologies. The transactions details of PCN technology are not stored on the distributed Ledger as records, but only used as documents in case of dispute [8]. The off-chain technology solves the problem that blockchain transaction time is too long and the number of transactions per second is too low, so it can solve the problem of large transaction request in the IoT data transactions, and does not need to store the blockchain main chain directly, which also conforms to the characteristics of limited computing and storage resources of most IoT devices. This paper should be the first solution that combines PCN technology and smart contracts for IoT data transactions.

3   PCN-based IoT Data Transaction Model

In this section, we will provide a framework for the PCN-based IoT data transaction model, which ensures the efficiency and privacy of IoT data transaction.

Figure 1 shows the overall structure and general entities of the Internet of things data trading market.

3.1 System Structure Overview

The IoT data transaction model in Fig. 1 include intelligent robots, smart cars, large servers, monitoring cameras, etc. Some devices have sufficient storage resources and computing resource, such as smart cars, etc. There are also quite a lot of devices that do not have sufficient storage or computing capabilities, such as surveillance cameras, etc. However, in PCN, they only need to store their own account information and smart contracts for PCN transactions, and the calculation is only the encryption algorithm for account funds transfer after establishing payment channels.

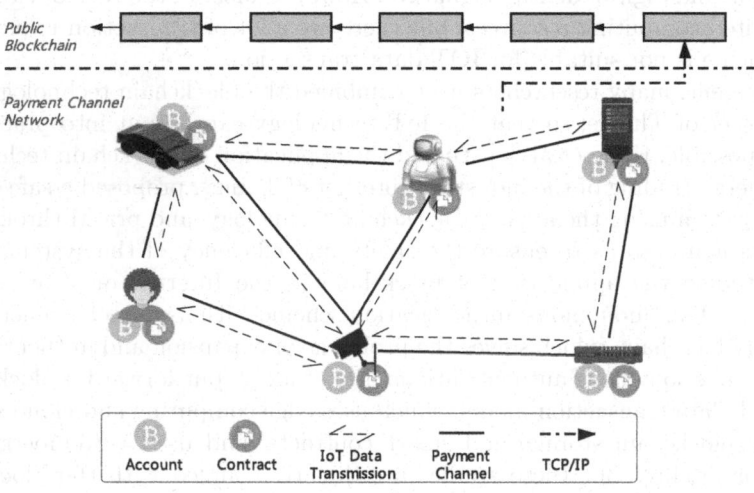

Fig. 1. System architecture of IoT trading market based on PCN.

Obviously, in our model, we have solved the problem that some IoT devices can't store blockchain and can't completely decentralize. In this model, transactions process shown as follows: First, two IoT devices establish peer-to-peer(P2P) payment channels in PCN, one for the data purchaser and one for the data owner. Payment channel will pass through other devices in PCN, and each passing device will charge fees agreed in advance to compensate for the cost of establishing the payment channel. If any participant violates the smart contract, the smart contracts will make corresponding punishment. If the transaction is completed, the payment channel will be closed and the transaction information will be sent to the blockchain, which will record the PCN transaction between the two blocks. If a party disputes the transactions, it can request the corresponding blockchain data for dispute determination. In our process, under normal circumstances, communication with the blockchain occurs only when the payment channel is established and closed, which greatly improves the transaction rate. In addition, smart contracts are used to restrict the behavior of participants, that is, decentralized peer-to-peer transactions are realized, and privacy security are guaranteed. As PCN is a kind of off-chain technology, this paper will mainly conduct research and discussion based on PCN technology, while PCN and blockchain communicate through TCP/IP, the specific details are not covered in this paper.

3.2   Payment Process of PCN

As shown in Fig. 2, a distributed PCN model can be regarded as a directed weighted graph G = (V, E). V represents all nodes in the graph, and each node has established a payment channel with at least one peer node. E represents all connections established in the network. A link denotes either a unidirectional channel from one user (the transferor) to another (the transferee), or one direction of a bi-directional channel between two users [2].

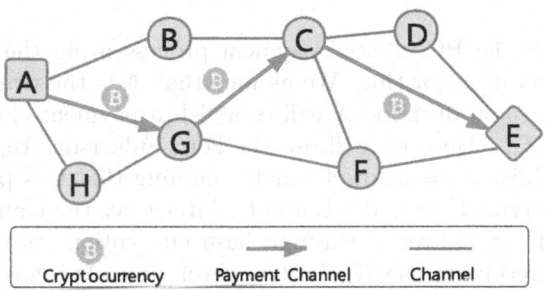

Fig. 2. A payment channel from A to D in PCN.

Each node $v_i \in V$ represents a user, each user has an encrypted currency account, and at least one payment channel connected with other nodes. Each side $e = (v_i, v_j) \in E$ represents a payment channel, v_i is the transferor and v_j is the transferee. Each payment channel has several attributes: First of all, each channel's own channel capacity c_e represents the total amount deposited by both parties in the channel account; At the same time, each edge $e \in E$ has the current balance b_e . If the channel is an one direction channel, c_e represents the maximum amount that the transferor can send before the channel is closed, and b_e represents the remaining amount that the transferor can send. If the channel is a bi-directional channel, then they are parallel. The c_e in the two channels is the same, which is the sum of the balance of both sides, that is, $b_{(U,V)} + b_{(V,U)} = c_{(U,V)} = c_{(V,U)}$. Obviously $b_e \le c_e$ has always been established in payment channels. In order to simplify the process, we assume that the balance is always positive. If the balance of a payment channel is 0, it cannot connect other nodes as the transferor, but it can still become the transferee. Only when it obtains new deposits or is recharged by the transferor, the node will restore the normal link.

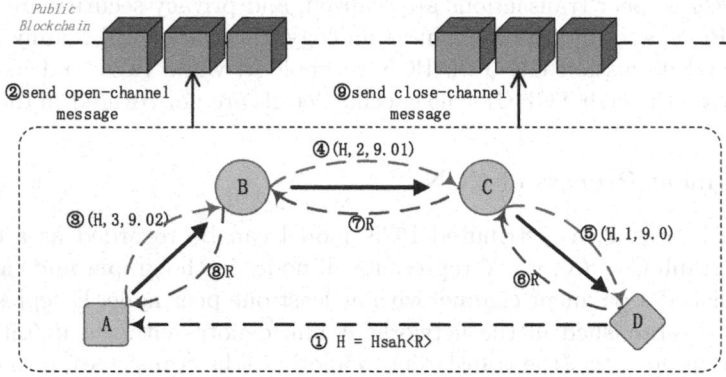

Fig. 3. A payment channel based on HTLC algorithm.

Figure 3 shows the PCN based payment process using the HTLC (hashed time lock contract) [9] algorithm. We assume that A is the transferor and D is the transferee. First of all, node A will establish a payment channel connected with node D in PCN. Here we will use the Ford-Fulkerson [10] maximum flow algorithm to establish a payment channel, assuming that this payment channel passes through intermediate nodes B and C. After that, the transferee generates a random value R, generates H through hash encryption, and sends H to the transferor; After receiving the H, the transferor uploads information of establishing the payment chain to the blockchain, and then the transferor begins to pay for the cryptocurrency. H is included in the smart contract, only when the transferor and intermediate node receive the random value R returned by the transferee, the transferor and intermediate node can really have the right to use it. In addition, each transaction is restricted by an HTLC tolerance, such that if the transferor does not receive R within the HTLC tolerance, the transferred fund will be refunded to the transferor. If HTLC lock time unit is δ, the maximum time for a payment chain transaction is $(n-1)\delta$, and n is the total number of nodes in the payment channel. For example, HTLC (H, 2, 9.01) from B to C in Fig. 3, only when B receives R sent by C within 2δ, C has the right to use the fund. The HTLC mechanism is used to ensure that the user can get payment from his predecessor after the successor got the payment. It needs to be clear that HTLC lock-in time is not the time required for payment channel transactions, but the worst-case transaction time. If users comply with the contract and respond quickly, the whole process only needs a very short time. HTLC also includes the transaction fees charged by the intermediate nodes for transferring the sender payment. The fees are significantly lower than blockchain transaction fees and largely due to the time-value of locking up funds in the channel, as well as paying for the chance of channels close on the blockchain [11]. After the payment is completed, PCN will send information to the public chain to confirm that the transaction has been completed, and blockchain will record the new account balance in PCN, at this time, the funds involved in the transaction can be used by users.

4   Smart Contract Design

In this section, we will describe the details of HTLC protocol implemented in this paper. We will use three core algorithms to explain how the contract enables all parties involved in the transaction to reach a consensus and complete the transaction.

The stage of transaction initialization will be described in the algorithm OpenChannel (Algorithm 1). The algorithm is based on the data returned after sending the HTTP request. We define it as $Message_{recive}$. The information is encrypted by the public key $pk_{\_a}$ of the payment node, which contains the result H of the random number R after hash encryption, the locking time t_l of the transaction completion, the transactions amount P and it cost $b_{\_c}$, as well as the attributes and data of the receiving node. The data structure of the node is shown in Table 1. As the main content of this paper is to clarify that the payment method based on PCN is superior to the traditional blockchain payment, so the existing technology is used in the communication between nodes and the establishment of routing. In this paper, the extended-routing protocol based on AODV [12] (Ad hoc On-demand Distance Vector Routing) is adopted, which is abbreviated as AODV-Ext protocol, through which the payment channel route $ListwlletAddress$ is obtained. The algorithm is implemented as follows:

This algorithm only runs when the sending node is initialized, and is used to create a payment channel and send a payment request, sendNode represents the sending node, reciveNode represents the receiving node, and the node data structure is shown in Table 1.

Table 1. Data structure of each node in payment network

Key	Description	Value
Name	Node's names	String
walletAddress	Address of HTLC	WalletAddress
ipAddress	Address of IP	IpAddress
Balance	Node account balances	Float
knownPeers	The wallet address of peer node	List<WalletAddress>
Channels	The channel have established	List<WalletAddress>
lockedFunding	Locked node account balance	Float

In the code, aBound represents the minimum amount of transactions allowed in the payment channel, and bBound represents the maximum amount of transactions allowed in the payment channel. Only when the balance of sending node is greater than the sum of the minimum amount and half of the transaction cost and the balance of receiver is greater than the sum of the maximum amount and half of the transaction cost, can the channel be established. If the sending node and the receiving node has been established the payment channel, the data will be obtained directly. If the payment channel is not established, the payment channel data will be obtained through AODV-Ext routing protocol. After obtaining the payment channel data, the sending node encrypts H, the amount of funds transferred, the transfer fee of the intermediate node, the unit lock time, and the payment channel routing data through the next node's public key encryption and sends it to the next node. The returned payment channel data will be submitted to the blockchain as evidence of establishing a payment channel and starting payment's activities.

After receiving the message sent by the former node, the intermediate node and the receiving node need to return the random number R within the locking time, then the transaction can be completed, otherwise the transaction fails. In the transaction data forwarding stage, the main algorithm is Transaction, and the algorithm code is as follows.

Algorithm 1. Transaction($thisNode, Transaction_{recive}$)

---

input: $Transaction_{recive} = Sig\_pk\_n < H, P, count - 1, fee, T\_l, routerList >$
  if $thisNode.walletAddress == routerList[-1]$ **then**
    $Response \leftarrow Sig\_pk\_p < R >$
    Send $< Response >$ to preNode
  else
    $H \leftarrow transaction.H$
    $count \leftarrow transaction.count$
    $P \leftarrow transaction.P - transaction.fee$
    $transaction \leftarrow Sig\_pk\_n < H, P, count - 1, fee, T\_l, routerList >$
    Send $< transaction >$ to nextNode
  end if
  $lockTime \leftarrow transaction.T\_l * count$
  if $getResponse == R\ in\ lockTime\ \&\&\ H == Hash(R)$ **then**
    $Response \leftarrow Sig\_pk\_p < R >$
    Send $< Response >$ to preNode
  end if

When the receiver receives the transaction request sent by the previous node, it first determines whether the receiver is the receiving node. If it is the receiving node, it does not need to continue to send the transaction request. P is the due fund of the receiving node. After the receiving node confirms that the transfer amount is correct, it sends R to the previous node. If the current node is an intermediate node, update the transaction request and send it to the next node. The specific update content is shown in the algorithm pseudo code. At the same time, the intermediate node starts to listen for the return value from the next node. If the return value is not received within the locking time, the transaction fails. If the return value R is received and hash (R) = H, send R to the previous node. Repeat this process until R returns to the payment node.

The payment node will start to monitor the return value after opening the payment channel. The logic is the same as above. When the payment node receives the correct return value R, it runs the CloseChannel algorithm. The algorithm is implemented as follows.

Algorithm 2. CloseChannel($thisNode, Response, routerList$)

---

input: $Response = Sig_{-pk_{-a}} < R >$
  if $H! = Hash(Response.R)$ **then**
    return paying failed
  end if
  if $H == Hash(Response.R)$ **then**
    $thisNode.funding \leftarrow thisNode.funding - P$
    $reciveNode.funding \leftarrow reciveNode.funding + P - B_{-c}$
    $midNode.funding \leftarrow midNode.funding + fee$
    $result \leftarrow Sig_{-pk_{-a}} Sig_{-pk_{-b}} < routerList >$
    Send $< result >$ to blockChain
  end if
  remove($routerList$)

Both CloseChannel and OpenChannel run in the sending node. When the sending node receives the correct R, it means that the payment transaction is successfully completed. At this time, the sending node allocates the funds to be transferred to the accounts participating in the transaction. The data involved in the allocation process is generated in OpenChannel. Then the sending node encrypts the updated payment channel data with its own public key and the receiving node's public key, then sends it to the blockchain, and finally removes the payment channel.

The above algorithms clearly show the advantages of this protocol: The first is security and privacy. Asymmetric encryption is used during transmission, so the security of transaction is guaranteed, and no transaction's information can be obtained by nodes and IoT devices that are not involved in the transaction; The second is flexibility. It can be deployed in various IoT devices, and it is very convenient to add and delete nodes in the network, which has no great impact on the whole networks; The third is efficiency. Payment transaction through this contract do not involve the operation of blockchain in transaction process. The blockchain is only used as a ledger to record the start and result of the transaction. When there is a dispute in the transaction, it is used as a judgment standard. Moreover, a node can participate in transactions of multiple payment channels at the same time, this is very characteristic of IoT transaction.

5   Algorithm Performance Evaluation

In order to verify the performance of our contract, we use Kotlin to build a PCN payment simulation platform based on Web. In this platform, we can set various parameters involved in the system transaction to simulate the transactions, so as to get the performance of our algorithm under different conditions, and make a comparison with the transaction rate of blockchain. Randomly generated nodes are connected according to the roles of nodes, and the whole network is distributed randomly. We set different account amounts and transaction limits for different roles of nodes, and set different transaction cost strategies and agent strategies to test the transaction speed and transaction success rate under different network sizes and network composition conditions.

5.1   Experimental Result

First of all, we use the blockchain simulation trading platform built by stoykov [13], etc. According to the comparison experiment of their paper settings, we can get the comparison of the transactions per second (tps) as shown in Fig. 4.

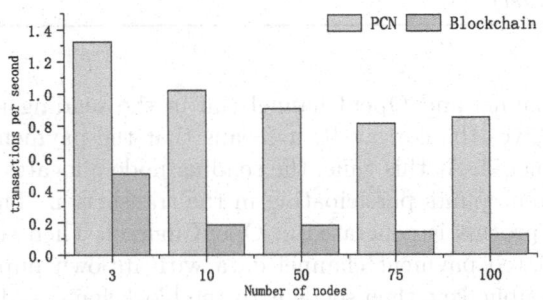

Fig. 4. This figure shows the number of single transactions that can be completed per second when using PCN transactions.

Obviously, the transaction rate of PCN is much higher than that of ordinary blockchain. It can be proved that the IoT data transaction system based on PCN is much more suitable than that based on blockchain. Next, we will test the trading success rate and trading rate of data trading system based on PCN under different circumstances, and test its stability and universality.

We set the node role as 10% routing node, 90% user node and 50 transactions. Using different routing protocols for simulation, the simulation results are shown in Fig. 5.

It can be found from the experimental results that the transaction success rate of AODV-Ext routing protocol is significantly higher than that of other protocols when the network scale is large, and the time required for each transaction is the least. Therefore, the AODV-Ext algorithm is the best choice under

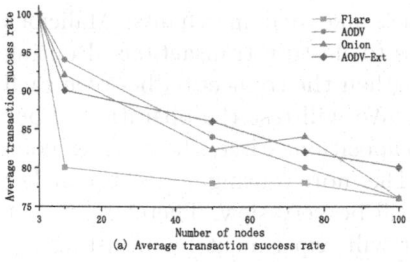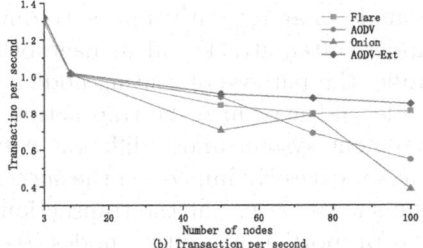

Fig. 5. The figure shows the comparison of transaction success rate and transaction speed of each transaction under different network size when 50 transactions are conducted with different routing algorithms.

the above conditions, and the transaction success rate and transaction rate under large-scale network conditions are better than other common routing algorithms. So in the next experiment, we will use AODV-Ext as the default routing algorithm.

During the simulation, there is no artificial designated transaction node connection, so a proxy system is designed in the simulator. The proxy system will generate payment channels according to different proxy policies. We keep the composition of the network unchanged, and the ratio of users to routers is still 9:1, using AODV-Ext routing algorithm, the simulation results using different proxy policies are shown in Fig. 6.

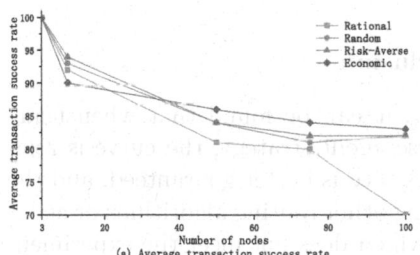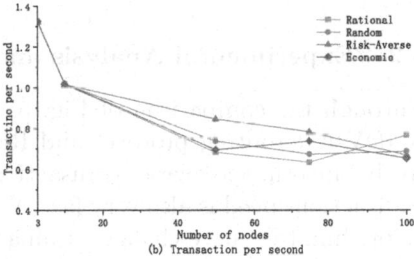

Fig. 6. It can be found that the gap above different proxy strategies is not very large. It can be seen that in this model, PCN algorithm and routing algorithm are the key factors affecting the success rate and transaction speed.

Analysis of Fig. 6 shows that when Risk-Averse strategy are adopted, the transaction per second are higher, while the difference between them in transaction success rate is very small, so we decided to use Risk-Averse agent strategy for experimental simulation.

According to the above simulation results, the next experiment will default to these two algorithms. Due to the diversity of IoT devices, we divide them into several types: Ordinary consumption node, which represents the users who conduct a large number of transactions in the payment network; Merchant node, a node that regularly opens trading channels like real merchants; Malicious nodes, often attack and damage other nodes to destroy transactions; Routing node, the purpose of routing node is to strengthen the connection between each node and maximize the transaction revenue. We will test the operation of our payment system under different network composition. First, the routing node has an excessive impact on the success rate. The more routing nodes, the higher the success rate, but the transaction speed will be very slow. Therefore, we set the proportion of routing nodes as 10%. We will experiment by adjusting the proportion of ordinary nodes and merchant nodes, as shown in Fig. 7.

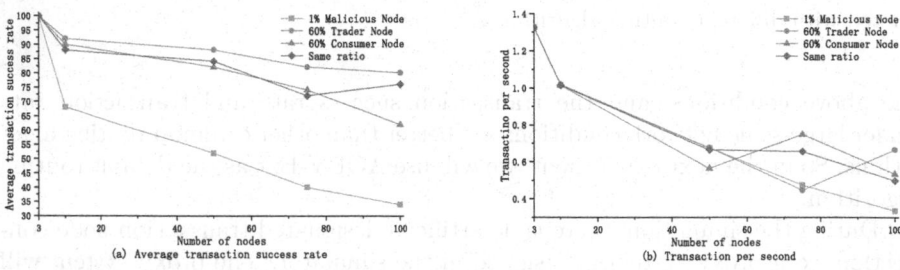

Fig. 7. In the case of fixed route proportion, the comparison of transaction success rate and transaction time between merchant nodes and common nodes is simulated when the ratio is 2:1, 1:2 and 1:1, and malicious nodes are added when the ratio is 2:1.

5.2 Experimental Analysis and Conclusion

Through the comparison of Fig. 5, 6 and 7, it can be found that when using AODV-Ext routing protocol and Risk-Averse agent strategy, the curve is relatively smooth, the overall transaction success rate is better guaranteed, and the transaction speed is also very fast. When using other routing algorithms or agent algorithm, the curve changes dramatically, which does not meet the experimental requirements. So when we use the above routing protocol and proxy strategy, the simulation can reflect the actual transaction state, but the success rate of the transaction is lower than the real success rate. This is due to the limitations of the simulator itself. Most of the transaction failures are due to the problem of the proxy algorithm. It fails when selecting the node to establish the payment channel, not during the transaction process. In the actual transactions, the agent strategy is not needed to select the transaction node, but the node spontaneously makes the transaction request, so the success rate of the transaction will rise significantly. The biggest difference between the commercial node and the ordinary node is that the commercial node limits the number of routing connections, so it can divide the large network into the small networks centered on the commercial node, which makes the routing structure more explicit. On the contrary, ordinary nodes do not limit the number of routing connections,

Table 2. Average number of links established under different network composition

Network composition	Numbers of node	Numbers of links
60%TraderNode	50	96
	100	199
60%NormalNode	50	110
	100	246
Same Ratio	50	113
	100	241

which leads to the complexity of routing, but reduces the transaction success rate and transaction speed. Table 2 can well prove this point of view.

In general, the above comparative experiments prove that PCN technology can be used in IoT data transactions. Compared with the data transaction system based on blockchain, the IoT data transaction system we proposed has higher transaction success rate, faster transaction speed, better privacy protection, lower hardware requirements. It can solve some of the key problem of IoT data transactions.

6   Conclusion

In this paper, we propose an IoT data transaction solution based on payment channel network, which solves the security, flexibility and efficiency problems of IoT transaction. A payment system based on PCN has been established, which not only ensures the transaction success rate but also greatly reduces the time required for the transaction, so that it can be well used in the IoT data transaction. Hannon, Christopher [14] and others also proposed to use payment channel for communication between IoT devices, they did not use HTLC technology but introduced third parties outside the transaction to supervise and mainly used blockchain transactions. Although it also reduced resource demand, but it was not suitable for large-scale IoT data transactions. Zhang Yu [15] and others proposed to apply the blockchain technology to the IoT data transaction, but it did not involve PCN technology, and more proposed a business model, pointed out a possibility. On the basis of the above two, this paper has conducted a more in-depth study, combining PCN technology with IoT data transactions, which proves its feasibility and advantages.

The solution proposed in this paper focuses on the establishment of payment system and the selection of payment technology. It does not take too much account of the data pricing and transaction costs in the IoT transactions and other commercial and economic problems. In the future research, we combine excellent business models and pricing strategies to improve the efficiency of the entire system, reduce payment costs, and reach a stage where it can be put into the market and practical.

Acknowledgments. This work is supported by the National Natural Science Foundation of China under Grants no. 61662042, 61262081, and 61462056; the Yunnan Provincial Key Project of Applied Basic Research Plan under Grants no. 2014FA028.

References

1. Poon, J., Dryja, T.: The Bitcoin Lightning Network: Scalable OffChain Instant Payments, Whitepaper (2016)
2. Yu, R., Xue, G., Kilari, V.T., et al.: CoinExpress: a fast payment routing mechanism in blockchain-based payment channel networks. In: 2018 27th International Conference on Computer Communication and Networks (ICCCN), pp. 1–9. IEEE (2018)
3. Liu, K., et al.: Optimal pricing mechanism for data market in blockchain-enhanced Internet of Things. IEEE Internet Things J. **6**(6), 9748–9761 (2019)
4. Cao, X., Chen, Y., Liu, K.J.R.: Data trading with multiple owners, collectors, and users: an iterative auction mechanism. IEEE Trans. Signal Inf. Process. Netw. **3**(2), 268–281 (2017)
5. Niu, C., Zheng, Z., Wu, F., Gao, X., Chen, G.: Achieving data truthfulness and privacy preservation in data markets. IEEE Trans. Knowl. Data Eng. **31**(1), 105–119 (2019)
6. Li, Z., Kang, J., Yu, R., Ye, D., Deng, Q., Zhang, Y.: Consortium blockchain for secure energy trading in industrial internet of things. IEEE Trans. Ind. Inf. **14**(8), 3690–3700 (2017)
7. Lu, Z., Wang, Q., Qu, G., Liu, Z.: Bars: a blockchain-based anonymous reputation system for trust management in vanets. In: 2018 17th IEEE International Conference On Trust, Security And Privacy In Computing And Communications/12th IEEE International Conference On Big Data Science And Engineering (TrustCom/BigDataSE), pp. 98–103. IEEE, August 2018
8. Yu, G., Nie, T., Li, X., Zhang, Y., Shen, D., Bao, Y.: Distributed data management technology in blockchain system-challenges and prospects. Chin. J. Comput. 1–27 (2019)
9. Poon, J., Dryja, T.: The Bitcoin Lightning Network: Scalable Off-chain Instant Payments (2016)
10. Ford, L.R., Fulkerson, D.R.: Maximal flow through a network. Classic papers in combinatorics, pp. 243–248. Birkhäuser Boston (2009)
11. Zhang, Y., Yang, D., Xue, G.: Cheapay: an optimal algorithm for fee minimization in blockchain-based payment channel networks. In: ICC 2019–2019 IEEE International Conference on Communications (ICC). IEEE (2019)
12. Perkins, C., Belding-Royer, E., Das, S.: RFC3561: Ad Hoc On-demand Distance Vector (AODV) Routing (2003)
13. Stoykov, L., Zhang, K., Jacobsen, H.-A.: Vibes: fast blockchain simulations for large-scale peer-to-peer networks. In: Proceedings of the 18th ACM/IFIP/USENIX Middleware Conference: Posters and Demos (2017)
14. Christopher, H., Jin, D.: Bitcoin payment-channels for resource limited IoT devices. In: Proceedings of the International Conference on Omni-Layer Intelligent Systems (2019)
15. Zhang, Yu., Wen, J.: The IoT electric business model: using blockchain technology for the internet of things. Peer-to-Peer Netw. Appl. **10**(4), 983–994 (2017)

Blockchain Based Trust Management in Vehicular Networks

Han Liu$^{(\boxtimes)}$ ⓘ, Dezhi Han, and Dun Li ⓘ

College of Information Engineering, Shanghai Maritime University, Shanghai, China
liuhanshmtu@163.com

Abstract. The development of Vehicular Networks (VANETs) is facing great challenges. In the open environment of VANETs, the fake information sent by malicious vehicles not only affect the fairness of information interaction, but also threaten the driving safety of normal vehicles seriously. Therefore, the study of trust evaluation and management in VANETs has become hot topics in recent years. This paper proposes a trust management model of VANETs based on blockchain. In this model, a Hidden Markov Model (HMM) based vehicle trust evaluation method is proposed, which can improve the accuracy for the detection of malicious behavior. Besides, we propose a trust management method based on alliance chain, which can greatly improve the efficiency of trust updating and querying on the premise of security. The results of comparative experiments show that the model is feasible and effective in the aspects of trust evaluation and trust management.

Keywords: Blockchain · VANETs · Trust management · Trust evaluation · HMM

1 Introduction

With the development of wireless communication technology and the progress of IoT, vehicles establish many types of VANETs by DSRC [1]. It provides three kinds of services for vehicles: driving safety, traffic efficiency and information entertainment [2], which greatly improves the driving experience of users and becomes an important part of smart city. Under the limitation of computing and energy, vehicles cannot support mass data storage and sharing [3]. Therefore, the VANETs move some computing tasks to the roadside unit (RSU) by using edge computing. RSU plays an important role in dealing with massive vehicle data, it can provide application services for vehicles, share the calculation work of vehicles and help vehicles communicate with each other efficiently [4].

However, some vehicles in VANETs compete with each other for lanes, passengers, traffic light resources, etc. Some dishonest vehicles in the network may seek personal benefits by tracking information of other vehicles and broadcasting fake information. Any third party may initiate dishonesty due to the openness of VANETs, In addition, RSUs are semi-credible, as they are usually distributed

© Springer Nature Singapore Pte Ltd. 2020
Z. Zheng et al. (Eds.): BlockSys 2020, CCIS 1267, pp. 333–346, 2020.
https://doi.org/10.1007/978-981-15-9213-3_26

around the roadside, the lack of reliable security measures makes it easy for attackers to hijack them. Therefore, how to effectively evaluate and manage the trust between vehicle and RSU are two important problems need to be solved.

Blockchain [5] is a public distributed ledger proposed by bitcoin in 2008. It guarantees data privacy through asymmetric encryption, and uses consensus algorithms such as PoW to maintain data consistency. These remarkable features of blockchain make it possible to build an ideal trust model in VANETs [6]. By deploying the blockchain to the RSU, the behavior of vehicle broadcasting and the activity record of RSU will be written into the non repudiation ledger in blockchain. Each entity in the network can verify and audit the transaction in ledger. In addition, even if the RSU is invaded and its data is tampered with, the integrity and correctness of the overall data will not be affected.

Based on the above considerations, this paper designs a trust (Management) model for VANETs based on alliance blockchain. The main contributions are as follows:

1) We analyze the practical problems, and put forward the system model, attack model and trust model of the VANETs, as theoretical supports.

2) We propose a vehicle trust evaluation algorithm based on HMM model, which is applied to the vehicle trust evaluation above RSU network. This algorithm has higher accuracy than the previous, and has a better application value in the current environment of excessive computing performance.

3) We propose a trust management method based on hyperledger fabric and applies smart contract to trust value querying and updating, which improves the overall efficiency of trust management, and ensures better security.

This paper is organized as follows. Section 2 introduces the related work. Section 3 states the problem definition and model design. HMM based vehicle trust evaluation method and alliance chain based trust management method are introduced in Sect. 4. The comparison and analysis of the experimental results are shown in Sect. 5 Section 6 is the conclusion of this paper.

2   Related Work

In the field of VANETs, trust management, limited vehicle privacy and malicious node detection have become three hot research topics. The continuous development of blockchain technology brings new ideas to distributed data storage and management, and becomes an effective method to solve the above problems.

Arkil Patel et al. [7] proposed a data transmission scheme called vehicle chain, which combined block chain with ECC to strengthen the security of the VANETs system without increasing the computing cost. According to Jian Kang et al. [3], as a vehicle edge computing server, the RSU cannot be fully trusted, and the attack or hijacking of the RSU will cause serious security and privacy challenges to the platform. Zhe Yang et al. [4] proposed a distributed vehicle network trust management system based on blockchain technology in which vehicles used the Bayesian reasoning model to verify the information received from adjacent vehicles and generate ratings, and then upload it to the RSU. Q. Feng et al. [8]

proposed an efficient and scalable blockchain assisted privacy protection authentication system (BPAS) based on the hyperledger fabric platform, which can provide automatic authentication in VANETs, protect the vehicle privacy, and allow the conditional tracking and dynamic revocation for misbehaving vehicles. Z. Lu et al. [9,10] proposed a blockchain-based anonymous reputation system (BARS) to establish the privacy protection model of VANETs. It used Merkle Patricia tree (MPT) to extend the blockchain structure, encrypted and stored the corresponding relationship between the certificate and the real identity in the tree, which can only be decrypted in case of dispute, thus conditional privacy is achieved. References [11,12] evaluated the impact of node mobility on the consensus algorithm. A consensus algorithm suitable for VANETs was proposed to solve the speed and efficiency problem for the pow or pos consensus algorithm on the public chain. References [13–15] focused on the application of blockchain in the mutual authentication mechanism between vehicle and RSU, maintaining the anonymity of vehicles and preventing RSU from being tampered with. Some scholars were inspired by the incentive mechanism in bitcoin and tried to issue "energy currency" and "information currency" in VANETs to encourage information exchange and energy sharing between vehicles and between vehicles and RSUs [16–18].

The above research provides an effective solution and reference for trust management in VANETs. However, there are still some deficiencies or defects in these studies. Firstly, most of these studies use probability and statistics as trust evaluation methods, which need to be improved in efficiency and accuracy. Secondly, most of these systems use public chain as the technology selection of blockchain. However, as we all know, the public chain has great defects in consensus efficiency and throughput performance.

3 Model Definition

In this section, we will define and analyze the trust related problems of the VANETs, and build models for these problems.

3.1 System Model

The system model designed in this paper mainly includes three parts, which are Vehicular Network Layer, Edge-Blockchain Layer, and CA Layer, as shown in Fig. 1.

Vehicular Network Layer. As the perception and application layer of the VANETs, vehicles play a dual role of producer and consumer. On the one hand, in the process of driving, vehicles continuously collect road conditions, traffic accidents, and other information, then broadcast them to the neighbor vehicles or RSUs. On the other hand, the vehicle receives information from other vehicles or RSUs and makes response actions.

Edge-Blockchain Layer. RSU relies on edge computing services and acts as a blockchain implementation layer. In this paper, alliance chain is proposed to be used as the selection of blockchain technology for the following reasons: Firstly, RSU belongs to different operators, so blockchain needs to support organization crossing. Secondly, RSUs are not open to the public. Only authorized RSUs can join the network. Finally, the efficiency of the alliance chain is much higher than public chain, which can meet the basic throughput needs of VANETs. In this layer, RSU verifies the messages broadcast by vehicles, evaluates the trust by analyzing the historical behavior of vehicles, and stores their trust values in the blockchain. As the peer node in the blockchain, RSU can store complete data copies, as redundant backups of other RSUs. Even if a part of the RSUs are hijacked or down, the consistency of data cannot be changed.

CA Layer. As a trusted organization, CA is mainly used to issue certificates and private keys for RSU and store public keys, providing authentication services for other entities. CA is strictly protected, ensuring strong service ability.

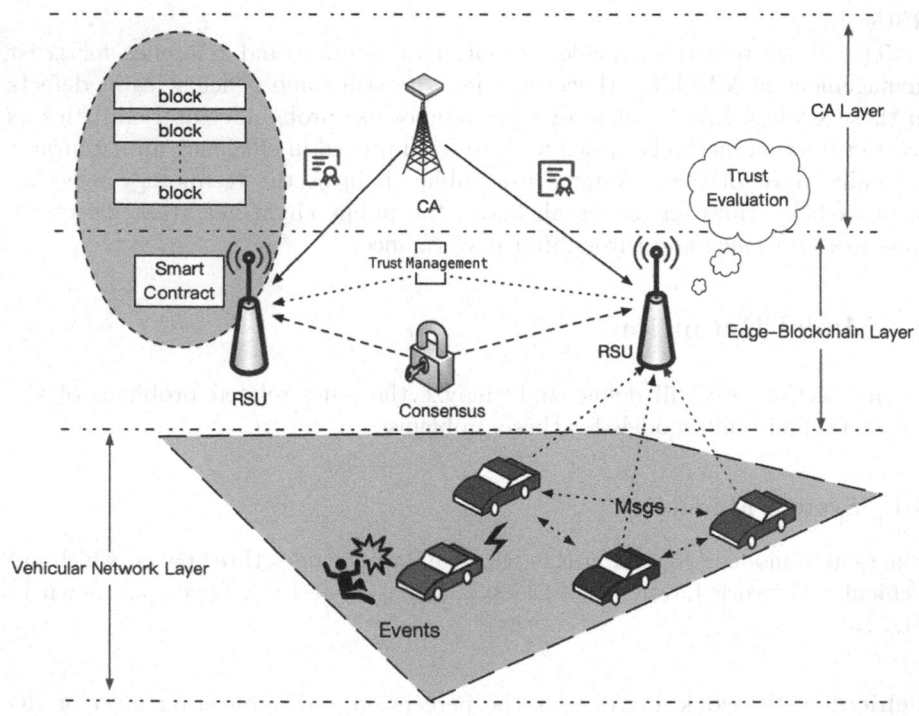

Fig. 1. System model

Based on the brief analysis of the first section, there is the possibility of malicious behavior in both vehicles and RSU in VANETs. Vehicles can send fake messages to neighbor nodes and RSUs to compete for resources, or attacked by hackers, than do that actively. The malicious behavior of RSU is usually due to illegal hijacking by hackers, which will lead to the disclosure of user privacy data and the tampering of vehicle information. The following is a specific analysis of malicious behaviors of vehicles and RSUs:

3.2 Malicious Behavior Model

Malicious Vehicle. The malicious behavior of vehicles is extremely harmful. Without supervision and punishment, once a few vehicles in the system gain the advantage of information or road resources through deception, other vehicles will follow this behavior. This paper attributes the malicious behavior of vehicles to two types of attacks.

a) message spoofing attack: For the purpose of self-interest, the attacker may deliberately broadcast fake information to occupy more traffic and information resources. For example, a malicious vehicle may deliberately broadcast a red light message to seize a lane when passing a green light intersection. In addition, attackers may broadcast harmful messages to disrupt traffic order and threaten the safety of other vehicles.

$$Vehicle \stackrel{broadcast}{\longrightarrow} \{MSG_{fake}|MSG_{danger}\} \tag{1}$$

b) reject cooperative attack: All the vehicles participating in the VANETs want to get more information but they tend to broadcast less information collected by themselves due to the consideration of fuel consumption, flow, battery and other costs. This kind of behavior will damage the fairness in VANETs.

$$Receive\{MSG_{outside}\} >> Provide\{MSG_{own}\} \tag{2}$$

Malicious RSU. RSU is located along the road and in a complex and change-able environment, which results in limited protection by network operators. Because of this unavoidable risk, RSU is considered to be semi-credible. Once the RSU is intruded, the attacker can tamper with and delete the privacy data stored in it. In this paper, the malicious behavior of RSU is classified into two types of attacks.

a) Denial of service attack: The hijacked RSU cannot provide normal services.

$$Rate(RSU_{Availability}) << 100\% \tag{3}$$

b) Data consistency attack: Attackers tamper with and delete the local data of RSUs, which leads to data inconsistency between different RSUs.

$$Data_{RSU1}\{...\} \neq Data_{RSU2}\{...\} \tag{4}$$

3.3 Assumptions

Assumption 1: Because the attacker's ability is not enough to control the whole RSU cluster (less than 50 %), the possibility of large-scale intrusion of RSU is very low. In addition, due to the regular security inspection of network operators, hijacked RSUs can be found and recovered in time. Based on above facts, it is assumed that an attacker can only invade a small number of RSUs in a short time.

Assumption 2: The existing PKI encryption system (such as RSA) cannot be brutally cracked.

Assumption 3: The computing power of RSU is excessive, and the memory and storage can be expanded as needed, which is enough to meet the diverse computing requirements.

Assumption 4: CA is trusted and well protected. It can store the certificate and public key of RSU completely.

The significance of the above four assumptions are: Assumption 1 is a prerequisite for the successful implementation of blockchain on RSU (the solution of Byzantine problem). Assumption 2 is the theoretical guarantee of RSU authentication and blockchain data security. Assumption 3 eliminates the limitation of RSU on computing performance and storage space, and provides physical support for the model and method proposed in this paper. Assumption 4 is a necessary condition for building alliance blockchain in RSU network.

4 Proposed Algorithms

This section describes the theory and algorithm in detail, which is divided into two parts: trust evaluation and trust storage.

4.1 HMM Based Trust Evaluation Algorithm

Hidden Markov Model. (HMM) is an extension of Markov model. For Markov model, the given observation sequence can determine the state transition sequence. However, in practice, given an observation sequence, it is often impossible to directly determine the sequence of state transition (for example, take out small balls of different colors from each jar, but it is impossible to know the sequence of jars), in which the process of state transition is hidden. This kind of stochastic process is called hidden Markov process, as shown in Fig. 2.

The hidden Markov model λ can be expressed as:

$$\lambda = (Q, V, A, B, \pi), \mathcal{O} \tag{5}$$

$Q = \{q_1, q_2, q_3, ..., q_N\}$ represents distinct states of the Markov process, N is number of states in the model.

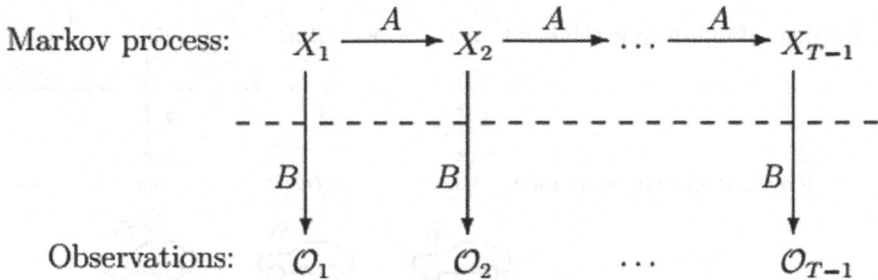

Markov process:

Observations:

Fig. 2. Hidden Markov model

$V = \{v_1, v_2, v_3, ..., v_M\}$ represents set of possible observations, M is number of observation symbols.

$A = [a_{ij}]$ represents state transition probabilities, which size is $N \times N$.

$a_{ij} = P(q_j \text{ at } t+1 | q_i \text{ at } t), 1 \leq i, j \leq N$ represents the probability of transition from time $t + 1$ to state Q when time t is in state Q.

$B = [b_j(k)]$ represents observation probability matrix, which size is $N \times M$.

$b_j(k) = P(v_k | j), 1 \leq k \leq M, 1 \leq j \leq N$ indicates the probability of outputting the symbol v_k in the state j.

π represents initial state distribution.

$\mathcal{O} = \{\mathcal{O}_1, \mathcal{O}_2, ..., \mathcal{O}_T\}$ represents observation sequence, and T is its length.

Hidden Markov model is mainly used to solve three basic problems.

Problem 1, probability calculation problem. Given the model $\lambda = (A, B, \pi)$ and a sequence of observations $\mathcal{O}$, find $P\{\mathcal{O}|\lambda\}$. In that case, we calculate the probability of observation sequence according to the given model.

Problem 2, prediction problems. Given the model $\lambda = (A, B, \pi)$ and a sequence of observations $\mathcal{O}$, find Q.

Problem 3, learning(training) problems. Given a sequence of observations $\mathcal{O}$ and the dimensions N and M, find the model $\lambda = (A, B, \pi)$ that maximizes the probability of $\mathcal{O}$.

Question of Trust Evaluation. Next, we will consider the issue of vehicle trust assessment in VANETs, as show in Fig. 3.

Vehicle V_i continuously collect traffic accidents, road conditions and other information in the process of driving, and broadcast it to the neighbor vehicle or RSU. We use the category of events as observation set $\mathcal{O}_i$. All event categories form status set V. The authenticity of information is the hidden value. Here, we use a set of discrete values $[-k, +k]$ as Q. The history of messages sent by the vehicle can be used as $\mathcal{O}$. According to the practical experience, the behavior of vehicles is regular, honest, and positive in most cases. The description of Trust-HMM is shown in Table 1.

Based on the above analysis, we can establish a HMM based vehicle trust evaluation method.

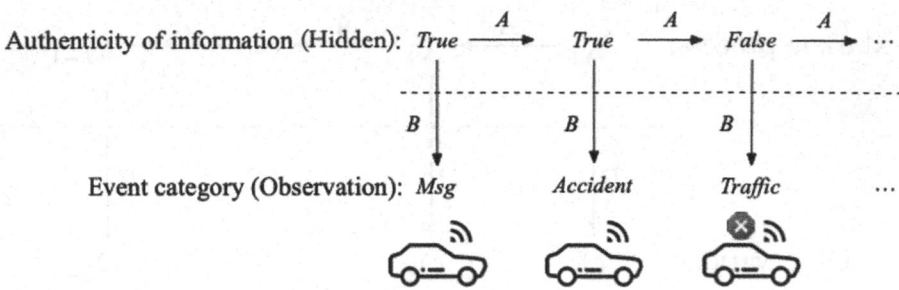

Fig. 3. HMM in trust assessment of VAENTs.

Table 1. Trust-HMM.

Q	Authenticity of message
V	Event category
$\mathcal{O}$	Message history
$\mathcal{A}$	Need training
$\mathcal{B}$	Need training
π	Need training

Step 1: RSU sets the trust value to the initial value of 100 for the vehicle.

$$VT_i \leftarrow 100 \qquad (6)$$

Step 2: the RSU collects the history of messages sent by each vehicle. According to the problem 3, the RSU trains the vehicle's trust assessment HMM model through the collected history.

$$MSG \xrightarrow{RSU} History \xrightarrow{train} HMM \qquad (7)$$

Step 3: when the model tends to be stable, the hidden value of the new message is calculated according to problem 2, then iterate the model use this message.

$$q \leftarrow HMM(MSG_{new}) \qquad (8)$$

Step 4: update the trust value based on the hidden value.

$$VT_i \leftarrow VT_i + q \qquad (9)$$

The trust threshold coefficient is $k, 0 < k < 1$:

$$isTrust = \begin{cases} 1, VT \geq k \cdot 100 \\ 0, VT < k \cdot 100 \end{cases} \qquad (10)$$

When the RSU finds that $isTrust = 0$ (standards for untrustworthy), the vehicle will be warned or punished.

4.2   Hyperledger Based Trust Management

Hyperledger fabric is an open source project sponsored by Linux foundation, which aims to provide a modular platform for blockchain solutions.

It overcomes the shortcomings of public chain, such as low throughput, low consensus efficiency and easy branching.

RSU can store privacy information, and keep a complete copy of other RSU by blockchain. When some RSUs down, other RSUs can provide services as backup immediately. In addition, the RSUs in the system endorse each other. Even if there are hijacked RSUs tampering with local data, the data security of the whole network cannot be affected. Other RSUs can also verify the authenticity of the message through the hash traceability feature of the blockchain. The system can generate multiple pseudonyms for the vehicle and store their corresponding relationship with the real ID into the blockchain to protect the privacy of the vehicle.

In this paper, all RSUs are regarded as peer nodes to build a blockchain network to jointly maintain blockchain data. RSUs of different operators can be divided into different channels (channel is a special concept in hyperledger, in the alliance chain, each channel maintains an independent ledger, and channels are isolated from each other).

$$Channel_n \leftarrow \{RSU_1, RSU_2, ..., RSUm\} \qquad (11)$$

There are three types of data to be stored in the blockchain system. The first is the relationship between vehicle's real ID and pseudonym.

$$Data_1 = (\{pse_1, pse_2, ..., pse_k\}, ID) \qquad (12)$$

The second is the history messages of vehicle.

$$Data_2 = (ID, \{VH_1, VH_2, ..., VH_n\}) \qquad (13)$$

The third is the vehicle's trust value.

$$Data_3 = (ID, VT) \qquad (14)$$

We use CouchDB (an open-source K-V database) as the blockchain database. The ledger in blockchain only records the key of the data, and the data is stored in CouchDB.

In addition, we implements two kinds of APIs with the smart contracts. One is the query function, which can query the vehicle trust value according to the vehicle pseudonym.

$$query(ID) \rightarrow VT \qquad (15)$$

The implementation of the smart contract is shown in Algorithm 1.

The other is the update function, which can modify the vehicle trust value according to the vehicle ID.

$$update(ID) \leftarrow VT_{new} \qquad (16)$$

The implementation of the smart contract is shown in Algorithm 2.

Algorithm 1 Query Vehicle's Trust Value.

Input: *ID*
Output: *VT or Error*
1: @implement SmartContractInterface
2: **while** Invoke() **do**
3:     CStub = ChaincodeStub
4:     State, err = CStub.GetState(ID)
5:     **if** err != null **then**
6:         **return** Error(err.Text)
7:     **else**
8:         VT = GetVTBy(State)
9:         **return** VT
10:     **end if**
11: **end while**

Algorithm 2 Update Vehicle's Trust Value.

Input: ID, VT_{new}
Output: *OK or Error*
1: @implement SmartContractInterface
2: **while** Invoke() **do**
3:     CStub = ChaincodeStub
4:     State, err = CStub.GetState(ID)
5:     **if** State == null **then**
6:         **return** Error('Not Found')
7:     **end if**
8:     err = CStub.PutState(ID,VT)
9:     **if** err != null **then**
10:         **return** Error(err.Text)
11:     **else**
12:         **return** OK
13:     **end if**
14: **end while**

---

5   Experiment and Analysis

The experimental environments of this paper are shown in Table 2.

Table 2. Hardware and software environment of the experiments.

CPU	i7 7500u 2.9GHz	Memory	8G
Hard disk	256G	OS	Mac OS 10.14
Docker	v19.03	Docker-compose	v1.24
Node	v12	Golang	v1.12
Hyperledger fabric	v1.4.3		

We designed two groups of comparative experiments to verify the effectiveness and performance of the trust management model proposed in this paper. The first group is a comparative experiment of HMM based trust assessment methods for VANETs. The second group is a comparative experiment of trust management model based on alliance chain.

5.1 Comparative Experiments of Trust Evaluation Methods

In some existing studies [4,19], the credibility of event is calculated by using Bayesian inference. These models use the distance between the vehicle and the receiver as the evaluation standard of message authenticity: the farther the distance, the lower the message credibility, and the closer the distance, the higher the message credibility. But we believe that this kind of evaluation method has a strong subjectivity, because vehicles with similar distance and vehicles with a long distance have equally possibilities in malicious behavior. In order to verify the advantages of the proposed method, we compared it with the distance based Bayesian inference method. In the experiment, these two kinds of methods are trained on 12 groups of data, and the correct rate is obtained with the test data included. We counted their accuracy on 12 sets of data. The comparison results are shown in Fig. 4.

It can be seen from the figure that the method proposed in this paper performs well and stably on different data sets. However, the method distance based Bayesian inference method is unstable in different data sets, which shows that this kind of model is not universal. This result just proves our previous judgment. The method we proposed can effectively reflect different situations and has a better practical value.

5.2 Comparative Experiments of Trust Management Model

Most of the existing blockchain based trust management systems in VANETs choose public chain as the underlying technology. We believe that the throughput of the public chain cannot meet the basic requirements of the vehicle network. The throughput of blockchain is directly related to the consensus mechanism. To prove the QoS advantages of our proposed model, we designed an experiment with the public chain represented by PoW consensus algorithm. The experiment simulates the time consumption of two kinds of blockchain systems to reach consensus on data consistency in different number of RSUs([5, 100]). The experimental results are shown in Fig. 5.

It can be seen from the figure that with the increase of the number of RSUs, the time consumed by the public chain to reach a consensus increasing geometrically on the premise of ensuring security, while the method we proposed tend to take a less time. It is proved that the trust management model based on alliance chain proposed in this paper is more efficient than the general public chain, which could meet the needs for corresponding speed in VANETs.

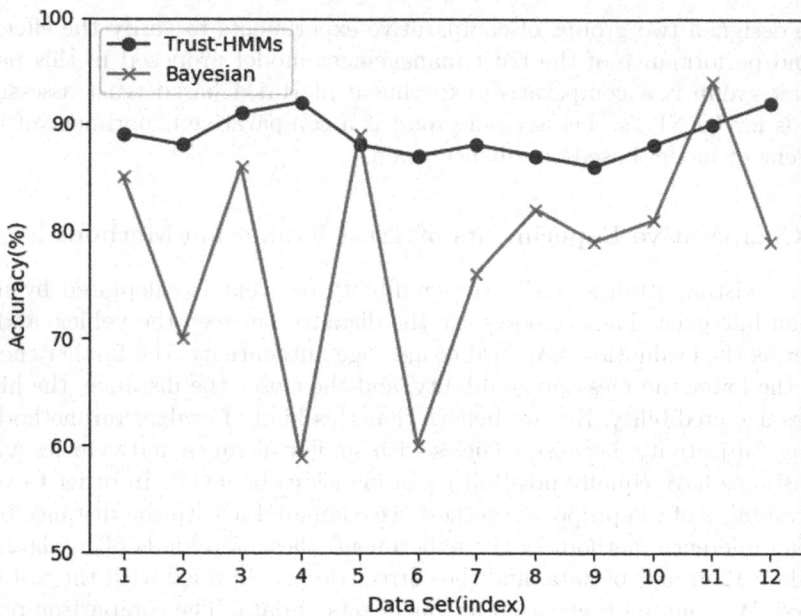

Fig. 4. Comparison of the accuracy between proposed method and distance based Bayesian inference method.

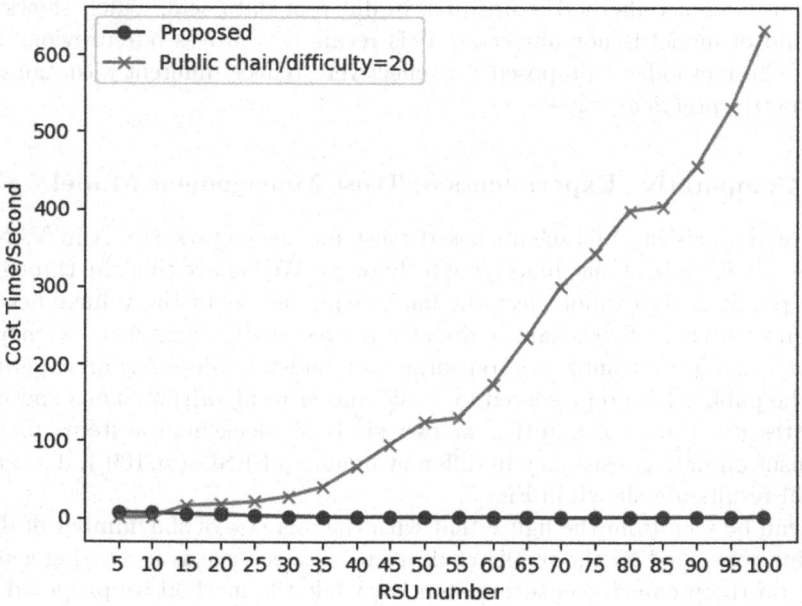

Fig. 5. Comparison of the consensus costs between proposed and public chain.

6 Conclusion

In this paper, we propose a trust management model based on blockchain. This model includes a HMM based vehicle trust evaluation method. According to the characteristics of collecting and sharing information in the process of vehicle driving, we regard the category of events as the observation value, and make all the event categories into the state value, so as to build a trust HMM model. It improves the detection accuracy of malicious behavior on the premise of the current computing performance surplus, and has good application significance. In addition, we propose a trust management model based on alliance chain to manage RSUs with different ownership in groups. rely on the good throughput of hyperledger, which can greatly improve the speed of trust query and update while ensuring security. In a word, this paper has a strong innovation on the trust management in VANETs, which has a certain application value.

Acknowledgments. This work was supported in part by the National Natural Science Foundation of China under Grant 61672338 and Grant 61873160.

References

1. Chen, S., Hu, J., Shi, Y., Peng, Y., Fang, J., Zhao, R., Zhao, L.: Vehicle-to-everything (v2x) services supported by LTE-based systems and 5G. IEEE Commun. Stand. Mag. **1**(2), 70–76 (2017)
2. Sun, S., Hu, J., Peng, Y., Pan, X., Zhao, L., Fang, J.: Support for vehicle-to-everything services based on LTE. IEEE Wirel. Commun. **23**(3), 4–8 (2016)
3. Kang, J., et al.: Blockchain for secure and efficient data sharing in vehicular edge computing and networks. IEEE Internet Things J. **6**(3), 4660–4670 (2019)
4. Yang, Z., Yang, K., Lei, L., Zheng, K., Leung, V.C.M.: Blockchain-based decentralized trust management in vehicular networks. IEEE Internet Things J. **6**(2), 1495–1505 (2019)
5. Satoshi, N.: Bitcoin–Open Source P2P Money. Accessed Nov 2019
6. Atzori, M.: Blockchain-Based Architectures for the Internet of Things: A Survey. Social Science Electronic Publishing (2017)
7. Patel, A., Shah, N., Limbasiya, T., Das, D.: Vehiclechain: blockchain-based vehicular data transmission scheme for smart city. In: 2019 IEEE International Conference on Systems, Man and Cybernetics (SMC), pp. 661–667. IEEE (2019)
8. Feng, Q., He, D., Zeadally, S., Liang, K.: BPAS: blockchain-assisted privacy-preserving authentication system for vehicular ad hoc networks. IEEE Trans. Ind. Inf. **16**(6), 4146–4155 (2020)
9. Lu, Z., Wang, Q., Qu, G., Liu, Z.: Bars: a blockchain-based anonymous reputation system for trust management in vanets. In: 2018 17th IEEE International Conference On Trust, Security And Privacy In Computing And Communications/12th IEEE International Conference On Big Data Science And Engineering (TrustCom/BigDataSE), pp. 98–103 (2018)
10. Lu, Z., Wang, Q., Qu, G., Zhang, H., Liu, Z.: A blockchain-based privacy-preserving authentication scheme for VANETs. IEEE Trans. Very Large Scale Integr. (VLSI) Syst. **27**(12), 2792–2801 (2019)

11. Kim, S.: Impacts of mobility on performance of blockchain in VANET. IEEE Access **7**, 68646–68655 (2019)
12. Yang, Y., Chou, L., Tseng, C., Tseng, F., Liu, C.: Blockchain-based traffic event validation and trust verification for VANETs. IEEE Access **7**, 30868–30877 (2019)
13. Sharma, R., Chakraborty, S.: B2VDM: blockchain based vehicular data management. In: 2018 International Conference on Advances in Computing, Communications and Informatics (ICACCI), pp. 2337–2343 (2018)
14. Zheng, D., Jing, C., Guo, R., Gao, S., Wang, L.: A traceable blockchain-based access authentication system with privacy preservation in VANETs. IEEE Access **7**, 117716–117726 (2019)
15. Kaur, K., Garg, S., Kaddoum, G., Gagnon, F., Ahmed, S.H.: Blockchain-based lightweight authentication mechanism for vehicular fog infrastructure. In: 2019 IEEE International Conference on Communications Workshops (ICC Workshops), pp. 1–6 (2019)
16. Liu, H., Yan, Z., Tao, Y.: Blockchain-enabled security in electric vehicles cloud and edge computing. IEEE Netw. **32**(3), 78–83 (2018)
17. Liu, H., Zhang, Y., Yang, T.: Blockchain-enabled security in electric vehicles cloud and edge computing. IEEE Netw. **32**(3), 78–83 (2018)
18. Wang, Y., Su, Z., Zhang, N.: BSIS: blockchain-based secure incentive scheme for energy delivery in vehicular energy network. IEEE Trans. Ind. Inf. **15**(6), 3620–3631 (2019)
19. Wang, T., Zhang, G., Liu, A., Bhuiyan, M.Z.A., Jin, Q.: A secure IoT service architecture with an efficient balance dynamics based on cloud and edge computing. IEEE Internet Things J. **6**(3), 4831–4843 (2019)

CMBIoV: Consensus Mechanism for Blockchain on Internet of Vehicles

Qiuyue Han[1], Yang Yang[1], Zhiyuan Ma[1], Jiangfeng Li[1], Yang Shi[1]([✉]), Junjie Zhang[2], and Sheng Yang[2]

[1] School of Software Engineering, Tongji University, Shanghai 201804, China
{qiuyuehan,1552712,1731542,lijf,shiyang}@tongji.edu.cn
[2] BAF (Shanghai) Technology Co., LTD., Shanghai 200092, China
{jj.zhang,s.yang}@baftj.com

Abstract. Both blockchain and Internet of Vehicles (IoV) are emerging technologies that attract interest from academia and industry. Deploying blockchain peers on vehicles enables corporation, coordination, trust, security, and privacy in the IoV. However, the peers are deployed on resource-constrained on-board computing devices, and have high mobility, which causes significant challenges on the blockchain. The blockchain's consensus mechanism must be efficient and energy-saving. In this paper, a proof-of-stake consensus mechanism is presented that uses tickets and sorters to address this issue. The proposed consensus mechanism prevents users from controlling the blockchain by hoarding a large number of coins, and reduces the cost of message communication during the election of the leader and verifiers. The performance of this mechanism could be further improved if the IoV was built over 5G communication channels.

Keywords: Blockchain · Consensus mechanism · Proof-of-stake · Internet of Vehicles · Mobile computing

1 Introduction

Internet of Vehicles (IoV) uses the new generation of communication technology [1–3] to make vehicles connect with other vehicles and various service providers, including automotive makers, automotive component manufacturers, authorized vehicle dealerships (4S chain stores), automotive service shops, usage-based insurance providers, gas stations, charging stations/poles, telecom operators, parking slots, and automotive spare parts distributors, dealerships, and agents. This ecosystem involves a large amount of data, users, and endpoints, such as on-board units and users' smartphones. Therefore, it is a challenge to support security, privacy, trust, corporation, and coordination in the IoV and the entire ecosystem.

As an example, adversaries can collect data from the IoV to predict user behavior or trace users' daily activities. Therefore, protecting the privacy of sensitive data in IoV [4–8] is a significant challenge. Because a blockchain is essentially a decentralized database of records [9], which can be used to protect the data owners' privacy, blockchain-based IoV can achieve both data collection and data protection efficiently.

© Springer Nature Singapore Pte Ltd. 2020
Z. Zheng et al. (Eds.): BlockSys 2020, CCIS 1267, pp. 347–352, 2020.
https://doi.org/10.1007/978-981-15-9213-3_27

Therefore, we aim to use a blockchain to address the issues of security, privacy, trust, corporation, and coordination in the IoV. Because of the limited equipment and energy supply in the IoV, proof-of-stake (PoS) is used as the consensus mechanism for the blockchain. To prevent users from hoarding many coins in PoS, we design tickets with certain trading rules. It is worth noting that although there have been some schemes to introduce ticket mechanisms in a blockchain, such as [10, 11], the nature of these schemes is different from the scheme in this paper. Moreover, in PoS, during the election of the block leader and verifiers, the communication cost among peers is quite high; therefore, we set up a sorting committee in the consensus mechanism to provide users' ranks in terms of the stake, and consequently enhance the efficiency of achieving consensus. An overview of the IoV combined with a blockchain is illustrated in Fig. 1.

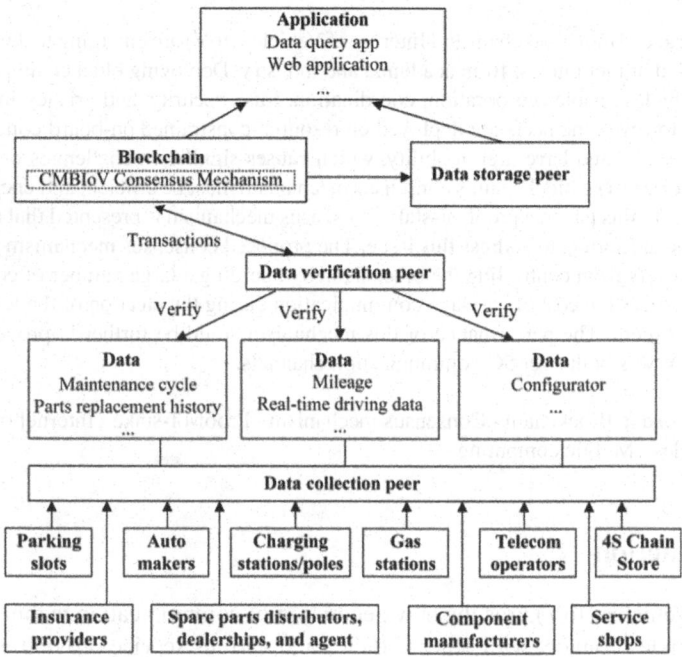

Fig. 1. Overview of the IoV combined with a blockchain

As shown in the figure, first, a data collection peer collects data from many places, such as maintenance factories, automotive equipment, and automobile dealers. Then, a data verification peer receives the data sent by the data collection peer and validates the data. Once the data is verified, the submission of the data is recorded in the blockchain. Additionally, as vehicles generate large amounts of data each day, the system stores the hash value of the vehicle data packet in the blockchain and stores the original data in data storage peers. The information collected from the IoV is added to the blockchain platform to form a decentralized and distributed data sharing market. After being authorized by users, the data is applied to intelligent transportation, insurance, and other fields. We propose a consensus mechanism for blockchains on IoV (CMBIoV), in which we design tickets with certain trading rules, set up a sorting committee, and use some of the techniques in Algorand [12], such as cryptographic sortition.

The main contributions in this paper are the following: (1) We propose a new CMBIoV to address the issues of security, privacy, trust, corporation, and coordination in IoV. For the CMBIoV, we design tickets with certain trading rules, which can prevent a user from controlling the entire blockchain by hoarding too many coins. (2) In the CMBIoV, we set up a sorting committee to provide users' ranks in stake, which decreases the communication cost during the election of the block leader and verifiers. (3) We use a threshold signature scheme to ensure that the peers in the sorting committee reach a consensus.

2 Proposed Scheme

2.1 Scheme Overview

The proposed consensus mechanism CMBIoV is a PoS mechanism for blockchains over IoV. In CMBIoV, we design stake tickets with trading rules and set up a sorting committee. Members in the committee reach a consensus through the threshold signature scheme. An overview of the CMBIoV is shown in Fig. 2.

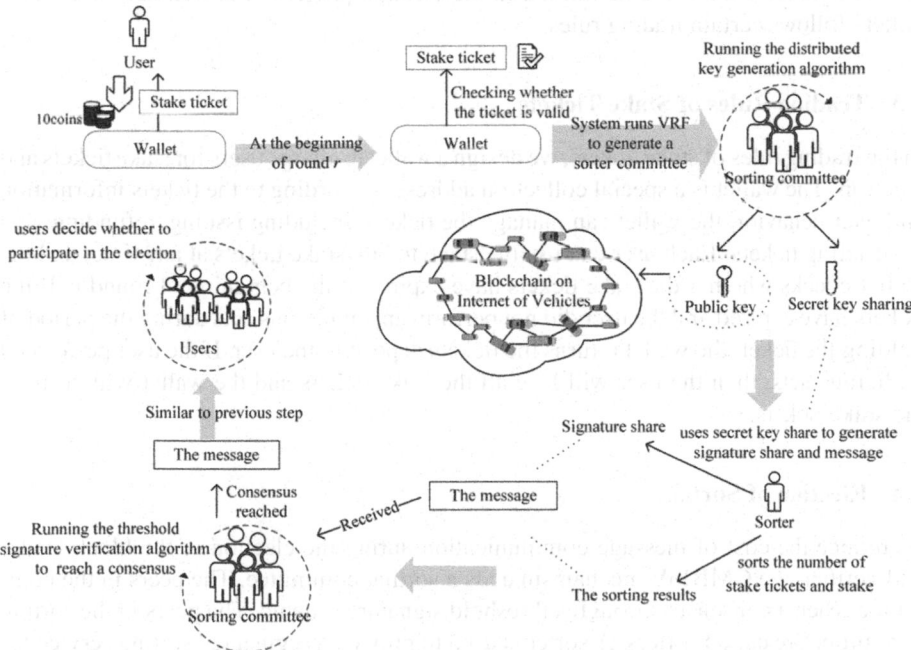

Fig. 2. Overview of the CMBIoV scheme

As shown in the figure, each user can use the stake to buy stake tickets from the wallet at any time, and each ticket is priced at 10 coins. At the beginning of round r, the wallet checks whether each ticket is valid. Then the system runs the cryptographic sortition algorithm based on the verifiable random function (VRF) to generate a sorting committee. The concept of VRF was first proposed by Micali et al. [13]. The VRF outputs a random value together with a proof value thereby proving that the random value is correct. After generating sorters, the distributed key generation algorithm is run by the sorters. For each sorter, this algorithm outputs the public key and a secret key sharing. Then each sorter sorts the number of stake tickets and stakes, and uses secret key sharing to generate the signature share and message. When the sorter receives messages from other sorters, the sorting committee reaches a consensus on the sorting results through the threshold signature verification algorithm. After obtaining the segmented sorting results provided by the sorting committee, according to the ranking of the stakes and the stake tickets, users in the blockchain network can decide whether to participate in the leader and verifier election.

2.2 Stake Tickets

To prevent users from hoarding many coins, and increase the possibility of being selected as a leader and verifier, CMBIoV uses stake tickets instead of stake, that is, the stake tickets held by users are time limited in the election process. The transaction of stake tickets follows certain trading rules.

2.3 Trading Rules of Stake Tickets

In the trading rules of stake tickets, we design a wallet to charge users for stake tickets and election. The wallet is a special collection address. According to the tickets information and user behavior, the wallet can manage the tickets, including issuing, refunding, and destructing tickets. Each user can use the stake to buy stake tickets at any time, and the wallet checks whether the stake tickets have expired at the beginning of round r. If the tickets have expired and the user did not perform any malicious acts during the period of holding the ticket, the wallet returns the tickets deposit to the user. If the user performed malicious acts, then the user will lose all the stake tickets and the wallet will destruct the stake tickets.

2.4 Election of Sorters

To reduce the cost of message communication during the election of the block leader and verifier, the CMBIoV mechanism adds a sorting committee. The peers in the committee reach a consensus through a threshold signature scheme. The peers in the sorting committee are called sorters. A sorter is used to provide a segmented sorting service for all peers in the system. Each peer is encouraged to compete for election. The sorting committee is changed every 10 rounds.

2.5 Segmented Sorting Algorithm for the Sorting Committee

The sorting committee calculates the sorted results of the stake and the stake tickets, and reaches a consensus on the sorting results through the threshold signature algorithm. The specific steps are as follows:

1. System generates sorters to form the sorting committee and the sorters run the distributed key generation algorithm to generate the public key and secret key sharing.
2. Sorting committee calculates the segmented sorting results.
3. Sorting committee reaches a consensus on the segmented sorting results.
4. Sorting committee broadcasts segmented sorting results.

2.6 Leader and Verifier Election

After obtaining the segmented sorting results provided by the sorting committee, according to the ranking of the stakes and the stake tickets, a user can decide whether to participate in the election. The election of round r generates the leader of round r and verifiers of round $r + 1$ simultaneously.

3 Discussion

In the above sections, we introduced a consensus mechanism CMBIoV. The CMBIoV mechanism has the following advantages: Using stake tickets instead of stake, that is, the tickets held by users, have timeliness in the election process, which can prevent users from hoarding a large amount of coins to increase the possibility of being selected as the leader and verifiers. Furthermore, we set up a sorting committee, which provides users with the segmented sorting results of the stakes and stake tickets, so that users can predict whether they can be elected as the leader and verifier in advance. Users with a high probability of winning the election can pay the service charge and submit an election request in advance. Users with a low probability of winning the election can choose not to submit an election request. Therefore, there will be fewer messages in the blockchain, which greatly reduces the network load. CMBIoV also has a limitation: because the verifiers for the current round have been elected in the previous round, some verifiers may be attacked since they were elected in the previous round, which may affect the reliability of the consensus. In the future, we plan to improve the proposed design to mitigate this threat.

4 Conclusion

To apply blockchain technology effectively and efficiently on IoV, we proposed a new consensus mechanism called CMBIoV. Because the peers are installed on resource-constrained embedded devices in vehicles or on the smartphones of drivers, the proposed consensus mechanism is PoS rather than PoW to mitigate energy consumption. The consensus mechanism sets up a sorting committee to provide users' ranks in stake. This decreases the communication cost incurred by requiring each peer to perform this task by itself, and thus enhances the efficiency of achieving consensus. Moreover, the consensus mechanism uses tickets with certain trading rules, which can prevent a user from controlling the entire blockchain by hoarding too many coins.

Acknowledgments. This research has been supported by the National Nature Science Foundation of China (Nos. 61772371 and 61702372), and BAF's research funding.

References

1. Gerla, M., Eun-Kyu, L., Pau, G., Uichin, L.: Internet of vehicles: from intelligent grid to autonomous cars and vehicular clouds. In: IEEE World Forum on Internet of Things (WF-IoT), pp. 241–246. IEEE (2014)
2. Yang, F., Wang, S., Li, J., et al.: An overview of Internet of Vehicles. China Commun. **11**(10), 1–15 (2014)
3. Alam, K.M., Saini, M., Saddik, A.El.: Toward social internet of vehicles: concept architecture and applications. IEEE Access **6**, 343–357 (2015)
4. Jiang, T., Fang, H., Wang, H.: Blockchain-based internet of vehicles: distributed network architecture and performance analysis. IEEE Internet Things J. **6**(3), 4640–4649 (2019)
5. Dorri, A., Steger, M., Kanhere, S.S., Jurdak, R.: BlockChain: a distributed solution to automotive security and privacy. IEEE Commun. Mag. **55**(12), 119–125 (2017)
6. Huang, X., Xu, C., Wang, P., Liu, H.: LNSC: a security model for electric vehicle and charging pile management based on blockchain ecosystem. IEEE Access **6**, 13565–13574 (2018)
7. Singh, M., Kim, S.: Branch based blockchain technology in intelligent vehicle. Comput. Netw. **145**, 219–231 (2018)
8. Kang, J., Xiong, Z., Niyato, D., et al.: Toward secure blockchain-enabled Internet of Vehicles: optimizing consensus management using reputation and contract theory. IEEE Trans. Veh. Technol. **68**(3), 2906–2920 (2019)
9. Crosby, M., Pattanayak, P., Verma, S., et al.: Blockchain technology: beyond bitcoin. Appl. Innov. **2**, 6–10 (2016)
10. Li, K., Li, H., Hou, H., et al: Proof of vote: a high-performance consensus protocol based on vote mechanism & consortium blockchain. In: Proceedings of IEEE 19th International Conference on High Performance Computing and Communications, IEEE 15th International Conference on Smart City, IEEE 3rd International Conference on Data Science and Systems (HPCC/SmartCity/DSS), pp. 466–473. IEEE (2017)
11. Wan, C., Tang, S., Zhang, Y., et al.: Goshawk: a novel efficient, robust and flexible blockchain protocol. Inf. Secur. Cryptol. **11449**, 49–69 (2019)
12. Gilad, Y., Hemo, R., Micali, S., et al: Algorand: scaling byzantine agreements for cryptocurrencies. In: Proceedings of the 26th Symposium on Operating Systems Principles, pp. 51–68. ACM (2017)
13. Micali, S., Rabin, M., Vadhan, S.: Verifiable random functions. In: 40th Annual Symposium on Foundations of Computer Science, pp. 120–130. IEEE (1999)

Blockchain and Mobile Edge Computing

Adaptive Edge Resource Allocation for Maximizing the Number of Tasks Completed on Time: A Deep Q-Learning Approach

Shanshan Wu[1]([✉]), Qibo Sun[1], Ao Zhou[1], Shangguang Wang[1], and Tao Lei[2]

[1] State Key Laboratory of Networking and Switching Technology,
Beijing University of Posts and Telecommunications, Beijing 100876, China
wshine3_533@163.com
[2] Autohome Inc., Beijing 100876, China
leitao8611@sina.com

Abstract. To relieve resource-limited mobile devices from computation-intensive tasks, reduce the transmission latency and mitigate the burden of the backhaul network for the centralized cloud-based network services, mobile edge computing (MEC) has been proposed to be a promising solution and draws increasing attention from both industry and academia. Traditional task offloading approaches focus on average-based metrics, and try to minimize the average service delay. The service delay of different tasks varies from each other, resulting in a low service reliability. To attack this challenge, this paper focuses on mobile users' computation offloading problem in wireless cellular networks for purpose of maximizing the number of tasks completed on time. Since the environment states, including available local resources, channel conditions and remaining computation resource of the edge cloud, will vary from time to time, we use the model-free reinforcement learning (RL) framework to formulate and tackle the computation offloading problem. The agent learns through interactions with the environment to decide executing task locally on the mobile device or offloading the task to the edge cloud via the wireless link for each mobile device user. Considering high-dimensional state spaces, we use deep Q-learning (DQN) which combines reinforcement learning method Q-learning and deep neural network (DNN) to obtain the optimal approach. Simulation results show that the effectiveness of the proposed approach in comparison with baseline approaches in terms of the total number of the tasks completed on time.

Keywords: Mobile edge computing · Computation offloading · Deep reinforcement learning · Deep Q-learning

1 Introduction

As the popularity of smart mobile devices in recent years, more and more applications, especially computation-intensive and latency-sensitive tasks such as face recognition, natural language processing, augmented or virtual reality (AR/VR), have been greatly affected by the limited on-device computation resources [1]. To tackle this problem, mobile devices choose to offload their tasks to the remote public cloud which are resource-rich (e.g., Amazon Elastic Compute Cloud (EC2) and Windows Azure Services Platform) at the beginning. But the transmission through the backhaul network may bring in intolerable latency [2,3].

Mobile edge computing [4] has been proposed to be a promising solution to relieve resource-limited mobile devices from computation-intensive tasks, reduce transmission latency and mitigate the burden of the backhaul network for the centralized cloud-based network services. Mobile edge computing enables the mobile user's device execute computation offloading by sending computation tasks to the MEC server through wireless cellular networks [5], which means the MEC server executes the computational task on behalf of the mobile device [6,7].

Thanks to the edge cloud, approaches aiming at improving the users' QoE (quality of experience) have been proposed these years and the overall energy consumption and time delay decrease afterwards. However, those approaches try to minimize the average service delay. When average-based metrics are employed to evaluate the offloading approaches, the service delay of different tasks may vary from each other. Considering that there are two tasks; the service delay of one task is high, and the task of the other task is very low. The average service delay is still low in this case. Therefore, those approaches may lead to a low service reliability and this paper will target at maximizing the total number of the tasks completed on time for higher service reliability.

Although the edge cloud can significantly augment computation capability of the mobile device users, it still remains challenging to achieve an optimal computation offloading approach for all mobile device users. One critical factor that greatly affects the performance of computation offloading approach is the wireless access [8]. If too many mobile device users decide to offload their computation tasks to the edge cloud via wireless link at the same time, severe interference to each other may arise, which causes low data rates for computation data transmission.

In this paper, we consider a general MEC system consisting of an MEC cloud, one base station and multiple mobile users as shown in Fig. 1, where each mobile user has tasks to complete on time and follows a binary computation offloading strategy. In particular, we aim to jointly optimize all the mobile users' offloading decisions at the same time. We propose a DQN based approach to maximize the number of tasks completed on time. Major contributions of this paper are as follows:

- We aim to maximize the number of tasks completed on time. Unlike other existing works about minimizing total overheads of all mobile users, including energy consumption and execution time, our proposed algorithm tries to enable tasks completed on time as possible as it can.
- The proposed approach can obtain a jointly optimized computation offloading strategy based on the observations from each mobile user and the outer

system. Compared with those approaches optimized by each mobile user' local observation from the environment to obtain agents making decisions for individual user independently of others, our approach can get more comprehensive information of current environment state and then make smarter decisions for all mobile users.

- To evaluate the performance of our approach, we conduct comprehensive simulation experiment. The experiment results show that our approach outperforms other approaches in terms of the number of tasks completed on time.

The remainder of this paper is organized as follows. We first present a review of related works about computation offloading optimization in literature in Sect. 2 and describe the system model and problem formulation in Sect. 3. We then propose the computation offloading approach based on DQN in Sect. 4. Numerical results are shown in Sect. 5. Finally, the paper is concluded in Sect. 6.

2   Related Work

There have been a number of works which discuss the computation offloading problem in mobile edge computing scenario. In [9–13], it is assumed that the computation resources of the edge cloud are rich enough to accommodate the offloaded tasks without delay, no matter how many tasks there are. In [14–16] finite remote resources are taken into account. [14] propose a framework to provide runtime support for the dynamic computation partitioning and execution of the application to optimize computation resources. [15] optimize the communication and computation resources by quasiconvex and convex optimization. [16] adopts heuristic local search to maximize the sum computation rate of all users by jointly optimizing the individual computing mode selection (local computing or offloading).

Inspired by the recent advantages of deep reinforcement learning (DRL) in handling Markov problems with large state spaces, some works [17–19] use DRL framework to optimize the computation offloading strategy. [17] adopts deep deterministic policy gradient (DDPG) to learn efficient computation offloading policies independently at each mobile user. [18] proposes a deep reinforcement learning-based online offloading framework to acquire an online algorithm that optimally adapts task offloading decisions and wireless resource allocations to the time-varying wireless channel conditions. [19] adopts DQN to minimize the total overheads in terms of computational time and energy consumption of all users in multi-user offloading scenarios.

The goals of the works mentioned above are mainly to minimize the overheads or maximize the computation rate between the local computing and offloading. However, this paper aims to enable tasks completed on time as possible as it can, which is quite important for the latency-sensitive tasks in financial filed.

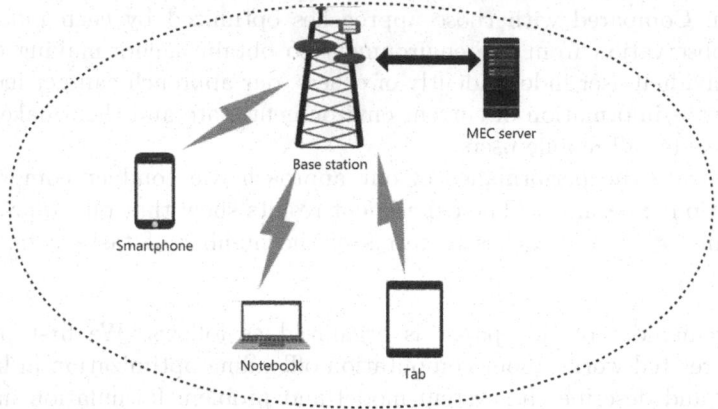

Fig. 1. Multi-user scenario in mobile edge computing.

3 Preliminary

3.1 System Model

As shown in Fig. 1, we consider a static multi-user MEC system, which consists of an MEC server, a base station b, and a set of mobile users $\mathcal{M} = \{1, 2, ..., M\}$. "Static" means that these users are fixed in their locations. A discrete-time model is adopted here where the operating period is slotted with equal-length t and it is assumed that for each user $m \in \mathcal{M}$, it has a computation-intensive and latency-sensitive task to be completed at each time slot t. Each mobile device can execute its task locally, but this may bring in overdue task due to its limited computation resources. Thus, mobile device may seek the help of the MEC server by offloading its task via the wireless link. However, it may reduce data rate if there are too many offloading tasks and the reason will be explained later.

3.2 Communication Model

The mobile device users are connected to the base station b via the wireless link. Let $a_{m,n} \in \{0, 1\}$ be the task offloading decision of the m-th mobile device user for its n-th task. Specifically, $a_{m,n} = 1$ denotes that the m-th user's n-th task is offloaded to the MEC server via base station b while $a_{m,n} = 0$ denotes that the task is computed locally on the mobile device. For these M mobile users and N tasks of each of them, there is an offloading decision sequence as $\mathcal{A} = \{a_{1,1}, a_{1,2}, ..., a_{m,n}\}$. We can get the uplink data transmission rate for computation offloading of mobile device user m as [20]

$$R_m(a_{m,n}) = a_{m,n} W \log_2 \left(1 + \frac{P_m H_{m,b}}{\sigma + \sum\limits_{i=1, i \neq m}^{M} \sum\limits_{j=1, a_{i,j}=1}^{N} P_i H_{i,b}} \right) \tag{1}$$

where W is the channel bandwidth, and P_m is the transmission of power user m which can be set by the user with a maximum transmission power constraint [21,22]. What's more, $H_{m,b}$ denotes the channel gain between the mobile device user m and the base station b, and σ is the additive white Gaussian noise.

From the communication model in (1), it can be seen that if there are too many mobile device users who choose to offload the computation tasks via the wireless link simultaneously, severe interference may arise, leading to low data rates.

3.3   Computation Model

We consider each mobile device user has one computation-intensive and latency-sensitive task at each time slot. Assuming that the total number of time slots is $T^{\max}$, then each mobile device user would have $T^{\max}$ tasks totally. For mobile user m, the computation task [19] arrives at time slot t is denoted by:

$$W_m^{(t)} \triangleq (D_m^{(t)}, C_m^{(t)}, T_m^{(t)\,\max}(t)) \tag{2}$$

where $D_m^{(t)}$ (in KB) denotes the input data size which includes program codes and input parameters. $C_m^{(t)}$ (in Megacycles) denotes the total number of the CPU cycles to complete the computation task $W_m^{(t)}$. $T_m^{(t)\,\max}(t)$ stands for the latest completion time for the computation task $W_m^{(t)}$ and it is as

$$T_m^{(t)\,\max}(t) = t + t_m^{\max} \tag{3}$$

where $t_m^{\max}$ represents for the maximum tolerable delay for completing task $W_m^{(t)}$. Next we will discuss the number of completed tasks for both local computation and MEC computation offloading cases.

Local Computing. Let $f_m^{(t)f}$ denote the free processor's computational speed (CPU cycles per second) of the mobile device user m at the time slot t. Especially, when there is only one task on the mobile device m, then $f_m^{(t)f} = f_m^l$ where f_m^l denotes the computational speed of the mobile device user m. The situation is allowed here that different mobile device may have different computational speed. When the local computation resource of mobile user m is free for the task $W_m^{(t)}$, namely $f_m^{(t)f} > 0$, then the computation execution time can be given as

$$T_m^{(t)l}(t) = t + \frac{C_m^{(t)}}{f_m^{(t)f}} \tag{4}$$

subject to

$$f_m^{(t)f} > 0$$

When $f_m^{(t)f} <= 0$, it means the mobile device m is busy with the past tasks and the task $W_m^{(t)}$ should queue up for its turn. Assuming that there is free local

---

Algorithm 1. Computation offloading approach based on DQN.

Input: the number of mobile users M, their location list L and tasks list J and computation speed list P, W and σ about the channel condition
Output: the weights θ^* of the target action-value function $\hat{Q}$

1: Initialize experience replay buffer B to capacity Z
2: Initialize action-value function Q with random weights θ
3: Initialize target action-value function $\hat{Q}$ with weights $\theta^- = \theta$
4: Initialize the task queue list K of all mobile users
5: **for** episode $= 1$, $E_{\text{train}}^{\max}$ **do**
6:     Initialize reward $r_0 = 0$
7:     **for** $t = 0$, $S_{\text{train}}^{\max}$ **do**
8:         Generate s_t from J, S, W, σ, K at index t
9:         With probability ϵ select a random action a_t
10:         Otherwise select $a_t = \arg\max_a Q(s_t, a; \theta)$
11:         Execute action a_t, receive an immediate reward r_t and observe the next state s_{t+1}
12:         Store transition $< s_t, a_t, r_t, s_{t+1} >$ in B
13:         Sample random minibatch of transitions $< s_j, a_j, r_j, s_{j+1} >$ from B
14:         Set
$$y_j = \begin{cases} r_j, & j = S_{\text{train}}^{\max} \\ r_j + \gamma \max_{a'} \hat{Q}(s_{t+1}, a'; \theta^-), & j < S_{\text{train}}^{\max} \end{cases}$$
15:         Perform a gradient decent on $(y_j - Q(s_t, a_t; \theta))^2$ with respect to the network parameters θ
16:         Every X steps rest $\hat{Q} = Q$
17:     **end for**
18: **end for**

---

computation resource for the task $W_m^{(t)}$ at time slot t' where $t' > t$, then the computation execution time of the task $W_m^{(t)}$ by local computing is then given as

$$T_m^{(t)l}(t') = t' + \frac{C_m^{(t)}}{f_m^{(t')f}} \tag{5}$$

subject to

$$f_m^{(t')f} > 0$$
$$t' > t$$

Cloud Computing. For the cloud computing approach, a mobile device user m will offload its computation task $W_m^{(t)}$ to the edge cloud and the edge cloud will execute the computation task on behalf of the mobile device user.

According to (1), we can compute the transmission time of mobile device user m for offloading the input data of size $D_m^{(t)}$ as

$$T_{m,off}^{(t)c}(a_{m,t}) = \frac{D_m^{(t)}}{R_m(a_{m,t})} \tag{6}$$

Let f_c be the computation speed of the edge cloud and n_c stand for the number of tasks which are computed by the edge cloud and not completed yet, then the computation speed assigned to user m by the cloud can be computed as

$$f_m^c(t, a_{m,t}) = a_{m,t} \frac{f_c}{n_c(t)} \tag{7}$$

$$n_c(t) = \sum_{m=1}^{M} \sum_{i=1}^{t} I(D_m(i) = 0, C_m(i) > 0) \tag{8}$$

After receiving the task data, the cloud will execute the computation task $W_m^{(t)}$. The execution time of the task $W_m^{(t)}$ of mobile device user m on the cloud can be then given as

$$T_{m,exe}^{(t)c}(a_{m,t}) = \frac{C_m^{(t)}}{f_m^{(t)c}(a_{m,t})} \tag{9}$$

The time overhead for the edge cloud to send the computation output back to the mobile device user would be neglected in this paper, similar to many works such as [23–27], since for many applications (e.g., face recognition), the size of the computation output is generally much smaller than the size of computation input consisting of program codes and input parameters. Therefore, the total time overhead for the offloading task $W_m^{(t)}$ of the mobile user m can be given as

$$T_m^{(t)c}(a_{m,t}) = T_{m,off}^{(t)c}(a_{m,t}) + T_{m,exe}^{(t)c}(a_{m,t}) \tag{10}$$

Assuming that the completion time for this task corresponding to its offloading decision $a_{m,t}$ is as

$$T_m^{(t)total} = (1 - a_{m,t}) T_m^{(t)l}(a_{m,t}) + a_{m,t} T_m^{(t)c}(a_{m,t}) \tag{11}$$

Let $G^{(t)}(a_{m,t})$ stand for the task arriving at time slot t of the mobile user m completed or not and it is as

$$G^{(t)}(a_{m,t}) = \begin{cases} 1, & T_m^{(t)total} \leqslant T_m^{(t)\,max}(t) \\ 0, & T_m^{(t)total} > T_m^{(t)\,max}(t) \end{cases} \tag{12}$$

We can model the optimization formulation of the problem as follows

$$\max_{a} \sum_{t=0}^{T} \sum_{m=1}^{M} G^{(t)}(t, a_{m,t}) \tag{13}$$

4   Task Offloading Based on DQN

In this section, we will develop a DRL based approach to maximize the number of tasks completed on time of all mobile device users. We model the computation

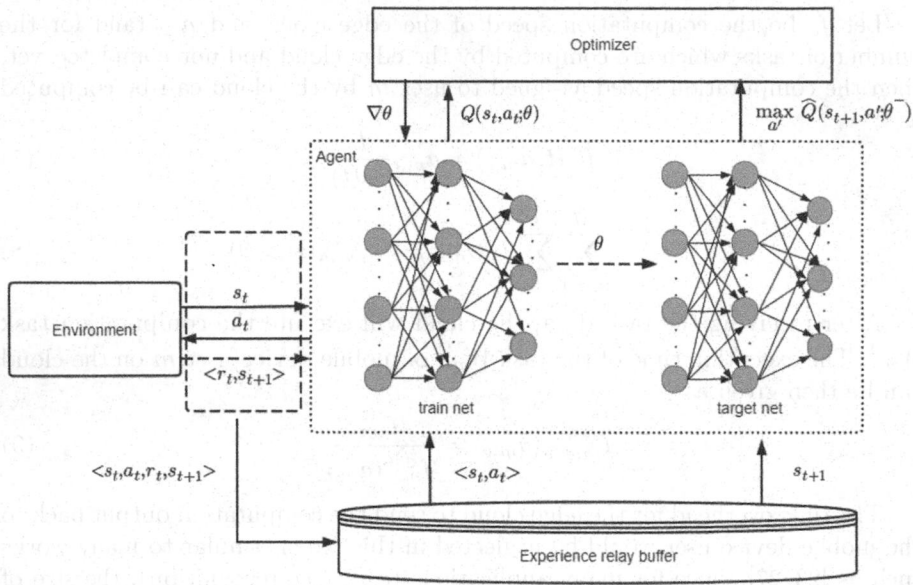

Fig. 2. Diagram of DQN.

offloading problem as Markov decision process (MDP) and the DRL framework developed as follows.

Agent: As shown in Fig. 2, the one who interacts with the environment and learns the optimal computation offloading policy for all M mobile device users.

Action: $a_t = \{a_1^{(t)}, a_2^{(t)}, ..., a_m^{(t)}\}$, a sequence which stands for the computation offloading decisions for all M mobile devices at the time slot t. Specially, $a_m^{(t)} = 0$ represents the mobile user m executes its task locally while $a_m^{(t)} = 1$ represents the mobile user m offloads its task to the edge at the time slot t. When the system begins to work, it is assumed that $a_m^{(0)} = 0, \forall m \in \mathcal{M}$.

State: Full observation of the system including the local computation resources of all M mobile device users, the channel conditions and the computation resource of the edge cloud. $s_t = \{s_1^{(t)}, s_2^{(t)}, ..., s_m^{(t)}, n_c^{(t)}\}$ stands for the state at time slot t. $s_m^{(t)}$ stands for the state of mobile device user m at the time slot t, and it consists of three parts as

$$s_m^{(t)} = <f_m^{(t)f}, W_m^{(t)}, R_m^{(t)}> \tag{14}$$

where $f_m^{(t)f}$ represents the free computation resource for the computation task $W_m^{(t)}$. Further, when $f_m^{(t)f} > 0$, it represents that the mobile device m has free computation resource for the current task, while $f_m^{(t)f} <= 0$, it represents that the mobile device m is busy with the past task and if the computation task $W_m^{(t)}$

is decided to be executed locally, then it will be put into the task queue of the mobile device user m and queue up for its turn. $W_m^{(t)}$ stands for the information of the computation task defined as (2). $R_m^{(t)}$ stands for the data rate of the mobile user m as (1).

$n_c^{(t)}$ denotes the number of the tasks which are offloaded and not completed yet. It reflects the busyness of the edge cloud and gives reference to the agent when it decides to offload or not. And it is as (8).

Reward: the reward for all M mobile device users at the time slot t which is given as

$$r_t = \sum_{m=1}^{M} G^{(t)}(t, a_{m,t}) \tag{15}$$

The framework of our approach is shown as Fig. 2. At the beginning of the time slot t, the agent is fed with state s_t from the environment, then it gives an action a_t back, finally, the environment gives a reward r_t and the next state s_{t+1} as a feedback at the end of the time slot t. $<s_t, a_t, r_t, s_{t+1}>$ is collected into the replay buffer and the agent begins to be trained from the experience sampled from the replay buffer after some steps. The optimizer tries to minimize the gap between current estimated Q-value and the target Q-value. The neural network can be updated as

$$Q(s_t, a_t) \leftarrow Q(s_t, a_t) + \eta(\hat{Q}(s_{t+1}, a') - Q(s_t, a_t)) \tag{16}$$

$$\hat{Q}(s_{t+1}, a') = r_t + \gamma \max_{a'} \hat{Q}(s_{t+1}, a') \tag{17}$$

where $\hat{Q}(s_{t+1}, a')$ denotes the target Q-value including current reward r_t and the maximum Q-value $\max_{a'} \hat{Q}(s_{t+1}, a')$ at the next state and $Q(s_t, a_t)$ stands for current estimated Q-value. γ stands for the discounted factor and η stands for the learning rate. The pseudocode of the approach is shown in Algorithm 1.

5   Numerical Results

In this section, we use simulation to evaluate the performance of the proposed approach compared with two baseline approaches. In the simulation scenario, we assume that there are $M = 10$ mobile device users randomly deployed within a radius of 50 m. For the wireless access, we set the transmission power $P_m = 100$ mW of the mobile device user m, the additive white Gaussian noise $\sigma = -100$ dBm and the channel bandwidth $W = 20$ MHz. Refer to [20], we set the channel gain $H_{m,b} = d_{m,b}^{-\alpha}$ where $d_{m,b}$ is the distance between mobile device user m and the edge cloud and $\alpha = 4$ is the path loss factor. It is assumed that the computing speeds of different mobile devices vary from each other, so we set the computing speed f_m^l of the mobile user m randomly from the set $\{0.1, 0.2, 0.3, 0.4, 0.5, 0.6, 0.7, 0.8, 0.9, 1.0\}$ GHz. The total computing speed of the MEC server is set $f_c = 100$ GHz. As for the information of the computation task W_m, the size of computation input data D_m (in KB) is in the range $[10, 100]$, the total number of CPU cycles C_m (in MegaCycles) is in the range $[10^8, 10^9]$, and the maximum tolerable latency $t_m^{\max}$ (in second) is in the range $[0.1, 0.2, 0.3, ..., 5]$. And we assume a time slot equals one second. In the testing stage, the total number of time slots $S_{test}^{\max} = 10000$ which means there are 10000 computation tasks for each mobile device user.

For comparison, these three offloading approaches are introduced as follows:

- Local computation approach. Each mobile device executes its tasks locally. When there are no free local computation resources for the arriving tasks of the mobile device users, these tasks should queue up for their turns.
- Edge computation approach. Each mobile device offloads its tasks to the base station b via the wireless link and the MEC server compute these tasks on behalf of the mobile device users.
- DQN based approach. The proposed approach based on DQN decides to offload or not according to the state observed by the agent. Specially, in the training stage, the maximum training episodes $E_{train}^{\max} = 300$, the total number of time slots $S_{train}^{\max} = 60000$, the learning rate $\eta = 0.001$, the discounted factor $\gamma = 0.99$.

5.1   Number of Tasks Completed on Time with Varying Number of Mobile Device Users

Figure 3 shows the relationship between the number of mobile users and the total number of tasks completed on time of all mobile users. Edge computation approach performs better than the local computation policy, especially when the number of the mobile device users is in the range $[3, 8]$. However, the gap between edge cloud computation and local computation is gradually decreasing when the number of mobile users is growing. It indicates that when there are many users which also means many computation tasks in the MEC system, the computation resource of the MEC server will be an important factor which should be taken into account when deciding to offload or not. Our proposed approach can effectively utilize the local computation resources and the computation resource of the edge cloud and performs better than the baseline approaches.

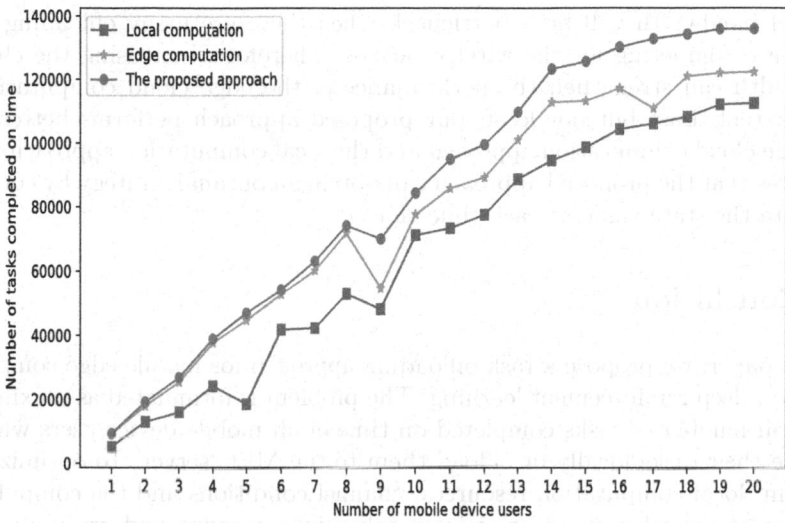

Fig. 3. Number of mobile device users versus total number of tasks completed on time with different approaches.

5.2 Number of Tasks Completed on Time with Varying Channel Bandwidth

Figure 4 shows the relationship between the channel bandwidth and the total number of tasks completed on time of all mobile device users. For edge cloud computation approach and the proposed approach, the total number of tasks completed on time increases gradually along with the increase of the channel bandwidth and the growth rate also slows down gradually. It indicates that the

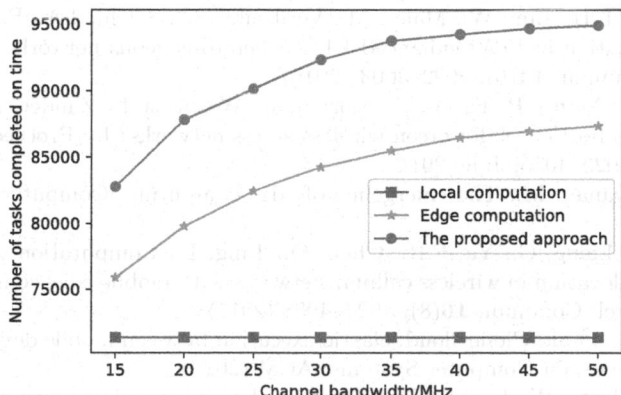

Fig. 4. Channel bandwidth versus total number of tasks completed on time with different approaches.

channel bandwidth will be a bottleneck when there are many offloading tasks which are competing for the wireless access. Therefore, increasing the channel bandwidth can strengthen the performance of the edge cloud computation to some extent. Last but not least, our proposed approach performs better than the edge cloud computation approach and the local computation approach which indicates that the proposed approach can obtain an optimal strategy by correctly estimate the state value at each time slot.

6   Conclusion

In this paper, we propose a task offloading approach for mobile edge computing based on deep reinforcement learning. The problem is formulated as maximizing the total number of tasks completed on time of all mobile device users who can execute their tasks locally or offload them to the MEC server. To optimize this problem, local computation resources, channel conditions and the computation resource of the edge cloud are jointly taken into account and we apply DQN to approximate state-action value $Q(s, a)$ to obtain an optimal mapping from the state to the action. The performance evaluation of the proposed approach is compared with two baseline approaches, and the simulation results show that the proposed approach can achieve better performance than baseline approaches in terms of total number of tasks completed on time.

Acknowledgment. This paper is supported by National Key R&D Program of China (Funding No. 2018YFB1402801).

References

1. Zhang, W., Wen, Y., Wu, J., Li, H.: Toward a unified elastic computing platform for smartphones with cloud support. IEEE Netw. **27**(5), 34–40 (2013)
2. Beyranvand, H., Lim, W., Maier, M., Verikoukis, C., Salehi, J.A.: Backhaul-aware user association in FiWi enhanced LTE-A hetero-geneous networks. IEEE Trans. Wirel. Commun. **14**(6), 2992–3003 (2015)
3. Tombaz, S., Monti, P., Farias, F., Fiorani, M., Wosinska, L., Zander, J.: Is backhaul becoming a bottleneck for green wireless access networks? In: Proceedings of IEEE ICC, pp. 4029–4035, June 2014
4. Satyanarayanan, M.: The emergence of edge computing. Computer **50**(1), 30–39 (2017)
5. Wang, C., Liang, C., Yu, F.R., Chen, Q., Tang, L.: Computation offloading and resource allocation in wireless cellular networks with mobile edge computing. IEEE Trans. Wirel. Commun. **16**(8), 4924–4938 (2017)
6. Chun, B.G., et al.: CloneCloud: elastic execution between mobile device and cloud. In: Conference on Computer Systems. ACM (2011)
7. Wen, Y., Zhang, W., Luo, H.: Energy-optimal mobile application execution: taming resource-poor mobile devices with cloud clones. In: Proceedings IEEE INFOCOM, Orlando, FL, pp. 2716–2720 (2012)

8. Barbera, M., Kosta, S., Mei, A., Stefa, J.: To offload or not to offload? The bandwidth and energy costs of mobile cloud computing. In: Proceedings of IEEE INFOCOM, pp. 1285–1293 (2013)
9. Zhang, W., Wen, Y., Guan, K., Kilper, D., Luo, H., Wu, D.: Energy-optimal mobile cloud computing under stochastic wireless channel. IEEE Trans. Wirel. Commun. **12**(9), 4569–4581 (2013)
10. Zhang, W., Wen, Y., Wu, D.: Energy-efficient scheduling policy for collaborative execution in mobile cloud computing. In: Proceedings of IEEE INFOCOM, pp. 190–194, April 2013
11. Zhang, W., Wen, Y., Wu, D.O.: Collaborative task execution in mobile cloud computing under a stochastic wireless channel. IEEE Trans. Wirel. Commun. **14**(1), 81–93 (2015)
12. Cheng, Z., Li, P., Wang, J., Guo, S.: Just-in-time code offloading for wearable computing. IEEE Trans. Emerg. Topics Comput. **3**(1), 74–83 (2015)
13. Lyu, X., Tian, H.: Adaptive receding horizon offloading strategy under dynamic environment. IEEE Commun. Lett. **20**(5), 878–881 (2016)
14. Chen, X.: Decentralized computation offloading game for mobile cloud computing. IEEE Trans. Parallel Distrib. Syst. **26**(4), 974–983 (2015)
15. Lyu, X., Tian, H., Sengul, C., Zhang, P.: Multiuser joint task offloading and resource optimization in proximate clouds. IEEE Trans. Veh. Technol. **66**(4), 3435–3447 (2017)
16. Chen, X., Jiao, L., Li, W., Fu, X.: Efficient multi-user computation offloading for mobile-edge cloud computing. IEEE/ACM Trans. Netw. **24**(5), 2795–2808 (2016)
17. Chen, Z., Wang, X.: Decentralized computation offloading for multi-user mobile edge computing: a deep reinforcement learning approach. ArXiv abs/1812.07394 (2018)
18. Huang, L., et al.: Deep reinforcement learning for online offloading in wireless powered mobile-edge computing networks. ArXiv abs/1808.01977 (2018)
19. Wei, Y., et al.: Deep Q-learning based computation offloading strategy for mobile edge computing. Comput. Mater. Continua **59**(1), 89–104 (2019)
20. Rappaport, T.S.: Wireless Communications: Principles and Practice, vol. 2. Prentice-Hall, Englewood Cliffs (1996)
21. Sardellitti, S., Scutari, G., Barbarossa, S.: Joint optimization of radio and computational resources for multicell mobile-edge computing. IEEE Trans. Signal Inf. Process. Over Netw. **1**(2), 89–103 (2015)
22. Sardellitti, S., Scutari, G., Barbarossa, S.: Distributed joint optimization of radio and computational resources for mobile cloud computing. In: Proceedings of 3rd International Conference on CloudNet, pp. 211–216, October 2014
23. Kumar, K., Lu, Y.-H.: Cloud computing for mobile users: can offloading computation save energy? IEEE Comput. **43**(4), 51–56 (2010)
24. Huang, D., Wang, P., Niyato, D.: A dynamic offloading algorithm for mobile computing. IEEE Trans. Wirel. Commun. **11**(6), 1991–1995 (2012)
25. Nguyen, P., Ha, V.N., Le, L.B.: Computation offloading and resource allocation for backhaul limited cooperative MEC systems. In: 2019 IEEE 90th Vehicular Technology Conference (VTC2019-Fall), Honolulu, HI, USA, pp. 1–6 (2019)
26. Zheng, X., Li, M., Tahir, M., Chen, Y., Alam, M.: Stochastic computation offloading and scheduling based on mobile edge computing. IEEE Access **7**, 72247–72256 (2019)
27. Li, Z., Du, C., Chen, S.: HIQCO: a hierarchical optimization method for computation offloading and resource optimization in multi-cell mobile-edge computing systems. IEEE Access **8**, 45951–45963 (2020)

Scheduling of Time Constrained Workflows in Mobile Edge Computing

Xican Chen[✉], Siyi Gao, Qibo Sun, and Ao Zhou

State Key Laboratory of Networking and Switching Technology,
Beijing University of Posts and Telecommunications, Beijing 100876, China
1103015686@qq.com

Abstract. Mobile edge computing is an augmentation of cloud computing, and helps to reduce latency and network traffic. It has become a promising solution for real-time or data-intensive mobile applications. A large amount of mobile applications, such as smart city application, are workflow application. Therefore, workflow scheduling in edge computing environment become one of the key issues in the management of workflow execution. We need to allocate suitable edge resources to workflow task so that the workflow task can be completed within the time constraint specified by end user. We will address this issue in this paper. We formulate the time constrained workflow scheduling problem in mobile edge computing as an integer programming. A workflow scheduling algorithm for mobile edge computing is derived by extending Differential Evolution Algorithm. We conduct simulation experiments by comparing our algorithm with existing algorithms. The results show the effectiveness of our algorithm.

Keywords: Workflow · Mobile edge computing · Deployment algorithm · Differential evolution

1 Introduction

With the quick development of computing technology, most of our smart devices are equipped with wireless sensors which help us collect data for further usage. Smart devices only have limited computing resources, which makes them incapable of performing computation-intensive tasks. In a cloud-based system, collected data will be transmitted to the cloud data center over the core network, and be processed there followed by some computing and transmission cost. However, cloud computing data centers are usually located far away from users, resulting in high delay and network resource consumption [3,6]. Mobile edge computing has some significant advantages in such condition. Mobile edge computing is at the network edge and in the middle layer between cloud and users [7]. Due to the proximity of the users to the edge cloud, the network traffic and network delay will be significantly reduced [1]. The mobile edge computing has aroused extensive attention, its current research includes resource alloction and resource management based on blockchain technology [10].

A large amount of edge applications, such as smart city application, are workflow application [5]. Generally, a workflow task is modeled as a Directed Acyclic Graph (DAG) in which nodes denote sub-tasks and edges denote dependencies among the sub-tasks. The weights on the nodes denote computation resource requirements, and weights on the edges denote communication resource requirements. For mobile edge computing, completing workflow tasks within the time constraint involving computation resources and network resources allocation. Due to the limitation of edge resources, resource allocation for workflow task is more complex compared with in cloud computing environment.

To address this issue, in this paper, we propose a novel algorithm which can efficiently manage task scheduling for workflow applications in mobile edge computing. Our key contributions in this work are as following: 1) We formulate the workflow scheduling in mobile edge computing as an optimization problem. We take both cost and time into consideration. The target is to minimize the execution cost while the execution time is within the requirement. 2) We design a scheduling algorithm for time constrained workflow applications by extending the DE algorithm. 3) We compare our algorithm with other existing algorithms, and the experiment results illustrate the effectiveness of algorithm.

The rest of the paper is organized as follows. Section 2 presents related work. In Sect. 3, we describe the task resource scheduling model. In Sect. 4, we present the detail of our algorithm. Section 5 presents the experimental results. Section 6 concludes the paper and discusses some future works.

2   Related Work

In the following, we present some well-known algorithms for workflow scheduling problems.

Myopic algorithm [9] assigns all sub-tasks in arbitrary order until all sub-tasks have been scheduled, and each sub-task is scheduled to a node which is expected to complete that task earlier than other nodes.

Min–Min [4] is a heuristic scheduling algorithm that assigns the task based on the task priority. The task priority is determined on the basis of its expected completion time on a resource. This algorithm divides the workflow sub-tasks into several independent groups. In every iteration, the algorithm takes all tasks in a group and calculates the minimum completion time for each task. Then, the task with minimum completion time over all tasks is selected to be scheduled first.

The max-min algorithm [4] is similar to min-min. The only difference between min-min and max-min is that the max-min algorithm gives the highest priority to the sub-task that requires the longest execution time rather than the shortest execution time.

Heterogeneous Earliest Finish Time (HEFT) [8] is a well-established scheduling algorithm. HEFT gives a higher priority to the sub-task with a higher rank value. This rank value is determined by the average execution time for each sub-task and average communication time for two successive sub-tasks.

Greedy randomized adaptive search procedure (GRASP) [2] is an iterative randomized search algorithm. In GRASP, a number of iterations are conducted to search the optimal solution for workflow scheduling. A candidate solution is generated at each iterative step, and current best solution is kept until the searching procedure terminates.

However, none of the current solutions considers the workflow scheduling problem in mobile edge computing environment. We will address this issue in this paper.

3   System Model

Since both the communication and computation aspects play a key role in mobile edge computing, we next introduce the communication and computation model in details.

3.1   Mobile Edge Computing

Resource Model. Let R,$\{r_1, r_2, r_3, ..., r_m\}$ denote the available mobile edge clouds. In mobile edge computing, the physical resources can be abstracted into virtual machines through virtualization technology. Assuming that there are m edge clouds, the $j - th$ edge cloud is represented by R_j, and its features are represented by $R_j = \{r_{id}, r_{comp}, r_{cost}, r_{vm}\}$. Here, r_{id} is the resource id, r_{comp} and r_{cost} are the computation capacity and computation cost, r_{vm} is the available vms that belong to R_j.

Task Model. A task can be represented by $T = \{t_{id}, t_{stor}, t_{data}\}$, where t_{id} is the task id, t_{stor} is the storage resource requirements, t_{data} is the size of data that needs to be processed.

Workflow Model. Workflow applications are commonly represented by a Directed Acyclic Graph (DAG). Formally, a workflow application is a DAG represented by $G = (T, E)$, where $T = \{T_1, ..., T_n\}$ is a finite set of tasks. E represents the set of directed edges. An edge (t_i, t_j) of graph G denotes the data dependencies between these tasks (the data generated by t_i is consumed by t_j). Task t_i is called the immediate parent of t_j if t_j is the immediate child task of t_i. We assume that a child task cannot be executed until all of its parent tasks are completed. In a given graph, a task without any precedents is called an input task, which is denoted by t_{input}. A task without successors is called an exit task, which is denoted by t_{exit}. Let $data[i, j]$ denote the amount of data required to be transmitted from task t_i to task t_j.

Let Γ be the finite set of tasks T_i ($1 \leqslant i \leqslant n$). Let Λ be the set of edges. Let D denote the time constraint specified by the users. Then, the workflow application can be denoted by a tuple $\Omega(\Gamma, \Lambda, D)$.

3.2 Computation Model

The edge resources can be virtualized to virtual machines, in that case, we need to assign each sub-task of workflow to a virtual machine. This allows workflow to be easily packaged and deployed. To execute a given workflow application (DAG), an infinite set of virtual machines can be used on-demand. The latter are represented as a directed graph denoted RG. Formally, a resource graph is represented by $RG = (VM, V)$, where $VM = \{VM_1, ..., VM_m\}$ is a finite set of virtual machines. V represents the set of directed edges. Each edge (VM_i, VM_j) corresponding to the link between these virtual machines.

Let ET be a $n \times m$ execution time matrix in which $EC(t_i, VM_j)$ gives the estimated execution time to complete task t_i on virtual machine VM_j.

Let UEC be a m-dimensional execution cost vector, where $UEC(VM_j)$ represents the cost per time unit incurred by using the virtual machine VM_j. Let EC be a $n \times m$ execution cost matrix in which $\text{EC}(t_i, VM_j)$ gives the execution cost to complete task t_i on virtual machine VM_j. $EC(t_i, VM_j)$ is defined by: $EC(t_i, VM_j) = ET(t_i, VM_j) \times UEC(VM_j)$.

3.3 Communication Model

Let B be a $m \times m$ matrix, in which $B[i, j]$ is the bandwidth between virtual machines VM_i and VM_j, where $B[i, j] \to -1$ means that there is no transfer cost, and the VMs are virtualized from the same mobile edge cloud.

Let $VM(t_j)$ denotes the virtual machine that executes task t_j. The transfer time $TT(VM(t_i), VM(t_j))$, which is for transferring data from task t_i (executed on $VM(t_i)$) is defined by: $TT(VM(t_i), VM(t_j)) = \frac{data[i,j]}{B[i,j]}$, if the $VM(t_i)$ and $VM(t_j)$ belongs to the same edge cloud, then $TT(VM(t_i), VM(t_j)) = 0$.

We assume that the data transfer cost $TC(VM(t_i), VM(t_j))$, which is the cost incurred due to the transfer of data from task t_i (executed on $VM(t_i)$) to task t_j (executed on $VM(t_j)$), is defined by:

$$TC(VM(t_i), VM(t_j)) = data[i, j] \times (C_{out}(VM(t_i)) + C_{in}(VM(t_j)) \quad (1)$$

where $C_{out}(VM(t_i))$ and $C_{in}(VM(t_j))$ represent the cost of transferring data from $VM(t_i)$ and the cost of receiving data on $VM(t_j)$, respectively.

Total Execution Time. Firstly, it is necessary to define two variables ST and FT, which are derived from a given partial task-to-virtual machine scheduling (i.e. a task t_i is assigned to virtual machine $VM(t_i)$). More precisely, $ST(t_j)$ and $FT(t_j)$ are the earliest start execution time and the earliest finish execution time of task t_j. The partial scheduling refers to the fact that for each task the ST and FT values are computed using only the tasks that must be performed before it. For the task t_{input}, $ST(t_j)$ and $FT(t_j)$ are calculated as follows:

$$ST(t_{input}) = 0 \quad (2)$$

$$FT(t_{input}) = ST(t_{input}) + ET(t_{input}, VM(t_{input})) \tag{3}$$

For the other tasks in the graph, the values of ST and the FT are computed recursively. In order to compute the ST of a task t_j, all immediate predecessor tasks of t_j must have been assigned and scheduled with the consideration of the transfer time:

$$ST(t_j) = \max_{t_p \in pred(t_j)} FT(t_p) + TT(VM(t_p), VM(t_k)) \tag{4}$$

where $pred(t_j)$ is the set of immediate predecessors of task t_j. If tasks with the same parent are scheduled to the same virtual machine, they have to wait until other tasks have freed the resource. The waiting time is denoted by $WT(VM(t_j))$. Otherwise, the waiting time is zero. FT is given by:

$$FT(t_j) = ST(t_j) + ET(t_j, VM(t_j)) + WT(VM(t_j)) \tag{5}$$

After all tasks in a graph are scheduled, the overall execution time will be the finish time of the exit task. The schedule length, also called *makespan*, is given by:

$$makespan = FT(t_{exit}) \tag{6}$$

4   Workflow Scheduling in Mobile Edge Computing

4.1   Problem Statement

The problem of finding the optimal task scheduling is considered to be an optimization problem in which the overall cost must be minimized while satisfying the time constraint. Formally,the optimization problem that we are addressing can be stated as follows:

- The overall cost is minimized.
- The completion time of the workflow is constrainted in order to meet our requirements, we call this time deadline. According to Eq. (6), we can define this constraint as:

$$makespan <= D \tag{7}$$

As workflow scheduling is an NP-complete problem, we rely on heuristic-based and meta heuristic-based scheduling strategies to achieve near optimal solutions within polynomial time. Then, we present an task scheduling approach based on an improved differential evolution to solve the problem.

4.2   Differential Evolution

Differential Evolution (DE) is a parallel direct search method which utilizes D-demensional parameter vectors to find the optimal solution. NP denotes the number of vectors.

$$x_{i,G}, i = 1, 2, ..., NP \tag{8}$$

NP does not change during the minimization process. The initial populations are chosen randomly and should cover the entire parameter space. DE generates new parameter vectors by adding the weighted difference between two population vectors to a third vector. This operation is called mutation. The mutated vector are then mixed with another predetermined vector. Parameter mixing is often referred to as "crossover" and will be explained later in more detail. If the obtained vector yields a lower cost value than the original vector, the obtained vector will replace the original vector in the following generation. This last operation is called selection.

More specifically DE's basic strategy can be described as follows:

Mutation. For each target vector $x_{i,G}; i = 1, 2, 3...NP$, a mutant vector is generated according to

$$v_{i,G+1} = x_{r1,G} + F \cdot (x_{r2,G} - x_{r3,G}) \tag{9}$$

with random integer indexes $r1, r2, r3 \in \{1, 2, 3...NP\}$ and $F > 0$. The randomly chosen integers $r1, r2$ and $r3$ are also chosen to be different from the running index i. F is a real and constant factor $\in [0, 2]$ which controls the amplification of the differential variation $(x_{r2,G} - x_{r3,G})$.

Crossover. In order to increase the diversity of the perturbed vectors, crossover is introduced. To this end, the trial vector:

$$u_{i,G+1} = (u_{1i,G+1}, u_{2i,G+1}, ..., u_{Di,G+1}) \tag{10}$$

is formed, where

$$u_{ji,G+1} = \begin{cases} v_{ji,G+1}, & randb(j) \leq CR \quad or \quad j = rnbr(i); \\ v_{ji,G}, & randb(j) > CR \quad and \quad j \neq rnbr(i); \end{cases}$$
$$j = 1, 2, ...D. \tag{11}$$

In (11), $randb(j)$ is the jth evaluation of a uniform random number generation with outcome $\in [0, 1]$. Cr is the crossover constant $\in [0, 1]$ which can be determined by the user. $rnbr(i)$ is a randomly chosen index $\in 1, 2, ..., D$ which ensures that $u_{i,G+1}$ gets at least one element from $v_{i,G+1}$.

Selection. To decide whether a vector should become a member of generation $G + 1$, the trial vector $u_{i,G+1}$ is compared to the target vector $x_{i,G}$ using the greedy criterion. If vector $u_{i,G+1}$ yields a smaller cost function value than $x_{i,G}$, then $x_{i,G+1}$ is added to $u_{i,G+1}$, otherwise the old value $x_{i,G}$ is retained.

4.3 Improved Differential Evolution

Encoding. For the workflow scheduling problem, a feasible solution is required to meet following conditions:

- A task can only be started after all its predecessors have been completed.
- Every task appears once and only once in the scheduling.
- Each task must be allocated to one available time slot of a virtual machine that is capable of executing the task.

Each individual in the population represents a feasible solution to the problem. Each task assignment includes four elements: taskID, vmID, startTime, and endTime. TaskID and vmID can map our task to a virtual machine. Start-Time and endTime indicate the time frame allocated for the task execution. However, evolving time frames during the genetic operation may lead to a very complicated situation. That's because any change made to a task could require adjusting the values of startTime and endTime of its successive tasks. Therefore, we simplify the operation strings used for genetic manipulation by ignoring the time frames. The operation strings encode only the allocation for each task and the order of tasks allocated on each virtual machine. As illustrated in Fig. 1, we use a 2D string to represent a solution. The first dimension represents the numbers of virtual machines while the other dimension shows the order of tasks on each virtual machine. Two-dimensional strings are then converted into a one-dimensional string for genetic manipulations. The number in brackets represents the ID of the virtual machine to which the task is allocated.

Fitness Function. The fitness function is the the total execution cost function in our problem. We now focus on the cost function, which is the total expense for workflow tasks execution. The cost consists of: i) the task execution cost and ii) the data transfer cost between the virtual machines. The cost function is defined as the sum of the costs of executing all workflow tasks, which is given by:

$$cost = \sum_{j=i}^{n}\{EC(VM(t_j)) + \sum_{p \in pred(t_j)} TC(VM(t_j), VM(t_p))\} \qquad (12)$$

Time Slot Assignment. Since we ignore the time frames during the mutation and crossover operations, we need to develop a time slot assignment algorithm in order to transfer an offspring string to a feasible solution. We should assign a time slot to each task. Algorithm 1 shows the details of the time slot assignment algorithm.

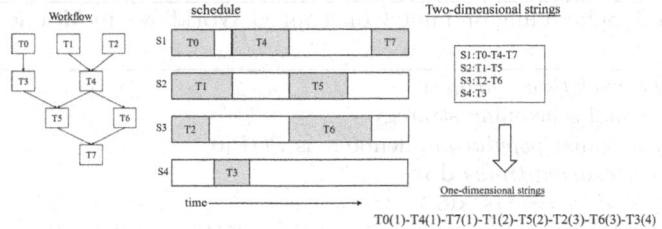

Fig. 1. Illustration of problem encoding

Algorithm 1. Time slot assignment algorithm

Input: A workflow graph Ω, two dimensional strings 2D
Output: A feasible schedule
1: *ready* ←get first level tasks in the workflow Ω
2: **while** *ready* ≠ ϕ **do**
3:   **for all** $S_i \in 2D$ **do**
4:     $T \leftarrow$ remove first task allocated on S_i
5:     **if** $T \in$ ready **then**
6:       compute the ready time of T
7:       query and assign a free slot on S_i for T
8:       remove T from ready
9:       $CT \leftarrow$ get ready child tasks of T
10:       **for each** $ct_i \in CT$ **do**
11:         **if** $ct_i \notin$ ready **then**
12:           ready ← put ct_i
13:         **end if**
14:       **end for**
15:     **end if**
16:   **end for**
17: **end while**

Workflow Scheduling Algorithm. The workflow scheduling algorithm is shown in Algorithm 2. Firstly, we randomly initialize the population. Secondly, we randomly choose two encoded strings, and start mutation and crossover process. Then, Algorithm 1 is adopted to assign time slots to each task. After obtaining time slot assignment, we can evaluate each strings by using cost function (12) and execution time (3, 4, 6). The process repeats until the algorithm converges.

The time complexity of the algorithm is $O(NG)$, where N describe the size of population and G stands for number of iterations.

Algorithm 2. Scheduling of Time Constrained Workflows in Mobile Edge Computing

---

Input: $DAG(workflow\ graph)$.
Output: the final scheduling strategy
1: randomly initialize $population$, denoted as $POP[0]$
2: **while** $g < iteration\_times$ **do**
3:    **while** $i < dimensions$ **do**
4:       randomly choose two strings, denoted as $POP[g]_j$ and $POP[g]_k$ where j and k are two random numbers between zero and $dimensions$, then start mutation process using Eq. (9)
5:       start crossover process using Eq. (10, 11).
6:       $i \leftarrow i + 1$
7:    **end while**
8:    start selection process using cost-objective function (12) and time function (3, ??, 4, 6)
9:    **if** $POP[g]$ meets our requirements **then**
10:       return $POP[g]$ as our final strategy
11:    **end if**
12:    $g \leftarrow g + 1$
13: **end while**
14: return $POP[iteration\_times - 1]$ as our final strategy

---

5   Experiments and Results

5.1   Experiments Parameters

We consider workflow with 26 layers and 106 tasks. Other parameters are shown in Table 1.

Table 1. Parameters

Dimensions	106 (equals to the number of the tasks)
Population	50
Amplification factor	0.5
Crossover probability	0.5
Iteration times	500
Lowest boundary	1
Highest boundary	10 (equals to the number of the virtual machines)

After choosing the right parameter, we compare Myopic, Min-min, Max-min, HEFT, GRASP, GA and PSO with our algorithm.

5.2 Results and Discussions

As is shown in Fig. 2, Fig. 3, Fig. 4 and Fig. 5, the cost increases with the increasing of the number of tasks. We can see that the cost of Myopic is the highest while the costs of GA, PSO and DE are much lower. The performance of our algorithm is the best among all algorithms. Since the number of tasks is relatively small, the difference of the algorithm may not be obvious.

The main reason is that it takes into account the computation cost and topology of all edge clouds in mobile edge computing, as well as the dependencies between them. When calculating the computation cost of a child task on a edge cloud, it considers the data transfer cost for transferring the output from its parent task to that node. This calculation is done for all the tasks in the workflow to find the near optimal scheduling strategy.

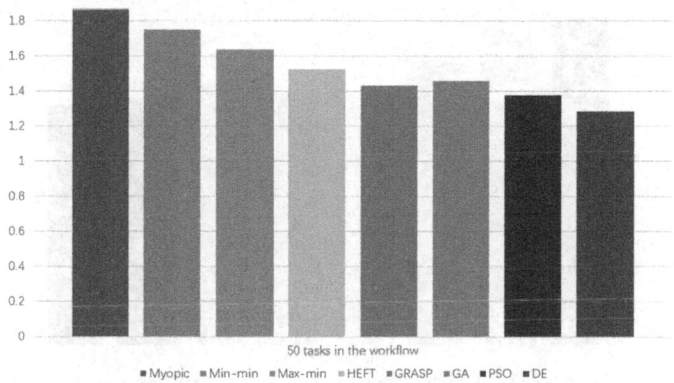

Fig. 2. Cost of different scheduling algorithms (50 tasks)

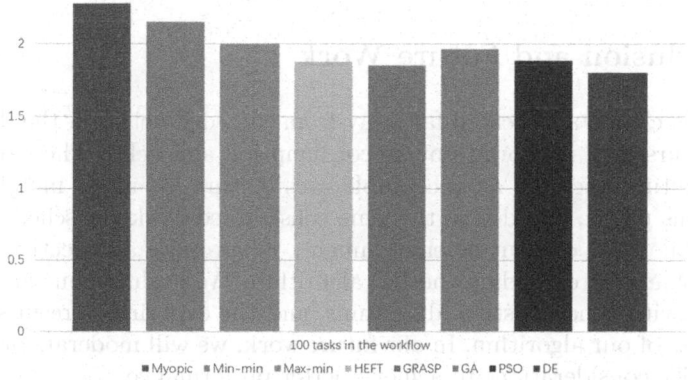

Fig. 3. Cost of different scheduling algorithms (100 tasks)

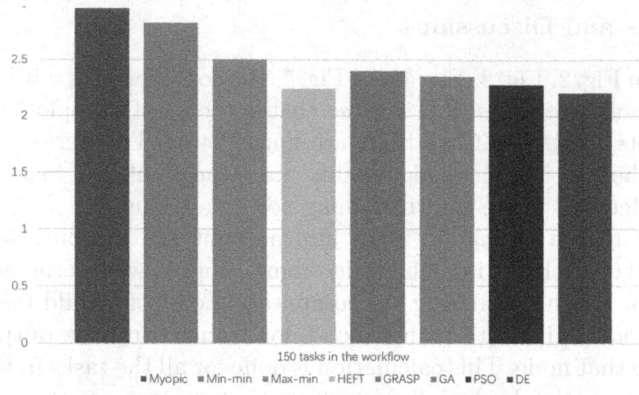

Fig. 4. Cost of different scheduling algorithms (150 tasks)

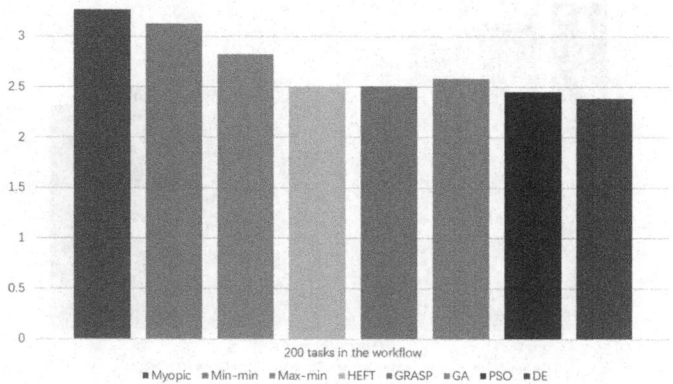

Fig. 5. Cost of different scheduling algorithms (200 tasks)

6   Conclusion and Future Work

Because the clouds are located far away from the edge network, the data transmission incurs high network resource consumption and delay. Therefore, mobile edge computing becomes an acceptable architecture for many mobile applications. In this paper, we address the time constrained workflow scheduling problem in mobile edge computing environment. We propose an effective algorithm for the problem by extending the DE algorithm. We evaluate our algorithm by comparing with other existing algorithms, and the experiment results show the effectiveness of our algorithm. In our future work, we will moderate our research with security considerations to achieve better performance.

References

1. Aazam, M., St-Hilaire, M., Lung, C.-H., Lambadaris, I.: PRE-fog: IoT trace based probabilistic resource estimation at fog. In: 2016 13th IEEE Annual Consumer Communications & Networking Conference (CCNC), pp. 12–17. IEEE (2016)
2. Blythe, J., et al.: Task scheduling strategies for workflow-based applications in grids. In: CCGrid 2005. IEEE International Symposium on Cluster Computing and the Grid, 2005, vol. 2, pp. 759–767. IEEE (2005)
3. Gupta, H., Dastjerdi, A.V., Ghosh, S.K., Buyya, R.: iFogSim: a toolkit for modeling and simulation of resource management techniques in internet of things, edge and fog computing environments. arXiv preprint arXiv:1606.02007 (2016)
4. Maheswaran, M., Ali, S., Siegal, H.J., Hensgen, D., Freund, R.F.: Dynamic matching and scheduling of a class of independent tasks onto heterogeneous computing systems. In: Proceedings of Eighth Heterogeneous Computing Workshop (HCW 1999), pp. 30–44. IEEE (1999)
5. Rahbari, D., Nickray, M.: Scheduling of fog networks with optimized knapsack by symbiotic organisms search. In: 2017 21st Conference of Open Innovations Association (FRUCT), pp. 278–283. IEEE (2017)
6. Rehr, J.J., Vila, F.D., Gardner, J.P., Svec, L., Prange, M.: Scientific computing in the cloud. Comput. Sci. Eng. **12**(3), 34 (2010)
7. Shi, W., Sun, H., Cao, J., Zhang, Q., Liu, W.: Edge computing-an emerging computing model for the internet of everything era. J. Comput. Res. Dev. **54**(5), 907–924 (2017)
8. Topcuoglu, H., Hariri, S., Min-you, W.: Performance-effective and low-complexity task scheduling for heterogeneous computing. IEEE Trans. Parallel Distrib. Syst. **13**(3), 260–274 (2002)
9. Wieczorek, M., Prodan, R., Fahringer, T.: Scheduling of scientific workflows in the askalon grid environment. Acm Sigmod Rec. **34**(3), 56–62 (2005)
10. Zheng, Z., Xie, S., Dai, H., Chen, X., Wang, H.: An overview of blockchain technology: architecture, consensus, and future trends. In: 2017 IEEE International Congress on Big Data (BigData Congress), pp. 557–564. IEEE (2017)

An Efficient Offloading Scheme for Blockchain-Empowered Mobile Edge Computing

Jin Xie, Fan Wu$^{(\boxtimes)}$, Ke Zhang, Xiaoyan Huang, and Supeng Leng

School of Information and Communication Engineering,
University of Electronic Science and Technology of China, Chengdu 611731, China
wufan@uestc.edu.cn

Abstract. Combining computation offloading with Mobile Edge Computing (MEC) is a research hotspot currently. In order to implement a trusted and reliable offloading system with MEC, blockchain technology provides a feasible approach with its features of security, transparency and decentralization. For the traditional blockchain with the linear data structure, the limited throughput seriously hinders the deployment in the practical offloading situation because it is unable to fulfill the requirements of being recorded timely from a tremendous number of offloading transactions. In this paper, we opt to apply a Directed Acyclic Graph (DAG) structure to promote the scalability of the blockchain-empowered offloading system. Specifically, due to the DAG structure, each MEC server can generate blocks consisting of the completed offloading transactions in parallel. In the novel system, an MEC server has to execute not only the offloading but also the mining with the limited computation resource. In this paper, we address the vital issue of how to strike the balance of computing resource allocation between the task offloading and the mining process. To this end, we first propose the Proof-of-Offloading (PoO) mining scheme to motivate the MEC servers to execute more offloading tasks by adjusting the mining difficulty according to its offloading load. Furthermore, we formulate the computing resource allocation as an optimization problem with the objective of minimizing the maximum offloading delay, subject to both the computing capacity and each offloading user's QoS requirement. Then, a two-layered algorithm is designed to solve this nonlinear problem, in which the original problem is decomposed into two subproblems, including the task selection and computing resource allocation. The simulation results demonstrate that the proposed algorithm has significant improvement over reference algorithms in terms of overall offloading latency.

Keywords: Blockchain · MEC · Computation offloading · DAG · PoO

1 Introduction

Mobile Edge Computing (MEC) has recently seen a surge in interest because it exhibits excellent potential on computation offloading, which is an efficient

© Springer Nature Singapore Pte Ltd. 2020
Z. Zheng et al. (Eds.): BlockSys 2020, CCIS 1267, pp. 380–393, 2020.
https://doi.org/10.1007/978-981-15-9213-3_30

approach to share idle computation and storage resources with the User Equipments (UEs) with the limited processing capability. More specifically, MEC pushes resources such as compute, network, and storage to the edge of the mobile network, which could be used to fulfil users' application requirements that are latency-sensitive, compute hungry [1]. For example, by introducing MEC to cloud-based vehicle networks, the vehicle services are improved in terms of latency and transmission cost [2]. Web-based augmented reality (Web AR) is a promising lightweight and cross-platform approach to augmented reality. However, the weak computational efficiency of current web browsers hampers the application of Web AR, so work [3] solves this problem by deploying Web AR applications at the edge of the network closer to users with MEC, which also promises the application performance in terms of latency. In light of the feature that MEC offloading always happens locally in proximity to users, the offloading system with MEC possibly prefers to be implemented in a distributed manner.

However, the distrusted and distributed environment of computation offloading in MEC brings some problems that are not well researched currently. First, there is no trusted third party in a distributed system to audit the process of computation offloading and withheld the payment for computation offloading in order to safeguard the legitimate rights of both sides involved in the computation offloading. Second, there is a contradiction between the privacy preservation and the authenticity of computation offloading because users are supposed to provide some identity information to testify the authenticity of the offloading request. Blockchain is a promising technology that stands out for its features of tamper-proof, traceability and anonymity as a distributed ledger. There are a few distinguished works combining blockchain with MEC networks in computation offloading [4–7]. These works can be divided by their methods of blockchain utilization in their designs. One of the two sorts uses blockchain to manage the behaviours of computation offloading [4,5]. More specifically, [4] introduces blockchain as an overlaid layer in the computation offloading system in MEC networks to manage and control the computation offloading. The other kind of utilization is offloading the demands for mining from computation constraint devices to MEC servers [6,7]. In work [7], mining tasks from UEs are offloaded to MEC servers. In this way, the users' demand is fulfilled, and the MEC server also gets steady income from mobile users.

Although the blockchain technology brings many benefits to the distributed system, the scalability is the bottleneck of deploying blockchain to real business environments. Throughput, storage and networking are three aspects of scalability. Particularly, throughput is of importance in the scalability of blockchain. Taking Bitcoin's throughput as an example, the throughput is restricted to seven transactions per seconds (TPS). However, trillions of transactions need to be recorded in IoT network [8]. The main reason for limited throughput is the linear structure of the traditional blockchain. More specifically, all the nodes in the blockchain network opt to publish their own blocks by referencing the latest block on the chain, which means that consequent transactions have to be suspended until the network reaches a consensus on the latest block of the chain.

Therefore, it is emergent to improve the throughput of blockchain. There are several methods to improve the throughput, such as increasing the number of transactions in a single block, or applying Sharding technology in the blockchain, which enables the throughput of blockchain to increase with the growing number of blockchain nodes [9]. Besides these methods, utilizing DAG is a revolutionary approach. In DAG-based blockchain protocol, transactions are enveloped in blocks, and blocks can be appended to the main chain concurrently. Although every block still needs to refer to the previous blocks, the referenced blocks are not restricted to the top block of the longest chain. Consequently, there are multiple blocks created at the same time referring to different previous blocks. Newly created blocks are legitimate if their transactions are valid and they refer to the valid previous blocks.

One of the typical instantiations of DAG-based blockchain is IOTA [10], and a pivotal part of IOTA is the data structure named Tangle. In Tangle, transactions are organized approximatively into a tree-like structure, and an arbitrary number of transactions could be published synchronously by approving two previous transactions. Besides, the heritage block structure in traditional blockchain can be applied in DAG as well. In work [11], a DAG-based blockchain protocol named CoDAG is proposed to promote the scalability of blockchain, where blocks are vertices in DAG, and every new advanced block is supposed to approve multiple previous blocks. It is worth noting that the TPS of CoDAG could reach 400. Introducing DAG-based blockchain to MEC offloading system may be a countermeasure. However, the DAG-based blockchain eliminates the bipartition of miner and transaction maker because of the absence of transaction fees. In other words, the service providers of computation offloading, which are MEC servers, are responsible for mining a block as well as computation offloading. The limited computing resource of MEC servers is the key factor affecting the DAG-based blockchain offloading system deployment in a practical scenario. For an MEC server to issue a block, the server must solve the PoW puzzle, which is similar to the mining process in Bitcoin. Running PoW mining algorithm may consume computing power of MEC servers prohibitively so that their computing ability to execute offloaded tasks will be weakened drastically. Consequently, there is a dilemma for MEC servers to reduce the latency of computing offloaded tasks or devoting more computing power to solve the PoW puzzle.

To cope with the problems mentioned above, we propose a DAG-based blockchain offloading framework with a novel mining algorithm in the MEC networks. In the PoO mining algorithm, the more offloading tasks are completed by the MEC server, the less computational intensity is required to solve the PoW puzzle. In this way, our approach meets the computation demands of UEs, and also records transactions of task offloading on the DAG-based blockchain with less computing resource. Different from the existing computing resource allocation schemes [12,13], MEC servers in our approach require computing power to solve PoW puzzles and computing offloading tasks simultaneously. Furthermore, we formulate the computing resource allocation as an optimization problem and design an efficient Dynamic Programming and Simplex method based two-layer algorithm (DPS) to find the optimal solution. Our contributions can be concluded into three folds.

1. We originally devise a framework of DAG-based blockchain for computation offloading in MEC networks. The DAG structure improves the throughput of blockchain in order to record a vast number of offloading transactions produced synchronously. The proposed PoO mining algorithm is able to balance the computing power allocation between offloading and mining on the MEC servers.
2. We formulate the computing resource allocation as a nonlinear mixed-integer programming problem with the objective of minimizing the maximum offloading delay, subject to both the computing capacity and each offloading user's QoS requirement.
3. A Dynamic Programming and Simplex method based two-layer algorithm (DPS) is introduced for task selection and resource allocation, which could lead to a lower latency of finishing both offloading tasks and mining process.

2   System Model and Procedure of Task Offloading

2.1   The Architecture of the System Model

As illustrated in Fig. 1, MEC servers and UEs consist of the DAG-based blockchain computation offloading system. We introduce a digital cryptocurrency named Offloading Coins (OCs) to the system, which is utilized as the payment of task offloading. The proposed system can be divided into two layers. Data transmission happens in the physical layer, and blockchain-related behaviours happen in the blockchain layer, which is built upon the physical layer. UEs are the provenance of offloading tasks. Each offloading task is described as an individual transaction.

MEC servers collect the offloading requests from the nearby UEs and further provide the offloading services. Due to the depletable computing resource, MEC servers only respond to partial requests. After the task is finished, the computing power released will be used to mine as shown CPU workload in Fig. 1. Besides, MEC servers maintain a local view of the DAG-based blockchain. According to the local data, MEC servers are able to check the validity of transactions.

2.2   DAG Based Blockchain Task Offloading

DAG Based Blockchain Structure. Unlike the heritage block structure in linear blockchain (e.g., Bitcoin), the block header in our scheme contains two previous blocks' hashes, which work as references to two previous blocks that this candidate block approves. We use the definition of tips in IOTA, which refer to the unapproved blocks now. When an MEC server attempts to add a new block to DAG, the MEC server has to verify two tips in DAG. Additionally, we stipulate that the MEC server always approves its own block superiorly, and the other tip will be selected by a Random Walk-based Tip Selection Algorithm

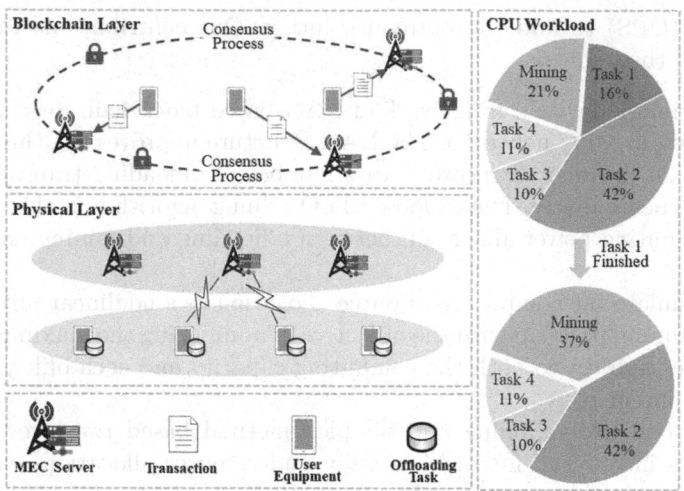

Fig. 1. System model

(RWTSA). In our scheme, a new block created by the MEC server always firstly approves the last block generated by this MEC server. For example, all the grey blocks in Fig. 2 are created chronologically by the MEC server with an id of 1, and the later created grey block always refers to the formerly created one. Before we introduce RWTSA, some notions need to be explained. We define the weight of a block, which is a constant value. The cumulative weight of a block equals the own weight of this block plus the sum weight of all blocks that approve this block directly or indirectly. For an MEC server, running RWSTA is based on the local view from itself. Although all the MEC server runs the same implementation code of RWSTA, they will get different tip selection results because of the unique local view of DAG. RWSTA starts a random walk from the very first block, which is the genesis block, and the next vertex on the path will be chosen randomly. However, the cumulative weight of a block determines the probability of this block being selected. The random walk stops until it finds a tip. The detail can be found in [10], which is not our focus.

Our strategy for choosing tips brings two benefits. First, by approving the previous block, which belongs to the same MEC server, the cumulative weight of this approved block increases steadily, which leads to a higher probability that this previous block could be approved by other blocks directly or indirectly. Besides, our strategy resists the bias from the MEC server on transactions with different rewards. If MEC servers publish new blocks by referring to two random blocks, new blocks can be set at any place in DAG, so there is no created order between blocks in time from the same MEC server. As a result, MEC servers could egoistically publish OTXs with higher rewards in advance of those transactions with lower rewards, even though the lower ones are constructed earlier.

In our scheme, once the MEC server decides to undertake an offloading task, the transaction of this task has to be published in this round of block update.

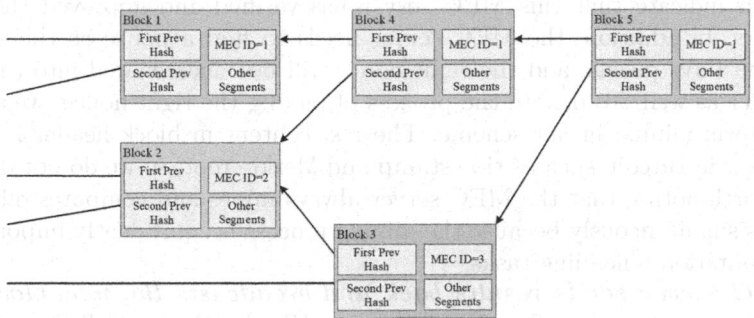

Fig. 2. DAG-based blockchain.

PoO Mining Algorithm. The PoO mining algorithm is an improvement of the original PoW mining algorithm [14]. The feature of PoO lies in that the difficulty of a PoW puzzle D depends on the total size of the offloading tasks completed by the MEC server. Therefore, D is defined as:

$$D = \text{int}(2^{(N_z - \exp(-\eta W - \lambda))}) \tag{1}$$

where $\text{int}(\cdot)$ returns an integral part of term in the bracket. The N_z denotes the bit length of the difficulty, and the W is the total size of offloading tasks contained in a block. The other two variables η and λ are preset parameters to control the changing rate of mining difficulty and the default difficulty.

The Procedure of Task Offloading. There are four steps of the task offloading process in our system:

1. *UEs construct and send OTXs to MEC servers:* UEs construct OTXs containing the value OCs as payment for task offloading, and the demand of QoS is described as the end time of returning a result. Besides, UEs utilize the multi-signature script to make sure that the MEC server will return the offloading results. Specifically, only when UEs get the computing result from the MEC server, will the MEC server get a digital signature from UEs to unlock the OCs in OTXs.
2. *MEC server chooses tasks:* After collecting the OTXs and tasks from UEs, the MEC server first checks the integrity of both task data and the transactions. Next, according to the end time included in the OTX, the MEC server ignores the tasks whose receiving time is close to the required end time to return the feedback. Then, after performing the task selection scheme, which will be detailed in the next section, selected OTXs will be enveloped into the body of a candidate block.

3. **MEC server constructs the candidate block:** The MEC server constructs the candidate block by packaging selected OTXs into a block body and generating a block header. The block header contains two previous blocks' hashes, which indicate that this MEC server has verified and approved these two blocks. In addition, the MEC server needs to find a nonce as the solution to the PoW puzzle, and the right nonce will be concatenated into the block header as well. To denote the process of finding the right nonce, we still use the term mining in our scheme. The rest content in block header is similar to that in Bitcoin such as timestamp and Merkle root, so we do not detail it. It worth noting that the MEC server always mines and computes offloading tasks simultaneously because the mining process is equivalently important as computation offloading tasks.

4. **MEC server sends results back and broadcasts the new block:** The MEC server keeps sending results back to UEs because not all the tasks will be finished at the same time. After constructing the new block with a right nonce, the MEC server will broadcast this block to other MEC servers in proximity.

3   Problem Formulation for Latency of Task Offloading

The transmission latency is not concerned in this paper because it is negligible compared with computing latency in our system. Assume that the system is slotted. At the beginning of each slot, the MEC server selects the tasks from an array of unselected offloading tasks $\mathcal{N}\{1, 2, \ldots N\}$. The selected tasks will be further executed by the MEC server. Define the offloading task indicator ρ_i to represent whether the task i is accepted as (2).

$$\rho_i = \begin{cases} 1 \text{ if choose the } i\text{th task} \\ 0 \qquad \text{otherwise} \end{cases}, \tag{2}$$

Let $\mathbf{T}(\rho)$ denote the set of the offloading tasks to be processed. Assume the cardinality of $\mathbf{T}(\rho)$ equals n. A task can be described as $\{s_i, d_i, \omega\}$. s_i represents the task size of ith task measured by bytes. d_i is the delay requirement, and the last element is computation intensity ω which is measured in terms of the number of CPU cycles need to compute one-bit data of the offloading task.

Let the computing capacity of the MEC is F, which is measured in terms of the number of CPU cycles per second. The computing resource allocation for each task is denoted as $\mathbf{f}^A \triangleq \{f_1^A, f_2^A \cdots f_i^A \cdots f_N^A\}$. If the task is not selected, the computation resource allocation for this task would be 0. The overall computing latency is:

$$d_{\max}^C = \max\{d_i^C\}, \forall i \in \{1 \cdots N\} \tag{3}$$

In (3), d_i^C is the computation latency of the ith task.

$$d_i^C(f_i^A, \rho_i) = \begin{cases} \frac{s_i \omega}{f_i^A}, \forall i \in \{1 \cdots N\}, \rho_i \neq 0 \\ 0, else \end{cases} \tag{4}$$

Algorithm 1: Dynamic Programming and Simplex method based two-layer algorithm(DPS)

Data: The set of unselected tasks $\mathcal{N}$, the maximum computing power F.
Result: The collection of selected tasks $\mathbf{T}$, and computing resource allocation $\mathbf{f}^A$.

1 **begin**

2   Initialize the number of attempts Λ to select tasks. Search the optimal task selection with different available computing power from F/Λ to F in line 20.

3   Initialize a two-dimensional array v, and set all value of v as -1. $v[n, AR]$ means the max total size of choosing tasks from the top n tasks in $\mathcal{N}$ when available computing resource is AR.

4   **Function** *Search(n, $\mathcal{N}$, AR)* **is**

5   **if** $n = 0$ or $AR < 0$ **then**

6   Update $\mathbf{T}$

7   **Return** an empty set

8   **if** $v[n-1, AR] = -1$ **then**

9   The value of $v[n-1, AR]$ is the total size of the returned set of executing $Search(n-1, \mathcal{N}, AR)$

10   **else**

11   **if** $s_{n-1}^O > AR$ **then**

12                 $v[n, AR] \longleftarrow v[n-1, AR]$

13   **else**

14   **if** $v[n-1, AR - (s_{n-1} * \omega/d_{n-1})] = -1$ **then**

15   Update $v[n-1, AR - (s_{n-1} * \omega/d_{n-1})]$ by executing $Search(n-1, \mathcal{N}, AR - (s_{n-1} * \omega/d_{n-1}))$

16   The value $v[n, AR]$ is the bigger one of $v[n-1, AR]$ and $(v[n-1, AR - (s_n * \omega/d_n)] + s_n)$

17   Update $\mathbf{T}$

18   **Return** $v[n, AR]$

19   **for** $j = 1..., \Lambda$ **do**

20         $\mathbf{S}^O \longleftarrow Search(N, \mathcal{N}, (F * j)/\Lambda)$

21   After getting the updated $\mathbf{T}$, execute the process of computing resource allocation via a simplex based minimax algorithm. And compare the latency of the current allocation scheme with former shortest one. If the latency of current scheme is shorter, then keep the allocation scheme and $\mathbf{T}$

22   **end**

Define that if an MEC server has done the average hash times of mining its candidate block with the specific difficulty, the mining process is finished. The mining latency is d^M. Denote the overall latency of task offloading as d, which equals the bigger one of computing latency and mining latency. We opt to find the optimal strategy of task selection and computing resource allocation to reduce the latency of task offloading in our system. So the problem is:

$$\underset{\mathbf{f}^A,\rho}{\mathrm{minimax}}(d_{\max}^C, d^M)$$

$$s.t. C1 : \sum_{i=1}^{N} f_i^A \rho_i \le F, \tag{5}$$

$$C2 : d_i^C \le d_i, \forall i \in \{1 \cdots N\}$$

The first constraint is the sum of allocated computing power should less or equal to the max computing power of the MEC server. The second constraint ensures that the computation latency of every offloaded task on the MEC server will not exceed the latency requirement of its owners.

If the mining process is finished before computation tasks, it is unnecessary to calculate the specific value of time spent on mining because the computation latency is the overall latency. However, if the mining process is finished after task computation, we can calculate the mining latency as:

$$d^M = \frac{W(\rho) + \bar{H}(\rho) * s^H * \delta}{f} \tag{6}$$

In (6), $W(\rho)$ is:

$$W(\rho) = \min\left(\sum_{i=1}^{N} \rho_i s_i, W_{\max}\right) \tag{7}$$

where $W_{\max}$ is the upper bound of the total size of tasks to reduce the difficulty of a block. The $\bar{H}(\rho)$ in (5) is the average hash times [15] to mine a block, which is:

$$\bar{H}(\rho) = \frac{2^{N_z}}{D(\rho)} \tag{8}$$

In (7), $D(\rho)$ is the mining difficulty of a specific candidate block that is related to ρ, which can be obtained by substituting W in (1) with $W(\rho)$ in (7). Further, transform hash times into CPU cycles. The number of CPU cycles needs to execute the hash function is associated with the input data size and the kind of hash function. As the block header is input, assume the size of block header is s^H that is measured in terms of byte. Moreover, let δ denote the number of CPU cycles that the MEC server needs to process the one-byte input of the hash function [16].

Substitute d^M in (5) with (6), and the objective of our problem can be transformed as:

$$\underset{\mathbf{f}^A,\rho}{\mathrm{Minimax}}(d_{\max}^C, \frac{W(\rho) + \bar{H}(\rho) * s^H * \delta}{f}) \tag{9}$$

As shown in Algorithm 1, we decompose this problem into two layers. At the lower layer, we define a recursive function Search($\cdot$) to choose tasks from $\mathcal{N}$. Since the lower layer provides the task offloading decision, the variable ρ is a known value to us. As a result, the right term in the bracket of (9) is a constant, and we can solve the problem with the method detailed in [17]. Transform the minimax problem into a minimum problem by using the overall offloading latency d:

$$\min_{\mathbf{f}^A} d$$
$$s.t. \text{C1, C2, C3} : \frac{s_i \omega}{f_i^A} \leq d, \forall i \in \{1 \cdots N\}, \rho_i \neq 0, \tag{10}$$

$$\text{C4} : \frac{W(\rho) + \bar{H}(\rho) * s^H * \delta}{f} \leq d$$

The third and fourth constraints ensure that the overall latency is bigger one of mining latency and computing latency. By now, the problem in (10) is a nonlinear constraint problem. Step by step, we opt to change the problem into a linear problem with standard form. First, we set the initial value of our variable $\mathbf{f}^A$:

$$f_j^{(1)} = \frac{\rho_i s_i \omega}{d_i}, \forall i \in \{1 \cdots n\},$$
$$\mathbf{f}^{(1)} = \{f_1^{(1)}, f_2^{(1)}, \cdots f_j^{(1)}, \cdots f_n^{(1)}\} \tag{11}$$

where $f_i^{(1)}$ is the initial computing power allocated to the ith task. The value of $f_i^{(1)}$ is the least computing power allocated to the task when the computation latency satisfies the UEs' requirement. Introduce a new set of variables $\mathbf{h} \overset{\Delta}{=} \{h_1, h_2, \ldots, h_i, \ldots h_N\}$, where $\mathbf{h}$ is a set of offset of allocated computing resource for each task. Substitute $\mathbf{f}^A$ in (10) with $\mathbf{h}$ and $\mathbf{f}^{(1)}$:

$$\min_{\mathbf{h}} d$$
$$s.t. \text{C1} : \sum_{i=1}^{N} \rho_i (f_i^{(1)} + h_i) \leq f, \forall i \in 1 \cdots N \tag{12}$$

$$\text{C3} : \frac{s_i \omega}{f_i^{(1)} + h_i} \leq d, \forall j \in \{1 \cdots n\}, \rho_i \neq 0$$

$$\text{C4, C5} : 0 \leq h_i, \forall i \in \{1 \cdots N\}$$

In (12), the second constraint of computing latency is removed by giving an initial value of computing resource allocation, which makes our problem simpler. However, the problem in (12) is still an optimization problem with nonlinear constraints. Therefore, we leverage linear approximation to transform the problem. First, define a function $G(\cdot)$ to represent the left side of the third constraint as follow:

$$G_i(f) = \frac{s_i \omega}{f} \tag{13}$$

$$G_i(f_i^{(1)} + h_i) \approx G(f_i^{(1)}) + h_i * G(f_i^{(1)})' \tag{14}$$

The exploitation of linear approximation is shown in (14). However, the value of h_i should be small enough, otherwise, the linear approximation is false, so we get the problem with linear constraints as (15):

$$\min_{\mathbf{h}} d$$
$$s.t. \, C1, C4,$$
$$C3 : G_i(f_i^{(1)}) + h_i * G_i(f_i^{(1)})' \leq d, \forall i \in \{1 \cdots N\}, \rho_i \neq 0 \qquad (15)$$
$$C5 : 0 \leq h_i \leq \varepsilon, \forall i \in \{1 \cdots N\}$$

where ε is a value small enough to make sure that linear approximation is always valid. Finally, the problem in (15) is a linear optimization problem with linear constraints that can be solved by the general simplex method. When we get the solution $\mathbf{h}$, compare the performance of new computing resource allocation $\mathbf{h} + \mathbf{f}^{(1)}$ with the last allocation $\mathbf{f}^{(1)}$ in terms of overall offloading latency. If the new allocation works better, then update the allocation by $\mathbf{f}^{(2)} \triangleq \mathbf{h} + \mathbf{f}^{(1)}$ and repeat this procedure until the largest element in $\mathbf{h}$ is smaller than a threshold (i.e., less than 1e–10), which means the scheme of resource allocation is already convergent in terms of computation offloading latency.

4 Performance Evaluation

We simulate the process of a single MEC server selecting offloading tasks and solving the PoW puzzle to create a block following our scheme in the Matlab platform. The analysis of our simulation shows that applying DAG-based blockchain into computation offloading in MEC is feasible, and the MEC server with limited computing power is able to record transactions into the blockchain while dealing with UEs' offloading requests. Moreover, we compare our approach to the offloading tasks selection and computing resource allocation with the greedy algorithm. The greedy algorithm is designed to choose as many tasks as the MEC server can to maximize the total size of the offloading tasks. For accuracy, every simulation is executed 100 times to get the average value.

4.1 Task Offloading Latency Analysis

In this section, we mainly present the task offloading latency for a single MEC server. The default parameters of these simulations are listed in Table 1.

Task Offloading Latency with Different CPU Frequency: We change the CPU frequency to observe the changes in latency. As shown in Fig. 3(a), when the MEC server works in the different capability of computation, our approach outperforms the greedy approach all the time in terms of latency. With the increase of computation capability, both our and greedy approaches work better. However, the greedy approach stops its downward trend at 13 GHz CPU frequency, while our approach still decreases the latency of task offloading until the max computation capability, which is 15 GHz. Moreover, the shortest latency of our approach is about 44 ms, which is about half of the shortest latency of the greedy approach.

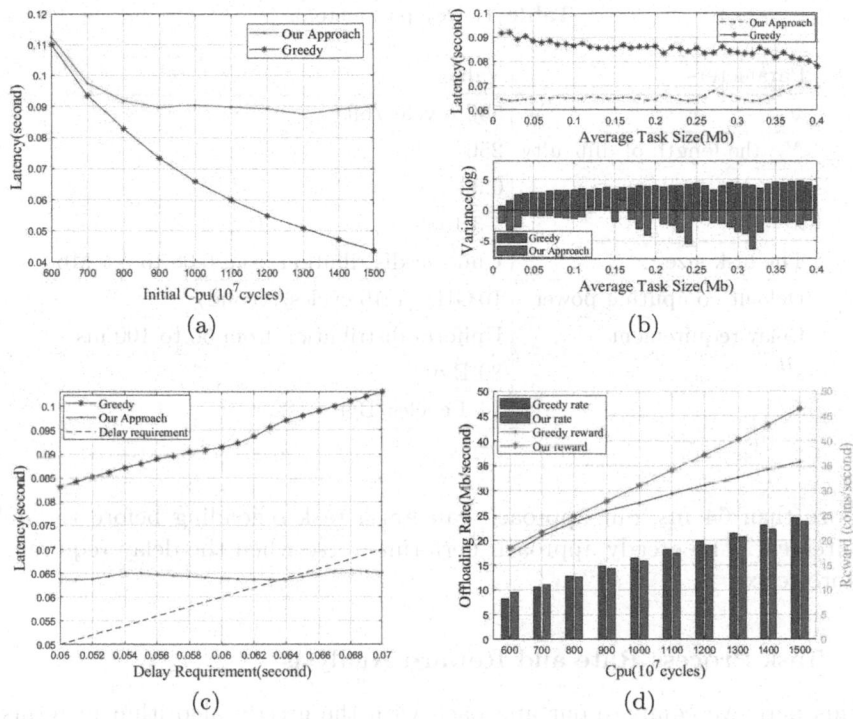

Fig. 3. Performance analysis.

Task Offloading Latency with Task Size: In this part, we generate tasks following a normal distribution with a variance of 0.005 and changing the average size. As illustrated in Fig. 3(b), our approach still outperforms the greedy approach. However, the greedy approach shows a downward trend of the latency, while our approach performs poorer at big data size than small data size. The reason is that the big size of data may lead to an overload on computing tasks, which breaks the balance of the mining process and computation offloading. Besides the latency, the variance of the 100 times experiments on every average size shows that our approach provides more consistent performance, which keeps variance less than 1 for most of the time.

Task Offloading Latency with Different Delay Requirements: In Fig. 3(c), we assume all the tasks' delay requirements are the same. We change the delay requirement from 50 ms to 70 ms. There is a baseline named delay requirement in Fig. 3(c). The reason why the task offloading latency is higher than the black dot line is that the MEC server is still mining after computing tasks. Although, in most instances of our approach can not finish the whole process of task offloading before the delay requirement, when the delay requirement

Table 1. Key parameters.

Parameters	Value
ω	500 (cycles/bit)
N_z, the length of difficulty	256
η	0.32
λ	-3.1355
The task size	Uniform distribution from 0.08 to 0.4 Mb
Default computing power	10 GHz (1e10 cycles/second)
Delay requirement	Uniform distribution from 50 to 100 ms
s^H	80 Byte
δ	14.4 cycles/Byte

is more than 64 ms, our approach can finish task offloading before the delay requirement. The greedy approach performs worse when the delay requirement is more relax.

4.2 Task Process Rate and Reward Analysis

In this part, we compare our approach with the greedy algorithm in terms of task processing rate. The processing rate refers to the bit size of data processed per second. Figure 3(d) shows that the processing rate of our approach is close to the greedy algorithm. However, we define the reward in this part, and we assume the MEC server will get one offloading coin for processing 1 Mb data task. Meanwhile, we also reward the MEC servers for reaching the mining target depicted in Sect. 3. As shown in Fig. 3(d), the reward of our approach grows linearly, while the greedy approach gets slower growth because our approach reaches the mining target much more quickly than the greedy algorithm.

5   Conclusion

In this paper, we proposed a DAG-based blockchain-empowered MEC task offloading paradigm. In order to balance the computing power allocation between offloading and mining at the MEC servers, the PoO mining algorithm was designed. We formulated the computing resource allocation as an optimization problem with the objective of minimizing the maximum offloading delay, subject to both the computing capacity and each offloading users' QoS requirement. At last, we proposed a two-layered approach to solving this problem.

Acknowledgments. This work is supported by the Sichuan Science and Technology Program under Grant (2019YFH0007), and Key Lab of Information Network Security, Ministry of Public Security.

References

1. Abbas, N., Zhang, Y., Taherkordi, A., Skeie, T.: Mobile edge computing: a survey. IEEE Internet Things J. **5**(1), 450–465 (2018)
2. Zhang, K., Mao, Y., Leng, S., He, Y., Zhang, Y.: Mobile-edge computing for vehicular networks: a promising network paradigm with predictive off-loading. IEEE Veh. Technol. Mag. **12**(2), 36–44 (2017)
3. Qiao, X., Ren, P., Dustdar, S., Chen, J.: A new era for web AR with mobile edge computing. IEEE Internet Comput. **22**(4), 46–55 (2018)
4. Guo, F., Yu, F.R., Zhang, H., Ji, H., Liu, M., Leung, V.C.M.: Adaptive resource allocation in future wireless networks with blockchain and mobile edge computing. IEEE Trans. Wirel. Commun. **19**(3), 1689–1703 (2020)
5. Liu, M., Yu, F.R., Teng, Y., Leung, V.C.M., Song, M.: Distributed resource allocation in blockchain-based video streaming systems with mobile edge computing. IEEE Trans. Wirel. Commun. **18**(1), 695–708 (2019)
6. Xiong, Z., Zhang, Y., Niyato, D., Wang, P., Han, Z.: When mobile blockchain meets edge computing. IEEE Commun. Mag. **56**(8), 33–39 (2018)
7. Zhang, K., Cao, J., Leng, S., Shao, C., Zhang, Y.: Mining task offloading in mobile edge computing empowered blockchain. In: 2019 IEEE International Conference on Smart Internet of Things (SmartIoT), pp. 234–239 (2019)
8. Zhao, L., Yu, J.: Evaluating dag-based blockchains for IoT. In: 2019 18th IEEE International Conference On Trust, Security And Privacy In Computing And Communications/13th IEEE International Conference On Big Data Science And Engineering (TrustCom/BigDataSE), pp. 507–513 (2019)
9. Yu, G., Wang, X., Yu, K., Ni, W., Zhang, J.A., Liu, R.P.: Survey: sharding in blockchains. IEEE Access **8**, 14155–14181 (2020)
10. Serguei Popov. The tangle. https://www.iota.org/research/academic-papers. (2018)
11. Yang, S., Chen, Z., Cui, L., Xu, M., Ming, Z., Xu, K.: CoDAG: an efficient and compacted dag-based blockchain protocol. In 2019 IEEE International Conference on Blockchain (Blockchain), pp. 314–318 (2019)
12. Liang, Z., Liu, Y., Lok, T., Huang, K.: Multiuser computation offloading and downloading for edge computing with virtualization. IEEE Trans. Wirel. Commun. **18**(9), 4298–4311 (2019)
13. Huang, L., Feng, X., Zhang, L., Qian, L.P., Wu, Y.: Multi-server multi-user multi-task computation offloading for mobile edge computing networks. Sensors **19**, 1446 (2019)
14. Yang, Z., Yang, K., Lei, L., Zheng, K., Leung, V.C.M.: Blockchain-based decentralized trust management in vehicular networks. IEEE Internet Things J. **6**(2), 1495–1505 (2019)
15. Ozisik, A., Bissias, G., Levine, B.: Estimation of miner hash rates and consensus on blockchains (draft), June 2017
16. Dai, W.: Crypto 5.6.0 benchmarks. https://www.cryptopp.com/benchmarks.html. Accessed 20 Mar 2020
17. Madsen, K., Schjær-Jacobsen, H.: Linearly constrained minmax optimization. Math. Program. **14**, 208–223 (1978)

Clustering Algorithm Based on Task Dependence in Vehicle-Mounted Edge Networks

Yixin Yu$^{(\boxtimes)}$ (iD), Xinyue Shi (iD), Yashu Yang (iD), Xiang Ren (iD), and Haitao Zhao (iD)

College of Communications and Information Engineering, Nanjing University of Posts and Telecommunications, Nanjing 210003, China

{b17010704,zhaoht}@njupt.edu.cn, Megrez_yue@163.com, 750727187@qq.com, 474048323@qq.com

Abstract. Mobile Edge Computing can shift computing tasks from cloud servers to mobile edge servers for processing so that data and applications located closer to users. However, traditional clustering algorithm was not adopted to deal with the case where similar tasks exist in the edge computing networks. In addition, the repeated computation of similar tasks will lead to high loading in the edge server. In this paper, we propose a task clustering algorithm based on task dependency in Vehicle-Mounted Edge Networks. And we study task adaptation algorithm based on task dependency in Vehicle-Mounted Edge Networks. We first introduce the task clustering algorithm to car edge network. Then, we propose a task arrival model in Vehicle-Mounted Edge Networks. By constructing similarity matrix to cluster tasks, different tasks with similar characteristics will be clustered based on the maximum value of task dependency. Next, tasks will be assigned to edge servers according to data perception scheduling. Finally, the simulation results show the proposed algorithm improves the overall efficiency of task processing in the Internet of Vehicles at the expense of a small amount of clustering effects.

Keywords: Vehicle-Mounted Edge Network · Energy consumption · Mobile Edge Computing · Task clustering algorithm · Task dependency

1 Introduction

Mobile clouding computing emerges to deal with the tension among resources, applications and terminals. However, the traditional cloud computing architecture [1] consists of few large data centers interconnected over long distance networks. The long distance between the cloud server and vehicles not only brings bigger return time, but also leads to instability of links.

In order to cope with these challenges, Mobile Edge Computing (MEC) [2] is introduced as a complementary example of cloud computing. Edge computing is located closer to the user, providing an intermediate node between the user and the cloud. The research on MEC server placement model, delay and energy consumption model and computing task offload [3] has made a great contribution to the application of edge computing in the Internet of Vehicles.

© Springer Nature Singapore Pte Ltd. 2020
Z. Zheng et al. (Eds.): BlockSys 2020, CCIS 1267, pp. 394–400, 2020.
https://doi.org/10.1007/978-981-15-9213-3_31

In addition, [4, 5] studied the performance of improved edge computing in the Internet of Vehicles. However, most of the studies did not consider the existence of similar tasks in the edge computing network. Repeated computing for similar tasks often causes huge pressure to the edge servers with less computing capacity than cloud computing. Based on the research of existing task clustering algorithms [6–8], we propose a task adaptation algorithm based on task dependency in Vehicle-Mounted Edge Networks.

Main contributions of this paper are shown as follows.

- We construct the composite model of vehicle arrival and task generation in the Internet of Vehicles.
- We learn the dependency between tasks and cluster the arrival tasks.
- We simplify the complexity of vehicle tasks and reduce the waste of resources caused by repeated processing of similar tasks.
- Simulation results show that the proposed algorithm can improve the overall efficiency of task processing in Internet of Vehicles.

Section 2 is the overview of system model. Section 3 analyzes our proposed model. Section 4 presents the simulation results. Section 5 gives a brief conclusion.

2   System Model and Problem Formulation

2.1   System Model

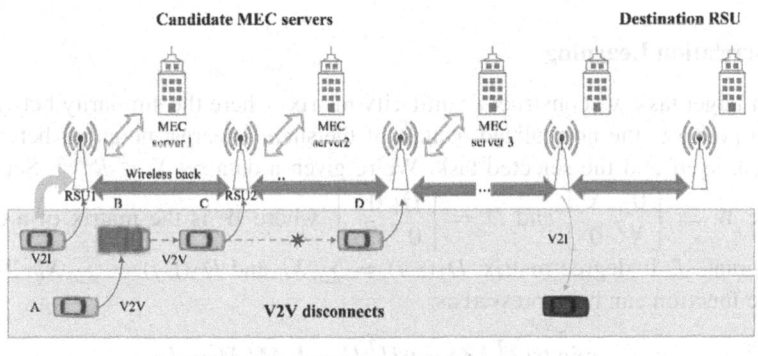

Fig. 1. Task arrival model in vehicle edge network.

In order to improve the efficiency of task processing in the Internet of vehicles, we use adaptive task clustering algorithm based on task dependence (ATCA) to cluster the tasks.

For the sake of brevity, Fig. 1 shows only the case of one-way road is considered in this paper. In one-way road, we set up N RSU, and between each of the two adjacent data centers we place a MEC server to provide task processing services for vehicles in the transmission range of the RSU. RSU communicates with each other via wireless backhaul, with a transmission range of L/2, ensuring that every car on the road is covered by at least one RSU.

Each vehicle terminal will generate task requests from time to time, and we use formula (1) to represent the distribution of vehicle tasks to the edge server, where is the number of vehicles in the section, is the number of tasks generated by vehicles within each time unit. As shown that the number of tasks generated in a unit of time follows a compound stochastic process.

$$Y(s) = ds \sum_{i=1}^{N(s)} D_i \tag{1}$$

The edge computing server processes it when the task arrives, we assume a sample set $D = \{x_1, x_2, \ldots, x_m\}$ includes m unlabeled samples, each tag sample represents a different task type, such as road information, in-vehicle multimedia entertainment, vehicle status and autonomous driving requests. Each sample $x_i = (x_{i1}, x_{i2}, \ldots, x_{in})$ is a n-dimensional eigenvectors, each vector represents a different task of the same type. We divide D into k unrelated clusters $\{C_l | l = 1, 2, \ldots, k\}$, where $C_{l'} \cap_{l' \neq l} C_l = \varnothing$ and $D = \cup_{l=1}^k C_l$. Correspondingly, we use $\lambda_j \in \{1, 2, \ldots, k\}$ as the 'cluster markers' of sample x_j, and $x_j \in C_{\lambda_j}$. We use cluster marker vector $\lambda = (\lambda_1, \lambda_2, \ldots, \lambda_m)$ included m elements represents the result of clustering. We can define each task x_{mn} as $x_{mn} = \{a^x, b^x\}$, where a^x represents a feature space composed of a set of features, b^x is the tag space for a set of potential tags. For different tasks i and j, if $b^i = b^j$, it's completely related. It's partially related when $b^i \neq b^j$ and $b^i \cap b^j \neq b^j$. And if $b^i \cap b^j = \varnothing$, it's not related.

2.2 Correlation Learning

For each target task we construct a similarity matrix, where the similarity between any two data points is the normalized weight of the shared nearest neighbor between the target task itself and the selected task. We're given a data set $X \in R^{d \times n}$, Set up two matrices: $W = \begin{bmatrix} 0 & X \\ X^T & 0 \end{bmatrix}$ and $D = \begin{bmatrix} D_1 & 0 \\ 0 & D_2 \end{bmatrix}$, where W is the matrix of a directed acyclic graph, D is degree matrix, $D_1(i, i) = \sum_j X_{ij}$ and $D_2(j, j) = \sum_i X_{ij}$. Then the objective function can be expressed as:

$$\min_Z tr(Z^T LZ), s.t. U^T U = I, M^T M = I \tag{2}$$

where $L = D^{-1/2}(D - W)D^{-1/2}$, $Z = [U; M]$, $U \in R^{d \times c}$ is comprised of eigenvector c, represents the division of features, $M \in R^{n \times c}$ is also comprised of eigenvector c, represents the division of the samples.

3 ATCA Algorithm

In this section, we want to add relevant task characteristics from source tasks to the cluster of target tasks and batch the tasks with highly identical features. To that end, we need to calculate the dependencies of tasks in the workflow based on conditional probabilities in the objective function.

Formula (3) is the probability of task t_i will occur when task t_j is assumed to be a common task based on the dataset. Consider the source task and the target task may be related, we use the conditional probability in formula (3) to calculate the dependencies of tasks in the workflow to determine the criteria to be followed for the transition to subtasks. After confirming the dependencies between tasks, we cluster the tasks with related characteristics.

$$P(T_i|T_j) = \frac{P(T_i \cap T_j)}{P(T_i)}, P(T_i) > 0 \tag{3}$$

The task clustering algorithm based on task dependency is described as follows: Line 2 to Line 4 is used to calculate the conditional probability of each pair of tasks and assign the value to divided samples. Line 5 to Line 10 is used to tag the most dependent task.

```
input: task list
output: all tasks processed by clustering
1 start
2 for each task t_i ∈ D_0 do
3 calculate the conditional probability of each pair of
tasks P(t_i|t_j)
4 if DM[i][j] = P(t_i|t_j) then
5 end if
6 index = 0
7 for each element ele(i, j) ∈ DM  D_0 do
8 choose the maximum value of ele(i, j) in the case of i ≠ j
9 tag i and task t_i and task t_j have the greatest depend-
encies
10 add t_i and t_j to CL_{index} and remove row DM, column i
from i
11 index = index + 1
12 end for
13 end
```

After clustering, tasks are assigned to the edge server according to the data-aware scheduling, and the edge server is used to calculate the task.

4 Simulation Results

We evaluate the performance of task clustering algorithm based on similarity in vehicle edge network and assume that all task clustering is handled by the edge server. As there are few clustering algorithms suitable for complex vehicle-mounted network environments, this part compares the ATCA algorithm with the non-clustering algorithm.

The simulation is performed in a moving edge computing scenario. The communication range of each RSU is set to 1000 m, the size of each task is 400–10000 Bytes, the CPU size required for the message is $1 * 10^6$–$6 * 10^6$ cycles/s, and the task arrival obeys Poisson distribution. The distance between RSU and the edge server is 100–1000 m, the transmission path loss is 3 dB, the communication bandwidth of the edge server is 1–3 MHz, and the calculation rate is 1–$15 * 10^8$ cycles/s.

In this section, Fig. 2 and Fig. 3 respectively show the changes of task processing delay and server energy consumption as the number of tasks increases.

4.1 Impact of Time Delay

Figure 2 shows when the number of tasks increases, the processing delay brought by ATCA algorithm is lower than that brought by the algorithm without clustering, especially when the number of tasks increases, the advantage of delay is more obvious. The time delay here consists of two parts, one is the time required for task clustering, and the other is the delay generated by server processing.

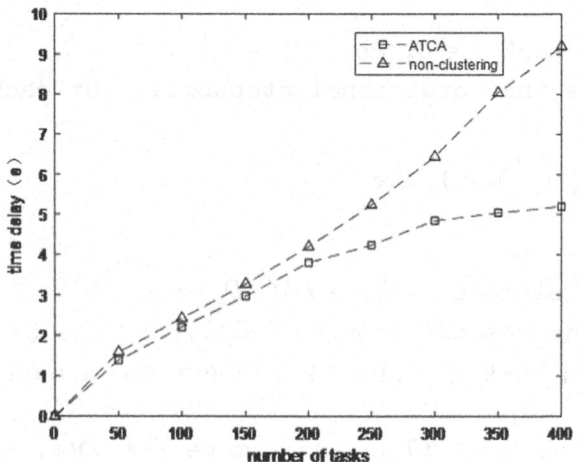

Fig. 2. Relationship between time delay and the number of tasks.

ATCA algorithm compared with non-clustering task clustering time, shorten the task processing time delay. When the number of tasks is not enough large, the number of tasks with the same characteristics is smaller, there is not particularly evident advantages, the ATCA algorithm still needs clustering processing, which takes a certain amount of time.

As the number of tasks keeps increasing, the number of tasks with similarity also keeps increasing, the algorithm in this section has an obvious advantage in terms of time delay. Through clustering, we can reduce the amount of time waste caused by repetitive processing of similar tasks, thus reducing the delay of task processing as a whole.

4.2 Impact of Energy Consumption

Figure 3 shows after the processing of ATCA algorithm, the energy consumption of the server is also lower than that of non-clustering. The ATCA algorithm causes two parts of energy consumption, including the energy consumption caused by task clustering and that caused by processing tasks.

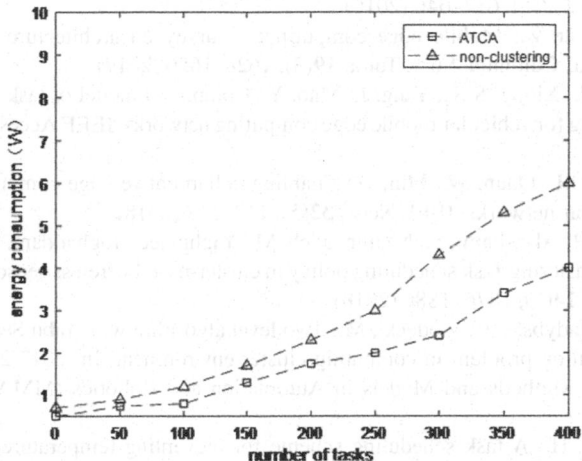

Fig. 3. Relationship between energy consumption and the number of tasks.

ATCA algorithm reduces the energy consumption of processing tasks by that of certain task clustering. When the number of processing increases, the energy consumption performance will become better. However, the advantage tends to be stable when the number of tasks arrives at a certain amount. As too many tasks sets will cause the energy consumption generated by task clustering greatly increased.

5 Conclusion

In this paper, we proposed an ATCA task clustering algorithm based on task dependency in Vehicle-Mounted Edge Networks. Task clustering with similar characteristics is carried out based on the maximum value of task dependencies, and tasks are assigned to edge servers according to data-aware scheduling. Through simulation experiments, it can be found that ATCA algorithm has shorter task processing time delay and lower energy consumption than that of other traditional clustering algorithms. We assume that all tasks are handled by the edge server, it can be found that the task set after ATCA clustering has good performance in terms of processing time delay and energy consumption in the heterogeneous Vehicle-Mounted Networks environment.

Acknowledgments. This work is supported by National Science and Technology Innovation Training Program (Project No.: 201910293004Z) and Nanjing University of Posts and Telecommunications Science and Technology Innovation Training Program (Project No.: SZDG2019004).

References

1. Gebremeskel, G.B., Chai, Y., Yang, Z.: The paradigm of big data for augmenting internet of vehicle into the intelligent cloud computing systems. In: Hsu, R.C.-H., Wang, S. (eds.) IOV 2014. LNCS, vol. 8662, pp. 247–261. Springer, Cham (2014). https://doi.org/10.1007/978-3-319-11167-4_25
2. Shi, W., Cao, J., Zhang, Q., Li, Y., Xu, L.: Edge computing: vision and challenges. IEEE Internet Things J. **3**(5), 637–646 (2016)
3. Mach, P., Becvar, Z.: Mobile edge computing: a survey on architecture and computation offloading. IEEE Commun. Surv. Tutor. **19**(3), 1628–1656 (2017)
4. Li, L., Zhou, H., Xiong, S.X., Yang, J., Mao, Y.: Compound model of task arrivals and load-aware offloading for vehicular mobile edge computing networks. IEEE Access **7**, 26631–26640 (2019)
5. Wang, K., Yin, H., Quan, W., Min, G.: Enabling collaborative edge computing for software defined vehicular networks. IEEE Netw. **32**(5), 112–117 (2018)
6. Neamatollahi, P., Abrishami, S., Naghibzadeh, M., Yaghmaee Moghaddam, M.H., Younis, O.: Hierarchical clustering-task scheduling policy in cluster-based wireless sensor networks. IEEE Trans. Ind. Inf. **14**(5), 1876–1886 (2018)
7. Bozejko, W., Nadybski, P., Wodecki, M.: Two level algorithm with Tabu Search optimization for task scheduling problem in computing cluster environment. In: 2017 22nd International Conference on Methods and Models in Automation and Robotics (MMAR), pp. 238–242 (2017)
8. Cao, Y., Wang, H.: A task scheduling scheme for preventing temperature hotspot on GPU heterogeneous cluster. In: 2017 International Conference on Green Informatics (ICGI), pp. 117–121 (2017)

Blockchain and Smart Contracts

How Similar Are Smart Contracts on the Ethereum?

Nan Jia[1], Queping Kong[3], and Haiping Huang[2(✉)]

[1] School of Management Science and Engineering, Hebei GEO University,
Shijiazhuang 050031, China
[2] Department of Basic Courses, Zhaoqing Medical College, Zhaoqing 526020, China
42036253@qq.com
[3] School of Data and Computer Science, Sun Yat-sen University,
Guangzhou 510006, China

Abstract. Ethereum is a programmable platform that allows everyone
to deploy and access the smart contracts on it. Such flexibility can lead
everyone to browse or reuse the source code of the existing smart contracts on the Ethereum. In this paper, to characterize the code clone
practice of the smart contract, we present a large-scale study on the
smart contracts coming from the Ethereum. We firstly collect more than
700,000 open-source smart contracts, and then we employ a highly effective approach (i.e., Locality-Sensitive Hashing, LSH) to cluster the similar smart contracts. At last, we conduct a qualitative analysis to characterize the clone practice of the smart contract, and further analyze the
reason why smart contracts are similar. Our analysis revealed that over
96% of the smart contracts can found similar contracts, which indicates
that the smart contracts on the Ethereum are highly homogeneous.

Keywords: Code clone · Smart contract · Locality-sensitive hashing ·
Code similarity · Blockchain

1 Introduction

Blockchain serves as a public ledger and transactions stored in blockchain are
nearly impossible to tamper [1,2]. Its purpose is to solve the credit problems
of both sides of the transaction in a decentralized environment, which can
greatly improve transaction efficiency and reduce costs [3,4]. Then, blockchain
has become a widely used technique to enable decentralized financial and business transactions [5].

As one of the most revolutionary and representative blockchain platforms,
Ethereum [6] has attracted a large number of participants, including developers
and users, and becomes one of the most active communities in the cryptocurrency world [7]. In Ethereum, developers are allowed to develop their own smart
contracts using high-level programming languages such as Solidity for various
domains [5,8–10], e.g., finance, game and healthcare.

© Springer Nature Singapore Pte Ltd. 2020
Z. Zheng et al. (Eds.): BlockSys 2020, CCIS 1267, pp. 403–414, 2020.
https://doi.org/10.1007/978-981-15-9213-3_32

The smart contract is a program that can be triggered to execute any task when specifically predefined conditions are satisfied [11,12]. The conditions defined in smart contracts, and the execution of the contracts, are supposed to be trackable and irreversible in such a way that minimizes the need for trusted intermediaries [13,14]. Due to the creditability of smart contract, more than millions of smart contracts have been deployed on the Ethereum until July 6th, 2019.

Since Ethereum is open platform, everyone can access the smart contracts without any constraints. Then, the source code of the existing smart contracts on the Ethereum can be reused by other developers. Meanwhile, the Ethereum applications are highly domain-specific, and the applications can share similar functionalities within the same domain [8], e.g., ERC20 applications implement the same interface for money transfer and balance inquiry [15]. As a result, the nature of Ethereum has provided convenience to create contract clones i.e., copying code from other available contracts.

The impact of contract clone is profound. Since many smart contracts are suffering from serious vulnerabilities, the copy-paste vulnerabilities would be inherited by the cloned contracts [15]. In this paper, we present a large-scale study to characterize the code clone of Ethereum smart contracts. Firstly, we collect a dataset from Ethereum that contains more than 700,000 open source smart contracts, which are deployed from July 30th, 2015 to July 6th, 2019. Then, we employ the Locality-Sensitive Hashing (i.e., LSH) [16] to quickly identify the similar smart contracts from the large-scale dataset. Specifically, we extract the syntactic tokens from the smart contracts in the dataset, and transform contracts into vector representation according to the syntactic tokens. LSH is employed to cluster the similar smart contracts based on the distances between the vectors.

We conduct quantitative analysis and qualitative analysis to characterize the clone practice of the smart contract. Fisrtly, our quantitative analysis reveals that over 96% of the smart contracts have similar contracts on the Ethereum, and this result suggests that the smart contracts on the Ethereum are highly homogeneous. Secondly, we further analyze the reason why smart contracts are similar. Some interesting reasons such as implementing the same "interface" have been found in our qualitative analysis.

The rest of the paper is organized as following. The background about blockchain and smart contract is introduced in Sect. 2. The data collection is presented in Sect. 3. Section 4 describes the LSH methodology we used to cluster the similar smart contracts. The setups and results of experiment are discussed in Sect. 5. We discuss the related works in Sect. 6. Section 7 presents the threats to validity. Section 8 summarizes our approach and outlines directions of future work.

2 Background

2.1 BlockChain and Smart Contract

Blockchain was first introduced by Satoshi Nakamoto in 2008 as the underlying data structure of Bitcoin [1]. As its name suggested, a blockchain is a chain of blocks, in which each block contains a number of transactions which are hashed in a Merkle Tree [17]. By storing the hash value of the previous block, each block refers to its previous block, forming a chain structure. Together with peer-to-peer communication, consensus between miners such as Proof of Work (PoW), asymmetric encryption and digital signature, a blockchain system can provide a temper-proof and immutable value-transfer network without relying on a trusted third party [17]. Hence, many people think blockchain tends to be another technology revaluation of the Internet, due to its unique security, trustworthiness and reliability [18].

In order to make blockchain suitable for more scenarios other than cryptocurrency, Ethereum, a blockchain platform, introduced smart contract which can be constructed with turing-complete programming languages such as Solidity (Solidity[1] is a contract-oriented, high-level language whose syntax is similar to that of JavaScript). Smart contracts are self-executing contracts where the terms of the agreement between multiple parties are directly written into lines of code [19]. The code and the agreements contained therein exist across a blockchain network. By developing different types of smart contracts, Ethereum can facilitate the construction and execution of complex applications such as financial exchanges, game, social and insurance contracts on the blockchain.

Any user can create a smart contract by publishing a transaction to a blockchain. Once a smart contract's program code has been deployed on the blockchain, it cannot be changed [20,21]. Therefore, even when the same contract creators may want to evolve the contract code and create new versions of the smart contracts, the older versions are still kept visible in the blockchain. As a result, the smart contract is similar with its evolving ones, and a code clone case exists on the Ethereum [22,23].

2.2 Locality-Sensitive Hashing

The Locality-Sensitive Hashing (LSH) algorithm was proposed by Aristides Gionis in 1999 [16]. The basic idea behind LSH is that: if two instances are similar in the original data space, then they have a high similarity after hashing conversion. On the contrary, if they are not similar, they should not be similar after hashing conversion. If a hash function $h(.)$ satisfies these two conditions, it is called a locality-sensitive hashing function. Mathematically, $h(.)$ should satisfy formulas (1) and (2):

$$if\ d(x,y) \leq d_1,\ then\ P(h(x) = h(y)) \geq p_1 \tag{1}$$

---

[1] http://solidity.readthedocs.io/en/develop.

$$if\ d(x,y) \geq d_2,\ then\ P(h(x) = h(y)) \leq p_2 \tag{2}$$

where x and y are two instances in the data space, $d(x,y)$ represents the distance between x and y. $h(x)$ represents the hashing value of x. $P(x)$ represents the probability of event x, and (d_1, d_2, p_1, p_2) is a set of thresholds. If both formulas (1) and (2) are satisfied, the locally sensitive hash function $h(.)$ is sensitive for thresholds (d_1, d_2, p_1, p_2).

3   Data Collection

Smart contract can be divided into open source and closed source categories. Open source contracts allow any user to download their source code from the Ethereum while closed source contracts only provide bytecode for users. To study why smart contracts are similar, we need to collect the source code of the smart contracts for further analysis. Therefore, we only collect the open source smart contracts as our dataset. We download the smart contracts from the Etherscan[2], which is an blockchain browser supported by Ethereum, and it provides the real-time transaction query.

Table 1 shows the statistical characteristics of the collected dataset. We collected 146,402 solidity files from Etherscan. There are a total of 703,565 smart contracts, which are stored in a local repository. On average, each smart contract involves around 4.8 individual contracts (ranges from 0 to 36), 20 functions, and 202 lines of code. And these smart contracts deployed on the Ehtereum mainnet from July 30th, 2015 to July 6th, 2019.

Table 1. Collected data

# Solidity files	146,402	# Contracts (total)	703,565
# Contracts (average)	4.8	# Contracts (maximum)	36
# Functions (average)	20	# Lines of Code (average)	212

An Ethereum smart contract can be created either by a user, or by another existing contract [6,7]. Then, we call them user-created contract and contract-created contract to distinguish these two types of contracts. Since we try to study the code clone practice in the two types of contracts, we distinguish the two types of contracts according to the address of the contract creator. If an address of the contract creator points to another contract, then this contract is a contract-created one, otherwise, it is a user-created contract. Table 2 shows the statistical characteristics of the user-created and contract-created contracts.

---

[2] https://etherscan.io.

Table 2. User-created and contract-created contracts

	# Solidity files	# Contracts (Total)
User-created	143,553	684,029
Contract-created	28,49	19,536

4   Clustering Similar Contracts

In this section, we employ LSH method to cluster the similar smart contract. To measure the similarity of smart contracts, the direct way is to compare the code syntactic similarity [24–27] between the smart contracts [2]. Therefore, we firstly extract the code syntax from the smart contracts. Then, a smart contract is transformed into a high-dimensional vector representation based on its syntactic tokens. At last, LSH is employed to map the high-dimensional vectors to the clusters in a low-dimensional space. The smart contracts in the same cluster is similar.

4.1   Code Syntactic Tokenizing

To obtain code syntax of a smart contract, we should identify the syntax of each code line containing in the smart contract. We employ the algorithm proposed in our previous study [2] to identify the main syntax tokens of smart contracts, such as *MappingExpression, ModifierDeclaration, IfStatement, AssignmentExpression, ReturnStatement, payable, Money*. Our algorithm parses abstract syntax tree to obtain the syntactic tokens of each code line. It's worth noting that a single code line may contain multiple types of syntax tokens. For example, a `if` code line "`if(_to == address(this))`" contains three types of syntax tokens: *IfStatement, BinaryExpression*, and *CallExpression*.

For all the user-created and contract-created contracts in our dataset, we extract the syntax tokens at code line level. Then, the syntax tokens containing in each code line is a token set, and we regard it as a token unit. For example, the token unit of code line "`if(_to == address(this))`" is $<IfStatement, BinaryExpression, and CallExpression>$. Then, the token units contained by a contract is the features that can be used to measure the similarity between the contracts.

Similar to the bag of words model [28], we can build a vector for each smart contract according to the token units its contained. Then, for all the contracts, a feature matrix is built. Two vector matrices based on the token units is built for the user-created and contract-created smart contracts, respectively. As Figure 1 shows, there are z user-created smart contracts, and we identify the token units contained in each contract. Then, we use matrix M to represent the token units that each contract contains. If a contract contains a certain token unit, it is labeled as 1 in the matrix. The matrix M is $z \times m$, and m is the number of the distinct token units.

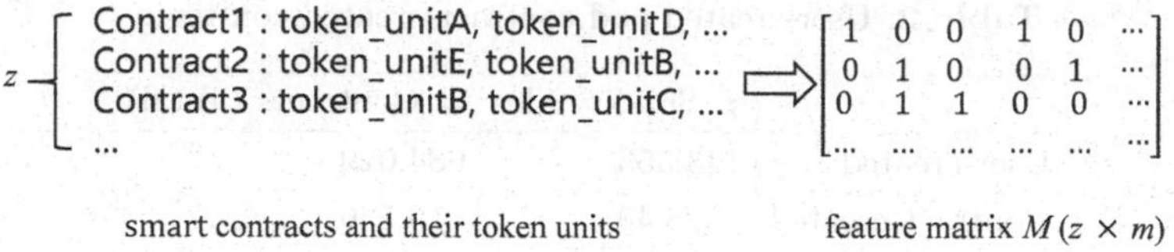

$$z \left\{ \begin{array}{l} \text{Contract1 : token\_unitA, token\_unitD, ...} \\ \text{Contract2 : token\_unitE, token\_unitB, ...} \\ \text{Contract3 : token\_unitB, token\_unitC, ...} \\ \text{...} \end{array} \right. \implies \begin{bmatrix} 1 & 0 & 0 & 1 & 0 & \cdots \\ 0 & 1 & 0 & 0 & 1 & \cdots \\ 0 & 1 & 1 & 0 & 0 & \cdots \\ \cdots & \cdots & \cdots & \cdots & \cdots & \cdots \end{bmatrix}$$

smart contracts and their token units   feature matrix $M (z \times m)$

Fig. 1. Transforming token units into vectors

4.2 LSH Clustering

We can use the LSH method to cluster the similar contract based on the feature matrix M. Specifically, we firstly randomly generate a zero-one matrix V with $m \times r$ dimensions. Then, we multiply matrices M and V, and obtain third matrix H. Each element $H(i.j)$ in H represent the product between the feature vector of a smart contract c_i and a random zero-one vector. If $H(i.j)$ is greater than a threshold t, the locality-sensitive hashing value $h(c_i)$ of the smart contract is 1. Otherwise, $h(c_i)$ is 0. Repeating the previous steps r times, we can get r locality-sensitive hashing values. If we splice these values together, and we can get a hashing sequence consisting of 0 and 1 with r length for smart contract c_i, i.e., $H(c_i) = (h^1(c_i), ..., h^r(c_i))$. Figure 2 shows the process of applying LSH to the feature matrix.

$$\begin{bmatrix} 1 & 0 & 0 & 1 & 0 & \cdots \\ 0 & 1 & 0 & 0 & 1 & \cdots \\ 0 & 1 & 1 & 0 & 0 & \cdots \\ \cdots & \cdots & \cdots & \cdots & \cdots & \cdots \end{bmatrix} \times \begin{bmatrix} 1 & 0 & \cdots & 0 \\ 0 & 1 & \cdots & 0 \\ \vdots & \vdots & \vdots & \vdots \\ 1 & 0 & \cdots & 0 \end{bmatrix}$$

feature matrix $M (z \times m)$ random matrix $V (m \times r)$

$$\begin{bmatrix} 1 & 0 & \cdots & 2 \\ 3 & 1 & \cdots & 0 \\ \vdots & \vdots & \vdots & \vdots \\ 0 & 4 & \cdots & 1 \end{bmatrix} \xrightarrow{\begin{cases} if\ H_{i,j} > t, then\ H'_{i,j} = 1 \\ if\ H_{i,j} \leq t, then\ H'_{i,j} = 0 \end{cases}} \begin{bmatrix} 0 & 0 & \cdots & 0 \\ 1 & 0 & \cdots & 0 \\ \vdots & \vdots & \vdots & \vdots \\ 0 & 1 & \cdots & 0 \end{bmatrix}$$

LSH matrix $H (z \times r)$ LSH matrix $H' (z \times r)$

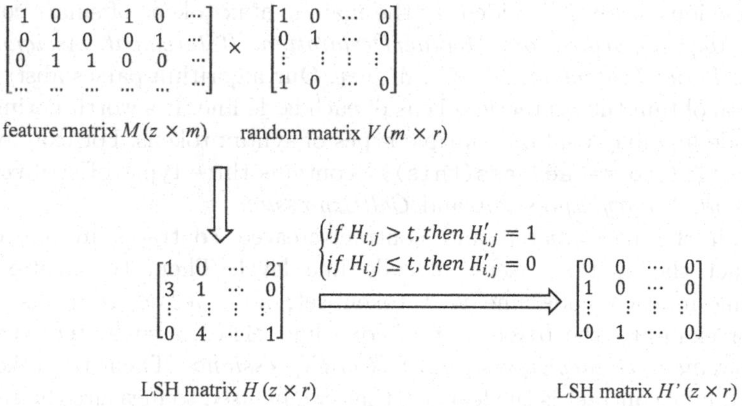

Fig. 2. Applying LSH to the feature matrix

According to the locality-sensitive hashing value $H(c_i)$ of smart contract c_i, we can map the smart contract to a bucket $[b_1..., b_k]$, where $[b_1..., b_k]$ is the existing buckets [16], and k is the number of buckets. As a result, the similar contracts are mapped to the same buckets, and these contracts in the same buckets are likely to involve code clone. We regard the smart contracts in the buckets as a cluster. Figure 3 shows the process of mapping smart contracts to the different buckets.

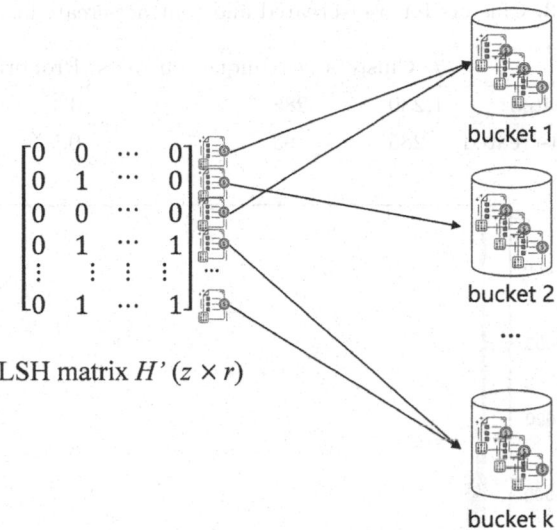

$$\begin{bmatrix} 0 & 0 & \cdots & 0 \\ 0 & 1 & \cdots & 0 \\ 0 & 0 & \cdots & 0 \\ 0 & 1 & \cdots & 1 \\ \vdots & \vdots & \vdots & \vdots \\ 0 & 1 & \cdots & 1 \end{bmatrix}$$

LSH matrix H' $(z \times r)$

bucket 1

bucket 2

bucket k

Fig. 3. Mapping smart contracts to different buckets

5   Results Analysis

When we apply LSH to cluster the similar smart contracts, the parameters t is 3 and r is 13. We cluster the similar smart contracts on the user-created and contract-created datasets, respectively.

5.1   Quantitative Analysis

Our observations from Table 3 show that LSH generates 1,230 clusters for user-created smart contracts. There are 288 unique contracts, which means they do not belong to any of the clusters. The proportion of the unique contracts is 4% (i.e., 288/684,029). This result suggests that 96% of user-created smart contracts can find at least one similar contracts in the dataset. For the contract-created contracts, there are 285 clusters created by LSH, and 93 contract-created smart contracts do not belong to any of the clusters, and this means that 99.5% (i.e., 19,443/19,536) of contract-created smart contracts can find at least one similar contracts in the dataset. Therefore, we can conclude that the code clone is a common practice in both user-created and contract-created smart contracts, and the result also reveals the homogeneity nature of the smart contract on the Ethereum.

Figure 4 shows the top 100 clusters for user-created contracts. We can observe that the biggest cluster contains 22,9224 contracts. In general, the clusters of user-created contracts follows a long-tail distribution considering there are 1,230 clusters in total. For all the user-created contracts, the top 20 clusters account for 87% of the contracts. The results suggest that the distribution of clusters follows

Table 3. Clusters for user-created and contract-created contracts

	# Clusters	# Unique contracts	Proportion (%)
User-created	1,230	288	4%
Contract-created	285	93	0.5%

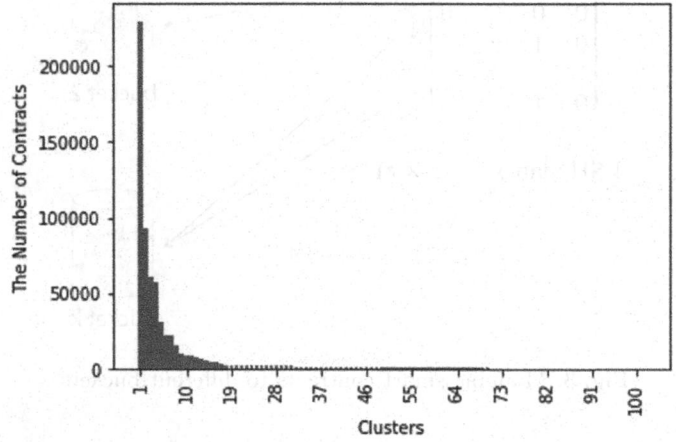

Fig. 4. Top 100 clusters of user-created contracts

a typical Pareto principle rule. Therefore, many smart contracts are concentrated in same cluster, and these contracts have similar code.

Figure 5 shows the top 100 clusters for contract-created contracts. The biggest cluster contains 5,994 contracts. The distribution of clusters also follows a typical Pareto principle rule, i.e., the top 20 clusters account for 90% of the smart contracts.

5.2 Qualitative Analysis

Since all the collected contracts are open source, we manually check these clusters and identify them according to the source code of the smart contracts. The largest clusters mainly fall into the following categories:

ERC Related Clusters. ERC related contracts take the majority of popular clusters. ERC standard[3] includes ERC-20, ERC-721, ERC-825, ERC-223. For example, to achieve the "issue currency", the corresponding smart contracts should implement the "interface" of ERC20. If a contract want to implement the ERC20 interface, it needs to implement the 6 functions, i.e., `totalSupply()`, `balanceOf()`, `transfer()`, `transferFrom()`, `approve()`, `allowance()`. As a result, all the smart contracts implements the ERC20 interface have similar

---

[3] A standard interface for tokens. https://eips.ethereum.org/EIPS/eip-20.

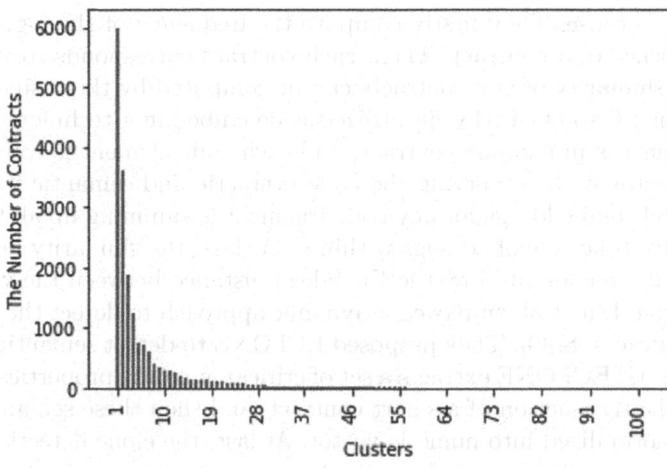

Fig. 5. Top 100 clusters of contract-created contracts

source code. The famous tokens implementing the ERC20 interface include: Huobi Token[4], FTX Token[5], USD Coin[6], etc.

Gambling Related Clusters. Many clusters are related to the gambling contracts. There are many gambling contracts on the Ethereum, and these gambling contracts often implement very simple and similar logic. Then, developers can directly copied and pasted the original open-source contracts to create similar gambling contract. As a result, the gambling contracts can be clustered together.

Other Clusters. We also observe other types of clusters, such as, game related cluster, social related cluster. These clusters have a strong industry orientation. The contracts belonging to the same industry are more likely to cluster together. These results suggest that the smart contracts on the Ethereum are highly homogeneous.

6 Related Work

The clone detection for smart contract can be divided into static [6,7,13,29] and dynamic ways [8,30]. He et al. [7] revealed that a large number of smart contracts are similar on Ethereum, which suggests that the smart contract is highly homogeneous. Our study is different from them in the clustering approaches. He et al. clustered any contract pair whose similarity score is greater than 0.7. Then, they build a weighted undirected graph by treating each contract as a node. At last, they traverse the graph and consider each connected component as a cluster. Kiffer et al. [6] found the smart contracts on Ethereum exhibit

---

[4] https://coinmarketcap.com/currencies/huobi-token/.
[5] https://coinmarketcap.com/currencies/ftx-token/.
[6] https://coinmarketcap.com/currencies/usd-coin/.

extensive code reuse. They firstly compute the frequency of the 5-grams in the opcode sequence of a contract. Then, each contract corresponds to vector of 5-grams. The similarity of two contracts can be computed by the cosine similarity of two vectors. Gao et al. [13,29] utilized code embedding technique to encode the code elements in a smart contract, and each code element is converted into numerical vector with preserving the code syntactic and semantic information. Then, the code embeddings for any code fragment is summing up all the vectors of the possible tokens' embeddings within it. At last, the similarity between two fragments can be computed by the Euclidean distance between the vectors.

In addition, Liu et al. employed a dynamic approach to detect the code clone in smart contracts [8,30]. They proposed ECLONE to detect semantic clones for smart contracts. ECLONE extracts a set of critical semantic properties generated from symbolic transaction of a smart contract, and then these semantic properties will be normalized into numeric vector. At last, the clone detection problem is modeled as a similarity computation of the numeric vectors. In summary, our approach is different from the existing studies. We extract the code syntactic tokens from each smart contract, and employ the LSH method to cluster the similar smart contracts and further analysis the code clone in smart contracts.

7   Conclusion and Future Work

Code clone is an essential and vital part of modern software development. Although studying the code clone has a long research history, we are the first to employ the LSH technique to analyze the similarity of the user-created and contract-created contracts, respectively. To evaluate our approach, we collect a datasets that contains more than 700,000 smart contract coming from Ethereum. The quantitative analysis shows that over 96% of the smart contracts are similar. The qualitative analysis reveals that the majority of popular clusters are ERC related contracts. The future research agenda mainly focus on extending the scale of the dataset. Firstly, we will take more open source smart contracts into consideration. Secondly, we will try to identify the code clone in the closed source smart contracts.

Acknowledgments. This research is supported by the National Natural Science Foundation of China (61902105), the Characteristic Innovation Project of Guangdong Province Office of Education (2019GKTSCX129).

References

1. Nakamoto, S.: Bitcoin: a peer-to-peer electronic cash system. Cryptography Mailing list, March 2009. https://metzdowd.com
2. Huang, Y., Kong, Q., Jia, N., Chen, X., Zheng, Z.: Recommending differentiated code to support smart contract update. In: 2019 IEEE/ACM 27th International Conference on Program Comprehension (ICPC), pp. 260–270, May 2019

3. Dinh, T.T.A., Liu, R., Zhang, M., Chen, G., Ooi, B.C., Wang, J.: Untangling blockchain: a data processing view of blockchain systems. IEEE Trans. Knowl. Data Eng. **30**(7), 1366–1385 (2018)
4. Zheng, P., Zheng, Z., Luo, X., Chen, X., Liu, X.: A detailed and real-time performance monitoring framework for blockchain systems. In: International Conference on Software Engineering Software Engineering in Practice - ICSE-SEIP 2018, pp. 134–143, May 2018
5. Norta, A.: Creation of smart-contracting collaborations for decentralized autonomous organizations. In: Matulevičius, R., Dumas, M. (eds.) BIR 2015. LNBIP, vol. 229, pp. 3–17. Springer, Cham (2015). https://doi.org/10.1007/978-3-319-21915-8_1
6. Kiffer, L., Levin, D., Mislove, A.: Analyzing ethereum's contract topology. In: Proceedings of the Internet Measurement Conference 2018, pp. 494–499 (2018)
7. He, N., Wu, L., Wang, H., Guo, Y., Jiang, X.: Characterizing code clones in the ethereum smart contract ecosystem. arXiv preprint arXiv:1905.00272 (2019)
8. Liu, H., Yang, Z., Jiang, Y., Zhao, W., Sun, J.: Enabling clone detection for ethereum via smart contract birthmarks. In: 2019 IEEE/ACM 27th International Conference on Program Comprehension (ICPC), pp. 105–115. IEEE (2019)
9. Christidis, K., Devetsikiotis, M.: Blockchains and smart contracts for the internet of things. IEEE Access **4**, 2292–2303 (2016)
10. Juels, A., Kosba, A., Shi, E.: The ring of gyges: investigating the future of criminal smart contracts. In: Proceedings of the 2016 ACM SIGSAC Conference on Computer and Communications Security, CCS 2016. ACM, New York, pp. 283–295 (2016). http://doi.acm.org/10.1145/2976749.2978362
11. Nick, S.: The idea of smart contracts (1997). http://www.fon.hum.uva.nl/rob/Courses/InformationInSpeech/CDROM/Literature/LOTwinterschool2006/szabo.best.vwh.net/idea.html. Accessed 2008
12. Chen, T., et al.: Understanding ethereum via graph analysis. In: IEEE INFOCOM 2018 - IEEE Conference on Computer Communications, pp. 1484–1492, April 2018
13. Gao, Z., Jiang, L., Xia, X., Lo, D., Grundy, J.: Checking smart contracts with structural code embedding. IEEE Trans. Softw. Eng. (2020)
14. Porru, S., Pinna, A., Marchesi, M., Tonelli, R.: Blockchain-oriented software engineering: challenges and new directions. In: 2017 IEEE/ACM 39th International Conference on Software Engineering Companion (ICSE-C), pp. 169–171, May 2017
15. Somin, S., Gordon, G., Altshuler, Y.: Network analysis of ERC20 tokens trading on ethereum blockchain. In: Morales, A.J., Gershenson, C., Braha, D., Minai, A.A., Bar-Yam, Y. (eds.) ICCS 2018. SPC, pp. 439–450. Springer, Cham (2018). https://doi.org/10.1007/978-3-319-96661-8_45
16. Gionis, A., Indyk, P., Motwani, R., et al.: Similarity search in high dimensions via hashing. Vldb **99**(6), 518–529 (1999)
17. Swan, M.: Blockchain: Blueprint for a New Economy, 1st edn. O'Reilly Media Inc., Newton (2015)
18. Wang, B., Chen, S., Yao, L., Liu, B., Xu, X., Zhu, L.: A simulation approach for studying behavior and quality of blockchain networks. In: Chen, S., Wang, H., Zhang, L.-J. (eds.) ICBC 2018. LNCS, vol. 10974, pp. 18–31. Springer, Cham (2018). https://doi.org/10.1007/978-3-319-94478-4_2
19. Parizi, R.M., Amritraj, Dehghantanha, A.: Smart contract programming languages on blockchains: an empirical evaluation of usability and security. In: Chen, S., Wang, H., Zhang, L.J. (eds.) ICBC 2018. LNCS, vol. 10974, pp. 75–91. Springer, Cham (2018). https://doi.org/10.1007/978-3-319-94478-4_6

20. Huang, Y., Chen, X., Zou, Q., Luo, X.: A probabilistic neural network-based approach for related software changes detection. In: 2014 21st Asia-Pacific Software Engineering Conference, vol. 1, pp. 279–286, December 2014

21. Kosba, A., Miller, A., Shi, E., Wen, Z., Papamanthou, C.: Hawk: the blockchain model of cryptography and privacy-preserving smart contracts. In: 2016 IEEE Symposium on Security and Privacy (SP), pp. 839–858, May 2016

22. Bartoletti, M., Carta, S., Cimoli, T., Saia, R.: Dissecting Ponzi schemes on Ethereum: identification, analysis, and impact. ArXiv e-prints, March 2017

23. Huang, Y., Jia, N., Shu, J., Hu, X., Chen, X., Zhou, Q.: Does your code need comment? Softw.: Pract. Exp. **50**(3), 227–245 (2020). https://onlinelibrary.wiley.com/doi/abs/10.1002/spe.2772

24. Huang, Y., Zheng, Q., Chen, X., Xiong, Y., Liu, Z., Luo, X.: Mining version control system for automatically generating commit comment. In: 2017 ACM/IEEE International Symposium on Empirical Software Engineering and Measurement (ESEM), pp. 414–423, November 2017

25. Huang, Y., Chen, X., Liu, Z., Luo, X., Zheng, Z.: Using discriminative feature in software entities for relevance identification of code changes. J. Softw.: Evol. Process **29**(7), e1859 (2017). e1859 smr.1859. https://onlinelibrary.wiley.com/doi/abs/10.1002/smr.1859

26. Huang, Y., Jia, N., Chen, X., Hong, K., Zheng, Z.: Salient-class location: help developers understand code change in code review. In: Proceedings of the 2018 26th ACM Joint Meeting on European Software Engineering Conference and Symposium on the Foundations of Software Engineering, ser. ESEC/FSE 2018, pp. 770–774. ACM, New York (2018). http://doi.acm.org/10.1145/3236024.3264841

27. Huang, Y., Hu, X., Jia, N., Chen, X., Xiong, Y., Zheng, Z.: Learning code context information to predict comment locations. IEEE Trans. Reliab. 1–18 (2019)

28. Jiang, H., Xiao, Y., Wang, W.: English explaining a bag of words with hierarchical conceptual labels. World Wide Web (2020). Bag-of-words models; Concept graph; De-noising algorithm; Explicit semantics; High-accuracy;Knowledge base; NAtural language processing; Rose tree. http://dx.doi.org/10.1007/s11280-019-00752-3

29. Gao, Z., Jayasundara, V., Jiang, L., Xia, X., Lo, D., Grundy, J.: SmartEmbed: a tool for clone and bug detection in smart contracts through structural code embedding. In: 2019 IEEE International Conference on Software Maintenance and Evolution (ICSME), pp. 394–397. IEEE (2019)

30. Liu, H., Yang, Z., Liu, C., Jiang, Y., Zhao, W., Sun, J.: EClone: detect semantic clones in ethereum via symbolic transaction sketch. In: Proceedings of the 2018 26th ACM Joint Meeting on European Software Engineering Conference and Symposium on the Foundations of Software Engineering, pp. 900–903 (2018)

Trustworthy Dynamic Target Detection and Automatic Monitor Scheme for Mortgage Loan with Blockchain-Based Smart Contract

Qinnan Zhang[1]([✉]) [iD], Jianming Zhu[1], and Yuchen Wang[2]

[1] School of Information, Central University of Finance and Economics, Beijing 100081, China
zhangqnp@163.com
[2] Software Development Center of ICBC, Beijing 100080, China

Abstract. Driven by technologies such as deep learning and blockchain, financial service industry has made rapid improvements in recent years. Mortgage loan is the main profit-making means of commercial banks, but there are many problems such as manpower cost, insufficient accuracy and evaluation of collateral. To cope with those problem, Artificial Intelligence (AI) and blockchain have been widely exploited. However, the monitoring of collateral is image recognition in dynamic video and it is difficult to avoid the risk of security attack. In this paper, we design a blockchain empowered method to achieve dynamic target detection and automatic monitor, which the change of target location and quantity can be detected by deep learning and recorded in blockchain. Meanwhile, if risk is detected, it will automatically trigger the alarm smart contract to realize automatic monitoring. We further implement a software prototype on fabric framework with real-world scenarios. Experiment results from real-world images show that the feasibility, usability and scalability of our proposed dynamic target detection and automatic monitor scheme for mortgage loan.

Keywords: Deep learning · Image recognition · Target detection · Automatic monitor · Blockchain · Smart contract

1 Introduction

Recently, the target detection and automatic monitor has drawn tremendous attention from financial service industry, in which the detection and monitoring of loan collateral has great potential application prospect. Mortgage loan is an important financial service for commercial banks to make profits. The advancements in technologies such as Internet of Things (IoT) [1], 5G, edge computing, deep learning and blockchain have paved the way for the rapid development of mortgage loan, resulting in an exponential growth of data generated by information of collateral. However, it is still facing the impact of risks such as high cost of manpower, low efficiency of collateral monitoring and inaccurate evaluation. Currently, most loan mortgage risk prevention and control mode mainly rely on manpower to analyze, distinguish and monitor. It not only consumes a lot of manpower, but also has the risk of miscalculation. Taking the financial mortgage

© Springer Nature Singapore Pte Ltd. 2020
Z. Zheng et al. (Eds.): BlockSys 2020, CCIS 1267, pp. 415–427, 2020.
https://doi.org/10.1007/978-981-15-9213-3_33

business as a breakthrough point, providing a more efficient, reliable and intelligent way for dynamic target detection and monitoring scheme has become an important research direction in financial industry.

In recent years, the application of artificial intelligence has developed in a variety of tasks, which significantly improves the efficiency of work. Among them, the improvement of deep learning [2] based on neural networks have witnessed unprecedented accuracy in various tasks, such as image recognition [3], speech recognition [4], drug discovery [5], cancer detection [6]. Artificial Intelligence (AI) is a powerful tool for addressing a great verity of complexity problems such as solving NP hard problems [7] and making predictions. The evolution of recognition algorithm for target detection improving the quality of mortgage loan services.

Image recognition based on deep learning has been developing rapidly in the field of target detection in recent years. In 2014, Ross Girshick, etc. [8] proposed R-CNN algorithm, which selected RoI (Region of Interest) as sample input by using selective search algorithm [9], which is supported by Support Vector Machine (SVM) [10] to classify and locate. In the same year, Ross Girshick [11] proposed Fast R-CNN algorithm and designed RoI Pooling layer structure, that effectively avoids the steps of image clipping and scaling in the same size in R-CNN processing, but it still does not get rid of the problem of excessive computational load caused by selective search algorithm to generate positive and negative sample candidate boxes. In 2015, Kaiming He, etc. [12] designed RPN (Region Proposal Network) to generate samples, and proposed Faster R-CNN algorithm. In 2017, Kaiming He, etc. [13] proposed Mask R-CNN algorithm, which replaced RoI Pooling layer in Fast R-CNN with RoI Align structure and added FCN branches for semantic recognition, thus enabling target detection network to have pixel-level image semantics segmentation capability.

Blockchain was first proposed as a core technology of bitcoin in 2008 [14], which constitutes the trust foundation of decentralized application [15]. At present, blockchain technology is regarded as the cornerstone of value internet, which has broad application prospects and opportunities [16]. However, blockchain also faces many application challenges. First, blockchain Ponzi scheme has caused serious negative impact, Edith Ngai, etc. [17] proposes an approach to detect Ponzi schemes on blockchain by using data mining and machine learning methods. Second, the current blockchain has low performance, Peilin Zheng, etc. [18] propose real-time performance monitoring framework for blockchain systems. Finally, the current blockchain scalability is poor, consensus algorithm will not be effective with the increase of nodes [19].

With the combination of distributed computing, cryptography, consensus algorithm, smart contract and other technologies, blockchain can guarantee that the system is tamper-proof, traceable and auditable without the credit endorsement of the third-party intermediary. However, there are some new challenges need to be tackled when deploy deep learning and blockchain in mortgage loan networks. First, existing deep learning algorithms are all based on static object detection and semantics segmentation on a single image and have not made an application attempt based on dynamic video stream type. Second, the centralized server for monitor is vulnerable to security threats, which can lead to the failure of the whole process of detection and monitor. Third, the process of data colloction may leak the private information of client. In this paper, we carries out the following tasks: modifying and adjusting the hyperparameters of Mask R-CNN network to adapt the dynamic target detection; giving dynamic flow processing of real-time mortgage video detection, which combine the information changes of the number, location and mask of mortgages; deploying it in consortium blockchain for recording detection results and automatic monitor collateral for mortgage loan business. To the end, our specific contributions are as following:

- We modify and adjust the hyperparameters of the mask R-CNN network to detect the dynamic target. Moreover, we design a real-time alarm algorithm based on the change of number, location and area of collateral.
- We propose a blockchian empowered collaborative framwork to target dectect over distributed node to reduce the risk of data leakage.
- We also evaluate the effectiveness of our proposed model with Hyperledger Caliper and CIFER-10 datasets for image detection.

The remaining of this paper is organized as follows. In Sect. 2, we introduce related preliminaries and system overview. In Sect. 3, the method of dynamic target detection is described in detail. The process of automatic monitor and alarm smart contract are further provided in Sect. 4. In Sect. 5, we present the security analysis and experimental evaluation of our proposed scheme on real-world datasets. Finally, we summarize this paper in Sect. 6.

2 Preliminaries

2.1 Mask R-CNN

Mask R-CNN is an instance segmentation algorithm, which can be used for target detection, target instance segmentation and target key point detection. Mask R-CNN achieves pixel-level instance segmentation expansion based on Faster R-CNN target detection, which predicts the segmentation mask by adding a mask branch to each RoI region and achieved excellent results. Moreover, it performs classification prediction and boundary box regression in parallel with the existing branches.

The first two steps of Mask R-CNN image processing process are the same as Faster R-CNN: the first step is to extract candidate regions from input images using Region Proposal Network (RPN). The second step, full convolution network(FCN) [20] applied to each RoI feature graph as the mask branch is added on the basis of its network structure at the same time of regression calculation, and the mask of the output candidate is predicted in parallel from pixel to pixel. The RoI of each sample is defined as a multitask loss function as follow:

$$L = L_{cls} + L_{box} + L_{mask} \tag{1}$$

The definition of classified loss function L_{cls} and location-box loss function L_{box} consistent with Faster R-CNN. The FCN branch uses sigmoid activation function for each pixel. In order to avoid the competition among masks generated by different classes, the average binary cross-entropy loss function L_{mask} is defined, and then k $m * m$ two value mask are output for each RoI to represent the spatial layout of candidate input objects of different k classifications at the pixel level.

Mask R-CNN uses Rectified Linear Unit (ReLU) as an activation function (2). Compared with sigmoid activation function, the ReLU activation function is more consistent with neuron excitation principle. There are many advantage including that small amount of calculation can accelerate the training speed of the model, shorten the convergence time of the model, and restrain the disappearance of gradient.

$$f(x_i) = \begin{cases} x_i & x_i > 0 \\ 0 & x_i < 0 \end{cases} \tag{2}$$

Region Proposal Network (RPN) outputs a set of candidate target areas and their scores on an arbitrary size image. It slides on the pre-network convolution feature image and takes the 3*3 windows on the feature map as input (each window is mapped to a 256-dimensional low-dimensional feature). Non-Maximum Suppression (NMS) [21] uses the idea of local maximum search to suppress the local non-maxima with the proportional threshold of IoU, and retains the candidate region of local maxima, that has the following steps: calculate the area of each box; rank the largest box according to the score; calculate the IoU of the remaining box and the current box; suppress the box that exceeds the IoU threshold, and repeat until the box queue is empty.

2.2 Blockchain-Based Smart Contract

In 1994, Nick Szabo [22] first proposed the concept of smart contract. He defined the smart contract as a computer program implementation of the contract terms, which can ensure the correct performance of the contract without the need for a trusted third party. With the development of blockchain technology, its decentralized trusted platform provides a natural distributed trusted execution environment for smart contracts, and realizes the expansion of blockchain technology application scenarios.

Ethereum smart contract development language is mainly solidity, which can support writing logic code in a special browser development platform Remix [23]. However, there are lots of repetitive codes on the Ethereum, in order to support smart contract update differentiated code is defined as the source code except the repeated ones in two similar smart contracts [24]. In addation, the security of smart contracts has always been a concern problems. In June 2017, a crowdfunding smart contract of the Ethereum platform [25] named the Dao was attacked.

2.3 System Overview

In this paper, we apply deep learning and blockchain in mortage loan for dynamic collateral detection and monitor. As depicted in Fig. 1, the consortium blockchain network consists of the banks and credit agencies, a number of camera equipment and moving collateral. Each collateral is monitored by GPS and camera equipment. The camera equipment has powerful computing and storage capabilities, which enables them to perform a large number of computing and caching tasks. Each GPS is connected to the camera equipment and is capable of computing and caching.

Consortium blockchain establishes secure and trustworthy records among all the end data collection devices through its encrypted and consensus process, which is maintained by the bank's servers with computing and storage resources. There are two types of transactions in our consortium blockchain: data record transactions and automatic alarm transactions. The data collection device packs the data after digital signature, and stores it on the blockchain after node consensus authentication. The training node collects data to start model training, and returns the detection results to the blockchain. For the privacy concerns, we encrypt the data, instead of to record the raw data. The credit agencies obtains the detection result and updates risk assessment criteria to the blockchain. If there is any risk in target, it will start the alarm equipment.

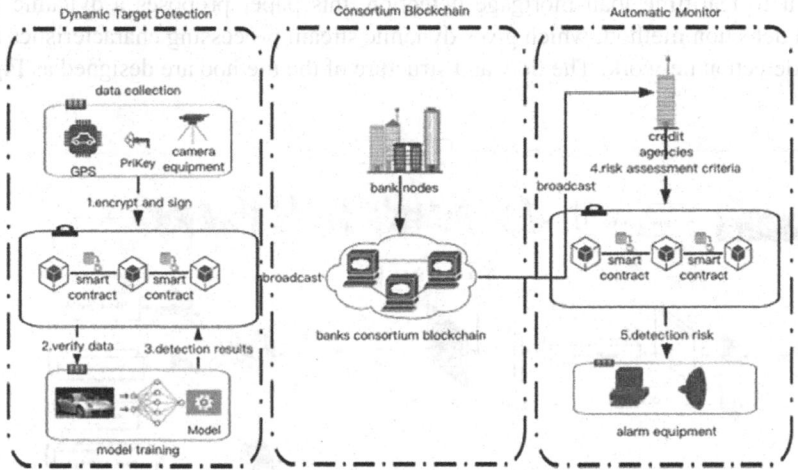

Fig. 1. Architecture of dynamic target detection and automatic monitor scheme

3 Dynamic Target Detection

3.1 Network Hyperparameters Design

ReLU activation function solves the problem of gradient dispersion of some sigmoid functions and speeds up the convergence of loss function. However, the feature of ReLU forcing negative values to zero often leads to the loss of many features of images. A new activation function, PReLU, is used in this paper. The expression is as follow:

$$f(x_i) = \begin{cases} x_i \ x_i > 0 \\ a_i x_i \ x_i < 0 \end{cases} \tag{3}$$

Compared with the ReLU function PReLU introduces a_i as a new parameter for negative input. The introduction of negative parameters avoids the loss of image features. PReLU only increases a bit computational complexity and the risk of over-fitting, which retains the advantages of ReLU in correcting data distribution and accelerating the convergence of loss function, and avoids the loss of negative features. Therefore, the PReLU activation function is used to replace the ReLU activation function in the original Mask R-CNN.

3.2 Dynamic Video Processing

Mask R-CNN network is designed for static processing of single image. In order to apply it to real-time loan mortgage detection, this paper proposes a dynamic video stream detection method, which gives dynamic stream processing characteristics to the target detection network. The flow and structure of the method are designed as Fig. 2.

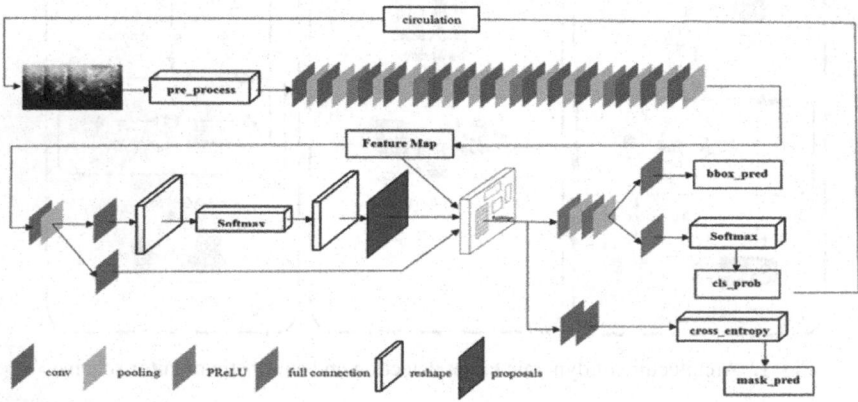

Fig. 2. The structure of network and the procession of simulate object detection on video data

1. Acquisition of real-time video stream data, frame interception operation, converted data for a single frame image set;
2. OpenCV is used to pre-process the intercepted single frame image, such as denoising, white balance, size transformation, etc.
3. The processed and processed single-frame image is transmitted to the network as input, and the network processes the image and outputs the result of image target detection.
4. Intercept the next video image and cycle the above operations.

3.3 Hash Conflict Resolution

In this paper, the target detection network outputs the type and probability score of the target object, the bbox of the target object coordinate frame and the mask set of the target object mask for a single frame image, as shown in Table 1. Each row in the table represents a complete array in the detection result structure. Hash Map structure is designed to store its detection information as baseline (Table 2) and comparison (Table 3). We use Hash algorithm principle to solve Hash conflict, in which the unique distinguishable individual ID is constructed for different target sharing unique category number.

Table 1. The detection results on one frame by this network

Cls	Car	Car	Airplane	......	Car
Prob	0.892	0.974	0.996	......	0.942
Bbox	(35, 46, 128, 256)	(12, 25, 311, 478)	(36, 48, 955, 948)	......	(49, 24, 312, 566)
Mask	[0.2536,0.3549, ..., 0.7748]	[0.3755,0.4546, ..., 0.65946]	[0.6465,0.6542, ..., 0.6455]	......	[0.6464,0.3546, ..., 0.64644]

Table 2. The structure of BaseLine

ID	Cls	Prob	Bbox	Mask
001	Car	0.892	(35, 46, 128, 256)	[0.2536,0.3549, ..., 0.7748]
101	Car	0.974	(12, 25, 311, 478)	[0.3755,0.4546, ..., 0.65946]
201	Car	0.942	(49, 24, 312, 566)	[0.6464,0.3546, ..., 0.64644]

Table 3. The structure of Comparison

ID	Cls	Prob	Bbox	Mask
001	Car	0.892	(35, 46, 128, 256)	[0.2536,0.3549, ..., 0.7748]
101	Car	0.974	(12, 25, 311, 478)	[0.3755,0.4546, ..., 0.65946]

4 Automatic Monitor and Alarm

4.1 Detection Results Consensus

Using consortium blockchain to record target detection results brings many benefits. First, the target detection results are stored on the blockchain after encryption and digital signature, which achieve the traceable and tamper proof information sharing. Moreover, the smart contract can automatic provide more reliable risk alarm results to banks, which can automatically monitor collateral. However, existing consensus in blockchain such as PoW, achieve consensus by consuming a lot of useless computing, resulting in waste of computing and communication resources. In order to reduce the waste of resources, we propose a proof of contribution protocol (PoC) for consortium blockchain transaction consensus. PoC utilizes worker's contribution to reach consensus, which can make better use of the workers' computing and communication resources. When a specific transaction request is coming, we select a leader from workers in transaction blockchain by contribution value in the blockchain. The leader is responsible for driving the consensus process and relay transaction information.

The factors can be considered as follows: first, only online nodes participate in the operation of the system online can ensure the normal operation of the blockchain. Second, the more users the system participates in the stronger the system availability. Therefore, this scheme makes the online calculation time of nodes as a contribution to promote the stable and safe operation of the digital currency transaction blockchain. The online contribution of nodes is obtained by calculating the online time of nodes and multiplying the coefficient α as follow:

$$OC = \alpha * \left(T_{lastblock} - T_{addtime} - T_{offline} \right) \tag{4}$$

Where OC is the online contribution value of the user; α is the online time coefficient of the system, which controls the proportion of OC value and the reward value of the overall contribution value, $T_{lastblock}$ is the block time stamp in the last block of the completed consensus; $T_{addtime}$ is the time stamp for each user to add to the network for the first time; $T_{offline}$ is the offline time of the server node.

4.2 Real-Time Alarm Process

The real-time monitoring and alarm has the following steps: In first step, system receives the comparison of the content information table of the image to be detected, and extracts the same kind of objects from the comparison and the reference standard information table baseline for number statistics, and detects whether the number of objects in the two frames has changed. In second step, system determines whether the number of comparison target objects is consistent with that of baseline. In addition, system determines whether the number of comparison target objects is consistent with that of baseline. Moreover, system extracts location information of ID individuals corresponding to comparison table and baseline table and detecting whether the position of the corresponding object in two frames has changed. Finally, system determines whether to terminate the operation. Algorithm 1 illustrates the overall process of real-time alarm smart contract

Algorithm 1: Real-time Alarm Smart Contract
Input: Comparison Table, Baseline Table
Output: *Risk result* $\mathcal{R}_a$
1: time ← Current Time
2: **for** *Tx cache list* ≠ ∅ **do**
3:      **while** *Current Time − time < Set$_t$* **do**
4:           **if** Comparison$_{num}$ < Baseline$_{num}$**then**
5:                output: $\mathcal{R}_{target\_loss}$
6:           **else**
7:                output: $\mathcal{R}_{target\_enter}$
8:           **if** Displacement > *threshold*
9:                output: $\mathcal{R}_{location\_change}$
10:          **else**
11:                output: target location unchanged
12:          **if** Target$_{area}$ > *Baseline$_{area}$*
13:                output: $\mathcal{R}_{area\_change}$
14:          **else**
15:                output: target area unchanged
16:      *time* ← *Current Time*
17: **end while**
18: **end for**
19: **return** *Risk result* $\mathcal{R}_a$

5 Experiment and Evaluation

5.1 System Prototype

In this paper, the model trains 13 epochs at a speed of 3.5 fps based on deep learning framework includes TensorFlow 1.4.6, gcc 4.8.3, GTX 1060 3G, MS COCO data set. The target detection network takes video single frame image (Fig. 3a) as input, after network recognition processing, outputs the result graph including target object type, probability score, coordinate frame and mask value (Fig. 3b). The result of the first frame image detection is used as the monitoring benchmark. This paper realizes real-time detection of the number and location of mortgage targets. Real-time alarm alert when the target type collateral enters and lost the monitoring area as shown in Fig. 4.

5.2 Performance Evaluation

This paper uses the consortium blockchain to build a trustworthy target detection and monitor system based on image recognition. In order to evaluate the practicability of the scheme in this paper, we use CIFER-10 dataset and deploy the simulation smart contract on the Hyperledger Fabric 1.4. In this section, Ubuntu 18.04. 3 system with 8 GB memory is used and the processor is Intel Core i5 3.2 GHz. In addition, we build a Fabric blockchain to simulate write transaction. we test the performance of the system by Hyperledger Caliper and the summary test result show as Fig. 5. Moreover, the training performance was tested on the CIFER-10 and Mnist datasets (see Fig. 6).

(a)input image

(b) output image

Fig. 3. The input image and output ((a) input image; (b) output image)

(a)target collateral lose

(b) target collateral object enter

Fig. 4. The results of detection and alarm information ((a) The results of detection and alarm information on object lose; (b) The results of detection and alarm information on object enter)

Test	Name	Succ	Fail	Send Rate	Max Latency	Min Latency	Avg Latency	Throughput
1	write	1000	0	100.2 tps	32.73 s	21.31 s	25.16 s	27.6 tps
2	query	100	0	101.2 tps	1.55 s	0.14 s	1.16 s	49.3 tps
3	invoke	89	11	50.5 tps	5.57 s	2.85 s	4.83 s	13.2 tps

Fig. 5. The summary of performance test result by Hyperledger Caliper

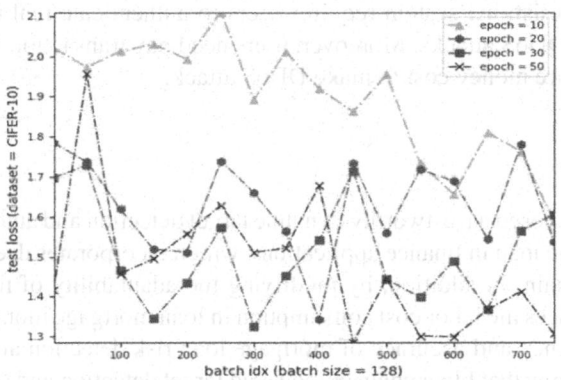

(a)   The results of training loss on CIFER-10

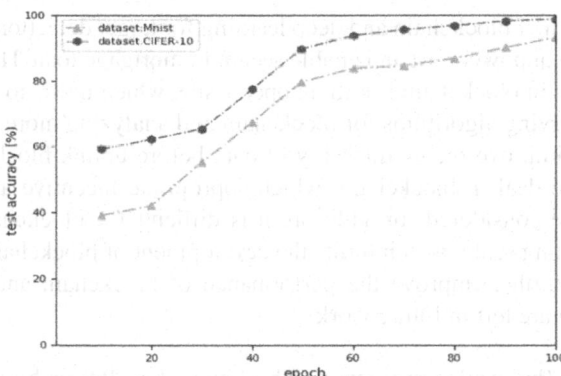

(b) The results of training accuracy on Mnist and CIFER-10 dataset

Fig. 6. The results of training performance ((a) The results of training loss on CIFER-10; (b) The results of training accuracy on Mnist and CIFER-10 dataset)

5.3 Security and Threat Analysis

In this paper, we build and deploy the consortium blockchain to establish an automatic monitor system for mortgage loan service. We integrate image recognition based deep learning and blockchain smart contract to address the security threats in the process of target detection and monitor.

- **Trustworthy results:** The consortium blockchain constructs a decentralized trustworthy detection and monitor mechanism, which stores detection results and performs smart contract. The decentralized detection and monitor scheme can guarantee the credibility and hard to tamper with the detection results, which can resist the risk of data leakage.
- **Transaction data security:** To prevent the dishonest user from detection transactions, the PoC consensus process validate the security of transaction data by the miners, and only the leader node can perform the smart contract.
- **DDoS Attack Resistant:** system requires users to authenticate real identity, which can resist major DDoS attacks. Moreover, users need pay transaction fees for miners so attackers require money cost to make DDoS attack.

6 Conclusions

In this paper, we proposed a trustworthy dynamic target detection and automatic monitor scheme for mortgage loan in finance applications, which incorporates deep learning and consortium blockchain. In addition, by modifying the adaptability of financial collateral, it not only reduces the labor cost consumption in loan mortgage monitoring but also improves the efficiency and accuracy of mortgage loan risk detection and control. The system prototype show that blockchain empowered target detection and automatic monitor scheme enhances the security during monitor process without requiring centralized trust.

The combination of blockchain and deep learning for target detection is a promising way to reduce the manpower cost and enable secure in mortgage loan. However, how to protect user privacy in blockchain is still an open issue, which needs to be explored by more privacy-preserving algorithms for blockchain and analyzing more security threat. Moreover, how to improve the creditability of data before uplink blockchain is still a problem need to be deal in blockchain, which appropriate incentive and punishment mechanisms can be considered. In addition, it is difficult for blockchain to adapt to the existing computing scale, which limits the development of blockchain applications. It is necessary to further improve the performance of blockchain and expand more applications, which are left in future work.

Acknowledgments. This work was supported by Nature Key Research and Development Program of China (2017YFB1400700), the National Natural Science Foundation of China (U1509214), the Central University of Finance and Economics Funds for the First-Class Discipline Construction in 2019.

References

1. Dai, H.-N., Zheng, Z., Zhang, Y.: Blockchain for internet of things: a survey. IEEE Internet of Things J. (IoT-J) **6**(5), 8076–8094 (2019)
2. LeCun, Y., Bengio, Y., Hinton, G.: Deep learning. Nature **521**(7553), 436–444 (2015)
3. Chan, T.H., Jia, K., Gao, S., et al.: PCANet: a simple deep learning baseline for image classification? IEEE Trans. Image Process. **24**(12), 5017–5032 (2015)

4. Hinton, G., Deng, L., Yu, D., et al.: Deep neural networks for acoustic modeling in speech recognition: The shared views of four research groups. IEEE Signal Process. Mag. **29**(6), 82–97 (2012)
5. Gawehn, E., Hiss, J.A., Schneider, G.: Deep learning in drug discovery. Mol. Inf. **35**(1), 3–14 (2016)
6. Danaee, P., Ghaeini, R., Hendrix, D.A.: A deep learning approach for cancer detection and relevant gene identification. In: Pacific Symposium on Biocomputing, pp. 219–229 (2017)
7. Bello, I., Pham, H., Le, Q.V., et al.: Neural combinatorial optimization with reinforcement learning. arXiv preprint arXiv:1611.09940 (2016)
8. Girshick, R., Donahue, J., Darrell, T., et al.: Region-based convolutional networks for accurate object detection and segmentation. IEEE Trans. Pattern Anal. Mach. Intell. **38**(1), 142–158 (2015)
9. Uijlings, J.R.R., Van De Sande, K.E.A., Gevers, T., et al.: Selective search for object recognition. Int. J. Comput. Vis. **104**(2), 154–171 (2013)
10. Press, W.H., Flannery, B.P., Teukolsky, S.A., et al.: Numerical Recipes: The Art of Scientific Computing. Cambridge University Press, Cambridge (1986). 839
11. Girshick, R.: Fast R-CNN. In: Proceedings of the IEEE International Conference on Computer Vision, pp. 1440–1448 (2015)
12. Ren, S., He, K., Girshick, R., et al.: Faster R-CNN: towards real-time object detection with region proposal networks. In: Advances in Neural Information Processing Systems, pp. 91–99 (2015)
13. He, K., Gkioxari, G., Dollár, P., et al.: Mask R-CNN. In: Proceedings of the IEEE International Conference on Computer Vision, pp. 2961–2969 (2017)
14. Nakamoto, S.: Bitcoin: a peer-to-peer electronic cash system (2008)
15. Zheng, Z., Xie, S., Dai, H., Chen, X., Wang, H.: An overview of blockchain technology: architecture, consensus, and future trends. In: Proceedings of IEEE 6th International Congress on Big Data (BigData), Hawaii, USA, pp. 557–564, June 2017
16. Zheng, Z., Xie, S., Dai, H., Wang, H., Chen, X.: Block-chain challenges and opportunities: a survey. Int. J. Web Grid Serv. (IJWGS) **14**(4), 352–375 (2018)
17. Chen, W., Zheng, Z., Cui, J., Ngai, E., Zheng, P., Zhou, Y.: Detecting ponzi schemes on ethereum: towards healthier blockchain technology. In: Proceedings of the 2018 World Wide Web Conference on World Wide Web (WWW), Lyon, France, pp. 1409–1418, April 2018
18. Zheng, P., Zheng, Z., Luo, X., Chen, X., Liu, X.: A detailed and real-time performance monitoring framework for blockchain systems. In: Proceedings of the 2018 International Conference on Software Engineering (ICSE), Gothenburg, Sweden, 134–143. ACM (2018)
19. Dinh, T.T.A., Wang, J., Chen, G., et al.: Blockbench: a framework for analyzing private blockchains. In: Proceedings of the 2017 ACM International Conference on Management of Data, pp. 1085–1100 (2017)
20. Long, J., Shelhamer, E., Darrell, T.: Fully convolutional networks for semantic segmentation. In: Proceedings of the IEEE Conference on Computer Vision and Pattern Recognition, pp. 3431–3440 (2015)
21. Neubeck, A., Van Gool, L.: Efficient non-maximum suppression. In: 18th International Conference on Pattern Recognition (ICPR 2006), vol. 3, pp. 850–855. IEEE (2006)
22. Szabo, N.: Smart contracts: building blocks for digital markets. EXTROPY: J. Transhumanist Thought (16), **18**(2) (1996)
23. http://remix.ethereum.org/
24. Huang, Y., Kong, Q., Jia, N., Chen, X., Zheng, Z.: Recommending differentiated code to support smart contract update. In: 2019 IEEE/ACM 27th International Conference on Program Comprehension (ICPC), pp. 260–270, May 2019
25. Buterin, V.: A next-generation smart contract and decentralized application platform. White Paper **3**(37) (2014)

Dynamic Gas Estimation of Loops Using Machine Learning

Chunmiao Li[1,2]($\boxtimes$), Shijie Nie[1], Yang Cao[3], Yijun Yu[4], and Zhenjiang Hu[5]

[1] National Institute of Informatics, Tokyo, Japan
{chunmiaoli1993,nsj}@nii.ac.jp
[2] SOKENDAI (The Graduate University for Advanced Studies), Hayama, Japan
[3] Kyoto University, Kyoto, Japan
[4] Open University, Milton Keynes, UK
[5] Peking University, Beijing, China

Abstract. Smart contracts on Ethereum can encode business logic and have been applied to many areas, such as token exchange, games, and others. Unlike general programs, the computations of contracts on Ethereum are restricted by the gas limit. If a transaction runs out of gas limit before execution finishes, EVM throws an out-of-gas (OG) exception, and the entire transaction fails, which reverts state before the transaction starts, but transaction fee is still deducted. It is essential to do gas estimation before sending transactions. Existing works mostly fail in estimating gas for loop functions because the iteration times of loops can not be statically decided. But we found that a quarter of all contracts have loop functions, and gas cost for loops is higher than for other functions. So it is necessary to do gas estimation for loop functions.

In this work, we propose a gas estimation approach based on transaction trace to estimate gas for loop functions dynamically. Our main idea is that we can learn the relationship between historical transactions traces and their gas to estimate gas for new transactions. We implement our approach in machine learning algorithms. The results show that random forest and K-nearest neighbors can achieve a better estimation accuracy rate than SVR and LSTM.

Keywords: Ethereum · Smart contracts · Gas estimation · Out-of-gas · Machine learning

1 Introduction

Ethereum [17] is the most popular public blockchain now, not only because it provides a decentralized, shared ledger, which allows all users to participant in the ledger update activities, but also it builds a "world computer" which can host and execute programs. These programs are so-called smart contracts [17]. Any user can deploy their contracts to Ethereum by sending a contract creation transaction. Concretely, users construct programs using Solidity, a widely-used programming language on Ethereum. Then these Solidity programs are compiled to bytecode and stored on the code field of a newly built contract account after

© Springer Nature Singapore Pte Ltd. 2020
Z. Zheng et al. (Eds.): BlockSys 2020, CCIS 1267, pp. 428–441, 2020.
https://doi.org/10.1007/978-981-15-9213-3_34

the contract creation transaction succeeds. One can send a transaction to the contract account when he wants to call a function on the contract. Once all Ethereum nodes verify the transaction, the Ethereum Virtual Machine (hereafter EVM) will run contract runtime bytecode on the transaction input data.

EVM is a stack-based, Turing-complete machine that can program any computation that a Turing Machine can execute, such as loops. To prevent resource waste due to infinite loop and make sure that contract programs can stop somewhere, the computation effort to execute EVM instructions are charged in the unit of gas. When a user sends a transaction, he needs to specify a gas limit attached to the transaction. *GasLimit* is the maximum available gas amount for transaction execution. But if transaction execution needs more gas than gasLimit, EVM will emit an out-of-gas exception immediately, and all executed operations are reverted. Meanwhile, the expenses for purchasing the gas limit are transferred to beneficiary accounts. The out-of-gas exception accounts for over 90% among all exceptions on Ethereum and causes substantial financial losses [11]. The leading root causes [11] for this exception are: 1. users are not familiar with the transaction execution mechanism; 2. there is no useful tool for gas estimation. There are mainly two ways to prevent out-of-gas exceptions. One way is to detect contracts with gas-focused vulnerabilities [9] to prevent users from calling vulnerable functions. The other one does gas estimation, i.e., given a transaction, we need to estimate its gas cost. Some work has devoted to gas estimation [1,12,13,16]. For example, Solc[1] statically predicts the gas cost for all contract functions. Marescotti et al. [13] apply symbolic model checking methods to detect the worst-case gas cost.

We found that a quarter of all contracts have loop functions, and gas costs for loops are higher than for other functions. So it is necessary to do gas estimation for loop functions. Unfortunately, existing methods mostly fail in estimating the gas cost for transactions to loop functions (i.e., functions containing loops). Static analysis cannot figure out the iteration times of any loops so that Gasol [1], a gas estimation tool, fails when the maximal number of iteration times is unbounded. Dynamic methods often send transactions to local testnet and observe the gas cost, but this gas is not the same as the actual transaction gas cost because the Ethereum mainnet may change and differs from the testnet.

In this work, we propose a novel approach to dynamically estimate gas for loop functions based on transaction execution trace. The insight is that gas costs for new transactions can be predicted based on analyzing history transactions. Our main idea is to learn the relationship between transaction trace and gas from historical transactions and apply this to gas estimation for new transactions. We consider using machine learning algorithms to determine these relations. As far as we know, we are the *first* to introduce machine learning ideas to gas estimation. But it is nontrivial to implement this idea because of two challenges: (1) how to collect traces for a lot of specific historical transactions; (2) traces for loop transactions are very long, and the longest trace we observed is 382, 552. It is hard to feed this long sequence to any existing learning models directly.

---

[1] https://github.com/ethereum/solidity.

To address the challenge (1), we instrument Ethereum-js virtual machine[2] to automatically record trace when replaying historical transactions in the forked chain. For challenge (2), we take two abstractions of the trace as features and feed them into different learning models. The first abstraction is frequency for 141 opcodes used on EVM, which are input to three learning models: random forest, K-nearest neighbors (KNN), and SVM for regression (SVR). EVM charges dynamic gas for 24 opcodes depend on runtime state. The second abstraction is dynamic opcodes sequence, which is sent to a Long Short-Term Memory (LSTM) model. The experimental results show that our approach is effective in gas estimation for loop functions. The Mean Absolute Percentage Error (MAPE) ranges from 0.59 to 168.77 in different learning algorithms. Generally, the random forest and KNN can achieve a better prediction accuracy rate than SVR and LSTM.

In summary, our contributions are list as follows.

- We provide a novel approach to estimate gas based on transaction execution trace. The main idea is that the relationship between transaction trace and gas from historical transactions can be learned to estimate gas for new transactions. As far as we know, we are the *first* using machine learning for gas estimation.
- We consider the random forest, K-nearest neighbors (KNN), SVM for regression (SVR), and LSTM learning models in our experiments. The results show that the random forest and KNN can achieve a better prediction accuracy rate than SVR and LSTM.
- We provide a dataset contain opcodes execution sequence and gas costs for 5718 transactions specially sent to loop functions. This dataset can be used for later research on studying the gas cost of transactions to loop functions.

2   Preliminary

2.1   Gas Mechanism on Smart Contracts

Blockchain is a decentralized, shared ledger, and Ethereum [17] is the most popular public blockchain now. There are two types of accounts on Ethereum: externally owned accounts (i.e., user accounts) and contract accounts. A contract account can store code (i.e., smart contracts) to encode business logic. Once a user sends a transaction to a contract account, the contract *opcode* will be executed in Ethereum Virtual Machine (hereafter EVM). Given a transaction, the executional *opcode sequence* in EVM is called a *transaction trace*. All transactions need to be performed on all blockchain nodes, to avoid network abuse and some inevitable issues (e.g., infinite loops) caused by the Turing-complete contract language Solidity, all EVM instructions in Ethereum are subject to fees [17]. The fee is measured by units of gas.

The gas limit is implicitly deducted from the sender's account balance at a certain gas price before the transaction starts. During the EVM working process,

---

[2] https://github.com/ethereumjs/ethereumjs-vm

the available gas is reduced by executing opcodes. Suppose the gas limit is G_1 and transaction actual execution cost is G_2. Note that there is another limit called the block gas limit G_b, which is the maximum amount of gas allowed in a block. In terms of relationships among G_1, G_2 and G_b, the different transaction execution scenarios are given below:

1. $G_2 < G_b$ and $G_1 >= G_2$: The transaction can be included to a block and succeeds. The gas remained at the end of the transaction is refunded to the sender's account.
2. $G_2 < G_b$ and $G_1 < G_2$: The transaction can be included to a block but fails with error. The EVM will emit an out-of-gas exception since there is no available gas to support further operations during the transaction execution. At this time, all gas cost is delivered to miner's account (beneficiary account), and all states done are reverted right before the transaction starts.
3. $G_2 > G_b$: The transaction cannot be included to a block and fails no matter how big G_1 is. For example, consider the contract function below. The gas requirements for executing `batchAirDrop` function is related to the length of transaction input `recipients`. The loop iteration times are decided by user input so the maximal gas cost for the loop is unbounded. If the length is too long, the gas cost to execute the loop function might become so huge that it exceeds the block gas limit, and this transaction will not be included in any block. In other words, no matter how much a user could afford, this transaction will always fail.

```
function batchAirDrop(address token_address,
            address[] recipients, uint256 ncash) {
    AToken token = AToken(token_address);
    for(uint i = 0 ; i < recipients.length ; i++) {
        address recipient = recipients[i];
        require(token.transfer(recipient, ncash));
    }
}
```

2.2   Learning Models

As far as we know, there is no previous work that applied learning algorithms on gas estimation. In this paper, we define gas estimation as learning a mapping $f : \mathbb{R}_N \to \mathbb{R}$, where $\mathbb{R}_N$ is N-dimension features, which is a representation of the transaction opcode sequence, and $\mathbb{R}$ is the predicted gas value.

The concept of machine learning is to learn a model from existing data with a performance measure metric and give a judgment or predictions on new data. Nowadays, machine learning algorithms are widely applied to various tasks, including computer vision, natural language processing, and recommendation systems. The feature space and regressor selection are entirely unknown, and there is no widely recognized evaluation metrics for gas estimation. To solve this challenge, we search for several machine learning and deep learning methods:

Random forest, K Nearest Neighbors (KNN), Support Vector Machine (SVM), and two different evaluation metrics: Mean Average Percentage Error (MAPE) and accuracy rate. The performance for each regressor is discussed in Sect. 4.

Random Forest. Decision tree learning algorithm can build a regression model in a tree structure. It is prone to overfitting when a tree is very deep. So random forest comes out to minimize this error. A random forest [3] is a group of decision trees and aggregates their results to a final result. Based on the voting strategy, the random forest may produce a better result from assembled models rather than individuals. The random forest model has advantages of overcoming overfitting and can be more interpretable because it can explicitly output weight for each dimension of features.

K Nearest Neighbors (KNN). KNN [14] is a common used supervised learning algorithm. Suppose the distance of samples is defined by a similarity measurement, for example, Euclidean metric, Minkowski distance, Manhattan distance, etc. KNN aims to find the closest K samples from the training set. Based on these K samples, the prediction result is the average with/without weights of their real output value. KNN methods usually have better performance on datasets with smaller size.

SVM for Regression (SVR). Support Vector Machine (SVM) [2] is a widely used machine learning method. SVM constructs a margin separator which finds a hyperplane that has the maximum distance between features. The SVM method is first proposed for the classification and can be extended to regression, called Support Vector Regression (SVR), although traditional SVM is based on the linear separable assumption. By defining the inner product of features in terms of a kernel function, the SVM also suits non linearly separable problem. Intuitively, gas estimation is not a linearly separable problem. This inspires us to use the Gaussian Kernel function in our experiments.

LSTM. As traditional neural networks can not handle the context information of time series data, recurrent neural networks are proposed to solve this. The information of history data is preserved by introducing the time-variant hidden state for each network cell, and the relationship between inputs can be learned during gradient descent. The Long Short-Term Memory (LSTM) Networks are a modified version of recurrent neural networks, which makes it easy to train by avoiding gradient vanishing and exploding problems. It contains input, remember, and output gate, which gives LSTM network cells the ability to decide which values to through and abandon others. We can treat the input opcode sequence as a time series sequence, and each opcode can be represented by an embedding word vector. The LSTM aims to give a prediction of gas based on the new input opcode sequence.

3   Our Approach

Now we give the workflow of the proposed approach. There are mainly three steps shown in Fig. 1. For simplicity, we refer the transactions sent to loop functions as loop transactions. First, we collect input and receipt for existing loop transactions. Then, we replay all loop transactions and extract their trace on local blockchain. Here *trace* means transaction executed opcode sequence on EVM. Last, we build a gas estimator model based on transactions trace using machine learning and deep learning algorithms. After gas estimator construction, for a new loop transaction, we can execute it on a local blockchain and get its transaction trace. By feeding this trace to the gas estimator model, the estimated gas cost is given.

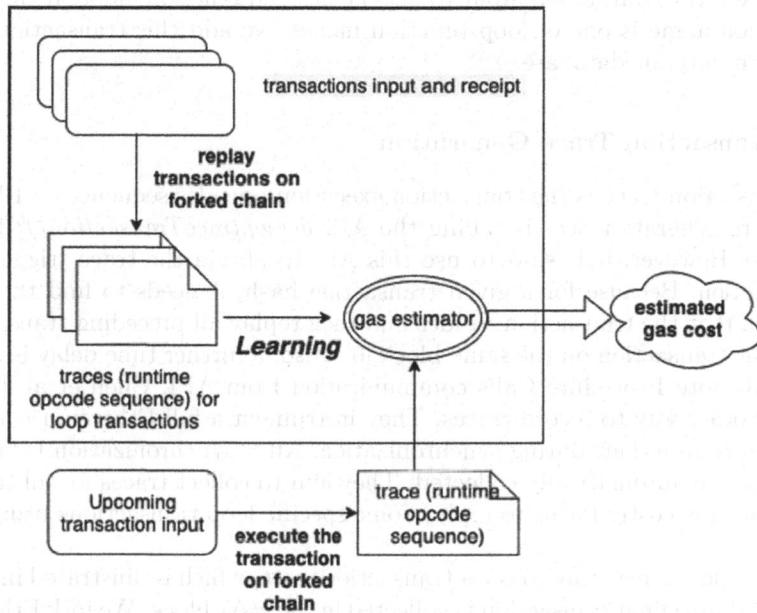

Fig. 1. Workflow of a trace-based approach

3.1 Loop Transactions Collection

A loop transaction is the transaction sent to a contract function containing loops. First, for a given contract, we need to select its functions having loops (hereafter loop functions). Next, we gather existing transactions sent to this contract. By analyzing inputs for existing transactions, we collect transactions which sent to loop functions. Details for the selection and analyzing steps are shown as follows:

1. **Select loop functions:** We first use Slither [8] to get the control flow graph (CFG) for functions in contracts. Slither is a static analysis framework, which can convert Solidity contracts to an intermediate representation called SlithIR. SlithIR has a node type called "IF_ LOOP" indicating the start of a loop. And we traverse all functions CFGs to collect loop functions that have at least one "IF_ LOOP" node.

2. **Gather transactions to a contract:** Etherscan[3] shows all transactions hashes to a contract address. For this study, We crawled recently no more than 2000 transactions hash for considered contracts from Etherscan. Then we pull the transaction detailed information (e.g., input, transaction sender) from a full node on Ethereum mainnet by calling *web3.eth.getTransaction()* API. Especially, we deploy a full node based on QuikNode's node service.

3. **Analyze transactions sent to loop functions:** The input of a transaction contains the invoked function name and parameters. We use abiDecoder[4]to decode every transaction input to get the invoked function name. If the called function name is one of loop function names, we add this transaction information into our database.

3.2 Transaction Trace Generation

The transaction trace is the transaction execution opcodes sequence on EVM. A method to generate traces is calling the API *debug.traceTransaction()*[5] from a full node. However, it is slow to use this API to obtain the trace triggered by a transaction. Because for a given transaction hash, it needs to find the previous block that the transaction resides and then replay all preceding transactions before the transaction on the same block [6]. Also, a further time delay is caused by the Remote Procedure Calls communication from API. Chen et al. [6] proposed another way to record traces. They instrument a full Ethereum node and replay all transactions during synchronization. After synchronization is finished, the traces are automatically collected. They aim to collect traces for all transactions. But it is costly for us to replay some specific loop transactions using their method.

We propose a new way to get a transaction trace, which is illustrated in Fig. 2. Suppose the original transaction is collected in the $\#N_b$ block. We fork Ethereum mainnet on $\#N_b - 1$ block to start a local testnet. Here we use **Ganache-cli**[6] and **Infura**[7] node service to implement this. Ganache-cli is part of the Truffle suite and the command-line version of Ganache. It can build a personal blockchain for development. Especially, it provides a fork command to allow users to fork from another running Ethereum client on the specified block, which allows us to send transactions to contracts on mainnet. Infura is a node cluster that free developers from synchronizing and maintaining an Ethereum node. Our study hosts an archive node because it can respond to API requests for any historical blocks. As shown in Fig. 2, our local testnet share the chain starting from the genesis block to $\#N_b - 1$ block. This is to construct the correct the same state before the original transaction. Especially, we revised the Ethereumjs-VM to collect trace when replaying transactions. Ethereumjs-VM is the Ethereum

---

[3] https://etherscan.io/.

[4] https://github.com/ConsenSys/abi-decoder.

[5] https://github.com/ethereum/go-ethereum/wiki/Management-APIs.

[6] https://github.com/trufflesuite/ganache-cli.

[7] https://infura.io/.

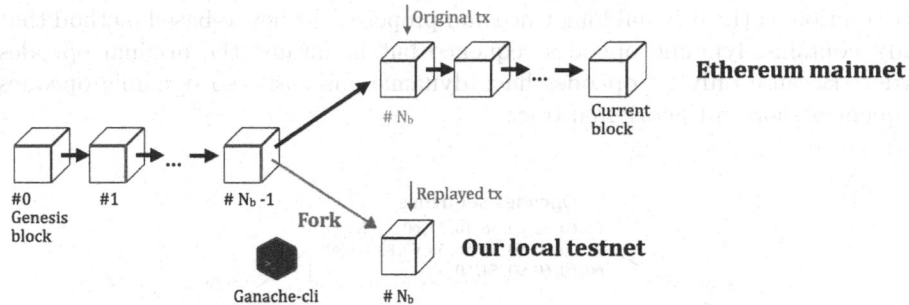

Fig. 2. Collect runtime trace by replaying a transaction

Virtual Machine (EVM) used in the Ganache blockchain. More concretely, EVM interpreter executes each opcode on **runStep** function, so we insert opcode recording code in this function. When EVM executes a transaction, the trace is automatically collected.

3.3   Build Gas Estimator Models

Trace for loop transactions are usually long. The maximal trace we collected contains 382,552 opcodes. Some works [10,15] using deep learning algorithms on malware detection based on input opcode sequence. In their practice, they only take the first L opcodes to meet the need for a deep learning network of the unified input length. As they observed, the larger the L is, the more memory and computation time is required to train the neural network. For gas estimation, we cannot simply follow this rule because each opcode contributes to the final predicted gas. Also, in our experiments, memory overflow error is raised due to the long sequence, even with batch size 1. It is hard to feed this long sequence into any existing learning models directly. So we propose two kinds of abstractions as features, i.e., opcodes frequency and dynamic opcodes sequence, shown in Fig. 3.

There are a total of 141 opcodes used on EVM. We checked go-ethereum[8] source code and divided them into three classes: constant cost opcodes, dynamic cost opcodes, and both constant and dynamic cost opcodes. EVM charges 117 opcodes and 10 opcodes in constant and dynamic gas costs, respectively. For example, **ADD** opcode costs 3 gas, and **EXP** gas cost can only be decided runtime. In addition to constant gas cost, a total of 14 opcodes also have dynamic gas, such as **SHA3**, which has fixed 30 gas cost and dynamic cost relating to memoryGasCost.

In Fig. 3, the frequency-based method extracts the frequency of all opcodes and feeds it to different learning models. For example, opcode 0x60 (i.e., PUSH1) occurred nine times in original trace (opcode sequence), so its frequency is 9. Here we consider three supervised machine learning models: random forest, K-nearest neighbors (KNN), and SVM for regression (SVR). Moreover, we have another

---

[8] https://github.com/ethereum/go-ethereum.

abstraction on the original long trace and propose a sequence-based method that only contains dynamic opcodes sequence but maintains the original opcodes order. Because only 24 opcodes have dynamic gas costs, so dynamic opcodes sequences shorten the original trace.

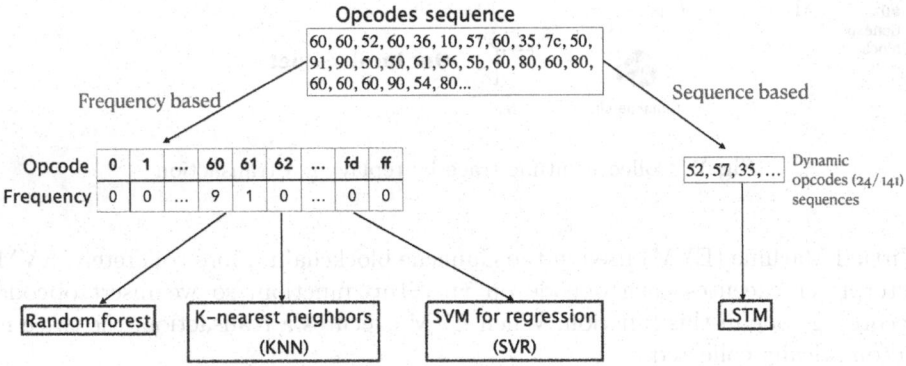

Fig. 3. Build gas cost models

After the gas estimator is learned, for a new transaction, we can first execute it on forked ganache blockchain and collect its trace, then get estimated gas by input its trace to the gas estimator.

4   Results

We use Smartbugs [7] contract dataset containing 47,398 unique contracts. As stated in Sect. 3, for each contract program, we employ Slither [8] to select its loop functions, i.e., functions that contain at least one loop. We observed that 10, 855 contracts have loop functions, which is 23% of all Smartbugs contracts. We crawled the recently 2000 transaction records to 10, 855 contracts from Etherscan and analyzed transaction inputs. The results show that there are 706 contracts with transactions to loop functions. Up to 50 transactions are sent to each of 457 loop contracts, which amounts to 64.7% of all loop contracts. Besides, 64 loop contracts range in loop transactions from 500 to 2000, which occupy 9.1% of all loop contracts. Almost a quarter of contracts have loop functions, but users do not often send transactions to them. The reasons behind this might be: 1. smart contracts might contain loop-related vulnerabilities, such as unbounded loop [9], but there is no effective tool that can remedy them. 2. There is no practical tool to estimate the gas cost for loop functions.

As state in Sect. 3, we need to replay loop transactions on forked testnet and collect their transaction traces. In our experiments, the average transaction replay time is about 30 s. For a very complicated transaction, it took 3 min to replay it. Considering time limits, we replayed recently *up to ten* transactions[9] for each loop contracts. Totally, we collect traces for 5718 transactions. The opcode length for these traces ranges from 43 to 382,552. The frequency-based method fixes 141 opcodes frequency as features. The sequence-based method maintains dynamic opcodes sequence as features and the maximal length is 14,267.

To evaluate the effectiveness of our approach, we consider two metrics:

- **Mean Absolute Percentage Error (MAPE):** it expresses the error as a ratio defined in this formula: $L = \frac{1}{n} \sum_{i=1}^{n} |\frac{g_{actual}^i - g_{pred}^i}{g_{actual}^i}| * 100$, i.e., the average difference between predicted gas and actual gas is divided by the actual gas, where the predicted gas is directly estimated by learned gas estimator. The smaller MAPE indicates the better prediction performance.
- **Prediction accuracy rate:** because the learned estimator may underestimate gas for some transactions, we compute this metric as different accuracy rates by adding additional gas on estimator provided gas. Here accuracy means that the predicted gas is higher than actual gas.

4.1 Frequency Based Method Performance

For frequency based method, besides collected 5718 transactions, we replayed transactions for four representative contracts, whose contracts hash are listed in Table 1. We first counted the opcodes frequency for each trace, then applied machine learning models (Random forest, KNN, SVR) on frequency vectors separately. The training set and testing set were randomly split into 70% and 30%, respectively. The training time is less then 2 s. The MAPE results are shown in Table 1. We have two observations:

- In general, gas estimation based on transactions to the same contract has a lower error rate than on transactions for different contracts. For example, if we use a random forest learning algorithm to estimate gas for transactions to contract 0x92240... and to combined four contracts transactions separately, the former MAPE is 0.78, and the latter is 1.99.
- In most cases, random forest and KNN can have a lower error rate than SVR. Consider contract 0x117cb..., the MAPE for random forest and KNN are 5.05 and 6.94, which is lower than 9.74 predicted by SVR.
- Recall that we replayed recent less than ten transactions for each loop contract and totally collected 5718 traces. The MAPE for these transactions is distinctly higher than that for combined four contract transactions.

Figure 4, Fig. 5, Fig. 6, Fig. 7, Fig. 8 and Fig. 9 list the prediction accuracy rate with incremented gas using random forest algorithm for six kinds of transactions on Table 1. Generally, the more gas is added to estimator provided gas, the more accuracy rate we can gain, where the accuracy rate means the percentage of the increased gas is higher than actual gas. For example, for transactions

---

[9] These ten transactions invoke the same loop function.

Table 1. MAPE results using Random forest, KNN and SVR

Contract hash	Loop transactions number	MAPE		
		Random forest	KNN	SVR
0x611ce695290729805e138c9c14dbddf132e76de3	2000	1.40	1.49	17.46
0x9224016462b204c57eb70e1d69652f60bcaf53a8	1238	0.78	0.59	0.96
0x117cb292e97a593fbca38b5cd60ec7144d4ca8c9	790	5.05	6.94	9.74
0x85b2949cea65add49c69dac77fb052596bc5ddd4	590	1.49	1.49	19.01
Combine above four contracts transactions	4618	1.99	1.94	110.90
706 contracts hash	5718	16.67	23.71	168.77

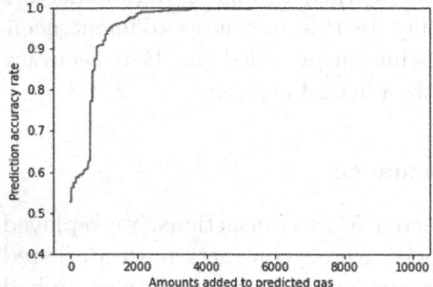

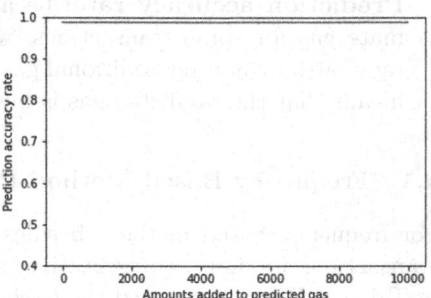

Fig. 4. Transactions to contract 0x611ce...

Fig. 5. Transactions to contract 0x92240...

to contract 0x117cb... , as seen in Fig. 6, if we add 2000 to predicted gas from gas estimator, the prediction accuracy rate can reach 70%, i.e., for 70% tested transactions, we can make sure that incremented gas is higher than actual gas. But if we add 6000 to predicted gas from gas estimator, the prediction accuracy rate can reach 82%,

4.2　Sequence Based Method Performance

For the sequence-based method, we chose 5718 transactions for 706 loop contracts as our dataset. We first extracted dynamic sequences (i.e., a sequence only contains dynamic opcodes) from each trace and fed these dynamic traces to LSTM models. The training set and testing set were randomly split into 70% and 30%. The training time is about three days. The MAPE for LSTM is over 800, which is far higher than MAPE for the random forest, KNN, and SVR.

Evaluate Our Method. Our methods are effective in estimating gas costs for loop transactions. The frequency-based method can have a distinctly lower

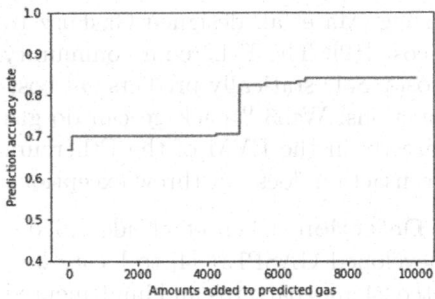

Fig. 6. Tranactions to contract 0x117cb...

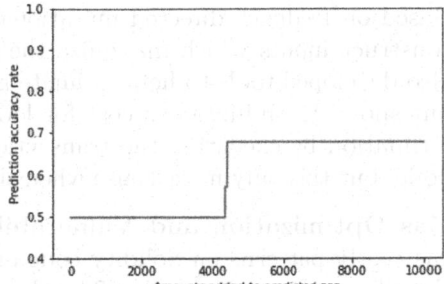

Fig. 7. Tranactions to contract 0x85b29...

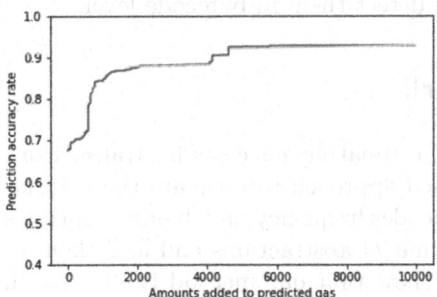

Fig. 8. Tranactions to four contracts 0x611..., 0x922..., 0x117..., 0x85b...

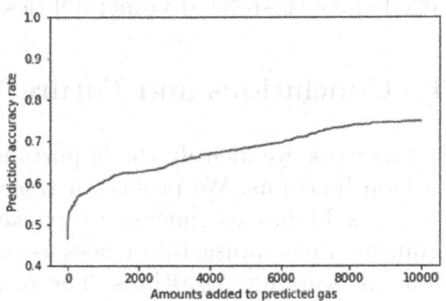

Fig. 9. Transactions to 706 contracts

prediction error rate (i.e., MAPE) than the sequence-based method. For the frequency-based method: 1. random forest and KNN have a better estimation rate than SVR. 2. prediction on transactions from the same contract is better than that from different contracts.

Limitation. As shown in Fig. 2, we assume that the Ethereum state on block $\#N_b - 1$ is the correct state before the execution of the original transaction. Suppose the replayed transaction is sent to contract C. Here, we consider that the preceding transactions in block $\#N_b$ don't change the state of contract C. To mitigate this, we will try to analyze the relationships among transactions in the same block.

5   Related Work

Gas Estimation. Albert et al. constructed a gas analyzer named GASOL [1], which can over-approximate the gas consumption of functions. Also, Marescotti et al. [13] presented two methods to decide the exact worst-case gas consumption. Signer provided Visualgas [16], a tool to visualize how gas costs relate to different parts of the code. However, none of them compare the actual transaction gas cost on mainnet with their predicted one to prove the effectiveness of their methods.

Based on feedback-directed mutational fuzzing, Ma et al. designed GasFuzz to construct inputs which maximize the gas cost [12]. The Ethereum community also developed tools to help estimate gas costs. Solc statically predicts gas cost, but shows the infinite gas cost for loop functions. Web3[10] package can do gas estimation by executing the transaction directly in the EVM of the Ethereum node, but this only make sense when this transaction does not throw exceptions.

Gas Optimization and Vulnerability Detection. Chen et al. identified 7 gas costly patterns on Solidity code and developed GASPER [4] to locate 3 of them by analyzing bytecodes. They later listed 24 anti-patterns and implemented GasReducer [5] to detect and replace them with efficient code. They focus on optimize gas usage whereas we want to do gas estimation. Grech et al. [9] surveyed three gas-related vulnerabilities and detect them in bytecode level.

6   Conclusions and Future Work

In this work, we identify the importance of estimating gas costs for transactions to loop functions. We propose a trace-based approach to estimate the transactions gas. In the experiments, we extract opcodes frequency and dynamic opcodes sequence from transaction traces as two kinds of abstractions and feed them to different learning algorithms. The results show that our method is effective in estimating gas cost for loop functions. Especially, random forest and KNN have a better estimation rate than SVR and LSTM. In addition, we provide a dataset that contains 5718 traces for transactions to loop functions. The dataset suggests more research and calls for attention to estimate the gas cost for loop transactions.

In the future, we would like to apply our idea to estimate gas costs for other functions besides loops. Also, since the prediction accuracy rate is not so high as expected, we will consider other trace abstractions to improve our results.

Acknowledgments. This work was supported partly by JSPS KAKENHI Grant Numbers JP17H06099, JP18H04093 and 19K20269. In addition, this work was partially funded by EU H2020 Engage KTN, EPSRC EP/T017465/1, EPSRC EP/R013144/1 and Big Code Forensic Analytics in Secure Software Engineering (Royal Society, IES\R1\191138).

References

1. Albert, E., Correas, J., Gordillo, P., Román-Díez, G., Rubio, A.: GASOL: gas analysis and optimization for ethereum smart contracts. In: 26th International Conference on Tools and Algorithms for the Construction and Analysis of Systems, TACAS 2020. Proceedings. Lecture Notes in Computer Science (2020, to appear)
2. Boser, B.E., et al.: A Training Algorithm for Optimal Margin Classifiers (2010). https://doi.org/10.1.1.103.1189

---

[10] https://web3js.readthedocs.io/en/v1.2.0/web3-eth.html.

3. Breiman, L.: Random forests. Mach. Learn. **45**(1), 5–32 (2001)
4. Chen, T., Li, X., Luo, X., Zhang, X.: Under-optimized smart contracts devour your money. In: 2017 IEEE 24th International Conference on Software Analysis, Evolution and Reengineering (SANER), pp. 442–446. IEEE (2017)
5. Chen, T., et al.: Towards saving money in using smart contracts. In: 2018 IEEE/ACM 40th International Conference on Software Engineering: New Ideas and Emerging Technologies Results (ICSE-NIER), pp. 81–84. IEEE (2018)
6. Chen, T., et al.: Tokenscope: automatically detecting inconsistent behaviors of cryptocurrency tokens in ethereum. In: Proceedings of the 2019 ACM SIGSAC Conference on Computer and Communications Security, pp. 1503–1520 (2019)
7. Durieux, T., Ferreira, J.F., Abreu, R., Cruz, P.: Empirical review of automated analysis tools on 47,587 ethereum smart contracts. arXiv preprint arXiv:1910.10601 (2019)
8. Feist, J., Grieco, G., Groce, A.: Slither: a static analysis framework for smart contracts. In: 2019 IEEE/ACM 2nd International Workshop on Emerging Trends in Software Engineering for Blockchain (WETSEB), pp. 8–15. IEEE (2019)
9. Grech, N., Kong, M., Jurisevic, A., Brent, L., Scholz, B., Smaragdakis, Y.: Madmax: surviving out-of-gas conditions in ethereum smart contracts. Proc. ACM Programm. Lang. **2**(OOPSLA), 1–27 (2018)
10. Karbab, E.B., Debbabi, M., Derhab, A., Mouheb, D.: Android malware detection using deep learning on API method sequences. arXiv preprint arXiv:1712.08996 (2017)
11. Liu, C., Gao, J., Li, Y., Chen, Z.: Understanding out of gas exceptions on ethereum. In: Zheng, Z., Dai, H.-N., Tang, M., Chen, X. (eds.) BlockSys 2019. CCIS, vol. 1156, pp. 505–519. Springer, Singapore (2020). https://doi.org/10.1007/978-981-15-2777-7_41
12. Ma, F., et al.: Gasfuzz: generating high gas consumption inputs to avoid out-of-gas vulnerability. arXiv preprint arXiv:1910.02945 (2019)
13. Marescotti, M., Blicha, M., Hyvärinen, A.E.J., Asadi, S., Sharygina, N.: Computing exact worst-case gas consumption for smart contracts. In: Margaria, T., Steffen, B. (eds.) ISoLA 2018. LNCS, vol. 11247, pp. 450–465. Springer, Cham (2018). https://doi.org/10.1007/978-3-030-03427-6_33
14. Peterson, L.: K-nearest neighbor. Scholarpedia (2009). https://doi.org/10.4249/scholarpedia.1883
15. Santos, I., Brezo, F., Sanz, B., Laorden, C., Bringas, P.G.: Using opcode sequences in single-class learning to detect unknown malware. IET Inf. Secur. **5**(4), 220–227 (2011)
16. Signer, C.: Gas cost analysis for ethereum smart contracts. Master's thesis, ETH Zurich, Department of Computer Science (2018)
17. Wood, G., et al.: Ethereum: a secure decentralised generalised transaction ledger. Ethereum Proj. Yellow Paper **151**(2014), 1–32 (2014)

A Data Integrity Verification Scheme Based on Blockchain and Blind Homomorphic Tags

Shuai Huang[1], Jing Xiao[1]([✉]), Hong-liang Mao[2], Mu-ran Su[2], Hai-bo Ying[3], and Shuang Tan[4]

[1] College of Electrical and Information Engineering, Hunan University, Changsha 410082, China
jxiao1985@hnu.edu.cn
[2] National Computer Network Emergency Response Technical Team/Coordination Center of China (CNCERT/CC), Beijing 100044, China
[3] Hunan Tianhe Guoyun Technology Co. Ltd., Changsha 410100, China
[4] National Defense Science and Technology University, Changsha 410003, China

Abstract. With the advent of big data, users' data is usually outsourced to the cloud. However, users will lose the absolute control over the data and its integrity is hard to be guaranteed. Currently, the most effective way to detect data corruption in the cloud is through data integrity verification that usually relies on third party. However, the third party is not always credible. This paper proposes a data integrity verification scheme based on blockchain and blind homomorphic tags to tackle the over-reliance on the third party auditor. Firstly, our approach is explored to weaken the centralization of the third party through the blockchain technology. Secondly, the smart contract is used to control the access of different auditors, and this allows users to change auditors freely. Lastly, blind homomorphic tags are proposed to avoid recomputing of tags when users change auditors. Based on the experiment results, our proposed scheme is more credible and has a higher recognition rate under the same computational overhead when compared with other mechanisms.

Keywords: Data integrity verification · Blockchain · Smart contract · Trusted third party · Blind homomorphic tag

1 Introduction

Data outsourcing becomes widely popular, with the emergence of new computing modes such as the cloud computing. However, it bears a number of defects due to the loss of absolute data control for users. Data integrity verification (DIV) is then brought into play as a solution. Earlier, the common methods used to depend on retrieving files and recalculating hash values. But it is no longer applicable with the increasing amount of data [1]. To match the increasing data

© Springer Nature Singapore Pte Ltd. 2020
Z. Zheng et al. (Eds.): BlockSys 2020, CCIS 1267, pp. 442–455, 2020.
https://doi.org/10.1007/978-981-15-9213-3_35

volume, Deswarte et al. proposed RSA homomorphic tags for DIV that effectively handles the retrieval of original data [2]. However, there are severe defects in computational and communication overhead. Later on, relevant scholars proposed improving schemes. Two of which put forward by Wang et al. inroduce a trusted third party to perform verification on behalf of users [3,4]. This scheme can tremendously alleviate the computational burden of users themselves. Nevertheless, this kind of public verification scheme still bears obvious shortcomings, such as the over-reliance on trusted third parties.

Due to the decentralized features of blockchain technology, a data integrity verification scheme based on the blockchain is proposed to overcome the shortcomings of the traditional public verification scheme. In our scheme, there are two phases (setup and challenge). In the setup phase, users split the data into sectors and generate homomorphic tags for each sector. A data preprocessing is done during this period to make the verification more precise. Then users upload the tag to the blockchain for storage so that the tags do not need to be generated repeatedly during the periodic verification. In the challenge phase, users can assign any third party to perform the verification on behalf of themselves, and the third party audit (TPA) is authorized by the user through smart contract.

Specifically, the contributions of this work are summarized as follows.

- Our scheme can alleviate the centralization of third party. Users can select any number of third parties in a verification process. At the same time, the corresponding TPAs can send their verification records to the blockchain as evidence. The final judgement of the data integrity can be determined by the user based on results returned by multiple TPAs.
- Our scheme can save the overhead for recomputing tags. Tags may be lost or damaged during the period of storage, and need to be recomputed after users change the TPA. Our scheme can avoid this puzzle by adding interference to former tags which are named by us as blind homomorphic tags. The blind homomorphic tags can also ensure that the previous auditor cannot infuence the subsequent verification after TPA changed.
- The blockchain can be used to ensure authentic and reliable verification results of TPA. The results can be traced back in the future and users are no longer dependent on a single third party. Users do not need to follow the fixed third party so as to make verification more transparent.

The remainder of this paper is organized as follows. In Sect. 2 we analyze both advantages and disadvantages of various schemes proposed by predecessors. In Sect. 3, we present our model and discussion in different adversary models. Our scheme based on blockchain technology is proposed in Sect. 4. Experiments and performance are discussed in Sect. 5. Conclusion is summarized in Sect. 6.

2   Related Work

Upon whether or not fault tolerant technology is adopted for the original data, the data integrity verification scheme can be divided into proof of data possession (PDP) and proof of retrievability (POR).

2.1 PDP Mechanism

PDP mechanisms include MAC authentication code, RSA signature-based scheme, BLS signature-based scheme, elliptic curve-based scheme, dynamic operation-enabled scheme, multi copy-enabled scheme and so on. Authentication code PDP is an earlier mechanism. This scheme is limited by verification times. Then, Deswarte et al. [2] proposed a PDP mechanism based on the RSA signature to address the shortcomings. No verification limit, while shielding the data content. But there are still great problems in the computational and communication consumption, and it cannot meet the dynamic environment. Later, Atteniete et al. considered a sampling strategy for data integrity verification in S-PDP and E-PDP mechanisms [5,6]. The concept of homomorphic verification tags is proposed to reduce communication consumption. Wang et al. proposed a PDP mechanism based on BLS signatures [3]. Compared with RSA signature-based scheme, BLS signatures have a shorter number of signature bits. Besides, the mechanism also uses the Merkle tree to ensure the correct location of the data block, and supports a dynamic operation. Subsequently, some scholars proposed various improvement strategies such as the PDP mechanism supported by the elliptic curve [7,8], PDP mechanism supported by multiple copies [9].

2.2 POR Mechanism

The PDP mechanism can effectively identify the integrity of data, but is unavailable to recover the damaged data. The POR mechanism is to recover the data integrity verification scheme of outsourced data files through fault tolerance technology while effectively identifying data corruption. The existing POR mechanisms include a sentinel-based mechanism, a compact mechanism, and a POR mechanism that supports dynamic operations, etc. Juels et al. first model the data recoverable proof, and propose a sentinel-based POR verification mechanism(SPOR) [10]. To address a limited number of verifications and large communication consumption of Juels' scheme, Shacham et al. respectively proposed a compact POR mechanism [11,12]. Later, scholars continue to make improvements on this basis, and come up with POR mechanisms that support dynamic operations [13].

With the emergence and development of blockchain technology, there is a wide spectrum of blockchain applications ranging from cryptocurrency, financial services, risk management, Internet of Things(IoT) to public and social services [14]. Related scholars have suggested combining blockchain with data integrity verification schemes to improve performance [15,16]. But both of their schemes ignored redundancy caused by recomputing verification tags when changing TPA. Given the low computational complexity of elliptic curve, we propose a scheme by combining the blockchain and the elliptic curve signature as an effective solution in this paper.

3   Problem Statement

3.1   Definitions and Preliminaries

Homomorphic Verifiable Tags (HVTs): Homomorphism is a kind of mapping from one algebraic structure to another which keeps all related structures unchanged. That is, a mapping exists here.

$$\phi : X \to Y \tag{1}$$

Which satisfied:

$$\phi(a \bullet b) = \phi(a) \times \phi(b) \tag{2}$$

In the equation, $\bullet$ is a kind of operation on X, $\times$ is another kind of operation on Y. Homomorphic tags are generated based on homomorphism. In the process of data integrity verification, the property of the HVTs can be used to verify the integrity of the data. The communication and computation consumption can be reduced in this way.

Bilinear Maps: Let G be an GDH (gap Diffie-Hellman)group, g is the generator of Group G. G_T is another multiplicative group which has the prime order p, mapping e:

$$G \times G \to G_T \tag{3}$$

This mapping is called a bilinear map. And it has bilinearity, non-degeneracy and computability.

Blockchain and Access Control Smart Contract: Blockchain technology is a new computing paradigm consisting of consensus algorithms, asymmetric encryption, distributed storage and other technologies [17]. The blockchain is linked by blocks generated by consensus algorithms, and the block contains transaction records of users' mutual transfers in the blockchain network [18]. Smart contract is a kind of code that can read and manipulate data on the blockchain. After Ethereum introduced the concept of a Turing-complete virtual machine [19,20], there are several types of smart contracts which are supported by different languages in different blockchain, connecting applications with the blockchain network. Some blockchains rigorously restrict access control for auditors by deploying relevant contracts that require the authorization from corresponding accounts, and those contracts are called access control smart contract.

3.2   System Model

In the paper, there are three different entities in our scheme: user, cloud server provider (CSP) and third-party audit (TPA). Users outsource data to CSP for convenient storage, while cloud service providers are sometimes unreliable. To reduce the computational burden, users would delegate data integrity verification to the TPA which, on the contrary, may also cheat users, such as counterfeiting the verification results, or procrastinating the verification. Particularly, in this paper we assume that all parties except user are not fully trusted, which indicates the possibilities for parties concerned to perform malicious operations.

3.3 Threat Model

In the threat model, we consider two situations of malicious operations.

Threat 1: CSPs cheat users. The cloud server provider is a semi-trusted entity. Probabilities exist that hardware corruption in cloud storage can compromise data integrity, such as hard disk track damage or storage hardware failure. It is also a hidden trouble that the data stored in the cloud storage system will be damaged when the system software is attacked by hackers. Cloud service provider may display malicious behavior such as deleting and modifying the data stored by users. In a word, data corruption can occur randomly in a cloud storage environment.

Threat 2: TPAs cheat users. TPA does not perform integrity verification or provide wrong verification results by colluding with cloud servers. When users are performing data integrity verification, the TPA delegated by users may not perform data integrity verification at all. TPAs would provide a false result out of interest. Furthermore, cloud server providers bribe auditors to cover up the fact that the data was corrupted.

4 The Proposed Scheme

In this section, we first give an overview of the model based on blockchain. Then we introduce the blind homomorphic tags proposed in our scheme. Lastly, we present the details of our scheme.

4.1 Architecture Overview

Figure 1 below shows the data verification model used in the cloud storage data integrity verification in this article. It comprises the user, cloud service provider (CSP), and third-party audits (TPAs).

Among them, users can leverage the services from cloud service providers to store data on remote nodes. Cloud service providers integrate storage resources to offer external storage or computing services. Trusted third-party audits are rich in audits. Traditional data integrity verification, which relies on third-party audits, cannot avoid inherent defects such as the waste of communication resources, cheat of audit institutions and repeated passing tags. In this case, we propose a method where the partial nodes on the blockchain or the entities are used to access the blockchain through RPC as distributed trusted third-party auditors. The results of each verification are recorded on the blockchain to ensure the authenticity and transparency. At the same time, we save the verification tag on the contract storage space of the blockchain and limit the access control authority of different TPA through smart contracts. During each verification process, users can select one or more TPAs to perform verification at the same time. In this way, users do not need to send tags to the auditor repeatedly, which saves the communication consumption between two parties. And when users change the verifier, the access right can be re-granted by modifying the contract.

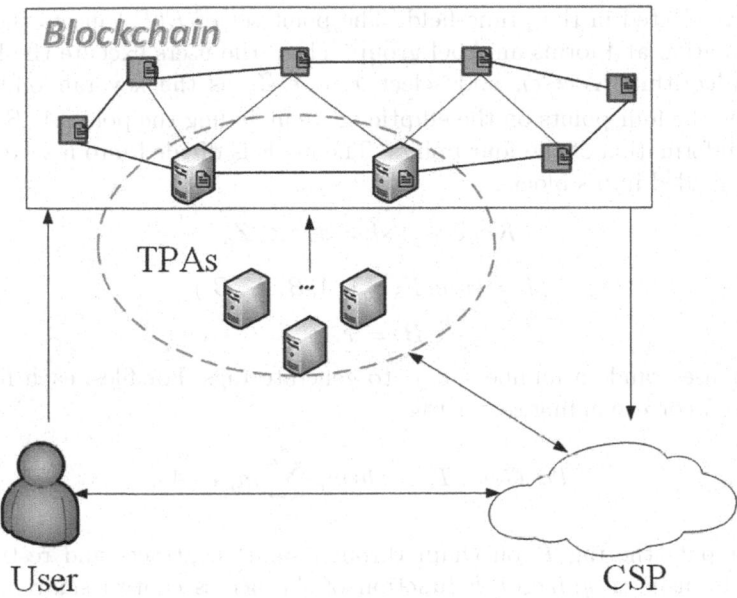

Fig. 1. Data integrity verification model

4.2 Blind Homomorphic Tags

Homomorphic tag is a general way in which users process the origin data with homomorphic encryption. In this way, TPA only needs to verify the encrypted homomorphic tags to reflect the integrity of the original data. But in public verification scheme, TPA needs to retain the homomorphic tags for multiple rounds. To avoid the interference of previous tags, we design a blind homomorphic tag in our scheme that can make the former tags invalid to ensure the security when changing TPA in next round. The specific operation is to add interference to the original tag. Here, we add interference by multiplying a random integer. If the original tag is T_i, the blind tags is $T_i' = rT_i, r \in [1, 2^t]$. This way makes the new tag invisible to the former TPA.

4.3 Construction of Our Scheme

This paper proposes a blockchain-based data integrity verification protocol by combining the PDP protocol based on the elliptic curve signature with blockchain technology, which is named as blockchain based PDP (BCPDP). The BCPDP data integrity verification protocol includes two phases, setup, and challenge.

• **Setup Phase**
First, the user determines the elliptic curve $E(F_q)$ generated by the base point $A \epsilon E(F_q)[p]$, where p is a large prime number. x, α are two private numbers

randomly selected in the prime field. The point set of $E(F_q)$ meets the Weierstrass equation and forms an Abel group. Then, the users execute the key generation algorithm $KeyGen$ and select x, $\alpha \in Z_p$ as the key randomly. They determine the four points on the elliptic curve including the points A, B, A', B', and the information of the four points. The file F is divided into n sectors, each block is divided into s blocks.

$$KeyGen : sk = x, \alpha \in Z_p \tag{4}$$

$$pk = (p, q, E(F_q), A, B, A', B') \tag{5}$$

$$B' = xA' \tag{6}$$

The user uses random numbers x, α to generate tags. For files, each file block generates a corresponding sector tag.

$$TagGen : T_i = xh(m_i) \sum_{j=1}^{s} m_{i_j} \alpha^j A \tag{7}$$

The user puts the tag T_i on chain through smart contracts and restricts the account by using $require\_auth$ function of the access control smart contract. Only CSPs and TPAs that meet the qualification for verification can obtain tags. Users store the data to a remote cloud service provider. When the user needs to change the verifier, the original T_i should be changed, and the original T_i is multiplied by a random number r to update the tag, making the original tag invalid. The new tags are:

$$T_i' = rxh(m_i) \sum_{j=1}^{s} m_i \alpha^j A = rT_i, r \in [1, 2^t] \tag{8}$$

In this way, without retrieving the data, we can directly perform the transformation on the former tag to save the new tag on the chain again.

• **Challenge Phase**
When a user needs to check data, a verification request will be sent to notify TPA to check data integrity. After receiving the users' request, the TPA queries the information of the homomorphic tags stored on chain through the smart contract to perform data integrity verification. TPA sends challenge information $chal$ to CSP, $Q : \{(i, \gamma)\}_{s_1 \le i \le s_c} \rightarrow chal$, i is the index of a data block, and γ is a random number. When CSP receives the challenge, the proof will be generated as follow:

$$ProofGen : T = \sum_{(i,\gamma) \in Q} \gamma^i T_i \tag{9}$$

$$\mu_i = h(m_i) \sum_{(i,\gamma) \in Q} m_{i_j} \gamma^i \tag{10}$$

The TPA will execute verification by the equation as follow:

$$VerifProof : e(\sum_{j=1}^{s} \mu_i (\alpha^j A) B') = e(T, A') \tag{11}$$

If the equation is true, the data will be complete, otherwise, the data integrity will be compromised. TPA sends the results of each verification to the user and saves them to the blockchain at the same time. The specific process of the data integrity verification protocol is shown in Fig. 2.

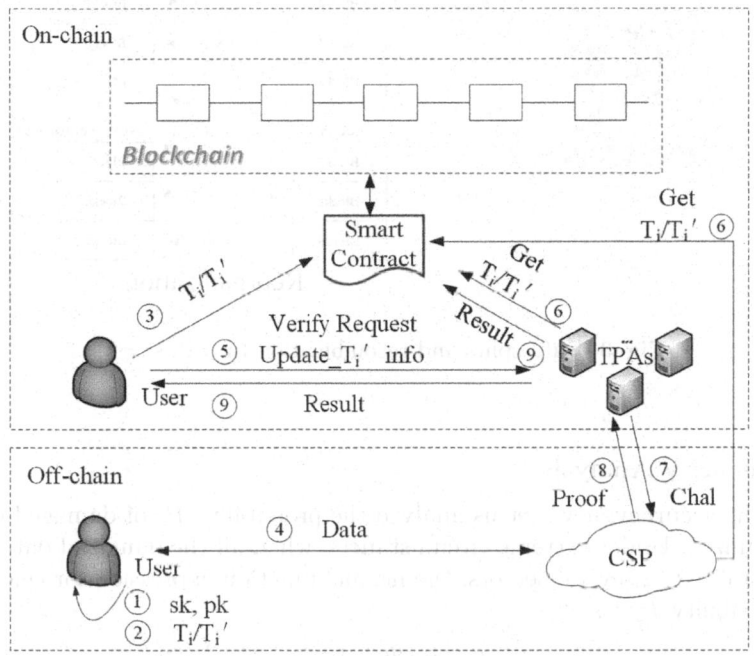

Fig. 2. Process of BCPDP protocol

5   Experiment and Discussion

5.1   Data Preprocessing

In order to reduce the computational complexity, our scheme adopts a data recombination strategy. We first split the data F into n sub-data sectors, with each sector divided into s blocks. Then the s blocks from different sub-data sectors are recombined to form a new sub-data sector as shown in Fig. 3. In this paper, the smallest unit of data verification is sector, with blocks as the smallest unit of data division. In order to increase the data corruption recognition rate and avoid the unidentification of data damaged in a continuous sector, the data processing should be done before next operation.

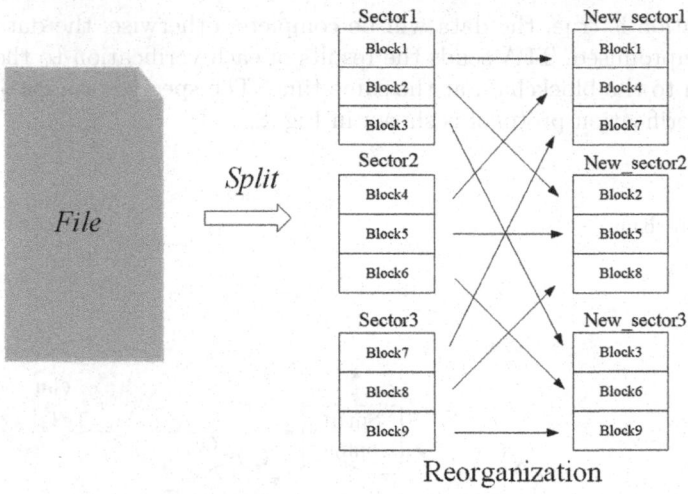

Fig. 3. Data splits and recombination (n = 3, s = 3)

5.2   Security Analysis

As for the accuracy, now, let us analyze the probability P_x of damaged data to be recognized. Under extreme circumstances, when all the damaged data blocks are centralized in several sectors. the normal function expression for calculating the probability P_x is:

$$P_x = 1 - \frac{n-p}{n} \cdot \frac{n-1-p}{n-1} \cdot \frac{n-2-p}{n-2} \cdots \frac{n-i-p}{n-i} \cdots \frac{n-k+1-p}{n-k+1} \tag{12}$$

In the above formula, n is the number of sub-data sectors, k is the number of sub-data sectors checked by the verifier, and p is the number of damaged sectors.

However, there is a smaller granularity in our scheme since the smallest unit of data division is a block. The damaged data blocks will be divided into s sectors on average. So the damaged sectors will be s times of normal schemes after data processing. The function expression for calculating the probability P_x is:

$$P_x = 1 - \frac{n-s\cdot p}{n} \cdot \frac{n-1-s\cdot p}{n-1} \cdot \frac{n-2-s\cdot p}{n-2} \cdots \frac{n-i-s\cdot p}{n-i} \cdots \frac{n-k+1-s\cdot p}{n-k+1} \tag{13}$$

From the above formula, we can conclude that our scheme can get higher recognition rate with the same number of sample. The following formula analyzes the probability of damaged data identified by the verification mechanism from the statistic. Let P_x be the probability of one damaged sector chosen by users at least. we can conclude that:

$$1 - (\frac{n - s \cdot p^k}{n}) \leq P_x \leq 1 - (\frac{n - k + 1 - s \cdot p}{n - k + 1})^k \qquad (14)$$

For example, if the whole data sectors of a data is 10^4 sectors, each sector will be divided into 10 blocks. The relationship between the rate of damaged data and the number of sectors need to be checked to make the corruption identified at a credibility of 99%, which can be obtained in Table 1.

Table 1. Recognition rate of damaged data

C1	C2	C3
0.1%	4603	10000
0.5%	919	9208
1%	459	4603
2%	228	2301
3%	152	1533
4%	113	1149
5%	90	919

C1: Rate of damaged data, C2: The minimum number sectors need to be checked with 99% credibility of our scheme, C3: The minimum number sectors need to be checked with 99% credibility of normal scheme.

According to Table 1, we give the minimum number sectors to be checked with 99% of two sample strategies. It is evident from the Table 1 above that the data is divided into 10^4 sectors. In our scheme, if 0.1% of the data in the original data is damaged, equivalent to damaged 10 pieces of sectors, then 4603 data sectors need to be checked before we considered 99% probability that the data corruption can be identified effectively. Similarly, when the damaged rate is 0.5%, equivalent to 50 bad sectors, then the number of random data sectors to be checked is 919 to ensure the precision. And the rest of rate of damaged data is likewise. Figure 4 showcases the relationship between the number of damaged sectors and the probability of successfully identifying data corruption P_x. The higher the rate of data corruption, the easier to detect the corrupted data. In particular, when $p = n$, it means that whole data is damaged. This scheme can find the corruption with a 100% probability.

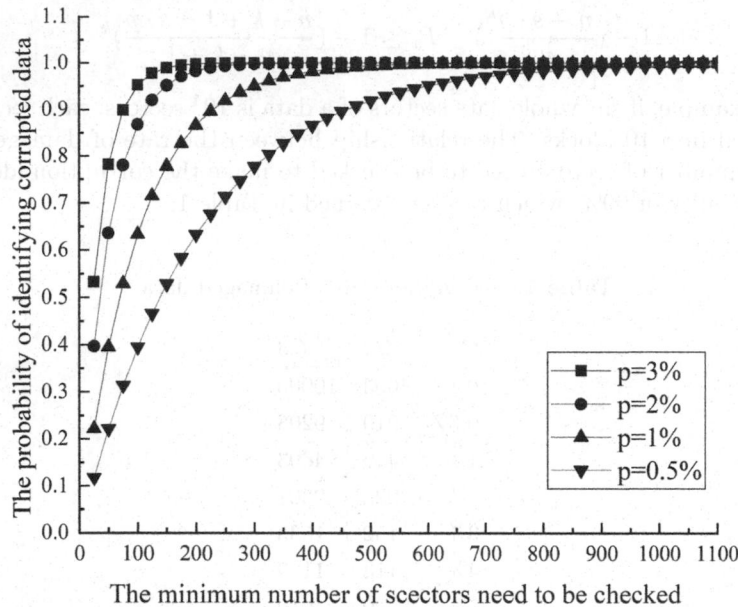

Fig. 4. Relationship between the number of the recognition rate and checked sectors.

5.3 Performance Analysis and Comparison

The experiment of our data processing and tag generation are implemented on Intel (R) Core (TM) i5-4200H @ 2.80 GHz personal computer with a RAM size of 12.0 GB. The system is Windows 10 Professional. The environment for building blockchain network is an Alibaba Cloud server with a 4-core CPU and 8 GB memory, with Ubuntu 16.04.3 LTS as the system. The parameters of the elliptic curve in the tag are generated by the OpenSSL library OpenSSL-1.1.1b. We deploy the blockchain service by setting up the node of Jungle, the test network of EOS. EOS is in version 2.0.4.

In setup phase, all procedures are completed at the side of users and the overhead mainly comes from the computation of data processing and tag generation. In challenge phase, the overhead comes from the communication between all parties and computation of validation. The performance of tag generation related to the file size is shown in Fig. 5. Obviously, the time of tags generation for our scheme is less than the S-PDP scheme.

In Table 2, we analyze the performance for different schemes in terms of blockchain technology, change of TPA and recombination block strategy. Additional performance comparisons of different schemes are shown in Table 2. Other schemes listed in the table bear inadequacies. For instance, even though the BB-DIS [16] takes a markov process sampling, but it still ignores the corrupted data in a continuous sector. Our strategy adopts the approach of recombination with smaller granularity. Though it increases some computational overheads in setup

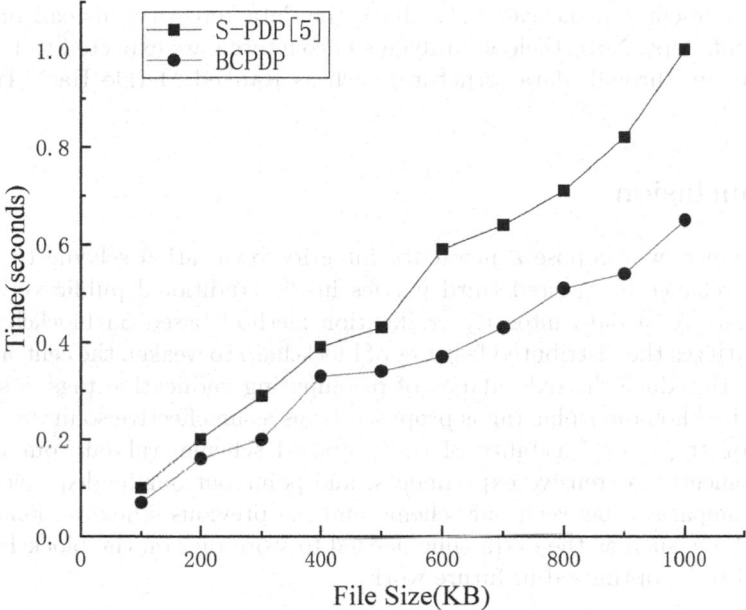

Fig. 5. Performance for tags generation

Table 2. Performance comparison of different schemes.

Scheme	C1	C2	C3	C4	C5
MHT-SC [3]	O(n)	O(c)	✗	✓	✗
S-PDP [5]	O(n)	O(c)	✗	✗	✗
E-PDP [5]	O(n)	O(c)	✗	✗	✗
BB-DIS [16]	O(n)	O(c)	✓	✗	✗
BCPDP	O(s · n)	O(c/n)	✓	✓	✓

C1: Setup Phase, C2: Challenge Phase, C3: Blockchain Supported, C4: TPA Change Supported, C5: Recombination Block Strategy Supported.

phase, the overhead caused by sample can be reduced in challenge phase and the recognition rate can be significantly increased. The Table 2 indicates that our scheme not only adopts the blockchain technology as a base but also supports the replacement of TPA. Most importantly, we use the sample strategy of dynamic recombination in data preprocessing to reduce the numbers that need to be checked during verification.

However, there are some insufficiencies in dynamic performance regarding our scheme with the unavailability of supporting dynamic inserts and deletes. In the mean time, our scheme does not focus on proof of retrievability, suggesting that the present scheme can only check the data integrity, instead of taking subsequent steps. Nevertheless, problems encountered are expected to be solved in the future through data structure, such as Ranked Merkle Hash Tree and sentinel.

6 Conclusion

In this paper, we propose a new data integrity verification scheme to address the over-reliance on trusted third parties in the traditional public verification mechanism. As a data integrity verification method based on blockchain, our scheme utilizes the distributed features of blockchain to weaken the centralization of TPA. To reduce the redundancy of recomputing verification tags, a strategy named blind homomorphic tag is proposed by us as an effective solution. Finally, we demonstrate the feasibility of the proposed scheme, validate our analysis by implementing extensive experiments, and point out our inadequacies based on the comparison between our scheme and the previous schemes. Some limits among those, such as the extra time needed to store tags on the blockchain, are expected to be optimized in future work.

Acknowledgments. This work was supported by the Changsha Science and Technology Commission (KH1902201).

References

1. Shuang, T., Yan, J., Wei-hong, H.: Research and progress of data integrity proof in cloud storage. Chin. J. Comput. **38**(01), 164–177 (2015)
2. Deswarte, Y., Quisquater, J.-J., Saïdane, A.: Remote integrity checking. In: Jajodia, S., Strous, L. (eds.) Integrity and Internal Control in Information Systems VI. IIFIP, vol. 140, pp. 1–11. Springer, Boston, MA (2004). https://doi.org/10.1007/1-4020-7901-X_1
3. Wang, Q., Wang, C., Li, J., Ren, K., Lou, W.: Enabling public verifiability and data dynamics for storage security in cloud computing. In: Backes, M., Ning, P. (eds.) ESORICS 2009. LNCS, vol. 5789, pp. 355–370. Springer, Heidelberg (2009). https://doi.org/10.1007/978-3-642-04444-1_22
4. Wang, C., Wang, Q., Ren, K., Lou, W.: Privacy-preserving public auditing for data storage security in cloud computing. In: 2010 Proceedings IEEE Infocom, pp. 1–9. IEEE (2010)
5. Ateniese, G., et al.: Provable data possession at untrusted stores. In: Proceedings of the 14th ACM Conference on Computer and Communications Security, pp. 598–609 (2007)
6. Ateniese, G., et al.: Remote data checking using provable data possession. ACM Trans. Inf. Syst. Secur. (TISSEC) **14**(1), 1–34 (2011)
7. Wang, H., et al.: An efficient provable data possession based on elliptic curves in cloud storage. Int. J. Secur. Appl. **8**(5), 97–108 (2014)
8. Chen, Y., Wang, F., Zhu, L., Zhang, Z.: A survey of remote data integrity checking: techniques and verification structures. Int. J. Grid Distrib. Comput. **8**(4), 179–198 (2015)

9. Curtmola, R., Khan, O., Burns, R., Ateniese, G.: MR-PDP: multiple-replica provable data possession. In: 2008 the 28th International Conference on Distributed Computing Systems, pp. 411–420. IEEE (2008)
10. Juels, A., Kaliski Jr, B.S.: PORs: proofs of retrievability for large files. In: Proceedings of the 14th ACM Conference on Computer and Communications Security, pp. 584–597 (2007)
11. Shacham, H., Waters, B.: Compact proofs of retrievability. In: Pieprzyk, J. (ed.) ASIACRYPT 2008. LNCS, vol. 5350, pp. 90–107. Springer, Heidelberg (2008). https://doi.org/10.1007/978-3-540-89255-7_7
12. Shacham, H., Waters, B.: Compact proofs of retrievability. J. Cryptol. **26**(3), 442–483 (2013)
13. Wang, C., Wang, Q., Ren, K., Lou, W.: Ensuring data storage security in cloud computing. In: 17th International Workshop on Quality of Service, 2009 IWQOS (2009)
14. Dai, H.N., Zheng, Z., Zhang, Y.: Blockchain for internet of things: a survey. IEEE Internet Things J. **6**(5), 8076–8094 (2019)
15. Yue, D., Li, R., Zhang, Y., Tian, W., Peng, C.: Blockchain based data integrity verification in P2P cloud storage. In: 2018 IEEE 24th International Conference on Parallel and Distributed Systems (ICPADS), pp. 561–568. IEEE (2018)
16. Wang, H., Zhang, J.: Blockchain based data integrity verification for large-scale IoT data. IEEE Access **7**, 164996–165006 (2019)
17. Zheng, Z., Xie, S., Dai, H., Chen, X., Wang, H.: An overview of blockchain technology: architecture, consensus, and future trends. In: 2017 IEEE International Congress on Big Data (BigData Congress), pp. 557–564. IEEE (2017)
18. Zheng, Z., Xie, S., Dai, H.N., Chen, X., Wang, H.: Blockchain challenges and opportunities: a survey. Int. J. Web Grid Serv. **14**(4), 352–375 (2018)
19. Wood, G., et al.: Ethereum: a secure decentralised generalised transaction ledger. Ethereum Project Yellow Paper **151**(2014), 1–32 (2014)
20. Huang, Y., Kong, Q., Jia, N., Chen, X., Zheng, Z.: Recommending differentiated code to support smart contract update. In: 2019 IEEE/ACM 27th International Conference on Program Comprehension (ICPC), pp. 260–270. IEEE (2019)

A Permissioned Blockchain-Based Platform for Education Certificate Verification

Hanlei Cheng[1,2], Jing Lu[1,3(✉)], Zhiyu Xiang[1(✉)], and Bin Song[1]

[1] Blockchain Laboratory of YGSoft Inc., Zhuhai 519085, China
chenghanlei@ygsoft.com
[2] Faculty of Science and Technology, Macau University of Science and Technology,
Macau SAR 999078, China
[3] Department of Computer Science and Technology, Hubei University of Education,
Wuhan 430205, China

Abstract. Distance education has become an important learning method for students. Nevertheless, online teaching is difficult to ensure the traceability of student activities. The difficulty in managing the non-instantaneous diploma verification and digital/paper files have always been severe problems in education management. The education information stored within the current centralized system is simply leaked and cannot be guaranteed in terms of impartiality and authenticity. In the present paper, a digital education certificate prototype is designed utilizing the permissioned blockchain of PKI-CA, digest algorithm, and interactive data authentication by digital signatures. The digital certificates can be issued by the system realizing the instant certificate verification between students and third parties via QR codes or dynamic authorization codes. The test results indicated that 100% correct work of the prototype, with the significant throughputs of getting and creating transactions are respectively 1982.6 tps and 263.9 tps on-chain during the test cycle.

Keywords: Permissioned blockchain · Smart contract · Certificates authentication · Data verification

1 Introduction

According to the latest monitoring and statistics of UNESCO, in April 24, 2020, the schools of more than 191 countries affected by the COVID-19 have been closed. Distance learning has become an important way for helping students to interact with teachers. Nevertheless, virtually integrated education poses challenges to tracking the learning process and the verification of learning results. Owing to the data island in education information systems within and outside the school, the students occasionally are forced by recruiting firms to get diploma certificate authentication from the school or even the Ministry of Education. Generally, the students should spend a long time and probably pay fees to obtain numerous translated supplements or original materials weakening the recruiting process, especially for the non-native student studying in other countries.

Z. Zheng et al. (Eds.): BlockSys 2020, CCIS 1267, pp. 456–471, 2020.
https://doi.org/10.1007/978-981-15-9213-3_36

For instance, the Chinese student studying abroad should get foreign diplomas legalized via the Chinese Service Center for Scholarly Exchange (CSCSE).

In this paper, the school-issued certificates were authenticated that are easy to damage or loss, and even not convenient to use since they need to be instantly validated. Within a point-to-point scenario, electronic education certificates under "Internet+" are not issued to students. However, they rely on a centralized specific education platform for inspection and storage. It indicates that the certificate registries are single failure points. If a third party should use the certificates, e.g., to verify claims in CV provided students for seeking jobs, they should verify and read each certificate individually and manually through a significantly time-consuming procedure [10]. The centralized registries accumulate a large number of precipitation data resources, resulting in risky data security and forcing the students to relinquish all control of their education data, especially the diploma.

Some blockchain-based electronic education projects emerged, with the emergence of blockchain technology. Although these projects adopted blockchain technology, the majority cases merely determine the hash or hash value (also known as a digital fingerprint, message digest, or digest) for the original version of the diploma PDF. It stores the hash value in a block in the blockchain instead of storing the SHA-256 hash of students' original education data [2]. They do not develop the mutual supervision and admission control mechanism in blockchain and do not focus on improving the authorized access and ownership of the diploma for the students. Hence, the universities are limited to share or even transfer their students' data to third parties owing to the administrative barriers [3]. Hence, this paper designs and builds an alliance blockchain-based digital foreign education certification prototype system, and identified the Macau University of Science and Technology (MUST) as the pilot university to solve the problem.

The main contributions of this paper as follows: it presents the detailed scheme of the prototype system allowing the blockchain digital certificates that cannot be forged using PKI-CA, digest algorithm, and interactive data verification. The MUST issues the authenticated certificates, received by the students, and verified promptly by any institutions with access to the blockchain without the intermediary parties.

2   Related Work

Blockchain technology can perform distributed encrypted storage after hashing data [16], and solve the trust and security problems when sharing and storing data [21]. It provides a reliable tamper-proof database to clarify the ownership and source of the education data [17]. Guy Zyskind et al. [27] demonstrates that users completely own and control their data, and others can collect the data through permissioned access on the Hyperledger Fabric. Students can get rid of the paper education certificates and use the distributed smart contracts ("chain code") to issue a student certificate as a blockchain transaction followed by inserting the corresponding school parameters like the course, degree level, the major, and graduation date.

In response to the current problem of the academic scheme, with the help of blockchain technology, some universities and technology companies use blockchain to develop electronic educational certificate storage systems hashing and encrypting the diploma document to protect its authenticity [3]. For example, Learning Machine was connected to MIT's Media Lab to create Blockerts-an open Ethereum-based platform to create, approach, and validate blockchain-based academic credentials. All students who graduated from the platform in February 2018 were awarded by MIT. Blockchain Digital Certificates. On 9th November 2018, the e-Scroll system as a blockchain application platform formerly introduced by the Ministry of Education of Malaysia started to obtain digital degree certificates for Ph.D. graduates in the country. It aimed to slow the frequent diploma fraud by blockchain. Educational blockchain contributes to alleviating the information asymmetry between the employers and applicants with transparent curriculum, competence assessment, and certification [6].

3   System Overview

To endorse and verify education data in real-time, the system uses certification authorities, universities, and employers as the organization nodes of the consortium blockchain (Fig. 1). The blockchain nodes joint monitor the entire authentication process of digital education certificates [18]. Through the system, schools are allowed to make an electronic diploma template before issuing a valid certificate. By applying a digital certificate for the issuance via a student, the system locates the proper digital diploma template automatically adapting to an education array input and generating a complete digital certificate. Then, the certificate is hashed to a digital fingerprint stored in an immutable mode on the blockchain [9]. When stakeholders tend to recognize the authenticity of the student's digital diploma, the system can run online authorization by sending a dynamic verification code to the terminal or scanning the QR code of the mobile client (Fig. 2).

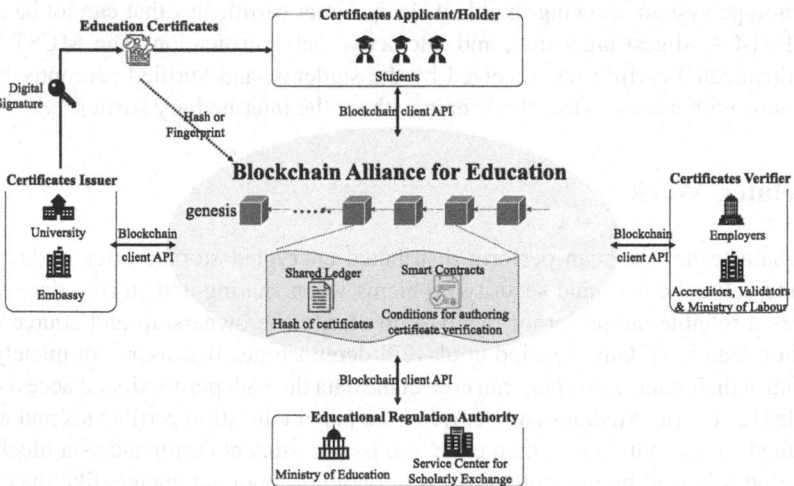

Fig. 1. The overview of the blockchain alliance for education

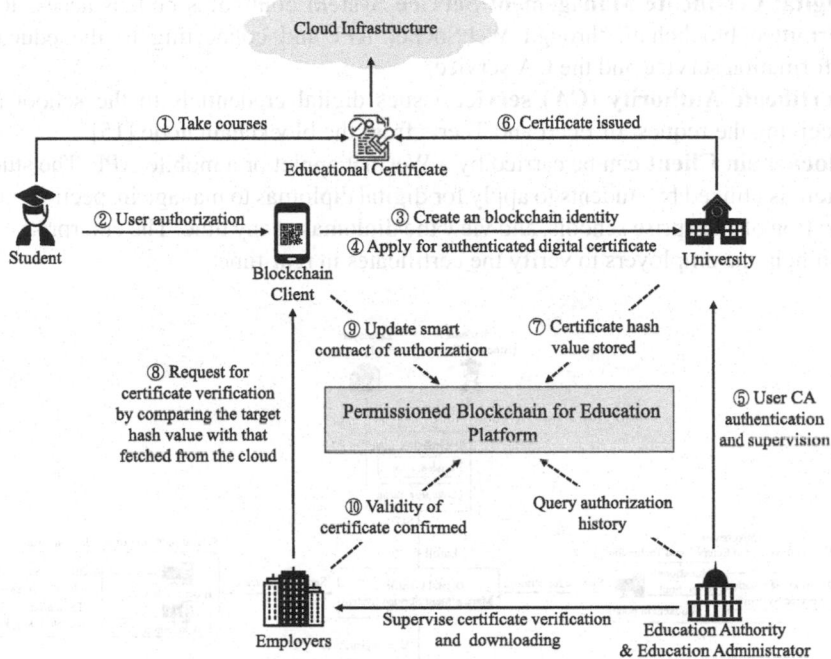

Fig. 2. The schematic diagram of the alliance digital education certification system

The prototype allows the students to actively apply to the school to generate digital diplomas based on their college professionals via the mobile terminal program (like WeChat Mini Program). The digital certificates are released by the school office after inspecting the students' identity and graduation status. When students are seeking employment or further study, other universities and companies can obtain a copy of digital certificates by seeking authorization from students instead of asking authenticity from the issuing organization. Moreover, students can authorize employers to search for their whole or partial schooling information [20].

3.1 Conceptual System Architecture

An overview of the prototype architecture is represented in Fig. 3, in which five parts exit as follows.

- **Permissioned Blockchain for Education** is responsible for the on-chain storage of different types of education data, such as learning history, course credits, and studying majors. The data stored on the chain are consensus and mutual supervision of the blockchain nodes of the alliance chain to ensure the credibility and security of data on the chain [26].
- **Education Information Service System for each university** supports the management of all digital certificates and critical education data, responding to the students' requests for issuing authenticated certificates.

- **Digital Certificate Management Service System** configures node.js access to the permitted blockchain through WebSocket API and connecting to the education information service and the CA service.
- **Certificate Authority (CA) service** issues digital credentials to the school after receiving the request of Ecert and Tcerts from the blockchain node [15].
- **Blockchain Client** can be carried by a WeChat applet or a mobile APP. The student client is utilized by students to apply for digital diplomas to manage inspection authorization of enterprise schools, and view the diplomas at any time. The enterprise client can help the employers to verify the certificates in real-time.

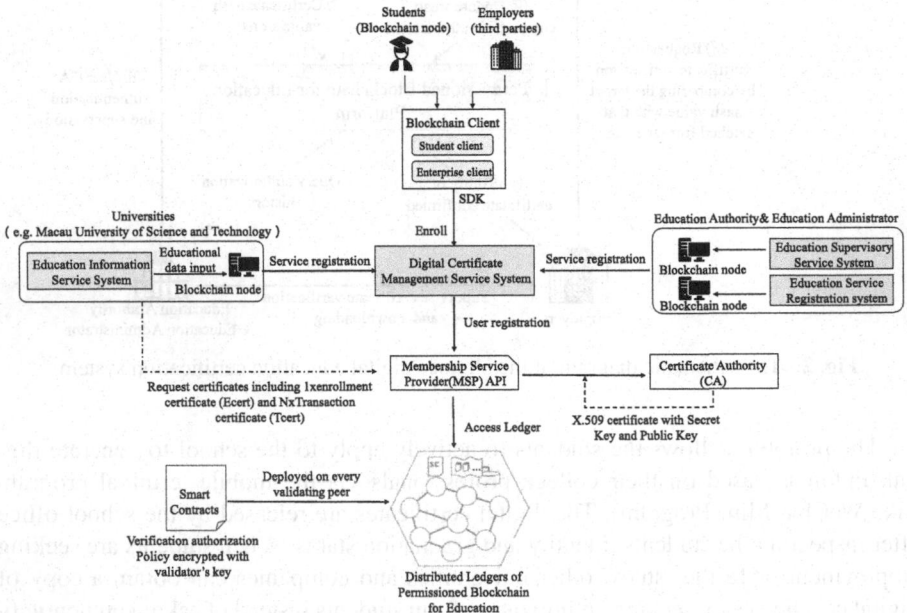

Fig. 3. The deployment topology diagram of the alliance digital education certification system

4   Prototype Implementation

4.1   CA Identification on the Permissioned Blockchain

On the permissioned blockchain, all nodes must be registered to obtain an X.509 identity credential) issued by a third-party CA authority, and have a legal identity before all operations on the blockchain [1].

4.1.1 Blockchain-Based PKI Certification Architecture

Membership services enable decentralized technologies and Public Key Infrastructure (PKI) to turn unauthorized blockchains into authorized blockchains [5]. Some typical certificate authorities are configured when setting up CA in blockchain to issue ECerts (Enrollment Certificates), TCerts (Transaction Certificates), and TLSCerts (TLS certificates), serving to transactions invoked on the blockchain, user enrolment, and TLS-secured connections between users or components of the blockchain [12]. The user enrollment process for obtaining TCerts, ECerts, and TLSCerts to membership service is represented in Fig. 4.

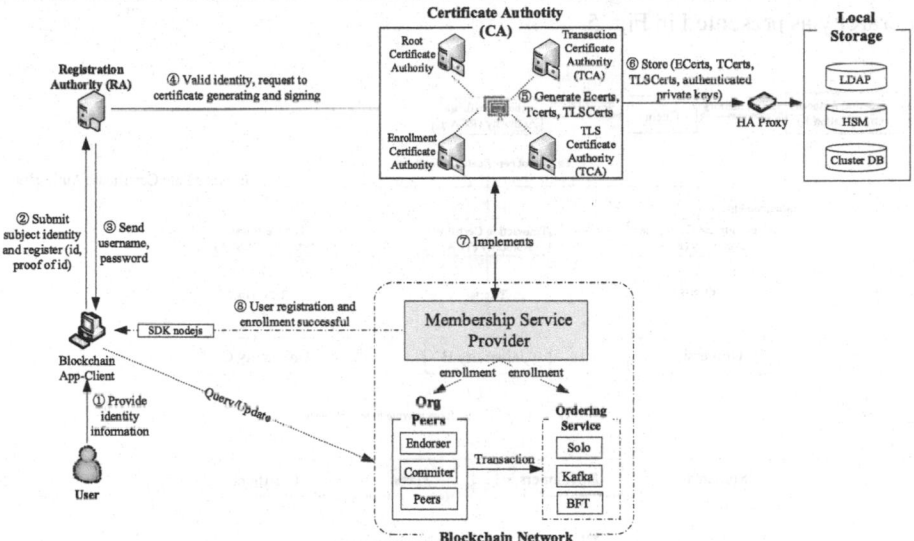

Fig. 4. The user enrollment process under the PKI architecture on the permissioned blockchain

- ECerts are long-term certificates including identities/enrollment IDs of their owners used to identity every registered user on the blockchain.
- The transaction certificates (TCerts) is disposal for each transaction over authenticated user-request authorizing nodes to submit the transaction selectively and securely not carrying information of the identities involved in the transaction.
- TLS certificates (TLSCerts) that the user utilizes the blockchain network securely to synchronize the data between other nodes.

4.1.2 CA Identity Hierarchy

The process of delegating identity credentials to users (or peer nodes including students, certifiers, developers, and other peers includes the root authority providing credentials to intermediate authority CA Server nodes are set in a tree structure comprising a root node and multiple intermediate nodes [4].

All members (root, intermediate authorities, and users/peer codes) should create their pairs of secret and public keys. A connection is created by an intermediate authority as the Level-1 delegatee to the root to attain a credential (a signature) to bind its public key to its attributes. When a Level-1 delegatee gets its credentials, it becomes a delegator itself, then it can issue credentials for the Level-2 delegates. Continuing this delegation process at any level, the length of the credential chain is increased to form an identity hierarchy as presented in Fig. 5.

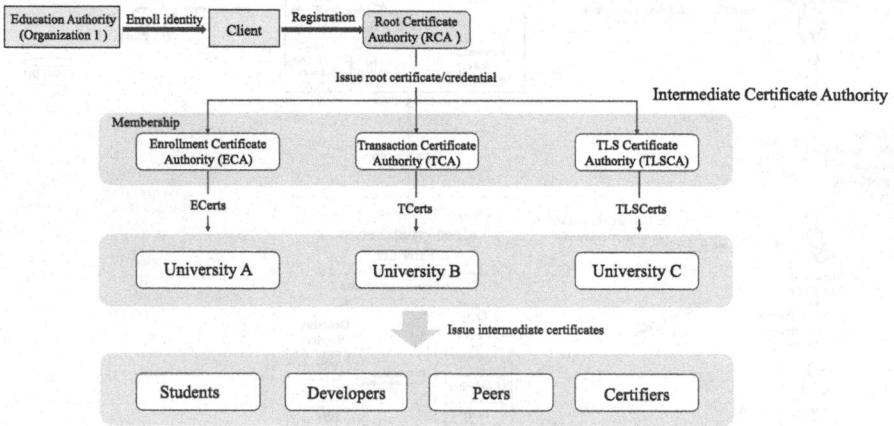

Fig. 5. CA identity hierarchy

By registering a new user in the permissioned blockchain, the platform should initially check whether the user already exists. If it is not present, then it should check whether there is an organization administrator to which the user belongs, as shown in Algorithm 1. If it exists, the CA authority registers the blockchain identity of the user through organization root CA, issuing a CA certificate for the user and generating the public key and private key through the Public Key Infrastructure (PKI) [25].

Algorithm 1: Check to see if already enrolled the user

```
if (userExists) {
        console.log('An identity for the user ' + user + '
already exists in the admin');
        return;
}
// Check to see if already enrolled the admin user.
if (!adminExists) {
        console.log('Run the enrollAdmin.js application before
retrying');
        return;
}
// Get the CA client object from the gateway for
interacting with the CA.
const ca = gateway.getClient().getCertificateAuthority();
const adminIdentity = gateway.getCurrentIdentity();
// Register the user, enroll the user, and import the new
identity into the admin.
const secret = await ca.register({ affiliation: 'education
org1.department1', enrollmentID: user, role: 'client' },
adminIdentity);
console.log('Successfully registered user ' + user + ' and
the secret is ' + secret );
process.exit
```

4.1.3 On-Chain Registration and Mapping of Digital Education Certificates

The digital education certificate is encoded on the blockchain to compute the "digital fingerprint or a hash value of the file," which is calculated by hash functions to a numeric value of a fixed length (typically size 256 bits in Bitcoin) identifying the data uniquely [15]. Each block in the blockchain technically includes transaction data, Merkle Root, and the hash of the previous block header. The hash value should be signed with a private key of file senders, like students and universities in this prototype, and then the receiver of the file such as employers can check its authenticity utilizing the corresponding public key [13]. It is important to note that the hash value of received data can be compared to the hash value of data when it was sent to determine the alteration of the data.

A blockchain consensus mechanism makes independent nodes reach a consistency on the data authentication based on consensus protocols. After verifying the hash value by a consensus mechanism, it is distributed to different devices for storage, and the electronic file itself is stored in the cloud. Hence, the file hash value will not be modified, even if a federation node exits or stops [11].

In this paper, smart contracts are designed and studied to register and map files on the chain and to verify changing the signed education certificates. When registering on the electronic file chain, first, the calculated hash of the file is linked to the block to which the hash is added, then the added method is used to accept the hash, store it in the map, and use the verified technique to return the hash Timestamp. The contract code of registering the education certificates is represented in Algorithm 2.

Algorithm 2: Contract certificate Registry of digital education certificates

```
contract DocumentRegistry {
  mapping (string => uint256) documents;
  address contractOwner = msg.sender;
  function add(string hash)
    public
    returns (uint256 dateAdded)
  {
    require (msg.sender == contractOwner);
    var timeAdded = block.timestamp;
    documents[hash] = timeAdded;
    return timeAdded;
  }
  function verify(string hash)
    constant
    public
    returns (uint256 dateAdded)
  {
    return documents[hash];
  }
}
```

4.1.4 The Process of Issuing Digital Education Certificate

The education information service of the school verifies the information submitted by the students. If the verification is successful, the digital finger-print of the electronic diploma certificate data is computed based on the digest algorithm [14].

Here, Digest of the data chunk file is utilized to provide the digital finger-print, among which, the electronic diploma certificate information is a character string composed of fields requiring to be backfilled on the electronic diploma certificate template. The data digest is created by hashing the data file for data integrity checks [2].

$Digest\,H(\cdot)$ $=$ $Digest(hash\,value\,of\,digital\,certificate\,data\,file)$, where $H(\cdot)$ denotes the cryptographic function [19]. The i_{th} hash digest is connected with $(i-1)_{th}$ hash digest to verify the authenticity of the data. $Sign_{sk_{uni}}(\cdot)$ represents the digital signature with the university public key. The transaction hash is a string generated by the school's education information service when is submitted to the chain based on the related rules of the blockchain. The certificate data file is identified by the channel ID of the university, the digital certificate stored in the cloud in terms of URL, the student public key, the university public key and the signature of data digest.

$$Digest\,H\,(file)\|Digest_{i-1} \tag{1}$$

$$Identity_i(channel_{id},\,URL_i,\,pk_{stu},\,Sign_{sk_{uni}}(Digest_i) \tag{2}$$

The education information service of the school will digitally sign the $DigestH\,(file)$ and submit it to the blockchain as a transaction. The hash value of the transaction will be recorded on the distributed ledgers via consensus mechanism [8]. Afterward, the school's electronic education service will issue the plain text data of the electronic education certificate to the student point-to-point. Then, the student can read the authenticated digital certificate via the mobile client.

4.1.5 The Process of Peer-to-Peer Verification for Digital Education Certificates

When the employers require to check the student's certificate, the student can activate the QR code including the transaction hash of the certificate on the blockchain and the student's blockchain account. The employer scans the student-presented QR code through the mobile device to initiate the authorization requests for the certificate validation. The student can select authorizing the employer to verify the certificate if it is permissioned, the client updates the student's authorization smart contract on the blockchain. The smart contract previously encodes authorization policies permitting certificates to be verified and viewed by the third party in an immutable and transparent manner.

After obtaining the verification authorization by the employer, its application client automatically requests the school's education information service for the unencrypted data of the certificate. The unencrypted data can be backfilled into the digital certificate template to generate a readable certificate. To further validate the certificate's authenticity, the application client should obtain the authenticated hash value of the certificate on the blockchain needing to be compared with the hash value calculated against the previously created certificate. If the hash values match, the authenticity of the certificate is validated. By altering a single file or bit in that dataset, an entirely new hash value is created. There is exactly one possible combination of numbers and letters corresponding to a digital file. In contrast, the inconsistent hashes indicated that the certificates provided by the student were corrupted.

Finally, the peers execute a consensus protocol to validate transactions, classify them into blocks, and build a hash chain over the blocks [23]. The ordering service ensures the delivered blocks on one channel are totally ordered and validated, and then locally stored in distributed ledgers updating the blockchain state.

5   Presentation of the Prototype

In this prototype, the Macau University of Science and Technology is considered as the university participating node to issue digital certificates. Educational stakeholders can manage the issuance of the certificates and control the authorization across the platform providing a comprehensive authorizing transactions' log to query (Figs. 6, 7, and 8).

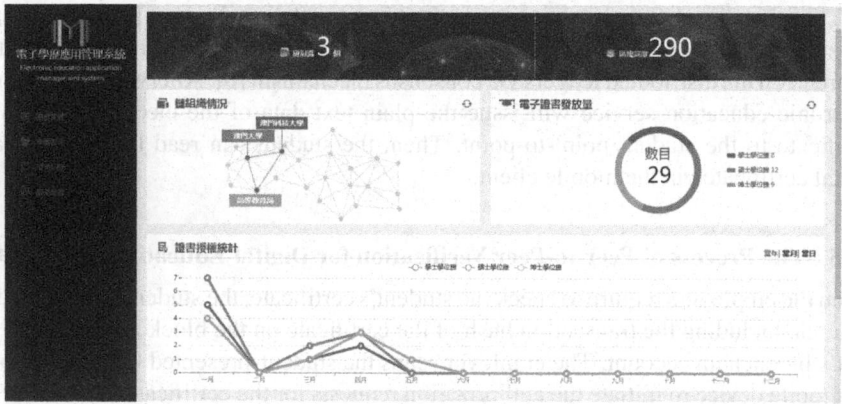

Fig. 6. The prototype interface of the Digital Certificate Management Service System

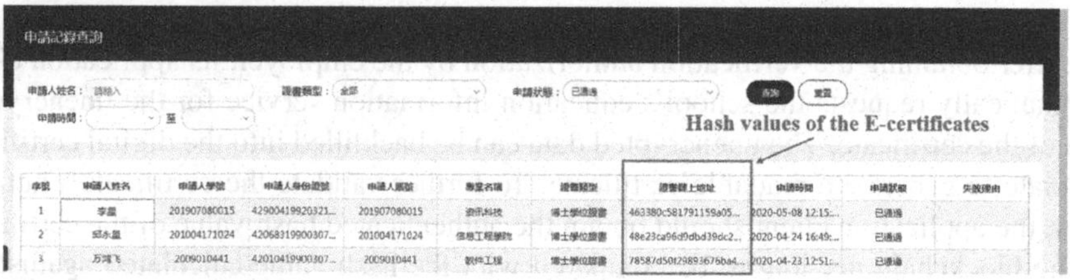

Fig. 7. Query the application history of the certificates

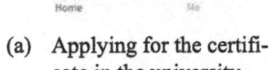

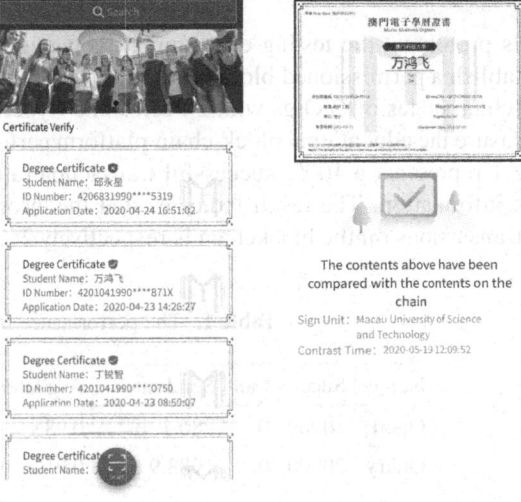

(a) Applying for the certificate in the university

(b) Scanning to verify the certificate

(c) Validating the certificate by hash comparison

(d) Certificate details

(e) Blockchain successful verification and E-certificate presented on the PC client

Fig. 8. The presentation of the prototype on the client

6 Hyperledger Fabric Experiments and Analysis

In this prototype, the testing environment is configured for Hyperledger Fabric V1.4 to establish a permissioned blockchain framework including the virtual deployment of blockchain nodes on 3 Orgs with 2 Peers. The Hyperledger Caliper instrument is used to measure the educational block-chain platform performance, scalability, and stability. Table 1 represents a 100% successful transaction rate of synchronizing and verifying block information. The result indicates that the throughput for creating and querying new transactions on the blockchain is respectively 263.9 tps and 1982.6 tps.

Table 1. The performance metrics

Name	Succ	Fail	Send rate	Avg latency	Throughput
Open	10000	0	280.1 tps	0.98 s	263.9 tps
Query	20000	0	1983.9 tps	0.01 s	1982.6 tps

Then, the experiment uses Win7 64bit as the PC client, CentOS Linux releases 7.4.1708 (Core) and Mysql 5.7.20 to examine the 6 key certificate verification scenarios. The response time of each transaction function is less than 5 s (Table 2), proving the higher efficiency than the traditional method of issuing and verifying the education certificates. The average CPU and memory utilization of database servers and application servers in all functions are less than the target values of 75% and 60% (Fig. 9).

Table 2. The response time

Transaction function	Concurrency	Average response time (s)	Transaction success rate
Generating check code	100	0.172	100%
Generating QR code	500	0.017	100%
Enterprise scan code	100	0.018	100%
Applying for the educational certificate	100	2.443	100%
Student certificate list certificate application	500	0.05	100%
Education certificates verified by enterprises	100	0.041	100%

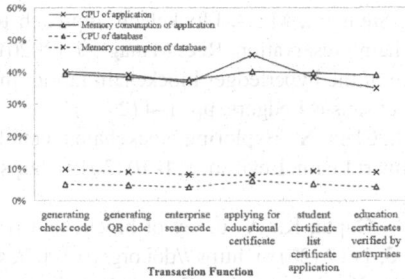

Fig. 9. CPU and memory consumption among the application and database servers

7 Conclusion and Future Work

The system was developed to realize the point-to-point issuance and verification of digital education certificates between students and schools, as well as third parties. We examine the performance and efficiency of verifying the education certificate criticized by the methodology in this paper. The results indicate that 100% correct work of the prototype, with the outstanding throughputs of storing and verifying the digital education certificate on the permissioned blockchain are respectively 1982.6 tps and 263.9 tps on average. Future work will further investigate the following tasks:

1. Deploying proper consensus mechanisms where multiple authorities control the data keep-recording rules and further enhance the credibility of data.
2. Considering to encrypt the education data by other encryption algorithms including SM4, homomorphic encryption, and zero-knowledge proof [24].
3. Enhancing on-chain storage performance practically through some techniques such as IPFS.

Acknowledgments. This research was funded by Natural Science Foundation of Hubei Province, 2018CFB571; Zhuhai Industry Core and Key Technology Research Project, ZH01084702180035HJL

References

1. Androulaki, E., Barger, A., Bortnikov, V., et al.: Hyperledger fabric: a distributed operating system for permissioned blockchains. In: Proceedings of the Thirteenth EuroSys Conference, pp. 1–15. ACM (2018)
2. Baza, M., Nabil, M., Lasla, N., et al.: Blockchain-based firmware update scheme tailored for autonomous vehicles. In: IEEE Wireless Communications and Networking Conference, pp. 1–7. IEEE (2019)
3. Bore, N., et al.: Towards blockchain-enabled school information hub. In: Proceedings of the Ninth International Conference on Information and Communication Technologies and Development, pp. 1–4 (2017)

4. Bralić, V., Stančić, H., Stengård, M.: A blockchain approach to digital archiving: digital signature certification chain preservation. Rec. Manage. J. (2020)
5. Cachin, C.: Architecture of the hyperledger blockchain fabric. In: Workshop on Distributed Cryptocurrencies and Consensus Ledgers, pp. 1–4 (2016)
6. Chen, G., Xu, B., Lu, M., Chen, N.: Exploring blockchain technology and its potential applications for education. Smart Learn. Environ. **5**, 1–10 (2019). https://doi.org/10.1186/s40561-017-0050-x
7. Dasgupta, D., Shrein, J., Gupta, K.: A survey of blockchain from security perspective. J. Bank. Financ. Technol. **3**, 1–17 (2019). https://doi.org/10.1007/s42786-018-00002-6
8. Deshpande, A., Stewart, K., Lepetit, L., Gunashekar, S.: Distributed ledger technologies/blockchain: challenges, opportunities and the prospects for standards. In: Overview report The British Standards Institution, pp. 1–34. BSI (2017)
9. Do, H.G., Ng, W.K.: Blockchain-based system for secure data storage with private keyword search. In: IEEE World Congress on Services (SERVICES), pp. 90–93. IEEE (2017)
10. Gräther, W., Kolvenbach, S., Ruland, R., Schütte, J., Torres, C., Wendland, F.: Blockchain for education: lifelong learning passport. In: Proceedings of 1st ERCIM Blockchain Workshop, pp. 1–8 (2018)
11. Hammi, M., Bellot, P., Serhrouchni. A.: Trust: a decentralized authentication blockchain-based mechanism. In: IEEE Wireless Communications and Networking Conference, pp. 1–6. IEEE (2018)
12. Kubilay, M.Y., Kiraz, M.S., Mantar, H.A.: CertLedger: a new PKI model with certificate transparency based on blockchain. Comput. Secur. **85**, 333–352 (2019)
13. Lemieux, V.: Trusting records: is Blockchain technology the answer? Rec. Manage. J. 110–139 (2016)
14. Li, J., Chen, L.: Block-secure: blockchain based scheme for secure P2P cloud storage. Inf. Sci. **465**, 219–231 (2018)
15. Mikula, T., Jacobsen, R.H.: Identity and access management with blockchain in electronic healthcare records. In: The 21st Euromicro Conference on Digital System Design (DSD), pp. 699–706. IEEE (2018)
16. Nakamoto, S.: Bitcoin: a peer-to-peer electronic cash system. https://bitcoin.org/bitcoin.pdf. Accessed 14 Mar 2020
17. Rouhani, S., Pourheidari, V., Deters, R.: Physical access control management sys-tem based on permissioned blockchain. In: International Conference on Internet of Things, pp. 1078–1083 (2018)
18. Seebacher, S., Schüritz, R.: Blockchain technology as an enabler of service systems: a structured literature review. In: Za, S., Drăgoicea, M., Cavallari, M. (eds.) IESS 2017. LNBIP, vol. 279, pp. 12–23. Springer, Cham (2017). https://doi.org/10.1007/978-3-319-56925-3_2
19. Shen, B., Guo, J., Yang, Y.: MedChain: efficient healthcare data sharing via blockchain. Appl. Sci. **9**, 1–23 (2019)
20. Skiba, D.J.: The potential of blockchain in education and health care. Nurs. Educ. Perspect. **38**, 220–221 (2017)
21. Swan, M.: Blockchain: Blueprint for a New Economy. O'Reilly Media, Inc (2015)
22. Turkanović, M., Hölbl, M., Košič, K., Heričko, M., Kamišalić, A.: EduCTX: a blockchain-based higher education credit platform. IEEE Access **6**, 5112–5127 (2018)
23. Vujičić, D., Jagodić, D., Ranđić, S.: Blockchain technology, bitcoin, and Ethereum: a brief overview. In: 17th International Symposium Infoteh-Jahorina (Infoteh), pp. 1–6. IEEE (2018)
24. Wang, Y., Kogan, A.: Designing confidentiality-preserving blockchain-based transaction processing systems. Int. J. Account. Inf. Syst. **30**, 1–18 (2018)

25. Yakubov, A., Shbair, W., Wallbom, A., Sanda, d., State, R.: A blockchain-based PKI management framework. In: The First IEEE/IFIP International Workshop on Managing and Managed by Blockchain (Man2Block) Colocated with IEEE/IFIP NOMS, pp. 23–27. IEEE (2018)

26. Zhang, X., Chen, X.: Data security sharing and storage based on a consortium blockchain in a vehicular ad-hoc network. IEEE Access **7**, 58241–58254 (2019)

27. Zyskind, G., Nathan, O.: Decentralizing privacy: using blockchain to protect personal data. In: Security and Privacy Workshops, pp. 180–184. IEEE (2015)

Blockchain and Data Mining

Exploring EOSIO via Graph Characterization

Yijing Zhao[1,2,3], Jieli Liu[1,2], Qing Han[1,2], Weilin Zheng[1,2],
and Jiajing Wu[1,2(✉)]

[1] School of Data and Computer Science, Sun Yat-sen University,
Guangzhou 510006, China
wujiajing@mail.sysu.edu.cn
[2] National Engineering Research Center of Digital Life, Sun Yat-sen University,
Guangzhou 510006, China
[3] School of Electronics and Communication Engineering, Sun Yat-sen University,
Guangzhou 510006, China

Abstract. Designed for commercial decentralized applications (DApps),
EOSIO is a Delegated Proof-of-Stake (DPoS) based blockchain system. It
has overcome some shortages of the traditional blockchain systems like Bitcoin and Ethereum with its outstanding features (e.g., free for usage, high
throughput and eco-friendly), and thus becomes one of the mainstream
blockchain systems. Though there exist billions of transactions in EOSIO,
the ecosystem of EOSIO is still relatively unexplored. To fill this gap, we
conduct a systematic graph analysis on the early EOSIO by investigating
its four major activities, namely account creation, account vote, money
transfer and contract authorization. We obtain some novel observations via
graph metric analysis, and our results reveal some abnormal phenomenons
like voting gangs and sham transactions.

Keywords: EOSIO · Blockchain · Graph analysis · Complex
network · Measurement

1 Introduction

Recent years, blockchain technology has become a buzzword and has aroused a
great deal of interests among researchers, developers and investors. Among the
blockchain systems, Ethereum is the largest one that supports smart contracts.
However, it suffers from high transaction-confirmation latency and low throughput problems since the employ of Proof-of-Work (PoW) consensus protocol [14].
And it gradually becomes unable to meet the demand of the rapid development
of decentralized applications (DApps), which needs higher scalability and quicker
response for transaction confirmations. Based on the Delegated Proof-of-Stake
(DPoS) consensus, a new platform EOSIO provides a solution for these problems. Built for commercial DApps, EOSIO has some outstanding features like
free for usage, high throughput and eco-friendly, having attracted much attention. Especially, the number of transactions in EOSIO has reached more than
four billion within two years, which witnesses the prosperity of EOSIO.

© Springer Nature Singapore Pte Ltd. 2020
Z. Zheng et al. (Eds.): BlockSys 2020, CCIS 1267, pp. 475–488, 2020.
https://doi.org/10.1007/978-981-15-9213-3_37

There are some studies about the performance [17], security [8], transaction data analysis [5,19] of EOSIO. For example, Xu et al. [17] presented a thorough analysis on EOSIO from the perspective of architecture, performance, and economics. Lee et al. [8] conducted the first study to analyze the security and possible attacks of EOSIO. Huang et al. [5] characterized the activities in EOSIO and developed techniques for detecting bots and fraudulent activities based on their insights. Zheng et al. [19] provided an overview of up-to-date on-chain data of EOSIO. However, existing studies investigating the EOSIO ecosystem from a graph analysis perspective are limited. And more in-depth analyses are needed to discover the user behaviors and understand EOSIO.

In this paper, we utilize graph analysis to explore the characteristics of the early EOSIO by investigating four kinds of user activities, namely account creation, account vote, money transfer and contract authorization. Firstly, according to these four kinds of activities in the first 15 million blocks, we construct the account creation graph (ACG), money transfer graph (MTG), account vote graph (AVG) and contract authorization graph (CAG) as weighted directed graphs. Secondly, we conduct an analysis on these graphs by measuring some graph metrics such as degree distribution, clustering coefficient, connected component, etc. Finally based on the investigation results, we discover some interesting insights about the EOSIO ecosystem, which would help people understand the user activities in the early EOSIO.

1.1   Related Work

Graph analysis assists people to understand the relationship between objects in complex systems. In 2012, Reid and Harrigan [15] first modeled the Bitcoin transaction data with graph representations. By combining some external information, they investigated a theft case of Bitcoin with flow analysis. Up to now, many researchers have conducted graph analysis on blockchain transaction data. Existing work on blockchain transaction graph analysis can be divided into describing the graph properties via some metrics, and conducting data mining tasks on graph-structure data. The former can give us insights into the blockchain systems and how their transaction graphs form and develop, while the latter mainly investigates some data mining tasks such as de-anonymizing the accounts [12], detecting illicit activities [3,4], examining link prediction [10], etc. And our work focuses on the former one.

There are many studies on investigating the blockchain transaction graph with graph metrics. For example, Lischke and Fabian [11] examined the Bitcoin transaction graph and economy during the first four years, and this analysis revealed the business distribution as well as transaction distribution across countries, and investigated the small world phenomenon in some subgraphs. Chen et al. [2] analyzed three major activities (money transfer, account creation and contract invocation) in Ethereum via graph analysis, and they discovered some new observations which help people have a full understanding of Ethereum. Motamed and Bahrak [13] investigated the graph properties of five kinds of cryptocurrencies and compared the evolution of these properties between different cryptocurrencies. Since EOSIO is a newly emerging blockchain system, studies on graph properties analysis related to EOSIO are few. Huang et al. [5] analyzed the money transfer, account creation and contract invocation activities of EOSIO, and further developed techniques to detect bots and fraudulent activities. However, our study are focused on characterizing four main activities (namely, account creation, account vote, money transfer and contract authorization) in the early EOSIO with graph property analysis, and we provide a deeper insight into the graph properties.

1.2 Contribution

In summary, we investigate the four major behaviors in EOSIO by conducting a graph analysis. Our major contributions are listed as follows:

(1) To the best of our knowledge, our work is the first systematic and comprehensive research on the early EOSIO via analyzing four major activities, namely account creation, account vote, money transfer and contract authorization.
(2) We construct four graphs for the four major activities in EOSIO, by measuring some graph metrics such as clustering coefficient, assortativity and so on, we obtain some interesting insights.
(3) We observe some abnormal phenomenons like voting gangs and sham transactions in EOSIO during our analysis, which helps the supervision enhancement of EOSIO.

The remaining sections are organized as follows. We introduce some background knowledge of EOSIO in Sect. 2. Then, we detail the procedure of data collection in Sect. 3. Next, we conduct graph construction and graph analysis in Sect. 4, where we list some analysis results. And finally, we conclude this paper in Sect. 5.

2 Background

This section introduces some background knowledge of EOSIO related to the following research. More details about the operation of EOSIO can be found in its white paper [7].

What's EOSIO? Released in June, 2018, EOSIO is a DPoS-based blockchain system designed for building commercial DApps. In DPoS, only 21 block producers are in charge of transaction verification and block production. These block producers are chosen by the vote from the token holders in EOSIO, which can guarantee the fairness and choose the most trusted 21 block producers. Compared with traditional blockchain systems, the DPoS-based EOSIO has much higher throughput per second (tps) that can generate a block with an average of 0.5 s. Like bitcoin in the Bitcoin system and Ether in Ethereum, the most common currency token in EOSIO is named EOS. Besides, EOSIO can also support

Turing-complete smart contracts, and it provides a more complete smart contract ecosystem. The complied bytecode of each contract is executed in EOSIO's WebAssembly-based virtual machine (EOSVM). Unlike many blockchain systems that use gas mechanism to solve halting problem [16], EOSIO is resources constrained (i.e., limiting the RAM, CPU and bandwidth). The resources can be obtained by token mortgage in EOSIO, and They are almost free for users because of the resources supplied from many DApps.

Transactions and Actions. In EOSIO, a block can contain multiple transactions and each transaction is made up of one or more actions. An action is an invocation of a contract that represents an operation in the system. There are mainly three types of actions, namely calling action, inline action and deferred action. A calling action represents a contract invocation from a user while an inline action represents an invocation triggered by a contract. And a deferred action is an action being scheduled to execute in a future transaction. Once a calling action or an inline action fails, the transaction would be rolled back, while the failure of a deferred action only affects the scheduled transaction. It's worth to mention that the detailed information of inline actions does not be packaged into transactions, which brings challenges in transaction data acquisition.

Accounts and Permissions. Different from Ethereum, the identity of an account is a unique string containing up to 12 characters, but not the public key. An account can be created only by an existing account in EOSIO, except the initial account in EOSIO named *eosio*. Each account can deploy only one contract on itself through the *setcode* interface of *eosio*, and can delete this contract by setting the contract code empty with the same interface. The basic actions are completed by interfaces provided from system accounts. For example, new accounts can be created by the *newaccount* interface of *eosio*, and the EOS transfer operation can be executed by the *transfer* interface of *eosio.token*. When invoking a contract, the related accounts should delegate appropriate permissions for the execution, namely assigning specific public/private keys and granting privileges to this action. The permissions are generally divided into owner permission and active permission, where an owner permission is the highest level of permission and it is designed for cold storage, and an active permission can perform all operations except changing the owner.

3   Data Collection

We collect all transaction data of the first 15 million blocks, which includes about 3 months transaction data from the launch of EOSIO on June 6, 2018.

Since the large volume of transaction data, it is infeasible to obtain all transaction data we need by directly crawling them from blockchain explorer [18]. We first utilize Nodeos, an EOSIO client provided by the official EOSIO development team, to synchronize the on-chain data. To speed up this process, we download blocks from some EOSIO backup service provider firstly and then start Nodeos from a certain specified block. Then the transaction information can be obtained through the RPC interface of Nodeos.

However, the details of inline actions are not recorded in on-chain data. To address this issue, we replay all transactions and utilize the action trace data, which is generated in EOSVM and records the detailed run-time information of actions. By calling the *history_file_plugin* interface provided by the EOSIO development team, we obtain the action trace data. Then, we extract the actions of activities including account creation, account vote, money transfer and contract authorization from the raw data. Note that the contract authorization activity refers to the permission to delegate behaviors for contracts belonging to common users rather than system users like *eosio.token*. After simplifying the representation of the raw data, we obtain the data that can be directly applied to graph analysis.

The statistics of actions for the four activities are shown in Table 1. As we can see, most of these activities are accomplished with calling actions. The proportion of calling actions in the actions of account creation and account vote is not surprising, since EOSIO provides interfaces for these activities from system accounts. Especially, we can conclude that the voting behaviors are relatively transparent in the early EOSIO because most of them are accomplished with calling actions whose records are public accessible in blockchain. Though money transfer activity can be conducted by directly calling the interface provided by *eosio.token* through calling actions, the proportion of inline actions in money transfer activity is relatively high, which means smart contracts are widely used in setting specific transaction rules by users. For contract authorization, it also has a small proportion of inline actions, and this phenomenon is caused by the selfinvocation between contracts.

Table 1. Statistics of actions.

Activity	Calling action (proportion)	Inline action (proportion)
Account creation	299,178 (99.053%)	2,860 (0.947%)
Account vote	129,800 (99.997%)	4 (0.003%)
Money transfer	4,557,498 (52.857%)	4,064,790 (47.143%)
Contract authorization	329,012,816 (99.241%)	2,515,729 (0.759%)

4 Graph Analysis

In this section, we explore the account creation, account vote, money transfer and contract authorization activity in EOSIO through graph analysis. By investigating several graph metrics, We obtain some interesting insights as follows:

Insight 1: In the early EOSIO, some accounts participate in transactions for testing or experiencing the platform.

Insight 2: Some risks exist in EOSIO, like the voting gangs in which the members vote for each other and the observing abnormal account for pressure testing.

Insight 3: EOSIO may exist spam transactions in its billions of transactions.

4.1 Account Creation

A new account is created by an existing account in EOSIO. To model the account creation activity, we define the account creation graph (ACG) as follow:

Definition 1 (ACG). *An account creation graph (ACG) is a directed graph $G = (V, E)$, where V is the set of nodes representing accounts in EOSIO and E is the set of edges, in which each edge (v_i, v_j), $v_i, v_j \in V$ represents the account creation relationship that v_i create v_j.*

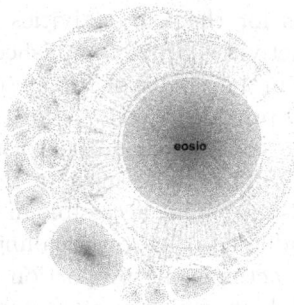

Fig. 1. Visualization of ACG.

There are total 302,039 nodes and 302,038 edges in the constructed ACG. We can see that the edge number is the same as the action number of account creation in Table 1, and the node number is one more than the edge number, which implies that each node except the initial system account *eosio* can be created once by its father account. Since a father account must be an existing account in EOSIO, the ACG is a tree-like graph with no circle.

We then visualize ACG by randomly selecting 8,000 nodes and applying union-find algorithm [6] to find out all connecting paths to the ancestor for each node. The visualization result of the graph including all selected edges via union-find algorithm is shown in Fig. 1. It is obviously that the graph is in a tree-like structure where most of the nodes have no outdegree, and every node has a connecting path to *eosio*, the ancestor of other nodes in the graph. In addition, there are several clusters in the graph and the cluster which includes *eosio* is the biggest one.

Figure 2 displays the degree distribution and outdegree distribution of ACG. Both of them satisfy the power law distribution and have a long tail. These distributions indicate that there are a few accounts creating many accounts with large degree. Besides, since the initial system account *eosio* has no indegree, and the indegree of other accounts is 1 because they can only be created once, we do not present the indegree distribution of ACG.

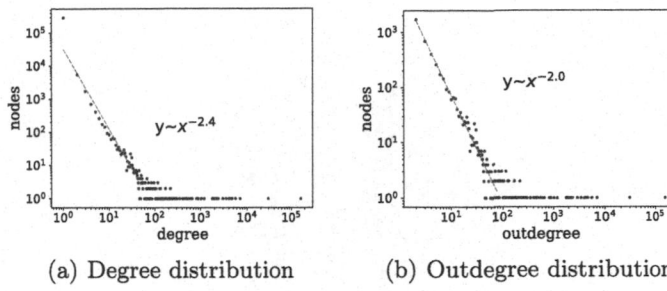

(a) Degree distribution   (b) Outdegree distribution

Fig. 2. Degree/Outdegree distributions of ACG.

Table 2. Metrics of Graphs

Graph	Cluster	Assortativity	Number of SCC	Largest SCC	Number of WCC	Largest WCC	Largest diameter	Smallest diameter
ACG	0	/	302,039	1	1	302,039	20	20
AVG	0.066	−0.221	28,750	18	3	28,766	6	1
MTG	0.259	−0.338	149,536	55,238	1	204,841	6	6
CAG	0.086	−0.160	35,462	3	223	35,086	10	0

Table 2 shows some graph metrics of ACG, including the values of the clustering coefficient, assortativity coefficient, number of strongly connected components (SCC)/weakly connected components (WCC), number of nodes in the largest SCC/WCC, and the largest/smallest diameter of WCC. We can see that the clustering coefficient is 0, because there is no account creation relationship between two accounts created by the third node. We have mentioned the fact that ACG is in a directed tree-like structure where each account can only be created by an existing account. Hence the number of nodes in the largest SCC is 1 and all nodes are in the largest WCC, which match our expectations. The largest diameter of WCCs is equal to the smallest one since ACG has one WCC, and the value of diameter indicates that the height of the tree is 20.

4.2 Account Vote

In EOSIO, each account can vote for others to choose the 21 block producers. To investigate the relationship between voters and candidates, we define the account vote graph (AVG) as follow:

Definition 2 (AVG). *An account vote graph (AVG) is a directed weighted graph $G = (V, E, W)$, where V denotes the set of nodes representing accounts enrolling in EOSIO's voting activity, E denotes the set of edges, in which each edge (v_i, v_j), $v_i, v_j \in V$ represents that v_i votes for v_j, and there is a mapping function $\varphi : E \to W$ that maps a weight from the edge attribute set W for each edge, which represents the corresponding voting times.*

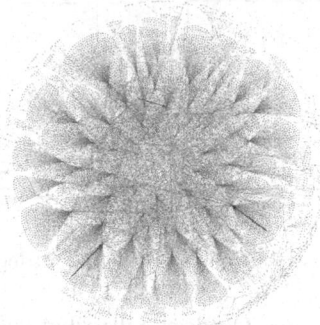

Fig. 3. Visualization of AVG.

For AVG, there are 28,769 nodes and 439,154 edges, and the total weight value of all edges in the graph is 1,519,464, which indicates that some voters often vote for the same producers in different actions. One possible explanation for this phenomenon is that some candidates are very trustworthy and have their faithful supporters.

Figure 3 displays the visualization result of AVG, which contains 10,000 edges selected from AVG. The thickness of each edge is proportional to its weight value. We observe that several edges are obviously thicker than others, which account for the continued supports to some candidates. There exist some hub nodes in the graph, representing some influential candidates. Besides, many edges are randomly distributed in AVG, which reflects that in the early EOSIO, some voters participate in voting for testing or experiencing.

As shown in Fig. 4, the degree distribution, indegree distribution and outdegree distributions of AVG can not strictly satisfy the power law distribution. We can observe that candidates with a large number of supporters occupy a small proportion of all candidates. And the voting times for most voters are few, which may be related to the rule that voters should mortgage a part of EOS tokens when voting.

The results of some graph metrics for AVG are shown in Table 2. As we can see, the clustering coefficient is 0.066, namely there are few triangles in AVG. If a voter votes for two candidates, these two candidates will barely vote for each other owing to their competitive relationship. The assortativity coefficient is negative, which implies that large-degree nodes tend to vote for or be voted by small-degree nodes. The number of nodes in the largest SCC is 18, indicating that there exist some few voting gangs in which the members vote for each other. More than 99.98% nodes in AVG participate in the largest WCC, which means that accounts are almost fully connected in AVG, and this phenomenon is similar in some other complex networks [1,9]. The largest diameter of WCC is 6, meaning that the distance between two nodes in AVG is small. Besides, none of the candidates votes for themselves, which is reflected by the smallest diameter.

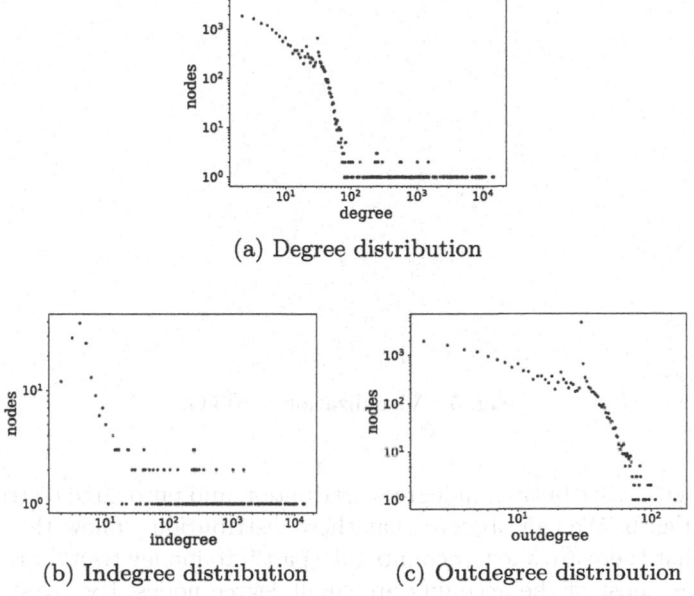

(a) Degree distribution

(b) Indegree distribution   (c) Outdegree distribution

Fig. 4. Degree/Indegree/Outdegree distributions of AVG.

4.3 Money Transfer

We construct a money transfer graph (MTG) to investigate the transfer relationship between accounts as follow:

Definition 3 (MTG). *A money transfer graph (MTG) is a directed weighted graph $G = (V, E, W)$ with a mapping function $\varphi : E \to W$ that maps a weight from the edge attribute set W for each edge, where V denotes the set of nodes which represent accounts participating in transferring EOS, E denotes the set of edges, where for $v_i, v_j \in V, w \in W$ each edge (v_i, v_j, w) represents that v_i totally transfers w EOS to v_j.*

MTG contains 204,841 nodes and 1,370,813 edges in total. According to Table 1, there are 8,622,288 actions related to money transfer, which is about 6 times more than edge number. That is, there exist repeated money transfer actions between two accounts.

We visualize MTG by sampling 10,000 edges from MTG, and make the thickness of each edge be proportional to its weight value. As shown in Fig. 5, the sampling subgraph of MTG exist significant community structures. It contains a few large-degree nodes, which are community centers and interact frequently with surrounding nodes, these nodes may be exchanges or accounts of some DApps in charge of their ledger. There are also a large number of small-degree nodes in MTG, the free for usage feature offers a low-barrier entry point for individual users.

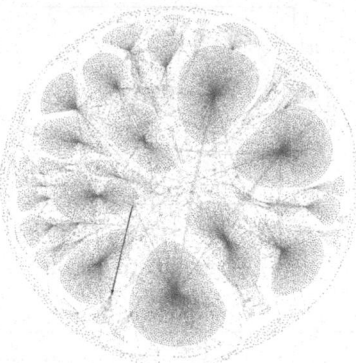

Fig. 5. Visualization of MTG.

The degree distribution, indegree distribution and outdegree distribution are shown in Fig. 6. We can observe that these distributions follow the power law, meaning that there are a few accounts take part into money transfer activities for many times, most of the accounts are small-degree nodes. By investigating the fitting line $y \sim x^{\alpha}$ we plotting, we can draw a conclusion that the distribution of outdegree is more variable than the distributions of degree and indegree, since the larger the α, the more variable is the degree.

As shown in Table 2, the clustering coefficient of MTG is 0.259, which is a relatively large value, indicating that if an account has transactions with other two accounts respectively, these two accounts tend to have money transferring relationships. The assortativity coefficient of MTG is negative, revealing that large-degree nodes tend to connect to small-degree nodes in MTG. The number of nodes in the largest SCC is 55,238, which accounts for about 26.97% of all the nodes in MTG. It indicates that some hub nodes (e.g., system accounts, exchanges) could contribute to large SCCs in MTG. Also another reason that cause large SCCs is sham transactions, which may be conducted by a group of accounts controlled by the same user. And since these transactions are used to increase the transaction volume by scalping, the interactions among the relative group of accounts would form SCCs to maintain the money flows. The largest WCC contains all nodes in MTG, since the EOS tokens are initially managed by the EOSIO's system accounts, and then they are distributed to the wallet of individual users by a series of processes. The diameter of MTG is small and the clustering coefficient is large, indicating a small world phenomenon in MTG.

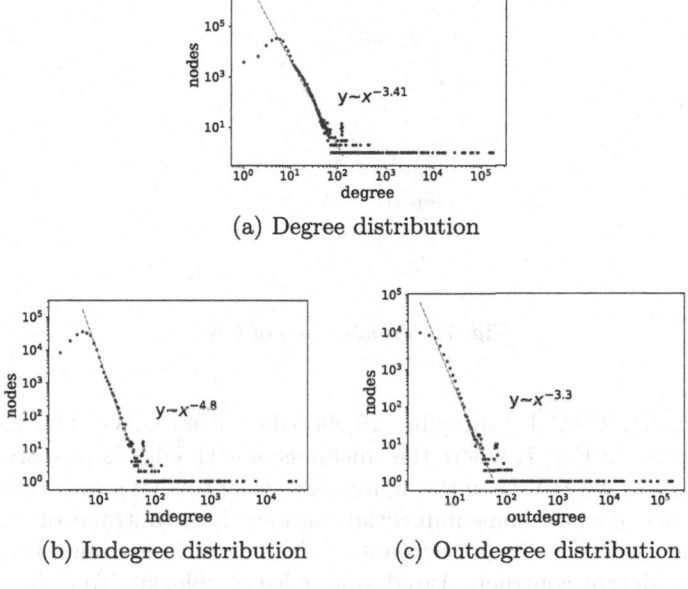

(a) Degree distribution

(b) Indegree distribution   (c) Outdegree distribution

Fig. 6. Degree/Indegree/Outdegree distributions of MTG.

4.4 Contract Authorization

According to the design of EOSIO, it is hard to know which account invokes the contract for a contract invocation. However, the information that which account delegate its permission for the execution of a contract can be extracted from the action trace data. We construct a contract authorization graph (CAG) to describe relationships in contract authorization activity. The definition is shown as follow:

Definition 4 (CAG). *A contract authorization graph (CAG) is a directed weighted graph $G = (V, E, W)$ with a mapping function $\varphi : E \to W$ that maps a weight from the edge attribute set W for each edge, where V is the set of nodes representing accounts taking part in the contract authorization activity, E is the set of edges, in which each edge (v_i, v_j, w), $v_i, v_j \in V, w \in W$ represents that v_i delegates its permissions to execute the contract of v_j for w times.*

There are 35,479 nodes and 126,918 edges in CAG. The total weight value of all edges in the graph is 331,530,705. However, we observe that the total weight value of edges belonging to an account "blocktwitter" is 316,579,248, which occupies a major part of the total weight in the graph. The contract of "blocktwitter" is reported to be an abnormal account that would periodically launch a great many of actions named tweets for pressure testing [19], and it behaves like a contract for denial of service attack.

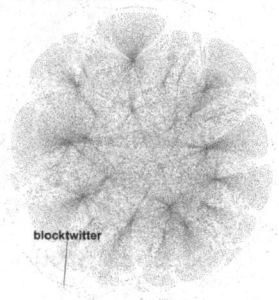

Fig. 7. Visualization of CAG.

We visualize CAG by sampling 10,000 edges from CAG. The visualization result is shown in Fig. 7, where the thickness of each edge is proportional to its weight value. As we can see in the figure, there exist some nodes with large degree in CAG, it may because some influential contracts (e.g. contracts of some popular DApps) are invoked by many accounts, or some active accounts invoke a large number of different contracts. Besides, an edge of "blocktwitter" is conspicuous in the graph with large thickness, which is consistent with our analysis.

Figure 8 shows the degree distribution, indegree distribution and outdegree distribution of CAG. All these distributions approximately follow the power law. From the indegree distribution, we can know that few contracts have been invoked for many times. That is, not all contracts are widely known and invoked by users. For the outdegree distribution, few accounts delegate their permissions to others for many times. Besides, there exists no long tail in the outdegree distribution, and the outdegree gap is small, which means that many users in the early EOSIO only interact with a limited number of contracts. Of course, this phenomenon may also be related to the small number of smart contracts in the initial phase of EOSIO.

Results in terms of several graph metrics for CAG are shown in Table 2. As we can see, the clustering coefficient is 0.086, which means if an account invokes two contracts respectively, these two contracts will barely invoke each other. The assortativity coefficient is negative, illustrating that large-degree nodes tend to interact with small-degree nodes in contract authorization activity. The number of nodes in the largest SCC is 3, which implies that there may exist some accounts belonging to the same owner (e.g., a DApp), and their contracts collaborate closely to complete some specific functions. More than 98.89% nodes are contained in the largest WCC. The smallest diameter of WCCs is 0 since some accounts invoke their own contract.

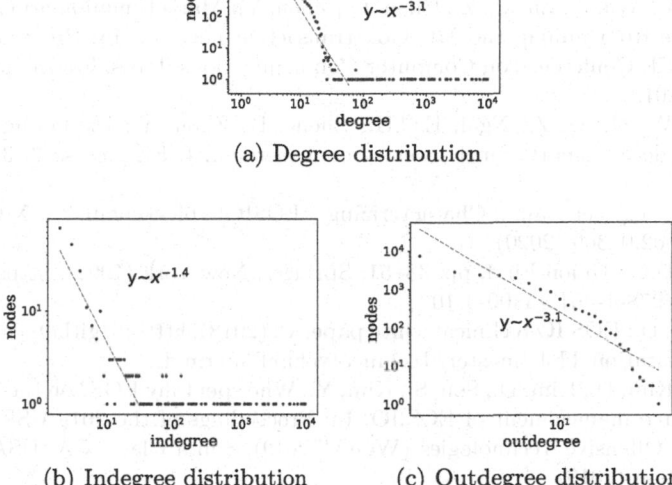

(a) Degree distribution

(b) Indegree distribution   (c) Outdegree distribution

Fig. 8. Degree/Indegree/Outdegree distributions of CAG.

5   Conclusion

In this paper, we have conducted a comprehensive graph analysis on EOSIO by considering four main activities in EOSIO, including account creation, account vote, money transfer and contract authorization. Via utilizing both the on-chain data and off-chain data, we have constructed four graphs for these activities. We then characterized these graphs using several complex network metrics, and obtained some interesting insights and observations such as there exist some few gangs in which the members vote for each other, which helps people have a deep understanding on EOSIO. For future work, we will focus on some abnormal behaviors revealed in our study, and provide constructive suggestions for EOSIO supervision.

Acknowledgments. The work described in this paper was supported by the National Natural Science Foundation of China (61973325, 61503420), the Fundamental Research Funds for the Central Universities (17lgpy120), and Key-Area Research and Development Program of Guangdong Province (2020B010165003, 2019B020214006).

References

1. Cha, M., Haddadi, H., Benevenuto, F., Gummadi, P.K.: Measuring user influence in Twitter: the million follower fallacy. In: Proceedings of the Fourth International Conference on Weblogs and Social Media. The AAAI Press, Washington DC (2010)

2. Chen, T., et al.: Understanding Ethereum via graph analysis. In: Proceedings of the 2018 IEEE Conference on Computer Communications, Honolulu, HI, USA, pp. 1484–1492. IEEE (2018)
3. Chen, W., Wu, J., Zheng, Z., Chen, C., Zhou, Y.: Market manipulation of Bitcoin: Evidence from mining the Mt. Gox transaction network. In: Proceedings of the 2019 IEEE Conference on Computer Communications, Paris, France, pp. 964–972. IEEE (2019)
4. Chen, W., Zheng, Z., Ngai, E.C.H., Zheng, P., Zhou, Y.: Exploiting blockchain data to detect smart Ponzi schemes on Ethereum. IEEE Access **7**, 37575–37586 (2019)
5. Huang, Y., et al.: Characterizing EOSIO blockchain. arXiv preprint arXiv:2002.05369 (2020)
6. Kozen, D.C.: Union-Find, pp. 48–51. Springer, New York (1992). https://doi.org/10.1007/978-1-4612-4400-4_10
7. Larimer, D.: EOS.IO technical white paper v2 (2018). https://github.com/EOSIO/Documentation/blob/master/TechnicalWhitePaper.md
8. Lee, S., Kim, D., Kim, D., Son, S., Kim, Y.: Who spent my EOS? on the (in)security of resource management of EOS.IO. In: Proceedings of the 2019 USENIX Workshop on Offensive Technologies (WOOT 2019), Santa Clara, CA, USA. USENIX Association (2019)
9. Leskovec, J., Kleinberg, J., Faloutsos, C.: Graph evolution: densification and shrinking diameters. ACM Trans. Knowl. Discov. Data **1**(1), 2-es (2007)
10. Lin, D., Wu, J., Yuan, Q., Zheng, Z.: Modeling and understanding Ethereum transaction records via a complex network approach. IEEE Trans. Circ. Syst. **67**, 1 (2020). II: Express Briefs
11. Lischke, M., Fabian, B.: Analyzing the Bitcoin network: the first four years. Future Internet **8**(1), 7 (2016)
12. Meiklejohn, S., et al.: A fistful of bitcoins: characterizing payments among men with no names. In: Proceedings of the 2013 Conference on Internet Measurement Conference, Barcelona, Spain, pp. 127–140. ACM press (2013)
13. Motamed, A.P., Bahrak, B.: Quatitative analysis of cryptocurrencies transaction graph. Appl. Netw. Sci. **4**(1), 131 (2019)
14. Han, Q., Wu, J., Zheng, Z.: Long-range dependence, multi-fractality and volume-return causality of ether market. Chaos Interdisc. J. Nonlinear Sci. **30**, 011101 (2019)
15. Reid, F., Harrigan, M.: An analysis of anonymity in the Bitcoin system. In: Altshuler, Y., Elovici, Y., Cremers, A., Aharony, N., Pentland, A. (eds.) Security and Privacy in Social Networks, pp. 197–223. Springer, New York (2013). https://doi.org/10.1007/978-1-4614-4139-7_10
16. Turing, A.M.: On computable numbers, with an application to the Entscheidungs problem. a correction. In: Proceedings of the London Mathematical Society. Wiley Online Library, London (1938)
17. Xu, B., Luthra, D., Cole, Z., Blakely, N.: EOS: an architectural, performance, and economic analysis. https://whiteblock.io/wp-content/uploads/2019/07/eos-test-report.pdf (2018)
18. Zheng, P., Zheng, Z., Dai, H.: Xblock-eth: extracting and exploring blockchain data from Ethereum. CoRR abs/1911.00169 (2019)
19. Zheng, W., Zheng, Z., Dai, H.N., Chen, X., Zheng, P.: Xblock-EOS: extracting and exploring blockchain data from EOSIO. arXiv preprint arXiv:2003.11967 (2020)

De-Anonymization of the Bitcoin Network Using Address Clustering

Changhoon Kang[1]([✉]), Chaehyeon Lee[1], Kyungchan Ko[1], Jongsoo Woo[2],
and James Won-Ki Hong[1]

[1] Department of Computer Science and Engineering, POSTECH,
Pohang 37673, Korea
{chkang,chlee0211,kkc90,jwkhong}@postech.ac.kr
[2] Graduate School of Information Technology, POSTECH, Pohang 37673, Korea
woojs@postech.ac.kr

Abstract. Bitcoin is the first cryptocurrency that was invented by a
pseudonymous person called Satoshi Nakamoto in 2008. Users of bitcoin are not required to provide any of their personal information, and
this pseudo-anonymity attracts people to exploit bitcoin for illegal transactions. A previous study tried to de-anonymize the bitcoin by using
P2P network traffic and find out an IP address of each bitcoin address'
owner. However, this method could only obtain the small number of reliable mappings between a bitcoin address and its owner's IP address.
To improve this study, we added a bitcoin address clustering process so
that we could suppose that all addresses in each cluster are owned by
one entity. We then mapped each cluster to an IP address and showed
that this change increased the percentages of reliable mappings that we
could find. We also suggested some ways to obtain improvements of our
method.

Keywords: Bitcoin · Pseudo-anonymity · De-anonymization · IP
address · Bitcoin address clustering

1 Introduction

Bitcoin [1] is a peer-to-peer network that records all transaction history in one
distributed ledger. Without providing any personal information, any person can
freely participate in the network by running a bitcoin node or simply generating
a wallet with its bitcoin addresses. This feature provides pseudo-anonymity on
the network so that no one knows an owner of each bitcoin address or a creator of
each transaction. By taking advantage of this pseudo-anonymity, many people
have used bitcoin as a means of payment in illegal trades. Silk Road, one of
the well-known but now-defunct black market, had exploited bitcoin to deal
with illegal transactions [2]. In addition, there was a study about the amount
of bitcoin that used in illegal activities, and this study argues that roughly one-
quarter of bitcoin users are related to illegal activities [3].

Z. Zheng et al. (Eds.): BlockSys 2020, CCIS 1267, pp. 489–501, 2020.
https://doi.org/10.1007/978-981-15-9213-3_38

De-anonymization of the bitcoin network is to find out information hidden behind anonymity by analyzing disclosed data. Previous studies have already suggested various methods to do this. For instance, some studies drew a bitcoin transaction graph to link bitcoin address to real entities [4,5], and some of them also used external information of users to uncover anonymity of the bitcoin network [6]. Another study obtained mappings between a bitcoin address and an IP address that was likely to own it [7]. Our study was inspired by this work and tried to improve the efficiency of their analysis method.

Bitcoin address clustering is a process to gather bitcoin addresses that are likely to be owned by the same entity into one cluster. We added this process to the previous method. This process is important in a statistical analysis that counts the number of each bitcoin address' usage in transactions relayed from a specific IP address because most bitcoin addresses are used only once and this frequency is insufficient to use them in the statistical analysis. By using bitcoin address clustering, we can even count bitcoin addresses that were used only once in the past together with other addresses in the same cluster. In other words, in contrast to the previous method, our method relates each cluster of bitcoin addresses to a specific IP address and each cluster represents one entity.

In this paper, we introduce some backgrounds about the bitcoin system and several previous studies that were attempted to de-anonymize the bitcoin network in the following two sections. We then give a detailed explanation of our method and show that our method could find out about 80–105 times as many reliable mappings as the method used in the previous study.

2   Background and Related Work

2.1   Bitcoin Network

The bitcoin network is a peer-to-peer network that consists of many nodes (Fig. 1). Each node can relay and generate blockchain-related data, including transactions and blocks. Once a node receives or generates these data, the node broadcasts them to the other nodes that are connected with this node. To operate the system, the network needs specific nodes called miners who validate received transactions and produce a new block with a certain volume of transactions. A distributed ledger called blockchain records all validated blocks so that every participant can access to the entire transaction history (Fig. 2).

Transactions of the bitcoin network are records of the flow of bitcoins. A structure of a transaction can simply be divided into input and output parts (Fig. 3). A creator of the transaction puts owned bitcoins that are outputs of an already confirmed transaction to the input and several sets of a receiver's bitcoin address and the number of bitcoins to send. If the transaction is validated and included in a new block, each of the output sets is called "Unspent Transaction Output (UTXO)" which is a unit of transaction input and output. Each receiver of new UTXOs can use them as the input of a new transaction that they create in the future.

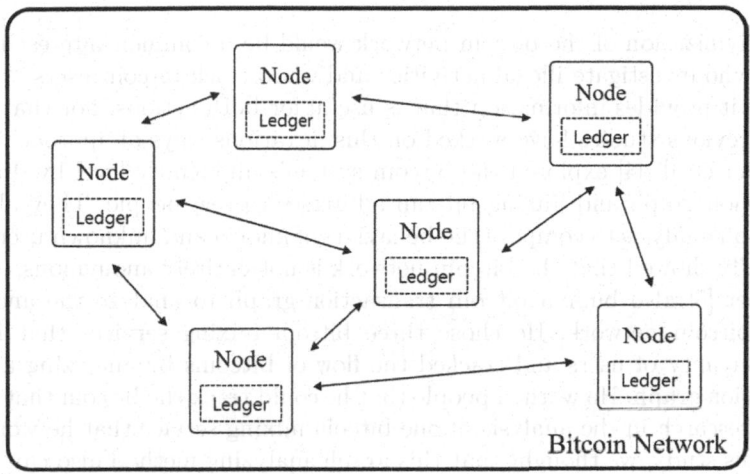

Fig. 1. A structure of the bitcoin network

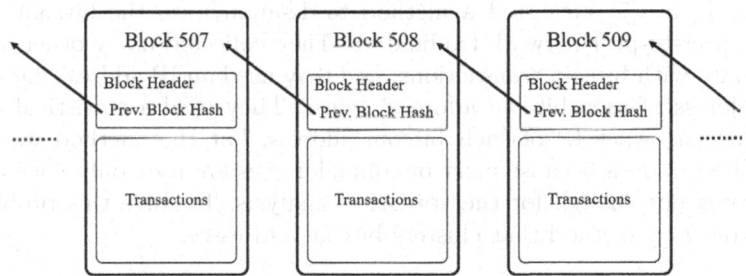

Fig. 2. A structure of a bitcoin blockchain

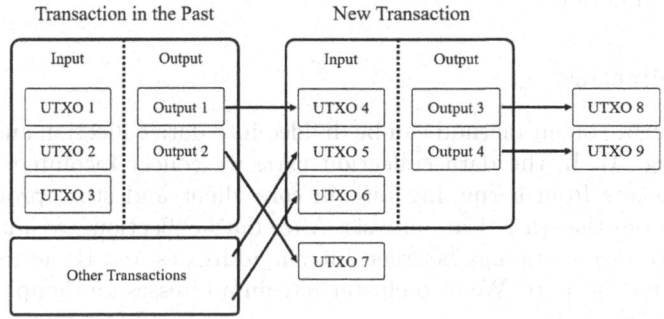

Fig. 3. A structure of a transaction and the use of UTXOs

2.2   Related Work

De-anonymization of the bitcoin network would be a common interest for both people who investigate illegal activities and who attack bitcoin users or system because it provides information that is useful for both actions. For that reason, many previous studies have worked on this in various ways of approaching.

Fleder et al. [4] explored the bitcoin system's anonymity level by drawing a transaction graph and linking bitcoin addresses to real people. They also used this graph analysis to compare the behaviors of known and unknown users. They eventually showed that the bitcoin network is not entirely anonymous.

Moser [5] also built a bitcoin transaction graph to analyze the anonymity of the bitcoin network. He chose three bitcoin mixing services that increase the anonymity of users and tracked the flow of bitcoins by analyzing a bitcoin transaction graph. He warned people that he could track the bitcoin that he used for the research in the analysis of one bitcoin mixing service that he worked on. From this study, we thought that this graph analyzing method also can be used for our study.

Reid et al. [6] created two network graphs derived from bitcoin's transaction history and analyzed their topological structure. They also showed the usage of external information and techniques to investigate an alleged theft of bitcoins.

Koshy et al. [7] suggested a method to de-anonymize the bitcoin network by using peer-to-peer network traffic data. They collected many other network-related data with bitcoin transactions, and they used an IP address data to find an IP address of each bitcoin address' owner. They used a statistical analysis on finding an owner IP of each bitcoin address, but this method wasted too much collected data because most bitcoin addresses are used only once and this frequency is not enough for the statistical analysis. To solve this problem, we propose our new method that clusters bitcoin addresses.

3   Bitcoin Address Clustering Method

In this section, we introduce the architecture of our method and explain each component in detail.

3.1   Architecture

The architecture of our method can be divided into data collection and statistical analysis (Fig. 4). In the data collection part, we collect incoming transaction message packets from a running bitcoin core client and store processed data that we need in the statistical analysis. After data collection, we analyze stored data and produce mappings between bitcoin addresses and IP addresses in the statistical analysis part. We also cluster bitcoin addresses and map each cluster on an IP address.

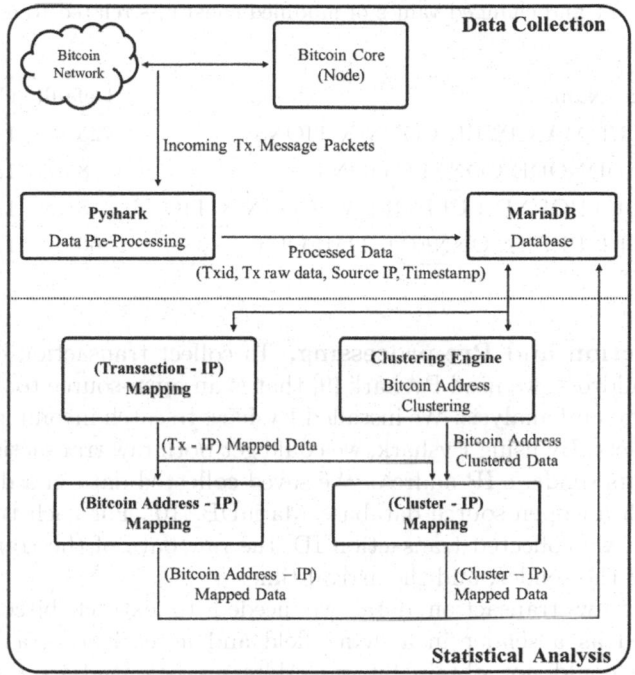

Fig. 4. The architecture of our method

3.2 Data Collection

Construction of a Custom Bitcoin Client. A bitcoin client is a software that makes a computer act as one node in the bitcoin P2P network. This means that a computer that is running the bitcoin client sends and receives messages that are necessary to operate a bitcoin blockchain system. We seek to collect transaction messages with their senders' IP addresses.

To do this, we first downloaded the open-source code of the bitcoin core client (Version. 0.19.1) from its GitHub [8]. We modified some network configuration related constants in the code to increase a default limitation on the number of connections that the client can make with other nodes. This step was necessary because we had to find a creator of each transaction by analyzing senders' IP addresses, so connecting directly with as many nodes as possible would increase accuracy. Thus, we changed the limitation on the number of connections from 125 to 1125. Besides, there were some other parameters that we also had to change the default value to make more connections (Table 1). Connections of a bitcoin node can be divided into inbound and outbound connections, and they work exactly in the same way after once the connection is made. The second and third constants of the table are related to the number of outbound connections. We also increased these values, as we increased the number of total maximum peer connections. The last constant in the table is for configuring the length of connection timeout. To keep being connected with other nodes, we extended this value.

Table 1. Default and changed values of modified constants related to network configuration

Constant Name	Default	Changed
DEFAULT_MAX_PEER_CONNECTIONS	125	1,125
MAX_ADDNODE_CONNECTIONS	8	1,008
MAX_OUTBOUND_FULL_RELAY_CONNECTIONS	8	1,008
DEFAULT_PEER_CONNECT_TIMEOUT	60	1,800

Data Collection and Pre-processing. To collect transaction data with its sender's IP address, we used Pyshark [9] that is an open-source tool for network packet capture and analysis. We installed Pyshark to catch incoming transaction message packets. By using Pyshark, we could get both raw transaction data from packets and its sender's IP address. We saved collected data in a database that we built with an open-source database MariaDB [10]. For each transaction in the database, we collected transaction ID, the raw data of the transaction, the IP address of the sender, and the arrival time.

For each raw transaction data, we needed to extract bitcoin addresses that are used as a sender in a "vin" field and a receiver in a "vout" field. However, we could not obtain bitcoin addresses belonged to a sender's side directly from raw transaction data, while a "vout" field contains exact bitcoin addresses of receivers. In a "vin" field, there are only a transaction id and a "vout" index of each UTXO used for input of the transaction. To find bitcoin addresses that owned these UTXOs, we used a Blockchain Data API served by BLOCKCHAIN.COM [11]. We could get single transaction data with its transaction id by sending the GET request of the HTTP protocol. With this transaction data, we got bitcoin addresses from UTXOs in defined "vout" indexes. Finally, for each transaction, we stored the transaction id, the source IP address, the arrival timestamp, and (bitcoin address, value) sets of input and output.

3.3 Bitcoin Address Clustering

We clustered bitcoin addresses extracted from all collected transactions. Two different heuristics that we planned to use in our method are introduced below (Fig. 5).

Multi-Input Addresses. We could assume that all bitcoin addresses that were used as input of one transaction belong to a single entity. This assumption is valid because a transaction creator has usually gathered his bitcoins that were owned by different addresses, and put them all together as input.

Transaction

Input	Output
Address 1	Address 4
Address 2	Address 5
Address 3	Address 1

Single Entity

Fig. 5. According to explained two heuristics, address 1, 2, and 3 are owned by the same entity, and address 1 is a change address.

A Change Address. We could also suppose that bitcoin addresses that were used both for input and output in one transaction are likely to be a change address of an entity who created the transaction. This assumption is valid because a transaction creator must spend all bitcoins in UTXOs used as input, he would return change to his bitcoin address again.

We described two different heuristics of bitcoin address clustering above. However, we only applied the "Multi-Input Addresses" heuristic in our method. This is because a change address is clustered as an input bitcoin address with the other addresses in the input.

3.4 Statistical Analysis

Except for applying bitcoin address clustering, we followed most processes in the previous method. To compare the improvement of the method, we conducted a statistical analysis twice with both the previous and our method.

Mappings Between Transactions and IP Addresses. We first had to infer an IP address of a user who was likely to create each transaction from its relayed pattern. We can divide relayed patterns into four different cases.

1. **Relayed by a Single IP**: In this case, only one IP address sent a transaction. We simply considered the IP address to be the transaction's creator (Fig. 6).

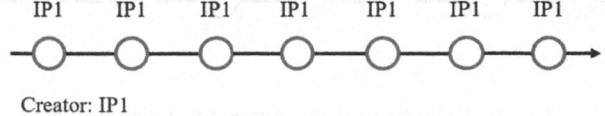

Creator: IP1

Fig. 6. Relayed by a single IP

2. **Relayed Once by Multiple IPs**: In this case, several IP addresses sent a transaction. We assumed that the sender of a transaction was the first one to receive it. This assumption may fail, because propagation delay may result in the transaction first reaching someone other than the real creator (Fig. 7).

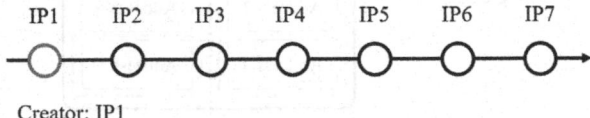

Creator: IP1

Fig. 7. Relayed once by multiple IPs

3. **Relayed Multiple times by a Single IP**: This case is the same as in the preceding case, except that one IP sends a transaction to our node multiple times. In this case, we selected the single IP that sent a transaction multiple times as the creator of the transactions. This assumption is reasonable because only a creator or bitcoin recipients of the transaction can relay the transaction multiple times and thus, the single IP address has the highest chance of being a creator of the transaction (Fig. 8).

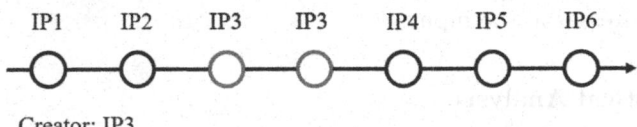

Creator: IP3

Fig. 8. Relayed multiple times by a single IP

4. **Relayed Multiple times by Multiple IPs**: In this case, multiple IPs send a transaction to us multiple times. There was no clear rule to choose one IP for the creator, and therefore, we did not handle this case in this study (Fig. 9).

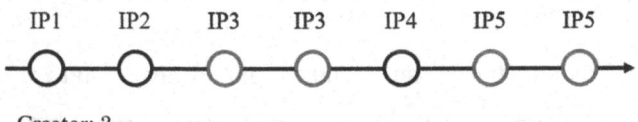

Creator: ?

Fig. 9. Relayed multiple times by multiple IPs

Mappings Between Bitcoin Addresses and IP Addresses. The previous study conducted this analysis with their method, and to compare the efficiency of the method with ours, we reconstructed this analysis with data that we collected in this study. From the previous stage, we obtained mappings between transactions and IP addresses. For each transaction, we could extract bitcoin addresses from input and output separately, and relate them to an IP address that was mapped to the transaction. We calculated two probabilities for each bitcoin address b and an IP address i pairs, and all notations and explanations below are from the previous study [7].

1. $N_I(b,i)$: The number of different transactions that are owned by IP i and contain bitcoin address b in their input.
2. $N_O(b,i)$: The number of different transactions that are owned by IP i and contain bitcoin address b in their output.
3. $N_I(b)$: The number of different transactions that contain bitcoin address b in their input.
4. $N_O(b)$: The number of different transactions that contain bitcoin address b in their output.

$$P_I(b,i) = \frac{N_I(b,i)}{N_I(b)}, \qquad P_O(b,i) = \frac{N_O(b,i)}{N_O(b)}$$

$P_I(b,i)$ is a probability that a transaction containing bitcoin address b in its input is owned by IP i. Similarly, $P_O(b,i)$ is a probability that a transaction containing bitcoin address b in its output is owned by IP i.

Mappings Between Clusters and IP Addresses. This is a method that we suggest in this paper, using bitcoin address clustering with the previous method. Most processes are the same as the existing method, except for some differences in notations. In our method, we also calculated two probabilities but this was for each bitcoin address cluster c and IP address i pairs.

1. $N_I(c,i)$: The number of different transactions that are owned by IP i and contain a bitcoin address belonged to cluster c in their input.
2. $N_O(c,i)$: The number of different transactions that are owned by IP i and contain a bitcoin address belonged to cluster c in their output.
3. $N_I(c)$: The number of different transactions that contain a bitcoin address belonged to cluster c in their input.
4. $N_O(c)$: The number of different transactions that contain a bitcoin address belonged to cluster c in their output.

$$P_I(c,i) = \frac{N_I(c,i)}{N_I(c)}, \qquad P_O(c,i) = \frac{N_O(c,i)}{N_O(c)}$$

$P_I(c,i)$ is a probability that a transaction containing a bitcoin address belonged to cluster c in its input is owned by IP i. Similarly, $P_O(c,i)$ is a probability that a transaction containing a bitcoin address belonged to cluster c in its output is owned by IP i. We can apply these probabilities of cluster c to each bitcoin address contained in the cluster.

Extracting Reliable Mappings. Finally, we extracted reliable mappings that satisfies the configured thresholds. We only picked pairs that have 50% or higher probability for $P_I(b, i)$ or $P_I(c, i)$. We also removed pairs if their $N_I(b, i)$ or $N_I(c, i)$ value is lower than 10.

4 Result

4.1 Data Collection

We started our bitcoin client on Mar.10, 2020, and collected data until May.09, 2020. Although we set the maximum number of connections to 1,125, the client software automatically reduced this number to 1,124 because of a lack of computing resources. After synchronizing with all previous blocks, the client started to send and receive bitcoin protocol message packets. We observed that during data collection, the client kept maintaining more than 1,025 connections. To increase accuracy, ideally, we had to connect with almost all bitcoin nodes, but we could not make more than 1,120 connections.

We collected incoming transaction data, pre-processed them, and then stored them in a database that we built. We could collect and save a total of 2,347,420 transactions. In the data collection stage, we had already filtered invalid transactions that have a wrong structure, but we again had to filter some of them that have invalid UTXOs as input. Eventually, we got a total of 2,081,891 valid transactions.

4.2 Bitcoin Address Clustering

We clustered bitcoin addresses in all collected valid transactions by using the simple heuristic explained in Sect. 3.3. From 2,081,891 transactions, we could extract 5,445,185 bitcoin addresses. After clustering, we got 4,474,624 clusters that represent each user entity. Because each cluster consists of some bitcoin addresses, we could use a large number of bitcoin addresses even if they were only used once.

4.3 Statistical Analysis

Mappings Between Transactions and IP Addresses. We mapped each transaction to an IP address that was likely to have created; for this purpose, we used analysis on a relaying pattern of the transaction. By using four relaying patterns that we had set earlier, we could map all transactions to such IP addresses. Eventually, we got 2,078,243 (Transaction - IP Address) mappings from 2,081,891 valid transactions. Overlap of transactions in our dataset reduced the total number of transactions.

Extracted Reliable Mappings from Each Method. We obtained mappings of (Bitcoin Address - IP Address) and (Cluster - IP Address) from each method. For each case, we counted the number of mappings that have reliability above each level (Table 2). As a result, we found that a method that clusters bitcoin addresses produced reliable mappings more than a method that maps bitcoin addresses separately onto IP addresses.

Table 2. The number of bitcoin addresses that could find their owner's IP address for each reliability level. ($N_I(b, i)$ or $N_I(c, i) \geq 10$)

Reliability threshold	Mapping object	
($P_I(b, i)$ or $P_I(c, i)$)	Bitcoin address	Addresses' Cluster
$\geq 50\%$	1,246	131,599
$\geq 60\%$	1,102	112,144
$\geq 70\%$	1,008	93,803
$\geq 80\%$	925	77,227
$\geq 90\%$	846	69,116
$\geq 95\%$	766	61,901
$\geq 99\%$	735	58,587

5 Discussion

We collected bitcoin transaction data with their senders' IP addresses, then clustered bitcoin addresses in transactions, and used statistical analysis to find reliable mappings between bitcoin addresses and IP addresses. We performed this study to improve the efficiency at which IP addresses of bitcoin addresses' owners can be found. The previous study that did not cluster bitcoin addresses could exploit only a few bitcoin addresses for statistical analysis because most of them were used only once in the whole record and this frequency was too low to allow reliable statistical analysis. Thus, we clustered bitcoin addresses and because of this, addresses in each cluster could be counted together as the same entity.

We found that adding the clustering of bitcoin addresses increased the number of reliable mappings between bitcoin addresses and IP addresses that were likely to own the bitcoin addresses. Our method with clustering found about 80–105 times as many mappings as the method used in the previous study. This result means that clustering reduced the number of bitcoin addresses that are unusable in the statistical analysis. However, in the clustering process, we only used a simple heuristic, and this method still left too many different small clusters. We expect that an improved clustering method might increase the number of reliable mappings.

The percentages of reliable mappings are still too low even though our method improved on the previous method. One possible reason for the low mapping rate is the limited number of connections that we could make with other bitcoin nodes. We only connected with some parts of bitcoin nodes and received transaction data from them, so the inferred IP addresses of the creators would be wrong for most of the collected transaction data. To overcome this problem, we must find a way to connect with most of the bitcoin nodes in the world. However, this study shows that there is a chance to improve the efficiency of finding an IP address of each bitcoin address' owner. New attempts with some improvements in the analysis process can be done in the following research.

6 Conclusion

We added a bitcoin address clustering process to the previous method that de-anonymized the bitcoin network by obtaining mappings between a bitcoin address and an IP address that was likely to own it. Unlike the previous study, we first made clusters of bitcoin addresses so that we could suppose all addresses in each cluster are owned by one entity. This change achieved a remarkable increase in the number of reliable mappings that we could find. Our method consists of several distinct analysis processes and thus, we have more chances to increase efficiency by improving each analysis process.

Acknowledgments. This work was supported by the ICT R&D program of MSIT/IITP [No.2018-000539, Development of Blockchain Transaction Monitoring and Analysis Technology] in Republic of Korea.

References

1. Nakamoto, S.: Bitcoin: a peer-to-peer electronic cash system (2008)
2. Huang, A.: Reaching within silk road: the need for a new subpoena power that targets illegal bitcoin transactions. BCL Rev. **56**, 2093 (2015)
3. Foley, S., Karlsen, J.R., Putni ņš, T.J.: Sex, drugs, and bitcoin: how much illegal activity is financed through cryptocurrencies? Rev. Financ. Stud. **32**(5), 1798–1853 (2019)
4. Fleder, M., Kester, M.S., Pillai, S.: Bitcoin transaction graph analysis. arXiv preprint arXiv:1502.01657 (2015)
5. Moser, M.: Anonymity of bitcoin transactions (2013)
6. Reid, F., Harrigan, M.: An analysis of anonymity in the bitcoin system. In: Altshuler, Y., Elovici, Y., Cremers, A., Aharony, N., Pentland, A. (eds.) Security and Privacy in Social Networks. Springer, New York (2013). https://doi.org/10.1007/978-1-4614-4139-7_10
7. Koshy, P., Koshy, D., McDaniel, P.: An analysis of anonymity in bitcoin using P2P network traffic. In: Christin, N., Safavi-Naini, R. (eds.) FC 2014. LNCS, vol. 8437, pp. 469–485. Springer, Heidelberg (2014). https://doi.org/10.1007/978-3-662-45472-5_30
8. Bitcoin core client. https://github.com/bitcoin/bitcoin/

9. Pyshark. https://github.com/KimiNewt/pyshark/
10. Mariadb. https://mariadb.org/
11. BLOCKCHAIN.COM. Blockchain data APIS. https://www.blockchain.com/en/api/blockchain_api/

Cryptocurrencies Price Prediction Using Weighted Memory Multi-channels

Zhuorui Zhang, Junhao Zhou, Yanan Song, and Hong-Ning Dai[✉]

Macau University of Science and Technology, Taipa, Macau
zhuorui.zhang@qq.com, junhao_zhou@qq.com,
ynsong@must.edu.mo, hndai@ieee.org

Abstract. After the invention of Bitcoin and a peer to peer electronic cash system based on the blockchain, the market of cryptocurrencies increases rapidly and attracts substantial interest from investors and researchers. Cryptocurrencies price volatility prediction is a challenging task owing to the high stochasticity of the markets. Econometric, machine learning and deep learning models are investigated to tackle the stochastic financial prices fluctuation and to improve the prediction accuracy. Although the introduction of exogenous factors such as macro-financial indicators and blockchain information helps the model prediction more accurately, the noise and effects from markets and political conditions are difficult to interpret and modelling. Inspired by the evidence of strong correlations among cryptocurrencies examined in previous studies, we originally propose a Weighted Memory Channels Regression (WMCR) model to predict the daily close price of cryptocurrencies. The proposed model receives time series of several heavyweight cryptocurrencies price and learns the interdependencies of them by recalibrating the weights of each sequence wisely. Convolutional Neural Network (CNN) and Long Short-Term Memory (LSTM) components are exploited to establish memory and extract spatial and temporal features. Moreover, regularization methods including kernel regularizers and bias regularizers and Dropout method are exploited to improve the generalization ability of the proposed model. A battery of experiments are conducted in this paper. The results present that the WMCR model achieves the state-of-art performance and outperforms other baseline models.

Keywords: Blockchain · Cryptocurencies price prediction · Weighted memory channels · Convolutional neural network · Long short-term memory · Deep learning

1 Introduction

The market capitalization of cryptocurrencies has been growing rapidly in recent years. As one of the best known cryptocurrencies, Bitcoin was invented in 2008 and defined as a peer to peer electronic cash system without central bank and administrators [23]. At the beginning of 2017, the Bitcoin market exceeded 10

© Springer Nature Singapore Pte Ltd. 2020
Z. Zheng et al. (Eds.): BlockSys 2020, CCIS 1267, pp. 502–516, 2020.
https://doi.org/10.1007/978-981-15-9213-3_39

billion dollars and rapidly hit 300 billion dollars by December 2017. Remarkably, with the unmatched advantages of transaction security, decentralization and transparency [29], cryptocurrencies as a new kind of digital assets, have received extensive attention than traditional currencies. Due to the significant value, the volatility prediction of cryptocurrencies has attracted lots of investors and researchers [1,21]. As a kind of virtual asset, the price of cryptocurrencies is influenced by many factors such as fake news, market manipulation and government regulation. Developing a model with high prediction accuracy helps investors make profits and reduce loss. Meanwhile, a sharp rise or fall in prediction reminds the investors to be aware of large price fluctuations in the short-term.

Cryptocurrencies such as Bitcoin are unique assets. Meanwhile, the price fluctuated characteristics of them are similar to both a typical commercial resource and a speculative asset [19]. The impact of factors such as trading volume on cryptocurrencies is complex and subjects to time [27]. Considering the high degree of uncertainty and stochasticity of financial forecasting, previous studies proposed various approaches. These approaches mainly include time series modelling based on historical price and modelling with exogenous drivers such as macro-economic indicators [28]. Conventional interpretable time series models including Autoregressive Integrated Moving Average (ARIMA) and Generalized Autoregressive Conditional Heteroskedasticity (GARCH) are leveraged to predict Bitcoin volatility by using the historical prices as the primary information [5,11]. Moreover, to tackle the intractable random changes of financial price, machine learning [21] and deep learning models are proposed in various sectors such as coal price, precious metal price and stock price prediction [2,20,30]. Neural networks with elements from Twitter and market data as input features by using sentiment analysis [11] and Bayesian neural networks based on blockchain information [16] are construct to study the latent driven factors.

Albeit numerous approaches and regression models for cryptocurrency prediction have been developed, the prediction accuracy of models with the only use of price time series has encountered bottleneck. In the context of having few systematic analysis on complex exogenous factors such as political and economic conditions, a natural problem arises: what kernel features are worth taking into account and how to extract those features when forecasting the cryptocurrencies price volatility? In [16], researchers find the evidence that the price of Bitcoin is mainly affected by the information of blockchain directly involved in fund and trade of Bitcoin rather than other macro-financial markets. Studies in the correlations among cryptocurrencies have been conducted in which the correlations are examined to be positive [4]. In particular, some authors investigated the price leadership dynamics of Ethereum (ETH) and Bitcoin (BTC). The result indicates that it has a lead-lag relationship between ETH and BTC [26] while other researchers examined the interdependencies between BTC and altcoin markets in short period and long period [9]. Although the interdependencies between cryptocurrencies have been investigated in different articles, few solutions are available to leverage and to modelling the correlations among cryptocurrencies.

Aiming to fully exploit the latent interdependencies between cryptocurrencies and recalibrate the importance of each cryptocurrency, we propose and develop a Weighted Memory Channels Regression model (WMCR model). Our proposed model is adapt to learn the correlations among several heavyweight cryptocurrencies price and extract both temporal and spatial features of time series after constructing the weighted memory channels. Inspired by the power of Long short-term memory (LSTM) in sequence learning [14] and the approach of dynamic channel-wise feature recalibration in Squeeze-and-Excitation Networks adapt for image processing task [15], we adopt an LSTM layer for each time series of cryptocurrency (which are also regarded as channels) to construct memory. Next we recalibrate the weights of channels by construct a Multi-Channel Weighting block. In addition, convolutional neural networks with kernel regularizers and bias regularizers are employed to extract temporal and spatial features. Non-linear activation functions such as ReLU [22], sigmoid and tanh have been exploited to add non-linear factors. These functions help to solve more complex problems and enhance the representation and the learning ability of neural networks. The implementation of our proposed model is based on Keras [7]. The main research contributions of this paper are summarized as follows:

- We originally propose a regression model based on deep learning framework to predict the daily close price of cryptocurrencies. It is worth mentioning that the WMCR model is efficient at modelling the non-linear correlations between cryptocurrencies dynamically and wisely, this process is novel and has not been used in other studies. It is also capable of extracting temporal and spacial features and establishing memories in short and long term.
- We compare the prediction accuracy and performance of our proposed model with a battery of econometric, deep learning and machine learning models. The WMCR model outperforms all baseline models in interpretable and commonly used evaluation metrics.
- We investigate the effect of three significant parameters on the WMCR model. Among these parameters, the number of convolutional neural network (CNN) layers impacts both the training loss and the validation loss noticeably. In addition, the factors of window length and number of neurons in each hidden layer mainly influence the convergence speed of validation loss.

2   Methodology

2.1   Model Overview

Based on the deep learning framework, we design a WMCR model to predict closing price of cryptocurrencies. The architecture of WMCR model is illustrated in Fig. 1 and the components of the WMCR model are listed in the following paragraphs.

LSTM Layers for Each Channel: To address the exploding and vanishing gradient problems in training the recurrent neural networks, LSTM is proposed

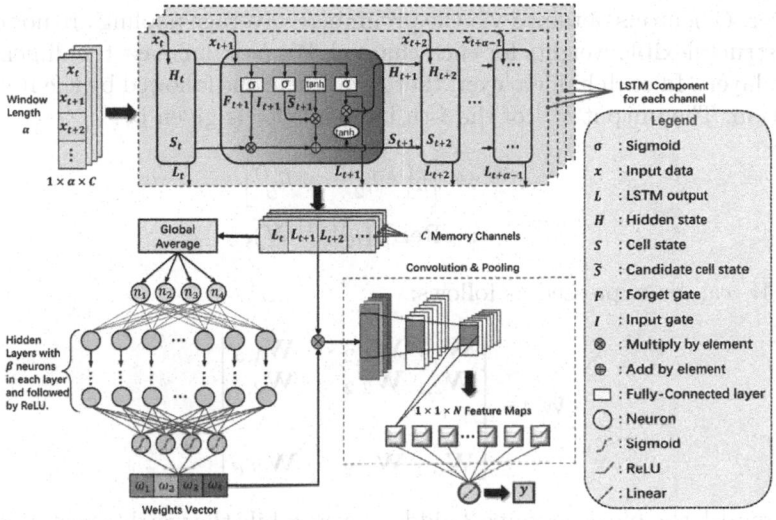

Fig. 1. The architecture of WMCR model.

by [14] and developed by [12]. Since the inputs of WMCR model consist of time series of several cryptocurrencies price after preprocessing, we employ an independent LSTM layer for each channel to filter the noises and memorize the important information of different sequences. In essence, this component can extract temporal features for each channel. In the LSTM component depicted in Fig. 1, the input gate I_t, forget gate F_t, LSTM output L_t, cell state S_t and candidate cell state $\tilde{S}_t$ are computed according to the following equations:

$$I_t = \sigma(\mathbf{W}_i x_t + \mathbf{W}_{hi} x_t + b_i), \tag{1}$$

$$F_t = \sigma(\mathbf{W}_f x_t + \mathbf{W}_{hf} x_t + b_f), \tag{2}$$

$$L_t = \sigma(\mathbf{W}_l x_t + \mathbf{W}_{hl} x_t + b_l), \tag{3}$$

$$S_t = F_t \odot S_{t-1} + I_t \odot \tilde{S}_t, \tag{4}$$

$$\tilde{S}_t = \tanh(\mathbf{W}_s x_t + \mathbf{W}_{hs} H_{t-1} + b_s), \tag{5}$$

where the weights matrices $\mathbf{W}$ are in $\mathbb{R}^{h \times \alpha}$. In addition, b_i, b_f, b_l, b_s are vectors of bias terms in $\mathbb{R}^{h \times 1}$. Moreover, σ is the sigmoid activation function.

Multi-channel Weighting Block: Inspired by the SENet architecture establishing weights for feature maps presented by authors in [15], we design a Multi-Channel Weighting block. This block is applicable for discriminating the importance of different time series. Given C channels, the Multi-Channel block starts with a global average pooling layer for each channel of L_i and generates C neurons. We denote the k-th channel of L_i by L_i^k. The value of the k-th neuron is n_k which is given by:

$$n_k = \frac{1}{\alpha} \sum_{i=1}^{\alpha} L_i^{(k)}. \tag{6}$$

However, C neurons obtained via the preliminary average pooling are not enough to construct flexible weights for each channel. We next increase the dimension in hidden layers. In each hidden layer, there are β neurons followed by the ReLU [22] activation. The output $h^{(i)}$ of the i-th hidden layer is given by:

$$
\begin{aligned}
h^{(i)} &:= \left[h_1^{(i)} \ h_2^{(i)} \ \cdots \ h_\beta^{(i)} \right] \\
&:= \mathrm{ReLU}(h^{(i-1)}\mathbf{W}),
\end{aligned}
\tag{7}
$$

where W can be expressed as follows:

$$
\mathbf{W} := \begin{bmatrix}
\mathbf{W}_{1,1} & \mathbf{W}_{1,2} & \cdots & \mathbf{W}_{1,\beta} \\
\mathbf{W}_{2,1} & \mathbf{W}_{2,2} & \cdots & \mathbf{W}_{2,\beta} \\
\vdots & \vdots & \ddots & \vdots \\
\mathbf{W}_{\beta,1} & \mathbf{W}_{\beta,2} & \cdots & \mathbf{W}_{\beta,\beta}
\end{bmatrix}.
\tag{8}
$$

In our model, the block contains 3 hidden layers while the weights vector contains 4 elements to perform the weighting for 4 channels correspondingly. In Fig. 1, the weights vector ω is given by the following equation:

$$
\omega := \left[\omega_1 \ \omega_2 \ \omega_3 \ \omega_4 \right] := \sigma(h^{(3)}\mathbf{W}^*),
\tag{9}
$$

where W^* is a weights matrix in $\mathbb{R}^{\beta \times C}$.

With the obtained weights vector ω, we multiply the original channels by elements of ω_k in the weight vector to rescale the memory channels generated by LSTM component. The rescaling channel $L^{*(k)}$ can be computed by $L^{*(k)} = \omega_i L^{(k)}$ and different k represents different channel. This block in WMCR model is responsible for modelling the nonlinear correlations between channels and identifying a reasonable weight vector for rescaling. While the interdependencies between different cryptocurrencies are challenging to identify, this block provides a succinct multi-channel weighting solution that is instrumental in improving prediction accuracy.

CNN Layers: The CNN is a representative feed-forward neural network in the field of deep learning. The CNN architecture brings the ability of representation learning. Motivated by the power of extracting spatial features and reducing parameters in CNN, we exploit a component mainly containing two CNN layers to extract the price characteristics of cryptocurrencies. In the second CNN layer, We double the number of convolution kernels to extract the features more sufficiently.

Fully-Connected Layer: We leverage a fully-connected layer to reduce dimensions by concatenating numerous feature maps into a single output neuron. This layer finally receives all the feature maps generated by CNN layers and connects with a single output neuron. After a linear activation function, the WMCR model ultimately outputs the price of prediction of the target cryptocurrency.

2.2 Weights and Memory Establishing for Multi Price Series

In finance, time series regression modeling is a challenging problem caused by the high stochasticity of market and the complex dependencies between latent driven factors. Inspired by the previous studies of relationships between cryptocurrencies and the SENet architecture, we design a WMCR model to adapt for modelling interdependencies between cryptocurrencies prices. As depicted in Fig. 1, the number of channels with α time steps in each sample is denoted by C, representing as channels. First, to remember the critical features for each channel, we employ C LSTM layers. The task in next phase is to modelling the interdependencies between these channels. Then, global average pooling layers are utilized to concentrate feature maps of each channel, generated by memory establishing process.

Next, we construct several full-connected hidden layers to generate different weights for every channel by exploiting the information aggregated in previous steps. In general, the number of channels or the species of interdependent cryptocurrencies is rare. In order to increase the dimension, the number of neurons in the first full-connected layer is much larger than C. To enable full-connected layers to make non-linear transformation, we utilize the ReLU as the activation function in each hidden layer. We also fix neurons as C in the last dense layer, to return to the dimension of the original channels.

Specially, we employ a sigmoid activation function after the last full-connected layer to generate the weights vector. In particular, the sum of C elements in the weights vector is 1. The generated weights vector is next multiplied with each channel by corresponding element.

2.3 Regularization Auxiliary

After the weights and memory establishing process for multi sequences, we build two CNN layers to extract spatial features of multi weighted memory channels. In this module, several methods of regularization are employed to tackle the problem of poor generalization and overfitting.

- **Dropout Method:** Dropout is a technique for preventing overfitting. It reduces training time by randomly dropping neurons along with their connections from the networks with a specified probability [13]. We set a Dropout rate as 0.55, representing that 55% neurons are dropped.
- **Kernel Regularizer:** In the model optimization process, the kernel regularizer allows to apply penalties on weight matrices W. Meanwhile, W also represents the convolutional kernels in convolutional layers. In the proposed model, we use the ℓ_2 regularization in the kernel regularizer.
- **Bias Regularizer:** Similarly, we use ℓ_1 regularization and employ a bias regularizer to apply penalties on bias terms b. We also conduct the combinations of ℓ_1 regularization and ℓ_2 regularization in both kernel regularizer and bias regularizer, showing the best performance.

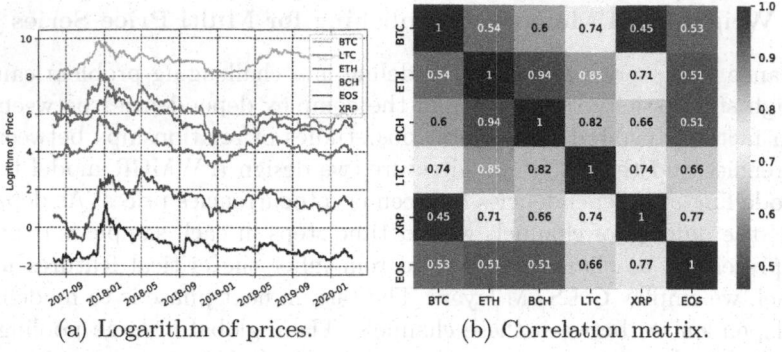

(a) Logarithm of prices.   (b) Correlation matrix.

Fig. 2. The similarity and correlation between price of popular cryptocurrencies.

The choice of different norm for kernel and bias regularizer is inspired by the Regularization Self-Attention Regression model in [30]. The loss function with regularization is computed as:

$$\mathbf{L} = \mathbf{L}_0 + \lambda(\sum_{i=1}^{N}\sum_{j=1}^{M} W_{ij}^2 + \sum_{i=1}^{N} |b_i|), \tag{10}$$

where $\mathbf{L}$ and $\mathbf{L}_0$ represent the loss before and after using the regularizers, respectively. And the elements in convolutional kernels are denoted by W_{ij} while b_i denotes the bias term and λ refers to the degree of punishment. In the proposed model, λ is taken as 0.01 and the loss function is computed according to the following equation:

$$\mathbf{L}_0 = \frac{1}{N}\sum_{i-1}^{N}(\hat{y}_i - y_i)^2, \tag{11}$$

where $\hat{y}_i$ represents the forecast value and y_i denotes the actual value.

3   Data Specification

According to the cryptocurrencies price released by CoinMarketCap at the website https://coinmarketcap.com/, we investigate and compare six popular and valuable cryptocurrencies including Bitcoin (BTC), Bitcoin Cash (BCH), Litecoin (LTC), Ethereum (ETH), XRP and EOS. Considering different prices at different time, we pick out the daily closing prices from July 23, 2017 to March 9, 2020. In Fig. 2(a), we take logarithm of prices to unify the scale. It can be noticed that the price curves show high similarity of fluctuation. To analyze the degree of similarity, we employ Pearson Correlation Coefficient (PCC) on paired price time series. The PCC value between two variables is computed as following,

$$\mathrm{PCC} = \frac{\mathrm{E}[(X - \mu_X)(Y - \mu_Y)]}{\sigma_X \sigma_Y}, \tag{12}$$

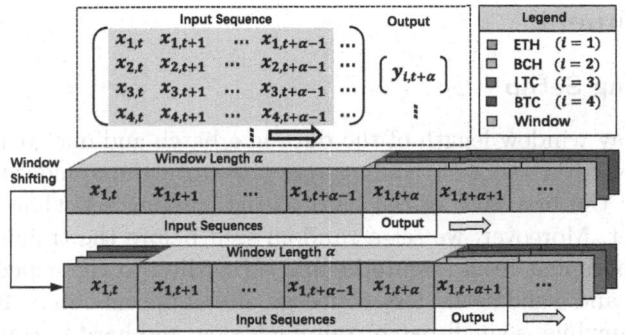

Fig. 3. Data preprocessing.

where X and Y are different variables and μ is the mean. In addition, σ is the standard deviation and E denotes the expectation. The numerator in Eq. (12) is essentially the covariance between X and Y. It is shown in Fig. 2(b) that PCC values between each pair in the prices of ETH, BCH and LTC are greater than 0.8. This result indicates the high correlations among them. In addition, the lowest PCC values of 0.45 and 0.51 are from the rows (or columns) of XRP and EOS separately. In Fig. 2(a), it shows the prices of XRP and EOS are orders of magnitude lower than other four cryptocurrencies. To the input of WMCR model, we choose the cyptocurrencies in similar price levels and have high PCC values with each other. This choice is conducive to construct more related channels in Fig. 1. We conduct the experiments mainly based on the prices of BTC, BCH, ETH and LTC. The preprocessing can be divided into two steps. First, we have employed the `StandardScaler` method from scikit-learn [24]. It standardizes features by subtracting the mean and scaling to unit variance (Fig. 3).

Next, a scrollable window is applied to move on the dataset. The number of time steps of each sample is regarded as the window length α. We use the previous data of the prices in α days to predict the price in day $\alpha+1$. Figure 2(a) shows the scrollable window concretely. As discussed in previous analysis of correlations, price of four kinds of typical cryptocurrencies are employed as the input of the proposed model. Specifically, these time series are combined and reshaped to a tensor with the dimensions arranged as batch size, time steps, features and channels. It is worth mentioning that the multi-channel price data is only applicable to our model while the dataset of baseline models merely includes single type of cryptocurrency. In this paper, we make price prediction primarily on ETH and LTC.

4   Experiment

4.1   Training Setup

We use a 7-day window length of the data in a batch and our goal is to predict the closing price in the 8-th trading day. To unify the standard of measurement, we use the first 80% of the data as the training set while the last 20% as the test set. Moreover, we set a random seed before the training process to make the experiment results reproducible. According to the experiments, both training loss and validations loss converge after approximately 100 epochs of training. Meanwhile, a small-batch training is slow and hard to converge while a large-batch training may converge to sharp minimizers and result in poor generalization [17]. Considering the efficiency and feasibility, the training epochs and batch-size are fixed to 100 and 80 empirically, respectively. In addition, we use the Adam optimizer [18] in the training process and the initial learning rate is 0.01.

4.2   Evaluation Metrics

To compare the performance of distinct models, we employ four commonly-used metrics to evaluate the prediction accuracy. There are the root mean square error (RMSE), the mean absolute error (MAE), the mean absolute percentage error (MAPE) and the R-squared. RMSE represents the square root of the average of squared residuals and the effect of each error is proportional to the squared error. Consequently, RMSE is susceptible to outliers. MAE measures the mean absolute errors between predicted prices and actual prices. MAPE usually expresses the accuracy as a ratio. It considers the ratio of the error to the actual value. R-squared (R^2) is a statistical measure of the regression model prediction. It indicates the extent to which the regression explains the change of dependent variable [3]. The R-squared measure is close to 1, meaning the better for the regression fittings.

4.3   Baseline Models

We employ six baselines to compare the performance with our proposed model. These baselines are the representative and prevailing methods from the fields of machine learning, deep learning and time series analysis.

   Autoregressive Integrated Moving Average (ARIMA) is an advanced method fit to time series data analysis and prediction [6]. It is widely applied to non-stationary financial data. Support Vector Regression (SVR) is an important application of SVM (Support Vector Machine). For non-linear separable datasets, SVR uses kernel functions to map data to high-dimensional space, and finds a hyperplane closest to the data [10,25]. Multilayer Perceptron (MLP) have achieved the state-of-art performance in various computer vision tasks. We construct an MLP with 2 dense layers and employ ReLU and sigmoid as the activation. The CNN structure is a type of feed-forward network with deep structure

Table 1. Influence of different parameters

Loss	Window length α			Dense Neurons β			CNN Layers γ		
	7	11	15	16	32	64	1	2	3
Training loss	0.1154	0.0882	0.0905	0.1162	0.1070	0.1197	0.1886	0.1031	0.1595
Validation loss	0.0419	0.0706	0.1182	0.0427	0.0160	0.0316	0.1792	0.0279	0.0594

and convolution computation. It mainly includes convolutional layers, pooling layers and fully-connected layers. In this baseline, we apply two CNN layers. LSTM neural network is specially developed to tackle the long-term dependence of general RNN. It is well-adapted for predicting time series data and can control the transmission state through three gates. Then it can remember the important features and forget the unimportant information. Two layers of LSTM are employed in this experiment. To capture the pivotal temporal information and to extract features simultaneously, we implement a mixed-structure baseline of LSTM + CNN. Gated Recurrent Unit (GRU) is a frequently used type of Gated Recurrent Neural Network [8]. It achieves a close performance to LSTM but is computationally much simpler. We also construct a baseline of GRU+CNN.

4.4   Parameter Study

To investigate the impact of multifarious parameters of WMCR model, we divide the previous training set in Sect. 4.1 into a new training set (the first 70% data) and a validation set (the remaining part of 30%). Moreover, both the training loss and validation loss are computed by Eq. (11). In addition, since predicting different cryptocurrencies influences on the performance slightly, to eliminate this effect, we all employ the dataset of ETH. Table 1 shows the training loss and validations loss after 500 epochs of training. The effect of three critical parameters are discussed as follow:

Effect of Window Length α. We perform the effect comparison between different window length α. Specially, the value of β in the multi-channel weighting block is fixed to 32 and γ is fixed to 2. Then, we vary α from 7, 11 and 15. Figure 4(a) shows the fluctuation of the training loss is not obvious with the change of α. In Fig. 5(a), while α is 7, the validation loss converges more rapidly. The reason is that our model shows the better generalization ability since a shorter sequence requires less memory cells in LSTM layers. Moreover, while we increase α to 11 or 15, the performance on validation loss drops sharply. This result indicates that establishing memory for a long sequence causes over-fitting. Therefore, we fix α to be 7 in the proposed model.

Effect of Number of Dense Neurons β. We next investigate the effect of number of neurons β in each hidden layer in multi-channel weighting block. We vary β from 16, 32 to 64 while the parameters of α and γ are fixed to 7 and 2 separately. Figure 4(b), the training loss with different β show similarity. It indicates that 16 neurons in each dense layer are capable of fitting the training

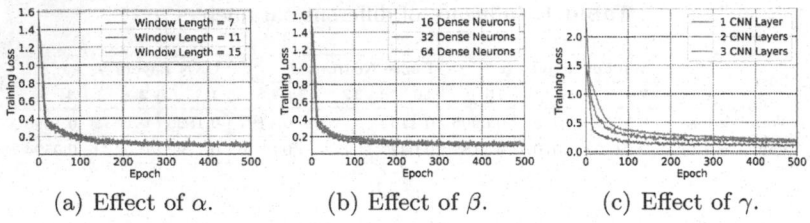

(a) Effect of α. (b) Effect of β. (c) Effect of γ.

Fig. 4. The impact of the significant parameters on training loss.

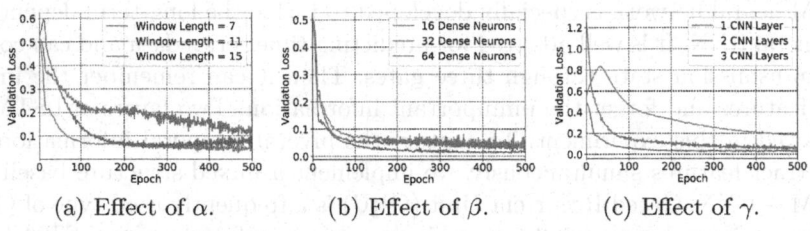

(a) Effect of α. (b) Effect of β. (c) Effect of γ.

Fig. 5. The impact of the significant parameters on validation loss.

set. However, Fig. 5(b) shows that the model with 32 dense neurons in multi-channel weighting block achieves noticeable lower validation loss and faster speed of convergence in the first 100 iterations. Combined with the results in Table 1, fixing β to 32 shows the superior performance.

Effect of Number of CNN Layers γ. To investigate the effect of number of CNN layers γ, we vary γ from 1, 2 and 3. Meanwhile α is fixed to 7 and β is fixed to 4. As shown in Fig. 4(c) and Fig. 5(c), the model with a single CNN layer generates obvious higher loss than other two groups with more CNN layers. In addition, the validation loss with 1 CNN layer increases notably at the beginning. This increment implies that a single CNN layer is insufficient to extract features and demands more iterations to acquire generalization ability. Meanwhile, as γ increases form 2 to 3, the curves of both training loss and validation loss exhibit the increased tendency. It implies that a deep convolutional neural network is not suit to our WMCR model.

4.5 Performance Comparison

We also perform the performance comparison between the WMCR model and baseline models. In particular, we set the parameter of α, β and γ to be 7, 32 and 2, respectively. Other parameters for all models in Table 2 retain consistency. For instance, we set the training ratio to be 80% and the number of training epochs is 100. Moreover, we make the prediction and regression on ETH and BTC datasets.

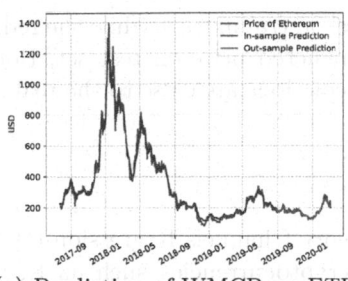
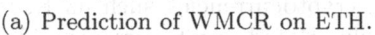

(a) Prediction of WMCR on ETH.

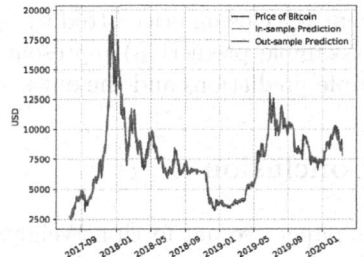

(b) Prediction of WMCR on BTC.

Fig. 6. Prediction on prices of different cryptocurrencies (Color figure online)

Table 2. Performance comparison

Models	Ethereum				Litecoin			
	RMSE	MAE	MAPE	R-squared	RMSE	MAE	MAPE	R-squared
SVR	1.24E + 02	1.15E + 02	7.09E − 01	−1.11E + 01	1.92E + 01	1.60E + 01	3.21E − 01	−2.14E + 01
ARIMA	1.56E + 02	1.48E + 02	8.45E − 01	−1.80E + 01	7.50E + 01	7.33E + 01	1.30E + 00	−4.69E + 01
MLP	2.45E + 01	1.89E + 01	1.15E − 01	5.30E − 01	5.71E + 00	4.76E + 00	8.21E − 02	7.22E − 01
LSTM	1.77E + 01	1.40E + 01	8.26E − 02	7.54E − 01	4.70E + 00	3.63E + 00	6.32E − 02	8.21E − 01
CNN	1.98E + 01	1.72E + 01	1.06E − 01	6.93E − 01	4.69E + 00	4.00E + 00	7.60E − 02	8.13E − 01
LSTM + CNN	2.09E + 01	1.68E + 01	9.81E − 02	6.57E − 01	6.37E + 00	4.84E + 00	8.87E − 02	6.54E − 01
GRU + LSTM	2.13E + 01	1.75E + 01	1.01E − 01	6.42E − 01	6.83E + 00	5.05E + 00	9.13E − 02	6.03E − 01
WMCR	**1.23E + 01**	**9.69E + 00**	**5.62E − 02**	**9.03E − 01**	**3.80E + 00**	**2.90E + 00**	**5.06E − 02**	**8.77E − 01**

First, we evaluate three typical machine learning models including SVR, ARIMA, MLP. As shown in Table 2, the evaluation metrics including RMSE, MAE, MAPE and R-squared have been computed for each model on ETH and LTC price datasets. For instance, the SVR achieves 1.24E+02, 1.15E+02, 7.09E+01, −1.11E+01 in RMSE, MAE, MAPE and R-squared measure, respectively on test set. Among these three machine learning models, MLP achieves better performance in both two datasets.

Second, we compare the performance of four deep learning models including LSTM, CNN, LSTM+CNN, GRU+CNN. The model of LSTM which consists of two LSTM layers shows superior performance. In particular, most of deep learning models have lower values of RMSE, MAE, MAPE and higher R-squared compared with conventional machine learning models. The reason of this improvement may lie in the distinguished ability of deep learning model in extracting features from highly stochastic data.

We then perform the evaluation of WMCR model. Table 2 shows the results of performance. Compared with other baseline models, the WMCR model achieves the lowest level of RMSE, MAE, MAPE and the highest value of R-squared. This result indicates our proposed model achieves better fitting and predicts more accurately on the price of ETH and BTC than the baselines. In Fig. 6, we show the real price curves and the predicted curves generated by our model on ETH and BTC datasets. The blue and green curves (in-sample prediction) represent the closing price fitted by our model on training set while the red curve (out-of-sample prediction) represents the predicted price on test set. Both the in-sample predictions and the out-sample predictions are close to the real prices.

5   Conclusion

In this paper, we put forth a Weighted Memory Channels Regression (WMCR) model to predict the daily close price of cryptocurrencies such as ETH and BTC by exploiting the price of four closely related cryptocurrencies. We use the WMCR model to establish the structure memory and to recalibrate the importance for different channels before extracting the temporal and spatial features of different price sequences. We also test the WMCR model on the dataset of historical prices of four heavyweight cryptocurrences (from July 23, 2017 to March 9, 2020). Based on the experiments, we show that our proposed model performs better than other baselines including prevailing econometric, machine learning and deep learning approaches. To improve this study, we are going to examine the use of more market information of cryptocurrencies in WMCR model such as market capitalization, volume and open price. We will also investigate how the weights vector generated by Multi-Channel weighting block affects the performance of WMCR model. Moreover, we intend to explore more reasonable numbers and types of channels in WMCR model to improve the prediction accuracy.

Acknowledgments. The work described in this paper was partially supported by Macao Science and Technology Development Fund under Macao Funding Scheme for Key R & D Projects (0025/2019/AKP).

References

1. Abraham, J., Higdon, D., Nelson, J., Ibarra, J.: Cryptocurrency price prediction using tweet volumes and sentiment analysis. SMU Data Sci. Rev. **1**(3), 1 (2018)
2. Alameer, Z., Fathalla, A., Li, K., Ye, H., Jianhua, Z.: Multistep-ahead forecasting of coal prices using a hybrid deep learning model. Resour. Policy **65**, 101588 (2020)
3. Anderson-Sprecher, R.: Model comparisons and R2. Am. Stat. **48**(2), 113–117 (1994)
4. Aslanidis, N., Bariviera, A.F., Martínez-Ibañez, O.: An analysis of cryptocurrencies conditional cross correlations. Financ. Res. Lett. **31**, 130–137 (2019)
5. Bakar, N.A., Rosbi, S.: Autoregressive integrated moving average (ARIMA) model for forecasting cryptocurrency exchange rate in high volatility environment: a new insight of bitcoin transaction. Int. J. Adv. Eng. Res. Sci. **4**(11), 237311 (2017)
6. Box, G.E., Jenkins, G.M., Reinsel, G.C., Ljung, G.M.: Time Series Analysis: Forecasting and Control. Wiley, Hoboken (2015)
7. Chollet, F., et al.: Keras (2015). https://keras.io

8. Chung, J., Gulcehre, C., Cho, K., Bengio, Y.: Empirical evaluation of gated recurrent neural networks on sequence modeling. arXiv preprint arXiv:1412.3555 (2014)
9. Ciaian, P., Rajcaniova, M., et al.: Virtual relationships: short-and long-run evidence from bitcoin and altcoin markets. J. Int. Financ. Mark. Inst. Money **52**, 173–195 (2018)
10. Drucker, H., Burges, C.J., Kaufman, L., Smola, A.J., Vapnik, V.: Support vector regression machines. In: Advances in Neural Information Processing Systems, pp. 155–161 (1997)
11. Dyhrberg, A.H.: Bitcoin, gold and the dollar-a GARCH volatility analysis. Financ. Res. Lett. **16**, 85–92 (2016)
12. Graves, A., Mohamed, A.r., Hinton, G.: Speech recognition with deep recurrent neural networks. In: 2013 IEEE International Conference on Acoustics, Speech and Signal Processing, pp. 6645–6649. IEEE (2013)
13. Hinton, G.E., Srivastava, N., Krizhevsky, A., Sutskever, I., Salakhutdinov, R.R.: Improving neural networks by preventing co-adaptation of feature detectors. arXiv preprint arXiv:1207.0580 (2012)
14. Hochreiter, S., Schmidhuber, J.: Long short-term memory. Neural Comput. **9**(8), 1735–1780 (1997)
15. Hu, J., Shen, L., Sun, G.: Squeeze-and-excitation networks. In: Proceedings of the IEEE Conference on Computer Vision and Pattern Recognition, pp. 7132–7141 (2018)
16. Jang, H., Lee, J.: An empirical study on modeling and prediction of bitcoin prices with Bayesian neural networks based on blockchain information. IEEE Access **6**, 5427–5437 (2017)
17. Keskar, N.S., Mudigere, D., Nocedal, J., Smelyanskiy, M., Tang, P.T.P.: On large-batch training for deep learning: generalization gap and sharp minima. arXiv preprint arXiv:1609.04836 (2016)
18. Kingma, D.P., Ba, J.: Adam: a method for stochastic optimization. arXiv preprint arXiv:1412.6980 (2014)
19. Kristoufek, L.: What are the main drivers of the bitcoin price? Evidence from wavelet coherence analysis. PLoS ONE **10**(4), e0123923 (2015)
20. Long, W., Lu, Z., Cui, L.: Deep learning-based feature engineering for stock price movement prediction. Knowl. Based Syst. **164**, 163–173 (2019)
21. McNally, S., Roche, J., Caton, S.: Predicting the price of bitcoin using machine learning. In: 2018 26th Euromicro International Conference on Parallel, Distributed and Network-based Processing (PDP), pp. 339–343. IEEE (2018)
22. Nair, V., Hinton, G.E.: Rectified linear units improve restricted Boltzmann machines. In: Proceedings of the 27th International Conference on Machine Learning (ICML 2010), pp. 807–814 (2010)
23. Nakamoto, S.: Bitcoin: A peer-to-peer electronic cash system. Technical report Manubot (2019)
24. Pedregosa, F., et al.: Scikit-learn: machine learning in Python. J. Mach. Learn. Res. **12**, 2825–2830 (2011)
25. Peng, Y., Albuquerque, P.H.M., de Sá, J.M.C., Padula, A.J.A., Montenegro, M.R.: The best of two worlds: Forecasting high frequency volatility for cryptocurrencies and traditional currencies with support vector regression. Expert Syst. Appl. **97**, 177–192 (2018)
26. Sifat, I.M., Mohamad, A., Shariff, M.S.B.M.: Lead-lag relationship between bitcoin and Ethereum: evidence from hourly and daily data. Res. Int. Bus. Financ. **50**, 306–321 (2019)

27. Sovbetov, Y.: Factors influencing cryptocurrency prices: evidence from bitcoin, Ethereum, dash, Litcoin, and Monero. J. Econ. Financ. Anal. **2**(2), 1–27 (2018)
28. Walther, T., Klein, T., Bouri, E.: Exogenous drivers of bitcoin and cryptocurrency volatility-a mixed data sampling approach to forecasting. J. Int. Financ. Mark. Inst. Money **63**, 101133 (2019)
29. Zheng, Z., Xie, S., Dai, H.N., Chen, X., Wang, H.: Blockchain challenges and opportunities: a survey. Int. J. Web Grid Serv. **14**(4), 352–375 (2018). https://doi.org/10.1504/IJWGS.2018.095647
30. Zhou, J., et al.: Precious metal price prediction based on deep regularization self-attention regression. IEEE Access **8**, 2178–2187 (2019)

Machine Learning Based Bitcoin Address Classification

Chaehyeon Lee[1]($\boxtimes$), Sajan Maharjan[1], Kyungchan Ko[1], Jongsoo Woo[2],
and James Won-Ki Hong[1]

[1] Department of Computer Science and Engineering, POSTECH,
Pohang 37673, Korea
{chlee0211,thesajan,kkc90,jwkhong}@postech.ac.kr
[2] Graduate School of Information Technology, POSTECH,
Pohang 37673, Korea
woojs@postech.ac.kr

Abstract. A bitcoin address is required for trading and maintaining pseudonymity for the owner. By exploiting this pseudonymity, various illegal activities are conducted around the world. To detect and deter illegal transactions, this paper proposes a method of identifying the characteristics of bitcoin addresses related to illegal transactions. We extracted 80 features from bitcoin transactions. Using machine-learning techniques, we successfully categorized addresses involved with illegal activities with a ~84% accuracy. We also examined the address features most affecting classification performance and compared two machine learning models. By applying the majority voting to the classification results of bitcoin addresses associated with a particular transaction, it will be possible to determine which category the transaction belongs to.

Keywords: Bitcoin · Bitcoin address classification · Illegal transaction detection · Address feature extraction · Bitcoin transaction analysis

1 Introduction

In 2008, Satoshi Nakamoto introduced Bitcoin, a peer-to-peer electronic payment system, to the world [1]. Blockchain [2] that is the basis of Bitcoin is a decentralized transaction technique in which participants maintain duplicate copies of temporally connected ledger data, called "blocks". Anyone in the network can duplicate the blockchain structure and can validate data on the network. Thus, the bitcoin network is autonomously maintained and operated by thousands of participating nodes without a central authority, assuring transparent transactions. This disintermediation has allowed cross-border value transfers between buyers and sellers having very low transaction fees and scant processing. Bitcoin employs a proof-of-work consensus algorithm that makes it impossible to maliciously delete, forge, or modify existing data. One must have a bitcoin address to send bitcoins, and a single user can have multiple addresses.

© Springer Nature Singapore Pte Ltd. 2020
Z. Zheng et al. (Eds.): BlockSys 2020, CCIS 1267, pp. 517–531, 2020.
https://doi.org/10.1007/978-981-15-9213-3_40

However, because it is nearly impossible to infer owner information from the bitcoin address, there are frequent cases of illegal transactions. In fact, there have been a variety of darknets that abuse bitcoin for illegal use [3,4] and statistics show that the total dollar value of bitcoin traversing the "dark net" has steadily increased since 2011 (See Fig. 1 [5]). By 2013, nearly 1M users were trading bitcoins. In 2017, when the trading value in darknet markets reached its highest value of USD 707M, most was traded through darknet markets. Silk Road [6] was one of the most famous online black markets, trading drugs, weapons, child pornography, stolen goods, and malicious code.

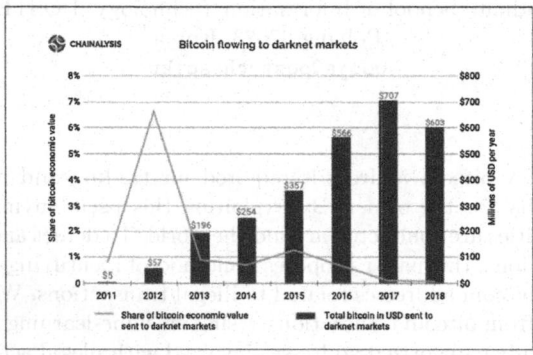

Fig. 1. Bitcoin values (in USD) sent to darknet markets from 2011 to 2018. Orange line graph shows the proportion of darknet Bitcoin transactions over all Bitcoin transactions (Source: Chainalysis)

In addition to illegal goods transactions, illegal activities such as money laundering and scamming are acting as a factor in hindering the enactment of cryptocurrency laws. Therefore, it is necessary to find a way to detect illegal transactions on blockchains. Although various cryptocurrencies such as bitcoin, Ethereum [7], and Monero [8] are used for illegal transactions in darknet, since bitcoin is the most widely used cryptocurrency on darknet, we focused on bitcoin and studied the methods to detect illegal transactions on the bitcoin network.

Because illegal users are likely to repeat transactions, and one user can leverage multiple bitcoin addresses, we analyzed the characteristics of bitcoin addresses to help detect illegal activities. The address characteristics associated with illegal transactions can be analyzed by collecting the transaction lists of known illegal trades. Machine learning classification models [9] can then be used to train the features so that such activities can be identified.

In this paper, we present a methodology for detecting illegal bitcoin addresses, and we then explain the detailed process of detection. Section 2 explains the background and several related work. Section 3 describes the classification process and its implementation. In Sect. 4, we present the results of several experiments. A broad discussion and conclusion with future work are provided in Sect. 5.

2 Background and Related Work

2.1 Background

Bitcoin Address. Digital cryptographic keys and signatures are used to prove ownership of bitcoin addresses [10,11]. Addresses can be infinitely generated, and the wallets can generate and maintain multiple bitcoin addresses indefinitely. When generating a transaction, the transmitter must specify the recipient's bitcoin address, which is shared with others. Bitcoin transactions transfer the ownership of bitcoin to the address of the recipient, and the blockchain is updated. During this process, personal information is neither collected nor transmitted.

Bitcoin Transaction. There are several types of bitcoin transactions having different input and output values. Fig. 2(a) shows the most common type of transaction: one output of bitcoin remittance from one input value, and another output that returns the remaining balance to the original owner. Because bitcoin lacks a mechanism that automatically returns remaining bitcoin to its original owner, the owner must generate an output that performs this function. The transaction of Fig. 2(b) sends multiple inputs to one address, and that of Fig. 2(c) allows multiple output values in one transaction for distributing and sending bitcoins to multiple addresses. The first transaction type can be included in the third type. As shown in Fig. 2(d), it is also possible to generate transactions having multiple inputs and multiple outputs.

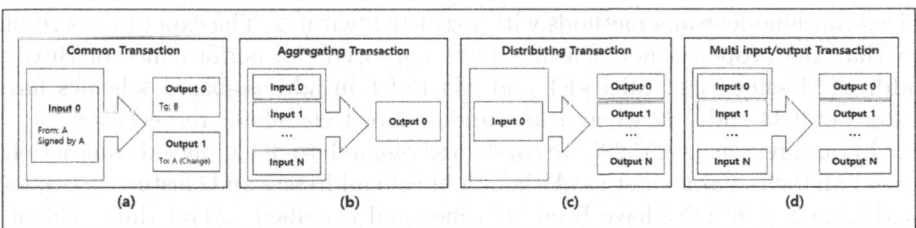

Fig. 2. The types of Bitcoin transactions

2.2 Related Work

Several authors have suggested methodologies for detecting types of bitcoin activities by using machine-learning methods, and they have evaluated their performance via experiments. By combining various features of bitcoin network and machine-learning techniques, they were able to determine whether or not activities were legal.

Zambre and Shah [12] proposed a machine-learning-based system that determined the characteristics of users related to bitcoin thefts and identifies those performing similar actions. To detect bitcoin thefts and fraudulent activities, they analyzed the transaction information of several famous thefts [13,14]. They extracted 22 features to segregate dishonest users from honest users and clustered them using a k-means [15] clustering algorithm to identify theft behaviors, achieving 76.5% accuracy.

Toyoda et al. [16] identified bitcoin addresses related to a high yield investment program (HYIP) by analyzing transaction patterns. They manually identified HYIP and non-HYIP addresses and extracted several features, such as the number of transactions associated with the bitcoin address and the number of blocks mined. A pattern was assigned to each transaction, and the frequency of each pattern was utilized as a key feature. They labeled the bitcoin address as "HYIP" or "non-HYIP" for classifying cybercrime groups via supervised learning. About 83% TPR (True Positive Rate) of the HYIP-related addresses were correctly classified.

Kanemura et al. [17] analyzed bitcoin transactions and addresses related to darknet markets and proposed a voting-based system that determined the labels of multiple addresses controlled by the same entity based on the number of the majority labels. They identified the characteristics of transactions related to darknet markets (DNM [18]) that could be used to identify newly generated DNM transactions. They extracted 73 features and used them to train the supervised classifiers. The proposed voting methods achieved an ~0.8 F1 score.

Yu-Jing et al. [19] proposed new features as well as commonly used features to detect abnormality of Bitcoin addresses. It includes numerous high orders of moments and summarizes the transaction history. They trained various supervised machine-learning methods with extracted features. The experiments result in that the proposed new features have improved the performance of Bitcoin address classification. Micro-F1 and Macro-F1 in address-based schemes have values of 0.83 and 0.82 when using random forest classifiers, respectively.

In our previous work [20], we conducted research to detect illegal transactions based on their characteristics. Although bitcoin addresses and clusters associated with criminal activity have been identified and classified several times, classification from transaction features alone has not been reported. Our previous work extracted nine features and added one label, giving 10 features for each transaction. We used them to train supervised-learning classification models, which ultimately achieved an F1 score of ~0.9. However, the test set may have been over-fitted, and the number of features used to determine the illegality of the transaction was probably too small.

Following these and previous studies, we have extended our scope to detect illegal transactions using the characteristics of bitcoin addresses rather than transactions. We increased the number of features to be extracted and checked which ones most affected the classification model.

3 Address Classification Methodology

To classify bitcoin addresses and detect illegal transactions, we designed a four-step methodology comprising transaction collection, bitcoin address feature extraction, machine-learning training, and testing (See Fig. 3). We collected several types of transaction hash lists and derived bitcoin transmission and reception addresses. We extracted 80 address features that were assigned different labels. Labeled data were learned by the machine-learning classification models, and the trained models were used to determine the classification to which the given bitcoin address belonged. The classification models were evaluated using the metric F1-score. The following subsections describe each step in detail.

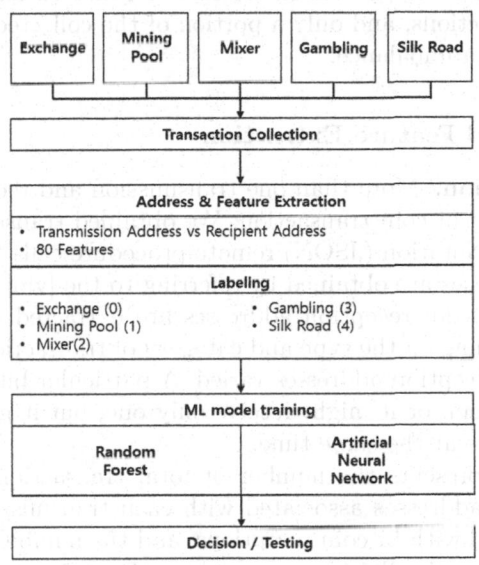

Fig. 3. Classification methodology

3.1 Transaction Collection

Before implementing the machine-learning model, we collected transaction hash lists from a publicly available forum, WalletExplorer.com [21], which discloses categories of data used for specific groups (e.g., exchanges, mining pools, services, dark nets). We focused on five categories: mixers, exchanges, gambling, pools, and Silk Road. We built a simple web crawler using Python and the Beautiful Soup library [22] to obtain a list of hash values for transactions. Data in all categories except Silk Road were collected beginning in January 1, 2016. For Silk Road, only data prior to 2018 was collected, because that is when the site was shut down. The number of transactions collected is specified in Table 1.

Table 1. The number of collected transactions by categories

Category	The number of collected transactions
Exchange	761,494
Mining pool	325,800
Mixer	93,200
Gambling	752,300
Darknet (Silk Road)	956,186

Note that experimental dataset does not necessarily reflect the proportions of real distributions in the bitcoin network. The collected data constituted only a fraction of transactions, and only a portion of the collected data were learned to alleviate any data imbalance.

3.2   Address and Feature Extraction

Address Extraction. More than one transmission and reception address can be extracted from a bitcoin transaction. We obtained transaction details using JavaScript Object Notation (JSON) remote-procedure calls (RPC) [23,24]. The transmission addresses are obtained by referring to the [vin] field of transaction details, and the bitcoin reception addresses are extracted by referring to the [vout] field. Depending on the type and category of transactions, the numbers of transmission and reception addresses varied. A particular bitcoin address might only serve one bitcoin, or it might receive only one, but it may also be used to transmit and receive at the same time.

Table 2 below presents the number of total transactions by category, the number of bitcoin addresses associated with each transmission, the number of addresses associated with bitcoin receptions, and the number of total addresses. Fig. 4 shows address distribution per category. For mining pools and darknet, a relatively small ratio of addresses were extracted, because certain addresses used for these services likely appeared repeatedly across the transactions.

Table 2. The number of extracted addresses by categories

Category	Transmission addresses	Recipient addresses	Total addresses	Transactions
Exchange	1,395,325	6,736,265	8,665,943	761,494
Mining pool	218,476	1,036,143	1,375,327	325,800
Mixer	178,721	480,754	718,915	93,200
Gambling	726,210	3,960,029	5,345,783	752,300
Darknet (Silk Road)	704,376	938,730	2,305,872	956,186

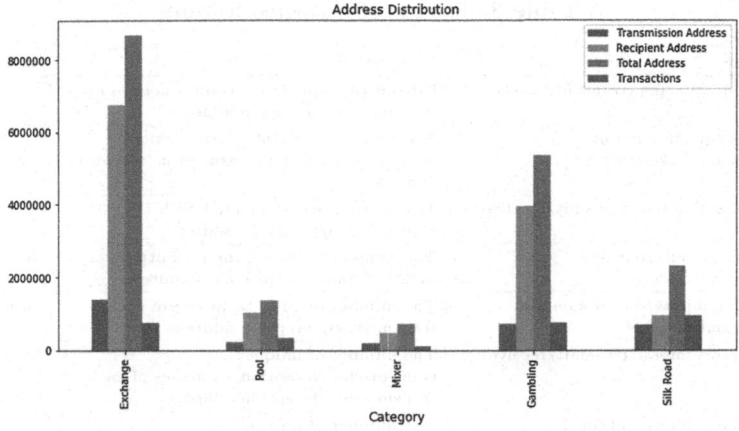

Fig. 4. Comparison of size distribution of extracted addresses by category

Feature Extraction. After extracting the transaction list, we extracted the key features for training. Illegal transactions exhibited common characteristics, such as high transaction fees in order to have them quickly included in blocks, multiple identical outputs inside one transaction (indicating money laundering), and multiple address distributions. To identify the common patterns associated with illegal transactions, we extracted features related to the addresses obtained from each.

We selected 26 features, and for some, we obtained four values: average, total, minimum, and maximum. When a specific bitcoin address appeared several times in a collected transaction, the feature values were updated per the incremental values and classified either as transmission or the reception. Depending on the category, some feature values were filled with −1. If a specific address was a transmission address, the feature values related to reception were set to −1, and, if a specific address was a reception address, the feature values related to transmission were filled with −1. A bitcoin address not having a value of −1 indicates that it transmitted or received bitcoins. We extracted 80 features, including those related to transmission and reception.

A Python script returned the transaction details of a given transaction hash from the JSON-RPC calls, extracting the relevant features (i.e., bitcoin transmission and reception amounts, transaction fees, number of inputs associated with transmission, number of outputs associated with reception, number of transmission addresses associated with transmission, number of reception addresses associated with reception). Table 3 provides simple descriptions of features extracted for bitcoin address classification.

Table 3. The list of extracted features

Name	Description	Etc.
Bitcoin amount (transmit/receive)	Bitcoin transmission/receipt amount of transmission/reception address	
Total bitcoin amount (transmit/receive)	Total bitcoin amount of transactions associated with the transmission/reception address	
Transaction fee (transmit/receive)	Transaction fees associated with the transmission/reception address	
Sibling inputs/outputs (transmit/receive)	The number of sibling inputs/outputs of each transmission/reception address	avg sum
Sibling inputs/outputs_out/in (transmit/receive)	The number of outputs/inputs of each transmission/reception address	min
Unique address (transmit/receive)	The number of unique transmission/reception addresses of each transmission/reception address	max
Unique address_out/in (transmit/receive)	The number of unique reception/transmission addresses of each transmission/reception address	
Transaction Size (transmit/receive)	Size of a transaction associated with transmission/reception address	
Block Interval (transmit/receive)	The interval between the block in which the transmission/reception address is included	
Relevant transaction (transmit/receive)	The number of transactions associated with the transmission/reception address	
Lifetime (transmit/receive)	Life time of the transmission/reception address	
First block (transmit/receive)	Block height where the transmission/reception address first appeared	
Total transaction number	Total number of transactions associated with the address	
Total life time	Lifetime of the address	
Label	Classification of the address	

Labeling. When training supervised-learning-based classification methods, training data must be labeled. Therefore, after extracting the features of each address, we manually labeled each according to the classification of the corresponding transaction (Table 4).

Table 4. The label of each categories

Category	Label
Exchange	0
Mining pool	1
Mixer	2
Gambling	3
Darknet (Silk Road)	4

3.3   Design of Machine-Learning Models

For classification, we used two machine-learning models: random forest [25] and Artificial Neural Network (ANN [26]). The addresses were classified into one of five categories. The models were implemented on the application programming interface provided by sklearn [27] and Tensorflow [28]. The ANN model comprised one input layer having 80 features, one hidden layers with 50 nodes, and one output layer.

3.4   Training and Testing of the Machine-Learning Models

After extracting the relevant address features, we trained our supervised-learning classification algorithms on the assigned labels. When the training phase was complete, the classification model could distinguish the associated feature values for each category. During the test phase, the classifier predicted where the classification of each address in the test set belonged using trained classifiers. To determine whether the model trained the training set well to enable the derivation of the correct classification results, we measured accuracy by comparing the initial labels with those predicted by the models. Fig. 5 shows the results of the trained machine-learning.

lifetime_recv	lifetime_total	init_trns_block	init_recv_block	curr_trns_block	curr_recv_block	label	predicted
28610	28610	-1	577060	-1	577060	0	0
81636	61	520045	519984	520045	519984	2	2
-1	349145	256237	-1	256237	-1	4	4
371568	76	233367	233291	233367	233291	4	4
26277	26277	-1	466699	-1	492976	2	2
153551	7747	456638	448891	456638	448891	3	3
143460	143460	-1	458148	-1	458148	2	2
-1	380784	224025	-1	224025	-1	4	4
-1	46194	558509	-1	558509	-1	0	3
169877	169977	-1	432065	1	122805	1	3
70557	70557	-1	531063	-1	531063	2	2
3716	3716	-1	548163	-1	551879	2	0
157921	157921	-1	444491	-1	444491	3	3
-1	33363	572057	-1	572057	-1	0	2
10887	10887	-1	595312	-1	595312	0	0
-1	378697	226127	-1	226127	-1	4	4
21590	21590	-1	584357	-1	584357	0	0
4763	4763	-1	438068	-1	442831	3	3
114093	114093	-1	493579	-1	493579	0	0
192875	192875	-1	408968	-1	408968	1	1

Fig. 5. Prediction results of the test set

4   Experiments and Results

4.1   Data Set Configuration

We collected several transactions for each category, and the number of addresses extracted from each transaction differed per category (See Fig. 6). The total extracted addresses was 18M, and, owing to hardware limitations, all data could not be trained. Therefore, the experiments were conducted by randomly selecting datasets. We set the datasets to different sizes to test the model and conducted the experiments several times. Prior to training, we defined the size of the training and test sets. The training:test split was set to 60:40 for each experimental dataset.

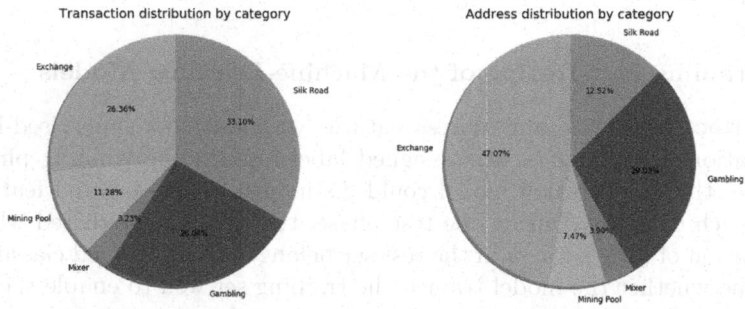

Fig. 6. Distribution ratio of transactions and addresses

4.2   Evaluation

Feature Importance. We investigated feature importance [29], of which 80 features most affected classification performance. We did not measure the feature importance of all datasets because of hardware limitations. Therefore, we collected 2,000 data items per category and examined feature performances of 10,000 datasets. Figure 7(a) shows the top 10 features that were most important. Figure 7(b) shows the importance of the top-20 features of the 80.

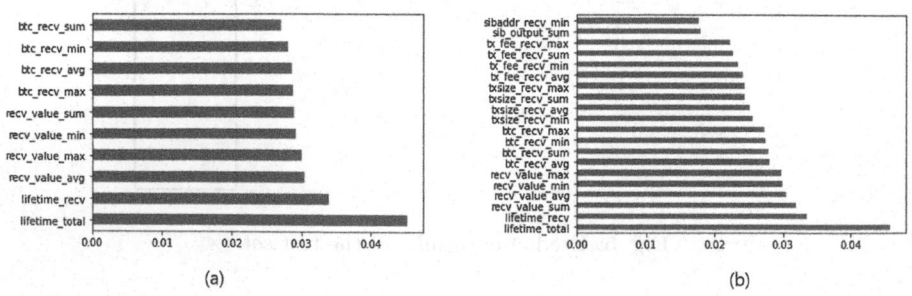

Fig. 7. Feature Importance; (a) the top 10 features (b) the top 20 features

The experimental results showed that the characteristics related to bitcoin reception were greatly affected. This can be attributed to the fact that the received address occupied a large part of the collected dataset. Lifetime was the most influential feature and indicated whether the address was used continuously and how long it was active. When a service having the same address is repeatedly used, it has a relatively long lifetime. Additionally, the second-most important feature was the amount of bitcoin received by the address. The third-most important feature was the total amount of bitcoin received by the transaction generated when the address received the bitcoin. The size of the transaction and the transaction fee had the greatest impact on the classification model.

Classification Performance Comparison. After training the extracted data, we used the two models to classify addresses. We repeated the experiment several times using different dataset sizes from the five categories, and we checked the differences of performance according to dataset size. We measured the accuracy as a performance index and checked whether the classification was well done using precision, recall, and F1 score values [30–32].

Random Forest Classifier: We randomly selected 1,000 to 200,000 data items for each category. Therefore, the accuracy of the random forest classifier was measured by setting the total dataset between 5,000 and 1,000,000. As a result of the experiments, we found that the accuracy increased steadily as the size of the dataset increased (Table 5). Our experiments showed an accuracy of ~0.84, and it is expected that the accuracy could be better if dataset size were extended.

Table 6 shows the precision, recall, and F1 scores of the results of the experiment from 200,000 data items for each category. These values show how well the classification was done for each category. In particular, in the case of the address corresponding to Silk Road, the scores had a value of 1.0, indicating that the address corresponding to Silk Road was well classified without error.

Table 5. Accuracy of the random forest classifier

Each data set	Accuracy
1000	0.741
3000	0.782
5000	0.789
10000	0.804
30000	0.825
50000	0.833
100000	0.838
200000	0.844

Table 6. Performance of random forest classifier by category

Category	Precision	Recall	F1-score
Exchange	0.82	0.74	0.78
Mining pool	0.86	0.85	0.86
Mixer	0.78	0.86	0.82
Gambling	0.77	0.77	0.77
Silk Road	1.0	1.0	1.0

ANN Model: We randomly selected 10,000 to 30,000 data items for each category to evaluate the ANN model. The total datasets were set from 50,000 to 150,000. The results are shown in Table 7. In the case of ANN, accuracy and F1 score were relatively lower than those of the random forest classifier. This shows that the result was not related to the increase of the size of the dataset, and the highest accuracy was 64%. Although the addresses associated with Silk Road were nearly as precisely classified as the random forest classifier, the mixer and gambling-related addresses were only classified at ~50% (Table 8).

Table 7. Accuracy of the ANN

Each data set	Accuracy
10000	0.646
20000	0.620
30000	0.614

Table 8. Performance of ANN by category

Category	Precision	Recall	F1-score
Exchange	0.62	0.52	0.56
Mining pool	0.77	0.56	0.65
Mixer	0.45	0.45	0.45
Gambling	0.51	0.46	0.48
Silk Road	0.99	0.98	0.99

5   Concluding Remarks

We classified various categories of bitcoin addresses using machine learning-based classification models. A transaction list was collected and sorted by five categories: exchange, mining pool, mixer, gambling, darknet. The associated bitcoin addresses were obtained from the transaction list. By extracting 80 features of bitcoin addresses and learning those extracted from the classification model, we successfully classified specific addresses. We used random forest and ANN algorithms as classification models, and the accuracy of random forest was 84%, which was relatively higher than that of ANN. We confirmed that the bitcoin addresses related to Silk Road were very well classified by both models.

There were some limitations to the study. First, the proposed ANN model delivered a low F1 score compared to the random forest classifier. This limitation might be overcome by adopting machine-learning based techniques. We could increase performance by adjusting the number of hidden layers or nodes. It is also possible to reevaluate the performance by training the model using characteristics having high importance without using all 80 extracted characteristics. We also could apply other available deep-learning methods. Second, the obtained transaction data had already been labeled prior to acquisition. The test dataset in our experiments was not exposed during model learning, but it might have been previously trained by similar algorithms through forum site we refered. In other words, the test dataset might have been exposed to a similar model. Because we obtained the test set using the same method as the training set, it may have been overfitted. Therefore, if we were to test the model on incoming/live transactions from the Bitcoin network, the measured F1 score might be lower than the experimental values reported here.

We should next predict address classifications associated with certain transactions by applying the proposed methodology while predicting the category of transactions by applying majority voting to the results. In future work, we plan to access the dark nets and collect a transaction list on currently operating sites, because the Silk Road has been closed for years. Then, we plan to apply the proposed methodology to check whether the addresses related to dark net markets are accurately classified and to check whether transactions are generated for those markets by adopting majority voting. Furthermore, we plan to predict whether a transaction is legal depending on the category of transaction.

Acknowledgments. This work was supported by the ICT R&D program of MSIT/IITP. [No.2018-0-00539, Development of Blockchain Transaction Monitoring and Analysis Technology].

References

1. Nakamoto, S., et al. Bitcoin: a peer-to-peer electronic cash system (2008)
2. Swan, M.: Blockchain: Blueprint for a New Economy. O'Reilly Media Inc., Newton (2015)
3. Harvey, C.R.: Bitcoin myths and facts. Available at SSRN 2479670 (2014)
4. Bitcoin Magazine: Bitcoin magazine: bitcoin news, bitcoin charts, events. https:// bitcoinmagazine.com/articles/darknet-markets-cant-live-with-or-without-bitcoin
5. Chainalysis. Chainalysis: The blockchain analysis company. https://www. chainalysis.com/
6. Wikipedia: Silk road (marketplace). https://en.wikipedia.org/wiki/Silk_Road_ (marketplace)

7. Wood, G., et al.: Ethereum: a secure decentralised generalised transaction ledger. Ethereum project yellow paper **151**(2014), 1–32 (2014)
8. Monero: Zero to monero. Technical report (2018). https://www.getmonero.org/library/Zero-to-Monero-1-0-0.pdf
9. Kotsiantis, S.B., Zaharakis, I., Pintelas, P.: Supervised machine learning: a review of classification techniques. Emerging artificial intelligence applications in computer engineering **160**, 3–24 (2007)
10. Brands, S.: Rethinking Public Key Infrastructures and Digital Certificates: Building in Privacy. MIT Press, Cambridge (2000)
11. Fischer, A.M.: Public key/signature cryptosystem with enhanced digital signature certification, US Patent 4,868,877, September 19 1989
12. Zambre, D., Shah, A.: Analysis of bitcoin network dataset for fraud. Unpublished Report (2013)
13. Bitcoin.com: Bitcoin history part 11: the first major loss of coins. https://news.bitcoin.com/bitcoin-history-part-11-the-first-major-loss-of-coins/
14. Techcrunch: Binance says more than $40 million in bitcoin stolen in ? Large scale??Hack. https://techcrunch.com/2019/05/07/binance-breach/
15. Hartigan, J.A., Wong, M.A.: Algorithm as 136: a k-means clustering algorithm. J. Roy. Stat. Soc.: Ser. C (Appl. Stat.) **28**(1), 100–108 (1979)
16. Toyoda, K., Ohtsuki, T., Mathiopoulos, P.T.: Identification of high yielding investment programs in bitcoin via transactions pattern analysis. In: GLOBECOM 2017–2017 IEEE Global Communications Conference, pp. 1–6. IEEE (2017)
17. Kanemura, K., Toyoda, K., Ohtsuki, T.: Identification of darknet markets??Bitcoin addresses by voting per-address classification results. In: 2019 IEEE International Conference on Blockchain and Cryptocurrency (ICBC), pp. 154–158. IEEE (2019)
18. Wikipedia: Darknet market. https://en.m.wikipedia.org/wiki/Darknet_market
19. Lin, Y., Wu, P., Hsu, C., Tu, I., Liao, S.: An evaluation of bitcoin address classification based on transaction history summarization. In: 2019 IEEE International Conference on Blockchain and Cryptocurrency (ICBC), pp. 302–310 (2019)
20. Lee, C., Maharjan, S., Ko, K., Hong, J.W.-K.: Toward detecting illegal transactions on bitcoin using machine-learning methods. In: Zheng, Z., Dai, H.-N., Tang, M., Chen, X. (eds.) BlockSys 2019. CCIS, vol. 1156, pp. 520–533. Springer, Singapore (2020). https://doi.org/10.1007/978-981-15-2777-7_42
21. WalletExplorer: Walletexplorer: smart bitcoin block explorer. https://www.walletexplorer.com/
22. BeautifulSoup: Beautiful soup documentation. Technical report. https://www.crummy.com/software/BeautifulSoup/bs4/doc/
23. Bitcoin.org: Bitcoin core. https://bitcoin.org/en/bitcoin-core/
24. Bitcoin.org: Bitcoin core json apis. https://bitcoin.org/en/developer-reference#bitcoin-core-apis
25. Pal, M.: Random forest classifier for remote sensing classification. Int. J. Remote Sens. **26**(1), 217–222 (2005)
26. Zurada, J.M.: Introduction to Artificial Neural Systems, vol. 8. West Publishing Company, St. Paul (1992)
27. Scikit learn.org: Scikit-learn: machine learning in Python. https://scikit-learn.org/
28. Tensorflow.org: Tensorflow: an end-to-end open source machine learning platform. https://www.tensorflow.org/?hl=en
29. Kursa, M.B., Rudnicki, W.R., et al.: Feature selection with the Boruta package. J. Stat. Softw. **36**(11), 1–13 (2010)

30. Davis, J., Goadrich, M.: The relationship between precision-recall and ROC curves. In: Proceedings of the 23rd International Conference on Machine Learning, pp. 233–240. ACM (2006)
31. Powers, D.M.: Evaluation: from precision, recall and f-measure to ROC, informedness, markedness and correlation (2011)
32. Goutte, C., Gaussier, E.: A probabilistic interpretation of precision, recall and f-score, with implication for evaluation. In: Losada, D.E., Fernández-Luna, J.M. (eds.) Advances in Information Retrieval. ECIR 2005. LNCS, pp. 345–359. Springer, Heidelberg (2005). https://doi.org/10.1007/978-3-540-31865-1_25

Deciphering Cryptocurrencies by Reverse Analyzing on Smart Contracts

Xiangping Chen[2], Queping Kong[1], Hao-Nan Zhu[1], Yixin Zhang[1],
Yuan Huang[1(✉)], and Zigui Jiang[1(✉)]

[1] School of Data and Computer Science, Sun Yat-sen University,
Guangzhou 510006, China
huangyjn@gmail.com, jiangzg3@mail.sysu.edu.cn
[2] Guangdong Key Laboratory for Big Data Analysis and Simulation of Public
Opinion, School of Communication and Design, Sun Yat-sen University,
Guangzhou 510006, China

Abstract. As the initial application of blockchain, Bitcoin is the most famous blockchain application as cryptocurrency and it has led to a misconception that blockchain can only be used to issue cryptocurrency. Meanwhile, the growing number of companies and organizations issuing their own cryptocurrencies based on blockchain has led to more confirmation that the main role of blockchain is to be used to issue cryptocurrency. However, blockchain is originally intended to achieve decentralized application, and cryptocurrency is just a byproduct of it. In this paper, we figured out how many smart contracts on Ethereum are involved issuing cryptocurrency, how many people are using these smart contracts and what is the revenue status of these smart contracts. To address these question, we collect more than 140,000 open source smart contracts and 16 million closed source smart contracts from Ethereum, and then identify the smart contracts that involve issuing cryptocurrency (called IC-contract) by determining whether the contract implements ERC20 standard. For the closed source smart contracts, we propose a reverse hash mapping method to determine the IC-contract at bytecode level. Additionally, we also obtain the transactions of all the IC-contracts and find that the open source IC-contracts have more users. Analyzing the IC-contracts based on transactions reveals that most of the IC-contracts have exceptionally low user activity, but most of them are profitable actually.

Keywords: Blockchain · Cryptocurrency · Bitcoin · Smart contract · Hash mapping

1 Introduction

As the first application of the blockchain, Bitcoin [1] has attracted much wider attention by the public. The market value of the Bitcoin reaches $149 billion until October 2019, and a single Bitcoin is worth more than $8,000. The Bitcoin blockchain data occupied more than 300G with the number continuing to

© Springer Nature Singapore Pte Ltd. 2020
Z. Zheng et al. (Eds.): BlockSys 2020, CCIS 1267, pp. 532–546, 2020.
https://doi.org/10.1007/978-981-15-9213-3_41

grow. Due to the popularity of Bitcoin, the public's initial understanding of blockchain technology is limited to Bitcoin [2], as well as Bitcoin is a kind of cryptocurrency, then the public equates the role of blockchain technology with issuing cryptocurrency.

Meanwhile, the proliferation of cryptocurrencies by various companies and organizations has reinforced the belief that blockchain technology is "equivalent" to issuing cryptocurrency. The popular cryptocurrencies include Bitcoin, Ether (Ethereum), EOS, LiteCoin, Ripple and Dash, etc. [3]. The big companies that have issued their cryptocurrencies include: Facebook, J. P Morgan, Bitmain, etc. Meanwhile, many small companies are also issuing even more cryptocurrencies. According to incomplete statistics, there are more than 4,000 cryptocurrencies[1]. Therefore, the public is increasingly convinced that blockchain technology is used to issue cryptocurrencies owe to the proliferation of cryptocurrencies.

However, blockchain, as an emerging technology, is originally proposed to eliminate centralization issue. To achieve the goal of decentralization, Satoshi Nakamoto came up with the idea of storing the ledger on a decentralized p2p network with consensus across the participants to keep consistent [1]. Participants are encouraged to write to the ledger with digital token as the rewards, which is known as cryptocurrency. Therefore, cryptocurrency is a means to encourage miners to work on the blockchain, which is just a byproduct of decentralization.

With the evolution of blockchain, blockchain technology has evolved from the original decentralized platform (such as Bitcoin) to a programmable decentralized platform (such as Ethereum). On Ethereum, users can customize smart contracts to suit their needs, and the smart contracts expand the functionality and usability of blockchain [4–6]. Users can issue their own cryptocurrencies, so-called tokens by implementing ERC20 standard [7] on smart contract. Ethereum community published the ERC20 standard to enable easier Initial Coin Offerings (i.e. ICO) [8].

Therefore, there are two types of cryptocurrencies in the market, i.e., one is the token implementing the ERC20 standard on Ethereum, and another one is the native asset of a blockchain [9], such as Bitcoin, Litecoin, XRP, EOS, etc. We call the smart contract implementing the ERC20 as IC-contract. Because the token cryptocurrency may rise expensive market values, the public is keen to issue one. Therefore, there are so many token cryptocurrencies in the market. We mainly focus on the token cryptocurrency in this paper, then the cryptocurrency in the remaining part of this paper refers to the token.

Although both the information of cryptocurrencies and smart contracts can be found in professional websites (e.g., CoinMarketCap (See footnote 1) and Etherscan[2]), many open questions remain: How many IC-contracts on the blockchain? How many people are using these cryptocurrencies? Are these cryptocurrencies traded frequently? What is the profit and loss status of the cryptocurrencies? Addressing these questions is meaningful to all stakeholders, end-users, developers and researchers.

---

[1] https://coinmarketcap.com/.
[2] https://etherscan.io/.

To answer these questions and more, this paper initiates the study of the IC-contracts on the Ethereum. With data of all the smart contracts (i.e., both of open source and closed source) from the Ethereum, we are able to measure the amount of the IC-contracts, the amount of users of the IC-contracts, and the revenue status of the IC-contracts, etc. To determine whether a closed source smart contract participates in issuing cryptocurrency, we propose a reverse hash mapping method that determines whether the contract involves the hash code of the ERC20 interface, and further analyze the characters of the IC-contract from its bytecode level. We also collect all the transactions from Ethereum to analyze the users and the profit and loss status of the IC-contracts. Our empirical studies show that 27.95% of open source contracts are IC-contracts, while only 0.93% closed source contracts are IC-contracts. In addition, more than 24% open source IC-contracts and 40% closed source IC-contracts have no user, the number of profitable IC-contracts is greater than that of losing IC-contracts.

This paper contributes the following:

- We are the first to perform a large-scale empirical study of cryptocurrencies from the perspective of smart contracts.
- We propose a reverse hash mapping approach to decode the function name at bytecode level.
- The empirical study reveals that the open source IC-contracts have more users.
- We also found that most of the IC-contracts are Less active but profitable.

The rest of this paper is organized as follows. Section 2 introduces background of cryptocurrencies and DApps. Section 3 presents the empirical study setup. The empirical results are shown in Sect. 4. Section 5 overviews the related works. Section 6 summarizes our study and outlines directions for future studies.

2   Background

In this section, we briefly introduce the background on ERC20 standard and blockchain-based decentralized applications, i.e., DApp.

2.1   ERC20

The potential use of Ethereum has increased endlessly due to its programmable character, i.e., smart contract [4,10,11]. To facilitate people create their own cryptocurrency, Ethereum introduces a token standard, i.e., ERC20. It was first proposed by Vitalik Buterin (a co-founder of Ethereum), then discussed and passed by the community. Users should adhere ERC20 if they want to create a smart contract to support the cryptocurrency on the Ethereum. ERC20 defines the main features of the cryptocurrency, such as token name, token abbreviation, and the maximum number of cryptocurrency that can be supported, as well as defining the query method and so on. If a contract want to implement the ERC20 interface, it needs to implement the 6 functions, i.e., `totalSupply()`, `balanceOf()`, `transfer()`, `transferFrom()`, `approve()`, `allowance()`, as shown in following. For a smart contract conform to ERC20, it will provide basic functionality to transfer tokens, as well as allow tokens to be approved so they can be spent by another on-chain third party.

Because of ERC20 standard, any company or individual can issue their own cryptocurrencies through implementing the ERC20 interface [7]. As a result, the cryptocurrencies have proliferated on Ethereum, and these cryptocurrencies circulate and serve all walks of life in society.

```
contract ERC20{
        function totalSupply() external view returns (uint256);
        function balanceOf(address account) external view returns (uint256);
        function transfer(address recipient, uint256 amount) external returns (bool);
        function allowance(address owner, address spender) external view returns...;
        function approve(address spender, uint256 amount) external returns (bool);
        function transferFrom(address sender, address recipient, uint256 amount)...;
        event Transfer(address indexed from, address indexed to, uint256 value);
        event Approval(address indexed owner, address indexed spender, uint256 ...);
}
```

People can learn about the common information of the cryptocurrencies from many websites, such as CoinMarketCap (See footnote 1), CoinGecko[3], and Binance[4]. These websites show detailed information such as the rankings, price tendency, market capitalization of the cryptocurrencies to public. But from a macro perspective people can get little knowledge about the market of the cryptocurrency, such as the profit and loss status, the activity level and the user profile of the overall cryptocurrency market. This information is important to get the whole story of the cryptocurrency market, especially for investors and researchers. To fill this gap, we empirically study the cryptocurrencies in this paper, and reveal the full picture of current cryptocurrencies on the Ethereum.

2.2 DApps

A decentralized application, i.e., DApp generally consists of two parts: web pages as front end, and smart contracts as back end. The front end is written in HTML, CSS, JavaScript, etc., and the back end is written in Solidity [12]. The key data and operations are kept in back end in a blockchain. DApps interact with smart contracts by transactions, namely contract requests, and provide services based on them.

Since the back end of a DApp is publicly run on the blockchain and the data cannot be modified easily, DApps have been widely adopted in different areas and trusted by more and more users [12]. The DApps can be found in some public websites, such as DappRadar[5] and StateOfTheDapps[6]. Each of them collects

---

[3] https://www.coingecko.com/en.
[4] https://info.binance.com/en.
[5] https://dappradar.com/.
[6] https://www.stateofthedapps.com/zh.

many decentralized applications and DApp developers can submit their DApps to the website and get them published. It is free and provides many services for users and developers, such as filtering DApps and user discussions.

3   Empirical Study Setup

3.1   Research Questions

RQ1: How many smart contracts are the IC-contracts on the blockchain?

IC-contracts are a special kind of smart contracts because they can be used to issue cryptocurrencies. The scale of the IC-contracts over the time on the Ethereum may show the rise and fall of the cryptocurrencies in history.

RQ2: How many people are using these cryptocurrencies?

To understand how prosperous the cryptocurrency market is today, we need to look at the acceptance level of the cryptocurrencies by the public and how many people are using them, and how active those users are.

RQ3: What is the revenue status of these cryptocurrencies?

Transaction is one of the most important features of the cryptocurrency, which means the cryptocurrency is transferred from one user to another. Then, the profit and loss status of the cryptocurrencies can be reflected by the transactions of the cryptocurrency.

3.2   Dataset Collection

Smart contract can be divided into open source and closed source categories. Open source contracts allow any user to download their source code while closed source contracts only provide bytecode. To identify the IC-contracts from all the smart contracts, we need firstly download all the open source and closed source smart contracts. We download the open source contracts from the Etherscan (See footnote 2), which is an blockchain browser supported by Ethereum, and it provides the real-time transaction query.

Blockchain can be considered as a ledger [13]. Because the transactions are validated by each blockchain peer, each blockchain peer can trust the ledger that maintained by himself. Thanks to the completeness of the ledger in each blockchain peer, researchers can run a blockchain peer to get all the data in the blockchain. Therefore, to collect the closed source smart contracts, we set up a blockchain node locally and through the JSON-RPC interfaces of parity, we can obtain the data in Ethereum blockchain. Table 1 shows the total number of open source and closed source smart contracts we collected.

We collect all the block data on the Ethereum. Each block consists of two parts: header and transaction. Block header contains basic information of a block, including the block hash, miner's address, timestamp, gas limit. Block transaction includes a set of transactions with each transaction recording the addresses of the sender and receiver, transfer amount, etc., which allows us to further analyze the revenue status of the IC-contracts. We synchronize full copy

Table 1. The total number of smart contracts

Open source	Closed source
147,218	16,594,370

of Ethereum before July 6, 2019 on Ethereum and the latest block number we synchronized is 8,099,999, with more than 1 billion transactions in total.

Meanwhile, to investigate the popularity of the IC-contracts in decentralized applications, we get several DApps from two open platforms, i.e., DappRadar (See footnote 5) and StateOfTheDapps (See footnote 6). Table 2 shows the total number of the contracts in DApps we collected. After dropping the duplication, there are 10,229 unique contracts in these two open platforms.

Table 2. The total number of the contracts in DApps

DappRadar	StateOfTheDapps	Unique
9,238	3,080	10,229

Although the smart contracts of the DApps are included in the open source and closed source contracts, we also separate them out for study. We do this for two reasons: firstly, DApp often has a graphical interface, then the threshold of operating DApp for user is lower than that of directly operating smart contracts, and this may led a difference in the user level. Secondly, most of the DApps are developed for Finance, Exchanges, and Gambling. Then, the IC-contracts in DApps may show different performance in the transactions when comparing with the general smart contracts.

3.3 Methodology

IC-contract Identification. Because one IC-contract should implement the ERC20 interface, then a IC-contract contains the 6 functions, i.e., `totalSupply()`, `balanceOf()`, `transfer()`, `allowance()`, `approve()`, `transferFrom()`. For the open source smart contracts, we can directly determine whether a contract implements the ERC20 interface by checking the 6 functions in their source code. However, it is different to determine whether a closed source contract implements the ERC20 interface because we can only get the bytecode of the closed source contract, which take the majority part in Ethereum.

To overcome the, we proposed a reverse hash mapping approach to determine whether a contract implements the ERC20 interface. Each function will be hashed when a smart contract is compiled into the bytecode, and the 6 functions of the ERC20 interface are hashed too. Then, we can determine whether a closed source contract implements the ERC20 interface by checking whether the bytecode of the contract contains the hash code of the 6 ERC20 functions.

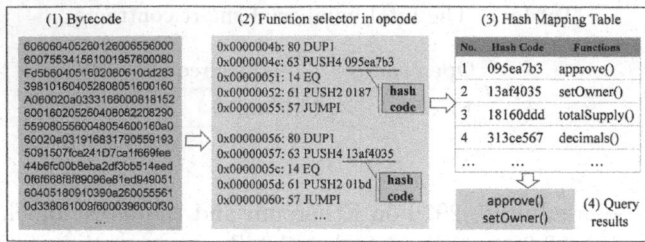

Fig. 1. The overview of our approach

We have collected the bytecode of all the closed source IC-contracts, and the bytecode of a IC-contract is hexadecimal string, which makes it difficult to know exactly what functions are defined inside a IC-contracts, as shown in the step 1 of Fig. 1. To overcome this issue, we employ the disassembler to convert bytecode to opcode, which is a low-level programming language of EVM, similar to assembly language. Then, we locate the function selector in the opcode which lists the hash code and memory addresses of all the functions defined in a IC-contract [14]. Therefore, we can get the hash code of all the functions via statically analyzing as the string with red underline shown in the step 2 of Fig. 1. At last, we can determine whether a closed source contract implements ERC20 interface by checking the hash mapping table, as shown in the step 3 of Fig. 1. It is noticeable that a closed source contract is regarded as IC-contract only if it contains all the 6 ERC20 function hash codes. Table 3 show the mapping relationships between the 6 ERC20 functions and their hash code.

Table 3. The hash mapping table

Functions	Hash Code
totalSupply()	0x18160ddd
balanceOf(address)	0x70a08231
transfer(address,uint256)	0xa9059cbb
allowance(address,address)	0xdd62ed3e
approve(address,uint256)	0x095ea7b3
transferFrom(address,address,uint256)	0x23b872dd

Transaction Extraction. For the analyzing of the revenue status of the users and the IC-contracts, it is needed to extract the transactions involved by the IC-contracts. Then, we calculate the profit and loss status of a user or a IC-contract from their transactions. Specifically, to calculate the profit and loss status of a user with a specific IC-contract, we firstly get all the transactions between the user and the IC-contract by their addresses, and then compute the user's revenue by amount the user receives from the IC-contract and the amount that he pays to the IC-contract. Similarly, the revenue of a IC-contract equals to the amount it receives minus the amount that it pays.

Sampling Closed Source Contracts. More than 99% smart contracts in Ethereum are closed source. If we analyze all the transactions of all the closed source contracts, there will be close to a billion transaction records, which will pose considerable challenges to our computing resources. Therefore, we randomly sample closed source contracts for analysis. At the same time, we should ensure that the sampled closed source contracts contain at least as many IC-contracts as open source contracts, because only in this way we can analyze the IC-contract in open source and closed source contracts on the same order of magnitude.

4   Empirical Study Results

4.1   RQ1: How Many Smart Contracts Are the IC-contracts on the Blockchain?

We identify the IC-contracts over the time from the open source and closed source smart contracts, as well as DApps. The overall distributions of IC-contracts in the three categories are shown in Fig. 2, and the blue lines represent the IC-contracts that implement the ERC20 interface, while red lines represent all the contracts. We count the number of newly released contracts every 15 days.

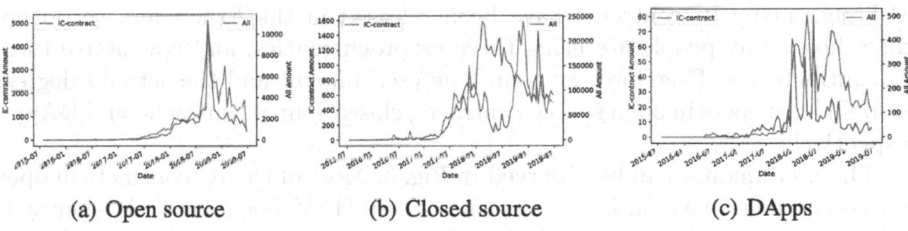

(a) Open source   (b) Closed source   (c) DApps

Fig. 2. The number of the IC-contracts (Color figure online)

There are 147,218 open source smart contracts in total, and we detect 41,160 IC-contracts from them, and IC-contracts account for 27.95% of all open source contracts. Figure 2 (a) shows the distributions of the IC-contracts and all the smart contracts in the history (It is worth noting that the scales of the vertical axis on the left and right sides of Fig. 2 (a) are different). It is obvious that the distribution of IC-contracts well fit the open source smart contracts on the timeline. We can observe from Fig. 2 (a) that when open source contracts are at their peak, IC-contracts are also at their peak.

Because there are 41,160 IC-contracts in open source smart contracts, we need to sample a certain number of closed source contracts so that they can contain about forty thousand IC-contracts. To do that, we firstly randomly sample

1% closed source contracts and found there are almost 1% closed source contracts are the IC-contracts. Then, according to this ratio, we randomly sample 4,500,000 closed source contracts, and detect 41,831 IC-contracts from them. The sampled contracts account for 27.12% of all closed source contracts, and the IC-contracts account for 0.93% of all the sampled contracts. This result shows that the proportion of IC-contracts in closed source contracts is much lower than that in open source contracts. Meanwhile, we can observe that the distribution of IC-contracts over the time does not fit the closed source smart contracts very well in Fig. 2 (b). For example, around July 2018, the creation of closed source contracts reaches a peak, but the creation of IC-contracts falls into a trough.

Meanwhile, we count the number of IC-contracts contained in the DApps. There are 10,229 smart contracts in the DApps, in which we detect 791 IC-contracts. These IC-contracts account for 7.73% of all the contracts in DApps. Figure 2 (c) shows that the distribution of IC-contracts basically fit the contracts of DApps on the timeline.

In summary, the number of IC-contracts in the open source smart contracts and DApps is much higher than that in the closed source contracts. It may be explained that in order to make the cryptocurrency more acceptable to the public, the contract owners need to open their code so that the public can have more confidence when investing the cryptocurrency.

4.2   RQ2: How Many People Are Using These Cryptocurrencies?

Although many IC-contracts have been released in the Ethereum, we do not know how many people are using these cryptocurrencies, and how active these IC-contracts are. Therefore, we count the user amount and the activity degrees of the IC-contracts in open source contracts, closed source contracts, and DApps, respectively.

The user amount can be observed in Fig. 3. Most of the IC-contracts in open source contracts have no users, i.e., more than 24.8% open source IC-contracts

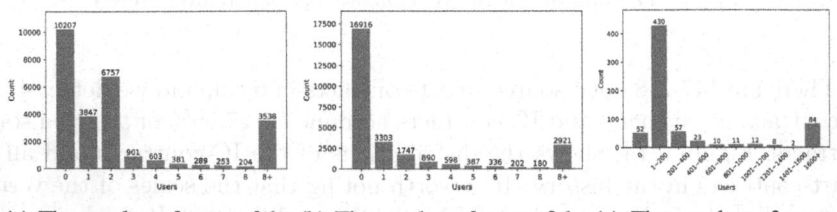

(a) The number of users of the open source IC-contracts

(b) The number of users of the closed source IC-contracts

(c) The number of users of the IC-contracts in DApps

Fig. 3. The number of the users of the IC-contracts

have no user (i.e., 10,207). In addition, most of the open source IC-contracts have only one or two users, and the proportion of such IC-contracts accounts for 25.76% of all open source IC-contracts. Only 8.6% of the open source IC-contracts have more than 8 users.

Similarly, more than 40% closed source IC-contracts have no user (i.e., 16,916), and only 6.98% of the closed source IC-contracts have more than 8 users. Different from the open source and closed source IC-contracts, the user base of the IC-contracts in DApps is much larger. Meanwhile, the user distribution of the IC-contracts in DApps is also different, and there are fewer contracts with no user, and most of the IC-contracts in DApps have 1 to 200 users. More than 10% IC-contracts have at least 1,600 users. This result is in line with our conjecture, i.e., DApp lowers the threshold of operating smart contract and it can attract more users to join it.

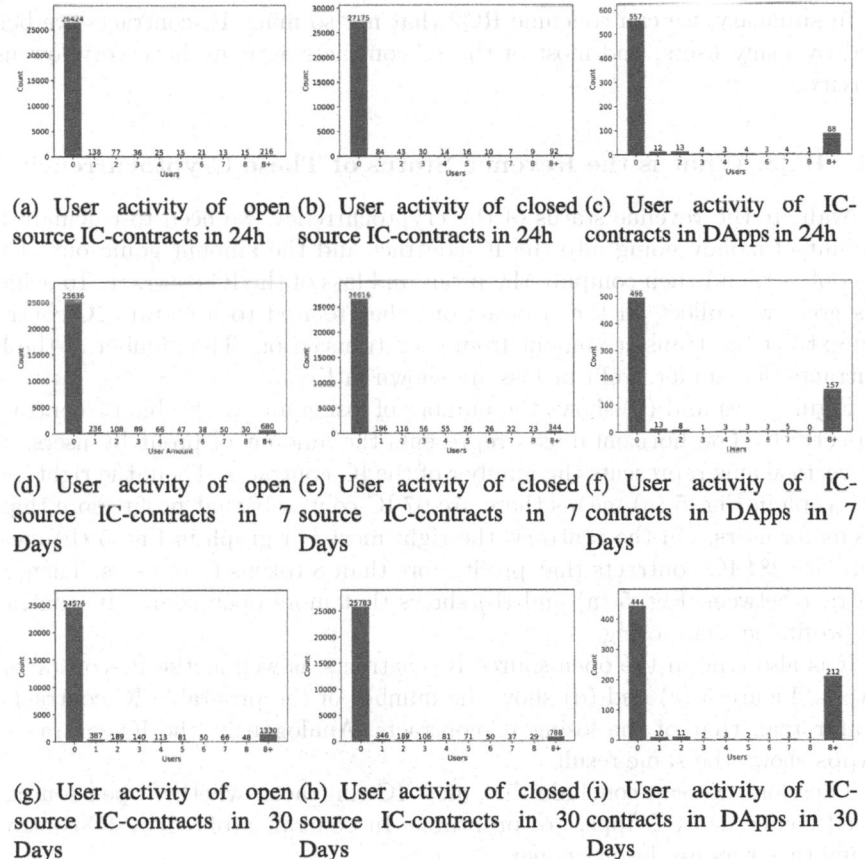

(a) User activity of open source IC-contracts in 24h

(b) User activity of closed source IC-contracts in 24h

(c) User activity of IC-contracts in DApps in 24h

(d) User activity of open source IC-contracts in 7 Days

(e) User activity of closed source IC-contracts in 7 Days

(f) User activity of IC-contracts in DApps in 7 Days

(g) User activity of open source IC-contracts in 30 Days

(h) User activity of closed source IC-contracts in 30 Days

(i) User activity of IC-contracts in DApps in 30 Days

Fig. 4. The activity degrees of the IC-contracts

The transaction amount can reflect activity of the IC-contracts. We count the number of the transactions of the IC-contracts within the last 24 h, the last 7 days, and the last month, respectively. These times are calculated from 8:00 pm on July 6, 2019.

Figure 4 (a), (b) and (c) show the activity of the three types of IC-contracts in the last 24 h. The horizontal axis shows the number of the transaction amount, while the vertical axis represents the number of IC-contracts involving the certain number of transactions. As the results show, most of the open source and closed source IC-contracts involve no transactions, and a small part of IC-contracts in DApps involve 1 to 2 transactions. In contrast, there are 88 IC-contracts in DApps involve more than 8 transactions in the last 24 h.

Similar tendency can be observed in the transactions of the last 7 days and 30 days. Namely, most of the open source and closed source IC-contracts involve no transactions, while more IC-contracts in DApps involve more transactions if the time range is stretched.

In summary, we can conclude RQ2 that not so much IC-contracts are being used by many users, and most of the IC-contracts actually have very low user activity.

4.3   RQ3: What is the Revenue Status of These Cryptocurrencies?

To evaluate the revenue status of the cryptocurrency, we need to calculate the amount of money going into the IC-contract and the amount going out of the IC-contract, and then compute the profit and loss of the IC-contract. To achieve this goal, we collect all the transactions that related to a certain IC-contract and extract the transfer amount from each transaction. The number of the IC-contracts that under profit or loss are shown in Fig. 5.

Figure 5 (a) and (b) shows the number of losing and profitable IC-contracts, respectively. The horizontal axis represents the amount of profit by users, and the vertical axis represents the number of the IC-contracts. Then, the right most bar graph in Fig. 5 (a) means there are 67 IC-contracts that profit more than 8 tokens for users. On the contrary, the right most bar graph in Fig. 5 (b) means there are 284 IC-contracts that profit more than 8 tokens from users. Then, the contrast between Fig. 5 (a) and (b) shows that more open source IC-contracts are profitable than losing.

It is also true in the open source IC-contracts as well as the IC-contracts in DApps. Figure 5 (c) and (d) show the number of the profitable IC-contracts is greater than that of the losing IC-contracts. Analogously, the IC-contracts in DApps shows the same result.

Therefore, we can conclude that most IC-contracts, whether open source or closed source or in DApps, are profitable. In general, profited by IC-contracts means the users are losing money.

Therefore, we can conclude RQ3 that most IC-contracts, whether open source or closed source or in DApps, are profitable. In general, profited by IC-contracts means the users are losing money.

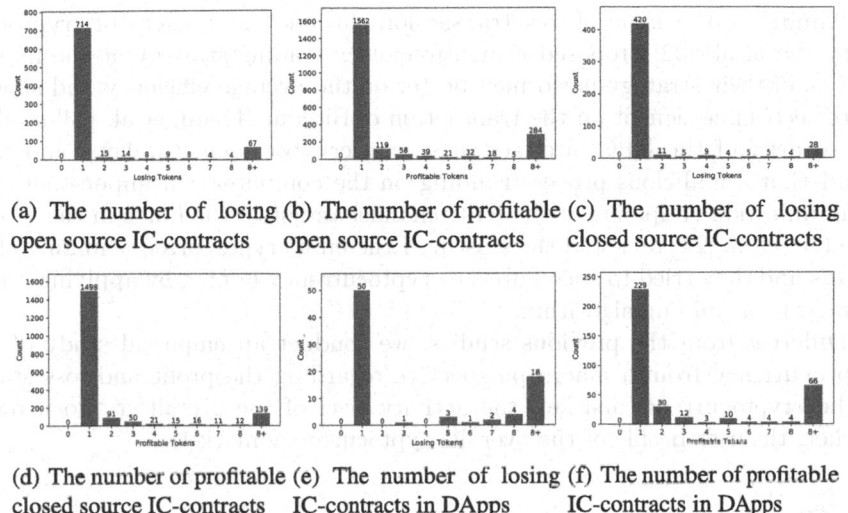

(a) The number of losing open source IC-contracts

(b) The number of profitable open source IC-contracts

(c) The number of losing closed source IC-contracts

(d) The number of profitable closed source IC-contracts

(e) The number of losing IC-contracts in DApps

(f) The number of profitable IC-contracts in DApps

Fig. 5. The revenue status of the IC-contracts

5 Related Works

In this section, we briefly review related studies. We review some previous empirical studies on cryptocurrency.

There has been extensive work towards empirically understanding various aspects of the cryptocurrency ecosystem, from the economic perspective [15–18], the sociological perspective [3,19–21] to the ecosystem efficiency and safety [22–24].

Johnson et al. [15] developed an economic model to capture the short-term incentives of cryptocurrency exchanges, and their model can derive a conclusion regarding an exchange's optimal economic decision. Olga et al. [16] studied what type of asset is closer to the cryptocurrency, and estimated which traditional methods of assessing financial assets are applicable to the cryptocurrencies. Liang et al. [17] analyzed the dynamics and systemic risk of the cryptocurrency market based on the public available price history, and they revealed that the cryptocurrency market is relatively fragile and unstable. Lesya et al. [18] proposed a method for technical analysis of cryptocurrency price differences to achieve the maximum number of transactions with minimal losses.

In addition, some researchers analyze the cryptocurrencies from the sociological perspective. Shaista et al. [3,19] utilized topic model along with public opinion mining approach to analyze the users concerns and their sentiment analyses on the cryptocurrencies, blockchain network, bitcoin, litecoin, and ethereum. Kaminski et al. [20] gathered 140 days of tweets for sentiment analysis and used it as input to get the correlation between social sentiments and cryptocurrency price fluctuations. Polasik et al. [21] performed the lexicon-based sentiment analysis for bitcoin price prediction in English articles, and regression is used to measure the relationship between the tone of the articles and the bitcoin popularity factors.

Aiming at the issue of low transaction efficiency and safety of cryptocurrency, Vo et al. [22] proposed a high-frequency trading strategy at the minute level, and their strategy performed better on the average efficiency and show a better economic benefit on the transaction of Bitcoin. Thanh et al. [23] studied the security of the RPC interface in several cryptocurrency wallets, and they found that a malicious process running on the computer can impersonate the communication endpoints of the RPC channel and steal the funds in the wallet. Pavel V. et al. [24] reviewed the existing Ethereum cryptocurrency mining algorithms and they tried to speed up the cryptocurrency mining by applying a new asynchronous mining algorithm.

Different from the previous studies, we conduct an empirical study of the cryptocurrency from a macro perspective regarding the profit and loss status of the cryptocurrency market, the activity level of the overall cryptocurrency market, the user profile of the overall cryptocurrency market.

6   Conclusion

To uncover the real veil of the cryptocurrencies on the blockchain, we conduct an empirical study on the IC-contracts that implement the ERC20 interface. To identify the IC-contract from the closed source smart contracts, we propose a hash mapping approach to decode the function name at bytecode level. Our study on the millions of smart contracts shows that most of the open source IC-contracts have a critical mass of users when comparing with closed source ones. We also reveal that most of the IC-contracts have very low user activity, but most of them are in a profitable position. In the future, we will further consider more closed source IC-contracts to make our empirical research more sufficient.

Acknowledgments. This research is supported by the National Key R&D Program of China(2018YFB1004804), the Key-Area Research and Development Program of Guangdong Province (2020B010164002), National Natural Science Foundation of China (61902441), China Postdoctoral Science Foundation (2018M640855), Fundamental Research Funds for University-Young Teacher Training Project (20lgpy129).

References

1. Nakamoto, S.: Bitcoin: a peer-to-peer electronic cash system. Cryptography Mailing list at https://metzdowd.com. Accessed Mar 2009
2. Christidis, K., Devetsikiotis, M.: Blockchains and smart contracts for the internet of things. IEEE Access **4**, 2292–2303 (2016)
3. Bibi, S., Hussain, S., Faisal, M.I.: Public Perception Based Recommendation System for Cryptocurrency, pp. 661–665 (2019)
4. Nick, S.: The idea of smart contracts (1997). http://www.fon.hum.uva.nl/rob/Courses/InformationInSpeech/CDROM/Literature/LOTwinterschool2006/szabo.best.vwh.net/idea.html. Accessed 2008

5. Nguyen, H.-L., Ignat, C.-L., Perrin, O.: Trusternity: auditing transparent log server with blockchain. In: Companion Proceedings of the Web Conference 2018, WWW 2018. Republic and Canton of Geneva, Switzerland: International World Wide Web Conferences Steering Committee, pp. 79–80 (2018). https://doi.org/10.1145/3184558.3186938
6. Huang, Y., Kong, Q., Jia, N., Chen, X., Zheng, Z.: Recommending differentiated code to support smart contract update. In: Proceedings of the 27th International Conference on Program Comprehension, ICPC 2019, pp. 260–270. IEEE Press, Piscataway (2019). https://doi.org/10.1109/ICPC.2019.00045
7. Somin, S., Gordon, G., Altshuler, Y.: Network analysis of ERC20 tokens trading on ethereum blockchain. In: Morales, A.J., Gershenson, C., Braha, D., Minai, A.A., Bar-Yam, Y. (eds.) ICCS 2018. SPC, pp. 439–450. Springer, Cham (2018). https://doi.org/10.1007/978-3-319-96661-8_45
8. Zheng, P., Zheng, Z., Dai, H.N.: XBlock-ETH: Extracting and Exploring Blockchain Data From Ethereum (2019)
9. Chen, T., et al.: Tokenscope: automatically detecting inconsistent behaviors of cryptocurrency tokens in ethereum. In: Proceedings of the 2019 ACM SIGSAC Conference on Computer and Communications Security, CCS 2019, pp. 1503–1520. ACM, New York (2019). http://doi.acm.org/10.1145/3319535.3345664
10. Luu, L., Chu, D.-H., Olickel, H., Saxena, P., Hobor, A.: Making smart contracts smarter. In: Proceedings of the 2016 ACM SIGSAC Conference on Computer and Communications Security, CCS 2016, pp. 254–269. ACM, New York (2016). http://doi.acm.org/10.1145/2976749.2978309
11. Parizi, R.M., Amritraj, Dehghantanha A: Smart contract programming languages on blockchains: an empirical evaluation of usability and security. In: Chen, S., Wang, H., Zhang, L.J. (eds.) Blockchain. ICBC 2018, pp. 75–91. Springer, Cham (2018). https://doi.org/10.1007/978-3-319-94478-4_6
12. Gao, J., et al.: Towards automated testing of blockchain-based decentralized applications. In: Proceedings of the 27th International Conference on Program Comprehension, ICPC 2019, pp. 294–299. IEEE Press, Piscataway (2019). https://doi.org/10.1109/ICPC.2019.00048
13. Wang, H., Zheng, Z., Xie, S., Dai, H.-N., Chen, X.: Blockchain challenges and opportunities: a survey. Int. J. Web Grid Serv. **14**, 352–375 (2018)
14. Wood, G.: Ethereum: a secure decentralised generalised transaction ledger EIP-150 revision (759dccd - 2017–08-07) (2017). Accessed 03 Jan 2018. https://ethereum.github.io/yellowpaper/paper.pdf
15. Johnson, B., Laszka, A., Grossklags, J., Moore, T.: Economic analyses of security investments on cryptocurrency exchanges, CoRR, vol. abs/1904.09381 (2019). http://arxiv.org/abs/1904.09381
16. Romanchenko, O., Shemetkova, O., Piatanova, V., Kornienko, D.: Approach of estimation of the fair value of assets on a cryptocurrency market. In: Antipova, T., Rocha, A. (eds.) DSIC18 2018. AISC, vol. 850, pp. 245–253. Springer, Cham (2019). https://doi.org/10.1007/978-3-030-02351-5_29
17. Liang, J., Li, L., Zeng, D., Zhao, Y.: Correlation-Based Dynamics and Systemic Risk Measures in the Cryptocurrency Market, pp. 43–48 (2018)
18. Lyushenko, L., Holiachenko, A.: Optimization of the method of technical analysis of cryptocurrency price differences movements. In: Hu, Z., Petoukhov, S., Dychka, I., He, M. (eds.) ICCSEEA 2019. AISC, vol. 938, pp. 388–397. Springer, Cham (2020). https://doi.org/10.1007/978-3-030-16621-2_36
19. Bibi, S.: Cryptocurrency World Identification and Public Concerns Detection Via Social Media, vol. Part F147772, pp. 550–552 (2019)

20. Kaminski, J.: Nowcasting the bitcoin market with twitter signals. Computer Science (2016)
21. Polasik, M., Piotrowska, A.I., Wisniewski, T.P., Kotkowski, R., Lightfoot, G.: Price fluctuations and the use of bitcoin: an empirical inquiry. Int. J. Electron. Commer. **20**(1), 9–49 (2015)
22. Vo, A., Yost-Bremm, C.: A high-frequency algorithmic trading strategy for cryptocurrency. J. Comput. Inf. Syst. **60**(6), 555–568 (2020). https://doi.org/10.1080/08874417.2018.1552090
23. Bui,T., Rao, S.P., Antikainen, M., Aura, T.: Pitfalls of Open Architecture: How Friends can Exploit Your Cryptocurrency Wallet, pp. 1–6, March 2019
24. Sukharev, P.V., Silnov, D.S.: Asynchronous Mining of Ethereum Cryptocurrency, pp. 731–735 (2018)

Blockchain Services and Applications

Blockchain-Based Distributed Machine Learning Towards Statistical Challenges

Mei Li[✉], Qigang Wang, and Wanlu Zhang

AI Lab, Lenovo Research, Beijing 100085, China
{limei8,wangqg1,zhangwl12}@lenovo.com

Abstract. Deep learning based artificial intelligence has made many breakthroughs. The training process of deep learning usually requires a lot of data. The availability of big data, especially privacy-sensitive data, is impeding the application of deep learning. Collecting the data may cause big privacy concerns. Some privacy-preserving deep learning methods have emerged in academia and industry. In this paper, we propose BDML+, a decentralized framework based on consortium Blockchain for privacy-preserving distributed deep learning. It focuses on statistical challenges such as different data distributions and data amounts among participants. Statistical challenges are tackled by several techniques. In the first block, a small amount of publicly shared data and a bootstrap warm-up model are given. During the training process, the local training epochs are automatically adjusted with an adaptive boosting method to prevent local training from non-convergence or overfitting. Besides, factors such as local data amount, the base block and the number of training steps are considered to avoid integrating parameter weights with large divergence. The experimental results show that BDML+ has strong adaptability to various data distributions and data amounts.

Keywords: Blockchain · Distributed machine learning · Collaborative learning · Privacy · Statistical challenges

1 Introduction

In recent years, deep learning [13] based Artificial Intelligence (AI) has made many breakthroughs, which greatly improve the accuracy of image recognition, natural language understanding, etc. Deep learning model training requires a lot of data. However, in many scenarios, such as healthcare and finance, collecting data may cause data privacy concerns and/or violate data protection regulations.

Many privacy-preserving deep learning training methods and systems have emerged in academia and industry. For example, differential privacy [2,19,26] adds appropriate noise to the data to eliminate personal identity. However, the noise may affect the model accuracy and data sharing between people/organizations are still needed. Federated learning [5,16,23] is a distributed machine learning framework, which enables training on decentralized data.

© Springer Nature Singapore Pte Ltd. 2020
Z. Zheng et al. (Eds.): BlockSys 2020, CCIS 1267, pp. 549–564, 2020.
https://doi.org/10.1007/978-981-15-9213-3_42

Although federated learning does not require sharing data, it relies on a (logical) central server to coordinate the training process and still raises privacy issues. There is a new trend to achieve privacy-preserving deep learning by leveraging Blockchain technology [21,22,24]. However, existing works face significant statistical challenges. A big challenge is data heterogeneity. Since model training in existing works relies on gradient descent and its variants [6] and gradients averaging, the training data with independent identical distribution (IID) is important to ensure that the stochastic gradient is an unbiased estimation of the full gradient. In practice, it is unrealistic to assume that the private data of each participant is always IID since the data of a participant is typically based on the usage of a particular person/organization. Besides, some people/organizations use certain services or applications more frequently than others, resulting in varying amounts of local training data.

In this paper, we propose BDML+, a decentralized framework based on consortium Blockchain for privacy-preserving distributed machine learning, which focuses on statistical challenges such as different data distributions and data amounts among participants. BDML+ assumes that although participants don't want to share data with others, they are honest and obey the BDML+ protocol. Since data distribution has a big impact on the accuracy of a model, data distribution will be adjusted before training. In the first block of the Blockchain, a small amount of publicly shared data and a bootstrap warm-up model are given. The amount of publicly shared data is far less than the total amount of data owned by all participants. Because the data amount and distribution of each participant may vary greatly, a fixed number of training epochs may lead to non-convergence or overfitting. During the training process, the training epochs of participants are automatically adjusted by an adaptive boosting method to prevent local training from non-convergence or overfitting. Furthermore, since participants receive knowledge by integrating (weighted averaging) parameter weights of other participants, factors such as the amount of local data, the base block and the number of training steps are considered to avoid integrating stale parameter weights with large divergence.

BDML+ has a wide range of application scenarios and is most suitable for data privacy-sensitive scenarios involving multiple people/organizations. For example, e-health researchers in different hospitals can train medical diagnostic models collaboratively. Mobile phone users can use privacy-sensitive personal data (photos, voice, text, etc.) to train image/language models for photo processing, speech recognition, next-word-prediction, etc. We implement the prototype system of BDML+ and evaluate it on image recognition tasks. The experimental results show that BDML+ has strong adaptability to various data distributions and data amounts. When data is non-IID and/or imbalanced, the convergence speed and model accuracy are significantly improved compared with existing methods [21]. When data is IID and balanced, the model accuracy is close to the centralized training and better than local training.

The main contributions of this paper are as follows:

- We propose BDML+, a privacy-preserving distributed deep learning framework based on consortium Blockchain, to enable different people/organizations to jointly develop one model without the need to expose their private data.
- We analyze the impact of data distributions, data amounts among participants and other statistical challenges on model training. BDML+ addresses statistical challenges by data distribution adjustment, adaptive boosting learning, and divergence aware parameter weights integration.
- We design and implement the prototype system of BDML+, and demonstrate that BDML+ has strong adaptability to various data distributions and data amounts with experimental results.

2   Background

2.1   Blockchain Technology

The concept of Blockchain was first proposed by Nakamoto [17] in 2008. As the public ledger of all transactions, Blockchain has become the core component of electronic currency Bitcoin. The Bitcoin design has become a source of inspiration for other applications of Blockchain [3, 7]. Blockchain is an immutable, shared, chronological distributed database system. A Blockchain consists of a series of blocks generated by cryptography. Blockchain networks are generally divided into public Blockchain, private Blockchain, and consortium Blockchain:

- *Public Blockchain* is completely open, which allows anyone to join, leave or contribute (e.g., read, write and audit) to the network freely.
- *Private Blockchain* is fully private, which only allows authorized participants to join the network, and the read/write permissions are strictly controlled.
- *Consortium Blockchain* can be regarded as a mixture of private and public Blockchain, which has customization options such as role and permission assignments.

The characteristics of Blockchain technology, such as decentralization, security, consensus and incentive mechanism inspire us to apply Blockchain technology to our collaborative training scenarios. The consensus model of Blockchain generates a trusted database. The incentive mechanism of Blockchain encourages participants to participate in collaborative training. The cryptography technology of Blockchain provides data confidentiality and computing auditability.

2.2   Deep Learning

The purpose of deep learning is to extract complex features from high-dimensional data and use them to build a model that correlates input and output. Deep learning architecture is usually constructed as a multi-layer neural network. Learning the neural network parameter is a non-linear optimization problem. Back Propagation (BP) is the most commonly used method for parameter optimization with respect to the loss.

When training a complex multi-layer neural network, the training process takes a long time. Distributed training [4,8,15] can effectively shorten the training time. Distributed training methods can be divided into three categories according to partitioning strategies: data parallelism (data), model parallelism (network structure), and pipelining (layer). Data parallelism deploys multiple copies of the same model, i.e., neural network, to different computing devices, with each device having different data. Results from all computing devices are periodically aggregated. Assuming there are N machines in the cluster, W represents the parameter weights of the neural network, λ is a scaling factor (e.g., learning rate). There are two popular merging methods: parameter averaging and gradient averaging, which are shown as follows:

- Parameter averaging: $W_{i+1} = \frac{1}{N} \sum_{j=1}^{N} W_{i+1,j}$
- Gradient averaging: $W_{i+1} = W_i - \lambda \sum_{j=1}^{N} \Delta W_{i,j}$

Model parallelism divides the model into multiple computing devices according to the neurons in each layer. Pipelining partitions the model according to depth and assigns layers to specific computing devices.

2.3   Related Work

Since deep learning model training needs a lot of data to achieve high accuracy and centralized data collection brings privacy concerns, some privacy-preserving deep learning models and systems have emerged in academia and industry.

Differential privacy [2,19,26] adds appropriate noise to data to eliminate personal identity. For example, [19] applied differential privacy to parameter updates using the sparse vector technique. [26] explored how to combine AI with differential privacy mechanisms and improve the performance of AI. However, the noise added by differential privacy may affect the accuracy of the deep learning model. Besides, data sharing between people/organizations are still needed, which may not be permitted by regulations such as the General Data Protection Regulation (GDPR)[1].

Federated learning [23] is a widely used framework in existing works [5,16, 18,27]. Federated learning is a kind of distributed machine learning approach that supports the training of large amounts of decentralized data residing on devices such as mobile phones. For example, [5] proposed a practical federated learning framework using TensorFlow to train a deep neural network on data stored on the phone without the need to transfer the data out of the device. [27] proposed federated reinforcement learning to consider the privacy requirement in reinforcement learning. Although federated learning does not require data sharing, it relies on a (logical) central server to coordinate the training process and still raises privacy concerns.

---

[1] General Data Protection Regulation (GDPR). https://gdpr-info.eu/.

There is a new trend to achieve privacy-preserving deep learning by leveraging Blockchain technology [21,22,24]. For example, BDML [21] and DeepChain [22] are two completely decentralized machine learning frameworks where the goal is to enable different people/organizations to jointly develop one model for a specific problem without the need to expose their private data sets. However, they suffer from significant statistical challenges, such as the heterogeneity of data and various amounts of local data from different sources. In this paper, we propose BDML+, a decentralized framework based on consortium Blockchain for privacy-preserving distributed deep learning, which solves these statistical challenges.

3   BDML+: Towards Statistical Challenges

BDML+ is a privacy-preserving decentralized deep learning framework based on consortium Blockchain, which benefits from the consensus model, incentive mechanism and cryptography technology of Blockchain, and aims at statistical challenges such as different data distributions and data amounts among participants.

3.1   Basic Protocol

As shown in Fig. 1, there are two types of roles: computational power providers (miners) and verifiers. In a BDML+ network, participants trust each other to some extent, that is, all participants are honest and will abide by the rules of BDML+, but cannot share data. The workflow of the basic protocol mainly includes the following three parts:

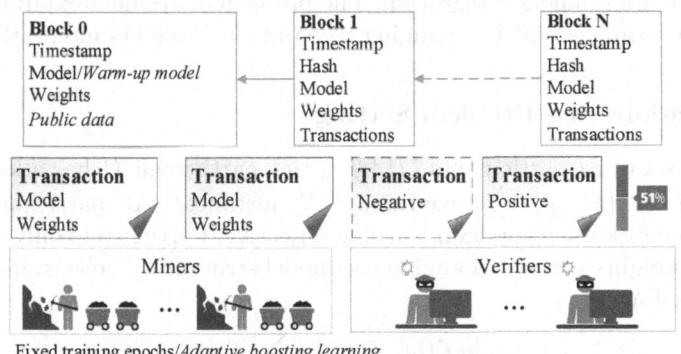

Fig. 1. Protocol of BDML+ (roman: basic protocol; italic: extended protocol)

Local Training. Miners first acquire the model structure and parameter weights from the latest block, then use local private training data to train and compete to generate new blocks. After training for a given fixed number of epochs, they send out the model and parameter weights through transactions to the BDML+ network.

Verification. Verifiers download transactions sent out by miners from the BDML+ network and verify them on the local private test data according to the following principles: if the model and parameter weights in a transaction perform better than the latest block, a positive vote will be given; otherwise, a negative vote will be given. They send out the vote result through transactions to the BDML+ network.

Consensus Strategy. Whether a new block can be generated depends on the verifiers' voting results and the speed of "mining". A new block is generated if most verifiers give positive votes (consensus) on a transaction (the model and parameter weights). A miner who gets consensus first is the new block creator. As a new block is created, the block creator, relevant miners and verifiers are issued incentives. In the case consensus is not reached, miners contribute their models and/or parameter weights to the BDML+ network. Other miners can integrate their models and/or parameter weights and continue training.

As described above, private training and test data are stored on each participant's local device, and all participants can only access their own data. In order to reach a consensus, only the model and parameter weights need to be exchanged among participants. In addition, technologies such as homomorphic encryption [9,18] and selective parameter update [19,24] can be used to further protect privacy. The basic protocol is similar to a previous work [21]. The main difference is that the gradient integration in that previous work is changed to parameter weights integration in BDML+ to prevent gradient expiration. Since BDML+ is a completely decentralized network, participants' local Blockchain are not always up-to-date. In the basic protocol, participants cannot know the starting point of the received gradient and cannot recover the actual parameter weights through gradient integration. The problem of gradient expiration can be alleviated to some extent by changing to parameter weights integration.

3.2 Notations and Problem Setting

Consider a set of M participants $\{P_i\}_{i=1}^{M}$, each participant P_i has a local private data set $S_i = \{(x_i^j, y_i^j)\}_{j=1}^{N_i}$ containing N_i instances. All participants in the BDML+ network use a common learning objective. Participants only update the parameter weights without changing the model structure. The learning objective is formulated as

$$\min_{w \in R} \mathcal{L}(w), \mathcal{L}(w) = \sum_{i=1}^{M} \mathcal{L}_i(w) \tag{1}$$

where $\mathcal{L}_i(w)$ indicates the loss on participant P_i's local private training data set with parameter weights w. The common learning objective generates a global model for all participants, covering various models from simple linear regression to deep learning. There are two types of transactions: updating parameter weights and voting.

Each participant P_i has both miner and verifier roles, who collects data in an IID/non-IID manner, with data on each participant being generated by a similar/distinct distribution $S_i \sim \mu_i$ over $\mathcal{X}_i \times \mathcal{Y}_i$. The union of local data conforms to a distribution μ over $\mathcal{X} \times \mathcal{Y}$. The number of instances N_i in private data sets of individual participants may vary significantly. S_i is split into the training set $S_i^{tr} = \{(x_i^j, y_i^j)\}_{j=1}^{N_i^{tr}}$ for the miner role and the test set $S_i^{te} = \{(x_i^j, y_i^j)\}_{j=1}^{N_i^{te}}$ for the verifier role.

3.3 Cause Analysis

We will analyze the statistical challenges faced by the basic protocol. Consider a standard multi-class classification problem, each input is divided into K mutually exclusive classes. Given a training set $\{x_i\}_{i=1}^N$ containing N instances, the binary target variables $t_k \in \{0, 1\}$ have a 1-of-K coding scheme indicating the class, and the network outputs are interpreted as $y_k(x, w) = p(t_k = 1|x)$, leading to the following cross-entropy loss function:

$$\mathcal{L}(w) = -\sum_{n=1}^{N}\sum_{k=1}^{K}\mu(t_k = 1|x_n)\ln y_k(x_n, w) \tag{2}$$

Parameter weights w' calculated by gradient descent are as follows (learning rate $\eta > 0$):

$$w' = w - \eta\nabla\mathcal{L}(w) = w + \eta\nabla\sum_{n=1}^{N}\sum_{k=1}^{K}\mu(t_k - 1|x_n)\ln y_k(x_n, w) \tag{3}$$

In the BDML+ network, participant P_i's local training (1 epoch on N_i^{tr} local training instances) using gradient descent is as follows:

$$w_i' = w_i + \eta_i\nabla\sum_{n=1}^{N_i^{tr}}\sum_{k=1}^{K}\mu_i(t_k = 1|x_n)\ln y_k(x_n, w_i) \tag{4}$$

According to the basic protocol, the closer w' and w_i' are, the more likely w_i' can pass the verifiers' votes. As shown in Eq. 3 and Eq. 4, the difference between w' and w_i' mainly comes from:

- *Cause 1:* Differences between the local data distribution μ_i and the overall data distribution μ.
- *Cause 2:* Differences between the number of local training instances N_i^{tr} and all training instances N.

Assuming participant P_i fails to pass verifiers' votes and has received parameter weights $\{w_i'\}_{i=1}^{M^r}$ from other participants during this period, it integrates received parameter weights according to Eq. 5 and continues local training.

$$w_i'' = \frac{1}{M^r}\sum_{m=1}^{M^r}w_m' = \frac{1}{M^r}\sum_{m=1}^{M^r}(w_m + \eta_m\nabla\sum_{n=1}^{N_m^{tr}}\sum_{k=1}^{K}\mu_m(t_k = 1|x)\ln y_k(x, w_m))$$

$$\tag{5}$$

According to the basic protocol, the closer w' and w_i'' are, the faster the model converges. As shown in Eq. 3 and Eq. 5, the difference between w' and w_i'' mainly comes from:

- *Cause 3:* Differences in initial training parameter weights among participants.
- *Cause 4:* Differences in local model convergence degree (influenced by the learning rate, training epochs and data amounts) among participants.

3.4 Extended Protocol

In order to solve the statistical challenges faced by the basic protocol, we extend the basic protocol according to the cause analysis. Algorithm 1 and Algorithm 2 provide the pseudo-code of the extended protocol for miners and verifiers respectively.

Data Distribution Adjustment. The basic protocol works well for IID data [21]. In practice, it is unrealistic to assume that the local data for each participant is always IID since the local training data of a participant is typically based on the usage of a particular person/organization. When non-IID data is trained using the basic protocol, the accuracy of the model will be greatly reduced since the stochastic gradient of each participant can no longer be regarded as the unbiased estimation of the full gradient.

To solve this statistical problem, we extend the basic protocol via data distribution adjustment. Consider a standard multi-class classification problem, each input is divided into K mutually exclusive classes.

According to *Cause 1*, in the first block (Fig. 1), a data set G that consists of a uniform distribution over K classes is given (the data set itself or a link to the data set), which is a data set distinct from the participants' data and the number of instances is usually much smaller than the total number of instances owned by all participants. Participants who join the BDML+ network need to download the publicly shared data and use it as training data together with their own training data. For participants with limited bandwidth or storage, they can only download a certain proportion of the publicly shared data. Given the download ratio $0 \leq \alpha \leq 1$, the training set of new participant P_i is as follows:

$$S_i^{tr'} = S_i^{tr} \cup G', G' \subseteq G, |G'| = \alpha|G| \tag{6}$$

In addition, the first block (Fig. 1) includes a warm-up model trained on the given publicly shared data G, that is, the parameter weights in the first block are no longer randomly generated as described in [21], but are trained with the publicly shared data set. Using the warm-up model is helpful to improve the convergence speed and accuracy.

Algorithm 1. Extended protocol: miner

Require:
     initial training epochs E and maximum training epochs E_{max};
     maximum acceptable difference d_{max};
     local training set $S_i^{tr'}$ (Eq. 6) and local test set S_i^{te};
Ensure:
 1: $w \leftarrow$ latest block;
 2: **while** no new block is generated **do**
 3:    $r \leftarrow 0$; $E_{total} \leftarrow 0$; $T \leftarrow$ received transactions from other miners;
 4:    $ACC_{median} \leftarrow$ test candidate weights in T on S_i^{te};
 5:    **repeat**
 6:      $w \leftarrow$ train on $S_i^{tr'}$ for E epochs;
 7:      $ACC_w \leftarrow$ test w on S_i^{te};
 8:      $r \leftarrow r + 1$; $E \leftarrow E - r + 1$; $E_{total} \leftarrow E_{total} + E$;
 9:    **until** $ACC_w \geq ACC_{median}$ or $E_{total} \geq E_{max}$
10:    wait for votes V from verifiers;
11:    **if** most V are positive **then**
12:      create a new block with w; add the new block to Blockchain;
13:    **else**
14:      $T \leftarrow$ received transactions from other miners;
15:      update w according to Eq. 7; $T \leftarrow [\,]$;
16:    **end if**
17: **end while**

The publicly shared data G is a data set different from participants' local private data and participants only need to download the publicly shared data G once when they first join the BDML+ network. Thus, the data distribution adjustment policy improves the basic protocol with no harm to privacy and little addition to the communication cost.

Adaptive Boosting Learning. In the basic protocol, before sending out the model and parameter weights through transactions to the BDML+ network, miners train with their own training data set until the number of training epochs reaches the preset value. However, the fixed number of training epochs may lead to unfitted or overfitted local models since the data distribution and data amount of each participant are different.

According to *Cause 4*, we extend the basic protocol based on the local test accuracy to adaptively boost the training process on participants who appear to be weak learners. As described in Algorithm 1, during the generation of two adjacent blocks Block b and Block $b+1$, participant P_i receives M^r transactions sent out by participants' miner role in the BDML+ network, where $w_m (m = 1, ..., M^r)$ represents candidate parameter weights. As shown in Algorithm 2, the verifier role of participant P_i needs to verify all the parameter weights in received transactions on local private test data set S_i^{te} and obtain the test accuracy $\{ACC_{w_m}\}_{m=1}^{M^r}$ to evaluate the quality of training.

Algorithm 2. Extended protocol: verifier

Require:
    vote threshold T_{vote};
    local test data set S_i^{te};

Ensure:
  1: $w \leftarrow$ latest block;
  2: $ACC_w \leftarrow$ test w on S_i^{te};
  3: **while** no new block is generated **do**
  4:    **if** transaction (w_j, n_j, b_j, e_j) received **then**
  5:      test w_j with S_i^{te};
  6:      **if** $ACC_{w_j} > ACC_w$ or $ACC_{w_j} \geq T_{vote}$ **then**
  7:        give positive vote V_{i2j};
  8:      **else**
  9:        give negative vote V_{i2j};
10:     **end if**
11:   **end if**
12: **end while**

Participant P_i needs to rank $\{ACC_{w_m}\}_{m=1}^{M^r}$ and calculate the median test accuracy ACC_{median}. Given initial training epochs E and maximum training epochs E_{max}, participant P_i takes the parameter weights on Block b as the starting point and uses local training data set $S_i^{tr'}$ to train E epochs, obtaining parameter weights w, then verifies w on local test data set S_i^{te} and obtains ACC_w. Since ACC_w is used to evaluate the quality of training, if $ACC_w \geq ACC_{median}$, it means the quality of participant P_i's parameter weights w exceeds most of the received candidate parameter weights, then the training process is complete. If $ACC_w < ACC_{median}$, then the training process continues for $E - r + 1$ epochs, where $r = 1, 2, 3, ...$, repeat these steps until $ACC_w \geq ACC_{median}$ or the total training epochs exceeds E_{max}. By continuous retraining for a decaying number of epochs as described above, an unfitted local model is adaptively boosted. In addition, only some participants will train until the total training epochs exceeds E_{max}, which not only saves the cost of local training, but also prevents model overfitting.

Divergence Aware Parameter Weights Integration. Since miners train local models via gradient descent and its variants [6], they receive knowledge by integrating (weighted averaging) parameter weights from other miners. It indicates that the accuracy of models may be affected by the number of instances in local training data set and the data distribution [11,20,25]. If miners integrate parameter weights that have big divergence with their own parameter weights, the convergence process will be slower or become unable to converge. This phenomenon is more serious when the miners' data are non-IID.

In order to improve the accuracy and convergence speed of the model, we consider factors such as the number of instances, the base block and the number of training steps to avoid integrating parameter weights with large divergence.

Based on this extension, a transaction sent out by a miner includes not only parameter weights, but also the number of training instances, the base block and training epochs.

As shown in Algorithm 1, during the generation of two adjacent blocks Block b and Block $b+1$, participant P_i receives M^r transactions $\{(w_m, n_m, b_m, e_m)\}_{m=1}^{M^r}$ sent out by miners, where w_m is the parameter weights calculated based on Block b_m using stochastic gradient descent (SGD) [6] to train e_m epochs on n_m local training instances.

Assuming that participant P_i trains E epochs based on Block b on N_i local training instances using SGD and obtains parameter weights w, but fails to pass verifiers' votes, then received parameter weights will be integrated. In the basic protocol, participant P_i integrates all received weights $w = \frac{\sum_{m=1}^{M^r} w_m}{M^r}$.

To solve the problem of imbalanced local training data, according to *Cause 2*, the amount of local training data is taken into account $w = \sum_{m=1}^{M^r} \frac{n_m}{\sum_{m=1}^{M^r} n_m} w_m$.

To avoid integrating parameter weights that have big divergence, according to *Cause 1*, *Cause 3* and *Cause 4*, miners integrate only those weights which have the same base block and have less difference in training steps instead of integrating all received weights. Miners can adjust acceptable step differences according to their own conditions (e.g., training losses, voting passage, etc.). Given maximum acceptable difference d_{max}, participant P_i integrates received weights as follows:

$$w = \sum_{m=1}^{M^r} \frac{(b_m - b)s_m n_m}{\sum_{m=1}^{M^r}(b_m - b)s_m n_m} w_m \tag{7}$$

where $b_m - b$ and s_m filter out weights with the same base block and acceptable step differences, s_m is as follows:

$$s_m = \begin{cases} 0, d_m > d_{max} \\ 1, d_m \leq d_{max} \end{cases}, d_m = |e_m n_m - EN_i^{tr}| \tag{8}$$

4 Evaluation

4.1 Settings

We design our own Blockchain based on application scenarios of BDML+. The system implementation is based on an open source Blockchain project[2] and Tensorflow [1].

We evaluate BDML+ with two popular data sets:

– *MNIST*[3] contains 60,000 training instances and 10,000 test instances. Each instance contains a handwritten digit, which has been size-normalized and centered in a 28 × 28 gray-scale image.

---

[2] A simple Blockchain in Python. https://gihub.com/dvf/blockchain/.
[3] The MNIST database of handwritten digits. http://yann.lecun.com/exdb/mnist/.

– *CIFAR-10* [12] contains 60,000 32 × 32 color images in 10 classes, with 6,000 images in each class. We use 50,000 images as the training set, and 10,000 images as the test set.

To prove the adaptability of BDML+ to simple and complex models, we use two popular deep learning models *LeNet-5* and *ResNet-32* as representatives respectively:

– *LeNet-5* [14] is a convolutional neural network (CNN) including 7 layers (conv → pool → conv → pool → fully connected → fully connected → output). We use *LeNet-5* for MNIST data set.
– *ResNet-32* [10] is a 32-layer deep network containing 5 residual blocks (batch normalization → ReLu → conv → batch normalization → ReLu → conv). We use ResNet-32 for *CIFAR-10* data set.

As described in Sect. 3.1, the basic protocol of BDML+ is similar to previous work [21]. As the main purpose of the extended protocol is to address statistical challenges and previous work [21] has proved the scalability, we only chose 10 participants according to data amounts.

4.2 Results

Basic Protocol vs. Extended Protocol. The training set is divided into two disjoint parts: publicly shared data (MNIST: 1%, CIFAR: 5%) and private data (MNIST: 99%, CIFAR: 95%). Publicly shared data consists of a uniform distribution over 10 classes. The download rate α is 1.0. The warm-up model is obtained by training 10 epochs on publicly shared data. The test set is private.

Figure 2 shows the test accuracy of Super_Data (centralized training with the full training set), Sub_Data (single participant training with 1/10 training set) and BDML+ on the full test set. For BDML+, private data are shuffled and evenly divided into 10 participants with IID data (each participant's data contains 10 classes). As shown in Fig. 2, when participants' data is IID and balanced, the model accuracy of BDML+ is close to the centralized training and better than that of any single participant.

Figure 3 shows the results of the basic protocol and the extended protocol of BDML+. When the number of instances of each participant is balanced, i.e., private data are shuffled and evenly divided into 10 participants. As shown in Fig. 3(a) and Fig. 3(c), for both LeNet/MNIST and ResNet/CIFAR, when participants' data is IID, the basic protocol performs well. If the extended protocol is used, the test accuracy can be further improved. However, when participants' data is non-IID (each participant's data only contains 2 classes), the performance of the basic protocol is poor, and the extended protocol can significantly improve the test accuracy. Compared with the basic protocol, the extended protocol improves the test accuracy by 4.73 times (from 0.2036 to 0.9624) and 5.03 times (from 0.1709 to 0.8589) for LeNet/MNIST and CIFAR/ResNet, respectively.

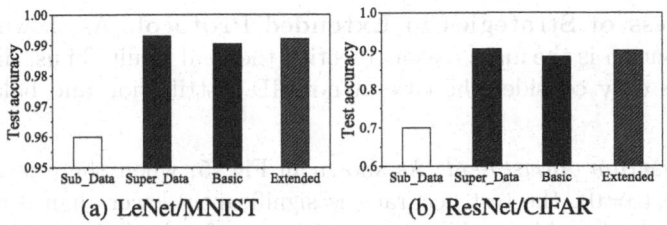

(a) LeNet/MNIST   (b) ResNet/CIFAR

Fig. 2. BDML+ accuracy

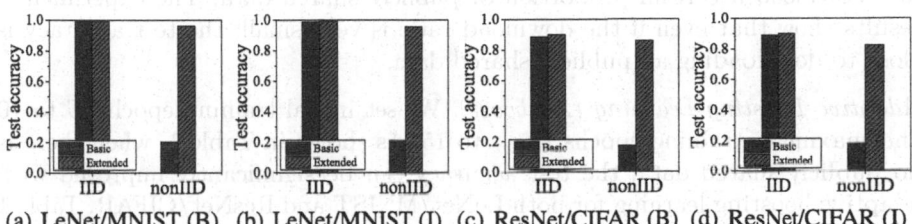

(a) LeNet/MNIST (B) (b) LeNet/MNIST (I) (c) ResNet/CIFAR (B) (d) ResNet/CIFAR (I)

Fig. 3. Basic protocol vs. extended protocol (B: balance, I: imbalance)

When the number of instances of each participant is imbalanced, i.e, private data are shuffled and divided into 10 participants according to the Poisson distribution. As shown in Fig. 3(b) and Fig. 3(d), for both LeNet/MNIST and ResNet/CIFAR, a conclusion similar to that of balanced data can be drawn, that is, when participants' data is IID, the basic protocol performs well. The test accuracy can be further improved by the extended protocol. When participants' data is non-IID, the test accuracy can be significantly improved by the extended protocol.

Figure 4 compares the test accuracy of each block when the number of instances of each participant is balanced and imbalanced with the non-IID distribution. As shown in Fig. 4, for both LeNet/MNIST and ResNet/CIFAR, when data is balanced, the model converges faster and the final accuracy is higher.

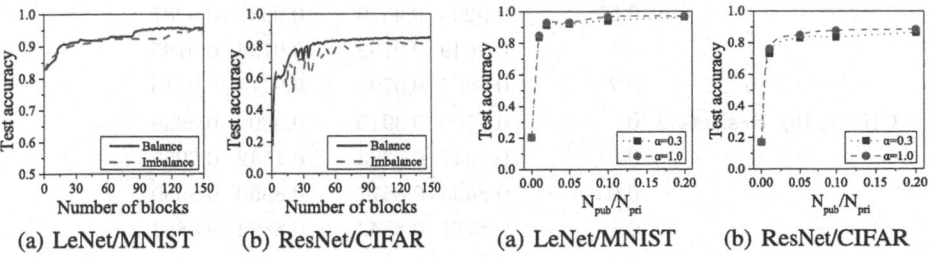

(a) LeNet/MNIST   (b) ResNet/CIFAR   (a) LeNet/MNIST   (b) ResNet/CIFAR

Fig. 4. Test accuracy of each block (non-IID)

Fig. 5. Data distribution adjustment

Effectiveness of Strategies in Extended Protocol. As shown in Fig. 3, data distribution is the main reason affecting the final result. Thus, the following experiments only consider the case of non-IID distribution and balanced data amount.

Data Distribution Adjustment. As shown in Fig. 5, when there is no publicly shared data ($\alpha=0$), the test accuracy is significantly lower than if only a very small amount of publicly shared data is given for both LeNet/MNIST and ResNet/CIFAR. For participants with limited bandwidth or storage, they can just download a certain proportion of publicly shared data. The experimental results show that even if the download ratio is very small, the test accuracy is close to downloading all publicly shared data.

Adaptive Boosting Learning (Adaboost). We set initial training epochs E to 10 and maximum training epochs E_{max} to 15. As shown in Table 1, when there is no publicly shared data, the test accuracy can be significantly improved with adaptive boosting learning for both LeNet/MNIST and ResNet/CIFAR. Table 1 also shows that this strategy can further improve the test accuracy when using publicly shared data and the warm-up model.

Divergence Aware Weights Integration (DAWI). As shown in Table 1, for both LeNet /MNIST and ResNet/CIFAR, when there is no publicly shared data, the test accuracy can be significantly improved with divergence aware parameter weights integration. In addition, this strategy can further improve the test accuracy on the basis of data distribution adjustment (publicly shared data and the warm-up model) and adaptive boosting learning.

Table 1. Results with Adaboost and DAWI for non-IID distribution and balanced data amount

Data/Model	N_{pub}/N_{pri}	Test accuracy			
		-	Adaboost	DAWI	Adaboost+DAWI
MNIST/LeNet-5	0	0.2036	0.4610	0.4759	0.4782
	0.01	0.8479	0.9600	0.9548	0.9624
	0.05	0.9295	0.9679	0.9637	0.9787
	0.1	0.9649	0.9752	0.9734	0.9795
	0.2	0.9683	0.9798	0.9774	0.9815
CIFAR-10/ ResNet-32	0	0.1709	0.3915	0.3899	0.3936
	0.01	0.7617	0.7793	0.7742	0.7955
	0.05	0.8493	0.8577	0.8560	0.8589
	0.1	0.8771	0.8843	0.8824	0.8884
	0.2	0.8840	0.8896	0.8887	0.8941

In all the experiments, each miner trained at least 10 epochs before launching a transaction. Since the training process took a long time (much longer than transaction transmission time), the cost of synchronization mechanism is acceptable. In the extended protocol, the training epochs of different miners are automatically adjusted, which can effectively reduce the cost of synchronization. In addition, the cost of synchronization can be further reduced by selective parameter update [19, 24].

5   Conclusion and Future Work

In this paper, we propose BDML+, a Blockchain-based decentralized framework for privacy-preserving deep learning to enable different people/organizations to jointly develop one model without the need to expose their private data. We analyze the impact of data distributions, data amounts among participants and other statistical challenges on model training. BDML+ addresses these statistical challenges by data distribution adjustment, adaptive boosting learning, and divergence aware parameter weights integration. We evaluate BDML+ on image recognition tasks. The experimental results show that BDML+ has strong adaptability to various data distributions and data amounts. In the future, we plan to extend BDML+ to support heterogeneous data. Furthermore, we plan to further protect the model and data privacy by using technologies such as homomorphic encryption and differential privacy.

References

1. Abadi, M., et al.: Tensorflow: a system for large-scale machine learning. In: USENIX Symposium on Operating Systems Design and Implementation (OSDI), pp. 265–283 (2016)
2. Abadi, M., Chu, A., et al.: Deep learning with differential privacy. In: ACM SIGSAC Conference on Computer and Communications Security (CCS), pp. 308–318 (2016)
3. Androulaki, E., Barger, A., et al.: Hyperledger fabric: a distributed operating system for permissioned blockchains. In: Proceedings of the 30th EuroSys Conference, pp. 1–15 (2018)
4. Ben-Nun, T., Hoefler, T.: Demystifying parallel and distributed deep learning: an in-depth concurrency analysis. ACM Comput. Surv. (CSUR) 52(4), 1–43 (2019)
5. Bonawitz, K., Eichner, H., et al.: Towards federated learning at scale: system design. In: Proceedings of the Conference on Systems and Machine Learning (SysML) (2019)
6. Bottou, L., Curtis, F.E., Nocedal, J.: Optimization methods for large-scale machine learning. Siam Rev. 60(2), 223–311 (2018)
7. Casino, F., Dasaklis, T.K., Patsakis, C.: A systematic literature review of blockchain-based applications: current status, classification and open issues. Telemat. Inf. 36, 55–81 (2019)
8. Chilimbi, T., Suzue, Y., Apacible, J., Kalyanaraman, K.: Project adam: building an efficient and scalable deep learning training system. In: Proceedings of OSDI 2014, pp. 571–582 (2014)

9. Gentry, C.: Fully homomorphic encryption using ideal lattices. In: Proceedings of the 41th Annual ACM Symposium on Theory of Computing (STOC), pp. 169–178 (2009)

10. He, K., Zhang, X., Ren, S., et al.: Deep residual learning for image recognition. In: IEEE Conference on Computer Vision and Pattern Recognition (CVPR), pp. 770–778 (2016)

11. Huang, L., Yin, Y., Fu, Z., Zhang, S., Deng, H., Liu, D.: Loadaboost: loss-based adaboost federated machine learning on medical data. arXiv preprint arXiv:1811.12629 (2018)

12. Krizhevsky, A., Hinton, G.: Learning Multiple Layers of Features from Tiny Images (2009)

13. LeCun, Y., Bengio, Y., Hinton, G.: Deep learning. Nature **521**(7553), 436–444 (2015)

14. LeCun, Y., Bottou, L., Bengio, Y., et al.: Gradient-based learning applied to document recognition. In: Proceedings of the IEEE, pp. 2278–2324 (1998)

15. Liu, T.Y., et al.: Distributed machine learning: foundations, trends, and practices. In: 26th International Conference on World Wide Web Companion (WWW), pp. 913–915 (2017)

16. McMahan, B., Moore, E., et al.: Communication-efficient learning of deep networks from decentralized data. In: Artificial Intelligence and Statistics (AISTATS), pp. 1273–1282 (2017)

17. Nakamoto, S.: Bitcoin: A Peer-to-Peer Electronic Cash System (2008)

18. Phong, L.T., et al.: Privacy-preserving deep learning via additively homomorphic encryption. IEEE Trans. Inf. Forens. Secur. **13**(5), 1333–1345 (2018)

19. Shokri, R., Shmatikov, V.: Privacy-preserving deep learning. In: ACM SIGSAC Conference on Computer and Communications Security (CCS), pp. 1310–1321 (2015)

20. Smith, V., Chiang, C.K., Sanjabi, M., Talwalkar, A.S.: Federated multi-task learning. In: Advances in Neural Information Processing Systems (NeurIPS), pp. 4424–4434 (2017)

21. Wang, Q., et al.: BDML: blockchain-based distributed machine learning for model training and evolution. In: Symposium on Foundations and Applications of Blockchain (FAB) (2019)

22. Weng, J., et al.: Deepchain: auditable and privacy-preserving deep learning with blockchain-based incentive. IEEE Trans. Dependable Secur. Comput. **PP**(99), 1 (2019)

23. Yang, Q., Liu, Y., Chen, T., et al.: Federated machine learning: concept and applications. ACM Trans. Intell. Syst. Technol. **10**(2), 12 (2019)

24. Zhang, W., Wang, Q., Li, M.: Medical image collaborative training based on multi-blockchain. In: International Conference on Bioinformatics and Biomedicine (BIBM) (2019)

25. Zhao, Y., Li, M., Lai, L., Suda, N., Civin, D., Chandra, V.: Federated learning with non-IID data. arXiv preprint arXiv:1806.00582 (2018)

26. Zhu, T., Philip, S.Y.: Applying differential privacy mechanism in artificial intelligence. In: International Conference on Distributed Computing Systems (ICDCS), pp. 1601–1609 (2019)

27. Zhuo, H., et al.: Federated reinforcement learning. arXiv preprint arXiv:1901.08277 (2019)

Research on a Blockchain Consensus Algorithm Based on Digital Copyright

Guo Jun[1](✉), Yang Lan[1], Zhou HongBo[1], and Guo Yang[2]

[1] QuanZhou University of Informaton Engineering Software College, QuanZhou, China
15980322638@139.com
[2] Jiangxi Academy of Agricultural Sciences, Nanchang, China

Abstract. Blockchain technology is a decentralized network structure based on the p2p network and cryptography technology as the core. It establishes trust relationships on the network with pure mathematical methods, without relying on intermediate platforms to establish trust relationships. In order to better protect the subjective rights and interests of digital copyright and reduce the occurrence of various infringement incidents, a digital copyright consensus algorithm based on blockchain technology is proposed. With the help of Map function conditions, the internal data transmission rate of the multi-channel model is improved, so as to obtain accurate time complexity values, and complete the design of the digital copyright blockchain consensus algorithm. Experimental results show that, compared with the APBFT algorithm, the maximum value of the DPA permission resistance index in this paper is increased to 83%, while the directional transmission time of data information is shortened to 0.08 s, which greatly reduces the probability of various digital copyright infringement incidents.

Keywords: Digital copyright · Blockchain · Consensus algorithm · P2P system · Signature certificate

1 Introduction

The essence of the blockchain is a shared database organization, which is a professional term in the field of information technology, For the information or data stored in it, it maintain a real-time traceability, openness, transparency, and common maintenance attitude. From the perspective of data connection, blockchain technology includes multiple processing methods such as point-to-point transmission, algorithm encryption, distributed storage, and consensus mechanism, etc., stipulating that each database can be used individually as a low-level information structure. Under the blessing of the principle of associated cryptography, the network information in the block can be divided into multiple parallel data packets and transmitted to the lower-level block organization [1, 2]. In the process of executing blockchain processing, the core host and the host must maintain the same action trend at all times. While transmitting data, we must also pay attention to the debugging and application of feedback receipt parameters.

© Springer Nature Singapore Pte Ltd. 2020
Z. Zheng et al. (Eds.): BlockSys 2020, CCIS 1267, pp. 565–574, 2020.
https://doi.org/10.1007/978-981-15-9213-3_43

The so-called digital copyright refers to the online copyright of information materials and publications. The practical application rights of disseminating text content with the help of emerging media such as digital media are composed of the copyright of publications such as mobile phone publications, e-magazines, and e-books. With the increase in the number of publications published online, which has seriously damaged the subjective rights and interests of digital copyright. In order to avoid the above situation, the APBFT algorithm establishes a strict admission mechanism with the support of digital certificates, and then improves the integrity of online copyright data by removing complex consensus information. However, the level of DPA permission resistance index of this method is too low, and it is easy to cause the directional transmission time of copyright information to be infinitely extended. In order to solve the above problems, a new digital copyright blockchain consensus algorithm is proposed. According to the connection requirements of hardware structures such as Java Spring framework and P2P network system, specific Map functions are designed to calculate the actual value of time complexity and effectively reduce the digital copyright invasion probability.

2   Blockchain Platform Technology

The blockchain platform uses the Java Spring framework and P2P network architecture as the basic execution structure. Under the function of digital signature certificates, the specific construction method of the blockchain platform is as follows.

2.1   Java Spring Framework

Java Spring framework is the foundation of the blockchain platform. It consists of a data coupling layer, a data access layer, a connection transmission layer, a load collection layer, and a detection and processing layer. The data coupling layer contains four types of data transmission elements with different execution functions and a Core information container, which can screen the infringement parameters in the blockchain organization according to the limited conditions of network digital copyright. The transmission element in the data access layer can control the connection behavior between the blockchain platform and digital copyright information, thereby collecting the infringing information parameters in a dispersed state into a beam-like transmission structure for direct adjustment by other blockchain-level units Access and use. The transmission connection layer is located in the middle of the blockchain platform, and can transfer the digital copyright information in the data coupling layer and data access layer to the load collection layer structure, which includes four types of physical nodes: Aspect, AOP, Data, and Access [3, 4]. Each type of node corresponds to only one type of digital copyright information, and can transmit the blockchain data analysis instructions, while establishing the signing certificate conditions necessary for the connection of the P2P network system. The loading collection layer mainly executes classification processing instructions related to digital copyright information, and temporarily stores the converted blockchain connection data in Beans, Context, and MVC nodes. The detection processing layer is located at the bottom of the Java Spring framework and can receive all digital copyright information in the upper-level blockchain organization, and arrange and process these information parameters according to the established consensus weight. The structure of Java Spring framework structure is shown in Fig. 1.

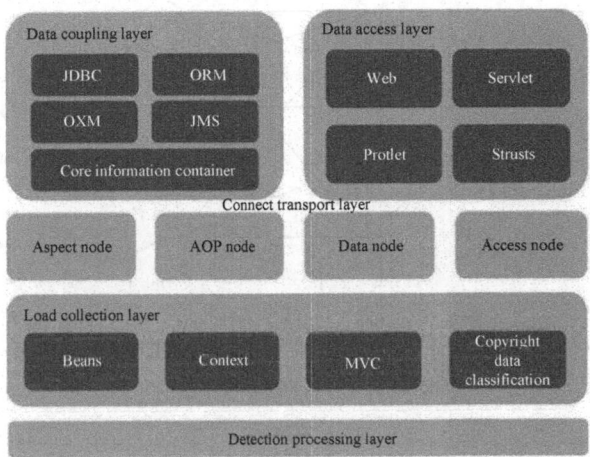

Fig. 1. Java Spring framework structure

2.2 P2P Network System

The P2P network system is the core structure of the blockchain platform, and describes the peer-to-peer relationship between data. In the Java Spring consensus concept, it is possible to establish a physical connection between conventional digital copyright information and various types of infringement information, and with the support of the client and server hosts, the application differences between the two are compared, so as to perform filtering and clearing processing on the established information data [5, 6]. For the P2P network system for digital copyright information, there is no independent central server or central node. Only the data host distributed in the Java Spring framework are used as the execution guarantee structure. During the entire consensus period, the associated network host always maintains the same connection trend, while the information connection loaded on the blockchain platform can only maintain the parallel transmission state between two peer hosts at the same time. In the case of irrelevant digital copyright information intrusion, all P2P network hosts can be used as subsidiary carriers of consensus data parameters. In order to comply with the connection requirements of the Java Spring framework, these information parameters are limited in the transmission behavior of the blockchain platform. And for the necessary digital copyright information, the blockchain platform composed of the P2P network system always maintains an open and good transmission state [7]. The P2P network architecture is shown in Fig. 2.

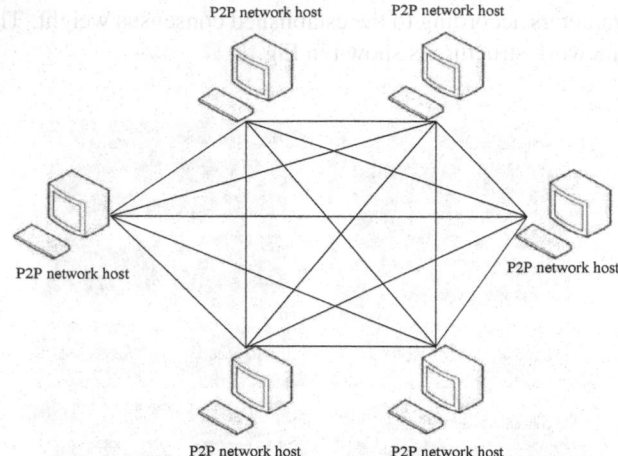

Fig. 2. P2P network architecture

2.3 Digitally Signature Certificate

A digital signature certificate is a extremely authoritative file or data structure. It is the subject of digital copyright information constraint body derived from the blockchain platform. It always maintains the form of electronic documents for consensus nodes in the Java Spring framework, and the public key form for the consensus hosts in the P2P network architecture. Since the certificate body structure contains the necessary copyright data public key information, and each public key corresponds to a matching information private key structure, the digital signature certificate in the P2P network system of the blockchain platform must undergo two processes of decryption and conversion before implementing data consensus. The so-called digital signature certificate decryption is a necessary processing method to limit the real-time location of the P2P network host. In the case of digital copyright infringement, all hierarchical units in the Java Spring framework are in a fast-moving state. On the one hand, it can realize the real-time conversion of key digital copyright information with the promotion of node organizations such as AOP. On the other hand, it can also strengthen the screening of irrelevant copyright information, thereby reducing the occurrence of various infringement incidents [8, 9]. Digital signature certificate conversion is a necessary method to remove irrelevant copyright information. It can control the output rate of digital copyright information according to the connection form of the P2P network host, so as to achieve the construction and maintenance of the blockchain consensus platform. Table 1 below reflects the design principle of a complete digital signature certificate.

Table 1. Design principle of digital signature certificate

Digitally signed certificate sort	Public key	Private key
Action location	Java Spring framework in a blockchain unit	P2P network architecture
Signature form	Decrypty	Transform
Target information structure	All digital rights information	Necessary digital copyright information
Conditions	Digital copyright infringement occurred	
Participation execution structure	AOP and other blockchain loading collection node structure	

3   Digital Copyright Blockchain Consensus Algorithm

With the support of the blockchain platform, the research of the digital copyright blockchain consensus algorithm is realized in accordance with the processing flow of Map function design, multi-channel model establishment, and time complexity calculation.

3.1   Map Function Design

Map function is a common form of blockchain consensus algorithm. It is a way to define the constraints relationship between key digital copyright information and intrusion of digital copyright information. Establish a data consensus space with a relatively large amount of stored values to meet the demand for the use of multi-channel models. It is assumed that in the blockchain unit, all input data belong to the category of digital rights information, and a P2P network node corresponds to only one type of information parameter, that is, all P2P network hosts in the blockchain unit always maintain a single correspondence. In order to ensure the stability of data information transmission, the encryption and decryption of digital signature certificates are artificially specified as two mutually opposite processing flows, and all digital copyright information can only be transmitted in the order of encryption and decryption. Without considering other interference conditions, the setting result of the Map function is only affected by the two physical quantities of the total amount of digital copyright information and the blockchain consensus cycle [10]. The total amount of digital copyright information is composed of two parts, the former represents the key digital copyright information, and the latter represents the intrusive digital copyright information. Under the condition of the same consensus, the actual value levels of the two do not interfere with each other. The blockchain consensus cycle is often expressed as $|\bar{t}|$, which can directly describe the unit processing time of the P2P network host. By combining the above physical quantities, the Map function of the digital copyright blockchain consensus algorithm can be defined as:

$$P = 1 - \sum_{\beta}^{\beta'} \frac{W_1^{e_1} W_2^{-e_2}}{|\bar{t}|!} \left[1 - \left(\frac{y}{u}\right)^{\varepsilon}\right] \tag{1}$$

Among them, β represents the lower bound data consensus conditions of the blockchain organization, β' represents the upper bound data consensus conditions of the blockchain organization, e_1, e_2 respectively represent the consensus coefficients of power terms related to key digital copyright information and intrusive digital copyright information, y represents the information output conditions. u represents information input conditions and ε represents Consensus calibration coefficient.

3.2 Multi-channel Model

The multi-channel model is a blockchain consensus structure established according to the Map function standard. According to the proportion of key digital copyright information in the total amount of information, an interconnection relationship is established between the control host assigned to execute the intrusion prevention instruction and the relevant host. Improve the data transmission process within the entire model [11, 12]. The complete multi-channel model includes at least eight blockchain hosts, which are arranged in a peer-to-peer manner. Generally, there are three kinds of connection relationships between the host and the host: direct transmission, facultative transmission, and progressive transmission. Among them, direct transmission mainly exists between peer hosts. When the value of the Map function is equal to the average limit condition, digital copyright information can freely realize the jump and connection between consensus nodes; facultative transmission mainly exists between the left parallel hosts. When

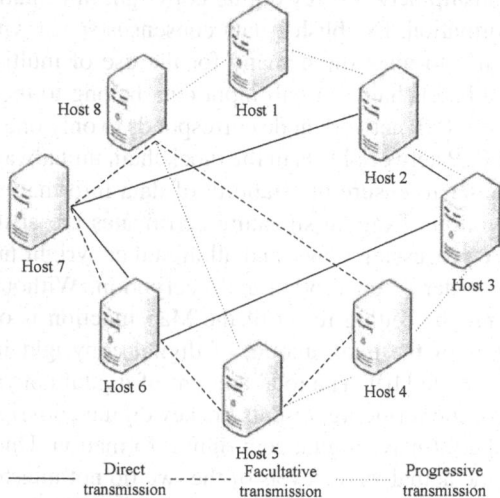

Fig. 3. Multi-channel model structure diagram

the value of the Map function is equal to the minimum condition, the digital copyright information can freely realize the jump and connection between consensus nodes. The progressive transmission mainly exists between the parallel hosts on the right. When the value of the Map function is equal to the maximum limit, digital copyright information can freely realize the jump and connection between consensus nodes [13]. The structure diagram of the multi-channel model is shown in Fig. 3.

3.3 Time Complexity Calculation

The time complexity calculation is the end process of building the digital copyright blockchain consensus algorithm. The practical added value of the Map function can be determined according to the actual connection relationship between the blockchain hosts, thereby the actual transmission range of copyright information can be obtained. Assume that $\sigma \downarrow$ represents the minimum digital copyright information consensus conditions that can be carried by a blockchain organization, and $\sigma \uparrow$ represents the maximum digital copyright information consensus conditions that the blockchain organization can carry. The simultaneous formula (1) can express the calculation result of time complexity as

$$a = \sum_{\sigma \downarrow}^{\sigma \uparrow} f^{\omega + \phi}(l_2 - l_1) \tag{2}$$

among them, f represents the information connection coefficient in a multi-channel model, ω, ϕ respectively represent consensus parameters of two different power-term consensus parameters. l_2 represents real value of maximum information power terms transmission per unit time. l_1 represents the minimum real value of information transmission per unit time. So far, the calculation and processing of various numerical parameters have been realized. So far, to achieve the calculation and processing of various numerical parameters, with the support of the Java Spring framework and P2P network system, complete the research of the digital copyright blockchain consensus algorithm.

4   Algorithm Applicability Analysis

In order to verify the practical application value of the digital copyright blockchain consensus algorithm, the following comparative experiment is designed. A certain amount of digital copyright information was intercepted as the experimental object. The detection host equipped with the blockchain consensus algorithm was used as the numerical recording element of the experimental group, and the detection host equipped with APBFT algorithm was used as the numerical recording component of the control group. Under the same experimental environment, the actual changes of the DPA permission resistance index and duration of the directional transmission of data information were analyzed.

4.1   DPA Permission Resistance Index

The DPA permission resistance index can reflect the probability of occurrence of digital infringement events. Generally, the larger the detection value of the index, the lower the probability of infringement. Table 2 below reflects the specific changes of the DPA permission resistance index of the experimental group and the control group.

Table 2. Comparison of DPA permission resistance index

Time/(min)	Experimental group DPA permission Resistance index/(%)	The control group DPA permission resistanceIndex/(%)
5	72.5	42.8
10	76.2	45.6
15	78.4	47.6
20	78.4	48.5
25	78.4	48.5
30	80.3	48.5
35	81.9	48.2
40	83.1	46.7
45	83.1	45.9

Analysis of Table 2 shows that the DPA permission resistance index of the experimental group has always maintained a gradual upward trend, and the global maximum value has reached 83.1%. The DPA permission resistance index of the control group has risen sharply first, and has begun to decline after reaching a stable value. The global maximum value is 48.5%, much lower than the numerical value of the experimental group. In summary, with the application of the digital copyright blockchain consensus algorithm, the value of the DPA permission resistance index has indeed been promoted to a certain extent.

4.2 Duration of the Directional Transmission of Data Information

Figure 4 below reflects the specific changes in the duration of the data information directional transmission of the experimental and control groups.

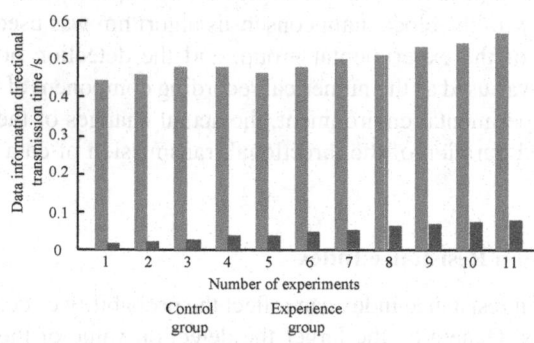

Fig. 4. Comparison of the duration of data information directional transmission

It can be seen from the analysis of Fig. 4 that although the duration of the directional transmission of data information in the experimental group keeps gradually increasing, the maximum value can only reach 0.08 s. In addition to the fifth recording result, the change trade keeps increasing gradually, but the maximum value has reached 0.57 s, which is much higher than the numerical value of the experimental group. In summary, the application of the digital copyright blockchain consensus algorithm can greatly shorten the directional transmission time of data information.

5 Conclusion

Under the influence of the Java Spring framework and P2P network system, digital signature certificate directly provides the numerical indicators required for the establishment of the Map functions. With the continuous improvement of multi-channel models, the calculation accuracy of time complexity has also been effectively improved. Compared with the APBFT algorithm, the digital copyright blockchain consensus algorithm can increase the DPA permission resistance index and shorten the directional transmission time of data information, which is in line with the original intention of protecting the subjective rights and interests of digital copyright.

References

1. Cheng, M., Liu, J., Xu, J.: Diverse search empire competition algorithm for solving traveling salesman problem. Comput. Appl. **39**(10), 2992–2996 (2019)
2. Liang, W., Lei, X., Li, K.-C., Fan, Y., Cai, J.: A dual-chain digital copyright registration and transaction system based on blockchain technology. In: Zheng, Z., Dai, H.-N., Tang, M., Chen, X. (eds.) BlockSys 2019. CCIS, vol. 1156, pp. 702–714. Springer, Singapore (2020). https://doi.org/10.1007/978-981-15-2777-7_57
3. Fang, Y., Deng, J., Cong, L.: Improved PBFT blockchain consensus algorithm based on ring signature. Comput. Eng. **45**(11), 32–36 (2019)
4. Xu, J., Meng, X., Liang, W., Peng, L., Xu, Z., Li, K.-C.: A hybrid mutual authentication scheme based on blockchain technology for WBANs. In: Zheng, Z., Dai, H.-N., Tang, M., Chen, X. (eds.) BlockSys 2019. CCIS, vol. 1156, pp. 350–362. Springer, Singapore (2020). https://doi.org/10.1007/978-981-15-2777-7_28
5. Ning, Z., Li, L., Liang, W., Zhao, Y., Fu, Q., Chen, H.: A novel exploration for blockchain in distributed file storage. In: Zheng, Z., Dai, H.-N., Tang, M., Chen, X. (eds.) BlockSys 2019. CCIS, vol. 1156, pp. 740–746. Springer, Singapore (2020). https://doi.org/10.1007/978-981-15-2777-7_60
6. Hao, X., Hanyu, D., Cheng, Q.: Recognition of FM fuze rough surface target and interference signal. J. Beijing Univ. Aeronaut. Astronaut. **45**(10), 1946–1955 (2019)
7. Liang, W., Long, W.H.J., Li, K.-C., Zhang, D.: Deep Reinforcement learning for resource protection and real-time detection in IOT environment. IEEE Internet Things J. 1–9 (2020)
8. Liu, G., Li, Q.: Blockchain data privacy protection mechanism based on searchable encryption. Comput. Appl. **39**(S2), 140–146 (2019)
9. Pan, X., Pan, X., Song, M., Ai, B., Ming, Y.: Blockchain technology and enterprise operational capabilities: an empirical test. Int. J. Inf. Manag. **52**, 101946 (2020)
10. Behnke, K., Janssen, M.: Boundary conditions for traceability in food supply chains using blockchain technology. Int. J. Inf. Manag. **52**, 101969 (2020)

11. Choi, T.-M., Feng, L., Li, R.: Information disclosure structure in supply chains with rental service platforms in the blockchain technology era. Int. J. Prod. Econ. **221** (2020)
12. Hawlitschek, F., Notheisen, B., Teubner, T.: A 2020 perspective on "the limits of trust-free systems: a literature review on blockchain technology and trust in the sharing economy". Electron. Commer. Res. Appl. **40** (2020)
13. Zhao, G., Di, B., He, H., Zhu, W.: Digital education transaction object authentication service based on blockchain technology. Internet Technol. Lett. **3**(2) (2020)
14. Information technology - data sharing; researchers from southwest jiaotong university describe research in data sharing (coordination of supply chain under blockchain system-based product lifecycle information sharing effort). Inf. Technol. Newsweekly (2020)

Blockchain-Based Dynamic Spectrum Sharing for 5G and Beyond Wireless Communications

Zuguang Li[1,2], Wei Wang[1,2]([⊠]), and Qihui Wu[1,2]

[1] College of Electronic and Information Engineering, Nanjing University of Aeronautics and Astronautics, Nanjing 211106, China
lizgnuaa@163.com, {wei_wang,wuqihui}@nuaa.edu.cn
[2] Key Laboratory of Dynamic Cognitive System of Electromagnetic Spectrum Space, Ministry of Industry and Information Technology, Nanjing 211106, China

Abstract. The blockchain technology written in smart contract has the advantages of the enabling intelligent settlement, value transfer and resource sharing, which provides a new secure and trusted platform for the dynamic spectrum sharing system. In this paper, we first summarize the application of blockchain technology in dynamic spectrum sharing considering the requirements of spectrum sharing. Then we discuss the key problems that need to be solved when applying blockchain to large-scale spectrum sharing system. After that, we analyze the key challenges in depth, and provide corresponding key technologies and possible solutions to the above problems.

Keywords: Dynamic spectrum sharing · Blockchain · Trusted spectrum ledger · Smart contract · Spectrum security

1 Introduction

With the wideband, ubiquitous, and syncretic development of wireless communications, the demand for spectrum resources keeps increasing explosively. However, the golden sub-6 GHz band that most suitable for wireless communications are almost exhausted, resulting in a serious structural supply-demand imbalance in spectrum resources. The shortage of available spectrum and low spectrum utilization caused by the static allocation mode forces us to adopt the dynamic spectrum sharing (DSS) technology. As a promising technology to improve the spectrum utilization, cognitive radio (CR) [1] technology has been developed almost 20 years, providing high levels of adaptivity to the communications environment with advanced spectrum sensing and sharing. However, the CR-based spectrum sharing still faces several problems that impede the implementation of DSS, such as lack of a spectrum sharing database that records the frequency information, lack of an effective incentive mechanism between primary and secondary users such that primary users cannot be compensated from sharing the idle spectrum, lack of a trusted platform that enables secure spectrum trading, and also severe security threats due to the open environment.

© Springer Nature Singapore Pte Ltd. 2020
Z. Zheng et al. (Eds.): BlockSys 2020, CCIS 1267, pp. 575–587, 2020.
https://doi.org/10.1007/978-981-15-9213-3_44

Blockchain technology provides a good solution for the security and incentive problems in DSS. Through cryptography technology [2] and consensus mechanism, blockchain establishes a peer-to-peer [3] trust mechanism in the uncertain cyberspace. The blockchain-based distributed ledger technology (DLT) and smart contract [4] can also enable intelligent settlement, value transfer, and resource sharing, which naturally promotes the integration of blockchain and DSS. With DLT, the spectrum transactions can be recorded with transparency, immutability, and traceability guarantee, reflecting the status of every link in the circulation, and thus establishing a trusted relationship for the spectrum transaction. Based on the consensus mechanism, the spectrum resources rights can be confirmed, registered, and stored before the transaction, each node on the network can verify the validity of the rights, and thus providing a guarantee for maintaining spectrum sovereignty. In spectrum transactions, by establishing rules with smart contract, transactions can be realized automatically with guaranteed benefits for each participant. Thus, the blockchain-based DSS technology has also been regarded as one of the key technologies of 6G. The Federal Communications Commission (FCC) and French national spectrum management agency have started the research on spectrum blockchain. Moreover, the IMT-2030 Spectrum Group of Ministry of Industry and Information Technology of China is also promoting the research on the blockchain-based DSS.

1.1 State of the Art

Different from the cryptocurrency applications, the complex hierarchical relationship, highly dynamic scenarios, and users' random behaviors impede the direct application of blockchain to the DSS system. Considering the requirements of DSS system and the limitations of blockchain technology, a thorough understanding of the architecture of the complex dynamic system is required. To achieve spectrum sharing between spectrum providers and users, Kim et al. [5] designed a spectrum sharing system with blockchain, which is consisted of users, communication services, and blockchain network, and the communication services have mobile network operators (MNOs) and micro operators (MOs). A unified and shared database among all participating nodes is built with blockchain to enhance the clarity of the spectrum situation. Maksymyuk et al. [6] introduced a blockchain-based distributed mobile network infrastructure where smart contract automatically executes all transactions to eliminate the need for complex and expensive billing system. Zhou et al. [7] proposed a spectrum-sharing framework based on blockchain for human-to-human (H2H) and machine-to-machine (M2M) communications, which solves the two-sided matching problem between users and devices through a low-complexity stable matching method based on Gale-Shapley algorithm. Chen et al. [8] established a centralized private blockchain operating environment and a consortium blockchain operating environment in parallel with a full-spectrum blockchain as a service architecture. A unified interface for the two operating environments is developed to meet the needs of users' own operating environment.

To improve the spectrum utilization, it is necessary to provide double incentives for the owners and demanders of spectrum resources to promote efficient trading. A double-chain system combining public blockchain and consortium blockchain was developed in [9]. The operators in consortium blockchain can trade spectrum directly. Moreover, game theory is used for operators to share the spectrum between each other. In [10], to encourage authorized users to share their own spectrum, authors proposed a secure spectrum auction program based on blockchain, where spectrum monitoring obtains the information of idle bands. At the same time, the program improves the efficiency of spectrum auctions and ensures its effectiveness through two sealed bids. The program has the advantages of decentralization, accessibility, verification of user identity, and fraud prevention. In [11], an iterative double auction mechanism was proposed to maximize the benefits of both traders, which can encourage data demanders to submit bids and determine the number and price of transactions.

To deal with the security issues in CR, Kotobi and Bilén [12] proposed a blockchain verification protocol, which adopts a security algorithm that ensures the secure spectrum sharing in mobile CR network by authentication mechanism and preventing malicious nodes from accessing the spectrum without paying. [13] proposed a solution to the privacy problem of the consortium blockchain, preventing attackers from obtaining the private information recorded on the blockchain through data mining algorithms. [14] proposed a blockchain radio access network (B-RAN) architecture, and developed a distributed, secure, and efficient mechanism to manage network access and essentially untrusted authentication between network entities.

It is worth noting that even though some works have started to investigate blockchain-based DSS, a theoretical unified framework is still missing. In order to meet the requirements of response delay, throughput, computing and storage costs of large-scale spectrum sharing system, it is necessary to further study the key issues such as the architecture, the trusted spectrum ledger model, the incentive mechanism, and smart contract for spectrum trading.

1.2 Organization

We first investigate the application of blockchain technology in DSS, and propose the key challenges that need to be solved to achieve efficient dynamic spectrum sharing in Sect. 2. Then, we propose the architecture of blockchain-based DSS in Sect. 3, followed by key technologies to solve the above problems in Sect. 4. Conclusions are drawn in Sect. 5.

2 Challenges in Blockchain-Based DSS

To meet the requirements of DSS while guaranteeing the availability, credibility, security, and efficiency of the blockchain based spectrum sharing, the following key issues need to be solved.

2.1 The Blockchain Architecture for Large-Scale DSS System

Among the services supported by the radio spectrum, there are not only public mobile communications, broadcasting and television-oriented services for daily life, but also civil aviation, railway, and meteorological services related to life safety and public welfare, as well as military defense, disaster relief, and other services related to national security. Different services have different requirements for quality-of-service (QoS), security, and bandwidth, which greatly increase the complexity of spectrum sharing system. At the same time, considering the specific property of spectrum resources, the auction and utilization of spectrum cannot be separated from the regulatory and administrative intervention of the radio management department. Therefore, when designing the architecture of blockchain-based DSS system, both the administrative approval and monitoring of the national radio management department, and the decentralized characteristics of multiparty participation such as private network operation departments, mobile operators, radio and television operators, and other relevant special departments. In addition, some services have very high level of security requirements. To achieve the strict management and efficient spectrum sharing, a hierarchical and heterogeneous hybrid blockchain architecture that includes administrative supervision and free marketing competition is required to combine consortium blockchain and private blockchain. Considering the requirements of DSS, blockchain technology should be improved through the optimization of modules. For example, the data structure, storage and query, and consensus mechanism of blockchain should be redesigned and optimized.

2.2 The Spectrum Ledger

In order to achieve efficient secure sharing and strict management of spectrum resources, the transaction process and usage status of spectrum should be recorded into the spectrum ledger to form a distributed spectrum database. The wide-area and dynamic characteristics of spectrum sharing, the diverse types of data, and the dramatic changes in data bring great challenges to the construction of the spectrum ledger. Considering the requirements of spectrum asset ownership, account information query, and circulation process records, we need to establish an account-based model with the account as the asset and transaction object. Compared with traditional databases, the blockchain ledger does not allow delete and modify operations. However, with the increase of the amount of block data, the storage space of blockchain nodes will become larger and larger. To reduce the storage space requirements of nodes while ensuring the performance, efficient data storage mechanism is required. In addition, efficient consensus is needed to ensure that only one node can write data to the ledger at the same time. Blockchain solves the trust of distributed nodes through the consensus mechanism, and ensures the immutability of information by using digital signature and hash operation for distributed unified storage, but the consensus mechanism cannot solve the problem of data fraud. In order to perform data inspection and quality evaluation provided by sensing nodes and also identify malicious nodes, advanced smart contract based spectrum sensing deserves more research efforts.

2.3 The Incentive Mechanism for Spectrum Sharing

Double incentives for the owners and demanders of spectrum resources is a prerequisite for spectrum resources trading so that the effective spectrum sharing can be achieved. However, it will also cause problems such as malicious encroachment, transaction congestion, and transaction fairness during spectrum trading. To this end, we need to create a payment mechanism suitable for spectrum transactions, construct an incentive model, and establish a secure spectrum sharing and leasing mechanism to ensure efficient completion of transactions. However, how to design the spectrum trading incentive strategy and the multi-user cooperative spectrum sharing incentive model to maximize the revenues of both the owner and demander is still a challenging issue.

2.4 Smart Contract for Spectrum Management

In CR, there is no trust between primary and secondary users, thus it is easy to cause fraud and lose the fairness of spectrum transactions. Meanwhile, a large number of illegal behaviors in the wireless network not only causes interference to primary users, but also increases difficulty for radio monitoring and management. In order to solve the implementation laws and regulations in the process of mutual trust and supervision between each node in the blockchain based spectrum network, smart contract cooperative spectrum resource management should be introduced. Smart contract is a programmable language that automatically executes the terms of a contract. It can establish rights and obligations for both parties to an agreement, then a computer or computer network can automatically run the smart contract script code. To this end, we need to weight the fairness of "first shipment" and "first payment" from the perspective of transaction initialization, payment transaction, withdrawal transaction, refund transaction, etc. Meanwhile, to achieve "face-to-face" trading of spectrum resources in the true sense, we should study the fair payment agreement based on smart contract to ensure the fairness of transactions. Considering the identity of the executor of laws and regulations in the supervision and management process, the operation process of laws and regulations based on smart contract should be studied. Therefore, in the spectrum cooperative management, both the fairness of transactions and regulations should be considered, so as to achieve a credible, automated, and coordinated spectrum management system based on smart contract.

3 The Architecture of Blockchain-Based DSS

The blockchain architecture has evolved three phases up to now. Blockchain 1.0 [15] is the architecture of digital payment system represented by Satoshi Nakamoto's earliest application of Bitcoin technology; Blockchain 2.0 [16] is the architecture typically represented by Ethereum which first introduces smart contract into blockchain; Blockchain 3.0 does not yet have a recognized representative, but it will go beyond the financial field and become a system architecture for enterprise-level applications that provide services to all walks of life. Although the architecture at each stage differs in specific performance, the basic architecture is usually divided to six layers: data layer, network layer, consensus layer, incentive layer, contract layer, and application layer.

The blockchain-based DSS should be considered to meet the requirements of availability, effectiveness, and security, so that the value transfer of spectrum information and digital assets can be achieved. However, the spectrum sharing system covers a wide range, including not only centralized regulatory agencies such as the National Radio Monitoring Center (NRMC), but also multi-party participants such as mobile network operators, railways, airplanes, satellites, etc., as well as multiple types of users such as mobile users, internet, cars, etc. In addition, it cannot meet the requirement of response time for the real-time performance and processing speed of the smart contract mechanism on the fully decentralized public blockchain. A pure private blockchain is not fundamentally different from the current distributed architecture and cloud platform architecture, but only adds a constant and trusted data function, which is not suitable for the entire chain and applications of multi-party participants. Therefore, the application of blockchain technology in the construction of a blockchain-based spectrum system should establish a consortium blockchain with a government regulatory department as the core. Based on this, the overall blockchain-based DSS model is shown in Fig. 1. NRMC has the monitoring rights to all nodes in the blockchain-based DSS system. The spectrum transaction information and the available spectrum usage of all nodes are open and transparent to NRMC, but NRMC is independent of other nodes.

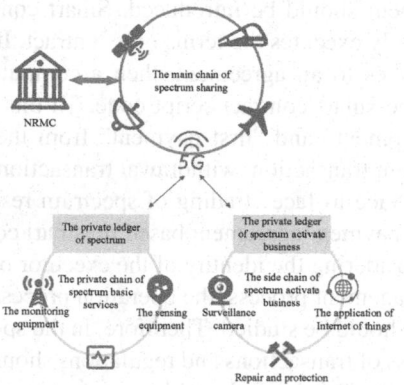

Fig. 1. The overall model of blockchain-based DSS.

Moreover, because the spectrum sharing system involves a large range and there may be cross-region transactions between different mobile network operators, it should be designed according to multi-level blockchains (main chain and side chain). Cross-region applications such as cross-region transactions are completed on the main chain, while intraregional applications are completed on the sidechain. In the local scope, the main services include distributed spectrum point-to-point [17] transactions, spectrum contracts, and spectrum data security. It is planned to consider deploying a sub chain in a local area, while the scenario of cross-region spectrum service plans to deploy the main chain of the blockchain-based DSS system. The main chain and the sub chain are side-chain relationships. The main chain mainly serves cross-region identity authentication, asset transfer, spectrum transaction, and data interaction, while the sub chain mainly serves blockchain application services in a single area. The sub chains between different regions realize flexible interconnection and disaggregation with the main chain according to channel conditions and functional requirements. There are different sub chains in multiple regions under a main chain of the complete blockchain-based DSS system. The sub chains do not directly exchange data with each other. All data interactions must be connected to the main chain through network security protection equipment (such as firewalls), and then the main chain completes the data interaction. Moreover, the operation security among the side chains, and that between the side chain and the main chain does not affect each other with flexible access and disassembly functions. In addition, the relationship between the spectrum blockchain and other activate business blockchains is the relationship between side chains.

The capacity of the public ledger will be increasing for the undeleted characteristic of blockchain. Thus, it's not necessary for each participating network node to maintain a complete ledger in practice, and the network node should be selectively classified according to the application scenario. Considering different requirements of the nodes on the main chain and the side chain, and the different authentication methods of the nodes participating in the blockchain, we divide the nodes into full nodes, relay nodes, and light nodes based on their functions. The full nodes are generally composed by the main and important participants in the blockchain, such as the telecommunications operators, which has the best communication resources and requires complete ledger records and consensus capabilities, completing data verification and synchronization functions. The relay nodes are generally composed by infrastructure in the network, e.g., communication base stations in local areas with data collection and forwarding capabilities. They can complete the data collection and allocation in the jurisdiction and provide this function for interactive information of other participants in the network. So the relay nodes own pretty good communication resources in the network. The light nodes are generally terminal equipment, such as mobile devices and civilian drones. They generally have the entry function for various applications and the ability to complete simplified authentication protocols, complete the collection and upload of raw data, and accept the interactive information of other participants in the network. But they do not have enough storage capacity of the entire blockchain data and only store neighboring node address information and block header information.

The blockchain-based DSS architecture is divided into system front-end and back-end. The front-end of the system is the user interface, including various user-oriented application interfaces, which can perform spectrum leasing and trading, asset transfers, etc. The back-end of the system is designed according to the basic framework of blockchain. The lowest-level includes the support system and the blockchain data layer. The distributed support system includes distributed computing, distributed storage, distributed network, and spectrum sensing. The data layer is responsible for encapsulating the underlying data blocks and related basic data and algorithms such as data encryption and time stamping. The core module includes four key functions: network layer, consensus layer, incentive layer, and contract layer. The network layer includes distributed networking mechanism, data transmission mechanism, and authentication mechanism. The consensus layer mainly encapsulates various consensus algorithms of network nodes such as Proof-of-Work (PoW), Proof-of-Stake (PoS), Practical Byzantine Fault Tolerance (PBFT) [18], etc. The incentive layer mainly considers the economic factors of the blockchain, including the spectrum coin issuance mechanism, allocation mechanism, and user reputation modelling and evaluation to inspire economic benefits. The contract layer encapsulates various programming languages, contract scripts and runtime environments to support the programmable characteristics of the blockchain. The top application layer encapsulates various application scenarios and use cases of the blockchain.

4 Key Technologies

In this section, we provide the key technologies in the blockchain based DSS system.

4.1 Trusted Spectrum Ledger

The distributed ledger provided by blockchain allows the spectrum transaction records to be open, transparent, immutable and traceable, which fully reflects the status of each link in the circulation, establishing a trusted relationship among various links in the circulation. It greatly promotes the implementation of spectrum sharing. Based on this, the blockchain-based DSS is essentially a distributed ledger which records spectrum information. Apart from the information such as spectrum auctions, spectrum transactions, and spectrum access, the spectrum ledger should also include sensing data from external spectrum sensing equipment. The information recorded in the spectrum ledger provides a basis for the efficient sharing of spectrum resources, fair transactions, and effective management and control, but it is also vulnerable to malicious node attacks. So, we should design and implement spectrum ledger data based on hash calculation to effectively solve the above problems. To this end, the spectrum ledger model is shown in Fig. 2. It should be noted that spectrum information usually has a large amount of data.

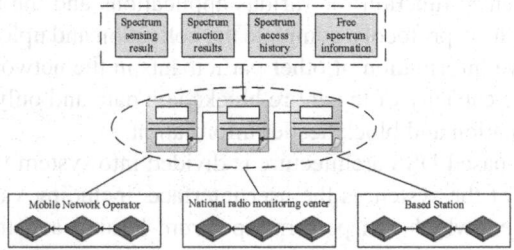

Fig. 2. The illustration of the spectrum ledger.

In order to ensure the storage in the block, on the one hand, data compression or pre-processing can be adopted. On the other hand, the original spectrum data can be uploaded to the edge storage server, and only the root hash value of the original data in the edge memory is stored in the blockchain. Figure 3 shows the architecture of the spectrum data block. The spectrum data generated in a certain period is hashed to generate a hash value. The hash value of each spectrum data is organized to form a Merkle tree, and thus any change in the spectrum data can be reflected on the root of Merkle tree.

At same time, the data in the wide-area with considerable values is helpful to understand the spectrum characteristics in the space. The monitoring and sensing network are established so as to obtain the spectrum sensing data [19]. Under the circumstance of limited sensing network resources, smart contract based spectrum sensing can be used, as shown in Fig. 4. First, the local spectrum management server deployed on the edge server or the cloud regularly releases spectrum sensing tasks, and proposes spectrum

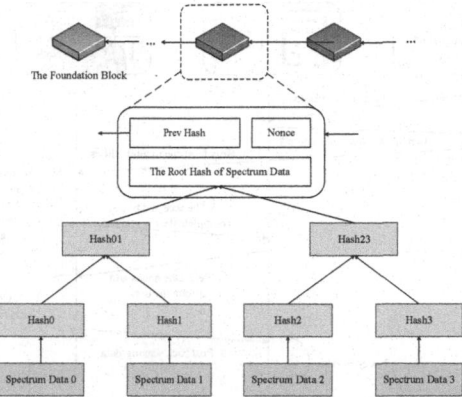

Fig. 3. The architecture of the spectrum block.

data collection task requirements including collection time, frequency band limits, and geographic area limitations. Spectrum data collection tasks are visible to all servers and nodes in the spectrum equipment network. When the spectrum management server issues a spectrum sensing task, it automatically generates and pre-stores the corresponding spectrum coin as a reward for the completion of the spectrum sensing task. Second, the sensing nodes decide whether to respond to the spectrum sensing task based on their own action plan, battery power, and geographic location. The nodes accepting the task complete registration on smart contract. Then smart contract completes the selection of nodes based on the location, price, and reputation. After that the smart contract informs the selected nodes. Finally, the sensing nodes complete the spectrum sensing task and upload the results. Smart contract completes the verification of the quality of the data, confirms whether it meets the contract requirements, and issues rewards according to the contract.

4.2 Smart Contract for DSS

By leveraging smart contract, spectrum trading can be completed automatically and securely by executing the contract terms without relying a trusted third party. In addition, the smart contract defined in the form of digital codes can be flexibly embedded in the spectrum management, asset transfer, and spectrum transaction information, which facilitates dynamic spectrum sharing. As shown in Fig. 5, the trigger conditions, response rules, and trusted data sources of the contract terms are preset in the codes of smart contract. The trigger conditions include specific trading time, data resources, and sharing institutions to ensure the orderliness of the system. Response rules include specific trading actions, legal agreements, etc., to ensure the legitimacy of transactions. Data sources mainly provide the information of spectrum data source that can be shared by both parties to a spectrum transaction. Secondly, smart contract is broadcasted to the nodes in the network along with the user-initiated transaction after mutual agreement and signatures by multiple parties. The miners verify them and stores them in the specific block after verification. The users can call the contracts by initiating a transaction after

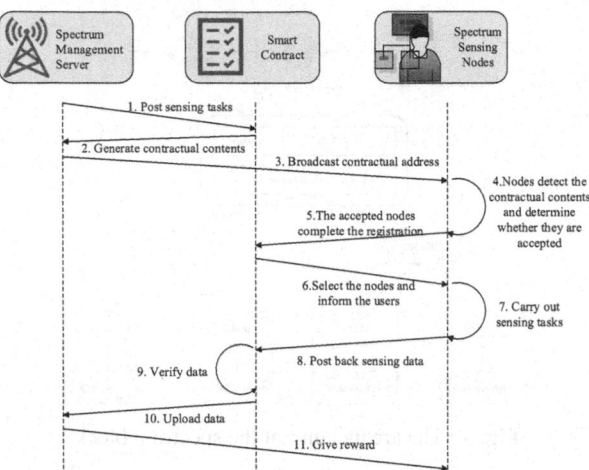

Fig. 4. The smart contract based spectrum sensing.

obtaining the returned contract address and contract interface. The miners are encouraged by the preset activating mechanism of the system, and provide their own storage and computing resources to verify the validity of the transaction. After receiving the contracts to create or call the transaction, the miners create contracts or execute the contract codes in the local sandbox execution environment. The codes automatically determine whether the current scene meets the contract trigger conditions based on trusted external data sources and inspection information to strictly enforce the response rules and update the world status. In the end, the trading verification is packaged and added to the new data block after being verified. The new block is authenticated by the consensus mechanism, and is linked to the main chain of the blockchain. All the updates take effect, and the miners get the block rewards.

4.3 The Spectrum Trading Mechanism

The status of each participants in the spectrum trading network is highly dynamic. Smart contract is added to each independent block to effectively separate the trading settlement of different participants. In [20], spectrum coin (SC) is used for spectrum trading settlement and mining rewards between UAV users and mobile operators. In [12], SC is used to pay for data transmission of cognitive radio networks, spectrum leasing between secondary users and primary users, and block rewards. SC is mainly used for spectrum transaction payment, transaction verification rewards and block rewards. In blockchain based DSS, SC can be used to facilitate the spectrum trading, including spectrum payment, trading verification rewards, and block generation rewards, etc. A possible spectrum trading scheme with SC is shown in Fig. 6. There are multiple spectrum authorized users forming part of blockchain. Primary spectrum users include spectrum authorization users and users who transfer spectrum resources, and secondary spectrum users include users who request or rent spectrum resources. The primary users and secondary users of the spectrum publish their spectrum resources and requirements to

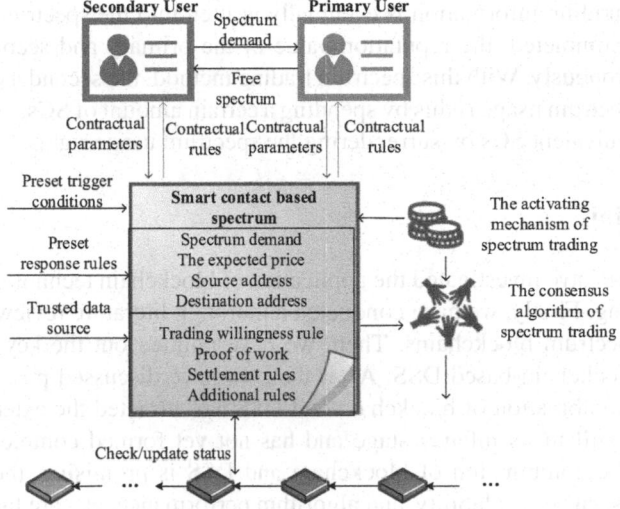

Fig. 5. The smart contract for DSS.

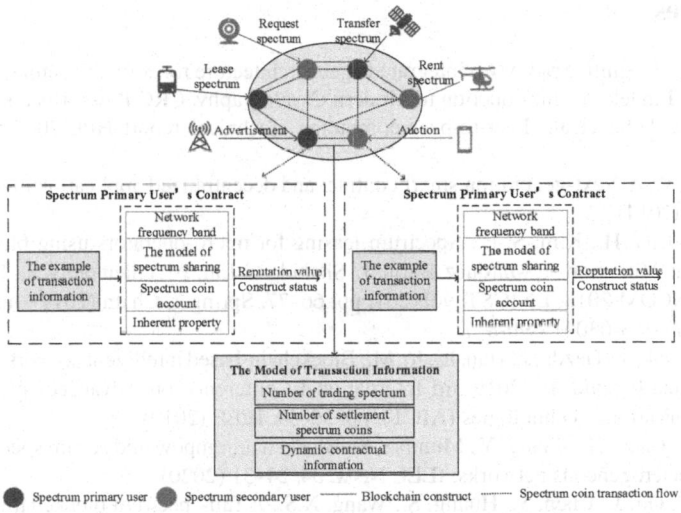

Fig. 6. The spectrum trading scheme based on SC.

all nodes in the network. Smart contract automatically communicates with users based on the request information, such as bidding, and frequency usage time. Once the information is matched, and the account balance meets the requirement. Then the agreement is automatically executed and the reputation value is updated. Smart contract determines whether to perform spectrum sharing trading based on the primary and secondary users' information matching results and reputation values. If the spectrum sharing trading is executed, smart contract establishes a transaction information model based on the number of spectrum trading, the number of settlement SCs, and dynamic contract information.

The spectrum trading information is eventually written into the spectrum ledger. After the trading is completed, the reputation value of the primary and secondary users is updated synchronously. With this spectrum trading method, the secondary users acquire the required spectrum usage rights by spending a certain amount of SCs, and the primary users obtain equivalent SCs by surrendering the spectrum usage rights.

5 Conclusion

In this paper, we have investigated the application of blockchain technology in dynamic spectrum sharing. Firstly, we have conducted a thorough literature review on the recent research on spectrum blockchains. Then, we have pointed out the key challenges in building the blockchain-based DSS. After that, we have discussed possible solutions. Although the combination of blockchain and DSS has attracted the extensive research attention, it is still in its infancy stage and has not yet formed completed standards. Even though the combination of blockchain and DSS is promising, the problems of blockchain on security, scalability, and algorithm performance, etc. are far from enough to be applied in DSS, which deserves more and more research efforts.

References

1. Mitola, J.: Cognitive radio. An integrated agent architecture for software defined radio (2002)
2. Katz, J., Lindell, Y.: Introduction to Modern Cryptography. CRC Press, Boca Raton (2014)
3. Milojicic, D.S., et al.: Peer-to-peer computing. Technical report HPL-2002-57, HP Labs (2002)
4. Buterin, V.: A Next-generation smart contract and decentralized application platform. White Paper **3** (2014)
5. Kim, J., Cha, H., Kim, S.-L.: Spectrum leasing for micro-operators using blockchain networks. In: Moerman, I., Marquez-Barja, J., Shahid, A., Liu, W., Giannoulis, S., Jiao, X. (eds.) CROWNCOM 2018. LNICST, vol. 261, pp. 66–77. Springer, Cham (2019). https://doi.org/10.1007/978-3-030-05490-8_7
6. Maksymyuk, T., Gazda, J., Han, L., Jo, M.: Blockchain-based intelligent network management for 5G and beyond. In: 2019 3rd International Conference on Advanced Information and Communications Technologies (AICT), pp. 36–39. IEEE (2019)
7. Zhou, Z., Chen, X., Zhang, Y., Mumtaz, S.: Blockchain-empowered secure spectrum sharing for 5G heterogeneous networks. IEEE Netw. **34**, 24–31 (2020)
8. Chen, Y., Gu, J., Chen, S., Huang, S., Wang, X.S.: A full-spectrum blockchain-as-a-service for business collaboration. 2019 IEEE International Conference on Web Services (ICWS), pp. 219–223 (2019)
9. Han, S., Zhu, X.: Blockchain based spectrum sharing algorithm. In: 2019 IEEE 19th International Conference on Communication Technology (ICCT), pp. 936–940. IEEE (2019)
10. Liang, Y.-C.: Blockchain for dynamic spectrum management. In: Liang, Y.-C. (ed.) Dynamic Spectrum Management. SCT, pp. 121–146. Springer, Singapore (2020). https://doi.org/10.1007/978-981-15-0776-2_5
11. Chen, C., Wu, J., Lin, H., Chen, W., Zheng, Z.: A secure and efficient blockchain-based data trading approach for internet of vehicles. IEEE Trans. Veh. Technol. **68**, 9110–9121 (2019)
12. Kotobi, K., Bilen, S.G.: Secure blockchains for dynamic spectrum access: a decentralized database in moving cognitive radio networks enhances security and user access. IEEE Veh. Technol. Mag. **13**, 32–39 (2018)

13. Gai, K., Wu, Y., Zhu, L., Qiu, M., Shen, M.: Privacy-preserving energy trading using consortium blockchain in smart grid. IEEE Trans. Industr. Inf. **15**, 3548–3558 (2019)
14. Ling, X., Wang, J., Bouchoucha, T., Levy, B.C., Ding, Z.: Blockchain radio access network (B-RAN): towards decentralized secure radio access paradigm. IEEE Access **7**, 9714–9723 (2019)
15. Nakamoto, S.: Bitcoin: a peer-to-peer electronic cash system. Manubot (2019)
16. Wood, G.: Ethereum: a secure decentralised generalised transaction ledger. Ethereum Proj. Yellow Paper **151**, 1–32 (2014)
17. Simpson, W.: RFC1661: the point-to-point protocol (PPP). RFC Editor (1994)
18. Castro, M., Liskov, B.: Practical byzantine fault tolerance. In: OSDI, pp. 173–186 (1999)
19. Bayhan, S., Zubow, A., Gawłowicz, P., Wolisz, A.: Smart contracts for spectrum sensing as a service. IEEE Trans. Cogn. Commun. Netw. **5**, 648–660 (2019)
20. Qiu, J., Grace, D., Ding, G., Yao, J., Wu, Q.: Blockchain-based secure spectrum trading for unmanned aerial vehicle assisted cellular networks: an operator's perspective. IEEE Internet Things J. 1 (2019)

A Decentralized Data Processing Framework Based on PoUW Blockchain

Guangcheng Li[1], Qinglin Zhao[1(✉)], and Xianfeng Li[2]

[1] Faculty of Information Technology, Macau University of Science and Technology,
Taipa, Macau 999078, China
guangcheng.li@hotmail.com, zqlict@hotmail.com
[2] International Institute of Next Generation Internet,
Macau University of Science and Technology, Taipa, Macau 999078, China
xifli@must.edu.mo

Abstract. Conventional master/slave-based data processing frameworks are vulnerable to single point of failure and performance bottlenecks of the master node. In contrast, blockchain systems adopt a decentralized framework and are capable of aggregating enormous computing resources. In this paper, we propose a blockchain-based data processing framework that utilizes the advantages of the blockchain for solving the drawbacks of the centralized framework. In our framework, the blockchain stores the task information and the adopted proof of useful work consensus enables nodes to process tasks using their computing resources, while competing for the leader (who dispatches pending tasks to the blockchain). Extensive simulations show that the proposed framework is better than the centralized framework in terms of the throughput and the task response time.

Keywords: Blockchain · Data processing · PoUW · Decentralized framework · Blockchain application

1 Introduction

Currently, most data processing platforms (e.g., MapReduce [5], storm [18], flink [4]) adopt a master/slave-based framework, where a master node centralizedly controls and manages numerous slave nodes. However, such a centralized framework generally has the following drawbacks: 1). the single point of failure or bottleneck occurring in the master node [1,2,11,15,20]; 2). high maintenance costs for expanding the scale of the cluster [6]; 3). throughput scalability issue when the cluster reaches a certain scale. In the era of big data, with the increase of real-time streaming data processing with high concurrency, the above problems become growingly serious. Hence, a fundamental solution is to adopt a decentralized framework.

The blockchain [17], originally designed for recording transactions, has been considered as a new decentralized computing framework that has great potential

Z. Zheng et al. (Eds.): BlockSys 2020, CCIS 1267, pp. 588–600, 2020.
https://doi.org/10.1007/978-981-15-9213-3_45

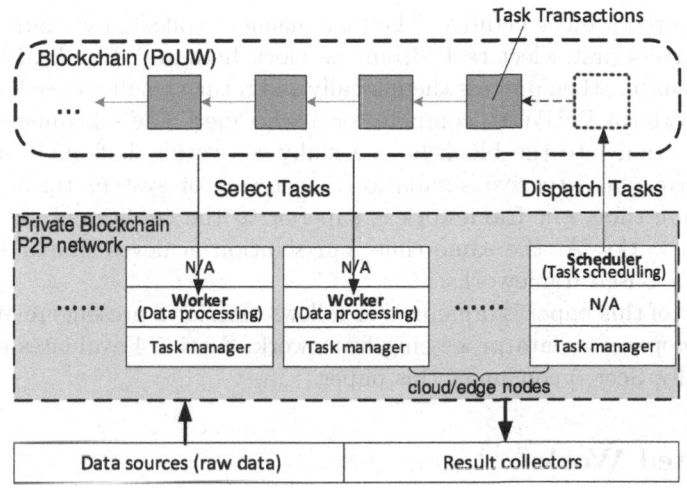

Fig. 1. The proposed blockchain-based data processing framework.

to meet various computing needs [17]. In this decentralized framework, there is no centralized entity, and all nodes are equivalent participants and maintain together the transactions consistency via a consensus mechanism [19]. The nature of the decentralization essentially allows infinite computing nodes to join the blockchain system, and therefore the system is capable of aggregating enormous computing resources. For example, as early as 2013, the Bitcoin network [14] was already more powerful than the top 500 supercomputers combined [13]. The decentralized characteristics and the aggregated enormous computing resources of the blockchain are what we imperatively need for solving the aforementioned drawbacks of the centralized framework.

Unfortunately, in the mainstream blockchain systems such as Bitcoin [14] and Ethereum [22], the enormous computing resources are mainly consumed in the consensus mechanism such as the proof of work (PoW), instead of solving meaningful practical problems (e.g., counting the number of cars in a streaming video). The proof of useful work (PoUW) [24] has therefore been proposed to overcome the drawback of PoW, whose idea is to let these computing resources solve practical problems, while reaching consensus as well. PoUW has stepped forward to utilize these potential enormous computing recourses for meaningful data processing. However, to use the blockchain for data processing, one challenge is to remold the transaction-recording blockchain for decentralized data processing. This paper is devoted to addressing this challenge. In this paper, for a private network (such as data center) where incentive mechanisms are not required and network latency can be ignored, we remold the transaction-recording blockchain framework to make it a data-processing framework with decentralized control. That is, we propose a blockchain-based decentralized framework for data processing. In our framework (shown in Fig. 1), the blockchain, adopting the PoUW consensus, stores task transactions. Each blockchain node plays three roles: task manager, worker, and scheduler. The task manager collects raw data from data source. Workers first select tasks from the blockchain and download tasks from the task manager, then process them locally and return result to result collectors, and then perform PoUW to compete for a scheduler. The scheduler dispatches task information into the blockchain. Finally, we verify that our framework is very effective via extensive simulations. In terms of system throughput and task response time, our framework is superior to the traditional master/slave-based frameworks. At the same time, our solution achieves similar fairness to master/slave-based frameworks.

The rest of this paper is organized as follows. Section 2 presents related works. Section 3 proposes a data processing framework. Section 4 evaluates our framework. Finally, Sect. 5 concludes this paper.

2   Related Works

This paper proposes a blockchain-based decentralized framework for data processing. It involves related works in the following two aspects.

Data Processing Framework. The master/slave based centralized framework is widely adopted in most data-processing platform such as MapReduce [5], flink [4], but it is vulnerable to single point of failure, performance bottlenecks, and etc. These drawbacks have received great attention. For example, the authors in [20] proposed a hot backup mechanism to solve the single point of failure (i.e., set up a backup node to take over the failed master node). The authors in [2,3] proposed a hierarchical master/worker (HMW) paradigm to overcome the performance bottleneck of the master node. However, all these improvements focus on the centralized frameworks. A fundamental solution is to adopt a decentralized framework as done in this paper. In the decentralized framework, all nodes are equivalent participants and therefore the single point of failure never occurs. Besides, the decentralized system is easily extended to a large scale, and therefore has good scalability in terms of the performance (such as throughput and security), and hardware upgrades.

Blockchain Applications. Blockchain is born with the decentralization feature, and therefore is attracting growing attention [10,16,21,23,25]. For example, the authors in [10] provided a blockchain-based decentralized framework for crowdsourcing, enabling a requester's tasks to be solved by a crowd of workers without relying on any third trusted institution. The authors in [23] proposed a blockchain-based decentralized trust management system for vehicular networks. The authors in [25] used blockchain for privacy protection while users share information among strangers. Different from the above work, we are the first to remold the blockchain for data processing. This study is very helpful to better design general decentralized computing frameworks for meeting various computing needs.

3   The Proposed Data Processing Framework

Here, we present a blockchain-based framework for data processing in a private P2P network.

In our framework shown in Fig. 1, the underlying blockchain P2P network consists of cloud/edge nodes. Each node, acting as a task manager, receives raw data from data source and organizes them into tasks, where each task (i.e., the most fine-grained processable data unit) is assigned a global unique ID and can be accessed through a uniform resource locator (URL). Tasks belonging to the same service can be regarded as a type of task, which have the same attributes (i.e., resource demand, time consumption in processing, arrival rate).

These nodes, when acting as worker or scheduler, will create and maintain a blockchain together via the proof of useful work (PoUW) consensus mechanism [24], where each block stores pending/processing/completed task transactions. That is, each worker keeps selecting pending task transactions from the blockchain and then processing the corresponding tasks locally; after finishing a task (i.e., finishing a certain amount of useful work), each worker first counts the number of its executed CPU instructions as the proof of completing useful work, and then competes for the scheduler by the number. Upon becoming a scheduler, the node will collect pending task transactions from task managers and processing/completed tasks transactions from workers, and then dispatch them into the blockchain.

Below, we will detail the blockchain transaction, the functionalities of the scheduler and the worker, and the workflow of the system sequentially.

3.1   Blockchain Transaction

In the blockchain, we use block to store task transactions, where a task transaction specifies the profile (such as ID and type) of a task. As shown in Fig. 2(a), each block consists of two parts: the block header and the block body.

The block header is used to identify a specific block on the blockchain and consists of the following fields:

- *hashPrevBlock*: the hash of the previous block header, through which we can connect a new block to the previous one.
- *time*: the generation time (timestamp) of the current block.
- *diff*: the difficulty coefficient d that the worker wins in executing the PoUW algorithm (explained in Algorithm 1). It controls the block generation rate of the blockchain, and is periodically adjustable to stabilize the rate.
- *PoUW*: the credential that the worker wins in executing the PoUW algorithm. A valid PoUW contains the useful work program attestation on the mining success and an attestation from the compliance checker of the program's compliance.
- *hashBody*: the hash of this block's body, upon which workers can verify the correctness and integrity of the block body.
- *transNum*: the number of transactions (included in this block body).

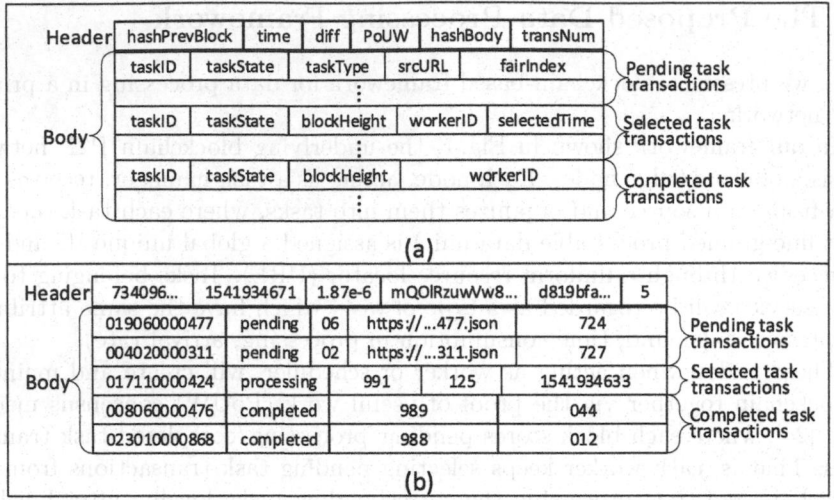

Fig. 2. (a) The data structure of a block. (b) An example block.

The block body stores task transactions. Each task is assigned a globally unique ID by its task manager. For example, assume 3 task managers: 001, 002, and 003. The task IDs assigned by these task managers can be 001109, 002087, 003272. Each task (and hence each task transaction) has three states: pending, processing, and completed. Each worker will select and process tasks according to the task attributes and its available resources. Whenever a worker selects or completes a task, it will create the corresponding task transaction. Upon receiving these transactions, workers will update the state of the corresponding tasks in their local task list, while the scheduler will collect these transactions into its newly created block, which will be linked to the blockchain.

A pending task transaction is used to notify workers of which task needs to be processed. It is composed of the following fields:

- *taskID*: the unique ID of the task.
- *taskState*: its value is set to "pending", indicating that this task needs to be processed.
- *taskType*: an integer representing the service type of a task. Each type of tasks has the same process flow, arrival rate, resource demand (e.g., CPU cores, memory, network bandwidth) and time consumption on processing.
- *srcURL*: the URL of the task, from which a worker can learn about whether the task has been selected by others when it tries to download the task, the arrival time of the task, the timeout within which the processing of the task should be completed, the collector URL (where to return the outcome of the task), and the download link of the task. Each task and its information are accessible and stored in the task manager until the processing of the task has been completed.

– *fairIndex*: A positive number indicated for fair task processing. If the system wishes to ensure a processing fairness among different task types, all tasks should be processed in ascending order of the fair index.

A processing task transaction is used to declare which task is being processed. It consists of the following fields:

– *taskID*: the unique ID of the task.
– *taskState*: its value is set to "processing", indicating that the task is being processed.
– *blockHeight*: the height of the block declares that the task is pending. If the processing of the task has not been completed after a timeout, the worker can find the block with hight = *blockHeight*, and acquire *srcURL* of the task for re-processing. For example, assume the *blockHeight* = *10*. Once the task is time out, the worker finds the 10th block and accesses the corresponding pending task transaction.
– *workerID*: the ID of the worker who selected the task.
– *selectedTime*: the time that worker selected the task. According to *selected-Time* and the current time, a worker can infer whether the processing of the task has timed out.

A completed task transaction is used to declare which task has been completed. It consists of the following fields:

– *taskID*: the unique ID of the task.
– *taskState*: its value is set to "completed", indicating that the task has been completed.
– *workerID*: the ID of the worker who completed the task.
– *completedTime*: the time that worker completed the task.

Figure 2(b) shows an example of a block, where there are 2 pending task transactions, 1 processing task transaction, and 2 completed task transactions.

3.2   The Scheduler

When a worker wins in PoUW, the corresponding node will act as a scheduler. At any time, the system only has one scheduler. The scheduler will conduct the following two operations.

Schedule Pending Tasks. Firstly, the scheduler collects newly arrived tasks from each task manager. Then, it calculates the fair index for each task by a scheduling algorithm. The scheduling algorithm under decentralized control is our future work.

Dispatch Block. First, the scheduler creates pending task transactions according to the scheduling result of the pending tasks. Then, it creates processing and completed task transactions according to its received processing and completed tasks which are broadcasted by workers since the last block. Third, it constructs the block body. Fourth, it creates a block header and splices it together with the block body to form an entire block. At last, it broadcasts the newly created block to the blockchain P2P network.

3.3   The Worker

Algorithm 1 PoUW Verification

1	**Input:** d: difficulty m: the number of executed CPU instructions for completing one task
2	**Output:** win: the competition result of the worker

3	$win \leftarrow 0$
4	$nonce \leftarrow \text{rand}(0,1)$
5	**if** $nonce \leq 1 - (1 - d)^m$
6	$win \leftarrow 1$

In our decentralized framework, each worker actively selects and downloads tasks from the blockchain and then processes them locally, instead of receiving tasks passively as in a centralized framework. Each worker keeps synchronizing its local blockchain with the blockchain of the system. Upon receiving a new block, the worker will conduct the following three operations.

Task Selection. First, each worker updates his own selectable tasks table, say, adding pending tasks, marking processing tasks, and removing completed tasks. Then, it invokes a task selection scheme to choose tasks according to some criterion such as processing fairness. Third, it broadcasts its selections to the P2P networks. When receiving these broadcasted messages, the other workers will choose other tasks, and the next scheduler will create a processing task transaction for each selected task (which implies that this task has been selected and in processing) and record it into a new block, and the corresponding task manager will change the state of each selected tasks (from pending to processing) once it finds that the related information of this task has been downloaded.

Task Processing. After downloading selected tasks, a worker processes them locally (say, counts the number of cars in a small video). Note that according to the PoUW consensus, tasks should be processed in a Trusted Execution Environment (TEE) [7,8], such as Intel SGX [12], to prevent any compromised workers from reporting more efforts than what it can actually perform. When completing one task, the worker will count the number of the executed CPU instructions, and send the outcome of the task to the collector, and finally broadcast the completed task to the P2P network.

Scheduler Election. Whenever a worker finishes a task, it will perform the PoUW consensus to compete for the scheduler by running Algorithm 1. Let m represent the number of executed CPU instructions for completing one task, and let d represent the current difficulty coefficient of the blockchain. In this algorithm, the worker generates a random number $nonce$ (line 4), and then checks whether the $nonce$ satisfies an inequality with respect to m and d (Line 5). If yes, the competition result win is set to 1, indicating that the worker wins the competition and hence will become a scheduler; otherwise, win is set to 0, indicating that the worker will not change its role.

3.4   Workflow

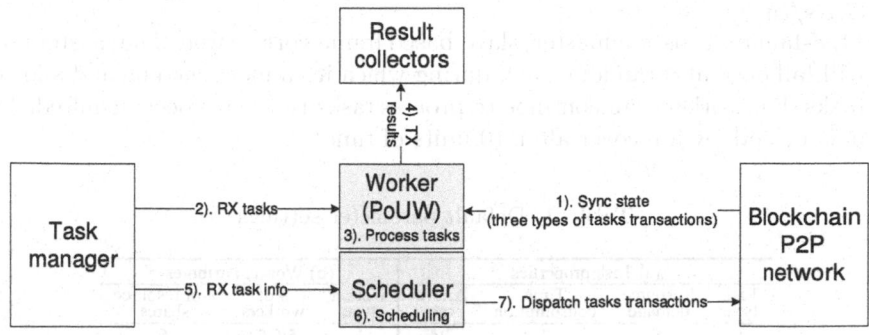

Fig. 3. The workflow of our decentralized system.

The complete data-processing workflow of our blockchain-based framework is illustrated in Fig. 3. We now explain the workflow steps as follows.

1. A worker constantly synchronizes the latest blockchain status with other workers and updates its selectable task table.
2. It acquires the related information of each selected task from task managers, according to the task table and a task selection scheme.
3. It then processes tasks.
4. It reports the data processing result whenever a task is completed, and then performs PoUW verification (explained in Algorithm 1) to compete for the scheduler. If the competition is successful, the node will switch from a worker to the scheduler; otherwise, it returns to the first step and keeps processing tasks.
5. The scheduler collects pending tasks from all task managers and the processing/completed tasks (broadcasted by workers).
6. The scheduler then performs a task scheduling algorithm to calculate fair indexes of pending tasks.
7. The scheduler packages the collected pending, processing, and completed task transactions and then creates a block, and dispatches it to the blockchain P2P network.

4   Evaluation

In this section, we evaluate our design via extensive simulations. We compare the following three frameworks in terms of system throughput, response time and fairness in the simulation.

– Decentralization. It is the framework proposed in this paper.

- M/S. It is a master/slave-based data processing framework, where the master node schedules and allocates tasks to workers. A master node has 12 shares of resources, and each share of resources is able to schedule or allocate 15 tasks/time.
- M/S-failure. It used a master/slave-based framework as well. The master node will fail once at a random time, during which it cannot schedule and allocate tasks, but workers can continue to process tasks that have been acquired. The master node will recover after 10 units of time.

Table 1. Default parameter settings

(a) Task properties				(b) Worker attributes		
Task type	Resource demand	Time consumption	Arrival rate	Worker type	# of workers	# of resource shares
1	5	2	24	1	5:5:50	5
2	5	3	8	2	5:5:50	8
3	4	4	15	3	5:5:50	9
4	4	5	12	4	5:5:50	10
5	3	6	14	5	5:5:50	16
6	3	7	12			
7	2	8	15			
8	2	9	13			

In the simulation, we fix task properties, and vary the number of workers. We assume that arrival rate of tasks follows Poisson distribution, and when a task is processed, it needs to occupy a part of the worker's resources and consumes some time. The default parameter settings are shown in Table 1. In Table 1(a), we list the properties of 8 types of tasks. In Table 1(b), we show the attributes of 5 types of workers. For example, when the "Worker type" is 1, the "# of type-1 workers" is set to "5:5:50". Here, the second parameter 5 in "5:5:50" stands for an increasing step of 5. Hence, "5:5:50" denotes that we increase the number of type-1 workers from 5, 10, 15, ..., to 50, sequentially. This corresponds to a simulation sequence, as the total worker number of all types increases from 25, 50, 75, ..., to, 250, which are labeled in the x-axis of Fig. 4 Fig. 5, and Fig. 6. Each simulation value is an average over 3 simulation runs, where each run lasts for 1200 s.

4.1 System Throughput

We measure the throughput by the number of atomic tasks per unit time (for short, tasks/time). The atomic task is a task that only needs to consume 1 share of resources and can be completed in 1 unit time.

Figure 4 plots the system throughput as the number of workers varies from 50 to 250. From this figure, we observe that the throughput of our scheme is always higher than those of M/S and M/S-failure. When the number of workers reaches 175, the master node has a performance bottleneck. Therefore, the system throughput of M/S and M/S-failure no longer increases with the number of workers.

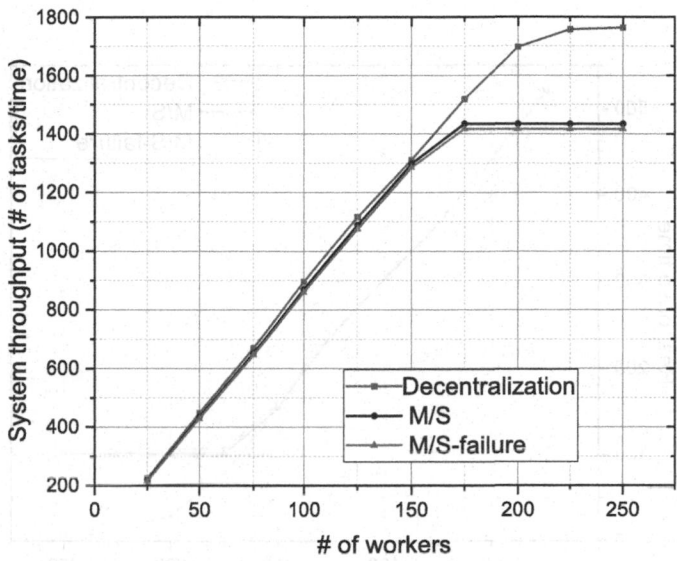

Fig. 4. System throughput as the number of workers varies

4.2 Response Time

Response time is the duration from the time when a task is generated to the time when it starts to be processed by a worker. The less response time, the more timely the task is processed.

Figure 5 plots the response time as the number of workers varies from 25 to 250. From this figure, we observe that when the number of workers is less than 150, the response time of the three schemes is almost the same, and it decreases almost linearly with the increase of the number of workers. When the number of workers is more than 150, the response time of our scheme drops faster. Due to the bottleneck of the master node, when the number of workers exceeds 175, the response time of M/S and M/S-failure no longer changes.

4.3 Fairness

In simulation, we measure the achieved fairness by Jain's fairness index [9], which is calculated as follows.

$$Fairness(x_1, x_2, \ldots, x_n) = \frac{(\sum_{i=1}^{n} x_i)^2}{n \cdot \sum_{i=1}^{n} x_i{}^2}, \tag{1}$$

where n represents the number of tasks' types, and x_i is the throughput of task type i. The result ranges from $1/n$ (in the worst case) to 1 (in the best case, where the throughput of each task type is equal).

Figure 6 compares the Jain's index among our framework, M/S, and M/S-failure. From this figure, we observe that the fairness of the decentralized framework is always lower than that of the two centralized framework. This is because

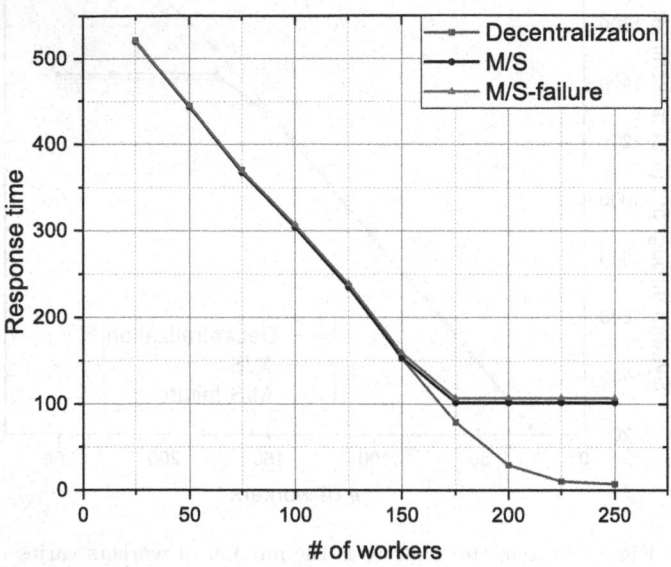

Fig. 5. Response time as the number of workers varies

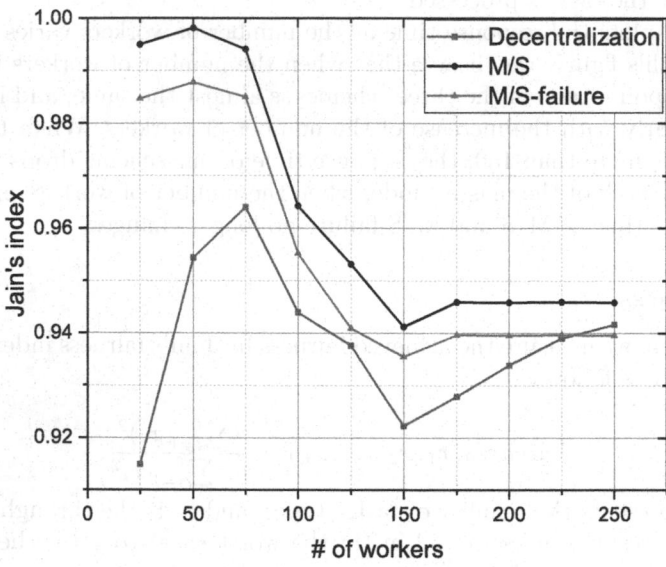

Fig. 6. Jain's index as the number of workers varies

in a decentralized framework, there is not a master node to allocate tasks, and workers choose tasks from the blockchain to process. Fairness therefore cannot be well guaranteed.

5   Conclusion

Conventional master/slave-based data processing frameworks are vulnerable to single point of failure and performance bottlenecks. To address these disadvantages, this paper proposes remolding the popular blockchain with decentralized framework for data processing. The blockchain was originally designed as a decentralized ledger, where each blockchain node adopts the proof of work (PoW) consensus, which consumes a great deal of computing resources primarily for competing for the leader. To avoid these resources wasting, we develop a blockchain-based decentralized framework for data processing, where we replace the PoW by the proof of useful work (PoUW) consensus and let the blockchain store data-processing tasks. By performing PoUW, the blockchain node can select and process tasks from the blockchain and at the same time compete for the leader who is responsible for dispatching pending tasks to the blockchain. A natural progression of this work is to present scheduling and task selection algorithms under decentralized control.

Acknowledgments. This work is funded in part by the National Nature Science Foundation of China (File no. 61872451 and 61872452), in part by the Science and Technology Development Fund, Macau SAR (File no. 0098/2018/A3, 0076/2019/A2 and 0037/2020/A1).

References

1. Aida, K., Natsume, W., Futakata, Y.: Distributed computing with hierarchical master-worker paradigm for parallel branch and bound algorithm. In: 2003 Proceedings of the 3rd IEEE/ACM International Symposium on Cluster Computing and the Grid, CCGrid 2003, pp. 156–163. IEEE (2003)
2. Archer, C.J., Mullins, T.J., Ratterman, J.D., Sidelnik, A., Smith, B.E.: Parallel computing system using coordinator and master nodes for load balancing and distributing work. US Patent 7,647,590, 12 January 2010
3. Bendjoudi, A., Melab, N., Talbi, E.G.: An adaptive hierarchical master-worker (AHMW) framework for grids-application to B&B algorithms. J. Parallel Distrib. Comput. **72**(2), 120–131 (2012)
4. Carbone, P., Katsifodimos, A., Ewen, S., Markl, V., Haridi, S., Tzoumas, K.: Apache flink: stream and batch processing in a single engine. Bull. IEEE Comput. Soc. Tech. Commit. Data Eng. **36**(4), 28–38 (2015)
5. Dean, J., Ghemawat, S.: MapReduce: simplified data processing on large clusters. Commun. ACM **51**(1), 107–113 (2008)
6. Genez, T.A., Bittencourt, L.F., Madeira, E.R.: Workflow scheduling for SaaS/PaaS cloud providers considering two SLA levels. In: 2012 IEEE Network Operations and Management Symposium, pp. 906–912. IEEE (2012)

7. Hoekstra, M., Lal, R., Pappachan, P., Phegade, V., Del Cuvillo, J.: Using innovative instructions to create trustworthy software solutions. HASP@ ISCA 11 (2013)
8. Hunt, T., Zhu, Z., Xu, Y., Peter, S., Witchel, E.: Ryoan: a distributed sandbox for untrusted computation on secret data. ACM Trans. Comput. Syst. (TOCS) **35**(4), 13 (2018)
9. Jain, R.K., Chiu, D.M.W., Hawe, W.R.: A quantitative measure of fairness and discrimination, pp. 2–7. Eastern Research Laboratory, Digital Equipment Corporation, Hudson (1984)
10. Li, M., et al.: CrowdBC: a blockchain-based decentralized framework for crowdsourcing. IEEE Trans. Parallel Distrib. Syst. **30**, 1251–1266 (2018)
11. Li, S., et al.: WOHA: deadline-aware map-reduce workflow scheduling framework over hadoop clusters. In: 2014 IEEE 34th International Conference on Distributed Computing Systems (ICDCS), pp. 93–103. IEEE (2014)
12. McKeen, F., et al.: Intel® software guard extensions (intel® sgx) support for dynamic memory management inside an enclave. In: Proceedings of the Hardware and Architectural Support for Security and Privacy 2016, p. 10. ACM (2016)
13. Mims, C.: The bitcoin network is now more powerful than the top 500 supercomputers, combined (2013). https://qz.com/84056/the-bitcoin-network-is-now-more-powerful-than-the-top-500-supercomputers-combined/. Accessed 09 Dec 2019
14. Nakamoto, S.: Bitcoin: a peer-to-peer electronic cash system (2008). https://bitcoin.org/bitcoin.pdf. Accessed 15 Dec 2019
15. Ren, Z., Xu, X., Wan, J., Shi, W., Zhou, M.: Workload characterization on a production hadoop cluster: a case study on taobao. In: 2012 IEEE International Symposium on Workload Characterization (IISWC), pp. 3–13. IEEE (2012)
16. Shrestha, A.K., Vassileva, J.: Blockchain-based research data sharing framework for incentivizing the data owners. In: Chen, S., Wang, H., Zhang, L.-J. (eds.) ICBC 2018. LNCS, vol. 10974, pp. 259–266. Springer, Cham (2018). https://doi.org/10.1007/978-3-319-94478-4_19
17. Swan, M.: Blockchain: Blueprint for a New Economy. O'Reilly Media, Inc., Newton (2015)
18. Toshniwal, A., et al.: Storm@ Twitter. In: Proceedings of the 2014 ACM SIGMOD International Conference on Management of Data, pp. 147–156. ACM (2014)
19. Vukolić, M.: The quest for scalable blockchain fabric: proof-of-work vs. BFT replication. In: Camenisch, J., Kesdoğan, D. (eds.) iNetSec 2015. LNCS, vol. 9591, pp. 112–125. Springer, Cham (2016). https://doi.org/10.1007/978-3-319-39028-4_9
20. Wan, J., et al.: Dual-JT: toward the high availability of JobTracker in hadoop. In: 2012 IEEE 4th International Conference on Cloud Computing Technology and Science (CloudCom), pp. 263–268. IEEE (2012)
21. Wilkinson, S., Lowry, J., Boshevski, T.: Metadisk a blockchain-based decentralized file storage application. Storj Labs Inc., Technical Report, hal, pp. 1–11 (2014)
22. Wood, G.: Ethereum: a secure decentralised generalised transaction ledger. Ethereum Project Yellow Paper **151**, 1–32 (2014)
23. Yang, Z., Yang, K., Lei, L., Zheng, K., Leung, V.C.: Blockchain-based decentralized trust management in vehicular networks. IEEE Internet Things J. **6**, 1495–1505 (2018)
24. Zhang, F., Eyal, I., Escriva, R., Juels, A., Van Renesse, R.: {REM}: Resource-efficient mining for blockchains. In: 26th {USENIX} Security Symposium ({$USENIX$} Security 17), pp. 1427–1444 (2017)
25. Zyskind, G., Nathan, O., Pentland, A.: Enigma: decentralized computation platform with guaranteed privacy. arXiv preprint arXiv:1506.03471 (2015)

Fabric-Chain & Chain:
A Blockchain-Based Electronic Document
System for Supply Chain Finance

Dun Li[✉][iD], Dezhi Han, and Han Liu[iD]

College of Information Engineering, Shanghai Maritime University, Shanghai, China
446838775@qq.com

Abstract. During the development of supply chain finance, the imperfection of credit system and financial service platform has been a major problem, which needs to be improved and improved through new technical means. The existing supply chain financial platform can not manage and store the financing information data with high credibility and reliability, and it is difficult to share data efficiently among multiple asset ends and fund parties, and also can not carry out automatic trial calculation and settlement of funds. This paper proposes a storage method based on blockchain and bloom filter, which is used as the storage model of electronic document data in the process of supply chain finance business. The simulation experiments show that the model proposed in this paper has greater improvement in both access efficiency and retrieval efficiency than the existing model.

Keywords: Blockchain · Hyperledger fabric · Electronic document system · Supply chain · Supply chain finance

1 Introduction

Supply chain finance is based on the real transaction background and self-compensation income of enterprises in the supply chain [1,2].

As Fig. 1 shows: It establishes a closed transaction structure based on capital flow, business information, etc. to provide comprehensive financial services for upstream and downstream enterprises in the supply chain [3]. The traditional supply chain financial platform can split the creditor's rights based on its limited credibility, and provide financing credentials for suppliers [4]. However, with the extension of the supply chain, this kind of trust will accelerate to decline [5]. The centralized information platform also has data tampering, data leakage, and other problems, which makes it difficult to prove the innocence of self-certification and increases the credit risk of banks. Therefore, it is necessary to ensure that the whole life cycle of the original transaction records can be traced and that the original transaction data has not been tampered with. To improve the authority of data, the platform usually needs to witness with the

© Springer Nature Singapore Pte Ltd. 2020
Z. Zheng et al. (Eds.): BlockSys 2020, CCIS 1267, pp. 601–608, 2020.
https://doi.org/10.1007/978-981-15-9213-3_46

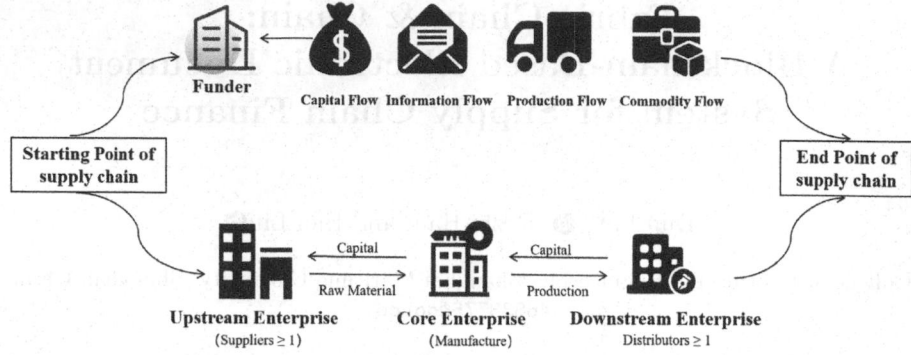

Fig. 1. Supply chain fiance system

help of a third-party authority such as notary office, but this mode will inevitably increase transaction costs, affect efficiency, and is not highly operable [6]. Thus, a safe, efficient, convenient, and low-cost multi-party storage solution is needed to ensure that all parties have completely preserved the data information while ensuring the security, authenticity, and reliability of the data.

The blockchain is maintained by the distributed consensus mechanism. Continuous blocks are connected by hash pointers, and all nodes participate in the verification [7].

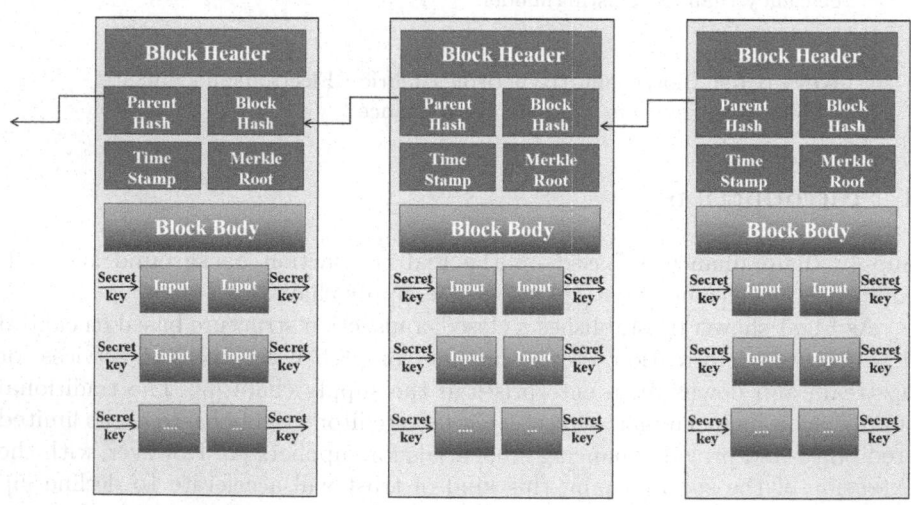

Fig. 2. Data structure of blockchain

As Fig. 2 shows, blockchain can completely solve the problem of verification and effective storage of existing credit vouchers [8]. Firstly, blockchain adopts a

P2P network structure. Any node enterprise with authority can obtain complete account book information related to it, and avoid data tampering and data disclosure through multi-party participation and joint management [9]. Secondly, the credit credentials generated by the core enterprises can be flexibly split on the blockchain according to different accounts receivable amounts. Any split behavior will be recorded on the chain through effective consensus broadcast and cannot be tampered with [10]. The bank can fully trust the business data on the chain.

This paper proposes a blockchain-based model for the transaction of supply chain finance and the storage, search and trust of electronic documents, in order to achieve mutual trust among participants and efficient access to relevant data.

The remainder of this paper is organized as follows:

In the second section, we summarize the document flow in supply chain finance. In the third section, we detail the specific system design. The experimental simulation is introduced in the forth section. In the fifth section, we give the final conclusion.

2   Document Flow in Supply Chain Finance

The supply chain finance solutions are mainly based on alliance chains with high controllability and high security, which combine the upstream and downstream core enterprises and suppliers of the supply chain, as well as financial asset enterprises such as financial institutions, banks, and securities companies [11]. The business data and trade data of each subject are linked and stored, and the blockchain technology is used as the basis of trust transmission to deeply empower each small and medium-sized micro-enterprise in the supply chain finance. The specific businesses include contract signing, creditor's rights confirmation, enterprise financing, creditor's rights transfer, capital clearing, ABS financing, etc.

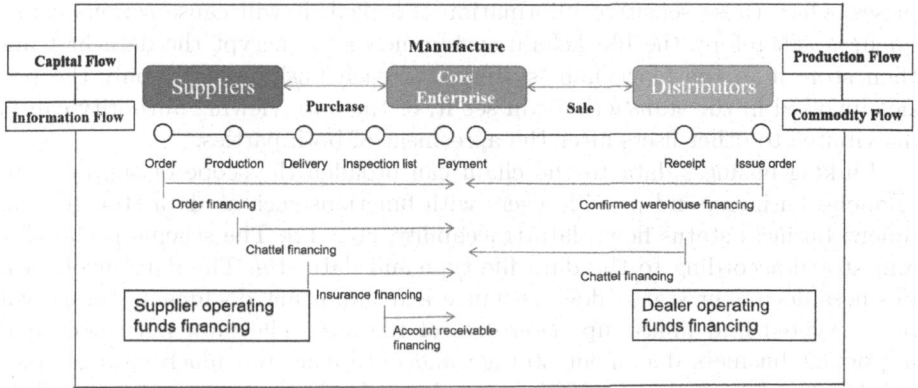

Fig. 3. Document flow

As Fig. 3 shows, the main participants of chain finance mainly include the following types of customers:

Core Enterprise. It plays a leading role in the whole supply chain business and helps the development of supply chain finance business through credit enhancement measures such as confirming the rights of accounts payable, providing repurchase, coordinating sales, etc.

Financing Enterprises. Including upstream suppliers and downstream distributors of core enterprise, all of which need financial services.

Financial Institutions. Including banks, securities companies, insurance companies, factoring companies, small loan companies, etc., which mainly provide financing, credit insurance, ABS, and other professional services.

Supply Chain Service Organizations. Including logistics enterprises, logistics parks, supply chain financial service platform, which provide technical and certificate keeping services to these enterprises and financial institutions.

This mode of supply chain finance can be summarized as "M + 1 + N" mode, that is, around the core enterprise "1" in the supply chain, it provides comprehensive financial services to the core enterprise, its upstream supplier "M" and its downstream distributors or customers "n" based on the transaction process. According to different financing collateral, financial institutions divide supply chain finance into receivables, prepayment, and inventory financing, among which the scale of receivables is particularly huge.

3 System Model and Design

3.1 Data Uplink on the Blockchain

This paper uses the form of fabric alliance chain for data storage, which only involves transaction and account information, not business data information of enterprises. The blockchain system contains the actual business data of enterprises. Once these sensitive information is leaked, it will cause serious consequences. Therefore, the blockchain system needs to encrypt the data first and then store it in the blockchain system. For each business data, only the parties involved in the transaction can see it, or the data viewing authority can be distributed to other users after the agreement of both parties.

Linking business data to the chain can broaden the scope of supply chain financial business, and provide users with functions such as data storage, document business status flow, data traceability, etc. [12]. The scheme is classified and stored according to the data file type and data size. The data involved in business document status flow, issuance and important document storage will be encrypted and linked up regardless of the size. The data not involved in important business document storage and occupying too much storage space will be stored in the local relational database. At the same time, the file will be encrypted and linked up after hash calculation. The specific process is as follows:

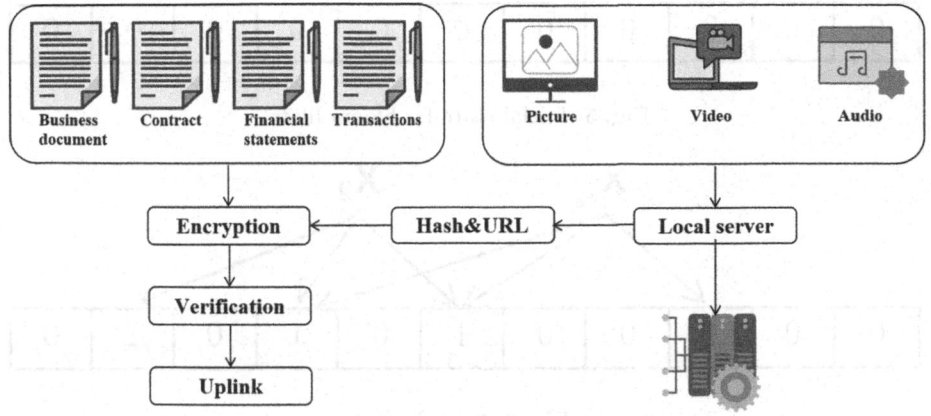

Fig. 4. Flow chart of data uplink

As Fig. 4 shows, for the data that does not involve important storage information and takes up a large space, the original data should be stored in the file server first, then the hash value and storage address of the file should be read, and the hash value and storage address of the file should be encrypted. The encrypted hash value and storage address are written into the blockchain through the smart contract. In addition, the message sender sends encrypted data to the blockchain system. The blockchain system verifies whether the transaction sender has permission. If it has permission, the data is successfully linked up. Otherwise, it prompts that the permission is insufficient and the link up fails.

3.2   Storage and Inquiry

To adapt to the change of business volume and keep the platform running efficiently, the platform needs to flexibly configure the basic parameters of blockchain, such as block time, block size, and single business content size. This paper introduces the bloom filter structure as the index of data storage, and searches it first in the query process.

The principle of the bloom filter is that when an element is added to the set, the element is mapped to k points in a group of digits through k hash functions, and they are set to 1. When retrieving, we just need to see if these points are all 1 (about) to know whether there is it in the collection: if these points have any 0, then the inspected element must not be present; if they are all 1, then the inspected element is likely to be present. This is the basic idea of the bloom filter.

As Fig. 5 shows, in the initial state, bloom filter is a group of bits containing m bits, and each bit is set to 0.

As Fig. 6 shows, to express $s = \{x_1, x_2\}$ For a collection of n elements, bloom filter uses k independent hash functions to map each element in the collection

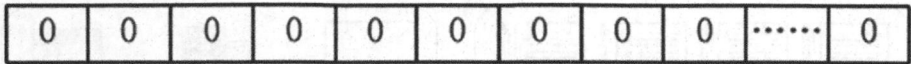

Fig. 5. Initial state for bloom filter

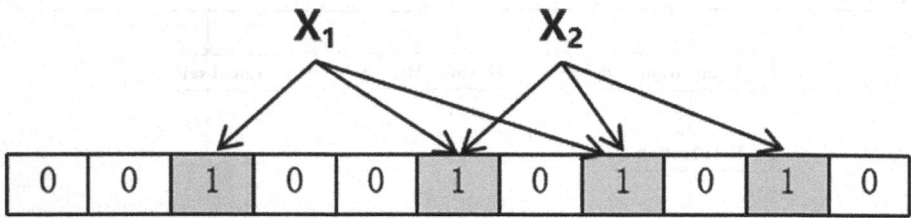

Fig. 6. Add element

to$\{1, m\}$. For any element x, the position $hi(x)$of the ith hash function mapping is set to 1 $(1 < I < K)$.

According to the characteristics of Bloom filter, only retrieving the summary information can greatly reduce the time needed for retrieval operation. Although there is a possibility of hash collision in the map summary of Bloom filter, but the summary length of Bloom filter is very sparse at present, so the possibility of map collision is so small that it can be ignored.

4   Experiment and Comparison

In this part, we will take experiments according to the theoretical to verify the advantages of the model proposed in this paper.

We implement bloom filter based electronic document API with smart contract of Hyperledger Fabric. API includes two functions: data record storage and data record query. Includes two parts: version and data.

Data Record Storage. In Hyperledger Fabric, the data is stored in status databases, which key is stored in ledger(blockchain). First, we calculate a hash of data by MD5 algorithm, which can uniquely identify the data. Next, we store the hash in a bloom filter and put the value of it to statusdb. In order to ensure the accuracy of the query, we adjust the length of bytes and the number of hash functions of bloom filter according to the estimated data size. Finally, we store MD5 value as the key, data as the value in status DB, and update the ledger.

Data Record Query. The steps to query a data record are as follows: First, we calculate a hash of data by MD5 algorithm, which can uniquely identify the data. Next, we take the bytecode of the bloom filter from the status BD, instantiate a bloom filter, and make hash matching according to the MD5 value obtained in the previous step. If the returned result is false (indicating that the data does not exist), a 404 error will be returned. Finally, we query the data by MD5 value from status DB, and return it.

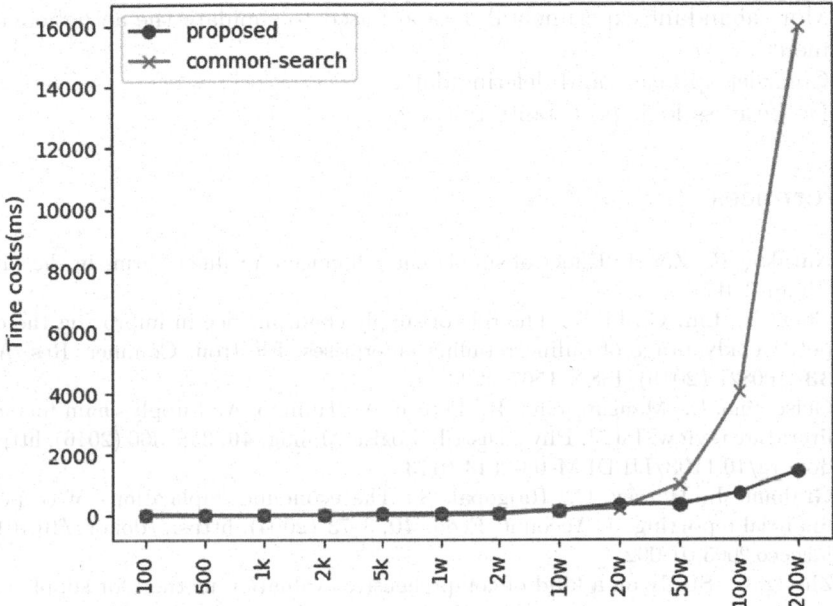

Fig. 7. Comparison between the proposed bloom filter-based method with the common search method

To verify the performance of this method, we compare the proposed bloom filter-based method with the common search method. The experimental results are shown in Fig. 7.

As can be seen from the figure, with the increase of data volume, the query time of our method is far less than that of the common query method. In addition, this paper is based on the hypeledgerfabric alliance chain, which has greater advantages over the public chain in system QoS.

5 Conclusion

This paper proposes a blockchain-based electronic certificate model of supply chain finance to adapt to the current business logic and development trend of supply chain finance. This model uses the distributed consensus mechanism of blockchain to ensure data maintenance, relies on the good throughput of hyperledger, uses MPT structure to ensure the reliable storage of data, and uses bloom filter structure to improve query efficiency. When the amount of data is large, this model can significantly improve query efficiency, and the accuracy is also guaranteed.

This paper is innovative in solving the bottleneck problem of the current supply chain financial development platform, which is worthy of reference for other researchers. Future work can be improved in the following areas:

1) More abundant experimental data are used to simulate the actual environment.
2) Consider updating and deleting data.
3) Do business logic portability research.

References

1. Karakuş, R., Zor, İ.: Effect of supply chain finance on value of firms in the supply Chain (2017)
2. Chen, X., Liu, C., Li, S.: The role of supply chain finance in improving the competitive advantage of online retailing enterprises. Electron. Commer. Res. Appl. **33**, 100821 (2019). ISSN 1567–4223
3. Gelsomino, L., Mangiaracina, R., Perego, A., Tumino, A.: Supply chain finance: a literature review. Int. J. Phys. Distrib. Logist. Manag. **46**, 348–366 (2016). https://doi.org/10.1108/IJPDLM-08-2014-0173
4. Graham, J., Harvey, C., Rajgopal, S.: The economic implications of corporate financial reporting. J. Account. Econ. **40**, 3–73 (2004). https://doi.org/10.1016/j.jacceco.2005.01.002
5. Zhong, C.: Study on a kind of comprehensive evaluation method for supply chain risk-extensive matter element with variable weight method. Sci. Technol. Manag. Res. (2012)
6. Patel, J.: An effective and scalable data modeling for enterprise big data platform. In: 2019 IEEE International Conference on Big Data (Big Data), pp. 2691–2697 (2019)
7. Zheng, Z., et al.: An overview of blockchain technology: architecture, consensus, and future trends. In: 2017 IEEE International Congress on Big Data (BigData Congress), pp. 557–564 (2017)
8. Zhou, T., et al.: EverSSDI: blockchain-based framework for verification, authorisation and recovery of self-sovereign identity using smart contracts. J. Comput. Appl. Technol. **60**(3), 281–295 (2019)
9. Jamal, A., et al.: Blockchain-based identity verification system. In: 2019 IEEE 9th International Conference on System Engineering and Technology (ICSET), pp. 253–257 (2019)
10. Huang, Y., et al.: Block chain network, branch node and block chain network application method (2017)
11. Hofmann, E., et al.: Supply chain finance and blockchain technology: the case of reverse securitisation (2017)
12. Katragadda, R.B., et al.: Systems and methods for blockchain security data intelligence (2020)

A Cross-border VR Technology for Blockchain Environment

Huiping Wang[(✉)], Alan Hong, and Xiaoyan Chen

The School of Software Engineering, Xiamen University of Technology, Xiamen 361024, Fujian, China

460131624@qq.com

Abstract. With the rapid development of blockchain and VR technology, great attention has been paid to researching these two technologies. Based on the analysis of the features of both technologies and literature review, this study expounds the combination and application of these technologies, and explores the necessity and feasibility of combining media digital assets. Then, suggestions would be made on further research into the sustainable development of these technologies.

Keywords: Blockchain · Virtual reality · Program development · The internet · Digital asset

1 Introduction

In an AI era, our life is being empowered by such technologies as artificial intelligence, genetic engineering, unmanned driving, blockchain and VR. With the rapid development of blockchain and VR technologies in various domains [1], exploring the edges of their integration and their cross-border combination would be significant for bettering our lives. Featured by distributed accounting and storage, blockchain technology is composed by equally-powering nodes and those that can jointly maintain the data blocks of the entire system. Though private information of all parties involved in transactions is encrypted, the data of the blockchain is open to all, making it and related applications accessible to everyone [2] and the whole system highly transparent. Also, the adoption of consensus-based specifications and protocols (a set of open and transparent algorithms) allows all nodes to exchange data freely and safely in a detrusted environment, making the machine reliable and free of human interventions. Once verified and added to the blockchain, the very information would be stored permanently; unless more than 51% of nodes in the system were under control at the same time, the modification of the database on a single node would otherwise be invalid, which makes the data of the blockchain highly stable and reliable [3]. As exchange between nodes follows certain algorithm, the program of the blockchain would judge the validity of any operation by itself, which makes one transaction party entrust his counterpart unnecessary and it very beneficial for credit accumulation [4]. As for the VR technology, it generates virtual environment by high tech and based on the characteristics of human senses, one that enables users to

© Springer Nature Singapore Pte Ltd. 2020
Z. Zheng et al. (Eds.): BlockSys 2020, CCIS 1267, pp. 609–615, 2020.
https://doi.org/10.1007/978-981-15-9213-3_47

embody an environment as if it were real. By wearing such VR devices as helmet displays and data gloves, users are in a virtual but extremely real-like situation [5], and any movements of body would generate corresponding change of VR images. For instance, the catch of one object in a VR environment would bring the feel of its existence, and this provides participants a mechanism for imagination, making any rational conception based on certain understanding of the environment broaden and deepen our knowledge.

2 Literature Review

2.1 Existing Researches on Blockchain

For a long time, countries have had layouts in terms of underlying platforms, application scenarios and solutions, mainly based on the following algorithms. According to the Byzantine Agreement, consensus can be achieved in a decentralized system; the asymmetric encryption algorithm use two different keys for encryption and decryption, that is, the public key and the private key that are normally in pairs. If one message was encrypted with the public key, the corresponding private key must be used for decryption, and vice versa. The consensus system composed of consensus nodes provides fault tolerance, and also security and availability [6], making it applicable to any network. Then, Paxos Algorithm is used to solve how certain distributed system achieve agreement on certain value or resolution. A typical scenario is that in a distributed database system, each node executing the same sequence of operations would reach a consistent state, if their initial state are the same. For this end, each instruction needs to execute the consistency algorithm so as to ensure the instruction consistent in each node. Consistency algorithm can be applied to many scenarios and is vital for distributed computing, one of which is Paxos Algorithm that functions based on the messaging model. Finally, Blockchain Consensus Algorithm is mainly for workload and rights proof. The data storing technology used is distributed storage that, by using the disk space on each computer through the network, makes those scattered storage resources a virtual storage device and data stored in all corners of the network. As such, distributed storage technology does not store the entire data in each computer but in different computers after cutting.

2.2 Existing Researches on VR

Researches on VR mainly fall into 4 groups: (1) Desktop VR. By simulating with PC and low-level workstations, it uses the computer screen as a window for users to observe the virtual reality. Through various input and external devices like a mouse, trackball, and torque ball, participants can fully interact with the virtual world, observe and operate the objects in the 360-degree virtual realm [7]. (2) Immersion VR. This technology provides users a new and virtually sensory space by enclosing their vision, hearing and other feelings, and provides a real and total immersion feeling by employing position trackers, data gloves, other hand-controlled input devices, and sounds among others. (3) Augmented reality VR can enhance the perception that cannot be or is uneasily be achieved in reality. A typical case is the head-up display of the fighter pilot, which can project the instrument readings and weapon aiming data onto a penetrating screen installed in front of the pilot, so that the pilot does not have to bow his head to read the data in the cockpit but concentrate on aiming at the enemy aircraft or navigation bias. (4) Distributed VR. With this, more users can observe and operate the same virtual world through the network to achieve collaboration.

3   Analyzing the Core of Blockchain

The core technology of blockchain lies in cryptography, consensus mechanism and P2P network technology. As shown in Fig. 1. The needs of blockchain for cryptography are determining ownership and protecting data privacy. As for the former, digital signature technology in cryptography is needed to prove the ownership of the digital asset, as e-data is easy to copy and digital assets cannot prove its ownership as easily as physical assets [8]. In terms of protecting data privacy, such cryptographic tools as asymmetric encryption, ring signature and zero-knowledge proof are needed for anonymizing transactions, because the account book in blockchain system is jointly maintained by all nodes of the network and the ledger data is open and transparent, and such public data records may cause privacy leaking. The second core technology, consensus based on machine algorithms is important for forming trusting [9], and consensus mechanism becomes possible, thanks to the reconstruction of currencies and value chains and the reorganization of production, with the ultimate goal of locking the reliable user with good wills in a reliable state with a reliable network. Finally, P2P network is a highly corresponding and efficient transmission protocol that enables thousands of nodes connected to each other in peer status and to freely enter and exit the network system, making the blockchain a distributed and decentralized system [10]. In summary, blockchain is essentially a decentralized distributed database and innovative model of applying such multiple technologies as distributed data storage, multi-center point-to-point transmission, consensus mechanism and encryption algorithm in the Internet age; with many edges, blockchain is significant in reshaping trust, so much that it greatly reduces transaction costs and thresholds and improves operational efficiency as well.

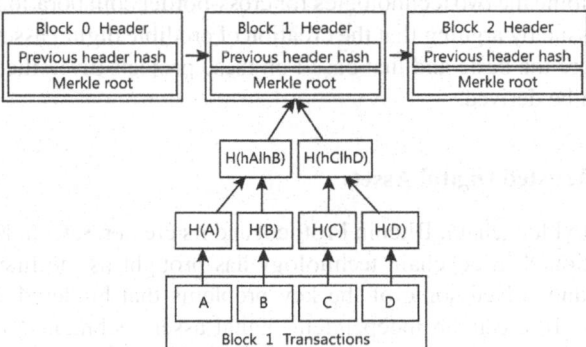

Fig. 1. Merkle tree connecting block transactions to block header merkle root

4   On the Development of VR Program

The major processes of VR program development are 3D modeling based on computer graphics technology, interactive setting in the engine and program designing. Excellent VR works are normally equipped with exquisite 3D models, to achieve which we must employ computer graphics technology, one important technology in VR field, to quickly, accurately and normally produce a large number of computer-aided designs, including mechanical drawings, architectural designs, circuit diagrams and geographic maps [11]. One of the interactive engines is an engine development software named Unity 3D, which is a multi-platform, comprehensive professional engine software developed by Unity Technologies and allows users to easily create interactive contents, like 3D video games and real-time 3D animations. It also boasts such advantages as a powerful editing interface and a powerful physics engine, as well as supporting a variety of authoring software and a wide range of common scripting languages. Also, Unreal Engine4 and Blueprint take up 80% of the global commercial game engine market share. Since its official birth in 1998, Unreal Engine has been developed continuously and become the most widely used engine with the highest overall application and powerful rendering effects in the entire game world. Blueprint, a visual language in Unreal Engine4, creates various executable processes in the form of nodes (shaped like blocks) in advance, and then can be programmed by simply arranging and connecting them with the mouse. The developers of Unreal Engine4 also position Blueprint and C++ as the two pillars of development. C# scripting, a programming language newly released by Microsoft Corporation, is designed to be "simple, modern, universal" and object-oriented programming language, with strong type checking, array dimension checking, uninitialized variable reference detection and automatic garbage collection (an automatic memory release).

5   Combining Blockchain and VR

By expounding blockchain and VR above, we can find their strong technical capabilities, then how to combine the two technologies for cross-border collaboration? This section is to address this issue by arguing that the creation of credible digital assets and the global VR ecosystem are the basic and that based on these projects diversified researches and applications can be derived.

5.1   Creating Trusted Digital Assets

When it comes to blockchain, Bitcoin Protocol and its creator Satoshi Nakamoto would always be mentioned. Blockchain technology has brought us the first digital asset in the real sense, and solved some of the key problems that hindered the development of digital assets. To create an independent digital asset, technicians must ensure that data not be copied, tampered with or forged [12], which sounds easy, but difficult to be done. For example, in this era of highly developing Internet, companies encounter huge challenges in preventing individuals from illegally downloading MP3 files, movies, and games. What if these documents were exchanged for money? So it is very difficult to prevent individuals from making profits by simply copying and pasting. Perhaps the above problem can be solved by storing all the resources on a platform strictly controlled by one company, like iTunes. However, this approach on the other hand brings the threats of exclusive control and manipulation. Before the advent of Bitcoin and blockchain, there were two ways to dispose of files on the Internet: either store them on a platform highly controlled by the enterprise, or expose them on the Internet to be illegally downloaded and used by others. Yet, blockchain came with a new framework by creating a credible platform, and this particular platform is the only one that makes assets valuable [13]. The download or copying of Bitcoin would generate no value at all, unless this is done on the public network of Bitcoin. Besides, the Bitcoin network is neither controlled nor maintained by any single entity, but relies on the distributed and decentralized combination between individuals and enterprises. In this way, the network can create assets that the controlling party cannot copy or manipulate [14]. Without Blockchain technology, independent digital assets, an important complement to another emerging technology (VR), cannot be issued.

5.2 Global VR

Like blockchain technology, VR is still in its infancy, which means that it is a long way to go before we get rid of reality and enter the virtual world. However, it can be seen from the past technology development cycle that VR would develop quickly. When the global business circle starts to adopt it, the decisive moment of VR would come. Pokemon Go (Pokemon), a smartphone game, is the first application that maps the virtual onto the real world; to interact with the game, players must constantly move in reality. The ideal global VR can be closely connected with the geographical environment and commercial space [15], but also can operate independently, which would become a huge drive for real economic value. The mapping of a common virtual network onto our corporate, home, and office would generate many possibilities. For example, if every enterprise has a virtual version of their corresponding physical location and can be accessed on a global virtual network, then we in Florida can meet someone in a coffee shop in Shanghai, and s/he can see and interact with the virtual person sitting opposite through a projector installed in the cafe or some special glasses. In addition, pure virtual space can also create huge utility and value. For example, a multinational company can purchase a virtual office building where employees around the world can access in a virtual form, which creates a tangible office environment for employees who are geographically far apart [16] to communicate rather than merely video calls. This can reduce the number of physical buildings purchased by the company and allow employees more geographical freedom, but this very idea also brings some problems; for example, how to purchase a virtual building? What about the ownership? Is it a building or a service like teleconferencing? When seriously exploring the potential meaning of virtual property and other commodities, we would naturally find that there is almost no difference between virtual and real buildings. Like the case in physical buildings, we also want to hire a virtual architectural designer to create an artistic and attractive space that can also be resold and refurbished if needed. Companies are probably providing an office-as-service model, limiting office owners' rights in designing and controlling their own spaces and hindering the development of secondary service providers, designers, architects and investors. This means that these buildings might vanish with the disappearing of the service providers. Therefore, as for virtual buildings (and all other forms of virtual assets or property), the best way is to let them exist in the form of actually tangible assets and personal assets. Within this model, the virtual asset market can own all the capabilities of the physical market. Companies and individuals can purchase, design, and sell these virtual buildings; designers can create virtual clothes (that might be more delicate) and sell them to online virtual persons; artists can design art exhibitions free from the limitations of the real world. By creating virtual goods or property that can exist in the form of tangible assets, the entire parallel economy would be activated, which would stimulate huge economic growth and bring more exciting possibilities. As shown in Table 1, Therefore, an essential aspect of creating secure digital assets is that these digital assets are actually owned by people, rather than simply authorized by a platform to someone else. When these digital assets are placed on the independent and secure global network of blockchain, they can bring real economic benefits to people.

Table 1. A comparison of various research

Research	Use digital assets	Use VR	Traceability
Literature [2]	Yes	No	Weak
Literature [7]	No	Yes	Weak
Literature [15]	Yes	No	Weak
Ours	Yes	Yes	Medium

6　Conclusion

The integration of VR into the blockchain is an innovation and revolution of digital media technology. The competition mechanism among the VR blocks in the blockchain would promote the content creation of collective participation in the future, but also avoid information redundancy and resource monopoly of VR in the era of big data, thereby making VR digital products more dynamic. Its distinctive technical features and structural advantages bring lights to the development of traditional VR technology and the overall VR industry into in-depth transformation. By proposing the adoption of VR in blockchain and the creation of global VR, we believe that various activities in the real can also be realized in the global virtual network through trusted digital assets, and this will break the limitations of physical space and achieve easy switching between virtuality and reality. Furthermore, the equalized supervision of the copyright protection of VR in the blockchain will also create a more favourable external environment for the development of the VR industry. In this way, a new era of VR and blockchain combination would surely come, when internal mechanisms and external environment develop in coordination.

References

1. Fan, Y., Lin, X., Liang, W.: TraceChain: a blockchain-based scheme to protect data confidentiality and traceability. Softw.: Pract. Exp. (2019)
2. Zhang, Y.: Design and analysis of digital asset management system framework based on blockchain. Comput. Sci. Appl. **9**(1), 28–37 (2018)
3. Zhaofeng, M., Weihua, H., Hongmin, G.: A new blockchain-based trusted DRM scheme for built-in content protection. EURASIP J. Image Video Process. **1**, 1–12 (2018)
4. Liang, W., Huang, W., Long, J., Li, K.-C., Zhang, D.: Deep reinforcement learning for resource protection and real-time detection in IoT environment. IEEE Internet Things J. 1 (2020)
5. Li, C., Yingfang, L.I., Zhiyuan, L., et al.: Gesture recognition in virtual reality interactive game. Technol. Innov. Appl. **13**(2), 262–271 (2019)
6. Liang, W., Li, K.-C., Long, J., Kui, X., Zomaya, A.Y.: An industrial network intrusion detection algorithm based on multi-characteristic data clustering optimization model. IEEE Trans. Ind. Inf. **16**(3), 2063–2071 (2020)
7. Wu, T.H., Wu, F., Liang, C.J., et al.: A virtual reality tool for training in global engineering collaboration. Univ. Access Inf. Soc. **18**(2), 243–255 (2019)
8. Salomon, R.: Digital Asset Traceability and assurance using a distributed ledger (2019)
9. Cho, C.-M.: Financial investment algorithm trading method and system based on blockchain smart contract (2020)
10. Liang, W., Fan, Y., Li, K.-C., Zhang, D., Gaudiot, J.-L.: Secure data storage and recovery in industrial blockchain network environments. IEEE Trans. Ind. Inf. 1 (2020)
11. Lv, C.: Analysis on the application and development of virtual reality technology (2019)
12. Zhani, M.F., ElBakoury, H.: FlexNGIA: a flexible internet architecture for the next-generation tactile internet. J. Netw. Syst. Manage. **28**(4), 751–795 (2020). https://doi.org/10.1007/s10 922-020-09525-0
13. Xia, L.: Research on virtual reality technology based on cloud computing (2019)
14. Wang, S., Ouyang, L., Yuan, Y., et al.: Blockchain-enabled smart contracts: architecture, applications, and future trends. IEEE Trans. Syst. Man Cybern. Syst. **49**(11), 2266–2277 (2019)
15. Zhengyu, Y., Information DO: The change of digital reality interaction mode of virtual reality technology. China Comput. Commun. (2019)
16. Jun, Z., Xiao, L.I., Kai, C., et al.: Using virtual reality to improve spatial cognition effect of urban planning scheme. Bull. Surv. Mapp. **9**, 108 (2019)

Trustworthy System Development

Data Ownership Confirmation and Privacy-Free Search for Blockchain-Based Medical Data Sharing

Cong Zha[1]($\boxtimes$), Hao Yin[1], and Bo Yin[2]

[1] Network and Big Data Technology R&D Center, The Department of Computer Science and Technology, Tsinghua University, Beijing 100084, China
chac16@mails.tsinghua.edu.cn, h-yin@mail.tsinghua.edu.cn
[2] The School of Computer Science, Beijing Information Science and Technology University, Beijing 100084, China
raul_yinbo@163.com

Abstract. With the development of data mining technology and the arrival of the era of big data, people can get more and more knowledge and information from the data. However, electronic medical data are stored in isolated data silos within each hospital due to the privacy and competition. Because of the complex interests of various groups, there is a lack of data flow between medical entities. On the one hand, this leads to difficulties for patients to obtain their own electronic medical data and to referral between different hospitals. On the other hand, it has led to serious lack of actual data for medical researchers. The realization of the determination of medical data ownership is the first condition for realizing medical data circulation. How to retrieve the required medical data while protecting privacy is the second problem to be solved.

In this paper, we design the medical metadata as the smallest subunit of data ownership confirmation and propose a blockchain-based medical data sharing Framework MDSF, which can be used for electronic medical data ownership confirmation and data search while protecting patient privacy. We use the petri nets to verify the system and prove its reachability and boundedness, which means it can realize its designed function and operate safely. The system provides users with a convenient and safe way to obtain their past medical data, also enables research institutions engaged in medical data mining to easily search and obtain the actual medical data needed after desensitization. Thereby the circulation of medical data between different hospitals, individuals and research institutions is realized.

Keywords: Blockchain · Electronic medical data · Data ownership confirmation · Data search · Petri nets

1 Introduction

Existing medical data require innovation. When patients go to different hospitals, their electronic medical data are scattered in isolated data silos in different hospitals, so they

Z. Zheng et al. (Eds.): BlockSys 2020, CCIS 1267, pp. 619–632, 2020.
https://doi.org/10.1007/978-981-15-9213-3_48

have difficulty to access old medical data. On the other hand, patients are willing to open their own data for better treatment [1]. In China, different hospitals use technology and data standards from different vendors to build their own hospital information systems. Interoperability issues between different hospital information systems present additional challenges for the sharing of medical data. Lack of coordinated data management and exchange means that health records are fragmented rather than cohesive [2]. In this condition, we can't organize medical data that is scattered among different hospitals.

The lack of medical data has also brought crisis to medical research. At present, the research institutions only have access to all medical data within the organization, which severely limits the integration of medical data and the development of medical data mining [3]. The ONC report emphasizes that "biomedical and public health researchers require the ability to analyze information from many sources in order to identify public health risks, develop new treatments and cures, and enable precision medicine" [4]. While some data is slowly passed from clinical research and teaching hospitals to researchers, we note that patients and regulators are increasingly interested in sharing more data to get better care and treatment [1].

Defining data ownership is one of the prerequisites for the sharing of medical data [5]. In order to clarify data ownership, we need to implement data ownership confirmation. In this paper, we designed the medical metadata as the smallest subunit of data ownership confirmation and realized the data ownership confirmation through the immutability of blockchain, which is the core component of the medical data sharing framework.

Helping patients and researchers find the medical data they need is necessary for data sharing. Traditional methods of data search, such as search engines, need to index data in advance. Because of the need for privacy protection of medical data, we can't use these methods directly. If data retrieval is performed in each medical data storage center, it will bring serious efficiency problems. In this paper, we propose a double-layer search mechanism to achieve a trade-off between efficiency and privacy.

Creating a decentralized data sharing framework for medical data faces many technical challenges. Firstly, because medical data contains lots of patients' private information, privacy protection is extremely demanding in the process of ensuring rights and circulation [6]. However, hiding all information will result in unreadable data, which makes research People can't find the data they need, so we need to build an adaptive medical metadata for the data sharing framework that satisfied three demands, which are protecting user privacy, retaining part of feature information and adapting to the different needs of different disease types. Secondly, because the system doesn't include a trusted center, users need to be able to trust the system without trusting any remote servers. Thirdly, we hope our medical data sharing framework has three features, which are secure, decentralized, and human readable. It was considered impossible according to Zooko's Triangle [7] to building a naming system with these three properties and most naming system only have two of the three features [8].

The main contributions of this article are:

1. Designing the medical metadata, which is the index of electronic medical data in the medical data sharing framework, as the smallest subunit of data ownership confirmation.

2. Proposing blockchain-based data ownership confirmation and double-layer search for medical data sharing and designing the incentive mechanism in the system.
3. Using petri nets to verify the reachability and boundedness of the system.

2   Related Work

Recently, blockchain technology has attracted extensive attentions from both industry and academia [9]. Blockchain technology isn't just only single one technique, but contains Cryptography, mathematics, Algorithm and economic model, combining peer-to-peer networks and using distributed consensus algorithm to solve traditional distributed database synchronize problem, it's an integrated multi-field infrastructure construction [10]. Blockchain can be considered as a distributed database containing value flows. All data is recorded in blocks and each block is chained by recording the hash value of the previous block. Figure 1 is an example of a typical blockchain structure. Any record in the blockchain cannot be changed unless someone controls more than 50% of the computing power in POW consensus algorithm.

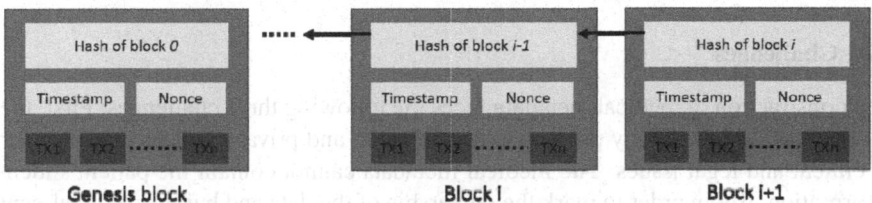

Fig. 1. An example of a typical blockchain structure.

Blockchain was proposed in 2008 and implement in 2009 by Nakamoto [11]. Bitcoin was the first cryptocurrency to use blockchain technologies. Then, Ethereum [12, 13], Zerocash [14, 15] and etc. provided more features such as smart contract or better security. Other work by Eyal et al. [16] and Wang et al. [17] modified the consensus mechanism of Bitcoin to improve system scalability.

There are many efforts involved in medical data on the blockchain. Zyskind et al. proposed a blockchain usage for access control management and secure data storage when using third party mobile services [18]. Factom [19] and MedVault [20] haven't publish specific methods or a summary of technical work. Azaria was the first to propose a system to manage and protect medical data based on blockchain technology [21]. Xia et al. proposed a blockchain-based system. The system provides medical data protection and management among big data entities [22]. But without incentives, the hospital may not be willing to share its own data. Dubovitskaya et al. proposed scenarios of blockchain technology application in different healthcare settings: primary care, medical data research, and connected health [23]. However, the efficiency of the system is easily restricted by using traditional public blockchain. Fan et al. resolved the problem of large-scale data management and sharing in an EMR system [24]. Patients can access their own records from different hospitals through their work. But researchers can't obtain the required data for scientific research.

In this paper, we designed medical metadata for data ownership confirmation and proposed a medical data sharing framework for sharing electronic medical data among authorized researchers and patients. The system is based on a self-built consortium blockchain which includes endogenous incentives. With self-built blockchain, we can give up unnecessary functions for better performance. By the system, we can enable patients to access their medical data in different hospitals, and also enable medical researchers to access the data they need when they are authorized.

3   Design of Medical Metadata

3.1   Design Goals

We use the medical data generated by the patient during a medical treatment as the basic data unit for data sharing, including but not limited to inspections, medication records, etc. We hope that generating medical metadata achieves four goals, which are clearing data ownership, facilitating the construction of a patient-centered medical record library, facilitating the exercise of data ownership and facilitating data search.

3.2   Challenges

The construction of medical metadata faces the following three challenges: First, medical data has a high privacy protection requirement, and privacy leakage causes a series of ethical and legal issues. The medical metadata cannot contain the patient's identity information. But in order to mark the ownership of the data and build a personal-centric case history library, the information recorded in the medical metadata needs to contain the identity information of the data owner. Secondly, in order to facilitate researchers to search for the required data in massive data, the label needs to retain some of the characteristic information of the electronic medical record. How to make the medical metadata structure adaptively adapt to the needs of different disease types for the characteristic information has become a problem to be solved. Finally, because the labels are generated independently within each hospital system, so they need to meet the requirements for distributed generation with the guarantee of uniqueness.

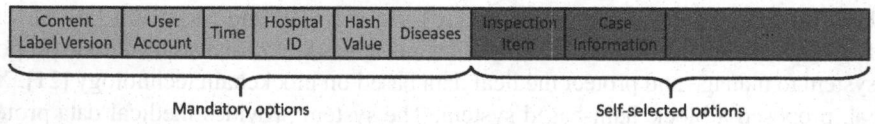

Fig. 2.   Structure of medical metadata.

3.3   Data Structure of the Medical Metadata

We propose the medical metadata structure based on the Json format to solve these challenges.

Medical metadata consists of both mandatory and self-selected options. The mandatory options include medical metadata version, time, user account, hospital id, diseases and medical metadata hash value. These mandatory options are required for each medical metadata. Self-selected options, which are used to flexibly record the required information for different characteristics of various diseases, includes adaptive information such as check items. The schematic is shown in Fig. 2.

We use 4 W (when, where, who, what), which are time, hospital, patient and diseases, to build a four-tuple that uniquely describes the patient's single treatment.

In order to increase the data payload ratio stored in medical metadata, we convert keys in Json format to short integers. For example, use short integer 0 for medical metadata version, 1 for time, and so on. The same version of the medical metadata has the same integer format, so that the user can distinguish the content of the key value corresponding to each integer according to the medical metadata version.

3.4 User Account Generation Method

The User Account is used to mark the patient's identifiable information but won't reveal the user's privacy. We use the public key in asymmetric encryption as the user account. The specific generation mode is shown in Fig. 3. The construction from UID to user account is divided into four steps. Firstly, we break the UID and add random number as salt. Secondly, we get Gx by calculating SHA256 algorithm with UID and salt. Thirdly, we use Gx as the private key and use base58check and secp256k1 to calculate the public key Gy. Finally, we use SHA256 and RIPEMD160 to operate on Gy in turn to get the user account.

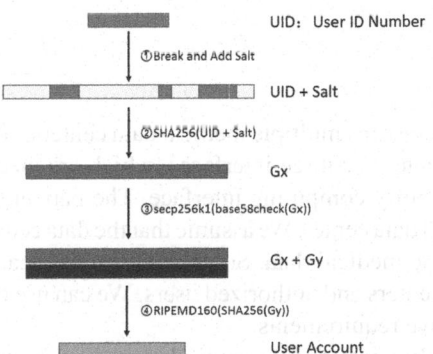

Fig. 3. User account generation method.

Through Fig. 3's method, we convert the readable user ID into unreadable User Account information, avoiding the leakage of user privacy. At the same time, it is convenient to follow the way of signature by asymmetric encryption to exercise the ownership of the data. Date owner can authorize data usage by signing and the process of ownership exercise achieves verifiability and non-repudiation.

4   Design of Data Ownership Confirmation and Privacy-Free Search

4.1   System Overview

Firstly, we propose medical data sharing framework MDFS. As shown in Fig. 4, we abstract the MDSF into the following four layers: data storage layer, blockchain layer, search layer, and user layer.

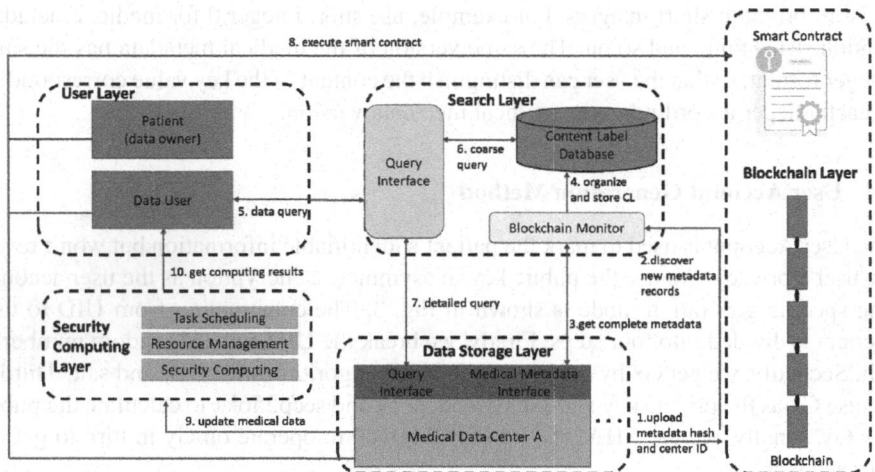

Fig. 4. MDSF structure diagram and flow chart.

Data Storage Layer

The data storage layer contains multiple medical data centers, corresponding to different hospitals. Each data center has three interfaces, which are medical metadata interface, query interface and security computing interface. The patient's complete medical data are stored in the medical data center. We assume that the data center has already processed and organized electronic medical data. So the medical data can be transmitted without barriers between data centers and authorized users. We can use the standard such as HL7 [25] to achieve the above requirements.

The medical metadata interface accepts the medical metadata hash value which comes from the search layer, and returns the complete medical metadata. The query interface accepts the medical metadata hash value and the query conditions, then uses 1 or 0 to return hit or miss. The secure computing interface is used to avoid medical data leakage. The interface sends processed data to authorized users.

Blockchain Layer

Blockchain layer contains a consortium blockchain based on PBFT consensus mechanism [26]. The blockchain consists of block head, transaction data and receipt data.

As shown in Fig. 5, there are seven fields, which are parent hash, timestamp, block height, coin base, extra data, logs bloom and state root, in block head. Parent hash is used to record the hash value of the previous block. Timestamp is used to record the timestamp when the block is generated. Block height is used to record the number of blocks so far. Coin base is used to record the user account of the block miner. Extra data is used to record the additional data. Logs bloom is used to store the Bloom filter of transaction data. The blockchain uses account mode rather than UTXO mode. State root is used to record the root hash value of the world state of all accounts, so we can use state root to determine whether the account status is the same between different blockchain nodes. Transactions root and receipt root record the root hash of the transaction data and the receipt data respectively.

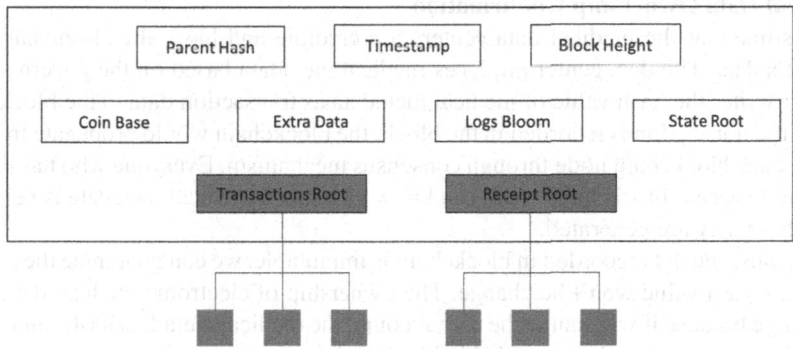

Fig. 5. The structure of block head.

There are two types of transaction data. One is token's transfer transaction on the blockchain, which includes transfer account, income account and transfer value. The other one is medical metadata release transaction, including the hospital ID and hash value of the medical metadata. The hospital ID is used to imply the location of the data and the hash value of the medical metadata is used to ensure data consistency and prevent data from being tampered by the data center.

The receipt data contains smart contract execution results which include data access and authorization results.

Search Layer

The search layer contains 3 modules, which are blockchain monitor, medical metadata database and query interface.

Blockchain monitor is used to monitor the addition of medical metadata on the blockchain. When detecting a new block, it sends a request to the medical metadata interface in data storage layer and accepts the medical metadata and sends it to the medical metadata database. medical metadata database, which is used to coarse query, stores the detailed medical metadata and creates index for the labels. The query interface is used to undertake the search request sent by the user layer and then executes a double-layer search.

User Layer

The user layer includes two roles: data owners and data users. Patients, who are Data owners, have the data ownership. Electronics medical data sharing requires authorization of the data owner. Data users may be medical researchers or patients themselves. They query the required data through the search layer, and then use rights to purchase data from the data center after authorization by the data owner.

4.2 System Flow

The process within MDSF consists of three parts, which are medical data ownership confirmation, medical data search and medical data transaction.

Medical Data Ownership Confirmation

We assume that the medical data centers are credible and have already managed the patient's data. The data center produces medical metadata based on the governed data. Then it writes the hash value of medical metadata as transaction data to the blockchain. When the transaction is recorded in the block, the blockchain would propagate information to each blockchain node through consensus mechanism. Everyone who has the permission to access blockchain nodes can know how much medical metadata is generated and where they are generated.

Because the data recorded in blockchain is immutable, we can guarantee the medical metadata hash value won't be change. The ownership of electronic medical data won't be change because if we change the user account, the medical metadata hash value would be different from the value recorded in blockchain.

Medical Data Search

We proposed a double-layer search strategy to achieve a trade-off between efficiency and privacy. The search process is shown in Fig. 6. Because of the different business priorities, different medical data centers store data on different types of diseases. If we use the search engine method to retrieve all data first, it is likely to cause privacy leakage. If we synchronize data search instructions indiscriminately to all medical data centers, this will greatly increase their load. We choice to use medical metadata database to filter

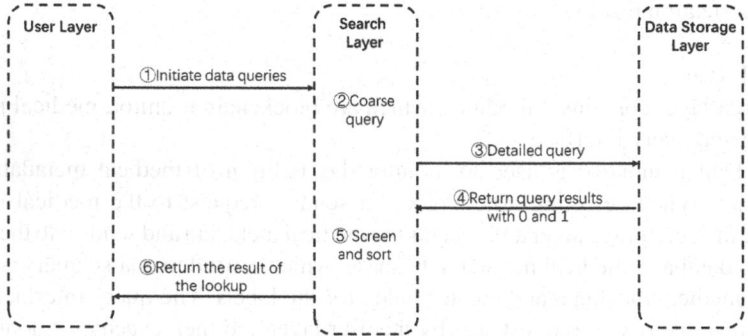

Fig. 6. The medical data search process.

in the search engine first. Then we transmit data search instructions to the corresponding medical data center.

Medical Data Transaction

The medical data transaction has two types. The first one is the data owner want to use his own data. In this condition, if the data center receives the data access request, it will verify that the signature of the requester is consistent with the user account of the medical data and send required data if they are consistent. The second type is some other people want to use medical data. In this situation, the data user needs to be authorized by the medical data center and data owner. The transaction process between different people is shown in Fig. 7.

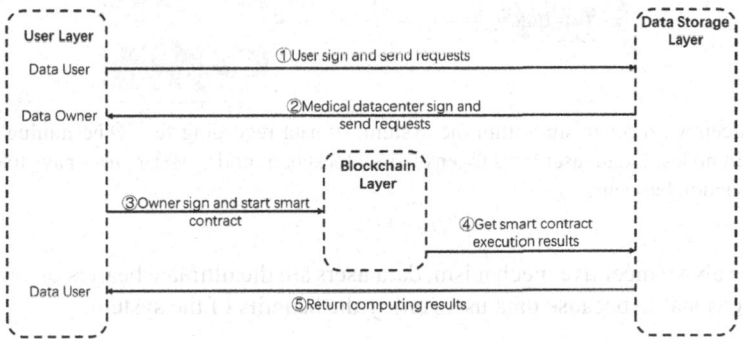

Fig. 7. The medical data transaction process between different people.

After data search, the data user would send its own account number, data receiving address, requested data and the signature of the above data to the medical data center. After the data center approves the data request, the data center signs the data request and sends it to the data owner. Then, the data owner checks the signature of the data center and the data user. If data owner agrees to the transaction, he would sign on the data request and send it to smart contract account on the blockchain. Blockchain nodes would check the signature of three roles and record contract execution results on the blockchain. If medical data center finds the data transaction was recorded on the blockchain, it would process the required data and send it to the data user.

4.3   System Incentive

It requires additional costs for Processing data and maintaining the blockchain, which means the system cannot run autonomously without economic incentives. In order to stimulate data sharing and promote data circulation, the system provides an endogenous incentive mechanism.

Blockchain nodes receive tokens as rewards during the mining process. These tokens will increase the enthusiasm of the blockchain nodes and improve the stability of the chain. When medical data centers upload medical metadata hash to the blockchain, they need to submit tokens to the blockchain nodes as a fee, because logging data requires consumption of storage and computing resources. Data users buy tokens from blockchain nodes and use these tokens to buy data usage rights from data owner and medical data center. Of course, the blockchain nodes which execute smart contract can also get rewards. The schematic diagram of incentives is shown in Fig. 8

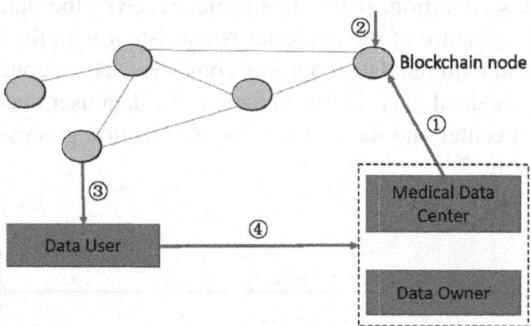

Fig. 8. Incentive mechanism within the system. ① data recording fee. ②the mining reward to blockchain nodes. ③data user buys tokens from blockchain nodes. ④data user pays tokens when data transaction happens.

In the above incentive mechanism, data users are the ultimate bearers of system fees. This is reasonable because data users enjoy the benefits of the system.

5   Formal Verification

We use petri nets to formalize the medical data sharing framework. Petri nets are basically composed of place P, transition T and token. In the process of modeling, the condition is represented by the place and the transition represents the event [27]. A transition (event) has a number of input and output places that represent the preconditions and post conditions. The tokens in the place represent resources or data that can be used. At any time, the distribution state of token in the system expresses the current state of the system, so that the system's change and development process can be clearly expressed through the flow of token in the graph.

There are 3 criteria to determine if the petri net model is correct [28]. The first one is the token can only start from the start place, then gradually be transferred to other places, and finally exists in the terminal place. Especially, only one token can appear in the terminal place. The second criterion is the tokens in the terminal place cannot coexist with tokens in other places. The final criterion is all the tokens in the start place must reach the terminal place.

5.1 Modeling and Formal Verification in the Medical Data Search

Process Modeling

We use the petri network to model the process of medical data search. The petri net of the process is shown in Fig. 9 and the meaning of each symbol is shown in Table 1. The letter P represents the place and the letter T represents the transition. P1 is the start place while P6 is the terminal place. For P2, if the search criteria are fully satisfied in the coarse search, the token jumps to T4. Otherwise, it would jump to T2. For transition T3, if the detailed search hits the target, the token would jump to P4, or it would jump to P5. All roads lead to terminal place P6. The model is correct.

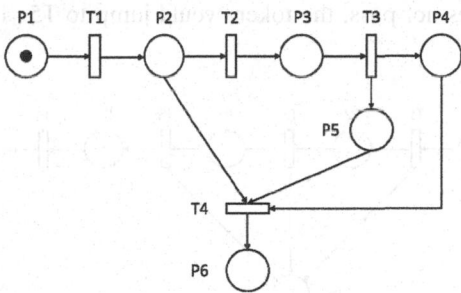

Fig. 9. PN_1. Petri net model for medical data research.

Table 1. The meaning of each place and transition of the medical data search in PN_1

Symbol	The meaning of each symbol
P1	The data user has a search requirement
T1	The data user initiates a search request and the search layer makes a coarse search
P2	Coarse search results
T2	The search layer makes a detailed search
P3	Detailed search results
T3	The data storage layer returns detailed search results
P4	Search hit
P5	Search miss
T4	The search layer sorts the search results and returns
P6	The data user gets data search results

The Proof of Reachability and Boundedness

We can easily find that all roads in the net lead to terminal place P6 and three criteria mentioned above are satisfied. The PN1 is reachable.

$$M_1[T_1 > M_2[T_4 > M_6 \tag{1}$$

Because there is no circle in PN_1, so the maximum value of M is smaller than the longest chain in the net, which means (2) is satisfied. The PN_1 is bounded.

$$\forall M \in R(M_0), M(p) \le 4 \qquad (2)$$

5.2 Modeling and Formal Verification in the Medical Data Transaction

Process Modeling

The PN2 is shown in Fig. 10 and the meaning of each symbol is shown in Table 2. P1 is the start place while P5 and P6 is the terminal place. For P2, P3 and P4, if they verify that the signature does not pass, the token would jump to T5. Then the transaction is cancelled.

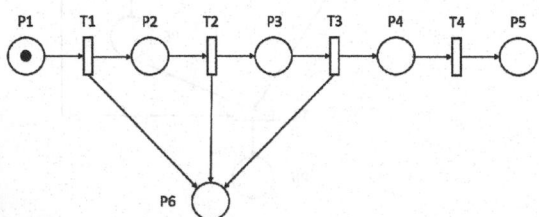

Fig. 10. PN2. Petri net model for medical data transaction.

Table 2. The meaning of each place and transition of the medical data transaction in PN_2

Symbol	The meaning of each symbol
P1	The data request signed by the data user
T1	The data center checks the signature and signs the request with his own private key
P2	The data request signed by the data user and corresponding medical data center
T2	The data owner checks the signatures and signs the request with his own private key
P3	The data request signed by the data user, corresponding medical data center and data owner
T3	The blockchain nodes verify the three signatures
P4	The data transaction is authorized
T4	The blockchain nodes executes smart contract and records the results to the chain. The data center sends required data to the data user
P5	The data transaction is succeeded
P6	The data transaction is canceled

There are only two terminal places, P5 and P6. Because all paths lead to these two places, the token finally would exist in terminal places. The PN2 model is correct.

The Proof of Reachability and Boundedness

For PN2, we can find that transition sequence T1 satisfy (3) and T1, T2, T3, T4 satisfy (4). From (3) and (4), the M6 and M5 is reachable from M1.

$$M_1[T_1 > M_6 \qquad (3)$$

To our petri net $PN_2 = (P,T;F,M)$, we can easily find transition sequence T1, T4 to satisfy (1). The M6 is reachable from M1. The PN_2 is reachable.

$$M_1[T_1 > M_2[T_2 > M_3[T_3 > M_4[T_4 > M_5 \qquad (4)$$

We can find there are no circle in PN_2, so the maximum value of M is smaller than the longest chain in PN_2, which is the path through P1, P2, P3, P4 and P5. It means (5) is satisfied. The PN_2 is also bounded.

$$\forall M \in R(M_0), M(p) \leq 4 \qquad (5)$$

6 Conclusion

In this paper, we design the medical metadata as the smallest subunit of data ownership confirmation and propose a blockchain-based medical data sharing Framework MDSF. The medical metadata can avoid revealing privacy, retain some of the data features and be generated distributed. Finally, we use petri nets to verify the reachability and boundedness of the framework which prove it can realize its designed function and operate safely. The system provides users with a convenient and secure way to obtain their past medical data and enabling research institutions engaged in medical data mining to obtain the actual medical data they need after desensitization. Thereby we achieve the circulation of medical data between different hospitals, individuals and research institutions.

Acknowledgments. This work was supported in part by the National Key Research and Development Program under Grant no. 2016YFB1000102, in part by the National Natural Science Foundation of China under Grant no. 61972222, 61672318, and in part by Purple Mountain Laboratory: Networking, Communications and Security.

References

1. Weitzman, E.R., et al.: Willingness to share personal health record data for care improvement and public health: a survey of experienced personal health record users. BMC Med. Inform. Decis. Mak. **12**(1), 39 (2012)
2. Mandl, K.D., et al.: Public standards and patients' control: how to keep electronic medical records accessible but private. BMJ **322**(7281), 283–287 (2001)
3. Santoro, E.: Artificial intelligence in medicine: limits and obstacles. Recenti Prog. Med. **108**(12), 500–502 (2017)

4. The Office of the National Coordinator for Health Information Technology, Report on health information blocking, U.S. Department of HHS, Technical Report (2017)
5. Kostkova, P., et al.: Who owns the data? Open data for healthcare. Front. Public Health **4**, 7 (2016)
6. Yang, J.J., Li, J.Q., Niu, Y.: A hybrid solution for privacy preserving medical data sharing in the cloud environment. Future Gener. Comput. Syst. **43**, 74–86 (2015)
7. Kaminsky, D.: Spelunking the triangle: Exploring Aron Swartz's take on zooko's triangle, January 2011. http://dankaminsky.com/2011/01/13/spelunk-tri/
8. Kalodner, H.A., et al.: An empirical study of namecoin and lessons for decentralized namespace design. In: WEIS (2015)
9. Zheng, Z., et al.: Blockchain challenges and opportunities: a survey. Int. J. Web Grid Serv. **14**(4), 352–375 (2018)
10. Lin, I.C., Liao, T.C.: A survey of blockchain security issues and challenges. IJ Network Secur. **19**(5), 653–659 (2017)
11. Nakamoto, S.: Bitcoin: a peer-to-peer electronic cash system. https://bitcoin.org/bitcoin.pdf
12. Buterin, V.: On public and private blockchains. https://blog.ethereum.org/2015/08/07/on-public-and-private-blockchains/
13. Wood, G.: Ethereum: a secure decentralised generalised transaction ledger. Ethereum Project Yellow Paper (2014)
14. Sasson, E.B., et al.: Zerocash: decentralized anonymous payments from bitcoin. In: 2014 IEEE Symposium on Security and Privacy, pp. 459–474. IEEE (2014)
15. Zhang, Y., et al.: Z-channel: scalable and efficient scheme in Zerocash. Comput. Secur. **86**, 112 (2019)
16. Eyal, I., et al.: Bitcoin-ng: a scalable blockchain protocol. In: 13th {USENIX} Symposium on Networked Systems Design and Implementation pp. 45–59 (2016)
17. Wang, J., Wang, H.: Monoxide: scale out blockchains with asynchronous consensus zones. In: 16th {USENIX} Symposium on Networked Systems Design and Implementation, pp. 95–112 (2019)
18. Zyskind, G., Nathan, O., Pentland, A.: Decentralizing privacy: using blockchain to protect personal data. In: Proceedings of IEEE Security and Privacy Workshops, pp. 180–184 (2015). https://doi.org/10.1109/SPW.2015.27
19. Factom, Healthnautica + factom announce partnership (2015). http://blog.factom.org
20. CoinDesk, Medical records project wins top prize at blockchain hackathon (2015). http://www.coindesk.com
21. Azaria, A., et al.: Medrec: using blockchain for medical data access and permission management. In: 2016 2nd International Conference on Open and Big Data (OBD), pp. 25–30. IEEE (2016)
22. Xia, Q., Sifah, E., Smahi, A., et al.: BBDS: blockchain-based data sharing for electronic medical records in cloud environments. Information **8**(2), 44 (2017)
23. Dubovitskaya, A., et al.: Secure and trustable electronic medical records sharing using blockchain. In: AMIA Annual Symposium Proceedings. American Medical Informatics Association, vol. 2017, p. 650 (2017)
24. Fan, K., Wang, S., Ren, Y., et al.: Medblock: efficient and secure medical data sharing via blockchain. J. Med. Syst. **42**(8), 136 (2018)
25. Dolin, R.H., Alschuler, L., Boyer, S., et al.: HL7 clinical document architecture, release 2. J. Am. Med. Inform. Assoc. **13**(1), 30–39 (2006)
26. Miguel, C., Barbara, L.: Practical byzantine fault tolerance. In: Proceedings of the Third Symposium on Operating Systems Design and Implementation, New Orleans, USA, vol. 99, pp. 173–186 (1999)
27. Petri, C.A., Reisig, W.: Petri net. Scholarpedia **3**(4), 6477 (2008)
28. Murata, T.: Petri nets: Properties, analysis and applications. Proc. IEEE **77**(4), 541–580 (1989)

A Survey on the Application of SGX in Blockchain Area

Hong Lei[1], Qinghao Wang[1,2], Wenbo Shi[2], and Zijian Bao[1(✉)]

[1] Oxford-Hainan Blockchain Research Institute, Chengmai 571924, China
{leihong,qinghao,zijian}@oxhainan.org
[2] Department of Computer Science and Engineering, Northeastern University, Shenyang 110001, China
shiwb@neuq.edu.cn
https://www.oxhainan.org

Abstract. As an emerging technology, blockchain is widely used in encrypted digital currencies and has an important impact in various fields such as finance, cloud storage, and Internet of things (IoT), etc. However, it faces various challenges in the process of its development and application: waste of resources, limited privacy protection, poor scalability, etc. Intel Software Guard Extensions (SGX), as a new trusted computing technology, brings solutions to the above challenges in the blockchain field. Based on the hierarchical structure of the blockchain, we are the first to systematically discuss the application status of SGX in the blockchian, including consensus layer, the ledger topology layer, the contract layer, and the application layer. Meanwhile, we summarize the advantages and challenges of SGX in the field of the blockchain, and look forward to the future development direction and the possible research topics.

Keywords: Blockchain · Intel SGX · Consensus algorithm · Smart contract · Privacy protection

1 Introduction

Blockchain is a technical solution that relies on distributed nodes to exchange, verify and store the network data without third parties. Bitcoin [1] is the first application of the blockchain, and its market capitalization is reaching 176 billion in June 2020 [2]. Ethereum [3] is another application of blockchain technology, which provides a platform for the operation of smart contracts to implement Turing-complete programming capabilities. At present, blockchain technology shows a wide range of application prospects. However, some issues restrict the development of the blockchain in nowadays. As we know, a large amount of power is consumed based on the proof of work mechanism. It restricts blockchain's application range severely. Meanwhile, the simple "Nakamoto" mechanism in blockchain can not completely guarantee the user's privacy. Some

Z. Zheng et al. (Eds.): BlockSys 2020, CCIS 1267, pp. 633–647, 2020.
https://doi.org/10.1007/978-981-15-9213-3_49

researches prove that the association between address and the user's identity can be obtained by analyzing the transactions on the blockchain [4,5]. Moreover, blockchain also suffers from other obstacles, such as poor scalability, lack of access to outside information, and centralization trend [6]. Therefore, how to solve the above issues becomes an essential step in the development of the blockchain.

Recently, employing Intel software guard extensions (SGX) to solve the problems in the blockchain has become a new research idea. SGX [7,8] is a trusted hardware technology developed by Intel corporation and has been added to Intel's CPU architecture. SGX provides a trusted memory range that preventing the code and data from being externally tampered and stolen. Meanwhile, the SGX built-in functions such as attestation mechanism, random number generation and monotonic counter provide the powerful efforts for solving security and privacy issues. The trusted execution environment (TEE) provided by SGX can ensure the correctness of execution (e.g., transaction verification, contract execution) and can protect private data from the outside world. An SGX-based party can be considered as a trusted party, which can replace complex cryptographic protocols to protect the security of schemes. Moreover, SGX can be used to simplify the process of protocols and enhance the security. However, due to the limitations of its design, SGX has certain deficiencies, such as performance load [9], memory restriction [10], side channel attacks [11]. These shortcomings limit the application of SGX technology in some scenarios and require researchers to combine effective scenarios to design effective solutions.

In general, TEE, especially Intel SGX technology, is a hot and highly developing field. Employing SGX to solve efficiency, privacy, and scalability problems in the blockchain still exist great challenges. In this work, we introduce existing schemes based on SGX in blockchain, abstract the functions and hidden dangers provided by SGX in these works, and suggest future directions in this area. In more details, our contributions are as follows:

1. *The first summary of SGX-based research of blockchain.* To the best of our knowledge, we propose the first systematic analysis on the application of SGX in blockchain system, which provides insight for employing SGX technology to solve the problems of the blockchain area. To introduce the existing works better, we divide the blockchain into six layers, which will be introduced in Sect. 2.1. We analyze the application of SGX in four of the above layers, which are associated with SGX.

2. *Systematic analysis of the functions and challenges of SGX in blockchain.* We summarize the practical functions of SGX employed in blockchain system. Meanwhile, we analyze the challenges caused by applying SGX to the blockchain and suggest the future directions in this area.

The rest of the paper is structured as follows. Section 2 presents an overview of blockchain's layers and Intel SGX technologies. Section 3 discusses the application of SGX in the consensus, ledger topology, contract, and application layers. We summary the advantages and disadvantages of SGX in the blockchain field in Sect. 4. Then, we discuss the open issues and show future directions in Sect. 5. Finally, we give the conclusion in Sect. 6.

2   Background

2.1   Blockchain Technology

Blockchain is a distributed ledger system. In the blockchain, nodes controlled by different users around the world form a vast P2P network to maintain the database system. The consistency is guaranteed by the consensus algorithm. For introducing the SGX-based schemes in blockchain field clearly, we introduce a hierarchical architecture of blockchain, as shown in Fig. 1.

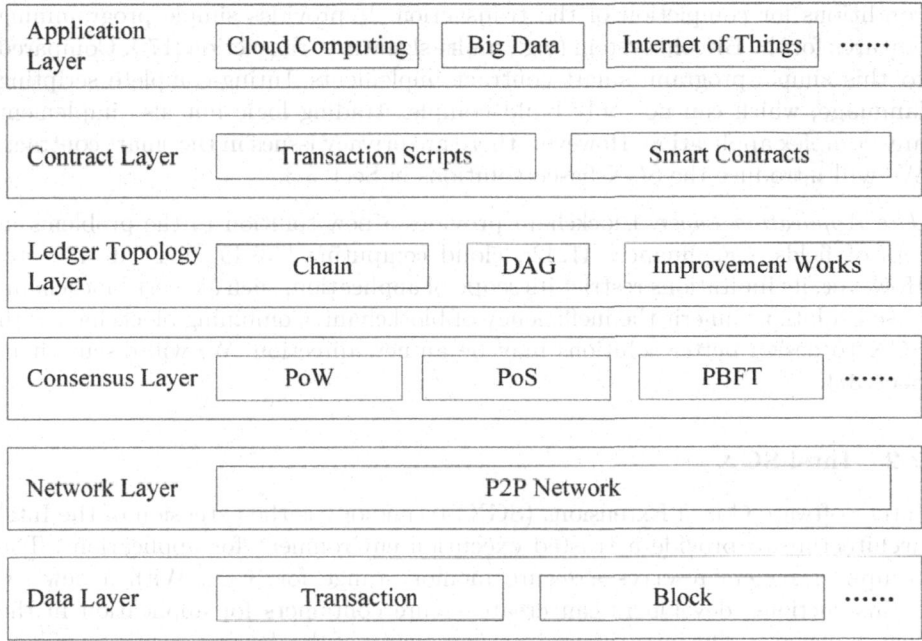

Fig. 1. The architecture of blockchain layer.

The Data Layer. The data layer mainly involves different data types recorded in blockchain, such as transactions, the hash value of block, smart contracts, etc.

The Network Layer. Nodes in the blockchain constitute a vast P2P network, and the functions of the nodes in the system are logically completely equal. Information is transmitted between the nodes in the form of flooding broadcasts.

The Consensus Layer. Blockchain uses a consensus algorithm to determine which node produces the next block, and maintaines the consistency of the blockchain. The mainstream consensus algorithms include Proof of Work (PoW) [1], Proof of Stake (PoS) [12], and Delegated Proof of Stake (DPoS) [13], etc. However, there are many limitations in existing consensus algorithm, such as resource waste (PoW), waste of resources (PoW), failure to provide provable security (PoS), and centralization trend (DPoS). We will discuss the SGX-based consensus algorithm in Sect. 3.1.

The Ledger Topology Layer. The ledger topology represents the state and structure of the data generated by the consensus layer, including chains, directed acyclic graphs (DAG), etc. Besides, the existing blockchain improvement efforts also produce some new ledger topologies by changing the organization, distribution, and status of the transactions, including payment channel [14], mix protocol [15], cross-chain transaction [16], etc. We will introduce the blockchain improvement schemes based on SGX in Sect. 3.2.

The Contract Layer. The contract layer includes simple trading scripts and smart contracts. In Bitcoin, the scripts contained in the transaction can preset the conditions for completion of the transaction. It provides simple programming features for the Bitcoin system (e.g., multi-signature transaction [17]). Compared to this simple program, smart contract implements Turing-complete scripting language, which can not only build complex trading logic but also implement any complex application. However, there are privacy issues in the smart contract. We will introduce the SGX-based solutions in Sect. 3.3.

The Application Layer. Blockchain provides a new solution to the problems in lots of fields, e.g., finance [41,42], cloud computing [43–45], IoT [46–48], etc. However, its limitations restrict its scope of application, such as most blockchain-based solutions inherit the inefficiency of blockchain. Combining blockchain with SGX to design better solutions may be an new direction. We will discuss it in Sect. 3.4.

2.2   Intel SGX

Intel Software Guard Extensions (SGX) technology is the extension of the Intel architecture to provide a trusted execution environment for applications. The computer system reserves a secure memory range for SGX. With a new set of instructions, developers can create secure containers for application in the secure memory. The integrity and confidentiality of the data in containers will be protected. SGX provides three major mechanisms: *secure container*, *attestation*, and *data sealing* [7,8].

Secure Container. SGX provides a secure container called **enclave**, which protects the execution of code and data in it from external influences (including privileged software such as OS and Hypervisor). To protect enclave, the access of enclave will perform additional check by the hardware. The access instruction that fails the above verification will return a reference error that the memory address does not exist. Additional memory access check enables the enclave to be isolated from the outside world.

Attestation. Attestation mechanism can prove that an enclave has deployed the correct code and the SGX-based platform creating this enclave is credible. SGX proposes two attestation schemes: **intra platform attestation** and **remote attestation**. Intra platform attestation is used by an enclave to prove to another enclave on the same platform, which can be used by calling the CPU instruction. Remote attestation process is based on intra platform attestation. It can be used to prove to the remote parties that it is trustworthy.

Data Sealing. Enclave data can be sealed out of secure memory for future use. SGX provides a special key called sealing key for data sealing to ensure the confidentiality and integrity of the data.

3   SGX-Based Schemes in the Blockchain Layers

3.1   SGX in the Consensus Layer

The principle and existing problems of these consensus algorithms have been introduced in Sect. 2.1. This section will discuss the schemes employing SGX to improve the existing consensus algorithms based on SGX.

Proof of Useful Work. PoW suffers from an enormous waste of resources, e.g., computing power, because nodes need to try to solve the computational puzzle each consensus round. To solve the problem, Zhang et al. [18] propose a new consensus scheme called Proof of Useful Work (PoUW). PoUW is an improvement to the PoW, which exploits SGX to transform the computing resources needed in PoW into useful works. In PoUW, every miner needs to support SGX, and get useful tasks from users each round. Miners will load those tasks into the enclave for execution. The enclave will determine if the execution wins the right to generate a new block in this round and provides certification. Finally, the winner can publish the new block and certification to the blockchain network by an agent. However, the security of PoUW will be destroyed by breaking the enclave in a miner node, because PoUW trusts the proof generated by each SGX-based miner node. For this problem, PoUW design a statistical analysis scheme based on newly generated blocks to detect whether SGX-based nodes are corrupted.

Secure Proof of Stake. PoS is another widely used consensus algorithm. In PoS, the possibility that a node obtains the right is related to the number and duration of assets it holds. Compared to PoW, PoS has less waste of resources and higher efficiency, but lower security [49,50]. Li et al. [19] propose the Secure Proof of Stake to improve the security of PoS. The scheme has the same way of obtaining rights generating new blocks as PoS, but it uses the nodes based on TEE (e.g., SGX) to provide security for the scheme. In the scheme, each node needs to generate a signature key pair in an enclave and configure the information in the blockchain network for joining the blockchain network. Since the signature key for the block is managed by enclave, the reliability of the block confirmation is ensured. Moreover, user's accounts are holden by the enclave, which improves security further. Considering the security problems of the PoS, the schemes implement a secure monotonic counter using SGX to ensure that the verifier generates at most one block at the existing block height. It prevents the verifier generating block for different branches to get more rewards at the same time.

Proof of Elapsed Time. Proof of Elapsed Time (PoET) [20] is a new consensus algorithm based on SGX, which is proposed in the Hyperledger Sawtooth Lake project. In the process of PoET, each node generates a random number, which represents the time that the node needs to wait. The node with the shortest waiting time will obtain the right to generate the block and receive the reward. The nodes of PoET only perform simple random number generation algorithm and corresponding waiting. Therefore, it does not need high computing resources. For security, the nodes need to execute protocol algorithm in the local enclave to ensure the correct generation of the random number and the correct execution of waiting time. The nodes will be verified with the remote attestation mechanism to ensure the reliability of the platform.

Proof of Luck. Based on the idea of PoET, Mitar et al. [21] propose a new consensus algorithm named Proof of Luck. The nodes in Proof of Luck are also based on TEE (e.g., SGX) and run the random number generation algorithm in the enclave to elect a leader. The smaller random number generated by the node, the sooner the new block generated by itself can be broadcast. After receiving the new block, nodes verify it and select the block with the smallest random number as the new block. To optimize performance, if nodes receive a block with a smaller random number before the broadcasting block of themselves, they will give up broadcasting their block to reduce network load. The scheme implements the SGX-based monotonic counter to prohibit concurrent calls of the enclave, which prevents individual nodes from running multiple consensus nodes concurrently to increase their competitiveness.

3.2 SGX in the Ledger Topology Layer

This section introduces the schemes based on SGX to enhance the improvement works of the blockchain.

Payment Channel. Payment channel [14] is one of the solutions to improve the throughput of blockchain. It can implement multiple off-chain transactions and only synchronize a settlement transaction in the blockchain. However, existing payment channel schemes rely on complex cryptographic protocols to ensure security, which results in inefficiencies and unfriendly to users. Lind et al. [22] propose Teechain, a secure payment channel solution. In Teechain, both parties that build payment channels are based on SGX. The enclave of both parties maintain the balance information, the address of transactions, and the corresponding private key. Before building the payment channel, both parties must deposit the funds that determining the transaction capacity of the payment channel. With remote attestation, each party constructs a secure communication channel for synchronizing the balance. During the transaction, the payment message is encrypted by the enclave and sent to the other party. The other party will receive the payment message and updates the balance. The balance maintained by the enclave of both parties and will not be affected by the users. Since both enclaves hold the key for the settlement transaction and the transaction based on the hash time lock, both users can settle the transaction separately after the timeout. Teechain takes the way that each user can only send the payment messages to ensure that neither user will reject the other party's messages to destroy the protocol. Meanwhile, Teechain employs hardware-based monotonic counters to prevent the replay attacks.

Mix Protocol. Transaction mix protocol is one of the solutions to solve the privacy problem in the blockchain. Most mix schemes use the centralized mix server model [15], which uses a single bitcoin address to receive the same amount of funds from multiple user addresses. Then, the server transfers the funds to the destination address. Since all user addresses have the same probability of being traded with the destination address, it is difficult for attackers to associate user and destination address. However, the centralized mixer has huge rights, and it is difficult for the protocol to constrain the malicious behavior of mixers. Tran et al. [23] propose a new privacy protection scheme. The scheme is based on the centralized model. The centralized mixer is based on SGX, and the mix operation will be load into the enclave to effectively prevent the malicious mix server from malicious behavior. To mix transactions, a user needs to construct a transaction (including information such as funds and destination address) to transfer funds to mixer's address. Enclave periodically get the transactions related to the mix and constructs the corresponding transfer transactions. Finally, the mixer will broadcast the transaction to the blockchain network. Since the mixer's address is generated and saved in the enclave, it can be ensured that the funds can only be spent by the enclave. The establishment of the secure communication channel between the user and the mixer ensures that the privacy of the mix information.

Cross-Chain Transaction. Atomic Cross-Chain Swaps (ACCS) achieve untrusted cross-chain transactions [16]. However, it relies on the parties to interact with the transactions continuously to ensure the security of the protocol. It is not only unfriendly to the user, but the complex interaction process seriously affects the performance of the protocol. Tesseract [24] is a cross-chain trading scheme that employing the secure execution features of SGX to implement real-time cross-chain transactions. In Tesseract, there is a central exchange based on SGX. The user who needs the service registers a Tesseract account and deposits a certain amount of balance into the exchange's address. The exchange enclave records the private key of the exchange's address and the balance of all users. In the transaction, the user makes orders by offering requests to the exchange. After receiving the message, the Tesseract enclave issues an order that is anonymous and visible to everyone. Other users choose the appropriate order to trade, and enclave updates the user's account balance based on the transaction information. Tesseract enclave will periodically synchronize settlement transactions to the blockchain network. The user can utilize the remote attestation mechanism to verify the program's validity in the enclave and build a secure channel to ensure the privacy of their transactions.

Light-Weight Client. Some researchers [25,26] propose the blockchain light-weight client schemes to support the node based on resource-constrained devices (e.g., mobile phones). In the scheme, there are two types of nodes: light nodes and full nodes. The light nodes only need to save a small amount of data on the chain and outsource most of the verification and storage work to full nodes. However, when full nodes work for light nodes, it needs to know all the transaction information from light nodes, which seriously affects the privacy of users. Matetic et al. [27] propose an SGX-based light-weight client scheme to protect the privacy of users. In the scheme, full nodes are based on SGX and load the transaction verification process into the enclave. When a light node sends a request to a full node, the enclave on the full node will scan the blockchain data and reply the Merkle path of the block. The light node verifies the correctness of the transaction through the Merkle path and the block header. They [27] also provides a variant scheme to improve the efficiency of verification. In the variant scheme, the enclave on the full node maintains a special version of the Unspent Transaction Outputs (UTXO) database. When receiving the verification request from a light node, the enclave will access the database and return the corresponding result directly. In both schemes, light nodes and the enclaves can construct the secure communication channel to protect the privacy of user.

3.3   SGX in the Contract Layer

The contract layer includes trading script and smart contract. The trading script can only build simple trading logic, while the smart contract has more programming power than general trading scripts. However, the contract codes on the blockchain are visible to all nodes, which undoubtedly affect the privacy of the smart contract. Some researchers [4,5] prove the feasibility of de-anonymization attacks by analyzing the transaction structure of blockchain. This section introduces SGX-based schemes to solve the privacy issue in the smart contract.

Kosba et al. [28] propose a smart contract system to protect the privacy of smart contracts. They design a manager to execute part of the user's smart contract, which includes private information. The manager will construct a zero-knowledge proof to prove the execution results. To ensure that manager is trusted and does not reveal sensitive data, they recommend that the manager can be loaded in a TEE (e.g., SGX). Yuan et al. [29] propose a scheme that protecting the security and confidentiality of smart contracts without breaking the integrity of existing blockchains. The scheme establishes a TEE-distributed storage platform (TEE-DS) as the execution platform of the smart contract. TEE-DS consists of the worker nodes based on SGX. To ensure the confidentiality of the smart contract code and data, the user needs to establish a secure channel with the TEE-DS before transferring the contract. The smart contract code will be transmitted using the secure channel. Users can be free to choose whether to become a worker node, which guarantees the scalability of the system. Cheng et al. [30] propose Ekiden to protect the privacy of smart contracts. Ekiden also separates execution of smart contact from consensus operations. The execution of smart contract is responsible for compute nodes, and consensus operations are responsible for consensus nodes. The consensus nodes are responsible for maintaining the blockchain system and updating the state of the smart contract. The compute nodes are based on SGX and will execute the smart contract in the enclave. Any node that supports SGX can join the system as a compute node. To reduce the impact of failed compute nodes, the scheme designed a key management protocol based on secret sharing [31,32]. Based on the design idea of Ekiden [30], Das et al. [33] implement a smart contract execution scheme based on Bitcoin. In the scheme, all users must submit the deposit into their contract before their contracts are executed, which is different from Ekiden [30]. At the same time, the execution node based on SGX must submit the margin equal to the sum of deposits. If the protocol fails, the party that misbehaves will lose the deposit. However, the scheme only supports the limited types of contracts and has security issues (e.g., multi-party collusion to secure margin).

3.4 SGX in the Application Layer

In this section, we will discuss the schemes in different application fields such as finance, cloud storage, and Internet of things (IoT) [34–36].

Distributed Cloud Computing Service. Most of the existing cloud computing models are based on centralized service models, which brings vast pressure of equipment to cloud computing servers and the trust problem between servers and users. Al-Bassam et al. [34] propose a distributed cloud computing solution, which allows execution nodes to rent their own trusted calculation time. It designs a fair trade protocol that combines the SGX remote attestation mechanism with smart contracts to ensure fairness in rental service. With the secure execution environment of the SGX and smart contract, the scheme ensures the correct execution of transactions and user' code. Meanwhile, it employs the distributed cloud computing model to ensure that users can continue to execute on other execution nodes if the current execution node is corrupted or offline. However, the scheme requires the separate construction of the payment channels between the user and the execution node, and it needs to maintain continuous communication during the rental process, which limits the availability of the scheme.

Data Ownership and Privacy Protection Data ownership and privacy protection have become one of the key researches in the era of big data. The existing schemes, including data access control [37] and data anonymization [38], cannot guarantee the proper use of data by authorized users. Yang et al. [35] combine smart contract with TEE (e.g., SGX) to enable privacy of data, which enables users to control other people's use of their private data. In the Privacy Guard, data owners use smart contracts to set usage policies for data, including data consumers, data usage conditions, and the purpose of the data. At the same time, the data usage record is stored on the blockchain to ensure the unchangeability and traceability. Privacy Guard delivers smart contract to the off-chain execution engine based on TEE. The correctness of execution does not depend on the consensus algorithm and does not require all blockchain nodes to execute the contract, which improves system efficiency. In general, Privacy Guard leverages TEE's isolation feature to protect the execution of smart contracts while reducing the consumption of smart contract consensus algorithms. The TEE remote attestation mechanism solves the user's trust in data storage.

IoT Data Security. Blockchain provides a new solution to the secure storage and management of IoT devices. However, the huge data flow of IoT far exceeds the throughput of existing blockchain systems. Meanwhile, the hybrid storage architecture, which stores data digests on the chain and stores the original data out of the chain, cannot guarantee the integrity and privacy of the IoT data. Ayoade et al. [36] propose a decentralized IoT data management solution. The scheme employs smart contracts to achieve data access control and SGX technology to store IoT data securely. The IoT device in the scheme is registered in the blockchain through the IoT gateway. It uses the smart contract to set the data access control algorithm to ensure that only authorized users can access the data. Moreover, the scheme uses the hybrid storage architecture to store data digests in blockchains, and the original data is stored out of the chain. To protect the off-chain data, the data will be encrypted by SGX. When a user wants to get the original data, he first proves his authority to the blockchain. A certificate will be obtained from the blockchain and submitted to the storage platform. The enclave of the storage platform performs integrity verification on the certificate and returns data to the user.

4   Discussion

At present, SGX has many applications in the blockchain field. Through the analysis of the previous sections, the functions of SGX in the field of blockchain can be summarized as follows.

1. *Secure execution.* An enclave is isolated from the external environment, so the execution logic of the code loaded into the enclave cannot be tampered by the external environment, which ensures the correctness of internal execution.
2. *Privacy protection.* The data in the enclave cannot be accessed and tampered by the outside world, so the privacy of sensitive data generated during execution can be effectively protected. Besides, the secure channel built between the enclave and the other party also guarantees the privacy of the data passed into the enclave.
3. *Simplify the protocol process.* Most cryptographic protocols often employ complex cryptographic tools, and cumbersome protocol flows to ensure security. The SGX-based role can act as a trusted party in the protocol to reduce the use of complex cryptographic tools and to simplify the protocol process, thereby improving the efficiency of the schemes.

4. *Trusted functions based on SGX.* Some trusted functions provided by SGX (such as trusted monotonic counters, trusted random number generation, etc.) can be implemented to provide trusted components for the solution, thereby improving the security of the scheme.

Obviously, SGX provides practical help to the research field of blockchain. Of course, there are still some problems in the application of SGX in the blockchain. Some of the issues are caused by the unique scenes of the blockchain, and the others are caused by defects of SGX. The details are as follows.

1. *Controlled communication.* The communication of SGX is controlled by the platform owner, so it is easy for the platform owner to intercept input of an enclave. Of course, the information passed into an enclave can be encrypted to ensure data security, but the interception cannot be stopped. It may lead to some network communication-based attacks (such as denial of service attacks, Eclipse attacks, replay attacks). Therefore, researchers have to design reasonable protocol to decrease the possibility that the SGX platform owner will intercept or tamper the input of the enclave. A reference is the Teechain [14], which introduces the beneficial results for an SGX platform owner to receive the correct inputs.
2. *Single point attack.* Most of the SGX-based solutions rely on the credibility of SGX. Once the SGX-based role is compromised, it is easy to cause the entire solution to crash. The problem is very conspicuous in the consensus schemes, which employ the SGX-based roles as the nodes in a P2P network (e.g., PoET [20], PoLK [21]). In those schemes, the SGX-based roles may maintain the large value relationship, which stimulates the attacker to launch attacks on the SGX, even the physical means. To tolerate such attack, a solution is to decentralize the benefit to reduce the possibility of attack. Meanwhile, it is possible that multiple SGX-based nodes cooperate to mitigate the attacks.
3. *Side channel attacks.* In recent years, some side channel attacks on SGX are exploded, which indicates that SGX indeed have some security holes. Although these attacks are relatively difficult to exploit, the attacker may use these means to attack the SGX with sufficient profit. To solve the problem, we can consider combining the scheme with the side channel attack defense scheme (such as Oblivious Random Access Machine [39], Address Space Layout Randomization [40]) to improve the security.

5 Future Directions

SGX provides the new solution to the problems of efficiency, privacy, and scalability in the blockchain. It has attracted much attention to academia and industry. We believe the following aspects should be noted in future research.

Security in Consensus Algorithms. In the blockchain, the consensus mechanism, while considered as a way to ensure fairness and trust in an untrusted system, provides a target for would-be attackers. We discuss the schemes using SGX to eliminate the attacks in existing consensus algorithms in Sect. 3.1. However, SGX has the potential to solve the more attacks in the consensus layer. For example, selfish mining attack is an attack strategy in PoW, which permits the miner to obtain more rewards of creating blocks. To implement the attack, a miner is not broadcast the generated block immediately and continue to generate the next block in a round, until a new block is broadcasted. Obviously, the miner based on SGX can be forced to broadcast the generated block, which prevents against selfish mining attack. Thus, it is a potential direction to solve the more attacks in the existing consensus algorithm using SGX.

Privacy Protection and Supervision. Privacy protection technology may provide a safeguard for the unlawful act. For example, offenders can anonymously achieve money laundering by anonymous digital currency. Thus, a splendid blockchain system should supervise the criminal acts while provides privacy protection. In this scenario, the SGX-based role can act as a qualified supervisor to hold the secret that can track the users. Thus, it is also a potential direction to build a trusted supervisor based on SGX.

6   Conclusion

This paper analyzes the application of SGX in the field of blockchain. Firstly, the blockchain layers and SGX technology are introduced. Secondly, the problems of blockchain and SGX-based solutions in the consensus layer, the ledger topology layer, the contract layer, and the application layer are elaborated. Finally, the functions of SGX in the field of blockchain are summarized, and the future directions have prospected.

Acknowledgements. This study is supported by Oxford-Hainan Blockchain Research Institute, the National Science Foundation of China (No. 61472074, U1708262) and the Fundamental Research Funds for the Central Universities (No. N172304023).

References

1. Nakamoto, S.: Bitcoin: A peer-to-peer electronic cash system (2008)
2. Bitcoin market value (2019). https://coinmarketcap.com/zh/currencies/bitcoin/
3. Buterin, V.: A next-generation smart contract and decentralized application platform. White paper (2014)

4. Bonneau, J., et al.: Sok: Research perspectives and challenges for bitcoin and cryptocurrencies. In: IEEE Symposium on Security and Privacy (2015)
5. Meiklejohn, S., et al.: A fistful of bitcoins: characterizing payments among men with no names. In: Proceedings of the 2013 Conference on Internet Measurement Conference. ACM (2013)
6. Zheng, Z., Xie, S., Dai, H., Wang, H., Chen, X.: Blockchain challenges and opportunities: a survey. Int. J. Web Grid Serv. (IJWGS) **14**(4), 352–375 (2018)
7. McKeen, F., et al.: Innovative instructions and software model for isolated execution. Hasp@isca10.1 (2013)
8. Anati, I., et al.: Innovative technology for CPU based attestation and sealing. In: Proceedings of the 2nd International Workshop on Hardware and Architectural Support for Security and Privacy, vol. 13 (2013)
9. Arnautov, S., et al.: SCONE: secure linux containers with intel SGX. In: 12th USENIX Symposium on Operating Systems Design and Implementation (OSDI) (2016)
10. Wang, W., et al.: Leaky cauldron on the dark land: understanding memory side-channel hazards in SGX. In: Proceedings of the 2017 ACM SIGSAC Conference on Computer and Communications Security. ACM (2017)
11. Hunt, T., et al.: Ryoan: a distributed sandbox for untrusted computation on secret data. ACM Trans. Comput. Syst. (TOCS) **35**(4), 13 (2018)
12. Seijas, P.L., Thompson, S.J., McAdams, D.: Scripting smart contracts for distributed ledger technology. IACR Cryptology ePrint Archive 2016:1156 (2016)
13. Seijas, P.L., Thompson, S.J., McAdams, D.: Scripting smart contracts for distributed ledger technology. IACR Cryptol. ePrint Archieve Technology (2016)
14. Poon, J., Dryja, T.: The bitcoin lightning network: Scalable off-chain instant payments (2016)
15. Valenta, L., Rowan, B.: Blindcoin: blinded, accountable mixes for bitcoin. In: Brenner, M., Christin, N., Johnson, B., Rohloff, K. (eds.) FC 2015. LNCS, vol. 8976, pp. 112–126. Springer, Heidelberg (2015). https://doi.org/10.1007/978-3-662-48051-9_9
16. Nolan, T.: Alt chains and atomic transfers. In: Bitcoin Forum, May 2013
17. Okupski, K.: Bitcoin developer reference. In: Eindhoven (2014)
18. Zhang, F., et al.: REM: resource-efficient mining for blockchains. In: 26th USENIX Security Symposium (USENIX Security 17) (2017)
19. Li, W., Andreina, S., Bohli, J.-M., Karame, G.: Securing proof-of-stake blockchain protocols. In: Garcia-Alfaro, J., Navarro-Arribas, G., Hartenstein, H., Herrera-Joancomartí, J. (eds.) ESORICS/DPM/CBT -2017. LNCS, vol. 10436, pp. 297–315. Springer, Cham (2017). https://doi.org/10.1007/978-3-319-67816-0_17
20. Intel Corporation. Sawtooth lake (2016)
21. Milutinovic, M., et al.: Proof of luck: an efficient blockchain consensus protocol. In: Proceedings of the 1st Workshop on System Software for Trusted Execution. ACM (2016)
22. Lind, J., et al. Teechain: a secure payment network with asynchronous blockchain access. In: Proceedings of the 27th ACM Symposium on Operating Systems Principles. ACM (2019)
23. Tran, M., et al.: Obscuro: a bitcoin mixer using trusted execution environments. In: Proceedings of the 34th Annual Computer Security Applications Conference. ACM (2018)
24. Tran, M., et al.: Obscuro: a bitcoin mixer using trusted execution environments. In: Proceedings of the 34th Annual Computer Security Applications Conference. ACM (2018)

25. Bünz, B., et al.: Flyclient: super-light clients for cryptocurrencies. IACR Cryptology ePrint Archive 2019:226 (2019)
26. BitcoinJ (2018). https://bitcoinj.github.io/
27. Matetic, S., et al.: BITE: bitcoin lightweight client privacy using trusted execution. In: 28th USENIX Security Symposium (USENIX Security 19) (2019)
28. Kosba, A., et al.: Hawk: the blockchain model of cryptography and privacy-preserving smart contracts. In: 2016 IEEE symposium on security and privacy (SP). IEEE (2016)
29. Yuan, R., et al.: Shadoweth: private smart contract on public blockchain. J. Comput. Sci. Technol. **33**(3), 542–556 (2018)
30. Yuan, R., et al.: Shadoweth: private smart contract on public blockchain. J. Comput. Sci. Technol. **33**(3), 542–556 (2018)
31. Herzberg, A., Jarecki, S., Krawczyk, H., Yung, M.: Proactive secret sharing or: how to cope with perpetual leakage. In: Coppersmith, D. (ed.) CRYPTO 1995. LNCS, vol. 963, pp. 339–352. Springer, Heidelberg (1995). https://doi.org/10.1007/3-540-44750-4_27
32. Schultz, D., Liskov, B., Liskov, M.: MPSS: mobile proactive secret sharing. ACM Trans. Inf. Syst. Secur. (TISSEC) **13**(4), 1–34 (2010)
33. Das, P., et al.: FastKitten: practical smart contracts on bitcoin. IACR Cryptology ePrint Archive 2019 (2019)
34. Al-Bassam, M., et al.: Airtnt: fair exchange payment for outsourced secure enclave computations. arXiv preprint arXiv:1805.06411 (2018)
35. Xiao, Y., et al.: Enforcing Private Data Usage Control with Blockchain and Attested Off-chain Contract Execution. arXiv preprint arXiv:1904.07275 (2019)
36. Ayoade, G., et al.: Decentralized IoT data management using blockchain and trusted execution environment. In: 2018 IEEE International Conference on Information Reuse and Integration (IRI). IEEE (2018)
37. Yu, S., et al. Achieving secure, scalable, and fine-grained data access control in cloud computing. In: 2010 Proceedings IEEE INFOCOM. IEEE (2010)
38. Li, N., Li, T., Venkatasubramanian, S.: t-closeness: privacy beyond k-anonymity and l-diversity. In: 2007 IEEE 23rd International Conference on Data Engineering. IEEE (2007)
39. Ahmad, A., et al.: OBFUSCURO: a commodity obfuscation engine on intel SGX. In: NDSS (2019)
40. Seo, J., et al.: SGX-shield: enabling address space layout randomization for SGX programs. In: NDSS (2017)
41. Tapscott, A., Tapscott, D.: How blockchain is changing finance. Harvard Bus. Rev. **1**(9), 2–5 (2017)
42. Hofmann, E., Strewe, U.M., Bosia, N.: Supply Chain Finance and Blockchain Technology: The Case of Reverse Securitisation. Springer, New York (2017)
43. Zheng, B.-K., et al.: Scalable and privacy-preserving data sharing based on blockchain. J. Comput. Sci. Technol. **33**(3), 557–567 (2018)
44. Gaetani, E., et al.: Blockchain-based database to ensure data integrity in cloud computing environments (2017)
45. Liang, X., et al.: Provchain: a blockchain-based data provenance architecture in cloud environment with enhanced privacy and availability. In: Proceedings of the 17th IEEE/ACM International Symposium on Cluster, Cloud and Grid Computing. IEEE Press (2017)
46. Dorri, A., et al.: Blockchain for IoT security and privacy: the case study of a smart home. In: 2017 IEEE International Conference on Pervasive Computing and Communications Workshops (PerCom Workshops). IEEE (2017)

47. Zhang, Y., Wen, Jiangtao: The IoT electric business model: using blockchain technology for the internet of things. Peer-to-Peer Networking Appl. **10**(4), 983–994 (2016). https://doi.org/10.1007/s12083-016-0456-1
48. Sun, J., Yan, J., Zhang, K.Z.K.: Blockchain-based sharing services: what blockchain technology can contribute to smart cities. Financ. Innovation **2**(1), 26 (2016)
49. Martinez, J.: Understanding proof of stake: the nothing at stake theory (2019)
50. Gaži, P., Kiayias, A., Russell, A.: Stake-bleeding attacks on proof-of-stake blockchains. In: 2018 Crypto Valley Conference on Blockchain Technology (CVCBT). IEEE (2018)

High-Accuracy Reliability Prediction Approach for Blockchain Services Under BaaS

Jianlong Xu[1]($\boxtimes$), Zicong Zhuang[1], Kun Wang[1], and Wei Liang[2]

[1] College of Engineering, Shantou University, Shantou 515063, China
{xujianlong,19zczhuang,19kwang}@stu.edu.cn
[2] College of Computer Science and Electronic Engineering, Hunan University,
Changsha 410082, China
weiliang99@hnu.edu.cn

Abstract. With the continuous evolution of service-oriented computing paradigm, block- chain as a service (BaaS) has emerged, which is crucial in the development of blockchain-based applications. To build high-quality blockchain-based system, users must select highly reliable blockchain services (peers) with excellent quality of service (QoS). However, owing to the large number of services and the sparsity of personalized QoS data, it is difficult to select the optimal services. Hence, we propose a QoS-based blockchain service reliability prediction framework (BSRPF) under BaaS. In this framework, we employ a matrix factorization-based method to perform accurate QoS prediction. To validate BSPRF, we conducted experiments based on large-scale real-world data, and the results show that BSPRF achieves high prediction accuracy and outperforms other popular methods.

Keywords: Blockchain · BaaS · Matrix factorization · Reliability prediction

1 Introduction

As an emerging distributed ledger technology, blockchain has received significant attention [1], and various blockchain-based applications are developing rapidly, such as smart contracts [2], Internet of Things [3], and security services [4]. Meanwhile, with the continuous evolution of service-oriented computing (SOC) paradigms, blockchain as a service (BaaS) has emerged, which can improve the productivity of blockchain-based applications development. BaaS is a concept mainly proposed by Microsoft and IBM [5], which aims to execute a certain blockchain node. In BaaS environments, users can quickly design blockchain-based applications by invoking a series of blockchain services (known as blockchain peers). These services are network-based software components that can provide search queries, transaction submissions, data storage, data analysis, and computation services. These services can be either centralized or decentralized to help developers (users) validate their concepts and models more quickly.

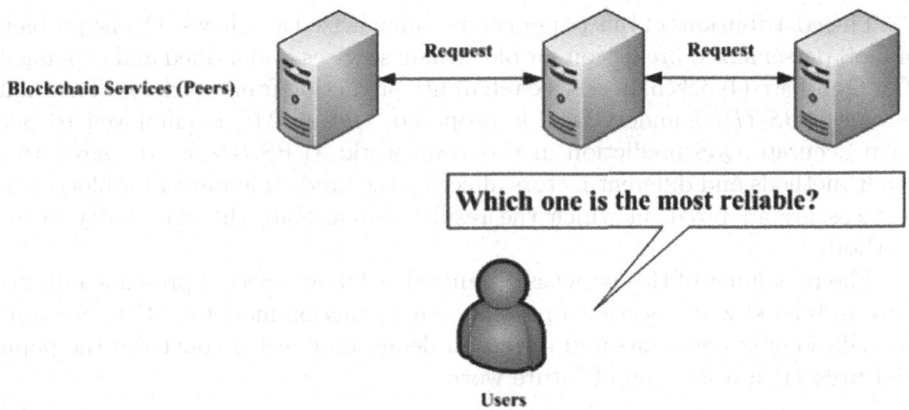

Fig. 1. An example of blockchain services selection

However, many services with similar functions exist on the Internet, and the method to select optimal blockchain services to build high-performance blockchain-based systems or applications is the main challenge for users. As shown in Fig. 1, for improved performance, users must select suitable blockchain services to form a better blockchain.

As a nonfunctional requirement, quality-of-service (QoS) is the most widely used evaluation criterion of optimal services in SOC [6,7]. To obtain the best service for users, one simple solution is to invoke each candidate service to obtain the QoS values (e.g., throughput and latency) of each service and then select the service with the best QoS values. However, this is both time and resource consuming. Meanwhile, owing to the unpredictability of the Internet environment, QoS values may vary for different users when the same service is invoked. Typically, another solution for obtaining unknown QoS is to perform predictions using historical QoS data at the client side, known as personalized QoS prediction [6–8]. Therefore, for blockchain service selection, the critical step is to obtain accurate QoS values of candidate services through personalized QoS prediction.

To obtain accurate QoS values, many approaches have been proposed by the service computing community in recent years [9,10]. The popular approaches are based on collaborative filtering, which can be categorized into memory-based collaborative filtering (CF) and model-based CF. As a model-based CF method, matrix factorization (MF) has achieved great success and has been employed for QoS value prediction in web services and cloud services, among others [9,10]. Inspired by the accomplishment of a matrix factorization algorithm for personalized QoS predictions, we herein propose a personalized QoS prediction framework for blockchain services ($BSRPF$) under BaaS. We utilized the QoS values (success rate data), which are from geographically distributed real-world blockchain services, and conducted extensive experiments; the experimental results demonstrated the effectiveness and efficiency of our approach.

The contributions of this paper can be summarized as follows: 1) The problem of QoS personalized prediction for blockchain services is identified and explained; 2) a QoS-based blockchain service reliability prediction framework for blockchain services $(BSRPF)$ under BaaS is proposed, and an MF is employed to perform accurate QoS prediction in this framework; 3) BSRPF is compared with other methods and different factors affecting the prediction model for blockchain services are analyzed, in which the results demonstrate the superiority of our method.

The remainder of this paper is organized as follows: Sect. 2 presents a discussion on related work. Section 3 presents our prediction model BSRPF. Section 4 describes our experiments and results in detail, and Sect. 5 concludes the paper and presents a discussion of future work.

2   Related Work

This section introduces related work in blockchain reliability prediction, including traditional software reliability research and blockchain-related reliability research.

Regarding traditional software reliability research, QoS prediction has been widely investigated in the past decade. CF methods are the most typical techniques for personalized QoS predictions. The main idea of CF is to determine a group of similar users or services based on the Pearson correlation coefficient (PCC). Subsequently, we predict the results according to the past QoS value. Typically, studies regarding CF start with memory-based methods. Memory-based CF can be classified into user-[11] and item-based CF [12]. User-based CF searches a set of nearest neighboring users with similar interests using the PCC, and item-based CF calculates the similarity of the items. Zheng et al. [13] proposed a neighborhood-based hybrid model that combines user- and item-based CF approaches. Later, model-based methods emerged. Model-based methods include CF based on a clustering model [14] and a latent semantic model [15]. MF is a model-based CF method that decomposes the user-item scoring matrix into a combination of several parts [16,17]. Zheng et al. [9] adopted a probability matrix factorization (PMF)-based approach for reliable, personalized predictions.

With regards to blockchain-related reliability, Xiao et al. [18] proposed a reliability-based evaluation method for circuit units, which avoids security and privacy vulnerable to hardware errors. Zheng et al. [19] proposed an approach to detect Ponzi schemes on blockchain using data-mining and machine-learning methods, which were used to detect Ponzi schemes even at the moment of its creation. Lei et al. [20] presented a reputation-based Byzantine fault tolerance algorithm that incorporates a reputation model to evaluate the operations of each node in a consensus process. Liu et al. [21] proposed a model to test the reliability of a blockchain-based Internet of Things application using a continuous-time Markov chain model. Kalodner et al. [22] proposed a multifunctional open-source software platform that supports different blockchain and analysis tasks. It parses the data of a P2P network and original blockchain data, and the analysis results are provided for users to analyze. Inspired by blockchain with distributed ledger technology, Du et al. [23] distributed consensus mechanisms and encryption algorithms, as well as proposed a personalized QoS prediction method for web services based on blockchain-based MF, which was more effective than traditional techniques. In recent years, BaaS has received significant attention from many scholars. For example, Lu et al. [5] proposed a unified blockchain-as-a-service platform, which aims to support both the design and deployment of blockchain-based applications. Zheng et al. [24] develop a BaaS platform called NutBaaS, which provides blockchain service in cloud computing environments, such as network deployment and system monitoring, smart contracts analysis and testing. IBM proposed IBM Hyperledger1 [1]for BaaS deployment solutions.

Inspired by the studies above, we herein study the reliability prediction method for blockchain services.

3   Reliability Prediction Method for Blockchain Services

In this section, the methodology of BSRPF is introduced, including the problem formulation and reliability prediction framework for blockchain services.

3.1   Framework of Blockchain Services Reliability Prediction

We propose a QoS-based blockchain service reliability prediction framework for blockchain services ($BSRPF$) under BaaS, as shown in Fig. 2. Our framework comprises four parts: collection of QoS values, success rate calculation, MF, and reliability prediction.

The framework includes the following main steps:

1) Users send requests to the blockchain services (peers), and the blockchain services respond to the requests and return the feedback QoS data to the users. The users submit these feedback data to the prediction server.

2) In the prediction server, the data collector collects QoS data regarding the success or failure of the request; next, the success rate data calculation module calculates the success rate based on the submitted data. The calculation results are used to form the user-service matrix of the success rate for MF.

3) Because users cannot request all services, this service matrix will not be extremely dense. With these known success rates, we can predict the unknown success rate values based on the MF module.

4) After MF, the request success rates of all users for all services are obtained, and the reliability of each blockchain service (peer) can be calculated by the reliability calculation module.

---

[1] https://www.ibm.com/blockchain/platform/.

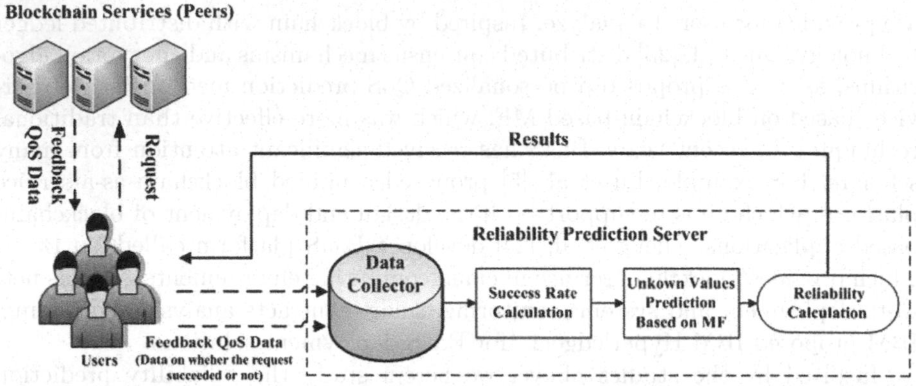

Blockchain Services (Peers)

Fig. 2. Framework of blockchain services reliability prediction (BSRPF)under BaaS

3.2   Reliability Prediction Method for Blockchain Services

We argue that blockchain services are the nodes or blockchain peers that can be composed of the blockchain application, and blockchain users are the developers of blockchain applications that can invoke blockchain services. For a group of users, each user can send a request to each blockchain service (peer), and the result of the request is the success rate. Because numerous blockchain peers exist in the real world, users cannot send a request to each peer; therefore, the success rate of users for blockchain services without requests should be predicted according to the similarity between peers.

Success Rate Calculation. After collecting data that signify the success or failure of a request, we can use these data to calculate the successful request rate for invoked blockchain services. First, we set a value as MaxBlockBack to denote the extreme value for the block backwardness of the peer in the blockchain. Subsequently, we set a value as MaxRTT to represent the maximum round-trip time for the peer [25]. The successful request rate can be calculated as follows:

For each user U_i and peer P_j, we used a counter for successful requests as $SuccessRequest_{i,j}$, and a failure counter as $FailureRequest_{i,j}$. As per [25], each batch of user sends requests to peer, and the peer will respond successfully if and only if it returns the correct block and the recent block height in time. If peer P_j responds successfully, then it is counted into $SuccessRequest_{i,j}$, else, it is counted into $FailureRequest_{i,j}$. The successful request rate of U_i and P_j is calculated using Eq. (1).

$$SuccessRate_{i,j} = \frac{SuccessRequest_{i,j}}{SuccessRequest_{i,j} + FailureRequest_{i,j}} \tag{1}$$

After calculating the successful request rate, we used the success rate to predict the unknown entries in the matrix and predicted the reliability of the blockchain services.

Low-Rank Matrix Factorization. Given a set of N users $U = \{u_1, u_2, \ldots, u_n\}$ and a set of M peers $P = \{p_1, p_2, \ldots, p_m\}$, N and P can form an $N \times M$ matrix R. The entry in R is indicated as r_{ij} which is on the ith row j^{th} column r_{ij}, representing the success rate of $user_i$'s request to $peer_j$. The value of r_{ij} is equal to null when u_i does not request p_j; otherwise it is not null. In this study, we used user success request rate as the QoS data.

According to the success rate matrix, we discovered that the distribution of the data deviated significantly. Therefore, applying the MF model directly to the original data may significantly reduce the prediction accuracy. To solve this problem, we applied the BoxCox transformation, a classical data transformation method, to the success rate matrix. This technique is used to stabilize data variance and yield data that are closer to a normal distribution to adapt to the matrix decomposition hypothesis. The transformation is rank preserving and is performed using a continuous power function defined as follows:

$$boxcox(x) = \begin{cases} (x^\alpha - 1)/\alpha & if \alpha \neq 0 \\ \log(x) & if \alpha = 0 \end{cases} \tag{2}$$

where the parameter α controls the extent of the transformation. For simplicity, we denote $\widehat{R_{ij}} = \text{boxcox}(R_{ij})$, $\widehat{R_{max}} = \text{boxcox}(R_{max})$ and $\widehat{R_{min}} = \text{boxcox}(R_{min})$ due to its monotonously nondecreasing property of Box-Cox transformation. R_{max} and R_{min} are the maximal and minimal values respectively. Similarly, $\widehat{R_{max}}$ and $\widehat{R_{min}}$ are the maximal and minimal values after data transformation. Then we map the data into the range [0,1] by linear normalization.

$$r_{ij} = (\widehat{R_{ij}} - \widehat{R_{min}})/(\widehat{R_{max}} - \widehat{R_{min}}) \tag{3}$$

To predict unknown entries in the matrix, it is necessary to fit the matrix into the factorization model and then use the factorization model for subsequent predictions. MF is a typical factor analysis model. In the same feature space, a high-dimensional matrix is decomposed into two low-dimensional feature matrices.

In this study, the success rate matrix $R \in \mathbb{R}^{N \times M}$ is assumed to have a low-rank structure, that is, it has a rank of $K \ll \min\{M, N\}$. R can be decomposed into two rank-K matrices $U \in \mathbb{R}^{K \times N}$ and $P \in \mathbb{R}^{K \times M}$. R can be calculated as $R = U^T P$. The column vectors of U and P have a natural interpretation. The ith column vector U_i of U is the potential factor that determines the behavior of user i and the jth column vector P_j of P is the potential factor that determines the features of ij. The dot product $U_i^T P_j$ is the model predicted score of u_i's success rate on ij.

We adopted PMF [26] and a probabilistic linear model with Gaussian observation noise. Our target was to maximize the posterior probability and minimize the following loss function

$$\mathcal{L} = \frac{1}{2} \sum_{i=1} \sum_{j=1} (R_{ij} - U_i^T P_j)^2 + \frac{\lambda_U}{2} \|U\|_F^2 + \frac{\lambda_P}{2} \|P\|_F^2 \tag{4}$$

In Eq. (4), R_{ij} is the available entry in the matrix. The first term is the squared loss. λ_S and λ_U are both small positive decimal numbers to control the extent of regularization which can avoid over-fitting problems, and $\|.\|_F^2$ represents the Frobenius norm. To minimize the loss function, we computed the gradients of the loss function with respect to U_i and P_j as follows:

$$\frac{\partial \mathcal{L}}{\partial U_i} = \sum_{j \in \mathcal{L}_i} (U_i^T P_j - r_{ij}) P_j + \lambda_U U_i \tag{5}$$

$$\frac{\partial \mathcal{L}}{\partial P_j} = \sum_{j \in \mathcal{U}_i} (U_i^T P_j - r_{ij}) U_i + \lambda_P P_j \tag{6}$$

Then alternative update on U_i and P_j can be done through:

$$U_i \leftarrow U_i - \eta \frac{\partial \mathcal{L}}{\partial U_i} \tag{7}$$

$$P_j \leftarrow Pj - \eta \frac{\partial \mathcal{L}}{\partial P_j} \tag{8}$$

In Eq. (7) and (8), η is the learning rate to control each iteration's change. After training, the prediction of u_i's success request rate of p_j as predicted by the model is the dot product $U_i^T P_j$:

$$SuccessRate_{i,j} \approx \widetilde{SuccessRate}_{i,j} = U_i^T P_j \tag{9}$$

Predict Reliability. After completing the steps above, we obtained the predicted success rate from blockchain requester U_i to blockchain peer P_j. To predict the reliability of P_j observed by U_i, we adopted a typically used exponential reliability function [27]:

$$Reliability_{i,j}(t) = e^{-(1-SuccessRate_{i,j}) \times t} \tag{10}$$

4   Experiment and Result

In this section, we describe our experiments to verify BSRPF and then discuss the parameters in the proposed model. By comparing the results with other methods and different parameters, we demonstrate the high accuracy of BSRPF. All of the experiments were conducted on an Intel(R) Core(TM) i7-4790 CPU @ 3.40 GHz, with 8 GB RAM, using Ubuntu 14.04 (64 bit) and Python 3.6.

4.1   Dataset

In our experiment, we used the real-world dataset proposed in reference [25]. It includes a 100 × 200 Success Rate matrix of 100 blockchain requesters and 200 blockchain peers. The blockchain peers are from 21 countries and the requesters are from 15 countries. In this dataset, more than 2,000,000 test cases were collected. To make our experiment more realistic, we mapped the success rate values from different requesters to peers into [0, 1].

4.2   Evaluation Metrics

In this experiment, we employ the root mean square error (RMSE) to measure the difference between the predicted and the measured values. It is defined as:

$$RMSE = \sqrt{\frac{\sum_{i,j}(R_{i,j} - \widehat{R}_{i,j})^2}{N}} \tag{11}$$

where $R_{i,j}$ is the known value, which denotes the success rate of requester i to peer j, and $\widehat{R}_{i,j}$ is the corresponding predicted value. N is the number of predicted values. The smaller the RMSE value, the higher the prediction accuracy we get.

4.3   Performance Comparison

To evaluate the performance of our method, we compared our method with three other methods for reliability prediction: user-based approach using PCC (UPCC) [28], item-based approach using PCC (IPCC) [29], and user-item-based approach (UIPCC) [30]. UPCC is a collaborative filtering method based on the request of the similarity between blockchain users to predict unknown values, and the request of similar blockchain users' PCC. The IPCC only employs similar blockchain peers for the prediction. UIPCC is a combination of UPCC and IPCC. In the experiment, these three methods were compared with our method to predict the same training success rate matrix.

For each round, we randomly deleted the entries in the generated success rate matrix to transfer it to the target density, and the deleted entries were set as the test values. The density was set as density = $\{30\%, 40\%, 50\%, 60\%, 70\%, 80\%\}$. We set the dimensionality K = 5 to decompose the matrix into two rank-K matrices. We set $\langle MaxBlockBack = 12, MaxRTT = 1000\rangle$ to evaluate the accuracy for situations with high requirements for confirming blockchain data. Such as cryptocurrencies wallet and cryptocurrencies exchange. Because these blockchain services need high requirements for confirming blockchain data. We set $\langle MaxBlockBack = 100, MaxRTT = 5000\rangle$ to evaluate the accuracy for daily usages. Such as ordinary blockchain users. Because they have high tolerances for block backwardness and latency. The experimental results are shown in Tables 1 and 2.

Table 1. Accuracy comparison of RMSE of blockchain reliability prediction method (MaxBlockBack = 12, MaxRTT = 1000)

Method	Density = 30%	Density = 40%	Density = 50%	Density = 60%	Density = 70%
UPCC	0.3646	0.3601	0.3623	0.3583	0.3547
IPCC	0.1022	0.1001	0.0963	0.0942	0.0889
UIPCC	0.1069	0.1045	0.1011	0.0985	0.0937
BSRPF	**0.0946**	**0.0895**	**0.0867**	**0.0818**	**0.0790**

Table 2. Accuracy comparison of RMSE of blockchain reliability prediction method (MaxBlockBack = 100, MaxRTT = 5000)

Method	Density = 30%	Density = 40%	Density = 50%	Density = 60%	Density = 70%
UPCC	0.4597	0.4566	0.4591	0.4550	0.4536
IPCC	0.0898	0.0858	0.0861	0.0819	0.0801
UIPCC	0.1003	0.0967	0.0969	0.0931	0.0916
BSRPF	**0.0890**	**0.0855**	**0.0851**	**0.0805**	**0.0801**

From Tables 1 and 2, we can infer the following:

1) BSRPF obtained lower RMSE values than the other methods in terms of the success rate, with different matrix densities. This indicates that BSRPF is more accurate than existing methods and further verifies the effectiveness of our method. Concretely, compared with the UIPCC, BSRPF achieved an improvement of 14.6% on average, as shown in Table 1; and 12.2%, as shown in Table 2.

2) Compared with the UPCC, IPCC, and UIPCC, BSRPF yielded more accurate predictions. This occurred because the PCC methods exclusively use the information for prediction, which is similar to the requesters and peers, whereas BSRPF uses all available information in the success rate matrix.

3) With the increase in density, BSRPF is more accurate than the PCC-based methods. For example, it achieved 8.0% higher accuracy than UIPCC when the matrix density was 30%, and 12.5% more accuracy when the matrix density was 70%.

4.4   Impact of Dimensionality

Dimensionality is the parameter K, which refers to the number of latent features used to the matrix. It is used to represent the rank of the low-rank assumption of MF. To demonstrate the impact of dimensionality, we set the dimensionality from 5 to 30 with a step increase of 5.

As shown in Fig. 3(a), with the different density, as the dimension increases gradually, the RMSE values fluctuate, and there is no upward or downward trend. Hence, we continue to explore, set the dimension from 1 to 5 with a step increase of 1, as shown in Fig. 3(b), with the increase of dimension, RMSE also fluctuates, but the overall trend shows a downward trend. The larger the dimension is, the longer the approach takes. In order to balance time and performance, we set the K to 5.

4.5   Impact of Matrix Density

Matrix density is the percentage of unknown entries in the matrix, which indicates the amount of available information for performing predictions. To demonstrate the effect of matrix density, we set the matrix density from 30% to 70% with a step increase of 10%.

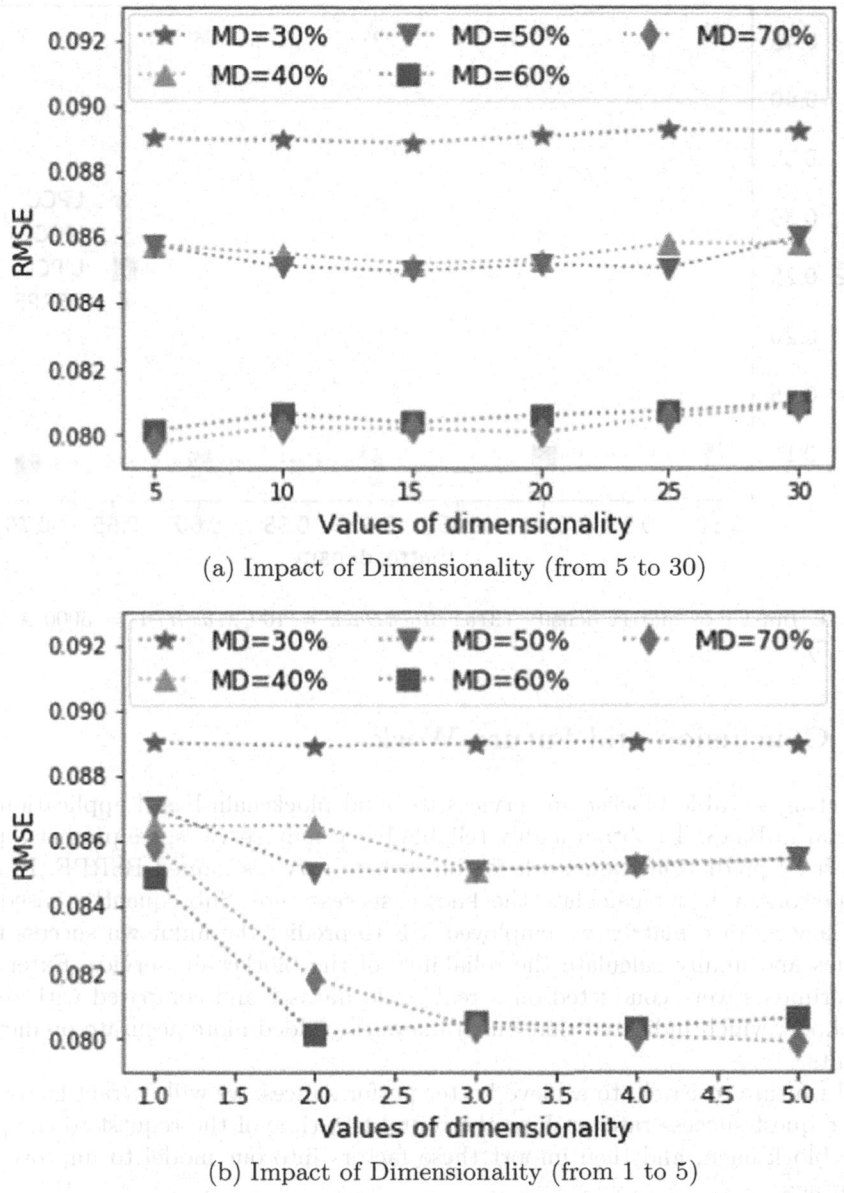

(a) Impact of Dimensionality (from 5 to 30)

(b) Impact of Dimensionality (from 1 to 5)

Fig. 3. Impact of Dimensionality($MaxBlockBack = 100, MaxRTT = 5000, \lambda = 1$)

As shown in Fig. 4, with the increase in the matrix density, the value of RMSE decreased slowly. This means that more accurate prediction results can be achieved by obtaining more blockchain information.

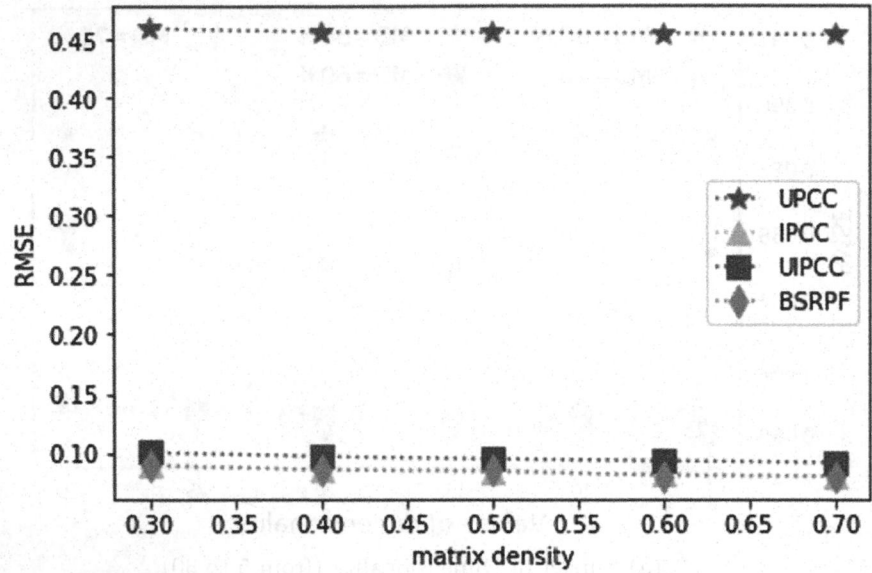

Fig. 4. Impact of matrix density ($MaxBlockBack = 100, MaxRTT = 5000, \lambda = 1, K = 5$)

5   Conclusion and Future Work

Selecting suitable blockchain services to build blockchain-based applications is crucial in BaaS. To obtain highly reliable blockchain services, we present a personalized prediction framework for blockchain services named BSRPF. In this framework, we first calculate the known success rate. Subsequently, based on the success rate matrix, we employed MF to predict the unknown success rate values and finally calculate the reliability of the blockchain service. Extensive experiments were conducted on a real-world dataset and compared with other methods, which indicated that our framework yielded more accurate prediction results.

In future research, to achieve better performances, we will extract factors of the request success rate, such as the round-trip time of the request to the peer and block hash, and then import these factors into our model to improve the accuracy.

Acknowledgment. This research was financially supported by the National Natural Science Foundation of China (No. 61702318), the Shantou University Scientific Research Start-up Fund Project (No .NTF18024),2018 Provincial and Municipal Vertical Coordination Management Science and Technology Planning Project (No. 180917124960518), 2019 Guangdong province special fund for science and technology ("major special projects + task list") project, and in part by 2020 Li Ka Shing Foundation Cross-Disciplinary Research Grant (No. 2020LKSFG08D).

References

1. Zheng, Z., Xie, S., Dai, H., Chen, X., Wang, H.: Blockchain challenges and opportunities: a survey. Int. J. Web Grid Serv. **14**, 352 (2018)
2. Kosba, A., Miller, A., Shi, E., Wen, Z., Papamanthou, C.: Hawk: the blockchain model of cryptography and privacy-preserving smart contracts. In: 2016 IEEE Symposium on Security and Privacy (SP), Los Alamitos, CA, USA, pp. 839–858. IEEE Computer Society (2016)
3. Liang, W., Tang, M., Long, J., Peng, X., Xu, J., Li, K.: A secure faBric blockchain-based data transmission technique for industrial Internet-of-Things. IEEE Trans. Ind. Inf. **15**, 3582–3592 (2019)
4. Liang, W., Fan, Y., Li, K., Zhang, D., Gaudiot, J.: Secure data storage and recovery in industrial blockchain network environments. IEEE Trans. Ind. Inf. 1 (2020). https://doi.org/10.1109/TII.2020.2966069
5. Lu, Q., Liu, Y., Weber, I., Zhu, L., Zhang, W.: uBaaS: a unified blockchain as a service platform. Future Gener. Comput. Syst. **101**, 564–575 (2019)
6. Guo, L., Mu, D., Cai, X., Tian, G., Hao, F.: Personalized QoS prediction for service recommendation with a service-oriented tensor model. IEEE Access **7**, 55721–55731 (2019)
7. Wu, J., Chen, L., Feng, Y., Zheng, Z., Zhou, M., Wu, Z.: Predicting quality of service for selection by neighborhood-based collaborative filtering. IEEE Trans. Syst. Man Cybern. Syst. **43**, 428–439 (2013)
8. Yang, Y., Zheng, Z., Niu, X., Tang, M., Lu, Y., Liao, X.: A location-based factorization machine model for web service QoS prediction. IEEE Trans. Serv. Comput. 1 (2018). https://doi.org/10.1109/TSC.2018.2876532
9. Zheng, Z., Lyu, M.R.: Personalized reliability prediction of web services. ACM Trans. Softw. Eng. Methodol. (TOSEM) **22**, 25–25 (2013)
10. Li, S., Wen, J., Luo, F., Cheng, T., Xiong, Q.: A location and reputation aware matrix factorization approach for personalized quality of service prediction. In: 2017 IEEE International Conference on Web Services (ICWS), Los Alamitos, CA, USA, pp. 652–659. IEEE Computer Society (2017)
11. Shao, L., Zhang, J., Wei, Y., Zhao, J., Xie, B., Mei, H.: Personalized QoS prediction for web services via collaborative filtering. In: IEEE International Conference on Web Services (ICWS 2007), Los Alamitos, CA, USA, pp. 439–446. IEEE Computer Society (2007)
12. Linden, G., Smith, B., York, J.: Amazon.com recommendations: item-to-item collaborative filtering. IEEE Internet Comput. **7**, 76–80 (2003)
13. Zheng, Z., Ma, H., Lyu, M.R., King, I.: WSRec: a collaborative filtering based web service recommender system. In: 2009 IEEE International Conference on Web Services, Los Alamitos, CA, USA, pp. 437–444. IEEE Computer Society (2009)
14. Zhu, J., Kang, Y., Zheng, Z., Lyu, M.R.: A clustering-based QoS prediction approach for web service recommendation. In: 2012 IEEE 15th International Symposium on Object/Component/Service-Oriented Real-Time Distributed Computing Workshops, Los Alamitos, CA, USA, pp. 93–98. IEEE Computer Society (2012)
15. Hoffman, T.: Latent semantic models for collaborative filtering. ACM Trans. Inf. Syst. (TOIS) **22**, 89–115 (2004)
16. Rennie, J.D.M., Srebro, N.: Fast maximum margin matrix factorization for collaborative prediction. In: Proceedings of the 22nd International Conference on Machine Learning, New York, NY, USA, pp. 713–719. Association for Computing Machinery (2005)

17. Salakhutdinov, R., Mnih, A.: Bayesian probabilistic matrix factorization using Markov chain Monte Carlo. In: Proceedings of the 25th International Conference on Machine Learning, vol. 25, pp. 880–887 (2008)
18. Xiao, J., Lou, J., Jiang, J., Li, X., Yang, X., Huang, Y.: Blockchain architecture reliability-based measurement for circuit unit importance. IEEE Access, 1 (2018)
19. Chen, W., Zheng, Z., Cui, J., Ngai, E.C.H., Zheng, P., Zhou, Y.: Detecting ponzi schemes on ethereum: towards healthier blockchain technology. In: Proceedings of the 2018 World Wide Web Conference on World Wide Web, Los Alamitos, CA, USA, pp. 1409–1418. ACM (2018)
20. Lei, K., Zhang, Q., Xu, L., Qi, Z.: Reputation-based byzantine fault-tolerance for consortium blockchain. In: 2018 IEEE 24th International Conference on Parallel and Distributed Systems (ICPADS), Lyon, France, pp. 604–611. IEEE Computer Society (2018)
21. Liu, Y., Zheng, K., Craig, P., Li, Y., Huang, X.: Evaluating the reliability of blockchain based Internet of Things applications. In: 2018 1st IEEE International Conference on Hot Information-Centric Networking (HotICN), Los Alamitos, CA, USA, pp. 230–231. IEEE Computer Society (2018)
22. Kalodner, H., Goldfeder, S., Chator, A., Möser, M., Narayanan, A.: BlockSci: Design and applications of a blockchain analysis platform, pp, 1–14. arXiv: Cryptography and Security (2017)
23. Cai, W., Du, X., Xu, J.: A personalized QoS prediction method for web services via blockchain-based matrix factorization. Sensors 19, 2749–2749 (2019)
24. Zheng, W., Zheng, Z., Chen, X., Dai, K., Li, P., Chen, R.: NutBaaS: a blockchain-as-a-service platform. IEEE Access, 134422–134433 (2019)
25. Zheng, P., Zheng, Z., Chen, L.: Selecting Reliable Blockchain Peers via Hybrid Blockchain Reliability Prediction, pp. 1–11. CoRR. abs/1910.14614 (2019)
26. Salakhutdinov, R., Mnih, A.: Probabilistic matrix factorization. In: Proceedings of the 20th International Conference on Neural Information Processing Systems, Red Hook, NY, USA, pp. 1257–1264. Curran Associates Inc., (2007)
27. Lyu, M.R.: Handbook of software reliability engineering. Softw. IEEE 18, 98–98 (1996)
28. Breese, J., Heckerman, D., Kadie, C.: Empirical analysis of predictive algorithms for collaborative filtering. In: Proceedings of the Fourteenth Conference on Uncertainty in Artificial Intelligence, San Francisco, CA, USA, pp. 43–52. Morgan Kaufmann Publishers Inc., (2013)
29. Sarwar, B., Karypis, G., Konstan, J., Riedl, J.: Item-based collaborative filtering recommendation algorithms. In: Proceedings of the 10th International Conference on World Wide Web, New York, NY, USA, pp. 285–295. Association for Computing Machinery (2001)
30. Zheng, Z., Lyu, M.R.: Collaborative reliability prediction of service-oriented systems. In: International Conference on Software Engineering, Los Alamitos, CA, USA, pp. 35–44. IEEE Computer Society (2010)

Analysis of the Randomness Generation for PoS-Based Blockchains with Verifiable Delay Functions

Liwei Liu$^{(\boxtimes)}$ and Maozhi Xu

School of Mathematical Sciences, Peking University, Beijing 100871, China
pkullw@pku.edn.cn, mzxu@math.pku.edu.cn

Abstract. With the development of Ethereum 2.0, the proof-of-stake-based blockchain has become more and more popular. Although not commonly deployed in existing blockchains, many PoS or its variants' consensus protocols have been proposed. As the same in many other cryptographic systems, the trustworthy randomness is crucial in PoS-based blockchains such as the selection of the block proposer. Since Boneh proposed the primitive of verifiable delay functions in 2018, it has received intensive attention and been used for many applications, among which the most interesting one is to make an unpredictable, unbiased and unstoppable randomness as the Ethereum Minimal VDF randomness beacon. In this paper, we analyze it in an algorithmic aspect, concentrating on the RANDAO scheme with verifiable delay functions to generate unbiased and public-verifiable randomness for such PoS-based blockchains. We analyze Pietrzak's verifiable delay function and give improvements to the Ethereum 2.0 Randomness beacon based on the benchmark results. We further propose some new ideas to prevent quantum attack and ASICs to break the scheme where verifiable delay functions are used.

Keywords: Public randomness · Proof-of-stake · Verifiable delay function · Blockchain · Trustworthy system

1 Introduction

The energy consumption of Bitcoin's proof-of-work (PoW) consensus protocol has been growing since its invention. This has motivated researchers to look into alternative blockchain consensus protocols which are more economic and efficient. Among all the candidates, the proof-of-stake (PoS)-based blockchain consensus protocols have been seen as the most promising and attracted much attention [5,7,10,19]. Such mechanism usually runs a computational inexpensive process to randomly select the next block proposer instead of spending intensive computation resources on solving hashing puzzles in PoW consensus protocols. While the difficulty adjustment in mining of the PoW consensus is due to the

© Springer Nature Singapore Pte Ltd. 2020
Z. Zheng et al. (Eds.): BlockSys 2020, CCIS 1267, pp. 661–674, 2020.
https://doi.org/10.1007/978-981-15-9213-3_51

computation power, the probability that a node is selected is set to be proportional to the stake it puts on the election phase. Besides the influence of differences of stakes, the public randomness is crucial to the safety and liveness of the PoS consensus protocol including use-cases for Byzantine agreement algorithms [6] and sharding on blockchain [17] thus require the randomness to be unbiased. Unbiased randomness which is public-verifiable is also important to construct trustworthy systems to protect the data security, such as generating public parameters for cryptosystems and decision of parameters in smart contracts.

Rabin introduces the randomness beacons to generate randomness [15]. This method requires a trusted third party to emit randomly chosen integers in public which doesn't meet our expect in a decentralized system. We concentralize on generating public randomness without a trusted party to make a decentralized trustworthy system. Rather than consider the entropy, we consider how to use random outputs from beacons or participants without introducing bias by an active adversary in an algorithm aspect. Priority approaches of this kind to randomness include slow cryptographic hash functions [11] and the RANDAO scheme [8] which we analyze in the following section.

From 2018 a new cryptographic primitive which is called verifiable delay function (VDF) was brought up [2] as an alternative to generate public randomness beacon. The main feature of VDF is its long sequential evaluation time to get a unique output and exponential-shorter verification time for any one to verify the correctness of the output with the proof. There are two practical VDF now: Pietrzak's VDF [14] and Wesolowski's VDF [18]. The Ethereum 2.0 uses a scheme combined with RANDAO and Wesolowski's VDF to generate public verifiable randomness [8].

In this paper, we analyze the Ethereum 2.0 randomness generation scheme in an algorithm aspect and fully explain the benefits for introducing verifiable delay functions to generate unbiased and public-verifiable randomness. Rather than using the Wesolowski's VDF in the original Ethereum 2.0 due to its small proof size [3], we choose to use Pietrzak's VDF due to its faster proof-computation time and smaller verification time when safety parameter is large and its potential to construct a continuous verifiable delay function [9] of which any intermediate state could be efficiently verified thus giving it the property to an outsourced verification procedure of which the start and the end could be any intermediate state in the evaluation chain. This makes it more suitable for a cloud-computing environment and a better choice to be a public randomness beacon. We have the following contributions:

- We analyze the last-revealer attack to the RANDAO scheme and introduce detailed methods to prevent such attack with verifiable delay functions, thus giving thorough analysis of randomness property of the Ethereum 2.0 scheme and ways to improve it.
- We analyze Pietrzak's VDF in both theoretical and practical aspects including fast proof-computation time by saving pre-computed values and present a detailed implementation [13] in C language. A precise benchmark is made

about the evaluation, proof-computation and verification against different time parameter and moduli.

- We propose some new ideas about the usage of verifiable delay functions for the randomness generation for PoS-Based blockchains such as Ethereum 2.0 by the above results including the algorithmic analysis and operating performances.

The remainder of this paper is organized as follows. In Sect. 2, the concepts of randomness and verifiable delay functions are introduced. Then we describe our strategy and analyze the Ethereum 2.0 scheme in Sect. 3. In Sect. 4 we analyze Pietrzak's VDF with benchmarking. We give our new variants and usages of the verifiable delay functions based on those in Sect. 5 and conclude the paper.

2 Preliminaries

2.1 Desired Properties of Randomness

We want to obtain randomness as random beacon values for a trustworthy system with the following properties:

- Liveness: Any single participant or a colluding party cannot prevent the progress.
- Unpredictable: Participants and attackers cannot predict or precompute values of the random beacon before it is revealed.
- Unbiased: Any single participant or a colluding party cannot influence future random beacon values to his bias.
- Public-verifiable: Participants which are not involved in producing the sequence of random numbers could also verify generated values based on public information only.
- Scalability: The number of supported participants could be large enough as desired.

2.2 RSW Time-Lock Puzzle and Verifiable Delay Function(VDF)

The RSW time-lock puzzle [16] is defined by a tuple (N, x, T) where $N = p \cdot q$ is an RSA modulus, $x \in \mathbb{Z}_N^*$ is a random number and $T \in \mathbb{N}$ is a time parameter. The challenge is to compute $y = x^{2^T} \pmod{N}$. This can be computed with two exponentiations using Euler's torsion function $\Phi(N)$: $y = x^e \pmod{N}$ where $e = 2^T \pmod{\Phi(N)}$. So a quantum computer can solve this puzzle easily by factoring N. The operation requires T sequential squarings if the group order is unknown and parallelism can not improve this complexity as squarings are sequential. One has ASIC with fast modular multiplication can accelerate this sequential computation. We make the puzzle public verifiable to construct a VDF. A VDF is a function $f : X \to Y$ that takes a prescribed time to compute even on a parallel computer. It implements a function which is a tuple of four algorithms [14] (where λ is a statistical parameter regarding safety):

1. VDF.Setup(1^λ) $\rightarrow$ **pp** – given an input statistical parameter 1^λ outputs a public parameter **pp**
2. VD.Gen(**pp**, T) $\rightarrow$ (x, T) – given an input time parameter T, samples an input x
3. VDF.Sol(**pp**, (x, T)) $\rightarrow$ (y, π) – given an input (x, T) outputs (y, π), where π is proof that the output y has been correctly computed
4. VDF.Ver(**pp**, (x, T), (y, π)) $\rightarrow$ {accept, reject} – given an input/output tuple (x, T), (y, π) outputs either accept if the proof is correct or reject otherwise.

A VDF has the following properties which we refer to be its security:

- Completeness: Correctly generated proofs will always be accepted.
- Sequentiality: A parallel algorithm using at most $poly(\lambda)$ processors that runs in time less than T cannot compute the function.
- Soundness: For a wrong output of the function, one cannot come up with an accepting proof (to convince others think this output is correct).

2.3 Halving Protocol

The Halving protocol [14] is an interactive protocol to verify the result recursively other than repeat the sequential squarings. In this protocol, the prover $\mathcal{P}$ has to convince the verifier $\mathcal{V}$ that it solved the RSW time-lock puzzle which means $y = x^{2^T} (\mathrm{mod}\ N)$. The Halving protocol has the tuple (N, x, T, y) as the input, where:

1. $N = p \cdot q$ is the product of two safe primes $p = 2p' + 1$, $q = 2q' + 1$ with two primes p', q'.
2. $\langle x \rangle = QR_N^+$ (i.e x generates the group $QR_N^+ = \{|z^2 (mod\ N)| : z \in \mathbb{Z}_N^*\}$).
3. $2^\lambda < \min\{p', q'\}$, where λ is the statistical security parameter.
4. $y = x^{2^T} \in QR_N^+$.

The Halving protocol runs as follow:

1. If T = 1 $\mathcal{V}$ outputs accept as long as $y = x^{2^T} = x^2$ and reject otherwise. If $T > 1$ do the next steps:
2. The prover $\mathcal{P}$ sends $\mu = x^{2^{T/2}}$ to $\mathcal{V}$
3. If $\mu \notin QR_N^+$ then $\mathcal{V}$ outputs reject, otherwise $\mathcal{V}$ samples a random r from $[2^\lambda]$(i.e.1, 2, ..., 2^λ) and sends it to $\mathcal{P}$
4. If $T/2$ is even, $\mathcal{P}$ and $\mathcal{V}$ output: ($N, x', T/2, y'$) where:

$$x' = x^r \cdot \mu$$

$$y' = \mu^r \cdot y$$

and if T/2 is odd, outputs: (N, x', ($T + 1$)/2, (y')^2)

In this recursive way Pietrzak is able to verify the RSW time-lock puzzle interactively. With the Fiat-Shamir heuristic he proposes a VDF. We analyze its details in Sect. 4.

3 Analysis of the Ethereum 2.0 Randomness Beacon

Randao [1] is a commit-reveal algorithm to generate a random number by a committee. It is used in Ethereum 2.0 combined with verifiable delay functions to generate unbiased randomness. Suppose we have a cryptographic hash function sha, we simplify the Randao contract as the following three phases:

- **1.Commit** Anyone who wants to participate in the random number generation needs to pick a secret number s. During a commit period, each member may commit to a secret s by publishing its hash sha(s).
- **2.Reveal** During a reveal period, each member may reveal their secret s corresponding to the hash sha(s).
- **3.Combine** Reveal secrets are combined into an output value. This combination could be a simple XOR of all the collected secrets or the output of any function of the collected secrets.

We usually assume this procedure as non-obligatory which allows members who fail to commit or reveal to be ignored when combining reveals to form the final output. This is for the liveness of this commit-reveal procedure as in the worst-case, the adversary may refuse to reveal. If all parties commit independently of other secrets and reveal at the appropriate time, then we consider there to be zero bias. We also assume that there is at least one honest participant.

In an asynchronous communication environment there could be ordered and non-ordered commit-reveal procedures. Non-ordered procedures are especially vulnerable if a non-honest member can delay their decision to reveal until the end of the reveal-step. If there is a party which controls the last several revealers, then they can reveal only certain ones and make more bias. These attacks can even be forced by blocking channels in the communication environment. So we consider ordered commit-reveal procedure here and the order is pre-defined or random(which can be derived by the last randomness-generation procedure).

Analysis of the RANDAO Scheme. Now we analyze how the malicious members could make bias in the commit-reveal procedure. Due to the property of the cryptographic hash function sha, no one can change their secret number in the reveal-step otherwise the RANDAO contract will throw their secret away from joining the third combine-step. Then it won't give bias on the final output.

However, as we mentioned, the last revealer could observe the others' secrets before he reveals his secret in the reveal-step. As they are in an asynchronous environment, there could be some time T between the time when the last revealer collects all the others' secrets and the end of the reveal-step. If T is long enough for him to calculate the two results: one is the output of the combine-step where the input are all the secret values including his committed secret and the other one without his secret, then he can choose his favoured result of the two results by revealing his secret or not thus making bias on the randomness of the output.

As we want the randomness to be scalable and the network latency is hard to estimate when there are many participants, we can't restrict the total time of the reveal-step too much. To prevent such last-revealer attack and generate unbiased randomness, we need to make the function in the combine-step complex enough so the last-revealer won't be able to calculate the output of the two cases we mentioned in time T. In other words, we want to make T too short for any member to calculate the output of the commit-reveal procedure. There could be two possibilities for the malicious member to accelerate the computation of the output of the function in the combine-step. One way is to use parallel computation with many CPU cores, GPU and other processors. The other is to use fast hardware like ASIC to make each non-parallel computation faster. The former one is always considered to be easier and we could make the function sequential in an algorithm-aspect to prevent the parallel computation. Also we want the output can be verified quickly by anyone rather than compute it sequentially again.

From the above analysis we can see a verifiable delay function perfectly meets our requirements to generate unbiased and public-verifiable randomness. We choose to use Pietrzak's VDF and give a both mathematical and computational view of it in the following section.

4   Analysis of Pietrzak's VDF

We first exhibit the detailed four algorithms of Pietrzak's VDF from [14] and then analyze the proof-computation. We keep the same mathematical setting and details on security proof are left out here.

4.1   Algebraic Setting

The algebraic setting of Pietrezak's VDF differs from the original RSW time-lock puzzle [16]. Firstly, it is required that $N = p \cdot q$ is the product of two safe primes (i.e., p is said to be a safe prime if $p = 2p' + 1$ is prime, and p' is also a prime) to remove elements of small order. Secondly, the operations are performed on the group of signed quadratic residues:

$$QR_N^+ = \{|z^2 (mod\ N)| : z \in \mathbb{Z}_N^*\}$$

and the group operation is defined as:

$$a \circ b = |a \cdot b (mod\ N)|$$

Membership in QR_N^+ can be tested efficiently as $QR_N^+ = J_N^+$ where J_N^+ is the group of elements with Jacobi symbol equal to $+1$.

VDF.Setup (1^λ). The statistical parameter λ of the VDF defines the security parameter λ_{RSA} of the time-lock puzzle. λ_{RSA} specifies the bit length of the RSA modulus and should be large enough so that it offers λ bit of security.

According to the security statement of the Halving protocol, it can be assumed that $\lambda < \lambda_{RSA}/2$ (i.e., $\lambda < \min\{p', q'\}$ where $p = 2p' + 1$ and $q = 2q' + 1$ and $N = p \cdot q$). The public parameter N returned by the setup algorithm is defined according to the aforementioned rule: two random $\lambda_{RSA}/2$ bit safe primes p, q are produced and the algorithm outputs $N = p \cdot q$.

VDF.Gen (N, T). This algorithm samples a random $x \in QR_N^+$ and outputs (x, T). It only makes sense to consider parameters T that are much smaller than 2^λ (say $T < 2^{\lambda/2}$).

VDF.sol $(N, (x, T))$. This algorithm computes sequentially $y = x^{2^T} \pmod{N}$ and proves to the verifier that y is the correct solution by outputting a proof π.

The verification of the time-lock puzzle is achieved by iterating through a modified version of the Halting protocol that is now presented. To reduce the number of interactions between the solver and the verifier to a single interaction, and to allow the prover to output a single proof π, Pietrzak uses the Fiat-Shamir heuristic which replaces the random numbers $r_i \in \mathbb{Z}_{2^\lambda}$ by a hash of the last prover's message. Concretely, the verifier outputs its hash [14]: $\mathbb{Z} \times \mathbb{Z}_N \rightarrow \mathbb{Z}_{2^\lambda}$ as r_i. Let $x_1 = x$ and $y_1 = y$. The proof $\pi = \{\mu_{i \in [t]}\}$ is then computed naively as in [14].

For $i = 1$ to t :

$$\mu_i = x_i^{2^{T/2^i}} \in QR_N^+ \tag{1}$$

$$r_i = hash((x_i, T/2^{i-1}, y_i), \mu_i) \in \mathbb{Z}_{2^\lambda} \tag{2}$$

$$x_{i+1} = x_i^{r_i} \circ \mu_i \tag{3}$$

$$y_{i+1} = \mu_i^{r_i} \circ y_i \tag{4}$$

VDF.Ver $(N, (x, T), (y, \pi))$. Firstly we check whether x, y and all the elements of the proof are in QR_N^+, if not output reject. If it is the case we do as follows and finally check whether: $y_{t+1} = x_{t+1}^2$ and output accept if this holds, otherwise output reject.

For $i = 1$ to t :

$$r_i = hash((x_i, T/2^{i-1}, y_i), \mu_i) \in \mathbb{Z}_{2^\lambda} \tag{5}$$

$$x_{i+1} = x_i^{r_i} \circ \mu_i \tag{6}$$

$$y_{i+1} = \mu_i^{r_i} \circ y_i \tag{7}$$

4.2   Complexity Analysis and Improvements

In this part we will go through the cost of proof-computation and verification. We show the origin method and explain an efficient method to compute the proof $\pi = \{\mu_{i \in [t]}\}$. This is origined from [14] while we analyze it more clearly here and conduct the complexity on one processor.

Cost of Computing the Proof. When computing the proof directly after the evaluation, one is required to iterate through t steps, where at each step $T/2^t$ squarings are computed. This defines a geometric series which sums up to approximately $T \cdot (1 - (1/2)^t)$. To improve the complexity, the prover saves 2^s values (where $s \in [t]$): $x^{2^{T \cdot j/2^s}}$ with $j \in [2^s]$ and use them when computing the proof. The prover computes $\mu_1, \mu_2, \ldots, \mu_s$ using stored values, and then fully recompute the remaining $\mu_{s+1}, \ldots, \mu_t$ in a brute-force fashion [14]. We will now show how pre-computed results are used to compute $\mu_{i \in [s]}$, then we will prove that computing the proof using pre-computed results has a complexity of $\sqrt{T} \cdot 11/8 \cdot \sqrt{\log_2(T) \cdot \lambda}$ on one processor and could be improved by parallelism. To understand the computation of $\mu_{i \in [s]}$ we introduce the following notation: $\bar{z}$, which denotes the z's log to basis x (i.e., $x^{\bar{z}} = z$). Hence, we can rewrite the exponentiations at each step of the proof computation as: $\bar{\mu}_i = \bar{x}_{i-1} \cdot 2^{T/2^i}$, $\bar{x}_{i+1} = r_i \cdot \bar{x}_i + \bar{\mu}_i$, $\bar{y}_{i+1} = r_i \cdot \bar{\mu}_i + \bar{y}_i$

As we can see in the structure of the latter serie, the $\mu_{i \in [s]}$ will at each iteration gain the value of the hash r_i and the exponentiation $2^{T/2^i}$, which is an already pre-computed result. So the exponentiation to $2^{T/2^i}$ is an already computed job, the only remaining task is to exponentiate this pre-computed result to the value of the hash r_i. The reason not using all pre-computed results to compute the proof lies in the heavier computation cost when s approaches t, for example $\mu_{s+1} = x_{s+1}^{2^{T/2^{s+1}}}$ only requires $T/2^{s+1}$ squarings. When computing larger $\mu_{i>s}$ the exponentiation required will be small. The exponent decreases exponentially in i: $2^{T/2^i}$. Hence we can compute these exponentiations directly. We can conduct that the perfect bound between these two types of computation is $s = t/2 - \log_2(t \cdot \lambda)/2$ and show that the complexity of the proof computation is $O(\sqrt{T} \cdot 11/8 \cdot \sqrt{\log_2(T) \cdot \lambda})$. Follow the details in [14] the time complexity calculated by squarings for $t = \log_2(T)$ and $s \in [t]$ is :

$$F(s) = \frac{3}{4} \cdot 2^s \cdot \lambda \cdot (s-1) + 2^{t-s} \qquad (8)$$

$$< G(s) = \frac{3}{4} \cdot 2^s \cdot \lambda \cdot t + 2^{t-s} \qquad (9)$$

We can choose $s = t/2 - \log_2(T \cdot \lambda)/2$ to minimize $G(s)$ at the value $2^{t/2} \cdot (\frac{\lambda(s-1)}{\sqrt{t \cdot \lambda}} \cdot \frac{3}{4} + \sqrt{t \cdot \lambda}) < \sqrt{T} \cdot \frac{11}{8} \cdot \sqrt{\log_2(T) \cdot \lambda}$ which is the complexity without parallellism.

Cost of Verification. The cost of running verification is dominated by $2t$ exponentiations (with λ bit of security). Exponentiations of a random λ bit exponent cost $1.5 \cdot \lambda$ and hence the cost of verification is around $3 \cdot \lambda \cdot t$.

4.3 Experiment Results

An implementation of Pietrzak's VDF is provided in C language. As our analysis above, the exponentiation of the μ_i's with precomputed results is calculated by the function `exponentiation_for_proof` in the *helper.c* file [13]. General operations as exponentiation, multiplication and subtraction are achieved with GMP library's functions and we use openssl library to give the hash function. The experiments are run on a computer with 16 GB of memory and a 2.5 GHz Intel Core i7 processor. The values are averaged after several trials. **All times are**

given in seconds. The most important thing is the running time of each algorithm of the VDF, and we could also benchmark the storage space against different parameters, and maybe more proof-construction methods. Here we mainly consider the elapsed time.

Time parameter T. The time parameter $T = 2^t$ was evaluated over the set $t \in [16, 30]$ with the security parameter $\lambda = 100$ bits and $\lambda_{RSA} = 2048$ bits. Table 1 presents the results for this configuration. The following components of the VDF were evaluated:

- time of evaluation (i.e., time to compute the output $y = x^{2^T}$)
- time to compute the proof π by brute force(naively)
- time to compute the proof π by saved values(optimally)
- time of verification

Table 1. Computation time for algorithms of VDF against t.

Time parameter t	Compute y	Compute π naively	Compute π optimally	Verification
16	0.049	0.045	0.021	0.006
17	0.080	0.089	0.030	0.006
18	0.160	0.166	0.059	0.006
19	0.325	0.320	0.080	0.007
20	0.627	0.641	0.194	0.007
21	1.257	1.269	0.244	0.008
12	2.542	2.533	0.332	0.008
23	5.156	5.249	0.780	0.009
24	10.593	10.497	1.000	0.009
25	20.703	21.088	2.396	0.010
26	41.150	41.777	3.029	0.010
27	85.247	83.089	7.293	0.010
28	165.610	163.754	9.531	0.011
29	331.248	327.373	23.139	0.012
30	661.588	660.961	35.524	0.012

As shown in Sect. 4, resolving the challenge takes $O(T)$ time complexity, while computing the proof is bounded by $O(\sqrt{T} \cdot \log(T))$ and verifying the proof takes around $O(\log(T))$. From the results above we could see directly: Firstly the proof-computation with stored values saves a lot of time comparing to that by brute force; Secondly, there are sharp decreases between the evaluation time and the proof-computation time, as well as the latter with the verification time. Thirdly, increasing the time parameter will almost linearly increase the evaluation time while the time of proof-computation and verification don't increase much.

Modulus N. We consider the influences of the RSA-modulus N with different binary length: the security parameter is fixed as $\lambda = 100$, λ_{RSA} is varying and $T = 2^{25}$. The following components of the VDF were evaluated:

- time to compute the output
- time to compute the proof π (with saved values)
- time of verification

The results are shown in Fig. 1. We could see that increasing the binary length of the RSA-modulus N will make the proof-computation time and verification time grow more significantly than enlarging the time parameter T.

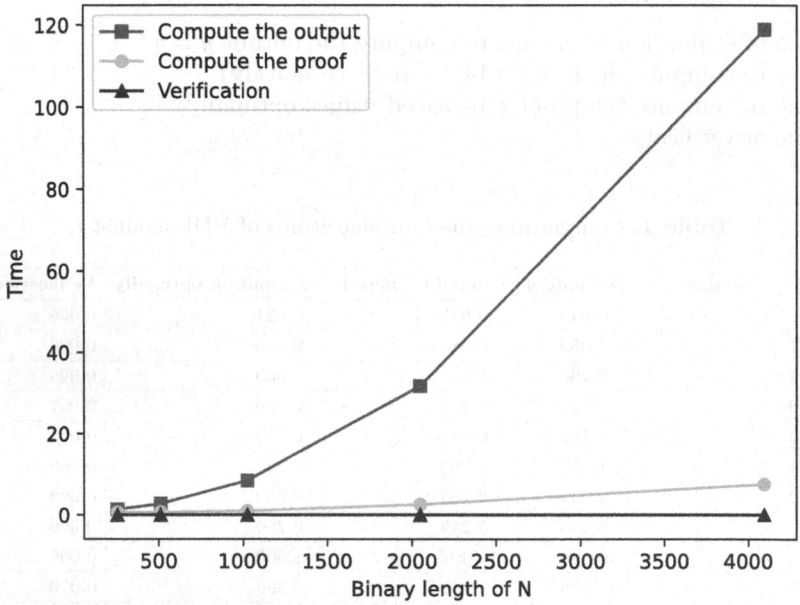

Fig. 1. Computation time for VDF's algorithms with different binary length of N

5 Security Issues and Variants

5.1 Quantum Attack and Trusted Third Party

In the security analysis of VDF made from RSW time-lock puzzle, the modulus parameter N and the "low order assumption" [3] are two key points for the sequentiality (which is also refer to be its soundness). The factorisation of N i.e., the order of the group should not be known by anyone, while N is always generated by a trusted third party or by some multi-party computation. This could bring trapdoor or extra work. Also it could suffer a quantum attack like the Shor algorithm (even in the class group setting of Wesolowski's VDF which doesn't need a trusted third party to generate the group).

To solve this problem, Ethereum deploys a method to change the group in a certain short time period which is impossible for the adversary to finish the quantum attack during this period. However with the development of quantum computers and pre-computation possibility, this method might be dangerous if potential attackers are quick enough or just have the factorisation of the public parameter N which may be pre-computed. Also, Pietrzak admits a low order assumption by his algebraic setting which means there will be no elements of small order which causes fake argument [3] and no loop in the squarings chain: $x \to x^2 \to x^4 \to x^8 \to \dots \to x^{2^T} (mod\ N)$. It means there do not exist two different integers i, j in $[T]$ with $x^{2^i} = x^{2^j} (mod\ N)$. The low order assumption is not a standardized cryptographic assumption like the factoring assumption or discrete logarithm assumption.

Here we adopt the low order assumption in a new interleaving squaring setting to answer part of the open problem in [3]. We try to solve the problem of quantum attack and remove the need for a trusted third party. As explained above, the public parameter N has an important role. Instead of using it, we choose to use two safe prime p, q which is 2048-bit long and change the T squarings with an input x in Z_p^* to be like:

The first squaring: $x_0 = x \to x^2 = x_1 (mod\ q)$. When we get the result x_1 in Z_q^*, we lift it as an integer x_1 in Z, and then reduce it to $\bar{x}_1 = x_1 (mod\ p)$, this is the input of the next squaring:

The second squaring: $\bar{x}_1 \to x_2 = \bar{x}_1^2 (mod\ p)$. As before we lift the result x_2 coming from Z_p^* in Z, and then reduce it to $\bar{x}_2 = x_2 (mod\ q)$, this is the input of the third squaring.

We repeat it for T times and finally get $x_T (mod\ q)$ as the output of the time lock puzzle. As we assume there is no element x of small order and therefore no loop in the squarings chain of length T (which can't be too large comparing to the safety parameter bound), this could be an alternative to the origin RSW time-lock puzzle as the squarings here are also sequential. We have implementation instances in the git repository [13] and we give a small example here with input $x = 3$ in Z_p^*, $p = 11, q = 23, T = 8$ as: $x = 2 \to 4(mod\ 23) \to 5(mod\ 11) \to 2(mod\ 23) \to 4(mod\ 11) \to 16(mod\ 23) \to 3(mod\ 11) \to 9(mod\ 23) \to 4(mod\ 11)$. So the output is 4. As these parameters are too small thus anything can happen, there is a loop begin with $4(mod\ 11)$ of length 4. The input x is a small order element and these p, q don't meet our assumption.

Now we can see there is no need for a trusted third party as we don't need to keep a secret factorisation here, and there will be no more quantum attack. With our assumptions the T squarings are sequential which means we can use it to generate unbiased randomness as it would take quite an amount of time to compute the result without shortcuts. The new problems come when making it public-verifiable: as the squarings are not commutative now, the methods used by Pietrzak or Wesolowski are no longer useful in the interleaving setting. However we could compute square roots now as we know p, q while we can't do it in modulus N before as the factorisation is unknown. To verify the result, we could store some intermediate values as some checkpoints to construct the proof, then verify the correctness of the output in parallel: from left to right we do the squarings while from right to left we compute the square roots. This measure can reduce the verification time by a constant comparing to the time for T squarings, thus achieves the same effect as the slow hash function [11] with checkpoints. We leave further research on good verification methods and conditions of the low order assumption of this new setting to future work.

5.2 Randomness with Different Inputs and Unknown T

The verifiable delay function itself has no randomness: given an input x, T, N, it always return an unique output y, π where $y = x^{2^T} \pmod N$. In this sense, the adversary with special hardware implementation of fast modular squarings can always get the output earlier than others, which gives advantage in situations like validator proposition in PoS-based blockchains. The Chia Network and Ethereum foundation launched ASIC competitions to give a upper bound on this acceleration ratio based on all potential implementations. The Ethereum 2.0 will adjust the difficulty due to the data submitted [4] to prevent such unfairness of hardware. However this method is not intrinsic. We want to explore if we could assign larger T to those ones with ASICS by giving different input of the VDF especially with different x, so they will have to do more squarings which eliminates their speed advantage on one squaring.

In [12] each competitor of the next validator gets its own input x of the verifiable delay function and solve its own "verifiable delay puzzle" by compute T squarings where T is the minimal integer satisfying $x^{2^T} < M \pmod N$, here M is a predetermined value which is relevant to the competitor's stake and N is the RSA-moduli which is equal to all competitors. They point out that with Pietrzak's VDF, one could quickly prove he solve the puzzle by verifying $y = x^{2^T} < M \pmod N$ with the proof computed in $O(\sqrt{T})$.

However there might be some problem of the complexity when computing the proof. The difference comes with the property that T is unknown here. In the RSW time-lock puzzle and Pietrzak's VDF, the time parameter T is known before the output of the function. As we show in Sect. 4, the proof-computation time can be reduced significantly by storing intermediate values $x^{2^{T \cdot j / 2^s}}$ with $j \in [2^s]$. We may always take this faster computing way for granted while it is not true in the case of verifiable delay puzzle. As T is not known before the computation ends, s is also unknown either, which makes it infeasible to directly use the method described by Pietrzak since we don't know which intermediate values to store. If we don't store any value until we find T, then computing the proof naively will take $O(T)$ times which slows down the whole network. As T could be rather large, it is always infeasible to store values comparable to T. We are doing further research on the efficient way of storing intermediate values for the proof.

To partially solve this problem (and also explore the randomness brought by different input in such puzzle schemes with non-defined T), we could try to guess the range of T. Firstly, we select some inputs randomly or in one range that we care most, and solve the verifiable delay puzzle above by computing a set of time parameter T. Secondly, we calculate the most promising value T_0 for T in this certain range. Finally when we do the computation of another verifiable delay puzzle, we save intermediate values with the T_0 value in the second step. After computing the actual T_1 of this verifiable delay puzzle we compare it with T_0 and then use the stored values to compute the proof. Hopefully the two values will be close so we could achieve the best complexity. We are further investigating the distribution of T with different inputs x in such inequality puzzles like the PoW hash schemes and will add implementations to the git repository.

6   Conclusion

In this work, we present a detailed implementation and optimization of Pietrzak's verifiable delay function with benchmarking, then show that enlarging the RSA-modulus is better than increasing the time parameter when adjusting the proof-computation time and verification time of the VDF. Combined with our analysis of the RANDAO scheme in the Ethereum 2.0 randomness beacon we point out that unbiased and public-verifiable randomness could be generated with VDF. Our results show that it is not wise to just adjust the time parameter or use a larger modulus. We propose to mix these two methods in the VDF evaluation while changing the modulus in an interleaving way, which makes a quantum computer have no significant advantage and no need for a trusted third party. We also explore other usages of verifiable delay functions to generate randomness which could potentially prevent adversary with ASIC and clarify some misuse of the VDF. These analysis and ideas could be useful to construct new verifiable delay functions and find better ways to generate reliable randomness for a decentralized trustworthy system with even a post-quantum feature, which could be very useful in the beacon chain of Ethereum 2.0.

Acknowledgments. Some parts related to implementation and benchmark utilize the work and report of Paul Mansat during his bachelor project. We thank him for his original coding and helpful discussions on the implementation. We thank the anonymous reviewers for their useful comments and suggestions. The authors were partially supported by the National Key R&D Program of China, 2017YFB0802000 and Natural Science Foundation of China, 61672059.

References

1. Randao git repository. https://github.com/randao/randao
2. Boneh, D., Bonneau, J., Bünz, B., Fisch, B.: Verifiable delay functions. In: Shacham, H., Boldyreva, A. (eds.) CRYPTO 2018. LNCS, vol. 10991, pp. 757–788. Springer, Cham (2018). https://doi.org/10.1007/978-3-319-96884-1_25
3. Boneh, D., Bünz, B., Fisch, B.: A survey of two verifiable delay functions. IACR Cryptology ePrint Archive **2018**, 712 (2018)

4. Buterin, V.: Vdf and attacks. ethereum research post (2018). https://ethresear.ch/t/verifiable-delay-functions-and-attacks/2365
5. Buterin, V., Griffith, V.: Casper the friendly finality gadget. arXiv preprint arXiv:1710.09437 (2017)
6. Cachin, C., Kursawe, K., Shoup, V.: Random oracles in constantinople: practical asynchronous byzantine agreement using cryptography. J. Cryptol. **18**(3), 219–246 (2005)
7. Chen, J., Micali, S.: Algorand. arXiv preprint arXiv:1607.01341 (2016)
8. Drake, J.: Minimal vdf randomness beacon. ethereum research post (2018). https://ethresear.ch/t/minimal-vdf-randomness-beacon/3566
9. Ephraim, N., Freitag, C., Komargodski, I., Pass, R.: Continuous verifiable delay functions. Technical Report, IACR Cryptology ePrint Archive, 2019: 619 (2019)
10. Kiayias, A., Russell, A., David, B., Oliynykov, R.: Ouroboros: a provably secure proof-of-stake blockchain protocol. In: Katz, J., Shacham, H. (eds.) CRYPTO 2017. LNCS, vol. 10401, pp. 357–388. Springer, Cham (2017). https://doi.org/10.1007/978-3-319-63688-7_12
11. Lenstra, A.K., Wesolowski, B.: Trustworthy public randomness with sloth, unicorn, and trx. Int. J. Appl. Crypt. **3**(4), 330–343 (2017)
12. Long, J., Wei, R.: Nakamoto consensus with verifiable delay puzzle. arXiv preprint arXiv:1908.06394 (2019)
13. Mansat, P. https://github.com/PaulMansat/Bachelor_Project_VDF_273856. Accessed 19 May 2020
14. Pietrzak, K.: Simple verifiable delay functions. In: 10th Innovations in Theoretical Computer Science Conference (ITCS 2019). Schloss Dagstuhl-Leibniz-Zentrum fuer Informatik (2018)
15. Rabin, M.O.: Transaction protection by beacons. J. Comput. Syst. Sci. **27**(2), 256–267 (1983)
16. Rivest, R.L., Shamir, A., Wagner, D.A.: Time-lock puzzles and timed-release crypto (1996)
17. Wang, G., Shi, Z.J., Nixon, M., Han, S.: Sok: Sharding on blockchain. In: Proceedings of the 1st ACM Conference on Advances in Financial Technologies, pp. 41–61 (2019)
18. Wesolowski, B.: Efficient verifiable delay functions. In: Ishai, Y., Rijmen, V. (eds.) EUROCRYPT 2019. LNCS, vol. 11478, pp. 379–407. Springer, Cham (2019). https://doi.org/10.1007/978-3-030-17659-4_13
19. Zheng, Z., Xie, S., Dai, H.N., Chen, X., Wang, H.: Blockchain challenges and opportunities: a survey. Int. J. Web Grid Serv. **14**(4), 352–375 (2018)

A Blockchain Based Scheme for Authentic Telephone Identity

Fuwen Liu[✉], Bo Yang, Li Su, Ke Wang, and Junzhi Yan

Department of Security Technology, China Mobile Research Institute, Beijing 100032, China
{liufuwen,yangbo,suli,wangkeyj,yanjunzhi}@chinamobile.com

Abstract. Authenticated telephone identity is an essential requirement to prevent spoofing attacks in VoIP systems. The framework STIR/SHAKEN provide a standardized method to ensure the authenticity of the calling number based on PKI. Unfortunately, it is not widely deployed due to its inherent weaknesses, such as the trust issue between multi-CAs. In this paper, we present a novel scheme used for VoIP systems to validate the telephone identity based on blockchain technology. The significant advantage of the proposed scheme is that these weaknesses presented in the framework STIR/SHAKEN are mitigated, as the certificates of all users are recorded on the trusted and unalterable blockchain. Moreover, an end-to-end trust on the calling identity can be achieved.

Keywords: Blockchain · Voice over IP (VoIP) · Public key infrastructure (PKI) · STIR/SHAKEN · Certificate authority (CA) · Blockchain certificate

1 Introduction

Voice telecommunication constantly plays a crucial role in the society since the telephone has been invented. The technology of voice telecommunication has experienced a huge change in the past two decades. It has been shifted from the circuits based technology to IP based technology to support voice communications. Although this change brings many benefits to operators, such as cost savings due to the unique IP network, it raises a great challenge to make the secure telecommunication. An adversary can forge the calling identifier in the IP network to launch a number of attacks, e.g. voice spam, cheat, and phish.

IETF has released a set of standards regarding authenticated calling identity for VoIP. STIR (Secure Telephone Identity Revisited) framework, consisting of RFC 8224 [1], RFC 8225 [2], and RFC 8226 [3], in order to ensure the authenticity of calling identity by applying the X.509v3 certificates [4], which are issued by a CA. SHAKEN (Secure Handling of Asserted information using toKENs) is an implementation based on STIR in practice.

The framework STIR/SHAKEN is not widely deployed due to its inherent weaknesses. The prerequisite of this framework is that PKIs are available. There is no global CA responsible for issuing certificates. Usually each operator has its own CA to manage the certificates. This raises the multi-CAs trust problem, i.e. it is difficult for one

Z. Zheng et al. (Eds.): BlockSys 2020, CCIS 1267, pp. 675–682, 2020.
https://doi.org/10.1007/978-981-15-9213-3_52

operator's CA to trust another operator's CA. Moreover, the framework STIR/SHAKEN achieves the authenticity of the calling number in a server-to-server fashion rather than in an end-to-end fashion.

In this paper, we present a novel scheme used for VoIP systems to validate the telephone identity based on blockchain technology. The significant advantage of the proposed scheme is that these weaknesses presented in the framework STIR/SHAKEN are mitigated, as the certificates of all users are recorded on the trusted and unalterable blockchain. Moreover, an end-to-end trust on the calling identity can be achieved.

The remainder of the paper is structured as follows. First the framework STIR/SHAKEN is briefly reviewed, and its weaknesses are analyzed (Sect. 2). Next, a novel scheme to validate the calling identity based on blockchain is proposed (Sect. 3). After that, the management of blockchain certificates is introduced (Sect. 4). Some final remarks conclude the paper.

2 Review of the Framework STIR/SHAKEN

The framework STIR/SHAKEN enhances the SIP protocol to verify whether the originator of a SIP call is valid or not by using digital signature technology, in order to mitigate the spoofing calls. This framework contains a series of protocols and procedures as follows:

- RFC 8224: Define how SIP Identity tokens are used to authenticate and verify the calling number in SIP signaling;
- RFC 8225: Define a method for creating and validating a token that cryptographically verifies a calling number;
- RFC 8226: Describe the usage of certificates in establishing authority over telephone numbers.

The basic idea of this framework is that an authentication server and a verification server are introduced to achieve the authenticated caller identity. The former is used to sign the caller identity related information (DATA field, FROM field, and TO field) in the SIP invitation message header, and creates the identity field to encapsulate the signature. The latter verifies the signature in the SIP invitation message based on the certificate of the caller.

2.1 Call Flow with the STIR/SHAKEN

The call flow with the STIR/SHAKEN is illustrated in Fig. 1.

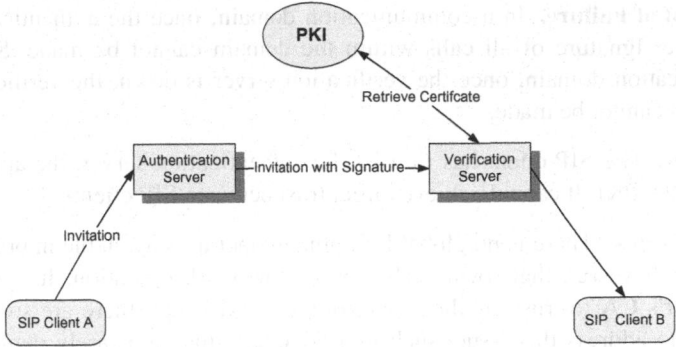

Fig. 1. Call flow with the STIR/SHAKEN

The detailed steps of call procedure are as follows:

1) SIP client A sends a SIP invitation message to the authentication server.
2) The authentication server checks the call source and calling number to determine whether the calling party is authorized to use this calling number.
3) The authentication server creates a SIP identity header as follows. It signs the DATA field, FROM field, and TO field in the SIP invitation message header. The FROM field contains the identity of the caller (SIP URI or phone number), the TO field contains the identity of the invitee (SIP URI or phone number), and the DATA field contains the timestamp of the SIP invitation message sent. The signature of the FROM field can ensure the authenticity of the caller identity, the signature of the TO field can ensure that the invitee's identity has not been tampered with, and the signature of the DATA field can prevent replay attacks. The authentication server places the signature and the address referring to the authentication server certificate into the newly defined identity field.
4) The authentication server sends a signed invitation message to the verification server.
5) According to the address of the authentication server certificate, the verification server connects to the PKI, and retrieves the certificate of the authentication server.
6) The verification server uses the public key in the certificate of the authentication server to verify the signature. After the verification is successful, the verification server forwards the SIP invitation message to SIP client B.

The framework STIR/SHAKEN utilizes the X.509v3 certificate to attest the authenticity of the authentication server. The authentication server attests the authenticity of the calling identity based on its register information. Thus this framework provides an implicit trust rather than a direct trust on the calling identity.

2.2 Weaknesses of the Framework

Introduction of the two servers to assure the authenticity of the calling identity and verification procedure relies on the availability of the PKI, may result in the following weaknesses.

Single Point of Failure. In a communication domain, once the authentication server is down, the signature of all calls within the domain cannot be made. Similarly, in a communication domain, once the verification server is down, the verification of all ingress calls cannot be made.

Trust Issues. The SIP client has to trust the authentication server, the authentication server, and the PKI. It cannot achieve direct trust between SIP clients.

Multi-CA Issues. There is no global PKI among operators available in practice. Most of operators have run their own PKIs for their network operation. It is difficult for one operator's CA to trust another operator's CA. Although there are some schemes attempting to address this issue, such as bridge CA, they are rarely deployed in the practical systems due to their complexity. There is no trusted authority that will like to establish a bridge CA among operators with fear to take the responsibility in the case of failure of the bridge CA.

3 Proposal

The origin of PKI comes from the security requirements of asymmetric key algorithms. If the authenticity of the public key used in the asymmetric algorithm is not guaranteed, the communication between the systems will be compromised by a man in the middle attack. X.509 v3 certificate is designed to address this issue, which is digitally signed by a trusted third party (CA: Certificate Authority). The main contents of a digital certificate include the public key, applicant's identity, CA's identity, and the CA's signature on all the contents of the certificate. Digital certificates can be transmitted using a public channel, since the contents of the certificate have been signed. The management of X.509 v3 certificate is accomplished by the PKI, which is usually composed of CA, RA (Register Authority), and CRL/OCSP (Certificate Revocation List/Online Certificate Status Protocol) server. The PKI is characterized as a centralized system, whose weaknesses include a single point of failure, multi-CA issues.

Blockchain is a technology that enables a number of untrustworthy participants to reach the agreement without relying on a centralized authority by leveraging cryptographic algorithms and consensus protocols. In the blockchain, once the data is recorded on the blockchain after the consensus progress, the data is recognized by all participants, and cannot be altered by anyone. The blockchain is characterized as a decentralized, tamper-resistant, and trustworthy system.

On the basis of above discussions, we propose a novel scheme based on the blockchain technology to overcome the weaknesses of the framework STIR/SHAKEN. In the proposed scheme, no authentication server and verification server are deployed. SIP client A generates the blockchain certificate which binds its public key with its identity. After the consensus procedure, this blockchain certificate is recorded on the blockchain, which cannot be tampered with. SIP client A initiates the call with the signed SIP invitation. After receiving the SIP invitation message, SIP client B fetches the blockchain certificate from the blockchain. SIP client B check the identity of the SIP client A by verifying the signature in the SIP invitation message with the public key in the blockchain certificate. Figure 2 illustrates the proposed scheme.

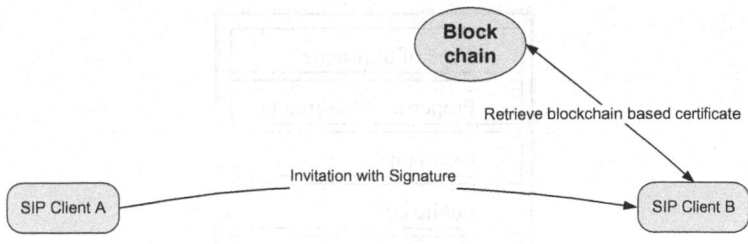

Fig. 2. Proposed scheme

The detailed steps of the proposed scheme are as follows:

1) SIP client A applies its own private key to sign the DATA field, FROM field, and TO field in the header of the SIP invitation message, and encapsulates the signature result into the identity field. The public key corresponding to the private key used for signing is recorded in the blockchain certificate of SIP client A.
2) SIP client A sends a signed invitation to SIP client B.
3) Upon receipt of invitation, SIP client B connects to the blockchain. It fetches the blockchain certificate of SIP Client A from the blockchain according to the identity in the invitation message. The public key in the blockchain certificate is used to verify the signature. If verification is successful, the authenticity of the identity of SIP client A is proved to be valid.

There is no single point of failure and trust issue for the proposed scheme, as it does not employ any servers to sign/verify the identity of the caller. Moreover, the proposed scheme does not have the multi-CAs issue, as the certificates are not issued by the CAs; instead they are recorded on the decentralized, tamper-resistant, and trustworthy blockchain.

4 Blockchain Certificate

Blockchain certificate is the key store of the proposed scheme. In the following, its format and management are introduced, respectively.

4.1 Format

The blockchain certificate can use the standard X.509 format. But this is not recommended for two reasons. First, blockchain certificate does not need the signature of the certificate information, as the authenticity and reliability of the blockchain certificate is guaranteed by the blockchain rather than the digital signature of a third party. If the X.509 format is applied, the unnecessary self-signed information has to be added to meet the requirement of X.509 format. Second, the message overhead of the X.509 format is too heavy in context of a blockchain certificate. Besides the unnecessary self-signed information, the signing identity (i.e. trusted third party) is surplus as there no trusted third party in the blockchain system. For this, we define an appropriate format for blockchain certificates, which is depicted in Fig. 3.

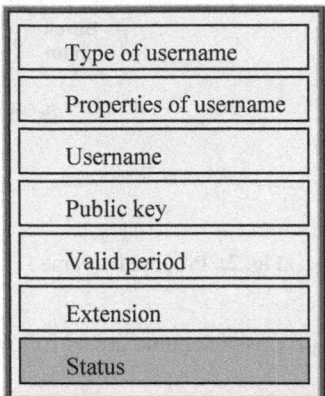

Fig. 3. Format of a blockchain certificate

- *Type of username*: A tag is used to distinguish different types of usernames, such as phone numbers, SIP URIs, etc.
- *Properties of username*: A tag is used to distinguish whether the username is anonymous or real. The anonymous username is used to protect the privacy of the user.
- *Username*: The name used by the user to apply for a blockchain certificate. For the VOIP system, if the username is a real name, it is the information in the FROM field in the SIP invitation message; if the username is anonymous, the username is a hash value of the information in the FROM field.
- *Public key*: It is generated by the certificate applicant, and its corresponding private key is kept secret by the certificate applicant. In order to make the length of the certificate as short as possible to save its storage space on the blockchain, it is recommended that Elliptical Curve Cryptography (ECC) is used to generate public/private key pairs.
- *Validity period*: It indicates the period that the certificate is valid.
- *Extension*: Reserve for future use.
- *Status*: A certificate has one of two statuses: valid or invalid.

4.2 Management

The management of a blockchain certificate is composed of two procedures: certificate application and certificate inquiry.

Certificate Application
The detailed steps for applying and issuing a blockchain certificate are as follows:

1) The user generates a blockchain certificate and marks the status of certificate as valid. If the username in the certificate is a real name, the user deals with the certificate information like dealing with transaction information on the blockchain, signs it with the private key of his account on the blockchain, and broadcasts the blockchain

certificate and its signature in the blockchain network. If the username in the certificate is anonymous, the user must sign the blockchain certificate and the user's real name (the username in the FROM field), and broadcast the blockchain certificate with the user's real name, as well as their signature on the blockchain network.

2) The accounting node is determined through the consensus mechanism used in blockchain.

3) The accounting node verifies the signature to ensure the integrity of the blockchain certificate and the user's real name.

4) The accounting node searches on the blockchain to check whether the username of the certificate applicant can be found on the blockchain. If the username is found, and the status of the certificate with the same name on the blockchain is valid, the accounting node rejects the application of certificate;

5) If there is a duplicate name, but the status of the certificate with the duplicate name on the blockchain is invalid, or there is no duplicate name, the accounting node checks the identity of the blockchain certificate by using the SMS (Short Message Service) module embedded in the blockchain software system. For verification, the blockchain systems sends an SMS verification code to the user applying for a blockchain certificate based on the username, and compares the SMS verification code returned by the user with the sent one. If they are the same, the authenticity of the username on the blockchain certificate can be determined. If the username is anonymous, an SMS verification code is sent to the user who applied for a blockchain certificate based on the user's real name (username in the FROM field).

6) After the identity of the blockchain certificate is successfully verified, the accounting node writes the blockchain certificate into the block, and the block is written into the blockchain after the waiting time required by the system is expired. This completes the application and issuance of the blockchain certificate. If the username is anonymous, the accounting node will only write the blockchain certificate into the block, and the user's real name will not be written into the block.

Certificate Inquiry

A user can fetch a certificate from the blockchain through the following steps.

1) To obtain the blockchain certificate of the SIP client, the user first initiate a query on the blockchain according to the username in the FROM field of the SIP message. If the username to be queried can be found on the blockchain, the blockchain system can get the certificate according to the username. If the status of the certificate is invalid, the blockchain system returns an error message to the user (the certificate exists but the status is invalid); if the status of the certificate is valid but the validity period has expired, it returns an error message to the user (the certificate exists but has expired); If the status of the certificate is valid and within the validity period, it is returned to the blockchain certificate that the user wants to obtain.

2) If the username to be queried cannot be found on the blockchain, an error message is returned to the user (the certificate with the queried username does not exist). The user imitates a query again based on the hash value of the username. The similar method as the step 1 is applied to acquire the certificate.

3) If the hash value of the username to be queried cannot be found on the blockchain, the query is terminated and an error message is returned to the user (the certificate with the queried hash value of the username does not exist).

5   Final Remarks

Authenticated calling identity is a premise to prevent spoofing attacks for VoIP systems. The framework STIR/SHAKEN is not widely deployed as its running relies on the availability of the PKI. The proposed scheme removes this limitation by using the decentralized, tamper-resistant, and trustworthy blockchain. It can provide end-to-end trust between SIP clients without relying on any servers. Thus the proposed scheme is well suited to be used in the VoIP system to achieve the authenticated calling identity for its simplicity.

References

1. IETF RFC 8224. Authenticated Identity Management in the Session Initiation Protocol (SIP)
2. IETF RFC 8225. PASSporT: Personal Assertion Token
3. IETF RFC 8226. Secure Telephone Identity Credentials: Certificates
4. ITU-T Recommendation X.509. Information technology – Open Systems Interconnection – The Directory: Public-key and attribute certificate frameworks, 10/2016

BDSS: Blockchain-Based Data Synchronization System

Rengang Liang[1,3], Qian He[1,2($\boxtimes$)], Bingcheng Jiang[2], Mingliu He[1,2],
and Kuangyu Qin[2]

[1] State and Local Joint Engineering Research Center for Satellite Navigation and Location Service, Guilin University of Electronic Technology, Guilin 541004, China
1184372550@qq.com, heqian@guet.edu.cn, 1179581668@qq.com
[2] Guangxi Key Laboratory of Cryptography and Information Security, Guilin University of Electronic Technology, Guilin 541004, China
jiangbc1990@126.com, 122669@qq.com
[3] CETC Key Laboratory of Aerospace Information Applications, Shijiazhuang 050081, China

Abstract. In view of the high-efficiency and security issues of data synchronization between cross-region remote cloud storage servers, such as the lack of consistency verification and the fact that most synchronization tools cannot achieve one-to-many data synchronization, a data synchronization system is proposed and implemented, and blockchain smart contract technology is introduced to achieve consistency verification of data synchronization between servers and traceability of data synchronization process; propose a data synchronization strategy based on Rsync and P2P to select the synchronization mode according to the threshold set by data synchronization system, reduce network overhead, and ultimately achieve efficient data synchronization; Experimental results show that: the blockchain-based data synchronization system can efficiently and securely achieve one-to-one or one-to-many data synchronization across regional servers.

Keywords: Data synchronization · Blockchain · Traceability · Consistency verification · Rsync

1 Introduction

With the rapid development of cloud storage and computer Internet technology, cloud storage-based applications continue to expand in various fields, and the depth of applications continues to deepen. The amount of data generated by cloud storage applications has shown explosive growth, and a single file can reach several GB or even dozens of GB. In the field of file synchronization tools, such as Rsync, Syncany, Unison, Dropbox, Hadoop, Rsync, etc. [1–3]. but these tools have been unable to effectively respond, for example: there is a hidden security risk in data synchronization, there is no visual interface for data synchronization, no Conducive to the management of the data synchronization process and other issues. MD. Ibrahim Khan et al. [4] used the blockchain [5, 6], and Rsync algorithm to achieve data synchronization, directly upload the file non-matching data to the blockchain, and the blockchain nodes download the non-matching

© Springer Nature Singapore Pte Ltd. 2020
Z. Zheng et al. (Eds.): BlockSys 2020, CCIS 1267, pp. 683–689, 2020.
https://doi.org/10.1007/978-981-15-9213-3_53

data for splicing, and finally achieve the data synchronization of each node. When the non-matching data is too large, there are too many blocks stored on the blockchain, resulting in low efficiency of data synchronization between nodes. Y. Wang et al. [7] proposed a folder and file synchronization model: ChainFileSynch, which involves a fast cloud storage file synchronization architecture, process, and processing algorithm based on blockchain. However, the synchronization method is to use the blockchain network to completely cover the files. When the large files are only modified parts, multi-node data synchronization causes network congestion.

This paper designs a blockchain-based data synchronization system architecture and stores data synchronization information in the blockchain to ensure the credibility of the data synchronization traceability information and facilitate the verification of synchronization data consistency and traceability information tracking and query. According to the actual data synchronization scenario, formulate a data synchronization strategy combining P2P and Rsync to reduce network overhead and achieve stable and efficient data synchronization between multiple servers across regions.

2 Implementation of BDSS

2.1 Overview

The blockchain-based data synchronization system (BDSS) consists of a data synchronization subsystem (DSS) and a traceability subsystem (TS). DSS includes differential synchronization mode based on the Rsync algorithm and full synchronization mode based on the p2p network; TS is used to verify the consistency of data synchronization and realize the transparency and security of synchronization between multiple servers. The system architecture of BDSS is shown in Fig. 1.

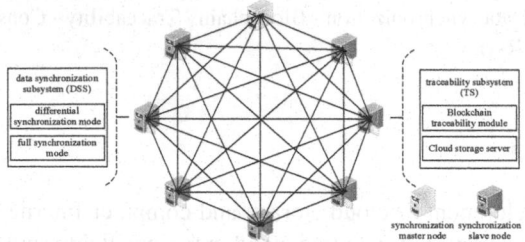

Fig. 1. The system architecture of BDSS.

The differential synchronization mode based on Rsync algorithm in DSS includes synchronization cluster, file monitoring module, synchronization control module, communication module, and blockchain module. The functions are described as follows:

1) **Synchronization Cluster**: The difference synchronization adopts the master-slave architecture mode. As an important part of DSS, the synchronization cluster is mainly composed of a synchronization master node and several synchronization slave nodes.

The synchronization master node serves as the control center of the synchronization cluster, it controls the synchronization source node (synchronization slave node where the local file changes) and the synchronization destination node (synchronization slave node that needs to update the local file system) to perform synchronization operations.

2) **File Monitoring Module**: This module is used to monitor the changes of the local file system of the synchronization slave node in real time (for example: file creation, modification and deletion).

3) **Synchronization Control Module**: The synchronization slave nodes in the cluster use the Rsync algorithm and select the appropriate block byte parameters for multi-server data synchronization under the control of the synchronization control module.

4) **Communication Module**: This module is mainly used for data communication between synchronization slave nodes.

5) **Blockchain Module**: The main function of the blockchain module is to interact with data synchronization information, including on-chain storage of data synchronization information and traceability information, and on-chain query process of data synchronization information.

DSS based on the p2p network [8, 9] full synchronization mode can provide an opportunity to use a large number of peer nodes' idle resources to improve data synchronization efficiency. The seed server generates a torrent file based on the resource file, and becomes a permanent Seeder for the synchronized slave nodes to download synchronously; The tracking server tracks all synchronized slave nodes in the system and collects and counts the status of all synchronized slave nodes in order to share file blocks between the synchronized slave nodes; the synchronized slave nodes obtain the seed list from the tracking server and communicate with the nodes in the seed list, request resources and communicate with the tracking server from time to time.

TS mainly includes two modules:

1) **Blockchain Traceability Module**: It mainly has the following functions: ① The synchronization source node uploads the data synchronization information to the data synchronization chain; ②The synchronization destination node performs data synchronization consistency verification; ③The synchronization destination node uploads relevant traceability information to the traceability information group.

2) **Cloud Storage Server**: Use the Sha-256 algorithm to calculate the DataHash value of the downloaded synchronization data and compare it with the DataHash value obtained from the data synchronization chain query. If they are not equal, the cloud storage server downloads the synchronization data again.

2.2 Workflow of the Main Information Exchange

The main information exchange process of the differential synchronization mode in DSS is shown in Fig. 2.

①: The Inotify tool monitors the changes of the local file system in real time, and the synchronization source node selects the data synchronization mode according to the file change status information and file size.

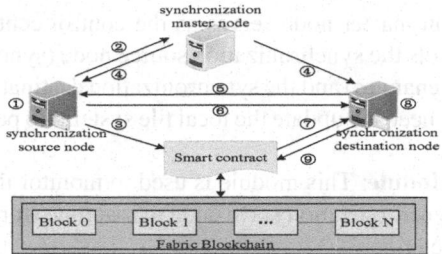

Fig. 2. The workflow of differential synchronization mode in DSS.

②: In the DSS differential synchronization mode, the synchronization source node sends a data synchronization request to the message queue of the message middleware deployed by the synchronization master node for caching.

③: The synchronization source node uses the Sha-256 algorithm to calculate the DataHash value of the requested synchronization data. The synchronization source node uploads data synchronization information (data synchronization ID, synchronization file list, DataHash, time, traceability information group, the IP of synchronization source node, etc.) to the data synchronization chain.

④: The synchronization master node obtains the data synchronization request cached in the message queue, and sends the data synchronization command to the synchronization destination node. The synchronization source node and the synchronization destination node start the data synchronization operation under the control of the synchronization master node.

⑤: The synchronization destination node queries the local file system according to the synchronization file list in the data synchronization command, and divides File_old into blocks according to the specified number of bytes, and calculate the weak check code and strong check code of all data blocks, and finally send the file check code set to the synchronization source node.

⑥: After receiving the check code set of File_old, the synchronization source node obtains the matching data information and non-matching data of the File_new and File_old files and sends them to the synchronization destination node. When the synchronization source node performs data block matching, it can compare the total amount of non-matching data with the difference data threshold to select the synchronization mode again.

⑦: The synchronization destination node uses the data sent by the synchronization source node and File_old to create and reorganize temporary files. Finally, the synchronization destination node queries the DataHash value from the data synchronization chain through smart contract.

⑧: The synchronization destination node calculates the DataHash value of the synchronized data and compares it with the DataHash obtained from the query on the data synchronization chain. If they are equal, the data synchronization is completed, otherwise the data synchronization download is performed again.

⑨: The synchronization destination node uploads the data synchronization traceability information (synchronization destination node's IP address, synchronization time, and synchronization file list) to the data synchronization chain through smart contract.

2.3 Data Synchronization Strategy Algorithm

The data synchronization strategy selects the data synchronization mode reasonably according to the file change status information, file size and the size of the difference data, to achieve the high efficiency of data synchronization between servers. The code for the data synchronization strategy algorithm is as follows:

```
Algorithm: data synchronization strategy
Input: FileChangeStatus,FileSize,DifferenceDataSize
Output: SynchronousMode
1.  if (FileSize >= FileSizeThreshold){
2.    if (Modify == FileChangeStatus)
3.      if (DifferenceDataSize >= DifferenceDataThreshold)
4.        SynchronousMode = P2PSynchronousMode;
5.      else
6.        SynchronousMode = RsyncSynchronousMode;
7.      end if
8.    else if (New == FileChangeStatus || Delete == FileChangeStatus)
9.      if (New == FileChangeStatus)
10.       SynchronousMode = P2PSynchronousMode;
11.     else
12.       SynchronousMode = RsyncSynchronousMode;
13.     end if
14.   end if
15.   end if
16. else
17.   SynchronousMode = RsyncSynchronousMode;
18. end if
19. return SynchronousMode
```

3   Experimental Evaluation

Full synchronization experiment of files through differential synchronization mode, the experimental results are shown in Fig. 3 below. In the full synchronization mode of DSS, the synchronization source node generates a P2P seed file named test.zip.torrent from the test.zip file through the seed server. The synchronization destination node is downloaded through the P2P client, the experimental results are shown in Fig. 4.

It can be seen from the analysis of Figs. 3 and 4 that the full synchronization mode based on the p2p network due to its cold start, in the full synchronization of small files, the differential synchronization mode is more advantageous; However, in the scenario of multiple nodes and large files, the full synchronization method based on P2P network

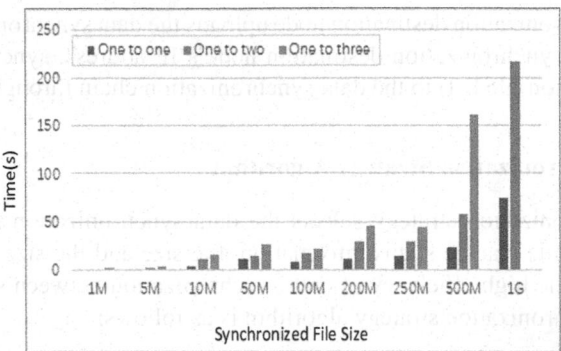

Fig. 3. Full synchronization of files through differential synchronization mode

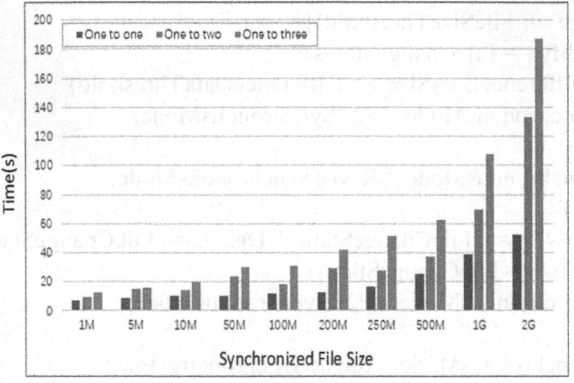

Fig. 4. Full synchronization of files through full synchronization mode

is more advantageous, in the full synchronization of 1G or 2G large files, the download speed of each node can be as high as 32 M/s. Even if the number of synchronization destination nodes increases, the synchronization speed for large files will not change much. Combining the advantages of the two synchronization modes through the data synchronization strategy, blockchain technology is introduced to achieve consistency verification and traceability of data synchronization, and to achieve efficient and safe synchronization between multiple nodes.

Acknowledgment. This work is supported in part by the National Natural Science Foundation of China (61661015,61967005), Guangxi Innovation-Driven Development Project (AA17202024), Guangxi Key Laboratory of cryptography and information security Found (GCIS201701), Guangxi Collaborative Innovation Center of Cloud Compu-ting and Big Data Found (YD1901), Innovation Project of GUET Graduate Education(2019YCXS046), CETC Key Laboratory of Aerospace Information Applications Found, Young and middle-aged backbone teacher of Guangxi colleges and universities Found and High Level of Innovation Team of Colleges and Universities in Guangxi Outstanding Scholars Program Funding

References

1. Shial, G., Majhi, S.K., Phatak, D.B.: A comparison study for file synchronisation. Proc. Comput. Sci. **48**, 133–141 (2015)
2. Stuart, A.: The dangers of file sync and sharing services. Comput. Fraud Secur. **2016**(11), 10–12 (2016)
3. Cui, Y., Lai, Z., Sun, L.: Internet storage sync: problem statement. IETF: draft-cui-iss-problem-03, Tsinghua University (2015)
4. Khan, M.I., et al.: Using blockchain technology for file synchronization. In: IOP Conference Series: Materials Science and Engineering, vol. 561, no. 1. IOP Publishing (2019)
5. Pradhan, S., Tripathy, S., Nandi, S.: Blockchain based security framework for P2P filesharing system. In: 2018 IEEE International Conference on Advanced Networks and Telecommunications Systems (ANTS). IEEE (2018)
6. Andoni, M., et al.: Blockchain technology in the energy sector: a systematic review of challenges and opportunities. Renew. Sustain. Energy Rev. **100**, 143–174 (2019)
7. Wang, Y., et al.: ChainFileSynch: an innovate file synchronization for cloud storage with blockchain. In: 2019 International Conference on Artificial Intelligence and Advanced Manufacturing (AIAM). IEEE (2019)
8. Chen, Z., et al.: Hypds: enabling a hybrid file transfer protocol and peer to peer content distribution system for remote sensing data. In: 2019 IEEE 25th International Conference on Parallel and Distributed Systems (ICPADS). IEEE (2019)
9. Li, X., He, Q., Jiang, B., Qin, X., Qin, K.: BTS-PD: a blockchain based traceability system for P2P distribution. In: Zheng, Z., Dai, H.-N., Tang, M., Chen, X. (eds.) BlockSys 2019. CCIS, vol. 1156, pp. 607–620. Springer, Singapore (2020). https://doi.org/10.1007/978-981-15-2777-7_50

Correction to: Scalable and Communication-Efficient Decentralized Federated Edge Learning with Multi-blockchain Framework

Jiawen Kang, Zehui Xiong, Chunxiao Jiang, Yi Liu, Song Guo,
Yang Zhang, Dusit Niyato, Cyril Leung, and Chunyan Miao

Correction to:
Chapter "Scalable and Communication-Efficient Decentralized
Federated Edge Learning with Multi-blockchain Framework"
in: Z. Zheng et al. (Eds.): *Blockchain and Trustworthy Systems*,
CCIS 1267, https://doi.org/10.1007/978-981-15-9213-3_12

In the originally published version of the chapter 12, the funding information in the acknowledgments section was incorrect. The funding information was removed.

The updated version of this chapter can be found at
https://doi.org/10.1007/978-981-15-9213-3_12

Author Index

Printed in the United States
by Baker & Taylor Publisher Services